2—
100

ECUADOR
& GALÁPAGOS ISLANDS
GUIDE

BE A TRAVELER - NOT A TOURIST!

OPEN ROAD TRAVEL GUIDES SHOW YOU
HOW TO BE A TRAVELER – NOT A TOURIST!

*Whether you're going abroad or planning a trip in the United States, take Open Road along on your journey. Our books have been praised by **Travel & Leisure, The Los Angeles Times, Newsday, Booklist, US News & World Report, Endless Vacation, American Bookseller, Coast to Coast**, and many other magazines and newspapers!*

Don't just see the world – experience it with Open Road!

ABOUT THE AUTHOR

Becky Youman and Bryan Estep are travel writers with extensive experience in Latin America. In addition to *Ecuador & Galapagos Islands Guide,* they are also the authors of Open Road's *Chile Guide.* Their work has appeared in various travel anthologies, including the critically acclaimed *In Search of Adventure.* They have also contributed to numerous periodicals such as the *Santiago News Review,Big World,* and *Transitions Abroad.* The husband-wife team lived in Latin America for nearly a decade, and are fluent in both Spanish and Portuguese.

BE A TRAVELER, NOT A TOURIST - WITH OPEN ROAD TRAVEL GUIDES!

Open Road Publishing has guide books to exciting, fun destinations on four continents. As veteran travelers, our goal is to bring you the best travel guides available anywhere!

No small task, but here's what we offer:

• All Open Road travel guides are written by authors with a distinct, opinionated point of view – not some sterile committee or team of writers. Our authors are experts in the areas covered and are polished writers.

• Our guides are geared to people who want to make their own travel choices. We'll show you how to discover the real destination – not just see some place from a tour bus window.

• We're strong on the basics, but we also provide terrific choices for those looking to get off the beaten path and experience the country or city – not just see it or pass through it.

• We give you the best, but we also tell you about the worst and what to avoid. Nobody should waste their time and money on their hard-earned vacation because of bad or inadequate travel advice.

• Our guides assume nothing. We tell you everything you need to know to have the trip of a lifetime – presented in a fun, literate, nonsense style.

• And, above all, we welcome your input, ideas, and suggestions to help us put out the best travel guides possible.

ECUADOR
& GALÁPAGOS ISLANDS
GUIDE

BE A TRAVELER - NOT A TOURIST!

Becky Youman & Bryan Estep

OPE ROAD PUBLISHIN

OPEN ROAD PUBLISHING

We offer travel guides to American and foreign locales. Our books tell it like it is, often with an opinionated edge, and our experienced authors always give you all the information you need to have the trip of a lifetime. Write for your free catalog of all our titles, including our golf and restaurant guides.

Catalog Department, Open Road Publishing
P.O. Box 284, Cold Spring Harbor, NY 11724

E-mail:
Jopenroad@aol.com

1st Edition

Front cover photo and top back cover photo©James Martin. Back cover photos©Frederick Atwood.

Maps by James Ramage.

TABLE OF CONTENTS

MAPS

SIDEBARS

SIDEBARS

SIDEBARS

ACKNOWLEDGMENTS

We'd like to acknowledge and thank the following people whose help and input added to the quality of this book: Miguel Larrea, Juan Cabrera, Stephanie Stevens, Lazlo Karoles, Karen Salinas, Frank Keifer, Margaret Goodheart, Nik Millhouse, Jorge Espinoza, Jacob Santos, Margarita Ponce, Enrique Portillo, German Ortega, Sergio Platonoff Maldonado, Miguel Ponce, Bolivar Lasso, Mignon Plaza, Paul Pinto, Pilar Medina, Olivier Currat, Francisco Cardenas, Hernan Jaramillo, Gloria Barba, Martha Pantin, Martin Santschi, Gino Luzi, Diego Viteri, Marena Moya de Montalvo and family, Eric Schwartz, Maria Genoveva Salem, Benny Ammeter, Lee Schel, Tomas Vargas, Helmut, Gabriela Donoso, Paulina Moreno, Jack Nelson, Wolfgang Boerchers, Lourdes Diaz Granados and Monica & Polo Navarro. We'd also like to thank the South American Explorer's Club

Jonathan Stein, our publisher, deserves kudos for putting up with us on another project.

A special thanks to American Airlines and Budget Rental Cars of Ecuador.

1. INTRODUCTION

Ecuador's compact territory offers a stunning composition of snow-capped mountains, tropical beaches, untamed jungle, and volcanic islands. The alluring geography is complimented by a wide array of activity, lodging and dining options. We offer you clear-cut recommendations to help shape your equatorial journey with confidence and ease.

You'll likely start your travels in the Andean Highlands, a lofty valley set amid a spectacular corridor of volcanoes. With the information we provide, you can time visits to the vibrant markets on the same mornings that the villagers arrive pulling pigs on leashes and toting bundles of richly woven garments. On the eastern side of the Andes lies the intriguing Amazon Basin rainforest. We offer insight on how to approach jungle travel and which jungle lodges are best for each budget. Soon you'll be gliding through lagoons in a dugout canoe paddled by a knowledgeable native guide and climbing a ten-story tree tower to marvel at monkeys, toucans and macaws.

A Galápagos cruise is an option that merits thorough consideration. We highlight important variables so that you can select the tour operator, vessel, and cruise length that are right for you. Whether you prefer a sleek sailboat, an elegant yacht, or a commodious cruise ship, our guidelines help you choose one that will be professionally staffed and outfitted with comfortable cabins and sumptuous meals.

If you seek outdoor adventure, we'll show you what mountains to climb, where to surf the glassiest waves, how you can safely dive among hammerhead sharks, and the best spots for hiking, birding, mountain biking, and horseback riding. After burning off all these calories, you will need to refuel. We point you to the best seafood and highland cuisine and superb international restaurants with delightful Ecuadorian hospitality.

Our strongest recommendations focus on unique Ecuadorian locales. We prioritize quality, regional culture, and personality. While both upscale travelers and backpackers will find reviews on establishments to fit their budgets, the often-overlooked mid-range traveler will benefit from our eclectic list of reasonably priced distinctive lodging alternatives. These include centuries-old, whitewashed haciendas; intimate, thatched-roof jungle lodges; and wonderful colonial inns.

Ecuador is an extraordinary destination – *buen viaje!*

2. OVERVIEW

Ecuador is a land endowed with staggering variety. The country, roughly the same size as the US state of Arizona, offers exotic Amazon jungle, remote Andean mountains, balmy tropical beaches and stark volcanic islands. To find these different ecosystems in any one country is amazing, but to have them all so near each other makes Ecuador truly unique.

Imagine yourself buying a richly embroidered garment from an indigenous woman whose bartering acumen is as keen as her beauty is exotic. Beyond her handicrafts stall is a crater lake graced with an undulating reflection of a snow-covered volcano. Within a 100-mile radius are lush tropical beaches and an astoundingly vast expanse of wild, pristine jungle.

The country not only offers amazing variety, but also excellent hotels and lodges from which to base your travels. You can explore the natural wonders that surround you and then return in the evening to first class service and tasty meals.

You will encounter an enchanting variety of animal life in Ecuador. The birds you can see in your travels, over 1500 species, include chatty pairs of brilliant scarlet macaws, dive-bombing blue footed boobies, and solitary Andean condors. Interesting mammals such as the tapir, looking like a cross between a pig and a rhino; and the pygmy marmoset, the world's smallest monkey, await you in the jungle. Other animals include the hideously compelling marine iguana and brilliant poison dart frogs.

It's not just natural wonders that make Ecuador so compelling. The country is studded with treasures of colonial art and architecture. A unique mix of European and indigenous elements marks this style, which flourished from the 16th to early 19th centuries. Entire sections of cities are remarkably preserved allowing you to walk back across centuries.

PEOPLE

Ecuador offers wonderful ethnic diversity for such a small country. More than thirteen indigenous groups share the land with mestizos, Afro-

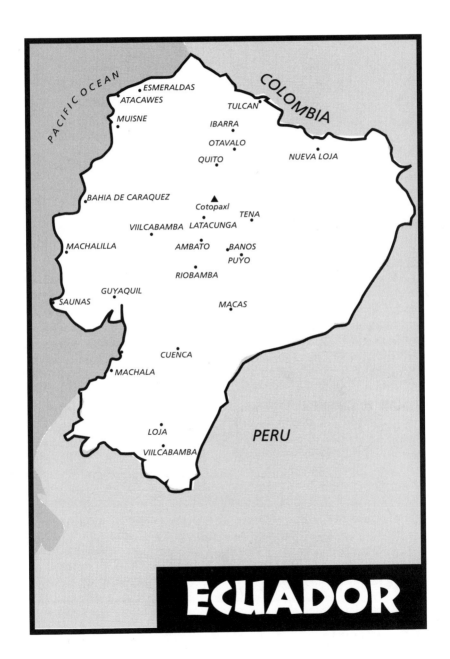

Ecuadorians and Caucasians. During your time in the country you will be exposed to an intriguing medley of customs, clothing, languages, art and food.

A composite sketch of the Ecuadorian personality would include traits from an effusively polite Quiteño, a carefree coastal inhabitant, a regal highland Amer-Indian, a hardworking colonist, and a unaffected jungle inhabitant totally in-tune with the rhythms of nature.

LODGING

The infra-structure for travelers is well developed, but not overly so. There are excellent accommodations in Ecuador that range from intimate colonial-style inns to sprawling haciendas. Remote jungle lodges only accessible by motorized canoe offer first class service in the heart of the Amazon Basin, while country getaways lie nestle at the bases of volcanoes.

SPORTS & RECREATION

There are plentiful sporting opportunities here. The twin spines of the Andes running the length of the country make Ecuador a paradise for mountain sports like hiking, mountain biking and climbing. The coast and Galápagos provide wonderful opportunities for surfing, swimming and scuba diving. Birders can't get enough of this small country with more bird bio-diversity per square kilometer than any other country in the world.

FOOD & DRINK

Ecuador is a seafood lover's dream. Tangy ceviche, shrimp the size of melon slices, tender stone crab and bountiful varieties of fish are all available at unbelievably low prices. Exotic fresh fruits are another Ecuadorian specialty. There are so many delicious and unique fruits that it will be hard to try them all during the course of your trip. Hand-squeezed juices are standard with every breakfast.

There are also some outstanding international restaurants in Ecuador. Offering unique décor, remarkable cuisine and excellent service, these world-class restaurants are a bargain for travelers with dollars.

ECUADOR'S REGIONS
Quito

We consider Quito to be the most beautiful capital city in all of Latin America. Folded between green pleats of rolling hills and the Pichincha volcano, the setting is spectacular. Terraced plots are decorative mosaics above the shiny metropolis. The whitewashed buildings and colonial masterpieces of Old Town give way to expansive parks and modern edifices as you move up the valley.

Intriguing museums, excellent hotels in all price categories and a wide array of dining options make it a city tailor made for the traveler. You can also enjoy superior shopping opportunities, unique colonial architecture and pleasurable excursions.

Northern Highlands

Dotted with lakes and volcanoes, the Northern Highlands offers quick access to a unique Amer-Indian cultures. The handsome Otavaleños, with luminous black braids and distinct clothing, will impress you with their regal manner.

Otavalo, the main city of the region, is home to an exotic market lineup that includes colorful fruits and vegetables, squealing piglets on leashes, bags full of guinea pigs and internationally acclaimed textiles. Hiking, horseback riding and biking opportunities abound.

The concentration of excellent hotels and haciendas in the Northern Highlands is unique in the country if not also the continent. Deciding where to stay may be one of the most difficult win-win decisions of your entire trip.

Central Highlands

The Central Highlands is also called the Avenue of the Volcanoes. Tall snow-covered mountains rise out of picturesque rolling hills. The perfectly conical Cotopaxi Volcano is the centerpiece of the popular **Cotopaxi National Park**. You can explore the park and its surroundings from one of a number of historic haciendas in the area.

Traditional Andean life still thrives in this part of the country. Colorful panchos and felt fedoras are more common than business suits even in province capitals like **Latacunga** and **Riobamba**. Unforgettable indigenous markets in towns like **Saquisilí** and **Pujilí** may inspire you to travel to more isolated high country locals where Quichua, not Spanish, is the lingua franca.

Ambato, a thriving commercial center, also offers interesting museums and spacious parks. It's just short drive from there to **Baños**, the city of lush greenery and waterfalls. Both Ecuadorian and foreign travelers flock to this popular destination.

Southern Highlands

Colonial **Cuenca** is the jewel of the Southern Highlands. With wonderfully maintained buildings, marvelous art, and cobblestone streets, Cuenca is a city to savor and enjoy. Surrounded by small artisan towns, this area also offers excellent shopping and day trips.

One of the most dramatic parks in the country, **El Cajas National Park**, is just a half-hour from the city. Stark buttes and hundreds of lakes offer endless opportunities for exploration. The country's largest Inca ruins, **Ingapirca**, offer a glimpse of that impressive civilization.

Further to the south **Podocarpus National Park** covers land ranging from high peaks to expansive plains and lush cloud forests. With hundreds of species of birds and orchids, it's well worth the trip.

Vilcabamba, the Valley of Longevity, is located just south of the park. This pleasant city is famous for its mild temperatures and easy-going way of life. With enjoyable hikes, moderately priced lodgings and inexpensive professional spa service, Vilcabamba is a hard place to leave.

Guayaquil & Southern Coast

Guayaquil, the country's largest city, is a sweltering port metropolis. Long the center of Ecuador's commercial and industrial growth, the city swaggers with a strangely attractive charisma. Some of the finest restaurants and museums in the country make a stopover here something to enjoy rather than avoid.

The **Santa Elena Peninsula**, specifically **Salinas**, is Guayaquil's oceanside playground. With tame, sparkling green water and a long sandy beach, Salinas fills with fun-seekers from the city on the weekends. High-rise condominiums and discos pulse with life at this coastal getaway.

Central Coast

The Central Coast is our favorite stretch of Ecuadorian beach. With verdant hillsides backing wide strips of white sand, this part of Ecuador sparkles in the sunshine. With excellent hotels in all price categories, there's something for everybody here. The section of coast around **Machalilla** National Park is especially attractive. Shimmering surf beckon as does the interesting natural history of **Isla de la Plata**.

Archeology buffs shouldn't miss **Chirije**, an eco-lodge in the middle of an important dig site. You can't help but trip over layers of the region's history here.

The seldom-visited area between **Canoa** and **Cojimíes** offers wide-open solitary beaches if you're willing to adjust to the lack of infrastructure. You have to time your visit with the tides as there are no roads here. Infrequent cars and buses just race along the edge of the sea.

Northern Coast & Lowlands

Crossing the Andes west to the coast, you pass through a number of different life zones. The subtropical cloud forests on the flanks of the mountains are one of the biological hot spots of the planet. Most commonly accessed from **Mindo**, this area houses a trove of unique bird and orchid species. An excellent range of lodging alternatives deservedly makes this a favorite excursion from Quito. The Northern Coast is the quickest beach access for Quiteños. **Atacames** rocks with partying Ecuadorians almost every weekend, but especially during the summer and holidays. **Same**, cleaner and prettier, offers the best lodging on this section of coast. For the truly unspoiled and unique, try the **Mompiche Lodge** on the **Muisne** peninsula. Accessed only by boat, your trip to the lodge will take you through silent mangrove swamps and across open ocean before you reach the isolated wide sandy beach.

Oriente

The jungles of Ecuador's Amazon basin are a vast expanse of intense and tangled tropical growth. Hundreds of species of birds, a variety of monkeys, amazingly disguised insects, surreal freshwater dolphins and other unique animals share this fascinating ecosystem reticulated with rivers, streams and lagoons.

Indigenous groups fight to maintain their traditional ways of life as they hurdle towards the 21st century. You can visit their homes and share *chicha*, fermented manioc, out of hand-carved bowls.

A stay in a jungle lodge is the best way to immerse yourself in the tropical rainforest experience. Comfortable lodging in pristine tracts of protected jungle offer fascinating activities coupled with excellent service.

Galápagos Islands

The Galápagos, thirteen large volcanic islands, four smaller ones and more than forty islets, are famous as a natural laboratory of geological and biological evolution. They're also beautiful. Black contours flow into dark lava beaches that lead to an emerald sea. Isolated swaths of powdery white sand stand in bold contrast to stark red landscapes.

It's the fearless denizens of the archipelago that make it such a compelling destination. Fat marine iguanas plop in piles on the rocks; sea lion pups clamber up to poke their noses at your toes; rays and eels slice through the water as you snorkel; giant land tortoises chew on juicy leaves; and blue-footed boobies perform their unforgettable mating dance.

You can choose among comfortable motorized yachts, sleek sailboats and commodious cruise ships to explore the wonders of the islands. Well-trained naturalists enrich your knowledge of the archipelago and help point out the natural wonders.

3. SUGGESTED ITINERARIES

Ecuador is so geographically diverse that your experience in the country will depend greatly on the regions you choose to visit. If you had time to hit each sector of the country you would find constant yet varied allure. More than likely you don't have that kind of enviable vacation schedule, so you are faced with narrowing down the destinations to those that will be most worthwhile for you.

What's the best way to go about doing that? Our strategy is to focus on the areas that are most strikingly unique, those that look the least like home. There are three regions of the country that have the most to offer travelers in this regard - the **Highlands**, **Oriente** and **Galápagos**.

In the Highlands you'll find fascinating indigenous societies, colorful market towns, outstanding crafts, spectacular scenery dotted with lakes and volcanoes, and the country's highest concentration of excellent hotels and haciendas. Activity options include long hikes, horseback rides, mountain biking trips, mountaineering, shopping outings and many chances to use those twenty rolls of film you brought.

There are three main traveler hubs in the Highlands. In the **Northern Highlands** you have the easily accessible **Otavalo** with world-class accommodations, excellent shopping and hikes galore. In the **Central Highlands** most people base themselves out of one of the wonderful haciendas near **Cotopaxi National Park**. Accessible in less than two hours from Quito, this area offers fascinating volcanoes and authentic markets in addition to excellent lodging. **Cuenca** is the heart of the **Southern Highlands**. This intriguing colonial city's highlights include interesting museums and wonderful restaurants. From here you can also visit Inca ruins and indigenous villages or trek through vast national parks.

The **Oriente** is a thriving tangle of tropical growth best experienced in isolated jungle lodges. Hundreds of species of colorful birds fly overhead, poison dart frogs hide at your feet and occasional monkeys chatter in warning at your approach. Dugout canoes transport you from point to point in this land where roads and cars do not belong. You can easily spend from three to six nights in this enchanting environment.

The **Galápagos** Islands are simply one of the most engaging ecosystems in the world. Famous for their geological and biological evolution, these starkly beautiful islands and their inhabitants are a highlight of any trip to Ecuador. Whether you're snorkeling nose to mask with a sea lion pup, snapping photos of a blue footed booby, or trying not to step on the unconcerned marine iguanas, you'll find yourself constantly amazed and bewitched with the wildlife on these hunks of lava. Your boat options cover the range from luxurious cruise ships to intimate yachts.

There's another factor to consider, however, when creating your itinerary and that is time. You need at least six days in the country to fit in a worthwhile visit to the Oriente and seven days is the minimum for a tour to the Galápagos Islands.

We offer itineraries below for five, seven, ten and fourteen days. If you have more time you might want to combine itineraries or focus more on a certain part of the country. If you're interesting in digging into a region, we highlight our favorite destinations at the beginning of each chapter.

FIVE-DAY ITINERARIES

Most international flights arrive to Quito in the evening or night and depart in the morning, stealing some of your precious vacation time. A five-day itinerary really only offers three days of exploring.

Northern & Central Highlands
Day 1
• Arrive Quito in the evening
• Dinner at one of the recommended Ecuadorian restaurants

Day 2
• Explore Old Town Quito (See *A Nice Day in Old Town* sidebar in Quito chapter)
• Dinner at one of the recommend international restaurants or drive to Northern or Central Highlands

Day 3
• Drive to Northern or Central Highlands if didn't do it the evening before
• Visit market or craft villages
• Overnight Highlands

Day 4
• Go on hike, horseback ride or mountain bike ride
• Return to Quito

• Visit Central Bank Museum or Mitad del Mundo
• Dinner at one of the recommended restaurants
• Overnight Quito

Day 5
• Leave Quito in morning

Southern Highlands
Day 1
• Arrive Quito in the evening
• Dinner at one of the recommended Ecuadorian restaurants

Day 2
• Fly to Cuenca
• Explore Colonial Cuenca (See the Colonial Walking Tour)
• Overnight Cuenca

Day 3
• Trip to El Cajas National Park; market villages or Ingapirca
• Overnight Cuenca

Day 4
• Visit Cuenca museums
• Return to Quito in evening
• Dinner at one of the recommended restaurants
• Overnight Quito

Day 5
• Leave Quito

SEVEN-DAY ITINERARIES

A seven-day trip to Ecuador gives you enough time to get into the jungle and explore Quito. If you take one of the larger ships that offer four-night cruises, the Galápagos is also an option. Alternatively, you could just extend one of the five-day itineraries to get a better feel for the Highlands.

Oriente
Day 1
• Arrive Quito in the evening
• Dinner at one of the recommended Ecuadorian restaurants

Day 2
• Explore Old Town Quito (See *A Nice Day in Old Town* sidebar in Quito
    chapter)
• Dinner at one of the recommend international restaurants

Day 3
• Fly to jungle lodge
• Overnight jungle lodge

Day 4
• Overnight jungle lodge

Day 5
• Overnight jungle lodge

Day 6
• Return to Quito
• Visit Central Bank Museum or Mitad del Mundo
• Dinner at one of the recommended restaurants
• Overnight Quito

Day 7
• Leave Quito in morning

Galápagos
Day 1
• Arrive Quito in the evening
• Dinner at one of the recommended Ecuadorian restaurants

Day 2
• Fly to Galápagos
• Overnight cruise ship

Day 3
• Overnight cruise ship

Day 4
• Overnight cruise ship

Day 5
• Overnight cruise ship

Day 6
• Return to Quito
• Visit Central Bank Museum, Old Town or Mitad del Mundo
• Dinner at one of the recommended restaurants
• Overnight Quito

Day 7
• Leave Quito in morning

TEN-DAY ITINERARIES

With ten days in Ecuador you can combine a Highlands visit with either the Oriente or the four-night Galápagos trip. This length stay also gives you the alternatives of taking one of the smaller boats on a longer cruise in the Galápagos; combining a 4-night cruise with a land-based stay in the Galápagos; or staying longer in the jungle.

Oriente & Highlands
Day 1
• Arrive Quito in the evening
• Dinner at one of the recommended Ecuadorian restaurants

Day 2
• Fly to jungle lodge
• Overnight jungle lodge

Day 3
• Overnight jungle lodge

Day 4
• Overnight jungle lodge

Day 5
• Return to Quito
• Dinner in Quito

Day 6
• Explore Highlands (See *Five-Day Itineraries*)
• Overnight Highlands

Day 7
• Explore Highlands
• Overnight Highlands

Day 8
• Explore Highlands
• Overnight Highlands

Day 9
• Return to Quito in morning to visit Old Town, the Central Bank Museum or Mitad del Mundo
• Dinner at one of the recommended restaurants
• Overnight Quito

Day 10
• Leave Quito in morning

Galápagos & Highlands
Day 1
• Arrive Quito in the evening
• Dinner at one of the recommended Ecuadorian restaurants

Day 2
• Fly to Galápagos
• Overnight cruise ship

Day 3
• Overnight cruise ship

Day 4
• Overnight cruise ship

Day 5
• Overnight cruise ship

Day 6
• Return to Quito
• Dinner in Quito or drive to Northern or Central Highlands

Day 7
• Explore Highlands (See *Five-Day Itineraries*)
• Overnight Highlands

Day 8
• Explore Highlands
• Overnight Highlands

Day 9
• Return to Quito
• Visit Central Bank Museum, Old Town or Mitad del Mundo
• Dinner at one of the recommended restaurants
• Overnight Quito

Day 10
• Leave Quito in morning

Galápagos in Yacht or Sailboat
Day 1
• Arrive Quito in the evening
• Dinner at one of the recommended Ecuadorian restaurants

Day 2
• Fly to Galápagos
• Overnight on boat

Day 3
• Overnight on boat

Day 4
• Overnight on boat

Day 5
• Overnight on boat

Day 6
• Overnight on boat

Day 7
• Overnight on boat

Day 8
• Overnight on boat

Day 9
• Return to Quito
• Visit Central Bank Museum, Old Town or Mitad del Mundo
• Dinner at one of the recommended restaurants
• Overnight Quito

Day 10
• Leave Quito in morning

14-DAY ITINERARIES

With a 14-day Itinerary you can extend stays on the 10-day itineraries or try to see a bit of the entire country. If you are going to do both, we recommend that you program your visit to the jungle to precede your trip to the Galápagos. That way you won't get spoiled by the exhibitionist animals of the islands before spending time spotting the more elusive jungle fauna.

Oriente, Galápagos and Highlands
Day 1
• Arrive Quito in the evening
• Dinner at one of the recommended Ecuadorian restaurants

Day 2
• Fly to jungle lodge
• Overnight jungle lodge

Day 3
• Overnight jungle lodge

Day 4
• Overnight jungle lodge

Day 5
• Return to Quito
• Drive to Highlands
• Overnight Highlands

Day 6
• Explore Highlands (See *Five-Day Itineraries*)
• Overnight Highlands

Day 7
• Explore Highlands
• Overnight Highlands

Day 8
• Return to Quito
• Visit Central Bank Museum, Old Town or Mitad del Mundo

- Dinner at one of the recommended restaurants
- Overnight Quito

Day 9
- Fly to Galápagos
- Overnight cruise ship

Day 10
- Overnight cruise ship

Day 11
- Overnight cruise ship

Day 12
- Overnight cruise ship

Day 13
- Return to Quito
- Dinner at one of the recommended restaurants
- Overnight Quito

Day 14
- Leave Quito in the morning

4. LAND & PEOPLE

LAND
Nature has taken the finest of what South America has to offer, hewn it into slabs and laid them in strips down Ecuador's tiny territory. Fit together like Inca masonry, these distinct geographical zones are the keys to the country's fabulous natural and cultural diversity. Ecuador's geological design includes a corridor of snow-capped volcanoes in the **Highlands**, dense tropical rainforest in the **Oriente**, miles of arid, then lush beaches along the **Coast**, and the volcanic islands of the **Galápagos**.

Ecuador, with an area of 283,000 square kilometers, is smaller than the state of Arizona. It is located in the northwestern part of South America. Bounded by the Pacific Ocean to the west, it shares borders with Colombia to the north and Peru to the south and east. The country is somewhat heart-shaped, with the wide band of the Andes running down the middle to separate the western portion, the coast, from the slightly larger eastern portion, the jungle. The equator, the nation's namesake, runs right across the upper third of the country.

The Highlands
The Highlands, or Sierra, is composed of lofty volcanoes and high altitude valleys. The mountains in Ecuador are part of the Andes system that rambles the entire length of the continent, from Tierra del Fuego to the Caribbean. Ecuador's portion of the Andes is composed of a set of parallel mountain chains that run down the country like a double spine. The *Cordillera Occidental*, or **Western Chain**, is generally the higher and wider of the two, boasting seven peaks over 4,500 meters. The **Eastern Chain**, the *Cordillera Oriental*, is older, and in most cases a bit shorter. The exception is **Chimborazo**, the highest mountain in the country at 6310 meters, being part of this Eastern Chain.

Both chains bulge with volcanoes. Perfectly shaped **Cotopaxi**, at 5900 meters, is considered one of the highest active volcanoes in the world. Both **Pichincha**, near Quito, and **Tungarahua**, near Baños, have been quite active in recent years. The volcanoes have expelled plumes of ash, but have not produced lava flow.

Transversal mountain chains cut the intervening valley into a series of ten basins. Over half of Ecuador's population lives in these basins known as *hoyas*. Potatoes, corn, beans, wheat, barley, and tea are grown in plots that climb the mountainsides to seemingly precarious heights.

With temperatures hovering around 60 degrees year round, the highlands are blessed with an eternal spring. Due to the thin air and exposure to vertical sunlight, however, daily variations in temperature can be extreme with hot days and cold nights. The rainy season lasts from October to May with most of the precipitation occurring in April. Average temperatures and rainfall drop as you move up from the low altitude subtropical level to the higher altitude temperate level where Quito and most other towns are located.

The **páramo** is a life zone found at higher altitudes. Dwarfed vegetation makes up an elfin woodland of spongy herbs, dry grasses, and a miniature, palm-like *fraileon* trees. Some elusive animals such as pumas frequent this area, but you are more likely to see condors and caracaras.

Cloud forests such as those that surround Mindo and Baeza are cloaked in a perpetual mist. Normally found as you descend the highlands, the trees here are loaded with mosses, orchids, ferns, and other epiphytes. The zone supports an extraordinary array of bird life.

THE CONTINENTAL SPINE

*The **Andes**, unlike the Himalayas, is not a single line of peaks, but rather a series of parallel and transverse mountain chains. The name Andes is believed to come from the indigenous Aymara word **anta**, which means copper colored.*

The Coast

Much of the coastal area near Guayaquil consists of an **alluvial plain** that begins at the western edge of the Andes and spreads forth to the Pacific. Three small mountain ranges are included in this territory, but none of them have peaks higher than 850 meters.

The fertile soil and warm climate ideally suit the region for production of bananas, palm, and cacao, which together make a significant contribution to the national economy. The marine areas south of Guayaquil provide appropriate conditions for shellfish production. Over 300,000 acres of shrimp farms make the crustacean one of the Ecuador's most important exports. The ecological cost, however, has been almost complete destruction of the mangrove forests in the area.

Ecuador's most popular beaches begin with the Santa Elena Peninsula almost due west of Guayaquil. This arid portion of the coast gives way to lush tropical hillsides and sandy white beaches about 100 km to the north. Fruits of the sea are abundant – oysters, shrimp, crabs, clams, and many varieties of fish support the numerous fishing villages along the coastline.

The coastal climate is influenced by the proximity to warm or cool ocean currents. The average temperature is 72 degrees. The rainy season that lasts from December to May is actually when you see the most sunshine because showers arrive in the afternoon. During the rest of the year, the weather is generally gray. Heavy rainfall occurs every six years or so due to El Niño conditions.

The Oriente

The Amazon River basin of the Oriente, which covers nearly half of Ecuador's territory, is endowed with a dense, biologically diverse **Neotropical rainforest**. Hundreds of tributaries flowing from the Andes merge to form three principal rivers – the **Aguarico**, the **Napo**, and the **Pastaza**, all of which eventually drain into the Amazon. A temperature of 77 degrees and 12 inches of rain per month is consistent year round. This is the perfect nurturing climate for life to flourish.

The Amazon ecosystem is considered to be one of the richest and most complex communities of plant and animal life in the world. Highly diverse flora and fauna characterize the region with extraordinary variations in their habitats and microhabitats.

The fertility of the tropical rainforest is primarily tied up in the trees rather than the surprisingly nutrient poor soil. Over 100 species of trees per acre have been recorded here, twice as many as in Central American rainforests, and five times as many as in the temperate forests of North America. Much of the plant life grows as epiphytes on branches and in nooks of the trees. About 1,500 species of birds live in a variety of forest habitats, lagoons, and open areas.

BUILD A BIGGER ARK

Attesting to the diversity of Ecuador's tropical rainforest is the staggering number of species that have been identified ... so far.

320 species of mammals
720 species of amphibians and reptiles
800 species of freshwater fish
1,500 species of birds

The majority of Ecuador's 1.6 million barrels of oil reserves is located in the Oriente. Exploitation of this resource is a highly charged issue due to the environmental damage that has occurred with repeated negligence. Additionally the development attracts colonists who clear-cut the rainforest to plant crops, which quickly exhaust the few nutrients in the soil.

Galápagos Islands

The Galápagos Archipelago, lying 1,000 kilometers west of Ecuador, consists of 13 principal islands, four smaller ones, and over 40 islets. These islands, among the most pristine areas left on the planet, are spread out over 300 kilometers in each direction. Created by a series of volcanoes, which are still quite active, the islands are rectilinear in formation.

The climate on the Galápagos is exceptionally dry for the tropics with distinct hot and cool seasons. Most years are very dry with wet years associated with moderate to major El Niño events. Gray skies are the norm during the *garua* season. The climate varies according to the altitude which is the also the major influencing factor of vegetation. While most of the lower altitudes are arid, the higher elevations are covered in cloud forest.

Galápagos plants and animals differ from mainland species due to millions of years of isolation. Wildlife includes giant tortoises, iguanas, and some famous birds such blue-footed boobies and Darwin's finches. The islands are also the home to the only penguin species that lives north of the equator. Other marine life includes sea turtles, sea lions, and fur seals. A variety of whales, dolphins, rays, and sharks inhabit the seas around the islands.

There are three major life zones, each with distinct plant life. The coastal zones on the shoreline host hardy, salt resistant plants such as mangroves. Several varieties of cacti grow in the extensive, desert-like arid zone. In the highest elevations of the biggest islands is the humid zone, which is kept moist by a cloud cover known as *garua*. Evergreen *scalesia* forests as well as several species of ferns, moss, and lichens make up the lush vegetation.

PEOPLE

Whether it's the courtly restaurant owner in Quito – the tacit, proud Otavalan couple in the Northern Highlands – the laid back hotel worker on the coast – the nimble-fingered Panama hat maker near Cuenca – the sharp-sighted native guide in the Oriente – or the gregarious, joking shopkeeper in Guayaquil, each of your interactions with Ecuadorians will weave the quilt that becomes your image of the country.

For a country so small, Ecuador enjoys startling ethnic diversity. There are more than thirteen indigenous peoples who share the land with Afro-Ecuadorians, Caucasians, and mestizos. It's precisely this cultural cornucopia that makes the country so interesting to visit. You will be exposed to a stimulating variety of customs, clothing, language, art and food.

With 12.3 million people, Ecuador is one of the most densely populated countries in South America. While in times past the vast majority lived in the Highlands, now the population is divided almost evenly between the Coast and the Highlands, with just a small percentage calling the jungles of the Oriente home.

ETHNIC COMPOSITION
Caucasians
Caucasians of European descent make up roughly 10% of the population. Based on a hierarchical social structure that can be traced to colonial times, most of the power and wealth of the country is concentrated in their hands. Exclusionary social arrangements (see *Social Classes* below) have perpetuated this system.

Mestizos
Fifty-five percent of the population is mestizo, of mixed Amerindian and Spanish blood. The roots of the Ecuadorian mestizo go back 500 years. Spain, wanting to protect its vast territorial holdings, sent large numbers of soldiers to the New World. They didn't, however, send any women. From the offspring of the conquistadors and Amerindian women grew what is now the heart of the Ecuadorian population.

Mestizo farmers along the coast are called *Montubios*. In the Southern Highlands around Cuenca, the mestizo artisans throughout the province are known as *cholos*. It's important to note that in other parts of the country the word *cholo* is often used disparagingly, but in Cuenca it is generally an affectionate term.

Afro-Ecuadorians
People of Afro-Ecuadorian descent comprise 10% of the country's inhabitants. There are two main population centers of Ecuadorian blacks. Along the north coast near **Esmeraldas**, they make up the majority of the people in the province. One of the chroniclers of the Spanish conquest, Cabello de Balboa, attributes their arrival in Ecuador to a 16th century shipwreck in which 23 African slaves managed to make it to shore and establish a settlement. Strains of this African heritage can be heard in the local music and tasted in the regional dining specialties.

The other center is in the middle of the Northern Highlands in the balmy **Chota Valley**. Their ancestors were brought to Ecuador as slaves to work the local sugar cane plantations.

INDIGENOUS GROUPS
Highlands

Today roughly 25% of Ecuadorian citizens are classified as indigenous. By far the largest indigenous group is formed of Quichua-speaking Highland Indians who identify themselves as *Runa*, The People. These Amer-Indians have had centuries of contact with Ecuadorian society, yet still maintain a distinct language and culture. Today many of them speak Spanish as well as Quichua.

These Quichua speakers can be divided into many subgroups. Each has a slightly distinct way of dressing, celebrating and making a living:

The **Imbabura** groups are found in **Otavalo** and the surrounding countryside. These people are known for their excellent woolen textiles and business acumen. The men wear a single, long braid down their backs, white pants and colorful panchos. The women wear embroidered shirts, dark skirts and rows of golden beads around their necks.

Tungarahua groups like the **Salasacas** and **Chibuleos** are mostly farmers. The Chibuleos are famous for growing garlic and onions. The Salasacas, also excellent weavers, can be recognized by their belts. The women wear several belts that when unwound measure over 20 meters long.

The Southern Highlands around Chimborazo has the largest percentage of indigenous people in the country. They live high in the mountains in ancient communities working the barren land. Each group is distinguished by the color of the women's dresses and the men's panchos.

Further south, the **Cañaris** live in the *páramo* zones cultivating cereals. Their embroidered belts are famous around the world. Close to Loja and the Peruvian border you can find the **Saraguro** Indians. Dedicated mainly to dairy farming, the Saraguros wear wide-brimmed white hats and black clothing.

Coast

The western lowland groups have mostly been assimilated into the mestizo culture. There are a few people of **Colorado** descent near Santo Domingo, but most share the lifestyle of the mestizos. The only ones with their hair dyed into the traditional red *achiote* paste helmet are those in the central plaza trying to earn a few bucks from tourists taking photos.

Oriente
The different indigenous groups of the Oriente had little contact with outsiders until the 1950s. Relying on migration to resolve conflicts and limit their impact on hunting grounds, they traditionally moved in small groups throughout the jungle.

In the 1950s the government started to build roads into the region to encourage settlement from the Highlands. Then, in the late 60s, substantial oil reserves were discovered in the zone, bringing in more people as well as ecological damage. The missionaries moved many of the groups to settlements and taught them to be ashamed of their traditional ways of life.

The Oriente indigenous people have suffered greatly from the damage done to their forests and cultures from colonists, oil companies and missionaries. Many of them have been forced to jump from the Stone Age to the 21st century in a matter of three decades. The repercussions of this shift have been devastating.

Land ownership and use are difficult subjects to tackle, because each faction involved has a legitimate demand for the resources of the Oriente. Ecuador is a poor country that desperately needs hard currency. Oil is, and will continue to be, the government's largest source of revenue. The settlers, coming from the over-crowded Highlands, also stake a claim to their right to try to scratch out an honest living. The indigenous groups, after living in the jungle for hundreds of years, have what many consider the most legitimate right to the land. The problem is that the indigenous groups were, and continue to be, disadvantaged in any conflicts because they have little knowledge of how to organize and work within the national bureaucracy.

The different groups of the Amazon are quite distinct, most having lived either in complete isolation from or at war with one another.

The **Cofans** live in the north along the Aguarico River. Most of them have been assimilated into Ecuadorian society through contact with oil companies, missionaries and mestizo groups, but a few remain in enclaves along the river in the Cuyobeno Reserve. Also found in the northern most reaches of the Cuyobeno Reserve are the **Siona-Secoya**.

Along the Napo and Pastaza Rivers are the **Jungle Quichuas**, related to the large group of Highland Quichuas. Separated from their Highland ancestors and living in a completely distinct environment, their culture and language have developed along unique lines.

Between the Napo and Curaray Rivers are the fiercely independent **Huaorani**. For years they managed to defend their territory from the intrusion of missionaries, settlers and oil companies. Known as terrific warriors, they continue to fight, now through political channels, for their autonomy.

The **Shuar**, established along the Upano and Zamora river valleys are the most numerous Amazonian indigenous group. They share many traditions and customs with the **Achuar** who live along the Pastaza River.

Social Classes

It is difficult for Americans and Europeans to comprehend the extent of the rigid social hierarchy present in Ecuador. Traditions of social interaction that are hundreds of years old continue to determine people's behavior in the present. This highly stratified society is divided between the elite, the middle class, the workers and the rural laborers. Money is not the only or even the most important factor when determining social class. Individuals fall into their respective categories on the basis of race, wealth and education.

The **elite** is comprised of financiers, industrialists, Highland land-owners and Coastal agro-exporters. This small group manages a stagger-ing 60% of the country's wealth. The **middle class** is the most diverse group, making up roughly 20% of the population. They are the businesspeople, professionals, government employees and army officers. The middle class can be divided into the upper and lower segments. The upper tends to identify with and emulate the elite while the lower finds more in common with the well-off members of the working class.

The **workers** are the fastest growing class. Originally linked to the artisans of colonial society, they are now largely comprised of immigrants to the cities from the countryside. Peddlers, craftsmen, artisans and unskilled wage laborers all fall into this class. Many live below the poverty line. The **rural laborers** are a large group with little political or economic power. They live in the countryside and are tied to the land. Access to farmable holdings assures their subsistence and defines their status within their community. The Elite control all the best tracts in the country, leaving the Rural Laborers to toil on the marginal plots. These plots often cannot support the family, forcing many of them to seek wage labor on the elite's farms or immigrate to the cities.

Then there are some people who don't even really enter into the system. Oriente indigenous groups live without much interaction with mainstream Ecuadorian society.

Regional Differences

Regional differences are another rift in Ecuadorian society, primarily between the people of the Coast and those of the Highlands. With differences in outlook, history and economies, both groups consider themselves superior to the other. This split is especially apparent among the elite.

Ecuador is unusual in Latin America in that there are two large population centers – Quito and Guayaquil. Both have contributed to the growth of the country, but each sees its contribution as more important than the other's. Guayaquil, the country's largest city with 1.8 million inhabitants, is the major port and commercial center. The majority of the country's export commodities are grown in the surrounding area. Quito, in the Highlands, is home to 1.2 million people. It is the country's capital and historical center as well as the site of its premier universities. The people from Quito characterize the people from Guayaquil as nouveau riche, money-grubbing liberals. The Quiteños in turn have reputations as conservative, uptight bureaucrats that spend all the country's tax money in the capital.

Language
The official language of Ecuador is Spanish, but there are other languages used throughout the nation. The native tongue of many Highlands as well as some Oriente Indians is Quichua, a form of the Quechua brought to Ecuador by Inca expansion. You also have A'ingaie-speaking Cofans, Paicoca-speaking Siona-Secoyas, Huao-speaking Huaoranis and Achuar-speaking Achuars.

Education
Formal education is divided into four stages. The first of these, two years of preprimary school, starts at age four. The next six-year stage, primary school, begins at age six. After that, secondary school is divided between a three-year general curriculum cycle and then a three-year specialization cycle. University study follows.

In theory, education is compulsory from ages six through fourteen. The reality is that economic pressures can be stronger than government laws, but most children attend at least primary school. Rapid population growth has put pressure on the education infrastructure, leaving some districts with under-qualified teachers in under-funded schools.

The general literacy rate, defined as those over the age of 15 that can read and write, is 90%. This government-provided statistic is considered high by many.

Government
Governing Ecuador is no easy task. There were 86 governments and 17 constitutions in the country's first 160 years of existence. Jose Maria Velasco Ibarra, elected president five times, stayed in office for his entire term only once.

The democratic government is composed of the executive, congressional and judicial branches. The president, elected for a four-year term, may not run for re-election. There are two classes of deputies, national and provincial, in the unicameral congress. Congress appoints judges. Bitter division between the executive and congressional branches has been the norm since Independence.

Due to Ecuador's history of *personalismo*, political parties have not developed as strong institutions. Voters are much more inclined to cast ballots for a candidate based on the office seeker's personality rather than his political party's platform.

The country is divided administratively into 22 provinces.

PROVINCES & THEIR CAPITALS

Azuay – Cuenca
Bolívar – Guaranda
Cañar – Azogues
Carchi – Tulcán
Chimborazo – Riobamba
Cotopaxi – Latacunga
El Oro – Machala
Esmeraldas – Esmeraldas
Galápagos – Puerto Baquerizo Moreno
Guayas – Guayaquil
Imbabura – Ibarra
Loja – Loja
Los Ríos – Babahoyo
Manabí – Portoviejo
Morona-Santiago – Macas
Napo – Tena
Pastaza – Puyo
Pichincha – Quito
Orellana – Coca
Sucumbios – Nueva Loja
Tungurahua – Ambato
Zamora-Chinchipe – Zamora

Religion

The Roman Catholic Church has played a central role in Ecuador's history from the time of the conquest. The conquistadors came not only in the name of the crown, but also the church. Until the 20th century you had to be Catholic to be a citizen of the country.

The Catholicism practiced by many is more of a folk Catholicism, combining indigenous beliefs with Catholic worship. With 95% of the country Catholic, many holidays commemorate important religious dates. Carnival is a time of crazy celebration, especially along the coast. In the Highlands it is certain saint's days that are the most important events. Evangelical and Pentecostal practices have recently made inroads in converting believers.

Family Life
The family is far and away the strongest and most esteemed social institution in the country. A typical household generally consists of the nuclear family as well as any number of people from a wider circle of kin. It is through this wide circle of kin, rather than any government programs, that most people receive assistance and support.

While there is always an obligation and responsibility towards blood relatives, a person's support circle is made even wider through the godparent, *compadrazgo*, relationship. Godparents are chosen for baptisms, confirmation, and weddings, cementing relationships and creating opportunities for assistance and advancement.

Ecuador is still a largely patriarchal society, even in many homes where the wife holds down a professional job. In general, although the man is the head of the household, he takes no part in the day-to-day functioning of the family. As long as things run smoothly, the home is the woman's domain.

Children traditionally live with their parents until marriage or even beyond. If they end up studying in another city, there is generally a cousin or *compadre* with whom they can live.

THE ARTS
Painting
Ecuador's art history, especially Quito's, commands great respect in Latin America. From the colonial period to the present day, Ecuadorian artists have achieved far-reaching fame for the quality and originality of their works.

During the colonial period a concentration of fine artists in the country's capital produced a body of work known as the Quito School of art. The paintings are greatly influenced by Spanish and Italian masters, but depict religious scenes grounded in the everyday life the artists knew. Paintings include images of Amerindian-faced disciples sitting down to a Last Supper of *chicha* and guinea pig.

Look for the works of Quito's most famous painter of the 17th century, **Miguel de Santiago**, in Quito churches and museums. The other artists of the "glorious trinity" of colonial Ecuadorian painting are **Pedro Bedon** and **Nicolas de Goribar**.

DYING TO MODEL

Miguel de Santiago's personal quest was to paint the agony of Christ on the cross with true emotion and realism. Stories say that he worked with model after model, but none could produce the authentic expression of suffering he sought. Finally one day, in a fit of frustration, he grabbed a spear and ran it through the model in front of him. Legend has it that Santiago sat in front of the dying man and finally achieved the painting he'd been after. He then spent the rest of his life in an Augustinian convent as punishment for his crime.

This story is probably apocryphal, but the over-the-top drama is so Latin we just had to throw in it.

Sculpture

The Quito school also produced a number of great sculptors, the most noteworthy being Bernado Legarda and Caspicara. **Legarda**, born in the early 1700s, was a man of enormous talents. Sculptor, painter, tiler, gold leafer, furniture designer and miniaturist, he is best known today for his delicate sculptures. Legarda transformed the sculpting material into something transparent and esoteric. His figures are famous for their smooth polychromatic robes – sinuous folds – and nostalgic, lifelike, facial expressions. He best known work, the Virgin of Quito, can be found in the San Francisco Church in Quito. An enormous copy of this Virgin stands on a hill overlooking the city.

Maneul Chili, known as **Caspicara**, also worked during the 18th century. Born of indigenous parents, he rose to become a sculptor of singular talent. His nickname is thought to come from the Spanish words *caspi*, log, and *cara*, face, in reference to his course features. Caspicara's works, displaying consummate perfection, are noted for their joyful compositions and masterly execution. His pieces reveal great religious sentiment as well as elegant baroque tendencies.

Modern Art

Modern Ecuadorian art is grounded in everyday life. Most of it tends to project images of people and scenes from the region. Indigenous expressionism, in which indigenous people are almost always present, is the medium for some of Ecuador's most famous modern painters, including **Oswaldo Guayasamín**, **Eduardo Kingman**, and **Antonio Paredes**.

OSWALDO GUAYASAMÍN

Guayasamín, considered one of the greatest modern Lain American painters, made his mark depicting the social ills of Ecuador. His works showed the pain and suffering of all people, but mainly focused on the indigenous people of his country.

Guayasamín, a mestizo raised in poverty, started peddling landscape sketches on the streets of Quito at age ten. He got his big break when Nelson Rockefeller, Coordinator for Inter-American Affairs, happened to attend his first show in Quito. Rockefeller not only spent hours looking at the paintings, he also bought a number of them.

After Rockefeller returned to the US, Guayasamín received an invitation to tour America's great museums. He visited the US, studied mural painting with José Clemente Orozco in Mexico and then traveled for two years through Central and South America sketching indigenous and marginalized people.

His murals grace both the Congress and Presidential Palace in Quito. He died at age 79 in March, 1999. You can visit his home, which is also a museum, in Quito.

Architecture

Quito is one of the best-preserved colonial cities in the world. Old Town, now a UNESCO world heritage site, features more than a hundred churches, monasteries, convents and plazas that were built during the colonial period.

Some of Quito's churches stand out as especially important or beautiful. The **Cathedral of Quito**, started in 1562, is considered by some art historians to be the oldest in South America. The **San Francisco Monastery**, one of the first religious monuments in the Americas, is an excellent example of the continents' Early Renaissance. The baroque style of the **Compañía de Jesus Church**, considered one of the richest Jesuit temples in the world, is completely intermixed with native art.

Other important architectural sites in the country include the pre-Inca ramp mounds called *tolas*, of the Northern Highlands, and the Inca walls of **Ingapirca** near Cuenca.

Writing

The most famous novel to come out of Ecuador is **Jorge Icaza's** *Huasipungo*, written in 1934. Depicting the difficult life of the Highland Indians, *Huasipungo* was one of the first Latin American novels to focus on social concern and protest as opposed to the romantic view of indigenous life.

Realism and the difficult situation of indigenous people have been common themes in works by the country's authors ever since. Other notable contemporary writers include **Javier Vásconez** and **Jorge Enrique Adoum**. The most famous 19th century author is **Juan Montalvo**, whose political essays supposedly inspired a man to assassinate then-president Gabriel García Moreno.

ROAD READING

We recommend the following books to enrich your travels in Ecuador. Some of them are out of print or hard to find. The website ***www.bibliofind.com*** *is your best bet for tracking them down at fair prices.*

The All-Star List
The Villagers (Huasipungo), *Jorge Icaza – An excellent depiction of life as a Highlands Indian.*
Savages, *Joe Kane – A sometimes humorous, balanced account of the lives and difficulties facing the jungle's indigenous people.*
Tropical Nature, *Adrian Forsyth and Ken Miyata – An entertaining and easy to read book on the amazing biology of the Amazon Basin.*
My Father's Island, Johanna Angermeyer *– A beautifully crafted account of one girl's experiences on the Galápagos Islands.*

Other Good Reads
The Panama Hat Trail, *Tom Miller – An entertaining journey tracing the people and processes involved in creating a Panama Hat.*
Travels Amongst the Great Andes of the Equator, *Edward Whymper – A collector's item outlining Whymper's 1879 exploration of Ecuador including the first ascent of Chimborazo. The book also has maps and 138 incredibly beautiful illustrations.*
The Encantadas, *Herman Melville – Ten sketches about the Galápagos authored by a man who knows how to write about the ocean.*
Living Poor, *Moritz Thomsen – On honest account of the lives of Ecuador's poor as experienced by the author during his time in the Peace Corps.*

Music

Ecuador's music reflects the country's multiracial character, influenced by Andean strains, African rhythms and jungle melodies. Andean wind instruments and the African marimba are both important components of the country's musical quiver. The *bomba*, a drum from the Chota Valley near Colombia, can also be added to the mix.

Popular folk music includes the *pasillo* from the lowlands, as well as the *yumbo* and *sanjuanito* from the Highlands. Modern music is influenced by both Caribbean *salsa* sound as well as Colombian *cumbia*.

By far the most famous singer to come out of Ecuador is Guayaquil's **Julio Jaramillo** (1935-1978). Jaramillo's songs, mainly *boleros* and *pasillos*, focus on alcohol, women and music. These are songs that induce people to get drunk and cry over lost loves. Just about every bar in the country will have at least one of his passionate songs on their play-list. Jaramillo's birthday, October 1, is official Ecuadorian *Pasillo* Day.

MUSIC TO YOUR EARS

We consider compact disks one of the best souvenirs around. They are light, easy to carry, and the music reminds us of our trip each time we hear it. You might want to expand your collection with LPs from some of Ecuador's best artists:

Julio Jaramillo *(Pasillo, Bolero)*
Pueblo Nuevo *(Andean folkloric)*
Seta Mar *(Tropical)*
Tercer Mundo *(Rock)*
Tranzas *(Pop/Rock)*
Audi *(Pop)*
Sobre Peso *(Heavy Rock)*

Folk Art

Ecuador has an immensely rich variety of crafts and folk art. Carving and painting, strengths since colonial times, are no less popular today. Many times entire communities focus on one particular craft. By visiting their markets and stores, you can see a wide range of works in the one medium. See the *Shopping* chapter for more details.

5. A SHORT HISTORY

While the only consistency in Ecuador's past is inconsistency, there are three phenomena that have shaped the country through the years. The first of these is Ecuador's highly structured and hierarchical society. Since colonial times a small group of privileged elite has controlled the destiny of the destitute voiceless majority. That societal structure continues even today.

The second phenomenon, called *personalismo*, involves strong personalities leading the country instead of institutions. You will see in the following history that time after time the power and antics of one person have determined the course of the country.

The last phenomenon is economic, but has had lasting historical force, and that's the dependence of Ecuador on a single commodity. This commodity's price, be it for cocoa, bananas, or oil, has been completely subject to the world market, leaving Ecuador without the ability to shape its own destiny. There have been times of boom, but they have always been followed by times of bust.

PRE-COLONIAL ERA
3000 BC-1552 AD

Some of the oldest pottery shards in the New World, dating back to 3000 BC, have been found on coast north of Guayaquil. Left by the **Valdivia** culture, they have helped archeologist trace the development of the culture from nomadic hunters and gatherers to more sedentary fishers and farmers. Of later indigenous groups, the **Cañari**, **Cara**, and **Quitu** became the strongest tribes in the Ecuadorian territory. They went through periods of harmony and war with each other before being dominated by the famous **Incas** in the 15th century.

In the late 1400s the Inca Empire began to extend its rule northward from its capital in Cuzco, Peru. The Cañari, Cara, and Quitu were all eventually conquered. This time period marked the height of Inca domination in South America, with their territory stretching the length of the continent from Chile to Ecuador. The ruler during this time of expansion was a king named **Huayna Capac**. While Cuzco was the empire's official royal and administrative center, he liked Ecuador so much that he ultimately set up his home in Tomebamba near modern day Cuenca, and named Quito a satellite capital.

The Inca domination over Ecuador was short-lived, but its impact has lasted centuries. The most important contribution was that Quechua, the Inca tongue, became the lingua franca for all the various Ecuadorian tribes. When the Inca conquered an area it was not uncommon for large groups of them to move into the subjugated land. They would then instill Quechua as the official language of the region. The Inca's were in charge in Ecuador for less than 100 years, but Quichua, a form of Quechua, is still the prevalent indigenous language in Ecuador today.

When the mighty Huayna Capac died he left his kingdom split between two of his sons. The older son, **Huascar**, was the legitimate heir out of Cuzco. The other, **Atahualpa**, born in what is present day Ecuador, was said to be Huayna Capac's favorite son.

Huayna Capac may have had good intentions in dividing control of the country, but neither of the half brothers was accustomed to nor willing to share. This inability to divvy up territory led to civil war in 1532. Atahualpa, the love child, won.

At just about this same time **Francisco Pizarro**, the Spanish conquistador, arrived to the continent. The Incas, weak from war, weren't prepared to properly deal with the Spanish invasion. After making his way down to what is now Peru, Pizarro invited Atahualpa to the Spanish camp. Showing none of the hospitality for which Spaniards are famous, he captured the new Inca ruler and slaughtered thousands of Inca warriors. Pizarro eventually had Atahualpa killed, but not until he had ransomed the Inca king for a room-full of gold and two of silver.

Meanwhile, in Ecuador some of the pre-Inca states were happy to see the Spanish, as it meant that they could now rid themselves of the Inca yoke. A few of them even fought on the side of the conquistadors. Little did they know they were trading bad for horrendous.

While Pizarro headed south to loot Cuzco, his lieutenant, **Sebastian de Benalcázar**, moved north to take Quito. By the time he had taken the city in it was completely in ashes, however, as **Rumiñahui**, a fierce Inca leader, burned it down rather than leave it for his conquerors.

COLONIAL PERIOD
1553-1821

The Colonial Period in Ecuador lasted for nearly 300 years. The goal of the conquistadors in South America was to exploit the continent for Mother Spain. The Spanish originally hoped that Ecuador be the same pot of silver and gold that they found to the south in Peru and Bolivia. It was not. When they struck out there, they hoped the country would have stores of spices. It did not.

AMAZON WOMEN

Francisco Orellana was lieutenant to Gonzalo Pizarro on a 1541 expedition to explore the unknown territory east of Quito. The men suffered terribly in the unforgiving jungle terrain. After they ran out of provisions, Pizarro sent Orellana and 50 soldiers ahead to search for more supplies.

As Orellana sailed further and further down the Napo River, his men convinced him that it would be impossible to return upstream. Drifting down the Napo, they reached the Amazon in August 1542. From there they floated the entire length of the Amazon before sailing around to Trinidad and then on to Spain.

When he got to Spain, Orellana told tall tales of gold, cinnamon and combat with Indians led by fighting women. This comparison to the Amazons of Greek mythology gave the great river its name.

Orellana returned to the Amazon to make his fortune. It didn't go very well. He lost both ships and men on the trip back to America and then his own ship capsized near the mouth of the river. He drowned in the famous waterway he had named.

The Highlands

The richness of Ecuador would lie in the one commodity it did have - land. A select few men were granted property by the King of Spain, which led them to live like royalty on huge feudal estates in the Highlands. In addition to the land, these estate owners were also granted title to the people who lived on these thousands of acres. In exchange, they were obliged to defend the region, indoctrinate its native peoples and collect the crown's tribute from their charges. These indigenous "charges", *huasipungos*, became virtual slaves, working for the hacienda owner in both the fields and textile mills. A form of this hacienda system lasted well into the 20th century, while the basic distribution of land ownership remains unchanged even today.

The Coast

The Pacific coast was ignored when the Spanish first arrived because it was an unhealthy place to live. Malaria made it difficult for the Europeans to make any inroads. Eventually one city on the coast, Guayaquil, became a center of vigorous illegal trade between the New

World colonies. All goods for export were legally bound to go through Spain. This assured that the crown could dip its fingers into all transactions. Smugglers from Guayaquil found it convenient, and lucrative to by-pass that step in the process.

The people of the coast were developing a distinct culture and mindset from that of the Highlands. Whereas in the highlands social rules were extremely rigid, they were much more lax on the coast. A smaller population and equal access to opportunity (smuggling) meant that people intermingled more. There were also not as many indigenous groups along the coast to force into slavery, which meant everybody had to work.

The Oriente

The Oriente, the land east of the Andes, was completely overlooked during this period. Hostile Indians and unfavorable living conditions kept all but the holiest and heartiest of priests out of there. A few adventuring expeditions, like Orellana's, were led in the area, but most of them met unhappy fates.

FAMOUS FOREIGNERS/1

During the time of Spanish rule, very few outsiders visited Ecuador. Spain, hoping to keep a tight rule over her subjects, was leery of allowing people with new, liberal ideas onto the continent. Through much cajoling and persuasion, the French were finally allowed in 1736 to send a group of men, headed by **Charles Marie de la Condamine***, to perform experiments and surveys along the equator.*

The Geodesic Mission arrived with the task of measuring one degree of the arc of the meridian, the earth's circumference at the equator. From this measurement they could prove that the earth, like many middle-aged people, bulged around its middle. It was also from this figure that the length of a meter was determined.

In addition to its equatorial work, the group studied archeological ruins and surveyed and attempted to climb many of Ecuador's famous volcanoes.

The Galápagos

The Galápagos Islands were mainly used as a hideout for pirates during the colonial period. It wasn't until Charles Darwin visited there in 1835 and wrote about his findings that the islands achieved worldwide fame as a natural biological laboratory.

FAMOUS FOREIGNERS/II

Alexander Von Humbolt, a German naturalist and explorer, arrived to Quito 1802 on an adventure of scientific discovery. He spent over a year in the country studying the Andean flora, volcanoes and archeological antiquities. One of his most famous feats was his attempt on the summit of 6310-meter **Chimborazo**. *While he did not reach the top, he set a new altitude record at the time. He also investigated and climbed Pichincha, Cotopaxi and El Altar.*

INDEPENDENCE

1822

The elite born in Ecuador, *criollos*, began to resent the many privileges of those born in Spain, the *peninsulares*. The *criollos*, seeking their piece of the *empanada*, sent pleas for support to both the liberator of the northern half of South America, **Simón Bolívar**, and the southern freedom fighter **San Martín.** Both leaders were sympathetic to the *criollo* cause and sent soldiers to Ecuador. Bolívar's favorite aid, **Antonio Jose de Sucre**, was among the men sent to fight. Sucre won a key battle against the Spanish on a mountain slope near Quito, leading to Ecuadorian Independence. This conflict occurred on May 24, 1822 and it celebrated every year as the Battle of Pichincha.

It is important to note that independence did not mean the liberation of the indigenous population. All it meant was a shift in power from the *peninsulares* to the *criollos*, or, for the indigenous, a new *patrón*. The *criollos* did not fight to change the system, but rather to benefit from it. They did.

GRAN COLOMBIA

1822-1830

A few months after Independence, Bolívar and San Martín met in Guayaquil where Bolívar maneuvered to have Ecuador become part of Gran Colombia along with Venezuela and Colombia.

Regional rivalries within Gran Colombia led to Ecuador's secession in 1830. Sucre and a Venezuelan General **Juan Jose Flores** led the fighting for Ecuador's independence. In 1830 the successful Flores was named the first president of independent Ecuador.

FLORES VS. ROCAFUERTE

1830-1845

When visiting Ecuador today it will quickly become apparent that there is a rivalry between the Coast, represented by Guayaquil, and the

Highlands, represented by Quito. Flores and Rocafuerte, two of the strong personalities that shaped Ecuador, personify that rivalry.

At the time of independence Quito and Guayaquil, separated by the massive Andes, were even further apart ideologically than geographically. Quito was the home of the landed aristocracy where not much had changed since 1533. A handful of important families owned huge haciendas worked by servile indigenous people. Not surprisingly, this aristocracy was a conservative lot, allied with the church and resistant to any change. Their leader of choice was **Juan Jose Flores**.

Guayaquil, on the other hand, was a busy, international port. A few wealthy merchants controlled the politics and economy there. They favored free trade and 19th century liberalism. A few of them even had less than obsequious attitudes toward the church. These men felt like they worked to create the country's income while the dolts in the national government, located in Quito, kept the tax revenue in the Highlands. The men from Guayaquil stood behind the leadership of **Vicente Rocafuerte**.

Flores and Rocafuerte waged an epic, seesawing battle for power for the first 15 years of the nation's independence. They could be quite rational at times; once even agreeing to alternate in the presidency. Any agreements they made would never last for long however. After a few months they would soon be vying for political dominance once again.

GABRIEL GARCIA MORENO'S THEOCRACY
1860-1895

After the Flores/Rocafuerte years the Ecuador went through another 15-year period of weak leaders fighting for power but doing nothing for the country in the meantime. Ecuador was a fractured mess. Seventy-five percent of the population was Amer-Indian, many of whom did not speak Spanish. Debt from the Wars of Independence was draining the national coffers. Infrastructure and schools were practically non-existent. Political cleavages made cooperation between parties out of the question. The stage was set for a dictator. **Gabriel Garcia Moreno** happily obliged.

Garcia Moreno was not your typical despot. Having been raised with a strong religious upbringing and studied in France, he was considered moral and cultured. Garcia Moreno saw Catholicism as a way to unite the country and move it forward.

He replaced the existing constitution with a new one that declared men could not be citizens of the country if they were not members of the Catholic church. Education, welfare, and the direction of much government policy were turned over to the church. During Garcia Moreno's reign, the opposition was ruthlessly quelled, but he always believed he was working for the good of the nation.

In some ways he was. Roads, schools, model prisons and hospitals were built and a railway was begun to link Quito and Guayaquil. On the other hand, his authoritarian heavy-handedness grew old in a time when liberalism was sweeping across the world. Liberals both at home and abroad began to grumble. An intellectual from Ambato, **Juan Montalvo**, was one of Garcia Moreno's most vocal critics. Garcia Moreno's tenure was brought to a quick halt when he was assassinated (hacked to death with a machete) on the steps of the government palace. He is still seen as a national martyr by conservatives.

Ecuador abolished slavery in the middle of the 19th century, but this act had little affect on the lives of the indigenous people. Instead of being virtual slaves, *huasipungos*, they now fell under a contract-labor system, *concertaje*, that kept them in permanent debt.

The peasants owed a certain yearly amount of labor to the hacienda in exchange for a small plot of land. The tract was often on terrible soil, unfit for growing much of anything. Because they could not support themselves off their land, they had to borrow from the *patrón*. The debt, impossible to pay-off, was transferred from generation to generation, creating a population of indentured servants.

FAMOUS FOREIGNERS/III

*Edward Whymper, a British vulcanographer, found much to study during is time in Ecuador in 1879-1880. He is best known for being the first man to summit **Chimborazo**, the highest mountain in Ecuador, which he did with two Italians in January of 1880. Whymper made seven other first ascents during his time in the country.*

His account of the trip, Travel Amongst the Great Andes of Ecuador, is an excellent book about late 19th century Ecuador and the remarkable man who traveled it.

JOSE ELOY ALFARO
1897-1911

After Garcia Moreno's death Ecuador limped through a time of power struggles and practical anarchy. The Liberals, however, began to dominate as one of their golden boys, **Eloy Alfaro**, rose to power. He represented the coastal reaction to Garcia Moreno's conservatism. As the standard-bearer for the liberals he removed much of the structure of the theocracy, working to separate church and state. Freedom of religion was instituted and divorce became legal. Much of the church's property was confiscated. Not surprisingly, most of wound up in the hands of Liberal leaders.

While the frosting changed, the flavor of the cake remained the same. The positive programs that had been started by García Moreno, such as road building and railways, continued. The negatives ones did as well. The central government kept its authoritarian bent, there was no land reform, and the lives of indigenous Ecuadorians stayed on the same wretched track. Alfaro overstayed his welcome in office and after some fighting was sent to one of the model prisons that Garcia Moreno had built years before. It undoubtedly was not as model as it had been, but that became irrelevant when a mob broke in, dragging Alfaro through the street and then burning his body.

EARLY 20TH CENTURY TURBULENCE
1911-1948

A short boom during immediately after WWI was followed by a depression. The nation, dependent on cacao as its single export commodity, was devastated when the crop was infected with a fungus called witches broom. The conservatives, not ones to let the memory of García Moreno's martyrdom die, called it "God's retribution."

The depression and ensuing urban discontent were punctuated with public riots as well as massacres by the army, who took over the government.

While the rest of the world was going through modernization and changes, Ecuador remained mired in its colonial structure of despotism, feudal estates, and poor infrastructure. Ironically, the higher prices for raw materials caused by WWII led to temporary prosperity and subsequent peacefulness in Ecuador. Ecuador sided with the Allies but played little role in the war.

The forties, however, were ushered in with a private war between Ecuador and Peru. Ecuador, due to lack of people and resources, had never settled its huge holdings in the Amazon territory. In July of 1941, after diplomatic wrangling failed to solve the conflict, Peru invaded, taking over most of the area. Ecuador's army, ill prepared for battle, was easily defeated. Part of this was due to the fact that the president, distrustful of political opponents, kept the best fighting forces in Quito for his personal protection.

The major world powers were caught up in WWII and did not want to deal with skirmishes between two small South American countries. Nor, however, did they want to disrupt the flow of important raw materials from both Ecuador and Peru. They brought the parties to the table at a peace conference in Rio de Janeiro in 1942 and basically strong-armed Ecuador into giving up the territory. Ecuador has claimed since then that the Protocol of Rio was forced on them and therefore invalid.

Bringing up this disputed territory has been an excellent way for politicians to distract the people from internal failings ever since.

THE DISPUTED ORIENTE

Many lives have been lost and resources wasted on the part of both Ecuador and Peru trying to control the disputed land. As recently as August of 1998 there were engagements between troops in the area. Finally, on October 26, 1998 both sides signed a treaty for peace. Peru kept most of the region except for 250 symbolic acres successfully defended by Ecuadorian troops in the 90s. The good news for travelers is that the treaty calls for both the creation of adjoining national parks and the opening of official border crossing areas in the zone.

THE VELASCO ERA
1944-1972

The period after WWII was full of upheaval. Constitutional rule and free elections would turn to chaos and be followed by military government. The most outstanding personality of the era was **Jose Maria Velasco Ibarra**. Velasco has been called the Huey Long of Ecuador, but he actually falls short of that comparison as he failed to at least make any of Long's accomplishments. A terrible administrator and a bundle of contradictory policies, Velasco's single strong point was his personal magnetism. He was elected president five times but served out his entire term only once.

During his time in office he would capriciously change economic programs, fly out of control in temper tantrums and outbursts, suspend civil liberties and then be ushered out by the military. When the military eventually bungled things, Velasco would step back into the picture, make all types of promises, mesmerize the electorate, and find himself back in office. He began to call himself *The National Personification*.

One of his more interesting quotes: "Ecuador is a very difficult country to govern."

Many contend that Velasco's continual presence in Ecuadorian politics retarded the country's political development and social and economic advancement. The power of his personality crossed party lines and made policy irrelevant. Any advances made by intervening governments were reversed by Velasco's time in office.

In 1961, during Velasco's 4th term, he literally fought with congress, including a gun battle in the chamber. No one was hurt, but the military stepped in and replaced Velasco with his constitutional successor. After a few years the military took over again, stepping down in 1966 when Velasco won his record 5th term.

MILITARY RULE

1972-1979

After major mismanagement on Velasco's part, the military stepped in again in 1972 and stayed in power for another seven years. The military government had the fortuitous timing to step into office during the world oil crisis in the seventies. Ecuador had oil, lots of it. Money came in hand over fist. Unfortunately, the country was ill equipped to handle the windfall.

While there were some infrastructure improvements and the middle class grew, inflation roared and debt mounted. The military government borrowed heavily against future oil earnings. As had been the case with cocoa and bananas, the price of oil eventually began to drop. At the same time, oil reserves proved to be much smaller than originally estimated. Simply servicing the interest payments on the government loans began to eat up much of the country's earnings. This is a legacy the country is struggling with today.

The military's time in office had little lasting positive effect. As had been the case every time there were changes in governments, the basic structure of the society stayed the same. The poor, enduring high prices under inflation, simply continued to suffer.

CHAOS IN THE '80s & '90s

The recent decades have been a period of economic hard times and presidents at odds with congress. Neither has led to much improvement in the status quo.

The end of the petroleum boom coupled with large debt has led to major financial crises. Two visits from El Niño in the last 15 years have exacerbated the situation, causing flooding, loss of life and significant infrastructure damage.

The last twenty years have been characterized by ugly conflicts between the executive and legislative branches. Outrageous political moves are standard and physical fighting in congress is not unheard of. The list of outlandish political events is a long one. One president, **Febres Cordero**, was taken hostage by the airforce until the government released a jailed airforce officer who had earlier tried to overthrow the presidency. For his troubles, a faction of the congress then tried to impeach the president for "allowing himself to be kidnapped."

Another president, **Abdalá Bucarám**, was known as *El Loco*, The Crazy One. Elected in 1996 he lasted all of six months before being voted out of office by congress due to "mental incapacity." In that time he had stolen from the state coffers, appointed his family members to a myriad of important positions and recorded a very bad CD.

In 1998, Jamil Mahuad, former mayor of Quito, won the national presidential election by less than 5%. His time in office has not been easy. He spent the first few months dealing with strikes and other backlash from austerity measures intended to get the economy back on track. The economy didn't recover, in fact it only got worse. Banks failed, worldwide oil prices fell and the *sucre* devalued by 100%. In August 1999 Ecuador became the first country to default on its Brady Bonds, causing the *sucre* to slide further. Un- and underemployment have reached record levels as there's just no work in these slow economic times.

LEAVING IN SEARCH OF A BETTER FUTURE

The migratory phenomenon that Ecuador is undergoing now has no precedent. In the southern provinces of Azuay and Cañar, an incredible one in four adults is working outside of the country. People are leaving in droves, searching for opportunities that just can't be found in Ecuador. The Unites States, Spain, Holland and Italy have large and growing numbers of Ecuadorian immigrants, both legal and illegal.

While it's common for men to leave, searching out positions as manual day laborers, they are not alone. Many times it's the woman of the family who strikes out to earn a better living, especially to Italy, finding a position as a maid or nanny.

Professionals, suffering from underemployment, are not immune to the promises of a brighter future either. Systems experts can often find employment in the United States, and for doctors it's Chile that offers better and higher paying jobs than they can find at home.

2000 & BEYOND

Politically and economically Ecuador is stuck in a familiar rut. The economy is in disarray and is precariously dependent on unstable world prices for oil and bananas. At the same time, Congress will not allow presidents to make the changes needed to bring Ecuador into the 20th much less the 21st century. It will take time and hard choices to get this country, so rich in resources, moving in the right direction.

Ecuadorian debt has grown to completely unmanageable proportions. The interest payments alone on the almost $20 billion dollars of debt have reached 125% of the country's GDP. Easy money during the heady days of high oil prices in the 1970s now has Ecuador in a hole that they won't be able to get out of on their own.

Perhaps Narziza de Jesus, an Ecuadorian woman who has been sainted because her body won't decompose, said it best when she foretold that Ecuador's future. She said that the country wouldn't be destroyed by fire or flood, regardless of El Niño and volcanic eruptions, but rather by bad government.

6. PLANNING YOUR TRIP

BEFORE YOU GO

WHEN TO VISIT

Ecuador's weather, due to its many microclimates, changes greatly from zone to zone. There is no ideal time to visit the country because each of these microclimates is going through its own weather cycle. If you are only going to visit one region, however, you can try to pick the best time for that particular area.

Because Ecuador straddles the equator, temperature is generally a function of altitude. As a rule it's hot at sea level and cool in the mountains. You can count on the temperature dropping about 10 degrees F for every 1000 meters you climb. The temperature at sea level is rarely above 90F, however, because the Humbolt current running up Ecuador's coast acts like an air conditioner in a bad hotel...it doesn't work perfectly but it does something to keep the temperature down.

Instead of four seasons, Ecuador has two – wet and dry. (Although they call them winter, *invierno* and summer, *verano*.) The rainy season is generally characterized by a build up of clouds during the day that lets loose in the afternoon. That seems simple, but there's an extra twist in the plot because every part of the country has its own distinct rainy and dry seasons. Also, in both the Galápagos and on the coast, the rainy season, winter, is actually warmer than the dry season.

If these seems confusing (it is), check the weather chart below.

Summer & Winter

The Galápagos is generally cooler, cloudy and dry from June to December and warmer, sunny, and wet from January through May. The coast follows this pattern somewhat, with its rainy season starting in January and lasting through April. Ecuadorians flock to the beaches during the rainy season, while foreign tourists tend to take their turn during the cloudy June through August months.

The Oriente experiences its rainy season from June through August. (Dry is a relative term when talking about the Oriente, as it is rainy all year.) This time slot, June through August, exactly corresponds to the highlands' dry season.

Rainfall Variation
The amount of rain in the rainy season differs dramatically from area to area. Wet in the Highlands means about 4-6 inches of rain a month, where as it's more like 11 inches a month during the coastal rainy season. In the Oriente, "dry" months average around 11 inches of rain with the wet ones topping out around 18 inches, causing mud slides and making many roads impassible.

All of this weather data is null and void if it happens to be a year of "El Niño." Every four or five years weather patterns are completely thrown off by this phenomenon.

EL NIÑO

Most of the world is familiar with the effects of El Niño after the bizarre weather of 1997/1998. Many people even know that the name El Niño comes from the Christ child, as the phenomenon generally occurs around Christmas time. What exactly is it the though?

El Niño is caused by a change in currents off the coast of Ecuador, Peru and Chile. Normally a current of cold water from the bottom of a very deep ocean trench runs along the Pacific coast of South America. About half way up Ecuador this giant underwater river, known as the Humbolt Current, takes a left and heads west.

About once every seven years however, things just get out of whack. A warm current from the north comes down and forces the Humbolt Current off the coast. The natural air conditioner basically goes on the blink and changes weather patterns all over the world. In Ecuador specifically, warm air from the ocean collides with air over the land, causing seemingly endless torrents of rain. Towns flood, roads wash out, crops are ruined and people lose their lives. Not a very nice Christmas present.

High Season
In terms of costs (and the number of people who will be sharing the sights with you), there are two high seasons. The first of these, from mid-December through January, is generally due to vacationing South Americans. The second high season, from June through August, is attributable mainly to gringos on holiday. Not only will costs go up, but you'll also have to plan ahead and make reservations during these months.

Easter is another time to expect crowds at the beaches and more popular Highland destinations.

The weather chart on the following page can help you plan your trip. The first line indicates whether it is the dry or rainy season. The second line shows the average daily temperatures. Remember that while temperatures don't vary much from season to season, there are can be wide differences between daytime and nighttime. You'll need a sweater at night even on the coast, and it will get warm during the day even high in the Andes.

WHAT TO PACK

You can get almost anything in Quito and Guayaquil that you can get at home, although sometimes at a price. Once you get away from the main cities, however, pharmacies, camera stores, and outdoor gear shops are under-supplied or hard to find. In addition to your trusty Swiss army knife and all the other travel items you normally pack, you'll want to bring:

• More film than you can imagine using - Especially if you're shooting slides.
• Insect repellent - 30-35% DEET.
• Sunscreen – Over 20 SPF is recommended.
• Motion sickness pills – A good idea if you will be cruising the Galápagos or flying in small planes.
• Binoculars – Imperative for wildlife viewing in the Oriente and Galápagos. Bring a set of binoculars for each person traveling. There's no reason to travel this far and then miss the monkeys because you were trying to share the binoculars.
• Flashlight – This will come in handy in jungle lodges with no generators and cities that have lost power.
• Snorkeling mask – For the Galápagos and coast; many boats will have gear but your own mask is always nice.
• Earplugs – Just take them. You'll be glad you did.
• Extra glasses – My Dad lost his in Argentina and had to wear his prescription sunglasses the whole trip. He looked like a movie star but it gave him headaches.
• Anti-diarrhea medicine – You know why.
• Iodine tablets – In case you get stuck somewhere without bottled water.
• Plenty of any prescription medicine - Also a copy of the prescription with both the brand and generic name of the medicine.
• Tampons - They are not commonly available.
• Toilet paper - This is something you can buy in Ecuador, but we're putting it on the list so you don't forget to have it with you at all times.
• Day pack – You'll need this to carry your camera, umbrella, sun screen, insect repellant, toilet paper and binoculars.

WEATHER & COST OF TRAVEL CHART

Area	Jan	Feb	Mar	Apr	May	Jun	Jul	Aug	Sep	Oct	Nov	Dec
Galap.	Rainy 78	Rainy 79	Rainy 80	Rainy 80	Rainy 79	Dry 75	Dry 74	Dry 73	Dry 72	Dry 73	Dry 74	Dry 75
Guaya-quil	Rainy 81	Rainy 81	Rainy 82	Rainy 82	Dry 81	Dry 78	Dry 77	Dry 77	Dry 78	Dry 78	Dry 79	Dry 81
Amazon	Rainy 70	Rainy 70	Rainy 70	Rainy 71	Rainy 71	Rainier 69	Rainier 69	Rainier 71	Rainier 72	Rainier 72	Rainier 72	Rainier 72
Quito	Rainy 58	Rainy 58	Rainy 58	Rainy 59	Rainy 58	Dry 58	Dry 58	Dry 58	Dry 58	Rainy 58	Rainy 58	Rainy 58
Cost of Travel	High	Low	High	Low	Low	High	High	High	Low	Lo	Low	High

Ecuador's diverse weather zones make each piece of clothing matter if you are going to cover the entire country. You will experience all four seasons as well as the rainy and dry ones. You'll want to pack clothes that layer for warmth, dry quickly, and are made of a fabric that breathes.

A sweater is appropriate at night even at the beach or the Galápagos, but shorts and t-shirts are fine during the day. In the Sierra, a coat and even hats and gloves are needed for the rainy afternoons at high altitude as well as for the chilly nights. Long pants are standard.

If you'll be visiting the coast or the Oriente it's important to have loose fitting long pants and long sleeved shirts to keep mosquitoes and other critters at bay. It's also a good idea to have at least one nice outfit for the city.

TRAVELING WITH CHILDREN

There are two types of lodging in Ecuador in regard to families. The first, created for foreigners, accommodate children but are not specifically set up with kids in mind. The second, created for vacationing Ecuadorian families, are much more child-friendly. These places, have the type of infrastructure that make trips more enjoyable for kids.

In the regions where Ecuadorians generally vacation, the coast and the Highlands, there is no lack of hotels, haciendas, with facilities set up for children. Most are like cabins with kitchens and bunk beds so that the whole family can stay together and save some money on meals. They also usually have swing sets, soccer fields, and other areas for kids to run around. Some of these places even have baby-sitting available.

The Oriente is generally not a spot for young vacationers as travel can be uncomfortable and facilities rustic. Most lodges recommend that children be at least ten before taking a trip to the jungle, but that all depends on the child.

It's important to take advantage of discounts offered for children throughout the country. Children under 12 only pay half fare on airplanes. Infants who sit in parents' laps ride free on buses and only pay 10% on planes. You should also bargain to get discounted prices for children in hotels.

Little blonde children are irresistible to many Ecuadorians. If your child falls into this category and is not comfortable with attention and pats to the cheek, you may want to wait a few years before taking the trip.

You can find plenty of baby paraphernalia in Quito and Guayaquil. Diapers, formula, baby toiletries, and clothing may cost more than they do at home, but are available for you in a pinch. Outside of these main cities you'll want to travel prepared with anything you might need.

VISAS & IMMIGRATION

United States and Canadian citizens traveling to Ecuador for tourism, business, or studies do not require a visa. You do however need a passport that is valid for six months from your time of entry into the country. Be sure to check yours now because it takes about six weeks to get your passport renewed (For passport information see the State Department's website at *http://travel.state.gov/passport_services.html*).

You also officially need a return ticket, proof of the economic means to support yourself during your time in the country and a tourist card. The only one we've been checked on is the tourist card, which you fill out when you enter the country. If you are dressed fairly neatly and behave respectfully, the customs agents will usually not ask to see your return ticket or money.

At the airport you will be issued either a 30 or 60-day tourist visa. If you will be staying up to the 90-day maximum, extensions up to the 90 days can be added at the **Immigrations office** in Quito: *Amazonas 2649, 2nd floor,* or in Guayaquil: *Migración del Guayas, Av. De Las Américas, frente al terminal terrestre (bus station).* They have some strange rules about the timing of granting extensions, so be sure to deal with it before it expires rather than after.

Visitors are allowed to be in the country a total of 90 days over any 12-month period. They are pretty inflexible about that one, so don't try to get in the country if you have already been there over 90 days in a year.

It's important to keep your copy of your tourist card safe because it will be requested upon leaving the country. You will also be asked to show it at military checkpoints, so keep it, and your passport, with you when you are on the road. If you lose your card you can get it replaced at the Immigrations office.

Ecuador goes through times when they are very vigilant about illegal immigrants. If a policeman or military officer in uniform asks for your passport and tourist card, just show them with a smile. If it's not somebody in uniform, be careful and don't get taken in a scam.

When you leave the country, along with handing over your tourist card, you'll have to pay a $25 departure tax.

To contact the **Ecuadorian Embassy in the US**: *2535 15th Street, N.W., Washington, D.C. 20009. Tel. 202/234-7200; www.ecuador.org.*

Ecuadorian Consulates in the US
• **New York**: *800 Second Avenue, Suite 601, New York, NY 10017. Tel. 212/808-0170*
• **New Jersey**: *30 Montgomery Street, Suite 1020, Jersey City, NJ 07302. Tel. 201/985-1700*

• **Philadelphia**: *100 South 6th Street, Suite 1015, Philadelphia, PA 19106. Tel. 215/925-9060.*
• **Baltimore**: *2925 Charles Street, Baltimore, MD 21218. Tel. 410/889-4435*
• **Washington**: *2535 15th Street, N.W., Washington, D.C. 20009. Tel. 202/ 234-7166*
• **Florida**: *1101 Brickell Ave., Suite M-102, Miami, FL 33131. Tel. 305/539-8214*
• **Houston**: *4200 Westheimer, Suite 118, Houston, TX 77027. Tel. 713/622-1787*
• **New Orleans**: *2 Canal Street, Suite 1312, New Orleans, LA 70130. Tel. 504/ 523-3229*
• **Chicago**: *500 North Michigan Avenue, Suite 1510, Chicago, IL 60611. Tel. 312/329-0266*
• **Michigan**: *136 State Street, Pontiac, MI 48341. Tel. 810/332-7352*
• **Los Angeles**: *8484 Wilshire Blvd., Suite 540, Beverly Hills, CA. Tel. 323/ 658-6020*
• **San Francisco**: *455 Market Street, Suite 980, San Francisco, CA 94105. Tel. 415/957-5921*
• **Las Vegas**: *3500 Paradise Road, Las Vegas, NV 89109. Tel. 702/735-8193*
• **Puerto Rico**: *Calle Recinto Sur 301, Oficina 401-A, Condominio Gallardo, Apartado 9020078*
San Juan, PR 00902-0078. Tel. 787/723-6572

Ecuadorian Embassy & Consulates in Canada
• **Ottawa**: *Embassy – 50 O'Conner St. #1311, Ottawa, Ontario K1P6L2. Tel. 613/563-8206*
• **Montreal**: *1010 St. Catherine Quest, Suite 440, P.O. Box H3B3R3, Montreal, Quebec H3B3R3. Tel. 514/874-4071*
• **Toronto**: *151 Bloor Street West, Suite 470, Toronto, Ontario M5S1S4. Tel. 416/968-2077*

CUSTOMS

All items that are considered a typical traveler's personal belongings are allowed in duty free. In addition, you can bring in 20 packs of cigarettes, 500 grams of pipe tobacco, 50 cigars, 1 liter of alcoholic beverages, and up to $200 of Duty Free purchases.

You can bring in a laptop computer, but they will tax you for a desktop model. Anything that appears to be commercial goods or falls outside of the category of traveler's personal belongings should be declared and is subject to duty. It is prohibited to bring firearms, ammunition or illegal drugs into the country.

When you leave, it is against Ecuadorian regulations to take any kind of plant or animal product. Archaeological artifacts are also a no-no.

You should check with the custom's office of your home country if you have any doubt about items that you will be bringing back from Ecuador. **US Customs**, *Tel. 202/566-8195*, generally allows two liters of alcohol and $400 of purchases duty free. The next $1,000 is taxed at 10%. Fresh food and Cuban cigars are illegal to bring into the United States.

ONE MORE MUY IMPORTANTE THING, SEÑOR & SEÑORA

Ecuador's official language is Spanish. There are also many indigenous languages spoken, but Spanish is a common tongue for most. Do yourself a favor and learn some basic phrases before you go. There are quite a few areas of the country where the person with whom you are trying to communicate won't speak English. Even if they do, it is just good manners to be able to greet them in their own language. You should buy a phrase book, but here's a start:

English	Spanish
Good morning	Buenos días
Good afternoon (12-8pm)	Buenas tardes
Good night (8pm-bed time)	Buenas noches
One	Uno
Two	Dos
Three	Trés
How are you?	Cómo está?
Please	Por favor
Thank you	Gracías
Excuse me	Perdón
Water	Agua
Beer	Cerveza
Bathroom	Baño
Awesome	Chévere

IMMUNIZATIONS

The Center for Infectious Diseases in Atlanta recommends the following vaccines for travel to Ecuador. You should visit your doctor at least six weeks before your trip to give the immunizations time to take effect.

• Hepatitis A or immune globulin (IG).
• Hepatitis B; only if you will have sexual contact with the locals, will be staying over six months in the region, or will be exposed through medical treatment.

- Rabies, if you might be exposed to wild or domestic animals.
- Typhoid.
- Yellow fever vaccination, if you will be traveling outside urban areas.
- Booster doses for tetanus-diphtheria and measles as needed.
- Mefloquine, sold in the US under the brand name Lariam, for malaria; only if you are going to the Oriente or the coast.

For more details and up to the minute recommendations, you can visit the CDC website at *www.cdc.gov/travel/tropsam.htm* or contact them at *Tel. 888/232-3228.*

TRAVELER'S INSURANCE

You should check your existing policies (health and home insurance) to see if your body and possessions are covered overseas. If they are not, you might want to inquire about the services of one of the companies listed below. Be sure to read the fine print so you know exactly what's covered.
- **American Express**, *Tel. 800/756-2639, www.worldaccess.com.*
- **Carefree Travel Insurance**, *Tel. 800/645-2424, www.berkely.com.*
- **International SOS Assistance**, *Tel. 800/523-8930, www.intsos.com.*
- **Travel Insured International**, *Tel. 800/243-3174, www.travelinsured.com*

BOOKING YOUR TRIP

There are a number of alternatives for you to consider when booking a flight to Ecuador. The best choice for you will depend on how much research you want to do yourself.

Travel Agents

Your local travel agent can easily book your flight to Quito or Guayaquil. You give him or her the dates and she comes back with a price. If you trust your travel agent and don't have time to shop around for bargains, this is any easy alternative.

Consolidators

Consolidators are basically high volume, low margin, low service travel agents. They buy airline seats at reduced rates and then pass some of the savings along to their customers. Tickets from consolidators are generally non-refundable and non-transferable, so you have to be sure about your dates before you book your tickets.

The savings to Ecuador when using a consolidator are not as substantial as they are to other locations like Europe and Asia, in fact many consolidators do not even handle South America. There are, however, some discounts available. **Airfare Busters**, *Tel. 713/961-5109*, and **Travac**, *Tel. 800/TRAV-800* are two consolidators that have flights to Ecuador. For more options you can check the **United States Consolidators Association** at *Tel. 916/441-4166, www.usaca.com* for a listing of its members.

On-line
You can search for bargains yourself with your computer. By using an on-line fare searching agent (such as *www.easysabre.com*) you can comparison shop yourself between airlines. You can also look for deals on sites that specialize in low airfares like *www.1travel.com*. To make your searching easier, the airport code for Quito's international airport is UIO and Guayaquil's is GYE.

With only three airlines, Continental, American, and SAETA, having direct flights to Quito, it's worth checking their websites for specials. Doing a check we did recently, the fare searching engine came up with $590 from Miami to Quito on SAETA, but the SAETA webpage had a $500 special for the same roundtrip flight. See *Getting to Ecuador* below for airline information.

Air Courier
Being a courier is a great, low cost way to travel the world. You have to be able to travel light though, because you are basically trading your luggage space for the discounted ticket. The only baggage you can take is a carry-on. Other rules include limited stays (although it can be up to a few weeks) and required round-trip travel.

You will check in with the courier agent at the airport where you take responsibility for the package and sign in. When you get to your destination there is another courier agent meeting your flight to receive the package and sign you out.

Couriers to Ecuador generally go through Miami. The flight costs around $200. Two of the largest courier booking companies in the US are **Discount Travel International**, *Tel. 212/362-3636*, and **New Voyager**, *Tel. 212/431-1616*.

Saving Money
There are some steps anybody can take to reduce travel bills. The best thing you can do is buy your ticket more than three weeks before your trip. The cheapest fares go quickly, so you want to buy it even further in advance if you can. Don't worry, if you miss a sale you can get a refund on the difference. Another money saver is to stay less than thirty days. Are you a senior citizen or student? Let the airlines know, as this can earn you additional discounts.

When looking to book your ticket, if price is a major issue, consider flying to Ecuador via Venezuela or Colombia, which can be less expensive than a direct flight.

STUDY TOURS/LANGUAGE LEARNING PACKAGES

Ecuador is an excellent place to learn Spanish. The Ecuadorian accent is clear and easy to understand and class prices are low. Many people have chosen Ecuador as their place to study, and as a result there are hundreds of language schools. This can be both good and bad. There are many options, but some schools are just not up the standards of others.

There are a number of factors you'll want to consider when choosing a language school. It's important to find the proper fit so that your experience is a positive one:

• Is the instruction private or in groups? How large are the groups? Over five in a group really starts to dilute personal attention.
• What is the curriculum? What is the main focus? Is it grammar, conversation, business Spanish, etc? Do they use aids like videos and taping or are all the materials written?
• What are the facilities like? Is it a large school compound, a small office, or somewhere in between?
• How many hours of class do you want to take a day? Many schools have minimum and maximum requirements. What is the cost per hour?
• What are the teacher's experiences? Do they have college degrees?
• Does the school organize excursions to cultural sights? How about weekend trips? Many times this is an excellent way to see the city and learn from a local.
• What is the average age of the other students?
• Are you expected to live with a family during your stay? What is the norm for these accommodations? Will you have your own bedroom, bathroom, desk? How far away will the homes be from the school? What is the cost?
• Do you want to study in a smaller town or in Quito?

Once you've figured out what factors are most important to you, the trick is to find a school that fits the bill. The schools listed below have all been recommended by people who have studied there as well as by the South American Explorer's Club.

• **Academia Latinoamericana**, *Jose Queri 2 between Eloy Alfaro and Los Granados. Tel. 2/452 824, Fax 2/433 820. E-mail: delco@spanish.com.ec.* Academia Latinoamericana is a full service school, offering free e-mail service, twice weekly excursions and volunteer internships. The grounds of the school itself include a swimming pool. hot tub and volleyball court.

• **Amazonas,** *Jorge Washington 718 and Amazonas, Rocafuerte building, 2nd floor. Tel. 2/527 509, Fax 2/504 654. E-mail: amazonas@pi.pro.ec.* Amazonas school can arrange for you to study Spanish in the jungle in addition to offering free e-mail service, salsa lessons and weekly excursions.

• **Cristóbal Colón School,** *Colón 2088 and Versalles. Tel. 2/506508, Fax 2/ 222964. E-mail colon@pi.pro.ec.* This Cristóbal Colón is consistently one of the most highly recommended schools with South American Explorer's Club members. They offer free e-mail, excursions and can arrange study in different parts of the country.

• **Instituto Superior de Español,** *Ulloa 152 and Carrión. Tel. 2/223 242, Fax 2/221 628. E-mail: superior@ecnet.ec.* The least expensive school on this list, the Instituto has free e-mail, salsa lessons, cooking classes and weekly excursions. They also have a campus in Otavalo if you prefer to hike and shop in your free time.

• **Diego Gortaire,** *Tel. 2/520 621.* If you're an advanced student looking to really hone your skills, you might prefer hiring a private tutor rather than registering with a school. Diego Gortaire is well recommended.

Another option is to organize your schooling though a reputable international company with schools around the world. A good periodical to consult that lists language schools for teaching opportunities as well as learning opportunities is *Transitions Abroad.* It's available on most magazine shelves in big bookstores.

• **Amerispan Unlimited,** *Tel. 800/879-6640, Website: www.amerispan.com*
• **Council Study Abroad,** *Tel. 888/268-6245, Website: www.ciee.org*
• **Spanish Abroad,** *Tel. 888/722-7623, Website: www.spanishabroad.com*
• **Language Link,** *Tel. 800/552-2051, Website: www.langlink.com*

BY AIR

Most people arrive to Ecuador by air, flying into Quito's Mariscal Sucre International Airport or Guayaquil's Simón Bolívar International Airport. Airfares will vary from $500 to over to $1000 round trip depending on the airline, departure city and time of year. The high seasons in terms of price are December-January and July-August. Miami has the most airlines departing to Ecuador so the flights from there are the cheapest. It is just over a four-hour flight from Miami to Quito.

It's worth noting that Quito airport actually closes at midnight, so if your departure from the US has been considerably delayed, you can count on a night in Guayaquil.

When you arrive, you will depart your plane and follow the signs to the immigration area. Make sure you filled out your tourist card on the plane. If you didn't get one, they are available in the immigration area. After filling it out, you go through the immigration line and on to customs.

After getting your bag in customs you will go through the lines there and out into the main airport. There is a currency exchange booth right outside the customs area. It is open as long as planes are landing.

There are only three companies that have direct flights to Ecuador from the United States. **American Airlines**, with service to 32 cities in 18 countries in Latin America, is pretty much king of the South American routes. They offer more non-stop service to Latin America from the US than any other airline. If you're a member of their frequent flyer program, American AAdvantage, it's worth staying on top of their specials because they often have Latin America promotions that let you cash in your miles at significant discounts.

- **American Airlines**: *Tel. 800/433-7300. www.aa.com.* Direct flights from Miami to Quito and Guayaquil.
- **Continental Airlines**: *Tel. 800/525-0280. www.flycontinental.com.* Direct flights from Houston to Quito with continuing service to Guayaquil. Flights from Newark to Guayaquil via Panama City.
- **SAETA** (Ecuadorian national airline): *Tel. 800/82SAETA.* www.saeta.com.ec. Direct flights from New York and Miami to Quito with continuing service to Guayaquil and other points in the country.

The following international airlines also service Quito:
- **Aeroperu**: Flights from Lima
- **Air France**: Flights from Paris
- **Avensa-Servivensa**: Flights from Lima and Caracas (Caracas via Bogota)
- **Avianca**: Flights from Bogota
- **COPA**: Flights from Panama City to Guayaquil and Quito
- **Ecuatoriana**: Flights from Quito and Guayaquil to 9 destinations in the Americas.
- **Iberia**: Flights to Madrid via Santo Domingo
- **KLM**: Flights from Amsterdam to Quito and Guayaquil (via Curacao)
- **LACSA**: Flights from San Jose, Costa Rica to Quito and Guayaquil
- **Lan Chile**: Flights from Santiago de Chile
- **Lufthansa**: Flights from Frankfurt via Bogota

BY BOAT

It is possible to take a freighter to Ecuador, but you need lots of time and a flexible schedule. The price is higher than a plane ticket and it takes quite a bit longer. You can contact **Freighter World Cruises**, *Tel. 800/531-7774, www.freighterworld.com* for more information. They are a travel agency for freighters as well as publishers of the *Freighter Space Advisory* newsletter.

BY BUS

You can enter Ecuador by bus from both Peru and Colombia. Bus service generally terminates at the border, so you will have to change buses after going through customs and immigrations. Some bus companies, like Pan-American International, offer service on both sides of the border and even have an attendant to help you get through the customs procedures. **Tulcán** is the Ecuadorian entry point from Colombia, and **Huaquillas** and **Macará** are the entry points from Peru.

BY CAR

You can enter Ecuador by car from the same official border points as you would by bus, **Tulcán** from Colombia and **Huaquillas** and **Macará** from Peru. To get through customs you need an international driver's license from AAA, a passport, and complete car registration papers in the driver's name. It wouldn't hurt to have the papers notarized, as the more stamps and signatures you can wave in the customs agent's face, the better. You should check these requirements with the embassy, as regulations fluctuate with country relations. Make sure you have insurance.

Many people have a dream of driving the whole way from North to South America. Read Tim Cahill's *Road Fever* for hilarious insight into the trip.

GETTING AROUND ECUADOR

Getting around Ecuador is not the huge time investment that it can be in some other South American countries. Ecuador's small size means that you can go from north to south by bus in under a day (a long day). That's good news for travelers. You can use your time enjoying destinations instead of stuck in a car or on a bus.

Having said that, the bad news is that 1998's El Niño was especially damaging to the transportation infrastructure. Many roads, as well sections of rail, have yet to be repaired. Travel in these areas, even though over short distances, can be time consuming. On the other hand, those roads that have been repaired have in most cases been upgraded as well, making quick transportation a breeze.

BY AIR

Flights within Ecuador are pretty reasonably priced and a good way to efficiently cover longer stretches. Quito and Guayaquil are the country's two air transportation hubs. Ecuadorians pay much less for the flights than foreigners, so don't be surprised if the person in front of you at the counter shells out less for his ticket.

Before you buy a ticket for a domestic flight, you should be pretty sure of your schedule, as tickets are non-refundable. On the other hand, until your boarding pass is issued you can change the date of your flight without paying a fee. After you book a ticket, be sure to reconfirm your reservation once before your flight. Twice would not be overdoing it.

On the day of your flight you should arrive to the airport an hour before your scheduled departure time. Check-in can be a zoo. Boarding is another interesting process as there are no seat assignments. If you've flown Southwest in the United States, you should be a pro at nabbing that good seat.

There are two national airlines in Ecuador.

• **TAME**, *Amazonas 1354 and Colon, 2nd Floor, Quito. Tel. 509382, 509383. Monday - Friday 9:30am - 1pm, 1:45pm - 5:30pm. Colon 1001 and Rabida, Quito. Tel. 554905 554274. Monday - Friday, 8:00am - 6:30pm, Saturday, 9am - 12pm* . From Quito they cover Guayaquil, Cuenca, Loja, Macas, Coca, Lago Agrio, Tulcán, Esmeraldas, Manta, Portoviejo, Bahía de Caráquez and Baltra (Galápagos). From Guayaquil they have flights to Cuenca, Loja, Machala, and Baltra (Galápagos).

• **SAN** (part of SAETA), *Republic de El Salvador 880 and Suecia, Edificio Almirante Colon, Quito. Tel. 254510. Amazonas 1429 and Colon, Edificio Espana, Local #6, Quito. Tel. 564969. Airport Tel. 456015, 452539, 440179. Both offices open Monday - Friday, 8:30am-6pm.* They have flights from Quito to Guayaquil, Cuenca and San Cristóbal (Galápagos) as well as flights from Guayaquil to San Cristóbal.

BY BOAT

You'll find boats and canoes taking the place of taxis on waters in both the Oriente and the coast. The same rules apply for these water taxis as for land ones – ask the price first.

BY BUS

Traveling by bus is the most common and least expensive means of transportation in Ecuador. All buses, however, are not created equal. For long distance rides you often have the luxury of opting for a first class bus with bathrooms, reclining seats, movies and drink service. Take it. Your body will thank you.

Shorter distance and cheaper buses are often converted school buses. Your knees didn't fit in them in 8th grade and they won't now. Many times you won't have a choice, but if you do, it's worth taking the more expensive ride. (Expensive is a relative term, as first class bus service from Quito to Guayaquil costs less than $20.)

The US Consulate advises against traveling in buses at night, and so do we. Accidents are common.

Passport checks on buses, especially in the Oriente, are widespread. It's not a big deal, just make sure you have yours within reach.

ECUADOR BUS BIBLE

We've gained some insights after riding our fare share of Ecuadorian buses, so we'll pass them onto you.

• *Buy your ticket the day before you travel.* It takes away the uncertainty and sometimes you can even reserve a seat. Stay away from the seats over the wheels.

• *Never sit in the back of the bus.* Worn out shocks, smelly bathrooms (when there are any), and swaying seats lead us to avoid what we endearingly call "the vomit zone."

• *Never sit by the exhaust pipe.* Some buses have exhaust pipes that expel their foul air and tremendous noise right next to the window. Avoid these seats.

• *Use the restroom before you get on board.* It is pure misery to wait three to four hours for a potty break when you have to go NOW.

• *Pay attention to your stuff.* Petty thieves lurk in bus stations and even on buses themselves.

• *Take your own food and water.* We have never regretted taking our own rations. We always regret it when we don't.

• *What you can't hear won't hurt you.* Take earplugs to block out the cacophony of people, animals, crying children and loud music.

Within cities, *colectivos* and *busetas*, Volkswagen vans and small buses, will be transportation alternatives. *Busetas* are even faster than regular buses because they stop less. When you went to get off the bus yell, "*esquina por favor*" and the driver will drop you at the next corner.

Out in the country, trucks, *camionetas;* and flatbeds, *rancheros,* get people to places in the surrounding area.

Buses depart either from the central bus station, *terminal terrestre,* or the bus company's office. Look under "Arrivals & Departures" in each chapter for the specific details for each town.

BY CAR

Driving in Latin America can be dangerous for those not accustomed to the rules of the road. In addition to hazards such as resting cows and crater-sized potholes, you'll find few road signs and much more aggressive drivers than on your highways at home. You'll end up having to ask for direction a lot, so if you don't speak Spanish you may want to opt for a taxi or hired driver.

It's helpful to think of the driving rules as completely dynamic, shifting with each person in every situation. Anticipate the moves of each driver by establishing one-on-one communication with them through eye contact and hand signals. Expect the car next to you to do the unexpected...turning right from the left lane is not an offense, so don't get upset about it. You should also never drive at night, avoid driving in cities, and wear your seatbelt.

Having said that, renting a car offers a great deal more maneuverability and time-saving than local buses, especially if you want to stop a lot along your route or get to remote attractions. Rental rates run about $30-$70 per day plus mileage. Four wheel drive vehicles, imperative for getting off the beaten track in the rainy season, are at the higher end of the scale, usually starting at about $50 plus mileage for the two-door vehicles.

For driving distances, see the driving distances chart on the next page.

FEMININITY AT THE FILLING STATION

The gas stations in Ecuador, as in most of Latin America, have only full service pumps. In order to attract truck drivers plying the Pan-American Highway, most of the stations are attended by young women. Nattily dressed in matching jumpsuits, they skillfully fill your tank without a scratch to those long acrylic nails.

To drive in Ecuador you need a valid driver's license from your state as well as an international driver's license. You can obtain the international licenses before you go for $10 from American Automobile Association offices, even if you are not a member. You'll also need the registration papers for your car. Keep these on your body, not in the car's glove

DRIVING DISTANCES

	Baños	Cuenca	Guayaquil	Loja	Otavalo	Puyo	Quito
Baños	—	6.5 hrs 309 km	4.5 hrs 288 km	9.5 hrs 514 km	6 hrs 271 km	2 hrs 61 km	3.5 hrs 176 km
Cuenca	6.5 hrs 309 km	—	5 hrs 250 km	6 hrs 205 km	13 hrs 537 km	9 hrs 370 km	10 hrs 444 km
Guayaquil	4.5 hrs 288 km	5 hrs 250 km	—	9 hrs 415 km	11 hrs 515 km	7 hrs 349 km	8 hrs 420 km
Loja	9.5 hrs 514 km	6 hrs 205 km	9 hrs 415 km	—	17 hrs 742 km	12 hrs 519 km	13 hrs 647 km
Otavalo	6 hrs 271 km	13 hrs 537 km	11 hrs 515 km	17 hrs 742 km	—	8 hrs 330 km	2.5 hrs 95 km
Puyo	2 hrs 61 km	9 hrs 370 km	7 hrs 349 km	12 hrs 519 km	8 hrs 330 km	—	6.5 hrs 237 km
Quito	3.5 hrs 176 km	10 hrs 444 km	8 hrs 420 km	13 hrs 647 km	2.5 hrs 95 km	6.5 hrs 237 km	—

compartment. It can be a huge hassle if they get stolen. If you are stopped at a military checkpoint you will need to show these papers along with your driver's license, passport and tourist card.

Read over all rental documents carefully and make sure everything is in writing. Then look over the car. All dings, scratches, or any other problems should be noted on the contract. Check that the spare has air and that the jack is in working order. After having had a starter go out on us in an isolated locale, we also always opt for manual transmission.

Once you've rented the car, there are some things you can do it keep it safe. Don't leave anything in the car that might tempt robbers. Many Ecuadorians even leave their glove compartments open and empty when the car is parked to satisfy thieves' slightest bit of curiosity. Also, always park your car in a guarded lot.

If your car does get broken into, you'll want to get a copy of the police report, *denuncia*, for the rental company and insurance purposes. Hopefully this won't happen, but if you have an accident be aware that some victims may see you as a target. Don't move anything and make sure some witnesses stick around the scene. If a pedestrian is hurt, it is your responsibility to pay for injuries, even if you are not at fault. Again, a copy of the *denuncia* is imperative.

You can find specific car rental information in the *Getting Around Town* section for each destination, but it's rare to find cars available outside of Quito, Guayaquil and Cuenca.

Another alternative is to hire a car and driver. Most of the major tour agencies and hotels are set up to arrange this. The cost is generally about $80 per day.

BY FOOT

Crosswalks are completely ignored and can therefore be dangerous terrain. You should wait for vehicles to stop before stepping in front of them.

BY TAXI

Taxis are a great way to get around town. They are inexpensive and generally know where they are going. In Quito cabs should, in theory, be metered. If they are not, agree on a price before you head towards your destination. It's a good idea to ask at your hotel how much it should cost to get to your destination in taxi, *cuanto debe costar ir al ____ en taxi*, so you won't get taken for a ride. Be aware that fares go up as much as 50% on weekends and at night.

If renting a car seems like too much of a responsibility or cost, hiring a taxi for day trips is an excellent alternative. Agree on an hourly or daily rate before you take off so you have the freedom to explore at your own pace. Remember you have to pay the cabby for the roundtrip even if you only go one way. About $6 an hour is a fair fare.

BY TRAIN

Even before the wrath of El Niño in 1998, train travel had become outdated for the typical Ecuadorian as the road infrastructure improved. Now, with kilometers of track completely wiped out, much of the country's train service has been suspended. Where trains do run, you'll find mostly fellow foreigners sharing the rails experience.

The trains in Ecuador are dog-eared and rusty at best. Many of them are simply old buses placed on train wheels. If you want the prime seats, wear layers and be prepared to scramble for the roof.

The most popular route with travelers is the Devil's Nose switchback near Alausí, which you access from Riobamba. See the destination write-up for more details. The famous Ibarra-San Lorenzo ride was still suspended when this book went to press, but ask around as that may have changed.

CROSSING THE BORDER

The border crossing into Colombia from Ecuador is at **Tulcán**. **Huaquillas** and **Macará** are the towns for crossing into Peru. It's not a good idea to cross in other places, no matter what the locals tell you, because you might not be able to get your passport stamped. Crossing into Peru from the Oriente has been asking for trouble with the border so ill-defined, but will hopefully get easier now that there is peace.

ACCOMMODATIONS

Accommodations in Ecuador cover the entire range from five-star international hotels to flea-ridden flops. We'll keep you away from the later. Mid-range travelers especially will find an excellent selection of clean, personable, unique and memorable lodging options. Many room prices include a continental breakfast, which usually consists of bread, jam, coffee, and juice. Occasionally eggs are included as well.

We used high season rates in our listings, so you should be quoted less than our indications during the off-season. It is always worthwhile to ask for an additional discount when inquiring about rates. Most establishments earn their bread and butter during the high season and are eager to attract clients when things are not so busy. We've even had the nicest hotels in some towns offer *un pequeño descuento* without any prompting.

Apart-hotels

Apart-hotels offer all of the services of a normal hotel but include extra living space, typically a small living room, a bedroom, and a kitchenette. The hybrid name is appropriate because the space isn't big enough to be called an apartment in most cases, but it is spacious enough to eliminate hotel room claustrophobia. Apart-hotels cost about the same as a double room of similar decor and quality. The kitchenettes allow for the advantage of eating a few meals in, or at least grabbing a simple, healthy breakfast on the run.

Boats

The most common way to visit the many sights of the Galápagos is via chartered boat or cruise ship. Puttering along from island to island, you get the chance to take in much of this incredible natural habitat. All boats are required to have on-board naturalists to keep tourists from spoiling too much of Darwin's laboratory.

Each boat has a different itinerary and the sleeping quarters range from cramped to commodious. Do your homework before you plop down your money. See our *Galápagos* chapter for more information on selecting your ship.

Cabañas

Cabins are another good option for extra space. The facilities are built with big families in mind, which is why the space and price tags are larger. The cabins are usually fully-equipped with cookware and all kitchen appliances.

Camping

Because some of Ecuador's most famous sites are contained within the national parks, you would think the park system would boast inviting places to stay. Unfortunately, the parks are badly under-funded and have little infrastructure. Sites are primitive and burglary is common.

If you are climbing one of the more popular volcanoes like Cotopaxi, there will be a place in the refuge to check your belongings while you climb. Use it.

Haciendas

When the Spanish conquered the Incas they parceled out huge tracts of land to be worked by the indigenous population. A large hacienda was the home of the *patrón* and his family. It took centuries, but these immense feudal estates were finally broken up by land reforms in the last few decades. Many of the large houses from these estates have been turned into fine country inns.

You shouldn't miss the chance to stay at a hacienda while in Ecuador. Sixteenth and seventeenth century homes have been opened up to the discerning traveler, many at affordable prices. The locations are usually lovely and the service excellent. Many sporting activities, especially horseback riding, are available to enjoy at haciendas.

Hostales

The direct translation of *hostal* would be hostel, but these aren't necessarily dormitory sleeping arrangements. Usually, they are simple inns, frequently a private house with the living room and dining room serving as common areas. Other *hostales* are as comfy as bed-and-breakfast inns in North America.

Hotels

Ecuadorian hotels run the gamut from no star to five star. Most of the five star hotels, especially the international ones, are located in Quito and Guayaquil.

Prices range from under $10 per night to over $200, but you can find a clean, comfortable hotel with private bathrooms starting at around $30. As you go up in price you are usually adding more space and amenities like a servibar, gym, swimming pool, sauna, and multiple restaurants.

Hosterías

Hosterías are inns that can range from simple to sumptuous. Usually they are in more remote locations, look like woodsy lodges, and have good country-style restaurants.

Lodges

Lodges are generally very simple, but all-inclusive. Usually in remote jungle areas, a stay at a lodge will include transportation, guide service, food, and board. Multi-day stays are normally required.

Motels

Motels in Ecuador are normally shelters for illicit rendezvous. They are located in city outskirts and surrounded by high solid fences to protect the identities of those frolicking within.

Youth Hostels

Ecuador's Youth Hostel system is run through the Ecuadorian Association of Youth Hostels (*albergues*). You can make reservations for the over 20 associated hostels at *Tel. 2/508 221, www.hostels.com/ec.html.* Check around because inexpensive *hosterías* often have similar pricing as youth hostels and far superior facilities.

7. BASIC INFORMATION

BUSINESS HOURS

It's difficult to write hard, fast rules for business hours in Ecuador. The times below are general guidelines, but don't be surprised if the particular business you are visiting is closed longer for lunch or kicks off twenty minutes early the particular day you need something.

• **Quito**: 9am-12:30pm; 2pm- 6pm; often open Saturday mornings
• **The Rest of Ecuador**: 9am-12:30pm; 2:30pm-6pm; occasionally open Saturday mornings
• **Restaurants**: Restaurants are open from 12:30pm- 4pm and again from 7 or 8pm-11 or 12pm. Snack bars and more informal places are open straight through from 8am-11pm. Restaurants are generally closed on Sunday evenings.
• **Banks**: 9am-1pm; open afternoons or Saturday mornings in larger cities.

COMPUTERS & INTERNET SERVICE

The local number for **American Online** users in Quito is *Tel.505 000*. The local number in Guayaquil is *Tel. 511 000*. You must change your network to the "aolglobalnet" at sign-on. Compuserve users can dial the same numbers for their service. Be aware there is a surcharge of $12/hour for both services.

There are scores of internet cafes popping up all over Quito as well as the larger tourists destination towns. These are listed as *Practical Information* in the destination chapters.

COST OF TRAVEL

Ecuador is a delightfully inexpensive country for people with dollars. The value of the *sucre* tends to fall and fall, leaving you able to buy more and more for that money. Even with the inflation that follows devaluation, our dollars always seems to buy more each time we're in the country. Restaurants, souvenirs and services like massages or laundry cost just of fraction of what they do at home.

You'll find however that some establishments, mostly hotels and travel agencies, set their prices in dollars as a hedge against currency fluctuation. These prices stay constant regardless of how the value of the *sucre* changes.

The biggest exceptions to the travel-in-Ecuador-is-cheap rule are the jungle lodges in the Oriente and boat trips in the Galápagos. They're expensive. That's not to say that some lodges and cruises aren't more economical than others however. You can probably find one to fit your budget.

It's hard to list prices because of the turbulent economic times that Ecuador is experiencing now. You may find some of the numbers listed in this book right on (for the establishments that charge in dollars) and others wildly off (for those that charge in *sucres*, which we converted to the current dollar price). If you find a place you want to stay it would be worth sending them a fax or e-mail to confirm their current pricing. Be aware that there is a two-tier pricing system in the country. You will be charged more for hotels and planes and trains than your Ecuadorian seatmate. Just keep in mind that it's cheaper than it would be at home anyway.

EARTHQUAKES

It is not unusual to experience the earth tremble during your time in Ecuador. Remember not to run out of buildings or use elevators during a quake, but rather stand under a doorway until the tremor is over. In modern buildings, lights will go out automatically to prevent fires if the quake is over a five on the Richter scale.

ELECTRICITY

Voltage in Ecuador is the same as in the United States at 110 with 60 cycles AC. The plug accepts two flat prongs, like those of the US. Generally there will not be a hole for the grounder prong, so you may want to bring an adapter.

EMBASSIES

• **American Embassy in Quito**: *12 de Octubre and Patria. Tel. 562-890. After hours Tel. 561-749, Fax 502-052. Tuesday-Friday 8am-11:30am, 1:30pm-5pm. Website: www.usis.org.ec*
• **Canadian Consulate in Quito**: *6 de Diciembre 2816 and James Orton. Tel. 543-214, Fax. 503108. Monday-Friday 9:30am-12:30pm*

EMERGENCY PHONE NUMBERS

The following numbers function in Guayaquil and Quito. Keep in mind that the person who answers the phone is unlikely to speak English.

• **Police** – *Tel. 101*
• **Fire Department** – *Tel. 102*
• **General Emergency** (like 911 in the US) – *Tel. 199*
• **Ambulance** – *Tel. 131*

ENGLISH LANGUAGE READING

The Explorer is a free booklet with information on Quito and the rest of the country issued monthly. It occasionally offers some good suggestions. You can find the English international editions of both *Time* and *Newsweek* on many newsstands for a reasonable price. Other magazines are available in larger cities, but cost as much as a hardback book. The *Miami Herald* is also available in Quito and Guayaquil.

The best place to go for books in English in Quito is **Libri Mundi**, *Juan León Mera 851*. They also have small shops in both the Hotel Colón and Hotel Oro Verde. In Guayaquil, travelers flock to **Librería Científica**, *Luque 223*, for their reading material.

ETIQUETTE

Latin Americans in general, and Ecuadorians in particular, exude politeness. It's a part of their cultural make-up that is very different from our "squeaky wheel gets the grease" philosophy. Ranting and raving may get results, but chances are that civility will get better ones.

It's basically considered good manners to greet anybody you're going to talk to with a pleasantry before moving onto business, even if you're just asking directions or telling the cabby where to go. It's a little hard to get used to, but once you do you'll appreciate how civil it is.

In terms of dress, Ecuadorians, mainly in the Highlands, are more formal than North Americans and even Europeans. In you don't want to stick out too much, observe those around you and dress accordingly. Blue jeans and tennis shoes are generally not normal attire for adults in the city, and shorts even less so. On the coast and in the jungle things are more casual.

HEALTH CONCERNS

The Center for Disease Control (CDC) in Atlanta has up-to-date information about Ecuador's disease concerns and risks. The number is *Tel. 888/232-3228*. You can also get information from their website at *www.cdc.gov/travel/tropsam.htm*.

The listing of diseases below is a large one. It should not scare you, but rather motivate you to take the simple precautions to prevent illness. When you get back home after your trip, stay attuned to your health and visit a doctor if you have any of the symptoms listed below.

Traveler's Diarrhea, Hepatitis, Typhoid Fever
Basically, food and waterborne diseases are the main cause of illness for travelers to Ecuador. Almost everybody will feel a little queasy at some point on their trip, but that's normal as you're exposed to different types of bacteria than you are at home. If you try to see that your food and water are safe, you've gone a long way towards preventing E. coli, salmonella, parasites, typhoid fever, toxoplasmosis and hepatitis.
The CDC offers this advice for staying off the injured reserve list:
• Wash hands frequently with soap and water
• Drink only bottled or boiled water or carbonated drinks. Avoid ice cubes.
• Eat only thoroughly cooked food, or fruits and vegetables that you have peeled yourself.
• Don't eat food from street vendors.
• Take your malaria prevention medication before, during, and after travel as directed (see below).
• Protect yourself from insects by using repellents and mosquito nets and wearing long-sleeved shirts and pants from dusk to dawn.
• Do not go barefoot.
• Always use condoms.

Many travelers live by the "boil it, cook it, peel it or forget it" rule. Others, like ourselves, are willing to take some chances if they think the quality of the food and preparation service merits it. Many people won't eat any salads, but we can't stand not having fresh vegetables. We just try to make good choices about where to order the chef salad and where to stick to the yellow food group - chicken, potatoes and bananas.
If you do experience vomiting or diarrhea just lay low, drink plenty of water and try not to eat much. You'll usually be fine by the next day.

Cholera
Cholera is an acute diarrheal illness, transmitted by ingestion of contaminated food or water. Although there was an outbreak of cholera in Latin America in the early 1990s, it has been mostly contained, leaving the risk of infection for travelers quite low.
Following the above suggestions, staying in decent hotels and eating in hygienic restaurants will help you avoid much of the danger. Of special concern to Ecuadorian travelers is the fact that raw and undercooked seafood is another major transporter of the disease. Ask whether or not the restaurant cooks its ceviche before you order it. Many do, helping eliminate part of the risk.
In the unlikely event you develop severe water diarrhea, go immediately to the hospital.

Malaria

Malaria, transmitted to people through the bite of an infected mosquito, is a serious disease that if not promptly treated can cause kidney failure, coma, and even death. The symptoms are flu-like including fever, chills, head and muscle ache and fatigue. If you have these symptoms for up to one year after your trip you should get prompt medical attention and tell your doctor that you traveled to Ecuador.

The risk areas for malaria in Ecuador include both the Oriente and the Pacific coast (including Guayaquil). Quito and the Highlands, as well as the Galápagos Islands, are not considered danger zones.

If you are going to travel to one of the risk areas, Mefloquine, sold in the US under the brand name Lariam, is the recommended drug. You will take one tablet a week starting the week before your trip, during the time you're in the infected area, and for four weeks after you return. Some people experience negative side effects to the medicine so ask your doctor about the pros and cons of taking it.

The best way to avoid malaria is to avoid mosquito bites. Protect yourself from mosquitoes by wearing clothing that covers most of your body, sleeping under bed netting when necessary, and using insect repellent with a concentration of 30-35% DEET. These same precautions can help prevent chagas, another disease caused by insect bites that causes heart problems later on down the line.

Altitude Sickness

Visitors to the Andes may experience some altitude sickness, also called acute mountain sickness or *puna*. Its symptoms include shortness of breath, difficulty sleeping, headache, nausea, and vomiting. These symptoms can last from two to five days. The best things to do if you feel this way, besides moving to a lower elevation, are to drink lots of water, avoid alcohol, and take ibuprofen or aspirin for pain relief. To avoid the situation all together, try to climb no more than 2000 meters for the first two days and then add another day of acclimatization for each additional 500 meters you climb.

High altitude pulmonary edema, swelling of the lungs, is a more advanced and dangerous state of altitude sickness. Its symptoms include repeated vomiting, staggering and confusion. It can be fatal within a few hours. If you suspect somebody in your group has pulmonary edema, you must move immediately to lower elevations.

Doctors, Hospitals and Pharmacies

If you do get sick, good medical care is available in Quito and Guayaquil. The American embassy has a list of well-trained doctors who speak English. In Quito, both the **Hospital Metropolitano**, *Mariana de*

Jesus and Avenida Occidental, Tel. 431520; and the **Hospital Los Andes,**
Villalengua 267, Tel. 241540 are recommended by the embassy.
  Pharmacies in Quito, especially the Fybeca chain, are well stocked.
You should bring your own prescription drugs with you, however, just in
case.

HOLIDAYS

  Ecuadorians love to commemorate events and honor people. You
could conceivably travel around the country from festival to celebration
for the entire year. The types of holidays can be divided into religious,
national, and regional celebrations. The religious celebrations include
both solemn processions and frenzied jubilation. Carnival, Easter, and
Christmas are the highlights of the religious calendar. National holidays
marking important dates in the country's history are usually accompanied
with brass bands and fireworks. Regional holidays usually combine a bit
of both and take on religious undertones even if they are marking
historical events.
  Special meals, too much alcohol consumption, closed businesses, and
excitement in the air are common with all three types of celebrations.
Book your transportation and hotel early.
  Ecuadorian businesses are closed on a national level for the following
historical and religious holidays:
• January 1: New Years
• Good Friday: Easter (most people take off the entire Holy Week, *Semana
  Santa*)
• May 1: Labor Day
• August 10: Independence Day
• November 2: All Soul's Day (Day of the Dead)
• December 25: Christmas

  Businesses are often closed for the following non-official holidays:
• January 6: Epiphany or Three Kings Day
• February 27: Patriotism Day
• Carnival Monday and Tuesday: Before Ash Wednesday
• May 24: Battle of Pichincha
• Ninth Thursday after Easter: Corpus Christi
• June 24: John the Baptist (Otavalo area)
• June 29: St. Peter and Paul (whole country but strongest in Northern
  Highlands)
• July 24: Simón Bolívar's Birthday
• July 25: Founding of Guayaquil (Guayaquil)
• September 1-15: Fiesta de Yamor (Otavalo)

- September 23-24: Festival of Our Lady of Mercy (Latacunga)
- October 9: Guayaquil Independence Day
- October 12: Day of the Indigenous Race (in place of Columbus Day)
- November 1: All Saints Day
- November 3: Cuenca Independence Day (Cuenca)
- November 11: Latacunga Independence Day (Latacunga)
- December 6: Foundation of Quito (Quito)
- December 24: Christmas Eve
- December 28-31: Day of the Innocents and New Year's Eve

If any of these holidays falls on a Thursday, you can bet that many businesses will be closed on Friday. Ecuadorians are accustomed to extending time off to the day that falls between a holiday and a weekend. They call it a *puente*, meaning bridge.

LAUNDRY

Most higher-end hotels will happily wash your clothes, at an exorbitant price. If you just have a few articles to be washed, it might be worth it for the convenience and quick turnaround.

If you've got a full suitcase full of dirty duds, we recommend finding the nearest laundromat. Cities will usually have at least one *lavandería* where you can drop off your clothes to be washed. You leave your bag of dirty clothes and come back in a few hours to find washed, dried, and folded finery. Some mid-range hotels have agreements with companies that will pick up and drop off your clothes for you.

Make sure they are not dry-cleaned, *lavaseco*, or your bill will be much heftier than you anticipated. Some laundry places will charge by the kilo and others by the load. If your clothes are wet, look for a place that charges by the load.

Small towns may not have a laundromat, but instead will have a woman who takes in people's wash and does it by hand. She'll never have a dryer, which means if it's not sunny you're taking a suitcase full of clean but wet clothes on to your next destination.

MONEY & BANKING

The current rate of exchange is **US$1 = 17,500 Ecuadorian sucres = Canadian $1.48**. All prices in this book are listed in US dollars. *Sucre* annual inflation historically runs at about 30 to 40 percent, but has been even higher recently. Dollar prices stay more stable. If you are going to be in Ecuador for more than two weeks, you might want to make your currency exchanges in small amounts, as the *sucre* could fluctuate rather wildly during your trip.

Coins come in 1,000; 500; 100 and 50 *sucre* denominations, but they are not good for much. Distinctly colored notes are issued for 100; 500; 1,000; 5,000; 10,000; 20,000 and 50,000 *sucres*. (*Sucres*, by the way, are named after a general who was a key figure in Ecuadorian independence from Spain.)

There are several different ways to access money in Ecuador and not one of them is fool-proof. We suggest traveling with a combination of cash, traveler's checks, credit cards, and your ATM card.

Traveler's Checks

Money exchange offices, *casas de cambio,* and banks will convert your traveler's checks to *sucres*. Money exchange offices are generally faster and more convenient than banks. American Express and Visa are the most widely accepted traveler's checks. If you need to exchange money after hours, both the Quito and Guayaquil airports have exchange offices that stay open until the last planes of the night arrive.

In remote places it can be hard to find anybody to cash traveler's checks, so be sure you have cashed some before you get out of the larger cities. Your hotel might exchange them, but at an unfavorable rate.

You will sometimes find moneychangers outside of the *casas de cambio.* The rate they offer is rarely better than that inside, and even if it is, they are known for passing off counterfeit bills. Just go inside and make the transaction.

There are two benefits to having traveler's checks in Ecuador. The first is that many remote hotels do not accept credit cards. With traveler's checks you can cover your bill without carrying around a lot of cash. The second benefit, and it is an important one with the petty theft in Ecuador, is that they can be replaced if stolen. Be sure to keep your check serial numbers in a different place than your checks.

ATM Cards

In Quito, Guayaquil and almost all other cities ATMs, on both the Cirrus and Plus systems, are the most convenient way to withdraw money from your home bank account. There is usually a fee for withdrawal, but that is outweighed by the favorable exchange rate and convenience. Make sure that your card is authorized for international withdrawals and that you know your pin. You can get money off your credit card out of the same machines.

The problem with relying exclusively on your ATM card is that sometimes you just can't get money out of the darn thing. Even if the machine says that it accepts your type of card you'll find it being rejected for no reason. Machines are also often out of money, especially on Sunday.

We depend primarily on ATMs, but have back-up cash and traveler's checks for those inevitable times when we need money and the ATM just won't give it up.

Credit Cards

Credit cards are widely used in Quito, Guayaquil and the main tourist cities. You may, however, find yourself paying a 6-8% surcharge to cover the merchant's transaction fee. That's standard in Ecuador. In the Galápagos that number jumps to 10%.

Diner's Card is inexplicably the most widely accepted card in the country, followed by MasterCard and then Visa. Just like a TV commercial, you might want to take a Master Card to the Galápagos because they rarely accept Visa or American Express.

Simply because a store displays a credit card logo does not mean that it will necessarily accept the card. It's a good idea to ask before you fill your shopping cart.

As another option, American Express offices will cash a personal check if you carry one of their cards.

Only American Express and Diners Club International have offices in Ecuador:

- **American Express Guayaquil**, *Ecuadorian Tours, Avenida 9 de Octubre 1900. Tel 4/287-111.*
- **American Express Quito**, *Ecuadorian Tours, Amazonas 339. Tel. 2/560-488.*
- **Diners Club Guayaquil**, *Urdesa, V.E. Estrada 306 and Las Lomas. Tel. 4/884-500.*
- **Diners Club Quito**, *Edificio Diners, Avenida de la República 710 and Eloy Alfaro. Tel. 2/553-211.*

Cash

Cash is your best friend in a pinch. Make sure you also have a reserve stash at all times, because you'll probably end up needing it. Try to have a supply of small bills on hand as you move around cities because cab drivers are famous for never having change. If you only have a large bill you might want to ask the cabby if he has change before getting in the car.

NEWSPAPERS & OTHER NEWS SOURCES

The most respected newspaper in Ecuador is *El Comercio* out of Quito. A conservative business paper, it provides good coverage of the country's political, economic, and cultural news. Our hope and dream is to make it in the daily "Airport" section, which is like a society page for travelers. If you want to preview the news before you go you can visit their web site at *www.elcomercio.com*. An alternative is *Hoy*, another daily, which has a more liberal editorial bias.

El Universo is the large, independent paper out of Guayaquil. You can find out about all the news on the coast as well as get the other side of some stories by going to its website at *www.eluniverso.com*. The country's most popular magazine, *Vistazo*, is also published in Guayaquil. It comes out every two weeks and is eagerly awaited by all. It's like Time magazine taken to extremes. The reporting on politics and business is generally more in-depth than you would find in Time, just as the stories on personalities and sports are more gossipy. It's our favorite news source about what is happening in Ecuador. Get the scoop before you go at *www.vistazo.com.ec*. The Ministry of Tourism in Ecuador maintains its own website at *www.ecua.net.ec/mintur/ingles*.

For all the recent AP releases and Washington Post articles concerning Ecuador, visit the Washington Post's excellent site at: *www.washingtonpost.com/wp-srv/inatl/longterm/worldref/country/equador.htr*.

POST OFFICE

The postal service is Ecuador is less than reliable. Not only wind, and rain, and sleet and hail will delay your packages, so will theft and riffling. Never send anything of value, either monetary or personal, in the Ecuadorian mail system. It might make it to its destination unharmed, but why take the chance?

If you need to send a package, we recommend sending it through an international courier that gives you a tracking number. It's more expensive, but we think it's worth it. Higher-end stores will many times offer to mail your items for you. It can be worth the extra expense to avoid the hassle of going to the DHL or FedEx office, just make sure they are using a reliable courier and call them a few days later to get the tracking number.

Post cards and letters usually make it, though you often wonder if they were delivered by one of the giant tortoises of the Galápagos. It costs about $1 to send a postcard to the US. Locals always insist on seeing their letters postmarked so that the postal employees can't steam the stamps off and resell them later.

You can have general delivery letters held at the post office. Your last name should be in capital letters and the letter should be addressed to *Lista de Correos, Correo Central*, and then the name of the city. If you are expecting a held letter, *poste restante*, and it's not there, look under your first and last names because you never know how the clerk has filed it.

The American Express office and South American Explorer's Club will hold mail for their members. The AmEx post office box address is **American Express**, *Apartado 2605, Quito*. The physical address for picking up the mail is *Avenida Amazonas 339*. See below for more information on the South American Explorer's Club.

SAFETY
Crime
There is relatively high incidence of non-violent crime in Ecuador. Pick-pocketing, burglary of personal items, and theft from vehicles are unfortunately common. You should be extra cautious in tourist areas, transportation sites and crowded markets. Bus stations and airports are favorite haunts of petty thieves.

On a more serious note, you should not walk on the beaches at night, even in resort areas. Crimes and assaults are known to take place with some frequency. The US Consul also advises against travel to the provinces of Sucumbios and Carchi, on the Colombian border, as tourist kidnapping and extortion are not unheard of.

Precautions
That's the bad news. The good news is that it's pretty easy to avoid being a victim. The most important thing is to remain alert to your surroundings and keep a watchful eye on backpacks and purses. Thieves usually work in groups, so don't let commotion around you distract you from your belongings. If you look confident and aware, you'll cut down your odds of being marked as an easy target.

We like to buy small locks to secure luggage and backpack zippers as an extra, although not perfect, barrier to entry. We also carry our day packs in front of us to keep an eye on them. Thieves have gotten awfully good at slashing the pack and stealing things out of it without the owner having the slightest idea.

For that same reason, it's not a good idea to keep your wallet in your back pocket. You might want to buy a neck, leg or waist pouch for traveling with your passport and valuables, but that's really not necessary if you are staying in nice hotels with safety deposit boxes and traveling in private transportation. We recommend dividing your money up so that you never have all of it in the same place.

Once you arrive to a town you should put everything into a safe deposit box, *caja de seguridad*, at your hotel if there is one available. If there is not one in your room, check at the front desk. Make sure you get an inventory list from the person handling your things to prevent any "misunderstandings." You should leave your expensive looking jewelry and watches at home.

We travel with copies of our passports, traveler's checks, and plane tickets. It's also a good precaution to write down credit card numbers and emergency replacement telephones so that they can be replaced quickly if they disappear. We even leave photocopies with somebody at home so that if everything gets stolen, a quick fax can get us on the way to having things replaced quickly.

WOMEN TRAVELERS

If you are a woman traveling solo, you are going to get special attention, both positive and negative. Foreign women, especially blondes, are rumored to be "easy" in this macho country. Be aware of that as you deal with Ecuadorian men.

Machismo can sometimes work in your favor. People can't understand why a nice woman would be traveling by herself and will invite you to join them – but they will view you as an oddity. Unfortunately there have been some cases of sexual assault cases against visitors, especially in beach resort areas. A woman should probably not walk anywhere at night alone.

*Less of a safety issue but more a pain, are the **piropos**. Even after years of living in Latin America, I find the propositions you get from men on the street irritating. The best thing to do is absolutely ignore it, but if somebody really bothers or physically touches you, a direct look in the face coupled with a loud "déjame in paz", leave me alone, will usually shame the culprit into slinking away. You can forget about trying to embarrass anybody at construction sites however - just walk on the other side of the street.*

SOUTH AMERICAN EXPLORER'S CLUB

The **South American Explorer's Club**, *Jorge Washington 311 and Leonidas Plaza, Tel. 2/225228, www.samexplo.org*, is a great resource for longer-term travelers in Ecuador. The services they offer their members more than justify the $40 membership fee. In their Quito clubhouse members can:
• Write and receive e-mail
• Obtain hotel and lodge discounts
• Use their excellent library and maps
• Buy books and maps
• Store extra luggage (of any shape and size for as long as you'd like)
• Receive mail
• Read trip reports
• Hang out with other travelers
• Trade books at the book exchange
• Organize trips

They also have clubhouses in Lima, Cuzco and New York. You can join through the New York office before your trip by mailing your check to *126 Indian Creek Rd, Ithaca, NY 14650, Tel. 607/277-048.*

STAYING OUT OF TROUBLE

Civil servants in Ecuador are paid appallingly low salaries, which often inspires corruption. It might be tempting, but it's really best not to pay a bribe. We've found that if you act like you don't understand any Spanish and keep asking dumb-sounding questions in English, the police will get frustrated and go hassle somebody else.

If you keep a low profile and don't break the law you should have no problems. Needless to say, but we will anyway, using drugs in a foreign country is stupid. You'll find little help or sympathy from your Embassy if you break the law.

TAXES

Standard tax rates in Ecuador are 10% and should be noted separately on the check. High and mid-range hotels and restaurants often charge an additional 10% service charge which is divided by the staff.

Make sure you haven't spent every dollar the day before you leave, because there is a $25 departure tax at the airport.

TELEPHONES

Calling from Ecuador

The phone system is Ecuador is not a model for the world, but it more or less works. There are a number of options for using the phone. The most convenient, and expensive in terms of long distance, is making calls directly from your hotel room. You can also make calls from the national phone company's, **EMETEL**, offices. You give the receptionist the number you want dialed, and when it's your turn, she'll direct you to a specific booth. She'll dial the number. If there is an answer she'll ring your booth, where you then pick up the phone and talk to your party. EMETEL offices are generally open from 8am-10pm.

There are two ways to make local calls from public phones. The most common is with tokens, *fichas*, that you can usually buy in a store near the phone. Other phones will except your coins. You'll also see people sitting on the street corner next to a regular telephone on a table. For about $0.50 you can pay them and make a call from there.

A phone service called Porto Alo is a good option for both national and international calls. The Porto Alo phones accept calling cards that you can buy wherever the phones are found. Another interesting option for international calls is the Net Phone service that functions through the internet. Available at many internet cafes, the connection isn't the greatest, but the cost is low.

If you need an operator for national calls dial *Tel. 105*, for international calls, *Tel. 116*. If you are looking for a phone number, you can try information at *Tel. 104*, although many times businesses are listed under corporate names.

To make national long distance calls you dial 0 and then the regional prefix code. To make international calls from Ecuador you dial 999 and then the country code. Canada's code is 175. The United States doesn't have a country code, but rather has carrier prefixes. AT&T is 119, 170 is MCI, and 171 is Sprint. Calls generally average around $2/minute to North America.

Calling to Ecuador

To dial Ecuador from the United States, you much first dial 011, then Ecuador's country code, 593, then the region code (without a zero), and then the number. For example, to call Quito you would dial 011/593/2/xxx xxx.

If you are trying to make travel arrangements and are finding communication a problem, you can use the **AT&T Language Line**, *Tel. 800/843-8420*, for translator service.

Regional Phone Codes

Quito, 2; Ambato, Baños, Puyo, 3; Guayaquil, 4; Manta, Bahía de Caráquez, Galápagos, 5; Esmeraldas, Otavalo, Ibarra, 6; Cuenca, Loja, Vilcabamba, 7.

TELEVISION

The 10 television channels in Ecuador seem to show a staggering array of soap operas and soccer games. We highly recommend the nightly soap operas, *telenovelas*, as a way to improve your Spanish. High-end hotels have cable, so you can get your fix of CNN, ESPN, and HBO.

TIME

Continental Ecuador is on Eastern Standard Time (GMT minus 5). The Galápagos are on Central Standard Time. There is no daylight savings time in Ecuador (it's on the equator, duh), so there is a one hour time difference with the east coast when the United States is on daylight savings time.

TIPPING

Non-mathematical people can relax because standard tipping in restaurants is 10%. Hand it directly to your waiter and tell him or her it is a tip, *propina*. Check your bill in nicer restaurants because many have already added a 10% service charge, *servicio*. This money is evenly divided between the entire wait staff. Even if the service charge is added, it's common to leave a little something (2-5%) for your specific waiter if you think the service merits it.

Airport porters and bellboys are used to receiving about $0.25-.50 a bag from Ecuadorians, but also know that Americans generally tip a buck a bag. It's up to you.

You generally don't tip cabs unless the change is very small or the cabby has helped you with your bags.

It's always difficult to know how much to tip tour guides. A private, English-speaking guide should receive about $10 for a day's work. If you're in a group, consider $5 per person to be split 60/40 between the guide and the driver.

The general rule for tipping on Galápagos boats and in lodges in the Oriente is $5-$10 per visitor per day for the guide and another $5-$10 per visitor per day for the crew or staff.

TOURISM OFFICES

Ecuador's governmental tourism agency, **CETUR**, has offices throughout the country. The helpfulness of their staff, as well as their resources, varies greatly from city to city. If the office in a certain town is especially good, we note that in the destination chapter.

WATER

Don't drink it. Ever. Even if an Ecuadorian tells you it's safe. Just buy bottled water either with, *con*, or without, *sin*, carbonation, *gas*. You'll have a better trip if you stay on the safe side.

Many people stay away from ice as well, but we don't have a problem with it in nice restaurants or tourist hotels.

WEIGHTS & MEASURES

Ecuador uses the metric system. A meter is 1.1 yards, a kilogram is 2.2 pounds, a liter is .26 gallons, and a kilometer is .6 miles. They also use the Celsius as opposed to Fahrenheit temperature system. An easy way to convert C degrees to approximate F degrees is 2C+30. (The accurate formula is 1.8C + 32.)

8. SPORTS & RECREATION

Here's a summary of Ecuador's sporting alternatives as well as the best areas in the country to enjoy the different options. The more specific information about where and how is included in the region chapters.

BEACHES

Ecuadorians cram onto the beach from December through March. Early morning joggers and walkers are replaced by cavorting kids around 10am. Late-night teens often don't show up until near lunchtime to catch rays and play soccer or volleyball.

There is an interesting phenomenon on the Ecuadorian beaches - tents. Even on overcast days you'll find many people settled in under a tent as protection from the sun. If not offered by the hotel, many times people will bring their own pup-tents and set them up right on the beach for the day.

You can find both hopping tourist centers and laid-back surfer spots along the Ecuadorian coast. Keep in mind that the reason Ecuadorians frequent the beach during the rainy season is that it is warmer during this time. Bright sunny mornings give way to afternoon thundershowers. If you go during the *verano*, summer, the skies are often overcast and the temperature cooler.

Best Regions: Central Coast, North Coast, Galápagos.

BIRDING

With over 1500 species of birds, Ecuador offers more bird diversity per square kilometer than any other nation in the world. The key to this diversity is the fact that the country, with its varied geographic melange, comprises eight distinct faunal zones. Each zone offers different birding possibilities. The most famous of these, the Galápagos, is home to many unique species. The Amazonian lowlands, however, is by most accounts, the most bio-diverse region in the world. The cloud forests around **Mindo** are also replete with a multitude of bird species. In terms of infrastructure, many lodges and haciendas in Ecuador specialize in hosting birders, with services such as professional guides and tree canopy towers.

Best Regions: Oriente, Galápagos, Northern Lowlands

FISHING

Though anglers are famous for stretching the truth, it's no lie to say that you can find a bit of everything in Ecuador. Trout have been introduced to streams in the sierra, while marlin, bonito, and sailfish are frequently caught off the coast. Jungle hauls include the infamous piranha and *barge*, huge catfish.

Best Regions: Southern Coast, Northern Sierra, Oriente.

JEFFERSON PEREZ – THESE LEGS WERE MADE FOR WALKING

Jefferson Perez, the only Ecuadorian to ever win an Olympic medal, brought home gold for the country in 1996. He outpaced his competitors in the 20-km speed-walking marathon in Atlanta and strolled into Ecuador's pantheon of heroes. Perez, 24 years old, is an official National Figure.

The entire country stopped what they were doing on July 26, 1996 to watch Perez as he maintained his position among the leaders of the race. After an hour of competition, most TV and radio stations in Ecuador had switched to coverage of the marathon. When he crossed the finish line in an hour and twenty minutes, the country exploded in a spontaneous wave of cheers, blaring horns and celebration. His success has inspired a whole group of young walkers, but more importantly has inspired the country. For once they have triumphed on an international level.

GOLFING

Golf is almost exclusively a country-club sport in Ecuador. There are few public courses but access comes at private course prices. The only golf course in South America designed by Jack Nicolas, just nine holes, can be found at the Club Casa Blanca near Esmeraldas.

Best Region: North Coast, Quito.

HANDBALL

Handball, also called *pelota nacional*, or national ball, is interesting to watch and difficult to master. Played with partners on a narrow slab, the idea is to advance along the lines drawn in the cement. As soon as a point is over, a new team steps in yelling, "pelota" to alert to other team to an incoming serve. The squishy ball is hit high in the air rather than put away

in smashes. Most visitors to Ecuador are introduced to the game when they see it being played on the far end of Pancho Plaza in Otavalo.
Best Region: Northern Sierra

HIKING & BACKPACKING

With Ecuador's backbone a set of parallel mountain chains, you can count on excellent hikes and dramatic scenery. The Andean *páramo*, a sub-alpine zone, features treks that pass by some of Ecuador's most famous volcanic peaks. You also have the option to hike back in time as you follow the Inca Trail to the country's last remaining Inca ruins. Guided hikes in the Amazon help reveal the splendor of the jungle.
Best Regions: Highlands, Oriente.

HORSEBACK RIDING

The conquistadors are gone, but both their haciendas and horses remain. Well, not their exact horses, but their horses' descendants anyway. These sturdy Andean mounts have adapted well to their high altitude homes. Many of the haciendas have been converted to excellent inns that offer horseback riding programs as their main sporting attraction. You could ride for weeks across the sierra. Those who are more prone to saddle sores can enjoy rides of just an hour or an afternoon in the Ecuadorian countryside.
Best Regions: Highlands.

MOUNTAIN BIKING

While many Ecuadorians use their bicycles as a source of transportation, there are plenty of gnarly adventures to be pedaled. The heights of the Andes mean steep climbs and all-out downhills. Most tour companies will haul you to the top of the mountain in a van and then let you loose for the ride down. Cheating...but fun.
Best Regions: Highlands.

MOUNTAINEERING, ROCK CLIMBING & ICE CLIMBING

Even the most experienced mountaineers can find a challenge in Ecuador. Geological forces have worked like a bad chiropractor on the country's spine to make each vertebra a high reaching mountain or volcano. It's an excellent place to train at altitude, as there are ten peaks over 5,000 meters. Short distances from city to mountain and roads up the skirts of the Andes make approaches and logistics simpler than you would imagine.

Only 60km south of Quito, perfectly conical Cotopaxi, one of the highest active volcanoes in the world, is probably the country's most popular climb. You can hire your guide and rent all the equipment you'll need in Quito. Summiting the country's highest peak, 6310 meter Chimborazo, requires more experience and technical skills.

Ecuador's big ten mountains are:
• Chimborazo – 6310 m
• Cotopaxi – 5897 m
• Cayambe – 5790 m
• Antisana – 5758 m
• El Altar – 5320 m
• Iliniza Sur – 5248 m
• Sangay – 5230 m
• Iliniza Norte – 5126 m
• Tungurahua – 5023 m
• Carihuairazo – 5020 m

Best Regions: Highlands.

RAFTING & RIVER KAYAKING

Where there are mountains with snow, there are rivers. Abundant rivers run both east and west off the Andes to create a playground for paddlers. Even the headwaters of the mighty Amazon are here. You can head to the east, through the heart of the jungle, or off to the tropical scenery of the west. Most trips are organized out of Quito although the rafting is actually on rivers a couple of hours away.

Best Regions: Quito, Oriente.

SCUBA DIVING & SNORKELING

Forget tropical reefs. The Galápagos gives you the chance to dive with an amazing assortment of practically fearless marine animals. You may have shared the waters with sea turtles and manta rays before, but how about penguins and hammerheads? All of these animals, and more, can be experienced by diving the Galápagos. Sea lions, dolphins, tropical fish and even sharks are seen at the roughly 25 dive sites. You can schedule a morning dive or spend a week on a specially outfitted dive ship exploring this fascinating ecosystem. Cold waters and strong currents are good reasons to make sure your diving skills are up to par.

Snorkeling is a must if you visit the area. Almost all boats have masks, fins and snorkels on-board, but you might want to bring your own for a custom fit.

Best Regions: Galápagos.

SURFING

Surfers have covered all of Ecuador's coast in the eternal search for the perfect wave. While perfection remains elusive, they have found some pretty good spots in their quest. Montañita is Ecuador's most famous surf town, but we prefer the breaks just up the coast from there.

Another popular surf destination is the 400-meter tube wave off of Muisne in the north. The Galápagos even has a swell during part of the year. The best months for surfing are December-May. The Surf Report from **Surfer Publications**, *US Tel. 714/496-5922,* has a report on Ecuador.

Best Regions: Central Coast, Northern Coast, Galápagos.

TENNIS

Andres Gomez' success on the men's professional tour made tennis a well-followed sport in Ecuador. The recent rise in the rankings of youngster Nicolas Lapentti has continued to feed that interest. Most of the courts are concentrated in Quito and Guayaquil as well as at resorts along the coast. The most common surface is red clay, which is a novel experience for Americans accustomed to hard courts.

Best Regions: Quito, Southern Coast.

NICOLAS LAPENTTI

Nicolas Lapentti, a professional tennis player from Guayaquil, has recently made great strides in his game. Ranked as one of the top ten players in the world, he's an Ecuadorian hero. Just 23 years old, he started his rise at the beginning of 1999 at the Australian Open, where he reached the semi-finals. Since then he has continued to climb in the rankings, gaining more news coverage and popularity in Ecuador.

The handsome Lapentti is also followed quite closely off the court. He received as much press for his special friendship with sex-pot Anna Kornakova as for any of his tennis successes.

VOLLEYBALL

This is not Olympic rules volleyball. With three players per side, a nine-foot net, and legal palming, Ecuador has recreated the game. It is not played with a volleyball, but rather a heavy soccer ball. You'll see the skinny macramé-looking nets strung up on poles through out the country. Even if a net is not available, that's not always a problem. We've seen kids playing it with a basketball over a set of monkey-bars. Unique in Latin America, Ecuadorians play as much volleyball as they do soccer. Give it a go when you're at the park or beach and see how you fair.

Best Regions: Entire country.

SPECTATOR SPORTS

BULLFIGHTING

Bullfighting is an extremely popular sport in Ecuador, often associated with festival celebrations. During the bullfight season, in December, matadors come from Spain to the large Plaza de Toros in Quito. In these fights, the bulls are killed as they are in Spain.

We prefer the more popular bullfights in towns around Ecuador. During the local festivals, the main plaza will be closed off and bleachers set up around the sides. Here the matadors do not kill the bulls but merely go through the earlier phases of the fight.

DAVIS CUP

Latin America Davis Cup matches are famous for being rowdy. Similar to soccer games, with drum banging, flag waving, and continual cheering, it's a great experience if you happen to be in town. Matches are on center court of the National Stadium in Guayaquil.

SOCCER

Soccer is the national sport of choice. Flip through the TV channels and you'll find two, three, or even four games on at the same time. Even if you know nothing about the sport, you should attend a game purely for the spectacle. Your first choice would be to see a National Team game. Fans are decked out to support their boys with passion. Your next best bet would be a professional game.

9. SHOPPING

In Ecuador, the shopping process is often as memorable and valuable as the item you actually end up buying. This is not to say that the country does not have excellent handicrafts, *artesanía* and textiles, but rather to emphasize the uniqueness of many buying experiences here.

Whether you are surrounded by a crazy kaleidoscope of over-burdened fellow customers, piles of hand-made woolen goods and bleating livestock in a Saturday morning market, or alone with a crafts-man in his home viewing his family's work, you will remember your shopping trips in Ecuador.

Another unforgettable facet of your search for souvenirs will be the prices. The strong dollar makes all but the most labor-intensive work by famous artisans easily within reach of the typical traveler. Some things are so inexpensive that you will find yourself calculating the price three or four times in your head to make sure you divided correctly. Chances are you did.

MARKETS

One of the most unique experiences in Ecuador is a morning at the market. The trick with visiting markets is to know what time to get there. Early in the morning, before the tour buses arrive, they act as thriving indigenous markets. Items that are of little commercial interest to tourists - food stuffs, animals and cookware - trade hands between locals while the cocks are still crowing. You should make sure you're up and at 'em then because this is really the most interesting time to be there. Especially at the most famous markets like Otavalo and Saquisilí, you want to get there before the tourist buses start in pull in around 10 or 11am.

By the time the buses roll in, around 11, most of the locals have done their shopping and gone home. This is the time for you to head to the textile section of the market or town to search for that sweater for your mom or the blanket for your nephew.

WHEN TO BUY

• **Monday** – *Ambato*
• **Tuesday** – *Latacunga, Guano, Riobamba, Salcedo*
• **Wednesday** – *Otavalo, Pujilí*
• **Thursday** – *Saquisilí, Riobamba, Guamote, Cuenca, Tulcán*
• **Friday** – *Ingapirca*
• **Saturday** – *Otavalo, Latacunga, Azogues, Zumbahua, Salcedo, Riobamba, Guano, Tambo*
• **Sunday** – *Cañar, Pujilí, Peguche, Saraguro, Cajabamba, Cotacachi*

WHAT TO BUY

Textiles

Ecuadorians have been experts in weaving textiles since before the colonial days. Hundreds of years of experience have created the wide variety of textiles found throughout the country today. Wool and cotton are the most popular yarns. Widespread woolen items include sweaters, hats, and gloves woven in colorful prints and solids. Wool carpets and wall hangings are another category of popular woven goods. Done by hand, each one is unique. We think the cotton shirts make great, lightweight gifts. The most sought out of these are either embroidered or trimmed with intricate and interesting designs.

Hammocks and shoulder bags, generally woven from nylon, are extremely popular, and functional. Brightly-colored hammocks are not just for looks, which you'll experience first hand in the lazy afternoon heat of the Coast or Oriente. The shoulder bags, called *shigras*, are the perfect satchel for toting your towel and sunscreen about.

Baskets are another popular woven item. Extremely inexpensive and good-looking, many of them can also stand up to the shmushing of the plane trip home.

Panama Hats

For the ultimate in shmushability, try a Panama Hat. One of the biggest surprises to most visitors to Ecuador (and Panama for that matter) is that Panama Hats are made in Ecuador. They are not called Panama Hats in Ecuador either, but rather *sombreros de paja toquilla*. Woven from plant fibers, these hats are famous for their tight weave, which fends off both sun and rain, and their ability to pop back into shape after the rigors of travel.

Custom says, although we've never seen it personally, that the highest quality Panama hat can be rolled up, passed through a wedding ring, and then spring perfectly back into shape when unrolled. A napkin ring seems more likely. Most Panamas are made in **Cuenca**, but some excellent ones are also woven just inland from Manta in **Montecristi** and **Jipijapa**.

PANAMA HATS

In the mid-1800s, with the California gold rush in full swing, boatloads of men seeking riches passed across Panama on their way to the West Coast. While there, many of them picked up straw hats made in Ecuador as protection against the strong rays of the sun. Not knowing any better, they called them **Panama Hats.**

Half a century later, swarms of Americans again descended on Panama, this time to work on the famous canal. Once again, those hats brought up from Ecuador were perfect to keep the worker's heads cool and covered. Poor Ecuador didn't get the credit for the hats this time either. To the continual consternation of Ecuadorians, the Panama name stuck.

Panamas became the height of fashion in the United States and Europe, worn by presidents, movie stars, and men who wanted to feel like them. In 1945, export sales for Panama hats represented 22% of total Ecuadorian exports. Although they have lost some of their popularity with the jet set, the hats are still a favorite Ecuadorian souvenir.

Woodwork

The tradition of fine woodworking in Ecuador has colonial roots. Just a peak inside any of the hundreds of churches around the country shows the fine work that can be produced with chisels and skilled hands. Religious art such as crucifixes and virgins, functional furniture master-pieces, sculptures of animals and exaggerated masks can be found in towns and markets around the country.

Leatherwork

Skilled cobblers can make you a pair of custom-fit shoes or boots while a leatherworker in another shop takes your measurements for a new jacket. Cowhide purses, belts, wallets and bags hang from shop stalls and windows at a fraction of the price that they can be found in other countries.

Painting

Colorful scenes of rural life, painted on stretched sheepskin, are prized folk art out of Ecuador. Named **Tigua paintings**, after the region from which they come, these beautiful works of art generally represent scenes of communal village life. Whether depicting festivals, crop harvests, market days or marriages, the incredibly detailed, vibrant paintings will capture your attention and imagination. Many of them come with decorated frames as well.

Other

The list of additional *artesanía* that comes out of Ecuador is a long one. Marzipan figurines, Christmas tree ornaments, jewelry, blowpipes, and metalwork add to the list of things that might make it back home with you. Tagua sculptures, whittled from the nut of a Tagua tree, make interesting gifts as they look and feel just like ivory.

WHERE TO BUY

There are three ways to go about buying your goods in Ecuador. The first of these is to visit large markets where items from all over the region, or even the country, are brought in for consumers. This is the best way to get a sense of the breadth of items available or to efficiently cover everybody on your gift list. The quality of items is generally high and the prices almost as good as they will be at the source.

The second is to go to the communities that specialize in creating certain types of work. Many artisan items come primarily from a certain village or region of the country. By traveling to that town you can usually find the greatest selection for that particular item. Even if you are not especially interested in buying, it's fascinating to see every home on the block dedicated to the same craft.

The third is to shop in stores that carry the handicrafts. This is many times an easy way to find some of the highest quality items because the shopkeeper has already done the culling for you.

Some villages are known and visited primary for the crafts and works of art they produce. The following list covers many of these:

• Woolen textiles - *Otavalo*
• Detailed weavings – *Cuenca*
• Embroidered clothing and linens – *Hacienda Zuleta near Otavalo*
• Panama Hats – *Cuenca, Montecristi, Jipijapa*
• Statues and other woodwork – *San Antonio de Ibarra near Ibarra*
• Religious woodwork – *Quito, Cuenca*
• Masks – *Cotopaxi*
• Leatherwork – *Cotacachi near Otalavo*
• Tigua Paintings – *Tigua/Chimbucucho near Latacunga*
• Blowguns - *Oriente*
• Dough figurines – *Calderón near Quito*
• Jewelry – *Chordeleg near Cuenca*
• Agave bags – *Riobamba*
• Carpets – *Guano near Riobamba*

WHAT NOT TO BUY

It is against the law to take animal products out of Ecuador, endangered or otherwise. This includes mounted butterflies, monkey paws and feather creations. It is also illegal to take any antiquities out of the country. Most of the ceramics being passed off as ancient aren't, but if they are, steer clear.

HOW TO BUY

There is a ritual to the buying process in many markets. You will first express interest in an item and ask how much it costs. The seller will then throw out a price she hopes you'll be willing to pay. You will then act as if that's too much and offer another price. She will act offended and make an offer lower than her original price but higher than yours...and so the dance goes on.

It's often fun to bargain in markets, but don't get so caught up in it that you forget the big picture. Many times I have gotten back home and kicked myself for not buying that great sweater simply because the asking price was $0.50 more than I was determined to pay at the time. Also, that $0.50 was really nothing to me, but could mean a lot to the person selling the item.

10. FOOD & DRINK

Ecuadorian food varies from province to province, but starch is consistently the main ingredient of most Ecuadorians' diets, be it potatoes, bananas, yucca, bread or rice. A traditional Ecuadorian meal might include a meat dish accompanied with boiled potatoes, potato cakes, and fried bananas.

The good news if you're not a fan of the yellow food group is that not all people eat that way. There are some excellent meals to be had in Ecuador. Bountiful seafood, delicious and exotic fresh fruit, and international twists on Ecuadorian fare offer the traveler a myriad of options for unforgettably tasty meals. This chapter will help you make the most of each time you sit down to dine.

OUR FAVORITE RESTAURANTS IN ECUADOR

In all of these places you'll find excellent food in an atmosphere that perfectly complements the location.
- *Villa Goya - Quito*
- *La Viña – Quito*
- *Magic Bean - Quito*
- *La Mirage – Otavalo, Northern Highlands*
- *Hacienda San Agustín de Callo – Cotopaxi, Central Highlands*
- *Marianne – Baños, Central Highlands*
- *Villa Rosa – Cuenca, Southern Highlands*
- *Caracol Azul – Guayaquil, Southern Coast*
- *Le Gormet – Guayaquil, Southern Coast*
- *Hostería Atamari – Machalilla, Central Coast*

WHAT & WHEN PEOPLE EAT

Ecuadorians generally start their day right before work with Nescafe, bread and scrambled eggs. Most of them will then work until lunch at about 1pm. The custom is that lunch, *almuerzo*, is the largest meal of the day. The typical fixed price meal - soup, an entrée with a starch, and dessert - is standard fare. When you order the *menú* at lunch it is called an *almuerzo* and at dinner a *merienda*. People normally won't eat again until around 8pm. Dinner, *cena*, at home is usually a lighter version of lunch.

Ecuadorians fall in the middle of the South American alcohol consumption ladder. Beer is the most common drink for many, even in nice restaurants. Wine, imported primarily from Chile, is quite expensive relative to other drinks.

Shellfish & Seafood
Mariscos y Pescado

Get ready to eat boatloads of seafood at bargain basement prices. Plentiful prawns, shrimp as big as melon slices, and loads of ceviche are yours for the feasting. It would be a crime for you to leave Ecuador without sampling the following treats from the sea:

• *Ceviche*: If there is a dish that typifies coastal Ecuadorian cuisine (besides bananas), this would have to be it. Ceviche is especially savory when you're sitting on the beach under a thatched umbrella listening to the waves crash on the shore. Take tender seafood marinated in lemon, onions, and cilantro, accompany it with cold beer and popcorn, and you've found paradise. You can choose from ceviche made of shrimp, *camarones*; fish, *pescado;* squid, *calamari;* shellfish, *concha*; or a mixture of all of them, *mixta*. To guard against cholera, you need to make sure they have cooked the seafood. As a quirky bonus, Ecuadorian ceviche is always served with popcorn, *canguil*. You'll also see ceviche spelled *cebiche*. It tastes the same either way.

• *Encocados*: Fresh seafood stewed in flavorful coconut milk wins our prize as the culinary highlight of the northern coast. A hint of Asia, a touch of Brazil, but 100% Ecuadorian delicious.

• *Camarones*: Ecuadorian shrimp are served in the finest restaurants around the world. Most of the largest shrimp are designated for export, but there are some restaurants in the country that serve the big guys. Regardless of the shrimp's size, their flavor is excellent. If it's possible to overdose on shrimp, you'll do it in Ecuador, simply because it's so inexpensive and available.

• *Langostina*: When you're going to splurge on a meal, check and see if the restaurant has fresh prawn. Whether it's grilled, *a la brasa*; or streamed, *al vapor* it's an exquisite treat. We go all out and dunk each tender morsel in rich, melted butter, *mantiquilla*.

• *Cangrejo*: Red mangrove crab, distinct from the blue crab we usually eat, is especially tasty when prepared in special *criollo* seasonings. If it's stone crab, *pangor*, season, we highly recommend ordering the meaty delight prepared any way it is offered.

You'll also want to sample the local fish. *Corvina*, sea bass is our favorite white fish. *Atún*, tuna; and *trucha*, trout, are also available. Smoked trout is a specialty of the Northern Highlands. *Pargo*, red snapper is best when served *a la plancha*, filleted and grilled. Most travelers to the Oriente like to try piranha, but it's more for show than flavor. *Bagre*, giant catfish, is one of the tastiest fish of the jungle.

Many times fish is served breaded, *apanado;* deep-fried, *brosterizado;* or pan-fried, *frito*. Watch out for food *a la mantiquilla*, swimming in butter (except the prawn of course) or *con mayonesa*, drowned in mayonnaise.

Soups & Stews
Sopas y Secos

Whether served as a first course with lunch or dinner or eaten as a light meal, soups are one of Ecuador's strong points. Don't miss *locro*, a full-bodied combination of cheese, avocado, and potato or *fanesca*, an Easter special full of onions, peanuts, fish, rice, and loads of vegetables. A delicious coastal soap is *encebollado*, fresh yellow fin tuna and yucca. It's traditional to plop a few spoonfuls of popcorn directly into your soup bowl. Are you brave enough to try the *caldo de pata*, pieces of cow hooves floating in a clear broth? People swear by both its flavor and Viagra-like qualities.

Seco, which means dry in Spanish, is inexplicably a term for a moist meat stew served over rice. The most common ones are *seco de pollo*, stewed chicken and *seco de chivo*, stewed kid.

Snacks & Pastries
Picadas, Pan, y Pasteles

Ecuadorian popcorn, *canguíl*, is one of our favorite snacks in Ecuador. Always served with ceviche, it also often accompanies soups. Street vendors sell bags of the stuff, which makes for a great post-museum treat. If it's natural looking it's probably salted, *salado*, and if it's pink it's sugarcoated, *dulce*.

Empanadas are ubiquitous snacks. These turnovers, stuffed with various ingredients and then fried, are handy and delicious. There are many different kinds of *empanadas* in Ecuador. Our favorites are the *empanada verde*, plantain dough filled with cheese, and the *morochos*, long skinny corn pastries filled with ground beef and carrots. Similar to *empanadas* are the *chiguiles*, corn flower pancakes with chicken breast and hard-boiled eggs.

Potato-based munchies are also popular. *Llapingachos*, a type of potato and cheese pancake, will definitely get you through until dinner or ever count as a meal, especially if served with *fritada*, bits of roasted pork.

LLAPINGACHOS

"Ophelia appeared with potato cakes with cheese melted in the centres. Tony called them 'yapping gauchos.' I imagined Argentineans camped out on the pampas sipping *maté* from gourds and howling at the moon while their potato cakes fried."
– Johanna Angermeyer in *My Father's Island*

Tortillas are not like the Mexican version of the same name. They are thick rounds that look like pancakes made either of wheat or corn. We like the corn ones best, as they taste like little cornbreads. *Humitas*, a *tamale*-like snack filled with cheese and steamed in plantain leaves, are delicious if moist.

Our stomachs just can't handle them, but Ecuadorians love *salchipapas*, a bag of greasy fries covered with hunks of hotdog and topped with mayo, ketchup, and mustard.

Ecuadorian bakeries are an excellent option for a quick, inexpensive nosh to get you to the next meal. Not only do they sell *empanadas*, but also scores of different kinds of breads and desserts. Just point at whatever strikes your fancy. Wheat bread is called *pan integral*.

Chifles, plantains fried like potato chips, are a favorite finger food on the coast. They go quite well with beer and seafood, as does *tostado*, toasted corn. More common in the Highlands, *tostado* is also reputed to take the smell of alcohol off your breath.

Fruit
Fruta

Ecuador's fruit, whether eaten straight off the stand or in a tall glass of juice, *jugo*, is outstanding. Exotic varieties we can't find at home are a dime a dozen here. Our favorites are *naranjilla*, a strange cross between a tomato and an orange; and *maracuya*, passion fruit. *Papaya* and *guanabana* are standard as are the old favorites, orange, *naranja*; blackberry, *mora;* and grapefruit, *toronja*. The strangest-looking-fruit-with-the-best-name award goes to *babaco*, whose excellent juice comes out of what looks like a yellow and green ridged football.

Bananas are not just fruit to Ecuadorians, but rather *oro verde*, green gold. One of the country's major exports, they also feed everything in the country. You'll see huge piles of green bananas along the highway in the highlands. They are used as livestock fodder. People also consume their fair share.

There are different kinds of bananas. *Oritos* are the little yellow ones. They are very sweet eating. *Bananos*, the bigger yellow ones that we call bananas at home, are also eaten raw, but they aren't as sweet as *oritos*. *Platanos*, what we call plantains, are used for cooking. They use green ones in salty dishes and ripe ones for sweet treats. We like the *patacones*, smashed and fried green plantains.

AVOID THE BUGS

Finicky stomachs are no fun on vacation. There are some common sense things you can do to make sure you don't end up spending your vacation in your hotel room or even the hospital.

*• **Take it slowly**. Let your body get used to the new germs you will encounter in any new place. Be especially careful your first few days and then, as your resistance grows, venture out to exciting new taste sensations.*

*• **Don't eat raw foods**. Yes, we just waxed lyrically about the ceviche, but make sure the ingredients are cooked, not just marinated.*

*• **Don't drink the water**. Drink only bottled or boiled water or carbonated drinks. Anything else will leave you doubled over faster than you can say, "Dónde está el baño?"*

MAIN COURSES
Segundos
Traditional Food
Comida Tradicional

Roasted guinea pig, *cuy*, is one of those dishes that you just have to try because it's so odd. Eaten by the Highland Indians for hundreds of years, it's a dish, like turkey in the United States, reserved for holidays and special occasions. Paintings from the Quito school even show the disciples and Jesus sitting down to a Last Supper featuring everybody's favorite childhood pet.

If you're really hungry, or had a bit too much *aguardiente* the night before, you might want to try the *churrasco*. Fried beef, fried eggs, fried potatoes, avocado, tomato and rice will get you up to your grease quotient for the day. Anything served *montañero* comes with a fried egg on top. You might want to avoid *guatita*, tripe, unless you're especially brave.

You can spice up any meal with Ecuadorian hot sauce, known as *ají*. You'll find this on every table in the country. If you want it even hotter you can ask for *más picante*.

Beef & Chicken
Carne y Pollo

Ecuadorian beef is generally pretty good, but it's no Argentina. *Un cuarto*, rare; *medio*, medium; *tres quartos*, medium-well; and *bien cocido*, well done, are the terms for how you like your steak cooked. A *parrillada* is an assortment of grilled meat that virtually offers every part of the cow. Sometimes it also comes with chicken and pork as well.

Pork, *chancho*, is generally served as *chorizo*, sausage or *chuletas*, chops. Tender suckling pig, usually roasted whole, is called *lechón*.

Chicken is everywhere. Most restaurants will have *pollo con papas fritas*, chicken and fries; *pollo al horno*, baked chicken; and *pollo con arroz*, chicken and rice on the menu.

YOU SAY POTATO, I SAY PAPA

The simple potato is one of the world's main food crops, and it got its start here in the Andes. Records indicate that potatoes were raised in South America as early as 1,800 years ago. The Spanish conquistadors exported the tuber to Europe, and now many people associate potatoes more with Ireland or Idaho than Ecuador. Keep your eyes open at village markets, where you can supposedly see as many as 20 varieties, but we can only differentiate about five or six.

*Keep in mind that this is one of those words in Spanish where the article matters...**la papa** is the kind you eat, el Papa is the Pope.*

Desserts
Postres

No meal is complete without a little sweet touch at the end. *Flan*, custard; *cocadas*, macaroon-like sweets; *bocadillos*, peanuts and honey; and *helado*, ice-cream, are typical restaurant options. We also like the *higos con queso*, figs dipped in honey served with cheese, and *pristiños*, honey wheat pastries.

Breakfast
Desayuno

The breakfasts that are included in the price of many rooms are usually light. Toast, *pan tostado*; marmalade, *mermelada*; butter, *mantequilla*; and tea or coffee, *te o café*, is somehow supposed to get you through until lunch. Occasionally places will serve eggs that you can order scrambled, *revueltos* or fried, *fritos*.

Coffee is always an adventure in Ecuador. You're never quite sure how you will get it. When you're lucky it's the good ground and brewed stuff. Other times it's Nescafe, which you can order *con leche*, with milk, or *pintado*, with water and milk. The last alternative, which you've probably never seen before, is called *esencia*, or essence. This essence of coffee is a super-thick, brewed coffee that sits at room temperature in a little pitcher on the table. You pour some of this in your cup and cut it with either hot water, hot milk or both.

Ludwig Bemelmans in his book *The Donkey Inside* says: "If you love coffee you must bring your own. They cook the coffee long in advance, brewing a foul ink of it which is kept in a bottle. Half a cupful of this dye is poured out, the sugar bowl emptied into it, and a little milk added on."

Fast Food
Comida Rápida

Ecuador is not unique in a world with McDonalds, Pizza Hut, Dominos, KFC, and Burger King sprouting up in the largest cities.

Non-Ecuadorian Food
Comida No Ecuatoriana

Quito, Guayaquil, and Baños are really the only cities that offer a range of ethic foods. Mexican, Thai, Japanese, Italian, Indian, and others can all be had if you're in need of a fix. Economical Chinese restaurants known as *chifa* are popular with the backpack crowd.

RESTAURANT LISTINGS IN THIS BOOK

In each restaurant listing we include the address and the phone number of the establishment. If the restaurant does not accept credit cards, or only accepts one type of credit card, we tell you that. If the listing says, "credit cards accepted," we mean they accept Visa, MasterCard, Diners, and American Express.

All listings fall into a price category of inexpensive, moderate, expensive, or very expensive. It's a lot cheaper in Ecuador than it is at home, especially if you eat the fixed meal, called menú, which is served at lunch or dinner.

To determine each restaurant's price category, we looked a meal that includes a main course, one drink, and either an appetizer or dessert. Wine, expensive in Ecuador because it is imported in small quantities, is not included in our price considerations.

*• **Inexpensive** – under $4*
*• **Moderate** – $4-$8*
*• **Expensive** – $9-12*
*• **Very Expensive** – over $12*

Non-Alcoholic Drinks
Bebidas Sin Alcohol

You can buy water and soft drinks everywhere. It's a good thing too, because you can't drink the tap water. Ecuador has all the international brands like Coke, Pepsi and 7-Up. Bottled water can be bought with, *con*; or without, *sin*; carbonation, *gas*. The major brand of carbonated water is called Guiteg. Many times when people are offering you water they will say *Guiteg* instead of *agua*. It can cause a double take because it sounds as if they are saying *whiskey*.

Juices are available throughout the country, but if you're buying it freshly squeezed from a café you need to be vigilant that they don't add tap water or non-pasteurized milk.

Yes, Ecuador is a coffee producing country, but Nescafe is also quite popular. If you seek it out, however, you can find a good cup of joe.

Alcoholic Drinks
Bebidas con Alcohol

Aguardiente, literally translated as "burning water" is a strong licorice-flavored booze. Made from sugar cane, it is often chugged straight from the bottle.

Ecuadorians, especially those from the coast, love beer. You would too if you lived in a sauna. There are just a handful of brands available. Many people consider the best Ecuadorian beer, *cerveza*, to be a brand called Club. Just make sure it's coming in bottle, not one of those wimpy 8 oz cans. Pilsner, another brand, comes in large bottles, which makes it a popular choice when quantity matters. Draft beer, called *choop*, pronounced "shoop," is quite inexpensive.

Chicha, fermented rice or manioc, has been quaffed since Inca times. In more remote areas the fermentation process is speeded along by chewing and saliva; you can pass on those batches, but it's good manners to act as if you are drinking it. Unless you are quite deep in the jungle, *chicha* sans-spit is what you'll normally be offered.

Cañelazo is a popular party drink. When there's a fiesta going on you're sure to encounter this mixture of boiled water, *aguardiente*, lemon, sugar, and cinnamon. We think it's great on chilly days.

Wine

Since Ecuadorian wine, *vino*, is not of high quality, Chilean labels invariably comprise the majority of the wine lists. Often it is the only origin available. In our dedication to assiduous research, we sampled a good number of Chilean wines while writing Open Road's *Chile Guide*.

Our preferences among the Chilean labels offered in Ecuador are as follows:

Casillero del Diablo will consistently be the best Cabernet Sauvignon for the money. It is usually priced at about $20 per bottle in restaurants.

Tarapacá and **Cousiño-Macul** are also excellent selections. Tarapacá is noted for its Sauvignon Blanc, especially the pricier *reserva*. Cousiño-Macul produces superior Cabernet Sauvignons.

The **Concha y Toro** label carries the vintner's name, but is of lesser quality than its Casillero del Diablo. This is often the most inexpensive wine offered and is on almost every menu. **Gato Negro** is of about the same quality as Concha y Toro. Both are less dry and lack a fullness of body compared to the others mentioned, but are still palatable.

Because restaurant food prices in Ecuador are so low, you will find that ordering a bottle of wine may more than double the cost of a meal for two. Some wines are available in half bottles. Wine sold by the liter in carafes, offered only in a few restaurants, is much less expensive. Ordering by the glass is another good option.

11. ECUADOR'S BEST PLACES TO STAY

HACIENDAS

HACIENDA SAN AGUSTIN DE CALLO, *Just north of Lasso on the left off the Panamericana, Cotopaxi, Central Highlands. Tel./Fax 3/719 160, Quito Tel. 2/242 508, Quito Fax 2/269 884. 4 rooms. Double $225. Breakfast and either lunch or dinner included. Three hours horseback riding included. Restaurant. Bar. Credit cards accepted.*

The hacienda at San Agustín de Callo is one of the most extraordinary properties in the country. The best preserved Inca ruins in Ecuador, gourmet food and extraordinary rooms are the perfect ingredients for a most memorable stay in the Central Highlands.

It's no mystery why the Inca chose this spot for building. Cotopaxi looms so big and close you feel like you can reach out and trace the contours of the mountain with your finger. Its size and majesty are enthralling. Once you pull your eyes away from the volcano, you'll notice you're in the hacienda's main courtyard. Thick yellow walls; red roof tiles; and abundant plants and flowers give the stone patio unexpected warmth. There might even be a shaggy llama or two hanging around the central fountain.

Although the hacienda merits a visit simply for the views and quality of the installations, it's the history that makes it unique. Built by the Incas in the 1400s, it was then converted by Augustan friars into a monastery. Notice as you enter the chapel, that three of the walls are the original Inca masonry. Large, perfectly chiseled stones fit together so tightly that that no mortar was necessary to keep them standing here over half a millennium.

First **La Condamine** and then **Humbolt** visited to study what Humbolt called, "The House of the Inca" during their respective expeditions in Ecuador. Famous landscape painter **Frederic Church** captured the majesty of Cotopaxi from here in the mid-1800s. Other distinguished guests include presidents and countless well-known 20th century Ecuadorian politicians.

There's a large living area for all guests off the corner of the courtyard. With multiple fireplaces, dark wooden floors, thick exposed beams and an original Inca wall, it's perhaps the most pleasant place on the property. Comfortable sofas and huge pillows are strewn about, offering plenty of space to sit down and go over some of the books from their collection of excellent Ecuador titles. Interesting antiques and family photos make you feel as if you have been invited into the weekend home of the country's elite. You have been. Owner Miñon Plaza has left this room basically intact from the days before the hacienda was open to guests.

The dining room, with two original walls, is probably the most spectacular setting for a meal in the entire country. Even if you're not staying at the hacienda, a meal here is a must. Both breakfast and dinner are included in the cost of a room. (See *Where to Eat* in the *Cotopaxi* section.)

The guestrooms at the hacienda, built around the courtyard, are each unique. All however feature exposed walls with sections of painted plaster, antique country furnishings, and at least two fireplaces. A Chilean muralist has interpreted the spirit of each room with whimsical illustrations. The large Geodesic Room features a vast picture window looking out at the countryside. The bathroom is marvelous, with a skylight above the tub, and glass-covered excavations in the floor showing sections of Inca wall.

If you envision yourself spending much time soaking in the tub, you might want to request the Fat Lady Room. Large women lounging at a Turkish bath cover the walls of the lavatory. As an extra bonus, the flickering light from the bathroom fireplace seems to make them dance. The Mural Room, so named because of its extensive wall decoration, is one of the only rooms with cable TV. This room, with thick eucalyptus mantles on the fireplaces, also reveals a piece of Inca wall. The room next door, without a private bathroom, is being re-designed to create a suite with the Mural Room.

The Presidential Suite is just that – a place where chief executives have stayed. Ex-President Leónidas Plaza Guttierez, great-grandfather of the woman who owns the hotel, bought the hacienda in 1921. In addition, Ex-President Galo Plaza Lasso was one of her uncles. The large, comfortable suite, with two rooms and hardwood floors, just feels like a president's bedroom.

If you want more privacy or want to cook a few meals for yourself, there is also a little house on a hill above the main complex available for rent. With a comfortable kitchen and living area in addition to the master bedroom, it's the perfect country cottage. There's only one fireplace here, but it's nice and big.

There are plenty of activities to fill your days. Three hours of horseback riding are included in the cost of a room night. They can also arrange mountain bike trips; trout fishing; 4WD tours to Cotopaxi, local Indian markets or other sights in the area; or even trekking using llamas to carry your provisions.

HACIENDA CUSIN, *Cusín, 15 kilometers south of Otavalo, Otavalo, Northern Highlands. Tel. 6/918013, Fax 6/918003; E-mail: hacienda@Cusín.com.ec; Website: haciendaCusín.com. 40 rooms. Double $98. Breakfast included. Restaurant. Bar. TV room with video library. Game room with billiards, darts, and Ping-Pong. Horseback riding. Mountain bikes. Squash court. Handicraft shop. Conference facilities. Credit cards accepted.*

To know your hacienda well, because at Cusín you really feel like you are the *patrón* of the estate, you should walk through it several times. The first time through you can get the feel for the big picture. You sense how its layout of white walls and terracotta tiles fits perfectly below the puckered green Imbabura Volcano; how the view of the local church harmonizes with the mountainside as if it were planned to be admired from the property, which it was.

On the next walk-through you can study the antique tapestries, indigenous Latin American textiles, and the exquisite colonial art, which is not merely hung on the walls, but rather, ingenuously placed to create a composition. It is composition that frequently indulges your sense of humor. Why is the life size wooden chicken standing near the diminutive crucifix? It is the cock that crowed. Period chairs and divans are placed at every turn so you shouldn't feel pressured to take it all in on foot, otherwise you might miss a monk peeping out of where you'd least expect. Sit down as often as necessary to absorb adequately the diorama of which you are now a part.

Wander through the grounds to admire the gardens bursting with the brilliant colors found in over fifty species of flowers, which attract nearly the same number of species of birds. This may take some time, as there are about four kilometers of trails meandering through this nine hectares of Eden. These will ultimately lead you to a vegetable garden, to a llama named Pedrito, to the horse stables, and to the monastery.

The hacienda's history dates back four centuries to 1602 when land was purchased at an auction from Phillip II, King of Spain. The Chiriboga family, which owned the hacienda for most of its existence, includes Don Pacifico, one of the founding fathers of Ecuador who ascended to the position of vice president. It was Clemintina Chiriboga, a petite lover of gardens and books that shrewdly managed the estate and endowed it with the spirit which it exudes today. In fact, the jasmine that she planted in the early part of the twentieth century still grows in the garden. The land was divided up among family members in the latter part of this century, and the buildings fell into disrepair until Nik Millhouse resurrected the estate, converting it into an elegant hotel. The Englishman is difficult to distinguish from the guests because he is usually having at least as much fun as they are.

The rooms retain their hacienda semblance through Andean craft furnishings, antique art, and beamed ceilings. Most of the rooms have fireplaces, as do the common areas such as the dining room, living room, and bar. Slipping into a comfortable sofa to read or chat while the fire is crackling nearby makes the grandeur almost homey. For yet more intriguing lodging, inquire about the cottage suites.

For diversion you can go horseback riding, mountain biking, or hiking in the nearby hills. Facilities on the grounds include a squash court, a well-equipped game room, and a great selection of movies in an extensive video library. The hacienda offers a reasonably priced Umbrella Plan, which includes a room with a fireplace, full board, and riding privileges.

A separate facility was added in the form of a monastery, linked to the main house by a walking bridge. Similar in style to the main house, this portion plays host to groups and conferences. You can take as the Ecuadorian government's endorsement of the facility, the signing of the new constitution here, which is known as la Constitución de Cusín. If nothing else, the monastery gives you another complex to explore, more art to ponder, and a perfect rooftop sitting area near the bell tower from which to observe the morning sun illuminate the rumpled volcano.

BEST MODERATELY PRICED HOTELS

Enjoy comfortable settings, good service and reasonable prices at the following excellent hotels:
- **Hostal de la Rabida**, Quito
- **Villa Nancy II**, Quito
- **Ali Shungu**, Otavalo, Northern Highlands
- **Hacienda Pensaqui**, Outside Otavalo, Northern Highlands
- **Hosteria Cienega**, Cotopaxi, Central Highlands
- **Mindo Garden**, Mindo, Northern Coast & Lowlands
- **Yachana Lodge**, Oriente

COLONIAL-STYLE INNS

MANSION DEL ANGEL, *Wilson E5-29 and Juan Leon Mera, Quito. Tel. 2/557 721, Fax 2/237 819. 49 rooms. 10 rooms. Double $99. Breakfast included. Cable TV. Credit cards accepted.*

We particularly recommend Mansión del Angel because it is a wonderful boutique alternative in a price category filled with aseptic, predictable hotels. Walking into this hotel is like stepping into the home of one of the Quito elite one hundred years ago. Decorated with unique and interesting antiques, oriental carpets, intricate inlaid wooden floors and original art works, La Mansión exudes elegance and style.

Mansión del Angel means "Mansion of Angels", which aptly describes one of the decorating motifs. Luckily, these are not the overly sweet angels of cheap mall knickknack shops worldwide, but rather stout Michelangelo-style seraphs. These portly cherubs cover the comfortable, custom-made pillows and comforters in each of the rooms.

As this is an old colonial home, each room has a different size and layout. All have soothing yellow walls with intricate molding, gilt canopy beds, a comfortable chair and ottoman, as well as an exotic cage for the television. Be sure to ask for one of the larger rooms, as the size varies considerably in the seven doubles. We particularly recommend spacious room 305 with the king-sized bed. The three singles are all small, but decorated with the same exacting attention to detail. The bathrooms, thankfully, are entirely modern. Every room has a very large shower as well as ample counter space, new blow dryers and big bars of soap.

The same people that created the incredible Hostería La Mirage near Otavalo own La Mansión. Many of the details that make La Mirage so special have been repeated here. Rose petals on the beds and sinks, nightly surprises on the pillows, and excellent service are hallmarks of the owners.

CAFÉ CULTURA, *Robles 513 and Reina Victoria, Quito. Tel. 2/504 078, Fax 2/224 271; E-mail:* info@cafecultura.com. *26 rooms. Breakfast not included. Double $58. Restaurant. Tour booking. Credit cards accepted but for an additional 10% fee.*

Ecuador has a plethora of delightful, intimate mid-range hotels, and the Cafe Cultura is one of the best. Housed in an old colonial mansion, which was used as the French Cultural Center in its previous life, the hotel is ideally located in New Town. Owned by English-Ecuadorian partners, Café Cultura sets a standard against which others are judged.

After passing under the bougainvillea-draped entrance, you walk through the small garden to the entrance of the house. Every part of the house is a treat and a pleasure. The reception area, with its high ceiling, immediately draws you in. Each room in the house was painted by a

Chilean muralist who has created a warm, artistic atmosphere. Rust colored walls lead up to blue ceilings. A giant Virgin hovers to the right of the front desk. It's hard to pull-off this kind of work without it looking tacky, but the painter has managed wonderfully.

To the left, through lovely French doors, the wood-panel library offers a relaxing refuge. A small bookshelf is available for guests, but we use the library mainly for hanging out after dinner. Dimmed lights, multiple candles and a well-attended fireplace make it the perfect place to unwind at the end of the night.

Candles, fresh cut flowers and fireplaces are standard in all common areas. Intriguing antiques hanging on the walls and comfortable couches make it hard to move along.

Each guestroom in the hotel is different. There are rooms both on the second and third floor of the house as well as in the back of the property. They too have been decorated by the same artist and share the same warm, comfortable tones. The owners have paid attention to details like natural light and have cut skylights into the ceilings of the rooms in back. We like pulling the skylight shade open each morning to have the bright Quito sunshine stream onto the bed. Tall people should be aware that the rooms on the third floor all have sloping ceilings. As far as the doubles go, take note that room eight has its own phone line, room ten has a fireplace, and room seventeen has both.

We think it's worth going for the honeymoon suite if it is available. For $78 you get a fireplace in your room and perhaps the most romantic bathroom we've seen. The free-standing tub surrounded by candles is like something out of a movie.

The rooms are only part of the story. The staff at the Cultura goes out of its way to make sure your visit is a pleasure. The Cultura Reservation Center, located in the hotel, can arrange guided tours, drivers, and hotel and plane reservations.

Lastly there's the restaurant. We rave about it in the Quito chapter, so suffice to say, we bet you'll have more than one meal here.

COUNTRY GETAWAYS

HOSTERIA LA MIRAGE, *Out 10 de Agosto just past the market in Cotacachi, Otavalo, Northern Highlands. Tel. 6/915 237, Fax 6/915 065. US Reservations Tel. 800/327 3573; Website: www.hosteria_la_mirage.com.ec; E-mail: mirage@mireage.com.ec. 23 suites. Double $220. Breakfast and dinner included. Restaurant. Bar. Tennis court. Mountain biking. Horseback riding. Heated pool. Steam bath. Jacuzzi. Massage. Conference room. Credit cards accepted.*

For absolute luxury and romance, Hosteria La Mirage is one of the best spots in the country. Fragrant hummingbird-filled gardens, large exquisitely furnished rooms, impeccable service, and gourmet food comprise the package that is the La Mirage experience.

Each of the unique suites is laid out so that you gaze at the gardens instead of at the room next door. One room may be L-shaped with crimson walls, while another will be decked out with a king-sized canopy bed and gold accents. All have marble floors with throw rugs, a separate sitting area, and a fireplace. You can relax on the sofa and watch birds feed outside your window.

It is the details of La Mirage that secure its position in the esteemed Relais & Chateaux group. From the time that you arrive you see that that every vessel that could possible hold water is filled with artfully arranged floating flowers. When you enter your room, your bed and bathroom are sprinkled with rose petals. A crimson rose blooms from a diminutive glass by your sink. The fresh cut flower arrangements in your room are changed daily. The bird list, included in the folder on your desk, is so beautiful that it deserves framing.

After enjoying your memorable dinner, your waitress will ask if you want your fire started. If you reply in the positive, it will be crackling by the time you get to your room. That toasty lump at the end of your bed is the hot water bottle placed to warm your feet. Along with the pressed flower bookmark on your pillow there is another small surprise. (We don't want to give everything away.)

The covered pool and spa area, decorated in overdone Roman style a la the Hearst Castle, should not be missed. La Mirage offers eight different types of massages including reflexology and aromatherapy. We consider the back, neck and shoulder massage the perfect anecdote to bouncing along Ecuadorian roads. The sauna, scented with eucalyptus branches, is another recipe for revival. Lap swimming is possible in the pool although it is a little short.

Your first activity at La Mirage should be a tour of the grounds. Wander through the extraordinary gardens where plants and flowers grow to prehistoric proportions. Bougainvillea, dahlias, hibiscus, roses and orchids are just a small listing of the flowers you'll find. Hanging baskets dangle from the trees to add to the lushness. The scent of flowers on the breeze is so heady it can stop you in your tracks.

Our tendency at the hotel is to slow down. We like to sit in garden nooks, read and relax. If you want activity, however, there's plenty of that to be had. Horseback riding, mountain biking, hiking and shopping are all recommended. Leave your tennis rackets at home however, because the court slants and has a barbed-wire fence on one side.

Both dinner and breakfast are included in the price of your stay and both are memorable experiences. (See *Where to Eat* in the *Otavalo* section.)

Breakfast is served in a sunny room that makes you feel as if you are in an aviary. Caged canaries sing all around you and only plate glass separates you from another room filled with birds. Again, it's the details that are overwhelming. The fire is popping, fresh flowers float in a bowl at your table, and you are presented with the *Miami Herald* upon arrival.

CASA MOJANDA MOUNTAINSIDE INN & FARM, *5 kilometers west of Otavalo, Otavalo, Northern Highlands. Tel./Fax 9/731 737 or via CRC in Quito 2/558 889; E-mail: mojanda@uio.telconet.net; Website: casamojanda.com. 9 cabins. $45 per person including breakfast, dinner, and afternoon tea. Horseback riding. Library. Credit cards accepted.*

The extraordinary cut of the windows is the greatest homage to the mesmerizing views from the Casa Mojanda. Whether you are in the eucalyptus finished dining room, the upstairs game room, or any of the cabins, your eyes constantly drift to the vista. The hotel is surrounded on three sides by verdant folds of terrain, much of which the local farmers have tilled, against the mighty force of gravity, into a rich, undulating checkerboard of green and earthen squares. If the windows aren't enough for you, simply slip down to the Japanese hot tub perched on the hillside to broaden the spectacular panorama.

The Casa Mojanda is an eco-tourism concern that seeks to exert minimum impact on the environment, while actively promoting local cultures and traditions. The amazing and inspiring accomplishment is that the objective is met while maintaining an extraordinary level of quality and comfort.

The architectural method used to design the main house and cabins is known as rammed earth. It is comparable to adobe in function, but the process is distinct. A framework of wood is filled with loose dirt, packed down solid, then the wooden frame is removed. Windows are cut out rather than built around. The cabin interiors are ample and homey, finished in eucalyptus, which is grown commercially in the area. Local weavers handcraft the eye-catching wool bedspreads. Most of the furniture is either handmade or antique cedar.

While the comfort and view from your room might seem too perfect to leave, there is compelling reason to do so, both on and off the property. The cedar shelves of the library are stocked with an excellent selection of books for guests to borrow. The game room draws guests in after their active days either to relax with a movie or to challenge each other in a board games. Vegetarian meals are served in the dining room by the flickering light of the fireplace. Much of the produce comes directly from the organic garden in the back yard. Guests gather in the dining room to socialize over afternoon tea or pre-dinner drinks or simply to gaze at the landscape from the pillow-covered window niche.

You will find enough hikes and walks throughout the countryside to keep yourself busy for several days. There are crater lakes in the area, as well as Otavalo's handicraft market. A small rodeo corral was built to help beginning equestrians learn before galloping off into the hills.

The owners of Casa Mojanda are an Ecuadorian/American couple that also created the Mojanda Foundation. The hotel donates a portion of its proceeds to this nonprofit organization that supports local social and environmental initiatives. You can learn more about their positive impact during your visit, which in itself contributes to the organization's success.

JUNGLE LODGES

SACHA LODGE, *Lower Napo River, Napo Province, Oriente. Quito office, Julio Zaldumbide 375 y Toledo. Tel. 2/566 090 or 509 504, Fax 2/236 521; E-mail: : sachalod@pi.pro.ec. Web site: www.sachalodge.com. 4 day/3 night package $577 per person including meals. Cabins have hot water and electricity. Does not include Quito/Coca roundtrip airfare of $110 per person. Credit cards accepted.*

When Tarzan dreams of his fantasy home, it must look like Sacha Lodge. Monkeys sometimes greet you upon arrival as you amble along a two-kilometer long boardwalk from the Napo River. During a short glide through a silky channel the dugout canoe rides so deep that your eyes are almost level with the water. The channel leads into a serene, ebony lagoon that spreads across four hectares. Only as you cross to the other side of this black mirror does the complex of huts slowly emerge from the lush jungle vegetation.

Sacha combines the most select ingredients of jungle adventure and native architecture then mixes in a handful of creature comforts. A day of jungle exploration - poking under leaves for frogs, trekking lush trails, swinging from vines, and paddling canoes - tends to build up a bit of dirt and sweat on your body. The natural coating feels good, but an even better sensation is scrubbing it off in a hot tiled shower. Afterwards you can relax in a bed blown cool by a ceiling fan. The rooms are big, well-lit, and just plain comfortable. Most rooms have a deck overlooking a tropically landscaped garden that hummingbirds and other bright fliers flock to. A nap in the hammock out here is divine.

A cold drink in the lofty bar overlooking the large lagoon is a nice transitional moment before dinner. Dinner itself is just right. Healthy portions of vegetables, fresh juices, and well-prepared fish and meat makes herbivores and omnivores alike content. The breakfasts are equally as good.

Sacha is an extraordinary arena for birders. It possesses the Empire State Building of tree towers, rising up 135 feet. You climb the sturdy steps thankful that you are finally going to see what the parrots and macaws see. When you reach the top gazing at the kapok trees like broccoli tops, the guide taps your shoulder indicating the telescope that he's packed with him. Through its lens you might see a pair of toucans mating, the stunning turquoise of green honey-creeper, or the silly grin of a sloth.

Getting to and from the tower is an adventure in itself. A native guide paddles a dugout canoe through a serpentine stream thick with fallen palm fronds. Vanilla vines dangle down from above. Golden dragonflies shimmer in the sunlight and tiny silver fish jump from the water, occasionally landing in the canoe. Some quick handwork sets them on their way through the tannin varnished water again. Green and white snail eggs cling to the bank as tiger and agami herons humorlessly survey their dinner prospects.

One of the best places to spend a few minutes after a day in the jungle is at the dock on the lagoon. You can launch yourself from the world's bounciest diving board into the refreshing water. It is an enchanting period each day as the sun sets beyond the lagoon and the surrounding vegetation turns into dark silhouettes.

The butterfly farm at Sacha is simply a wonderful place to observe these colorful creatures. While the biologist's hard work takes place in the main portion of the facility, there is well thought out area for visitors on the opposite side of the net wall. Here you idle on a bench by a little pond as these vibrant origami creatures flit about or land on your arm to lap up some salt. Other excursions that you have to look forward to include medicinal tours, night walks, canoe rides searching for caimans, and a trip to a parrot salt lick.

Sacha's 2,000 hectares of primary rainforest is one of the most well protected private areas on the Napo River. You have an excellent opportunity for observing a wide variety of wildlife.

Your journey to Sacha begins in the Quito airport with a 45-minute flight to Coca. You board a motorized canoe in the nearby Napo River for two-hour motorized canoe to Sacha's property.

LA SELVA, *Lower Río Napo, Napo Province, Oriente. Quito office: 6 de Deciembre 2816. Quito Tel. 2/550 995. Quito fax 2/567 297; Website: : www.laselvajunglelodge.com. 19 cabins. Four day/three night package $550 per person, all meals included. Cabins have cold water showers and gas lamps, no electricity. Does not include roundtrip airfare from Quito $110 extra per person. Credit cards accepted.*

If you want an intimate jungle experience with first class service, La Selva is one of the best. Open for 14 years now, this prototype tropical rainforest lodge gets you about as close to the jungle as you can be while still sleeping in a comfortable bed.

The layers of civilization begin to peel away as soon as you step off the dock in Coca to take a motorized canoe up the Napo River. When you arrive to La Selva, you walk on an elevated boardwalk through the rainforest to the edge of the Garzacocha Lagoon. From there you board a small dugout canoe that is paddled softly across the lake to the entrance of the lodge. An awed silence overcomes your group as you glide across the black water to the dock.

You enter the lodge through the main common areas, which are the bar and dining rooms. Crackling, blue-eyed *oropendulas*, a type of oriole, fly past your nose in flashes of black and yellow. A cold exotic fruit drink and delicious snacks await. That's indicative of the La Selva experience – you tromp around in the jungle utterly fascinated and then return to the lodge for mouth-watering food and refreshing drinks.

The common areas, as well as the cabins, are built in the style of the homes of the indigenous people of the region. Twin beds in the cabins are outfitted with mosquito netting and the air circulates so well through the screens that you may need to use your blanket at night. You'll have two kerosene lamps for your cabin – one to light the way outside and one to use inside. It's quite romantic to brush your teeth by the flickering light.

Make no mistake that the cabins here are very simple. The beds are comfortable, but small, and you have to tuck the mosquito netting in at night. The bathroom has a bamboo floor, which gets wet when you take your cold shower and stays that way for a while. If you're not cut out for that type of roughing it, know it and go elsewhere.

One of the reasons that Selva has not introduced a generator for the cabins is so guests can really immerse themselves in the natural jungle sounds. The birdcalls are especially enchanting. Their songs, which sound like stones being dropped in a bucket of water, children's slide whistles and gravely squeaks, will be your alarm clock.

The real draw to Selva is the isolation in the jungle. While there is no guarantee, you have excellent odds of spotting many exciting animals such as different types of monkeys, parrots, macaws, tanagers, and our personal favorite, pygmy marmosets. The eerie sound of howler monkeys around the lake is absolutely unforgettable, as is the sight of thousands of colorful birds flying around the parrot salt licks.

The skilled guides collaborate with you to figure out your priorities. Birders are sent out with native guides who can identify birds simply by the way the air rustles. Generalists have their choice of a wide array of activities. You should not miss the tree tower, a 45-meter wooden structure built around a beautiful kapok tree. From the excellent vantage point above the canopy you can see so many species that it will automatically make a birder out of you. Other activities include drifting slowly down black water streams, walking through the jungle to learn about medicinal plants, swimming in Garzacocha, and visits to the Butterfly Farm.

If you happen to catch a big piranha, they'll cook it up for you for dinner. If not, you're in luck anyway as the food is outstanding. When the bamboo horn signals that the meal is ready, you can look forward to fresh juices, fruit and marmalade at breakfast, followed by three and four course lunches and dinners. Served family-style around tables lit with kerosene lamps, the excellent flavor and variety of the food is remarkable, especially given the logistical considerations. Much of it is flown in from Quito to Coca and then brought by boat from there. Don't miss the chance to try veal Milanese a la Amazon.

La Selva also offers a separate safari trip called the Light Brigade. On the this point-to-point six day camping trip you get to enjoy some more remote parts of the jungle and then wine and dine in typical Selva style.

Your journey to La Selva begins in the Quito airport with a 45-minute flight to Coca. You board a motorized canoe in the nearby Napo River for a two-and-a-half-hour motorized canoe to La Selva's property.

KAPAWI, *Pastaza River, Morona Santiago Province, Oriente. Guayaquil Tel. 4/285 711, Guayaquil Fax 4/287 651; E-mail: eco-tourism@canodros.com.ec; Website: : www.canodros.com. 20 cabins. Four day/three night package $750 per person including meals. Cabins have solar-heated lukewarm showers and solar electricity. Does not include roundtrip airfare from Quito, $150 round-trip per person. Credit cards accepted.*

Kapawi, the newest entry in the up-scale jungle lodge category, is a remote, marvelous place to experience the wonder and mystery of the rain forest. The facilities are spacious and comfortable, designed to fit perfectly into the jungle yet offer a haven for travelers.

The adventure begins in Quito, where you board a chartered plane to the jungle. The plane flies low along the country's spine, bringing you eye-to-crater with volcanoes. You then take a left and soar over the jungle finally to drop down onto a dusty red-dirt runway hacked out of the expanse of green. Met by your Achuar and naturist guides, you walk 10 meters to the water's edge where you board a motorized canoe and head down the Capahuari River for one-and-a-half-hours.

Once you arrive to the lodge, an elevated walkway leads to the main buildings, which house the bar and dining areas. These buildings, as all the others on the property, are built from wood in the typical Achuar elliptical style. The bar and dining area, although built in traditional fashion, are enormous. Light and airy, with high ceilings, they are extremely comfortable and elegant in their simplicity. The bar area has plenty of low couches with comfortable pillows as well as the most extensive Amazon library we've seen in a lodge. There is a large porch out front with well-positioned hammocks.

The dining room serves excellent food in a unique setting. The chairs, *tutánes*, are the wooden stools with carved animal heads common in Achuar homes. Guests eat family style around square, candlelit tables. Menus feature homemade bread, flavorful dishes, crisp vegetables and lots of fresh fruit. The service-level is amazing, especially when you consider that the person waiting on you may never have been to a restaurant in his life. Make sure that you get the chance to try their traditional Achuar meal one night, featuring fish cooked in banana leafs.

All of the buildings overlook a clearing that is a lake when there is enough rain. This is the only drawback to Kapawi. When the lake is low, the view from your cabin is basically a big field. When there is water however, it is absolutely gorgeous. The amazing thing is that all it takes is one or two days of strong rains for the water to lap at the edges of the lodge.

The cabins, built without nails, are rustic yet very comfortable. They are larger and lighter than the cabins at most lodges, yet very much retain a jungle feel. The bark is left on the planks used for the walls and floor. Soft cotton sheets and comforters make the twin beds a pleasant place to listen to the symphony of birds and frogs. Mosquito netting is not necessary as large screened windows provide plenty of breeze while keeping insects at bay. A nice deck overlooking the lake has both a hammock and lounge chair. From here you can watch egrets, cardinals and hummingbirds feed among the nearby water plants. Solar power provides lighting for all the facilities.

The tiled bathroom is spacious, but only cold water is available from the tap. A bag of water heated by the sun is hung in your shower each afternoon providing warm water. (If it's not sunny, then your water is not that warm.) Don't worry about bringing shampoo as they request that you use only the biodegradable soap and shampoo they provide.

You can plan as busy or relaxed an agenda with your guides as strikes your fancy. There are several walks, trips to lakes and other outings available. Many of Kapawi's guests look forward to the chance to be even closer to the jungle by spending one night in tents. Some activities that you can do on your own include a self-guided walk, paddling a dugout canoe around the lake, and piranha fishing. Birders will delight in the 520 species of birds found in the area. Although Kapawi has not yet built a canopy tower, one is in the works.

Another highlight is the visit to an Achuar home. Kapawi has figured out that the way to get the most out of the visit is through two-sided interaction. You really feel like an invited guest and get a chance for personal communication.

As is the case anytime except in a zoo, there is no guarantee of the animal life you'll see here. You have very good chances of finding pink river dolphins, gigantic morpho butterflies, pre-historic hoatzins and screaming macaws. You might also spot howler monkeys, squirrel monkeys, capuchin monkeys, hundreds of cobalt-winged parakeets, bats, caimans, poison dart frogs or even a kinkajou.

One of the most intriguing aspects about Kapawi is the way it has managed to produce a healthy relationship between private enterprise and the local indigenous community. In fact, the ambitious plan is to entirely hand over the lodge to the Achuar in 2012. This partnership is seen as a model for sustainable use of indigenous land throughout the country. The respect that Canodros, the owners of Kapawi, exhibits for the Achuar and their way of life is passed on to guests through every aspect of the lodge experience.

ONE-OF-A-KIND HOTELS

While these hotels didn't make our best places to stay list, we thought they deserved to be singled out for sheer uniqueness.

• *El Otro Lado*, *Baños, Central Highlands. You can bicycle from Baños to these three huts by an amazing waterfall.*

• *Hostal Dillon* , *Ballenita, Southern Coast. Stay in a maritime museum hotel with an incredible view of the coastline.*

• *Casa Grande*, *Bahia de Caraquez, Central Coast. A fashionable house with high-class art is yours.*

• *Chirije*, *Bahia de Caraquez, Central Coast. These rustic cabins are located at a rich archeological dig. Pottery shards are everywhere.*

• *Mompiche Lodge*, *Muisne, Northern Coast. Travel by boat through mangrove swamps and open sea to arrive to this remote haven.*

• *Flotel*, *Cuyabeno Reserve, Oriente. It's a riverboat cruise in the jungle with plenty of interesting excursions.*

BEACH ESCAPES

RED MANGROVE INN, *Avenida Charles Darwin, Puerto Ayora, Santa Cruz, Galápagos. Tel/Fax 5/526 564; E-mail: redmangrove@ecuadorexplorer.com; Website: www.ecuadorexplorer.com/redmangrove. 4 rooms. Double $88. Breakfast not included. Cafe. Bar. Hot tub. Bicycle and kayak rental. Master card only for 10% additional fee.*

The Red Mangrove is a small, extremely comfortable hotel looking out over the blue waters of Academy Bay. You can watch the waves break on the black volcanic rocks in front of the salmon-colored Mediterranean style building from almost everywhere in the hotel. The main gathering area/bar/dining room is open and airy with a touch of the Greek Islands. Lots of puffy, batik-covered throw pillows tempt you to plop down and relax right there, as do the hammocks. The welcoming fire in the evening makes it even harder to budge.

The honor bar opens up to a guest kitchen area where you're invited to start the coffeepot if you get up before the breakfast staff arrives. Breakfast choices include fresh yogurt with granola and thick pancakes. You'll be drinking your morning brew out of beautiful ceramic mugs made by Monica, one of the owners. She also made all the wonderful nautical and Galápagos ceramic vases, plates, pitchers, door handles, soap dishes and towel hangers that you'll find throughout the hotel.

It's this personal touch that gives the Red Mangrove much of its charm. Both Polo and Monica are interesting, artistic people, who have decorated the hotel as an extension of their home. The toilets in the upstairs rooms, for example, are elevated in order to look out majestically over the Bay. Large showers with in-laid bits of colorful tiles and hand-decorated mirrors complete the bathroom ensemble.

The spacious rooms all have lots of windows in order to take advantage of the views and refreshing sea breezes. Even though it gets cool at night, you stay warm under the alpaca wool blankets. Rattan mats and throw pillows give the rooms an informal, mellow charm.

Even though the hotel is extremely relaxing, that doesn't mean there's not much to be done for the more activity-inclined. Polo is working on opening up what he calls "The Other Galápagos." By that he means the things that people on programmed boat trips don't get to see or do. He can arrange mountain biking, kayaking, scuba diving, and surfing, as well as mountain tours and trips to other islands. At the end of the day you get to come back to the hotel and sink into the hot tub while gazing at the stars.

The Red Mangrove has perfected a winning combination, offering large, comfortable rooms in a small boutique hotel on a beautiful site.

HOSTERIA ATAMARI, *Kilometer 83 on the Ruta del Sol, Machalilla, Central Coast. Tel. 4/780 430. Quito tel. 2/228 470. Quito fax 2/234 075. 12 rooms. Double $60-120 depending on type of room. Restaurant. Bar. Pool. Tours arranged. Airport transfer. Credit cards accepted.*

Perched on a point high over the sea, the Atamari is one of our favorite coastal oases. The thing that first catches your eye as you enter the grounds is the gardens. Bird of paradise plants reach towards the sun, orange bougainvillea spring over fence posts, plump aloe plants avail themselves for treating sunburns, and color coordinated butterflies float from plant to plant.

From the gardens your view is automatically drawn out to sea. Waves break for kilometer after uninterrupted kilometer on the pale coast below. Turquoise waters shift to indigo as the ocean deepens. Darting frigate birds and squadrons of pelicans fly by at nose level.

One of our favorite things about the Atamari is its feeling of privacy. It's only around the pool or in the restaurant that you realize other guests are enjoying this small paradise with you. The rest of the time it's only the birds that interrupt the sound of crashing surf.

All of the buildings, with the exception of the pool and restaurant, are tucked away in the folliage. There are twelve cabins on the grounds that range from small, comfortable rooms with private but downstairs baths to large suites complete with balconies and hanging hammocks. All of the options are in excellent condition and include such luxuries as comforters and daily delivered tea.

Each room has superb views of the ocean, but some are simply breathtaking. Room number two, a suite that includes a sofa and small refrigerator, has a bank of windows looking out over the edge of the property and up the coast. Room number 12, a bungalow, is spacious, private and our personal favorite. Atamari is one of the few places in all of Ecuador that has realized that two people need two hammocks for serious lounging.

When mealtime comes around you won't be disappointed. Specializing in seafood, the Atamari makes some of the best, albeit expensive, dishes on this section of coast. We highly recommend starting with *picaditos de cameron frito*, popcorn shrimp, outside in the bar at sunset. Because of supply issues they don't always have all the items on the menu, so ask for what's fresh and go with that as an entree. The chef is also willing to create things off the menu when it's not too crowded. We requested a fish sandwich and received a delicious grilled sole fillet on thick slices of German bread.

Although the Atamari is perched above the sea, they have created beach access via a steep stepped pathway. It only takes about five minutes to get down to kilometers of flat beach, excellent for walking. Make sure you go at low tide however, because strong surf cuts the Atamari cove off from the main beach when the tide is up. You can always get back via the road, but that's about a thirty-minute walk.

Most people spend their first few days at the Atamari just unwinding, enjoying the pool and walking on the beach. When you're ready for more action however, the hotel arranges excursions to Isla de la Plata or Isla de Salango, Los Frailes Beach, or even mountain biking.

BEST INEXPENSIVE & BUDGET HOTELS

There are some great inexpensive and budget hotels in Ecuador. The ones on this list are the cream of the crop.

- *La Casona de Mario, Quito.*
- *Villa Nancy I, Quito.*
- *Crossroads, Quito.*
- *Hostal Esther, Otavalo, Northern Highlands.*
- *CEA, Mindo, Northern Coast & Lowlands.*
- *Black Sheep Inn, Chugchilán, Latacunga Excursions & Day Trips, Central Highlands*
- *Hostal Macondo, Cuenca, Southern Highlands.*
- *Madre Tierra, Vilcabamba, Southern Highlands.*
- *Ruinas de Quinara, Vilcabamba, Southern Highlands.*
- *Alandaluz, Machalilla, Central Coast.*
- *Liana Lodge, Oriente*

Note that Madre Tierra and Alandaluz offer lodging in both the inexpensive and moderate price ranges.

12. QUITO

Quito is, in our estimation, the most visually attractive of all the Latin-American capitals. Set in a valley at the foot of the Pichincha volcano, the city is surrounded by fertile green hills. Terraced plots cover the contours of these mounds, creating an enchanting contrast with the shiny city below. With pretty whitewashed buildings, excellent examples of colonial architecture, expansive green parks and an excellent tourist infrastructure, Quito is a pleasant introduction to Ecuador.

The two parts of Quito, **Old Town** and **New Town**, almost feel like two different cities. Old Town, with its well preserved colonial structures and cobblestone streets, seems to have been frozen in time. Very few of the building are less than a hundred years old, adobe is more common than concrete, and Highland Indians sell many of the same wares around the main plaza that their ancestors did centuries ago. Only the car traffic and blaring CD stands bring you back to the 21st century. During the day the avenues crackle with the energy of street vendors, business people and shopping pedestrians.

Traveling north up the valley brings you to modern Quito, known as New Town. Actually a mixture of the old and the new, it's not unusual to see a modern high-rise next to a restored colonial home in this part of town. Most of the city's fine hotels and restaurants are located here, as well as much of the shopping and bars.

North of New Town you'll find the even more modern financial district. With sparkling office buildings and wide grassy spaces, this is also where many of the city's upper-class citizens live.

Although Quito certainly does its fair share of commerce, especially today, it has historically considered itself above having to work. With a past based on landed lords ruling their haciendas from afar, Quito is a city where culture, politics and education have always ruled the day. The Quiteños are content to leave the dirty work of capitalistic growth to Guayaquil.

Despite the fact that it is situated just 22 kilometers south of the equator, Quito enjoys a year-round temperate climate because of its altitude at 2,850 meters. Mornings and evenings are always cool, while the equatorial sun heating thin mountain air means warm afternoons. As is the case with many mountain cities, pollution can sometimes get trapped in the basin through thermal inversion. More often however, especially in the mornings, the city is bathed in a strong, clear light. Both snow-capped volcanoes and tall office buildings glitter in first rays of the sun.

History

Quito, although not a large city, was a significant political and spiritual center for the Incas. **Atahualpa**, the famous Inca ruler and warrior, lived here with his beloved Cañari princess governing the northern half of the Inca empire.

Quito was defended by the Inca warrior **Rumiñahui** during the war with the conquistadors. As it became apparent that the Spanish were going to take the city, Rumiñahui set Quito ablaze and headed to the hills with the city's treasure, leaving little for the conquerors.

The Spanish, led by conquistador Sebastián de Benalcázar, determined to rebuild. The new Quito was founded on December 6, 1534. The site was chosen not only because it was already an important market and crossroads, but also for its abundant water, good wood supplies and healthy, malaria-free environment. The ravines around the site also helped defend from Indian attacks.

Benalcázar paced off the main plaza and adjoining blocks that still delineate Old Town today. During the Colonial Period, the city was officially governed by both the Peruvian and New Granada viceroyalties of Spain. The truth is however, that the city was really controlled by the church. Command of construction, education and arts fell primarily into Catholic hands. The city was a flurry of building during the 17th and 18th centuries, with distinct religious orders competing to construct the mightiest symbols of their faith..

The society of Quito at this time functioned under what was basically a caste system. The landed elite lived off the labors of hundreds of indigenous people virtually enslaved on the haciendas. Social norms and appearance were very important to the upper-class of colonial Quito and still are today.

Quito first declared Independence from Spain on August, 10, 1809. The revolt was subdued and its leaders violently killed. Another attempt was made in 1822, where the tide turned permanently towards independence at the Battle of Pichincha.

In terms of geography, Quito stayed mostly confined to what is today *Quito Antiguo*, Old Town, until the early 20th century when the railroad arrived. This permitted transportation of construction materials, which allowed the city to grow at a much faster pace. Not until the mid-1940s, however, did the most important families move from downtown to the new, tony Mariscal in *Quito Moderna*.

ARRIVALS & DEPARTURES
BY AIR
All flights from Quito go through either the domestic or international terminal of Quito's **Mariscal Sucre International Airport**, *Tel. 440 083.* The conveniently located airport, ten to fifteen minutes from New Town, is simple but certainly adequate.

International Flights
When you arrive from abroad, you will depart your plane and follow the signs to the immigration area. Before you get in the line for immigrations you will need to grab a T3 tourist card if you didn't get one on the plane and fill it out. This becomes your tourist visa, so you'll need to keep it with your passport at all times. After filling it out you go through immigrations and on to customs.

After getting your bag in customs you will come up to what looks like a traffic light. Hit the button to see whether or not you get the green go ahead. If you get the red light, step to the side and put your luggage up on the table for somebody to inspect it. Once you get through the lines you are in the main airport building. There is a currency exchange booth to the right when you exit, as well as ATM machines in the outdoor corridor between the international and domestic terminals.

THE MANY FACES OF MONEY
You've just gotten your first fistful of Ecuadorian money. Take a minute to check out the historical figures on the bills.
• *10,000 – Vicente Rocafuerte; An educator, writer and politician, Rocafuerte was president of Ecuador from 1835-1839. A liberal from Guayaquil, he was always pitted in battle against Quito conservative Juan Jose Flores.*
• *20,000 – Gabriel García Moreno; García Moreno, a conservative icon, was president of Ecuador a number a times between 1861 and 1875. He is famous for involving the Catholic Church in governing the country. Moreno was assassinated on the steps of the government palace in 1875.*
• *50,000 – Eloy Alfaro; A soldier and politician, Alfaro rose to power as a coastal military chief. Fighting to break the conservative hegemony, he headed the liberal revolution in 1895. Dismissed after a term as president, he staged a coup in 1906, removing the ruling president. Elected again as president in 1907, he himself was ousted and murdered five years later.*

Official yellow airport taxis should be waiting outside the terminal door. If there are not any, walk down twenty meters to the domestic terminal, where there are usually some waiting. It shouldn't cost more than $6 to get to New Town, even at night.

Domestic Flights

There are two main airlines that cover the country, **TAME** and **SAN**. **Aerogal** has smaller, mostly charter flights into the Amazon Basin.

It's a good idea to confirm your reservation on any of these airlines twice before you fly. Once 72-hours before departure and another time 24-hours before. Arrive to the airport at least an hour before your flight in order to check your luggage and get your boarding pass. There are no seat assignments on domestic flights so embarking the plane can be a bit of a free for all.

If you are flying to Guayaquil, they have a unique system called *aeropuente*, air bridge. You buy a ticket to Guayaquil and it is good for any flight on any day. You then just show up before the flight and try to get space on a first-come, first-serve basis. If you really want to be assured space you have to show up a couple of hours early. It's terribly inefficient, but that's how they work it.

Airlines

• **TAME**, *Amazonas 1354 and Colón, 2nd Floor.. Tel. 509 382, 509 383. Monday – Friday 9:30am – 1pm, 1:45pm – 5:30pm. Colón 1001 and Rábida. Tel. 554 905 554 274. Monday – Friday, 8:00am – 6:30pm, Saturday, 9am – 12pm*. From Quito Tame covers Guayaquil, Cuenca, Loja, Macas, Coca, Lago Agrio, Tulcán, Esmeraldas, Manta, Portoviejo, Bahía de Caráquez and Baltra (Galápagos).

• **SAN** (part of SAETA), *Republic de El Salvador 880 and Suecia, Edificio Almirante Colón. Tel. 254 510. Amazonas 1429 and Colón, Edificio España, Local #6. Tel. 564 969. Airport Tel. 456 015, 452 539. Both offices open Monday – Friday, 8:30am-6pm.* SAN has flights from Quito to Guayaquil, Cuenca and San Cristóbal (Galápagos).

• **Aerogal**, *Amazonas 7797 and Juan Holguín. Tel. 441 950*

Many international airlines have offices in Quito. Most are closed on Sunday, so if you need to make any travel arrangements then, you'll have to go to the airport.

• **American Airlines**, *Amazonas 367 and Robles. Tel. 561 144*
• **Aeroperu**, *Jorge Washington 718, 3rd floor. Tel. 561 699*
• **Air France**, *World Trade Center, Tower A, 12 de Octubre and Cordero. Tel. 527 374*
• **Avianca**, *780 República de Salvador. Tel. 264 392*

- **British Airways**, *1429 Amazonas and Colón. Tel. 540 000*
- **Continental Airlines**, *Naciones Unidas and Amazonas, Banco La Previsora building, 8th floor. Tel. 261 503*
- **Copa**, *910 Veintimilla and Juan Leon Mera. Tel. 228 740*
- **Iberia**, *Amazonas 239 and Jorge Washington. Tel. 560 546*
- **KLM,** *12 de Octubre and Lincoln. Tel. 986 828*
- **Lan Chile,** *18 de Septiembre 238 and Reina Victoria. Tel. 541 300*
- **Lufthansa**, *18 de Septiembre 238 and Reina Victoria. Tel. 508 396*
- **United Airlines**, *República del Salvador 880. Tel. 254 662*
- **Varig**, *Portugal 794 and República del Salvador. Tel. 254 662*

BY BUS

The main bus station in Quito, the *terminal terrestre, Maldonado 3077 and Cumandá, Tel. 570 670*, is located just southeast of Old Town. You can find buses leaving from here to just about everywhere in the country, or at least to the cities that then connect to out of the way places.

Keep a close eye on your belonging here. Pickpockets and swindlers have had lots of practice with unaware gringos. We've talked to quite a few people who were "helped" by seemingly official attendants who managed to be just distracting enough to allow partners to swipe backpacks and handbags.

SAMPLE TIMES & FARES FROM QUITO

Travel time and fares for one-way trips from Quito to the following cities:

	Bus Fare	Bus Travel Time	Airfare	Air Travel Time
Guayaquil	$8	8 hours	$40	40 minutes
Manta	$7	8 hours	$35	30 minutes
Cuenca	$9	10 hours	$40	40 minutes
Loja	$11	14 hours	$45	50 minutes
Lago Agrio	$8	8 hours	$60	30 minutes

Bus Companies & Destinations
- **Flora Imbabura** – Cuenca, Tulcán, Manta
- **Turismo Oriental** – Cuenca
- **Transportes Latacunga** – Latacunga
- **Transported Chimborazo** – Riobamba
- **Zaracay** – Esmeraldas, Tena, Lago Agrio, Ambato, Baños
- **Panamericana** – Guayaquil, Santo Domingo
- **Los Lagos** – Otavalo
- **Trans Andina** – Ibarra

· **Transportes Loja** – Loja
· **Transportes Amazonas** - Puyo

BY CAR

With cabs as cheap as they are, there's no reason for you to deal with renting a car to get around in the city. Some trips however, especially into remote areas of the highlands as well as the Central Coast, are much easier and more convenient if you have your own transportation.

If you rent a car in Ecuador, we highly recommend going with a reputable international company. If you were to have a breakdown, these companies are prepared to assist you with 24-hour help lines and more than one office in the country. We have used Budget out of Quito and been quite happy with the results.

Car Rental Companies

· **Budget**, *Colón 1140 and Amazonas. Tel. 545 761. Hotel Colón branch Tel. 525 328. Airport branch Tel. 459 052*
· **Ecuacar**, *Colón 1280 and Amazonas. Tel. 523 673*
· **Localiza**, *6 de Diciembre 1570 and Wilson. Tel. 505 986, Fax 506 005*
· **Avis**, *Colón 1741 and 10 de Agosto. Tel. 550 238*
· **Dollar**, *Ascaray 281 and 10 de Agosto. Tel. 430 777*

BY TAXI

We have seen much of Ecuador by taxi. The costs are so reasonable and the time savings and freedom so great that we recommend taking cabs for trips of up to a four hours. It usually costs about $6 per hour for trips out of Quito. If you hire a cab for a one-way trip, remember that the driver has to get back to Quito, so you will be charged for both ways. We recommend the taxi company at *Tel. 500 600*. Ask for one of the newer station wagon cabs with backseat seatbelts that are very comfortable for road trips.

BY TRAIN

The **Estación Central**, *Sincholagua and Maldonado, Tel. 656 144*, is the departure point for trains. The train runs south to Riobamba once a week. You have to really be a train buff to take this route because it is more expensive and takes far more time than going by bus. There are often delays due to mechanical failures as well.

ORIENTATION

Quito, ringed by volcanoes, is located in the northern quarter of the country on a high plateau nestled between the twin spines of the Andes mountain chain. It is practically sitting on the equator, which is why is was chosen by the Geodesic Expedition from France as the city from which to measure the circumference of the globe. (See the *History* chapter). Although an equatorial city, Quito's altitude of 2,850 meters means that you can forget grass skirts and balmy breezes here.

From Quito it is 240 km north via the Pan-American Highway to Tulcán on the border with Colombia, and 837 km south to Macará on the southern border with Peru. (There is another border crossing with Peru at Huaquillas, 578 km southwest of Quito via Guayaquil.)

The city runs basically north to south, with the oldest sections of the city where you'll do much of your sightseeing being on the southern end. As you travel north you move through New Town, where most travelers spend end up staying and eating the majority of their meals, and up through the financial district to the wealthier suburbs. Hemmed as it is by tall mountains and steep valleys, Quito just keeps getting longer rather than wider as it grows. It is 35 km long and only 5 km wide.

The main traffic arterioles running the length of the city are *America, 10 de Agosto, Amazonas* and *6 de Diciembre*. You can often use the large statue of the Virgin of Quito at the Panecillo to identify south.

Many of the streets in Quito, and the country for that matter, are named to commemorate important dates in Ecuador's history. Here's what some of the more common ones celebrate:

• **24 de Mayo**: Anniversary of the Battle of Pichincha
• **10 de Agosto**: National Independence Day
• **9 de Octubre**: Guayaquil Independence Day
• **12 de Octubre**: Columbus Day or Indigenous Peoples Day
• **6 de Diciembre**: Founding of Quito

GETTING AROUND TOWN

Taxis are one of the delights of Quito. We're not saying they are all in excellent shape and that some drivers won't up the fare, but in general they are a great, inexpensive way to get around town. You can either flag a yellow cab off the street, or have your hotel or restaurant call you one from a taxi stand, *sitio*. When you get in, make sure that your cab has a taxi-meter and that it is turned on before the driver takes off.

The drop rate for street cabs is about $0.30, but most will charge a $1 minimum for rides that end up less than that on the meter. Tipping is not common unless the driver helps you with your luggage, but most people just round fares up for simplicity sake. Our favorite Quito taxi stands are **Fedetaxi**, *Tel. 494 444*; and **Radiotaxi**, *Tel. 500 600*.

If you prefer to get around town by **bus**, we recommend taking the bus-like electric **trolley**. It's quieter, faster and cleaner than your standard bus and runs almost the entire length of the city. You'll see the green trolley stations along 10 de Agosto and into Old Town. A ride on the trolley costs about $0.25

Buses run on most of the main streets. The best thing to do is pick a place on the correct side of the street to go in the direction you want and then ask a driver or somebody waiting which bus to take. The reader boards on the bus display the final destination and some routing points. Bus fare is for standard *popular* buses is about $0.10 and for more spacious *executivo* buses $0.30.

Driving in Quito can be a bit of a headache unless you've spent some time here and really learned your way around. If you rent a car for a trip out of the city, make sure you get detailed directions on leaving town. If you're going north, 10 de Agosto turns into Gallo Plaza Lasso which becomes the *Panamericana*. If you're headed south, the easiest thing to do is take Sucre until it also turns into the Pan-American Highway.

WHERE TO STAY

Hotel choices in Quito run the range from luxurious to bare-bones, but we can definitely say that there will be something to make you happy in each price category. In fact, the hard thing in Quito is narrowing the good choices down. We would send friends and family, according to their budgetary constrictions, to all of the hotels listed below. The couple of exceptions are the hotels that have been given positive reviews in the past that are now past their prime.

Even though all of the hotels listed are good, that does not mean that some aren't better than others. Within each price category we have ranked the hotels according to our preferences. The first hotels on the list are our top choices for the category and we work down from there. The hotels at the top of the list are not necessarily the most expensive. Rather, they are the hotels that provide excellent accommodations for the category in addition to offering something special. The distinguishing quality might be location, size, décor, friendliness of the staff, or if you're lucky, all of the above.

The prices we quote are the walk-up rack rates including tax. If you make your reservation in advance, you should definitely ask for a corporate discount. Send a fax on company letterhead or an e-mail requesting the reduction.

Almost all of the hotels are in New Town, between Avenida Patria and Orellana. If they are not, we note that in the write-up.

Very Expensive

Most of the hotels that fall into the Very Expensive category, over $150 a night, are affiliated with international chains. You will find the same comfortable rooms and well-trained staff here that you would in their affiliates in Boston or Bangladesh.

SWISSOTEL, *12 de Octubre 1820 and Cordero. Tel. 2/566 464, Fax 2/ 569 189. 240 rooms. Double $260. Cable TV. Restaurant. Café. Bar. Gym. Pool. Sauna. Casino. Beauty salon. Business center. Credit cards accepted.*

The Swissotel, formally the Oro Verde Quito, is a suberb hotel. As soon as you walk through the doors you are greeted by a flurry of staff bearing hot towels and refreshing tropical fruit juice. It is this high level of service that distinguishes the Swissotel from the competition.

The rooms are spacious and comfortable, decorated with local art and ceramics. Ask for a room on a high floor to get excellent views of Quito. On clear days the panorama gets even better, as you can see many of the volcanoes ringing the city. One cloudless morning we rode up and down the glass elevator snapping photos of snow-covered Cotopaxi.

One of the things that we appreciate most about the Swissotel is its large gym. Lifecycles, Stairmasters and treadmills are all available, as is a Universal weight station. There is a separate room for aerobics and step classes. The heated pool, half indoors and half out, is another plus. Comfortable lounge chairs ring its edges, but most people vie for the freestanding hammocks.

When it comes time to dine, there's no reason to leave the premises. The Swissotel has by far the best restaurants of any hotel in the city. You have the option of French, Italian, Japanese and Ecuadorian food in the hotel's four excellent eateries. If you're more in the mood for propping your feet up and vegging in front of the TV you're in luck, as some of the best pizza in Quito can be ordered from room service. Just make sure to open your door for the turndown service as a different sweet niblet is delivered to your pillow each night.

MARRIOTT, *Amazonas and Orellana. Tel. 2/972 000, Fax 2/972 050. 257 rooms. $150. Cable TV. Restaurant. Café. Bar. Gym. Heated pool. Spa. Business center. Credit cards accepted.*

The Marriott is the newest entry in the Quito luxury hotel category. While the building looks like a bleached pyramid from the outside, it's a nice change from the cookie-cutter, boxy hotels once you step through the doors. The impressive yet comfortable lobby is bathed in light. Glass-paneled, geometric steel tubing acts as a giant skylight illuminating the polished marble floors. The soothing sound of trickling water comes from the multi-level, indoor waterfall that leads out to the pool. Incredible flower arrangements decorate tables and pedestals.

The rooms are exactly what you would expect from any Marriott in the world, but the dual line telephones and PC jacks are a luxury in Quito. The separate bath and shower lend an air of extravagance to the bathrooms. For the best views, ask for a room on one of the higher floors

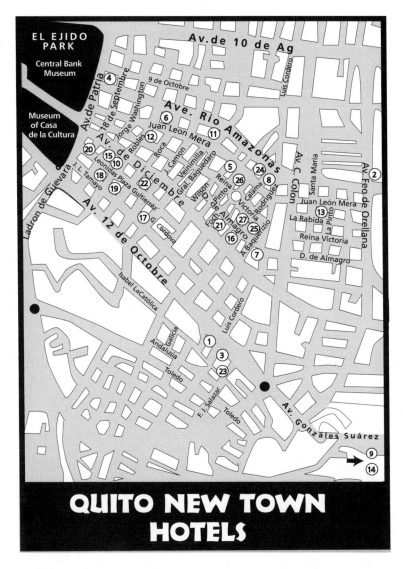

QUITO NEW TOWN HOTELS

1. Swisshotel	11. Hotel Reina Isabel	21. Casa Sol
2. Marriot	12. Café Cultura	22. Hostal Villa Nancy I
3. Radisson	13. Hostal de la Rábida	23. Floresta
4. Hilton Colón	14. Villa Nancy II	24. Orange Guest House
5. Mansión del Angel	15. La Cartuja	25. Cayman Hostal
6. Hotel Almeda Real	16. Hostal ds la	26. Magic Bean
7. Hotel Sebastion	17. Sierra Madre	27. Loro Verde
8. Hotel Rio Amazonas	18. Hostal Los Alpes	
9. Hotel Quito	19. Hostal Villantigua	
10. Amaranta Aparthotel	20. Hotel Plaza Internacional	

looking out at the Pichincha volcano. When it comes to relaxing, this is an excellent place for it. The outdoor pool is designed to look like multiple ponds in a jungle-like setting, while the health club includes full spa services. If it's nighttime entertainment you're after, try the lobby bar with live jazz music and 20 types of martinis before retiring to the library for a game of snooker. The main restaurant, La Hacienda, offers Mediterranean food in a colonial hacienda environment featuring antique furniture and beautiful decorative tiles.

The Marriott's location is great if you are here for a combo business/pleasure trip as it is right between New Town and the uptown business area, yet only about 15 minutes from the historical center.

RADISSON ROYAL QUITO HOTEL, *12 de Octubre y Cordero 444. Tel. 2/233 333, Fax 2/235 777. Toll free 800/333-3333. 112 rooms. Double $100. Cable TV. Bar. Cafeteria. Restaurant. Business center. Conference facilities. Gym. Sauna. Credit cards accepted.*

The Radisson is an outstanding value in the category. Joined at the hip to the World Trade Center, this hotel offers first class comfort and quality at a reasonable price. Fresh cut tropical flowers burst forth from vases in the lobby and stairwells. The rooms are impeccable and include the simple and sublime touches you would expect from the Radisson such as fine furnishings and well-appointed bathrooms. The restaurants here include the La Terraza Steak Grill specializing in juicy cuts hot off the *parrillada*. Business people and upscale travelers alike will be more than satisfied with the superior service.

HILTON HOTEL COLÓN INTERNATIONAL, *Amazonas and Patria. Tel. 2/560 666, Fax 2/563 903. E-mail: hiltonre@impsat.net.ec. 399 rooms. Double $225. Non-smoking rooms. Cable TV. Restaurant. Café. Bar. Pool. Sauna. Gym. Casino. Business Center. Beauty salon. Travel agency. Rental car. Free parking. Credit cards accepted.*

The Hilton Colón is big, big, big. You can easily get lost wandering around the shopping area and lobby as you try to make your way to the gym. Excellent phones, voice mail, cable TV and computer connections make it extremely popular with business travelers. While there is no questioning the high level of service, we prefer the more personal Swissotel and sparkling Marriot over this aging giant.

SHERATON FOUR POINTS, *República de El Salvador and Naciones Unidas. Tel. 2/970002, Fax 2/433906. 140 rooms and suites. Double $204. Cable TV. Restaurant. Café. Bar. Gym. Business Center. Credit cards accepted.*

If you're coming to Quito strictly on business will spend all your time in the financial district north of Naciones Unidas, you might as well stay up in the same neighborhood. The new Sheraton, bordering Parque La Carolina, is the up-town hotel of choice.

If it is full, you can try the near by **Holiday Inn Crowne Plaza**, *Los Shyris 1757 and Naciones Unidas, Tel. 2/252114, Fax 2/251985* for $250 a night for a double.

Expensive

The Expensive category, $80-150, is mainly comprised of nationally owned hotels that offer many of the same services furnished at international chains. With the exception of the **Mansión del Angel**, these are mostly large, square hotels. What they have in their favor are telephones, cable TV and dependable hot water, making them popular with Ecuadorian business travelers and tour groups.

MANSION DEL ANGEL, *Wilson E5-29 and Juan Leon Mera. Tel. 2/ 557 721, Fax 2/237 819. 49 rooms. 10 rooms. Double $99. Breakfast included. Cable TV. Credit cards accepted.*

We particularly recommend Mansión del Angel because it is a wonderful boutique alternative in a price category filled with aseptic, predictable hotels. Walking into this hotel is like stepping into the home of one of the Quito elite one hundred years ago. Decorated with unique and interesting antiques, oriental carpets, intricate inlaid wooden floors and original art works, La Mansión exudes elegance and style.

As this is an old colonial home, each room has a different size and layout. All have soothing yellow walls with intricate molding, gilt canopy beds, a comfortable chair and ottoman, as well as an exotic cage for the television. Be sure to ask for one of the larger rooms, as the size varies considerably in the seven doubles. We particularly recommend spacious room 305 with the king-sized bed. The three singles are all small, but decorated with the same exacting attention to detail. The bathrooms, thankfully, are entirely modern. Every room has a very large shower as well as ample counter space, new blow dryers and big bars of soap.

The same people that created the incredible Hostería La Mirage near Otavalo own La Mansión. Many of the details that make La Mirage so special have been repeated here. Rose petals on the beds and sinks, nightly surprises on the pillows, and excellent service are hallmarks of the owners.

Selected as one of our *Best Places to Stay* – see chapter 11 for more details.

HOTEL ALAMEDA REAL, *Roca 655 and Amazonas. Tel. 2/562 345, Fax 565 759; E-mail:* apartec@uio.satnet.net. *www.apartec.com.ec. 145 rooms. Double $110. Cable TV. Restaurant. Café. Bar. Business Center. Beauty Salon. Gym. Parking. Travel agency. Bookstore. Credit cards accepted.*

The Alameda Real costs half the price of the larger international hotels yet offers almost all the amenities. Its five star rating makes it a good value for people who need those types of services.

The noise of the street fades away when you walk into the lobby with its sun-drenched atrium. The other parts of the hotel, decorated in pastel florals, are also nice and light. The rooms are of the expected high quality for a hotel of this caliber. For an additional $20 the junior suites are a spacious alternative. You should definitely request a room on a higher floor for views of the surrounding hills. The staff is helpful and the service level is high.

HOTEL SEBASTIAN, *Almagro 822 and Cordero. Tel. 2/222300, Fax 2/222500. E-mail: hsebast@hsebastian.com.ec. 56 rooms. Double $96. Cable TV. Restaurant. Bar. Cafe. Conference facilities. Credit cards accepted.*

The Hotel Sebastian is a ten story Swiss chalet complete with cheery flower boxes outside of every window. This four star hotel is a cut above the rest in its price range due to its attention to details like finely finished wood and exquisite throw rugs in all of the rooms. The location is central, but peaceful, fronted against a small park. The coffee shop and restaurant downstairs are convenient, or you can walk to one of the many excellent, nearby restaurants.

HOTEL RIO AMAZONAS, *Cordero 375 and Amazonas. Tel. 2/556 666 or 556667, Fax 2/556670. Website hotelrioamazonas.com. 55 rooms. Double $96. Cable TV. Restaurant. Credit cards accepted.*

This gleaming glass and steel high-rise structure is comfortable, but with the better hotels offering doubles for the same price, it can't compete. The strongest attribute is that it towers over the neighboring buildings so rooms on the west side have impressive views of the verdant Pichincha mountainside.

HOTEL QUITO, *Gonzales Suaréz N27 142. Tel. 2/544 600, Fax 2/567 284. E-mail: emil.raschle@orotels.com. 212 rooms. Double $90. Cable TV. Restaurant. Café. Bar. Pool. Sauna. Casino. Business center. Beauty salon. Credit cards accepted.*

The Hotel Quito is starting to show its age, but there's not another property in town with better views. All of Quito stretches out below, as does the fertile Cumbayá Valley. The hotel is built around a nice sized swimming pool with a large yard area, which is a big plus if you've got kids. We like the hotel's location up above the town of Guapulo, yet just a five minute cab ride from New Town. Even if you don't stay here, you should consider a meal or drink in the top floor restaurant. Lunch is a nice hour to come because you can see everything, but dinnertime is especially romantic because of the twinkling lights below.

AMARANTA APARTHOTEL, *Leonidas Plaza 194 and Jorge Washington. Tel. 2/543 619, Fax 2/560586. 40 rooms. Double $70. Breakfast included. Cable TV. Credit cards accepted.*

The Amaranta is a highly functional place that fits the bill if you need space. The boxy, six story building is nothing special on the outside, but each apartment includes a large living area, comfortable bedroom, separate bathroom and small but well-stocked kitchen. The spacious rooms have a lot of ugly green carpet, but they are spotless. The staff is friendly and very helpful as well. Ask for a room up top to get nice views of the surrounding hills.

HOTEL REINA ISABEL, *Amazonas 842 and Veintimilla. Tel. 2/544 454, Fax 2/221 337. 120 rooms. Double $70. Breakfast included. Cable TV. Credit cards accepted.*

This new four star hotel on Amazonas lacks character, but makes up for that with its modern facilities and comfortable rooms. Direct phone lines, cable TV and blow dryers in the bathroom can all be found here. The rooms are clean and nice and hallways bright. We love the coastal accent of the doorman who turns *hasta luego,* see you later, into *'tal'ego.*

HOWARD JOHNSON, *Alemania E5-103 and La República. Tel. 2/265 265, Fax 264 264. 94 rooms. Double $80. Cable TV. Restaurant. Bar. Business Center. Gym. Credit cards accepted.*

Howard Johnson is popular with mid-level business people making calls in the financial district, as it is located near Parque Carolina. The plain square building offers no surprises, which exactly it's appeal for those who seek dependable service.

Moderate

It is in the Moderate category, $40-80, that Quito really shines. There are so many unique, comfortable and interesting places to stay in this price range that we recommend most of these hotels over some of their more expensive counterparts.

Many of these hotels are converted from old colonial homes, so there are some things to keep in mind – most don't have central heat or telephones in the rooms. If there's a real cold spell that space heaters can't overcome or you have lots of calls to make, you might be more comfortable in one of the less charming but more functional options above.

CAFÉ CULTURA, *Robles 513 and Reina Victoria. Tel. 2/504 078, Fax 2/224 271; E-mail:* info@cafecultura.com. *26 rooms. Breakfast not included. Double $58. Restaurant. Tour booking. Credit cards accepted but for an additional 10% fee.*

Ecuador has a plethora of delightful, intimate mid-range hotels, and the Cafe Cultura is one of the best. Housed in an old colonial mansion, which was used as the French Cultural Center in its previous life, the hotel is ideally located in New Town. Owned by English-Ecuadorian partners, the Café Cultura sets the standard against which others are judged.

After passing under the bougainvillea-draped entrance, you walk through the small garden to the entrance of the house. Every part of the house is a treat and a pleasure. The reception area, with its high ceiling, immediately draws you in. Each room in the house was painted by a Chilean muralist who has created a warm, artistic atmosphere.

To the left, through lovely French doors, the wood-panel library offers a relaxing refuge. A small bookshelf is available for guests, but we use the library mainly for hanging out after dinner. Dimmed lights, multiple candles and a well-attended fireplace make it the perfect place to unwind at the end of the night. Candles, fresh cut flowers and fireplaces are standard in all common areas. Intriguing antiques hanging on the walls and comfortable couches make it hard to move along.

Each guestroom in the hotel is different. Sky lights, fireplaces and private phone lines are amenities found in some of the rooms. We think it's worth going for the honeymoon suite if it is available. For $78 you get a fireplace in your room and perhaps the most romantic bathroom we've seen. The freestanding tub surrounded by candles is like something out of a movie.

The rooms are only part of the story. The staff at the Cultura goes out of its way to make sure your visit is a pleasure. The Cultura Reservation Center, located in the hotel, can arrange guided tours, drivers, and hotel and plane reservations. Lastly there's the restaurant. We rave about it below in our *Where to Eat* section, so you really ought to try at least one meal here.

Selected as one of our Best Places to Stay – see chapter 11 for more details.

HOSTAL DE LA RABIDA, *La Rábida 227 y Sta. Maria. Tel. 2/222169, Fax 2/221720; E-mail: larabida@uio.satnet.net. 11 rooms. Double $60. Cable TV. Restaurant. Bar. Credit cards accepted.*

Gracefully robed in whitewashed walls and stately French doors, La Rábida exudes elegance and refinement. The eleven-room inn is located in a quiet residential neighborhood, but within easy walking distance of the restaurants and activity in New Town. You should opt for at least one meal in the cozy dining room as the menu, although as diminutive as its residence, offers more enticing Italian fare than many of Quito's *trattorias*. You can select from specialties like pasta in tomato, chili, and bacon sauce or chicken breast in orange sauce. Breakfast includes homemade breads and marmalade, fresh juices, and other delights that range from healthy to hearty.

Admire the two-foot thick walls as you pass from room to room. The den is furnished with tasteful, comfortable sofas from which you can be entranced by a crackling fire. The next room is the bar and library where guests enjoy pre-dinner drinks and animated conversation surrounded by European naturalist prints. The dining room follows and then leads out into the courtyard and luxuriant garden. Most of the rooms surround this small piece of Eden.

The Italian owner has done an extraordinary job with the limited space of the rooms by focusing on sleekness of line in furnishings and adding the warmth of the European countryside. All of the beds have comforters and some include a flourish of wrought iron in the headboard. Our favorite room here is number eleven, which includes a small, private atrium with a circular lead glass window that channels light into it, making it a perfect reading nook.

HOSTAL VILLA NANCY, *Los Muros 146 and Gonzales Suarez. Tel. 2/ 550 839. E-mail: nancita@pi.pro.ec. 12 rooms. Double $48. Breakfast included. Airport transfer included. No credit cards.*

Villa Nancy is probably the homiest hostel in Quito. As soon as you walk in the door you feel the welcoming influence of your hostess Nancy, who lives here with her husband and young son. Located up by the Hotel Quito on the way to Guapulo, Villa Nancy is out of all the hubbub of New Town, but only five minutes away by taxi.

We like this hotel. Gleaming hardwood floors, a comfortable breakfast room and spotless quarters are all appreciated, but it's the warmth of the home that gives Villa Nancy its real charm.

A few of the rooms are actually suites, with separate living and bedrooms. Room 12 is our personal favorite with its large lounging area and sweeping views of Quito below. If the Pichincha volcano happens to be in one of its active stages you'll get a great look at that as well. If you are going to spending much time in the hotel, we say that it's definitely worth an additional $12 for extra space a suite affords.

Villa Nancy is located in a residential neighborhood, but there are a number of good restaurants within walking distance, so you don't feel at all stranded.

LA CARTUJA, *Leonidas Plaza 170 and 18 de Septiembre. Tel. 2/523 577, Fax 2/226 391. E-mail: cartuja@uio.satnet.net. Website: www.ecuadorexplorer.com/ lacartuja. 12 rooms. Breakfast included. Restaurant. Double $40. No credit cards.*

This cheery yellow house is one of the excellent new entries in the mid-range hotel category. Painstakingly remodeled, the colonial-style home turned hotel was formerly the site of Great Britain's embassy. The house features high ceilings, intricate white molding and polished parquet floors.

The lodgings are extremely pleasant, making this a place you won't mind settling in and staying for a while. The Cartuja especially stands out amongst it peers in terms of amenities. Each room sports many features that are not standard in hotels in this price category including phones, televisions and safety deposit boxes.

There is a tranquil green courtyard behind the main house with additional guest rooms. While these rooms don't have the tall ceilings and expansive feel of the main house, they are nice and quiet.

The young Spanish couple that owns the hotel sees that only excellent international and Spanish homemade food makes it way out of the kitchen. All in all, La Cartuja offers great personality and comfort for the money.

ANTINEA APART-HOTEL, *Juan Rodriguez 175 and Almagro. Tel. 2/ 506 838, Fax 2/504 404. E-mail: hotelant@uio.satnet.net. 15 suites and apartments. Double apartment $58. Restaurant. Cable TV. No credit cards.*

If you want a little more room, but still like the idea of staying in a colonial-style building, this big rambling house is the place for you. The double apartments here are really little more than rooms with a small kitchenette, but having the extra space can make an amazing difference in your comfort level. So can the freedom to slap together a sandwich or have a bowl of cereal without leaving the room. The kitchenettes all have burners, refrigerators, cookware and utensils.

If you're tired of hanging out in your room, you can always sit around the fireplace downstairs or enjoy reading a book one of the three sunny patios. The Antinea is also a good option of you are traveling in a larger group or family as they offer bigger, two-story apartments with multiple bedrooms.

SIERRA MADRE, *Veintimilla 464 and Tamayo. Tel. 2/505 687, Fax 2/ 505 715; E-mail: htsierra@hoy.net. 21 rooms. Double $50. Breakfast not included. Restaurant. Bar. Credit cards accepted.*

The Sierra Madre is deservedly known for its tasty breakfast buffet and its balconies. While the pleasant rooms are similar to those in many of the New Town hotels, with hardwood floors and medium sized bathrooms, five of them have the luxury of a private balcony. Don't despair if they are all taken though. Even if you don't get one of those rooms, you can enjoy the views of Quito from the large roof-top terrace. The Mediterranean-style café offers more than just breakfast, but the homemade bread, fresh fruit and granola and yogurt are what we look forward to most. Veintimilla gets quite a bit of traffic, so ask for one of the quiet rooms in back.

HOSTAL LOS ALPES, *Tamayo 233 and Jorge Washington. Tel 2/561 110, Fax 2/ 561 128. 24 rooms. Double $58. Breakfast included. Restaurant. Credit cards accepted.*

Located on a quiet street near the American Embassy, this family-run hostel is clean and friendly, but also a bit dark and old in decor. The house, red-roofed and white-walled, looks like it was transplanted from the center of Old Town. A tree-covered entrance, with a small cafe area in the garden, leads into the colonial home. Stained wood and wrought iron, combined with garish colors and shag carpets, give at a 70's-conquistator style inside. There is a light-filled atrium upstairs that's nice for reading. The rooms are decent-sized and there is some common space in the house in front of the fireplace or in the garden. The Italian heritage of the owners means that the restaurant downstairs serves good *manga*.

HOSTAL VILLANTIGUA, *Jorge Washington 237 and Tamayo. Tel. 2/ 227 018, Fax 2/545 663. 12 rooms. Double $48. Breakfast not included. Credit cards accepted.*

The Villantigua is located in an old house near the South American Explorer's Club. The house is decorated in a dated style, but it is clean and the Ecuadorian owners are likable. As is the case with many older homes, the rooms are large with high ceilings. There is an inviting, although small, fireplace nook downstairs. The Villantigua is often recommended, but we think it a bit overpriced for what you get.

HOTEL PLAZA INTERNACIONAL, *Leonidas Plaza 150 and 18 de Septiembre. Tel. 2/524 530, Fax 2/505 075; E-mail: hplaza@uio.satnet. net. 54 rooms. Double $45. Breakfast not included. Restaurant. Bar. Travel agency. No credit cards.*

The grand, iron, arched entrance that greets your arrival to the Hotel Plaza promises more than the inside offers. The original building, a colonial home, houses the restaurant, travel agency and a few of the guestrooms. A flimsy high-rise behind the main building comprises the majority of the rooms. These more modern facilities are smaller than the ones in the main house. The location, close to Patria Avenue, can be loud. Either take earplugs or knock this one off your list.

Inexpensive

The Inexpensive category, $15-40, is also filled with strong options if this is your price range. Many of these personality-rich locales are run by their owners. The rooms and bathrooms are a bit on the small side and can be chilly at night sometimes, but you'll get a pretty comfortable bed and hot water.

CASA SOL, *Calama 127 and 6 de Diciembre. Tel. 2/230 798, Fax 2/223 383; E-mail: casasol@ecuadorexplorer.com. Website ecuadorexplorer.com/casasol/ home. Double $30. Suite $43. 10 rooms. Breakfast included. Restaurant. Credit cards accepted.*

As bright as its name, this Ecuadorian run B&B shines among other Quito locales in its price range. Earth-toned ceramic tiles inlaid with smaller blue squares lead you to the front porch. Inside, each wall in the cozy common areas is a bold stroke of color. The rooms surround a diminutive courtyard where guests relax and chat. Though not the largest of rooms, they are cheery enough that it is easy to overlook this shortcoming. The reasonably priced suites include a small living area and a kitchenette. Vibrant photos of colorfully painted tribal faces adorn the sunlit breakfast room. The one drawback to this intimate hotel is a bit of traffic noise off the busy street behind it. It's pretty quiet at night though.

HOSTAL VILLA NANCY, *Carrion 335 and 6 de Diciembre. Tel. 2/563 084. E-mail: nancita@pi.pro.ec. 8 rooms. Double $20 with shared bath. Breakfast included. Airport transfer included. No credit cards.*

This is the original and less expensive Villa Nancy. While not as nice as Villa Nancy no. 2, it is a very good choice for the money. It becomes an ever better deal when you consider that the round trip airport transfer, included in the price of a room, is an $8 value. While located in New Town, it is not right in the thick of things, which makes it a pleasant quiet option.

The best thing about this Villa Nancy is the plethora of pleasant spill-over space. Not only is there a small veranda out in front of the house, but there is also a tree shaded garden in back. Both spots include a table and patio chairs, making them perfect places for writing postcard, catching up in your journal or just taking in some morning sunshine. Inside the house there is also both a common living and dining area. The house itself is spotless, with polished hardwood floors and neat rooms.

FLORESTA HOTEL, *Isabel La Catolica1015 y Salazar. Tel. 2/225 376 or 236874, Fax 2/500422; E-mail: floresta@impsat.net.ec. Double $38. 20 rooms. Cable TV. Cafeteria. Credit cards accepted.*

This cheery small hotel feels like a cozy bed and breakfast except breakfast isn't included. The homey rooms are done tastefully in bright pastels. The living areas downstairs and the small sundeck upstairs are good places for lounging. The hotel is located a stone's throw from New Town, just behind the Swissotel.

THE ORANGE GUEST HOUSE, *Foch 726, corner of Amazonas. Tel. 2/ 221305 or 569 960, Fax 2/569956; E-mail: angermeyer@accessinter.net. Website angermeyer.com. 12 rooms. Double $28. Breakfast included. Credit cards accepted.*

This pleasing inn is situated in the back portion of an old home. The rooms are tastefully finished with blonde wood floors and furniture, and whitewashed walls framed in royal blue. Thick comforters and perfect reading lights enhance bedtime. The Orange Guesthouse is one of the most solid options for the price. The complimentary breakfast is served in the small dining nook. Since the hotel is located in the heart of New Town, several of the rooms catch disco noise. Ask for one on the bottom floor for more peace and quiet.

CAYMAN HOSTAL, *Juan Rodriguez 270 y Reina Victoria. Tel./Fax 2/ 567 616; E-mail: hcayman@uio.satnet.net. Double $22. 12 rooms. Breakfast included. Cable TV. Cafeteria. No credit cards.*

This newly opened hotel is located in a refurbished old house, smartly painted in light yellow with green shutters. The hotel's mascot is a backpacking caiman crocodile. This backpacker inn will even satisfy suitcase carriers with its tidy rooms that, amazingly for the price, all include private baths. Parquet floors are underfoot throughout the house. Breakfast is served in a covered, tiled courtyard. There is also a nice garden on the side of the house to catch afternoon rays.

MAGIC BEAN, *Foch 681 and Juan Luis Mera. Tel. 2/566 181. 4 rooms. Double with bath $26. Shared room $8 per person. Breakfast included. No credit cards.*

The Magic Bean deserves rave reviews for its restaurant. (See *Where to Eat* below). It also offers some decent digs for the price. Teal walls, polished wood molding and hardwood floors lend this place a classiness that the price does not indicate. There is a living area with tons of travel information for trip planning as well. The best part of staying here is that the restaurant is only a flight of stairs away.

Another good, cheap option attached to an excellent eatery is **El Cafecito**, *Cordero 1124 and Reina Victoria, Tel. 234-862.*

LORO VERDE, *Rodriguez 241 and Almagro. Tel. 2/226 173. 19 rooms. Double $16. Breakfast included. No credit cards.*

The Loro Verde is a good old stand-by in the inexpensive category. The house, although not exactly sparkling, has the kind of comfortable, lived-in character that comes with age. Another good thing about the place is its kitchen access. The rooms all have private baths. Ask for one in back if you're a light sleeper.

HOMESTAYS IN QUITO

Some people want to really dive into the Ecuador experience and stay with a local family during their time in Quito. It's great for the Spanish practice. If that seems appealing, you might want to try one of these families recommended by members of the South American Explorer's Club:
- *Blanca Aguirre, Toledo 1498 and Coruna. Tel. 2/523 297*
- *Maruja Jeria de Narvaez, Sevilla 210 and Vizcaya. Tel. 2/237 810*
- *Marta Cabezas, Salazar 476 and Zaldumbide. Tel. 2/235 659*

Budget

Even in the Budget category, under $15, there are some great options. You'll be sharing a bathroom, but usually will have kitchen privileges and the run of the house.

LA CASONA DE MARIO, *Andalucía 213 and Galicia. Tel. 2/544036, Fax 2/230129. 15 rooms. Double $12 with shared bath. Breakfast not included. No credit cards.*

Mario is a cool, laid-back guy and his hostel mirror's his personality. The great old house, with high ceilings and hardwood floors, is one of our favorites in the category. This is a place where you can feel at home, hang out and meet other travelers. The rooms are simple, but there is tons of spill over space, including both an upstairs and downstairs living area with cable TV, a pleasant garden, and a patio. Both people on a tight budget and those tired of eating out will appreciate the two fully outfitted kitchens available to Casona guests 24 hours a day. Facilities for clothes washing and a storage area are other pluses here.

The hostel is located in the mellow Floresta neighborhood, behind the Swissotel. It's a nice safe place away from, but within walking distance of the Mariscal hustle. If you stay longer than two weeks, which is a tempting thought, he'll give you a discount.

CROSSROADS, *Foch 678, corner of Juan Leon Mera. Tel. 2/234-735; E-mail: jbrummel@uio.satnet.net. 30 rooms. Double w/ shared bath $14. Dorm bed $5. Cafe. No credit cards.*

This impressive, burnt orange manor-turned-hotel is one of Quito's best options in the budget category. Long hallways of hardwood floors polished till they squeak lead to spacious, simple rooms, also outfitted with the lustrous floors. Attractive lounging areas include a small court-yard with an outdoor fireplace, a nice cafeteria, and a front yard garden. There is also a small guest kitchen for those that prefer to prepare their own meals. Since this place is in heart of the nightlife area and on a corner of a fairly busy street, ask for an interior room for a better prospect of undisturbed slumber.

HOSTAL EL TAXO, *Foch 909. Tel. 2/225 593; E-mail: acordova@rant.com. Double with shared bath $16, or $8 per person. 10 rooms. Cafeteria. No credit cards.*

This funky budget option has been around longer than most, which speaks highly of its appeal, but unfortunately it's starting to show its age. Every time we turned a corner we would spot something intriguing that kept us interested, such as original artwork on the walls, or the garden patio that hosts musicians on the weekends. This place somehow whispers "mellow" enticingly.

LA CASA DE ELIZA, *Isabel La Católica 1559. Tel. 2/226 602. 6 rooms. Double $12 with shared bath. Breakfast included. No credit cards.*

Eliza's house is your house as long as you're a guest. Wash your clothes, cook your meals, feel right at home. We are fans of the Floresta neighborhood and this is a decent budget choice in the area. You can get information on the Cerro Golondrinas Trek through the cloud forest, as Eliza is very involved in the foundation.

EVA LUNA WOMEN'S HOSTAL, *Pasaje de Roca 630 and Amazonas. Tel. 2/234 799; E-mail: admin@safari.com.ec. 3 rooms. $4 per person for shared room. Breakfast not included. Women only. No credit cards.*

The bright yellow flower on the door marks the spot of this unique hostel. Catering to women only, it offers a nice place to relax in macho

Latin America. A shared kitchen and small patio are surprising extras for the price. Each room has two sets of bunk beds. There are lockers available to store your stuff. The only drawback is that if the hotel is full, 12 women are sharing one bathroom.

AMAZONAS INN, *Joaquín Pinto 471, corner of Amazonas. Tel. 2/225 723 or 2/222 666. Cable TV. Double $10. 25 rooms. Cafe. No credit cards.*

This place scores zero in personality, but it is clean and quiet, despite its epicentral location, and has a color TV in each room.

HOSTELLING INTERNATIONAL, *Pinto 325. Tel. 2/543 995. 20 rooms. Double room with shared bath $14. No credit cards.*

This international hostel is a wreck. Quito has too many places with personality and hygiene to be lured in by the comforting International Hostel logo. Try elsewhere.

Old Town

HOSTAL LA CASONA, *Manabí 255. Tel. 2/954 764, Fax 2/563 271. 30 rooms. Double $10. No credit cards.*

The La Casona is a charming, ancient home, that reaches toward the sky from an inner courtyard. Exaggerated stone columns that climb 10 meters highlight the first floor, while the columns on the second and third floors are finished in opaquely varnished wood. The courtyard floor is oddly inlaid with smooth stones and unidentified animal vertebrae. The rooms are bare except beds, but they are good ones. This hotel should not be confused with the La Casona de Mario in New Town, which we include on our *Best Inexpensive Hotels* sidebar.

LA POSADA COLONIAL, *Paredes 188 and Rocafuerte. Tel. 2/282 859, Fax 2.505 240. 15 rooms. Double $9. No credit cards.*

Some people like the vibe of Quito's colonial center so much that they want to stay there. If you're one of those people, La Posada is one of the only good inexpensive options. The old building, beautifully renovated, makes you feel like you've stepped into the past.

HOTEL PLAZA DEL TEATRO, *Guayaquil 8-75, Plaza del Teatro. Tel. 2/959 462 or 952 980, Fax 2/519 462. 25 rooms. Double $11. TV. Restaurant. No credit cards.*

The Plaza del Teatro is a clean, solid entrant in the Old Town budget category. It has few features of note, except a polished marble entrance and its location on the last stop of the electric trolley line.

WHERE TO EAT

You can find almost any kind of food in Quito. If you are just in Ecuador for a short time however, you should focus in on Ecuadorian food to really get the flavor of the country. There are many good options from which to choose.

If you are spending more than a week here, you'll get to the point where you can't stand to see another potato. When that happens (and it will), you're in luck because there are excellent international and ethnic options in Quito.

A smart choice if you're watching your pennies or in a bit of a hurry is the lunch *menú*. Many restaurants offer this fixed meal that usually consists of soup, a main course with potatoes and/or rice, dessert and a drink. It usually costs less than $3 and gets to your table in minutes.

As a reminder, many restaurants are open from 12pm-4pm and again from 7 or 8pm-11pm. Snack bars and more informal places are open straight through from 8am-11pm. Many restaurants are closed on Sunday evenings, when it can be very hard to find a place to eat. Some of our favorite Sunday night dining options (other than room service) are **Il Risotto**, **Hunters** and **Clancy's**.

When we calculate costs we consider a meal that includes a salad or appetizer; main course; dessert; and a water, soft drink or beer. We don't include wine because, as all wine is imported, it is rather expensive relative to the rest of the food here. Our price categories are broken down as follows (prices are per person):
• Inexpensive: under $4
• Moderate: $4-$8
• Expensive: $9-$12
• Very Expensive: Over $12

You'll notice that meals considered expensive in Ecuador could be thought of as moderately priced in many other parts of the world. We recommend that you take advantage of that and try some of the outstanding international restaurants in Quito while you're here.

Ecuadorian Food
Ecuadorian food varies from the Highlands to the Coast. Much of the Highlands food is based on meat and potatoes. On the Coast, it's bananas and seafood. Some of the restaurants below serve dishes from around the country, while others focus on either the indigenous food of the Andes or the rich bounty from the sea.

LA QUERENCIA, *Eloy Alfaro 2530 y Catalina Aldaz. Tel. 461665. Expensive.*

La Querencia is our favorite dinner spot for Ecuadorian cuisine. The wood planked floors and ceilings and sturdy wooden furnishings accent the coziness of this elegant house. A fireplace crackles on chilly evenings to set the room aglow.

For appetizers the dilemma will be choosing between the six varieties of ceviche and the three types of *humitas*. Whether you order the shrimp

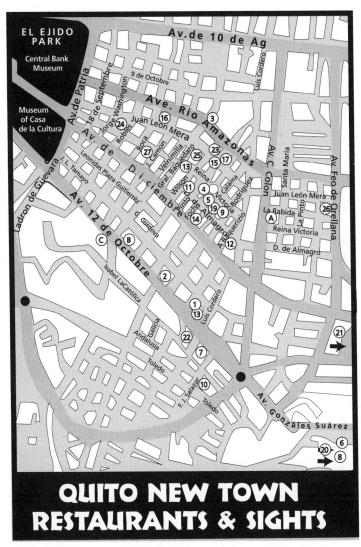

QUITO NEW TOWN
RESTAURANTS & SIGHTS

1. La Choza
2. Marc Nostrum
3. Las Redes
4. Viejo Jose
5. Mama Chlorindas
6. Villa Goya
7. La Viña
8. Avalon
9. Boca del Lobo
10. Clancy's

11. Il Risotto
12. Il Grillo
13. Pavarotti
14. La Bettola
15. Pizzaiolo
16. La Guardia del
    Coyote
17. Red Hot Chile
    Peppers
18. Tex-Mex
19. Shorton Grill
20. Hunters

21. Sake
22. Happy Panda
23. Magic Bean
24. Cafe Cultura
25. Grain Cafe
26. Crepes and Waffles
27. El Holandes

ATTRACTIONS
A. Viverium
B. Museo Amazonica
C. Museo Jijon and
   Caamaño

154 ECUADOR & GALÁPAGOS ISLANDS GUIDE

or seabass or other type of ceviche, it will be accompanied by an overflowing bowl of popcorn. A cold *cerveza* is the recommended wash for this combo. *Humitas*, a corn cake similar to Mexican tamales, are usually sold in street carts, so this is a good chance to order one in a restaurant. For a main course, if you have yet to try *seco de chivo*, you should do it here. This typical Ecuadorian dish of lamb stew is anything but "dry" as the name indicates. At La Querencia the meat is particularly moist and the sauce especially flavorful. The *fritada Quiteña* is also superb. While the direct translation of fried pork does not seem that appealing, it really is a succulent preparation that you should give a chance early on in your visit, because you will probably order it again.

LA CHOZA, *12 de Octubre 1955 y Cordero. Tel. 230 839. Credit cards accepted.*

La Choza is an excellent option to indulge in finely prepared Ecuadorian cuisine. The high walls of the main dining area painted in brilliant yellow and burnt orange. A variety of tastefully positioned antique farm utensils and woodcarvings stand out against this high-energy background. Frequently tour groups line several tables pushed end to end, but this is not a commentary on the quality of the food, and in fact, enlivens the atmosphere when the Andean musicians appear. A more intimate dining area is located on a balcony overlooking the main room.

This is a good place to try one of the Ecuadorian cocktails such as the *azadon – chicha* (corn cider), vodka, and fresh fruit; or an *Atahualpa – naranjilla* juice (a tart orange), and rum. The *plato típico La Choza* is a sampler plate that allows you to taste a wide range of Ecuadorian fare. It is better to order and share this as an appetizer rather than as a main course as it's listed on the menu. The *llapingacho montado* is a flavorful indulgence, semi-jerkied, surprisingly tender pork served on a corn fritter, topped with an egg.

MARE NOSTRUM, *Mariscal y Tamayo E10-5. Tel. 528 868 or 237 236. Expensive. Credit cards accepted.*

Housed within a ceramic-tiled, ivy-walled Spanish style house, the Mare Nostrum is a seafood lover's sanctuary. The high sky-lighted ceilings and lanky walls provide a light, airy atmosphere that is perfect for lunch. All of the food is presented on beautiful, heavy pewter often so hot to the touch that the wait staff builds their biceps as they serve the plates with industrial sized prongs.

The delectable stoned crab crepe is the only way we can imagine starting a meal here. It is absolutely delicious. For the main course, most patrons steer the ship toward one of the seafood entrees. Squid, prawns, shrimp, clams, and mussels join forces in flavorful platters prepared in paella, butter and garlic sauce, coconut sauce, or grilled. All but the heartiest eaters could split one of these ample servings and be satisfied. The seafood is perfect in freshness and tenderness. Garlic or chili fanatics should ask the waiter to crank up the normal intensity a bit.

BAMBU BAR, *Almagro 22-13 and Andrade Marín. Tel. 237-436. Moderate. Credit cards accepted.*

It is worth the quick cab ride to have lunch at the cheery Bambu Bar Restaurant. A wall of windows makes the garden appear to be part of the dining room. Meanwhile, suspended from the ceiling is a fern so expansive you will feel like a rainforest is hovering overhead. This locale is a favorite of Ecuadorians for homegrown fare with an international accent. The food is creatively prepared without being overly nouveau.

It is difficult to read past the tempting appetizers. You can begin your meal with a traditional Ecuadorian starter like *locro de queso,* potato and cheese chowder, or go for the flaky, rich stone crab prepared in crepes or bisque. Many of the Ecuadorians who dine here prefer to indulge in the ceviches, loading on the popcorn, the aroma of which fills the room. The *empanadas de morocho* are also excellent. If you actually get to the entrees without ordering enough starters to fill you up, consider the delicious pork in plum sauce or the flaky sea bass sprinkled with capers.

RINCON LA RONDA, *Bello-Horizonte E8-45 and Almagro. Tel. 540 459. Moderate. Credit cards accepted.*

This popular restaurant serves refined versions of the best of dishes found all over the country. Widen your horizons and order something you've never heard of. The service is excellent, the décor traditional and the food memorable.

LAS REDES RESTAURANT, *Amazonas 845 and Veintimilla. Tel. 525 691. Moderate. Credit cards accepted.*

This bright and cheery restaurant is a fun place to enjoy some of Ecuador's fruits of the sea. Your dining options here are shellfish, fish and more fish. If you can't decide what you want, you can go for the *Gran mariscada,* a grab bag of sea creatures cooked on the grill, or the *mariscal,* the same creatures sautéed in garlic. If you like strong flavors, ask them to go heavy on the garlic. This is also a good place to sample *ceviche,* one of Ecuador's most delicious and traditional dishes.

EL VIEJO JOSE, *Reina Victoria and Pinto. Inexpensive. No credit cards.*

You can find yourself forgetting you're in the Highlands when you walk into this *cevichería.* With a mainly seafood menu, Viejo Jose is a favorite for inexpensive dishes from the coast. Close your eyes, listen to the salsa music, take a bite of the excellent ceviche and you're transported right to the beach. This restaurant stays open until 5pm on Sunday, but is closed on Monday.

MAMA CLORINDAS, *Reina Victoria 1144 and Calama. Tel. 544 362. Inexpensive. No credit cards accepted.*

This restaurant is a good choice for low cost Ecuadorian food in New Town. You can get almost all the typical food of the Highlands, including *llapingachos, empanadas* and *fritadas.* The décor leaves something to be desired, but you're here for the food.

If it's just an *empanada* that you're after, we recommend **Frutería de Monserrat** at *Eloy Alfaro and 6 de Diciembre.*

OUR FAVORITE RESTAURANTS IN QUITO
- *La Querencia* – *Ecuadorian*
- *Mare Nostrum* – *Ecuadorian*
- *Villa Goya* – *International*
- *La Viña* – *International*
- *El Mero Mero* – *Mexican*
- *Magic Bean* – *Café*
- *Café Cultura* – *Café*

Other Types of Food

Ecuador has been a popular spot on the backpacker route for years. Some of them usually end of sticking around and starting businesses, which means you can get just about any type of health or ethnic food that exists.

On the more expensive end, there are some excellent restaurants serving the type of high quality international fare that can only be found in the world's large cities. With the sucre as weak as it is, a gourmet meal that might cost $80-100 in San Francisco ends up costing about half that in Quito.

International

VILLA GOYA, *Ana de Ayala 2734, corner of Avenida de los Conquistadores, in Guapulo. Tel. 558 277. Expensive. Credit cards accepted.*

Culturally, you might feel the obligation to eat fine Ecuadorian cuisine if you only have one meal in Quito, but the Villa Goya should make you think twice about it. Located in the village of Guapulo, but less than ten minutes from New Town by taxi, you feel like you've left Quito. A magnificent, luminous church on a small plaza, about a half block away from the restaurant, creates the *pueblito* ambience. The feeling continues as you pass through the hacienda-like entryway of the restaurant, but one look at the ultra hip bar tells you that this isn't the *campo.*

The dining room should be entitled *Passion and Purity*. Passion for the brazen, deep red walls which wrap seductively around the ten tables; purity for the high contrast, virginal white highlights elsewhere. No matter which direction you face, you gaze at a visual splendor. An undulating, white fireplace, hemmed in by blocky white bookshelves dominates one red wall. The next facade is unadorned except a single, wrought iron candelabra. Another wall is entirely consumed by a row of French doors, with white windowpanes of course, that exhibit a waterfall of luscious, green vines. The last wall contains the blackboard with the menu, the daily offerings of which are all so inviting, that trying to choose among them might cause schizophrenia.

The eggplant stuffed with smoked trout is delectable, as is the shrimp in sherry sauce, which we sopped up to the last drop with our bread. Potent cracked black pepper accentuates a flawlessly prepared filet mignon. For dessert, you can opt for the Mocha Delight, dark chocolate ice cream in a Baileys and coffee sauce, served in an oversized martini glass.

The service at Villa Goya is as superlative as the ambience and cuisine. Reservations are necessary.

LA VINA, *Isabel La Católica and Cordero. Tel. 566 033. Expensive. Credit cards accepted.*

La Viña is simply one of the finest restaurants in Quito, or Ecuador for that matter. The restaurant is actually a house in La Floresta with simple yet elegant décor. Basically one large room, the dining area holds about 15 tables. The décor is understated yet classy, leaving the focus on the food. Rich hues of navy blue curtains against yellow walls lend La Viña an Old World stateliness.

You can't go wrong with anything you order here, but we highly recommend the organic house salad as a starter. Fresh lettuce, crispy green beans, tomatoes, mushrooms and warm cheese coated with sesame seeds create a symphony in your mouth. The *lomo con tres hongos*, three types of wild mushrooms in a sublime sauce on a thick juicy steak, is one of our favorite main courses, as is the ravioli stuffed with spinach and covered with a flavorful yet mellow Roquefort sauce. Each dish is artfully presented on a plate that contrasts in color with the food to make your entree the center of attention. Dessert, even if you're stuffed, is a must. While some might prefer the bananas baked in phyllo covered with Bailey's, or the passion fruit tart, we go for the *Marquesa de Chocolate* every time. The dense slab of chocolate presented on a plate dusted with cocoa powder and powered sugar is absolute ambrosia.

AVALON, *Av. Orellana E-12-278 y 12 de Octubre. Tel. 229 993. Expensive. Credit cards accepted.*

Avalon is one is an excellent upscale restaurant in Quito. The interior features modern art hung on feisty, colorful walls, while the entire building is surround by lush gardens. The international cuisine includes delicious soups such as lobster bisque and New England clam chowder. The Nicoise salad and the stone crab *au gratin* are also superb. The specialty of the house is seafood highlighting the meatiest of fishes – wahoo, swordfish, and tuna – prepared in tantalizing sauces such as passion fruit. This is an excellent chance to indulge in *langostina*, prawn as big as bananas. We also highly recommend the fettuccine prepared with this scrumptious shellfish.

TECHO DEL MUNDO, *Hotel Quito, Gonzales Suaréz N27 142. Tel. 544 600. Expensive/Moderate. Credit cards accepted.*

The restaurant on the top floor of the Hotel Quito offers a mesmerizing view and solid international cuisine. The lights of Quito spread out surreally below as the folds of hills warp the grid pattern. Everyone can find an attractive entrée on the menu that features a variety of seafood and meat dishes with a French accent. The bar shares the same view, so you might consider stopping by for a drink, then walking over to the Avalon for dinner.

LA BOCA DEL LOBO, *Calama 284 y Reina Victoria. Tel. 234 083. Moderate. Credit cards accepted.*

This bar and restaurant is cutting edge chic with an artistic flair. The cuisine is on the lighter side - a creative variety of soups, *empanadas*, and personal pizzas. While appetizers like Camembert with honey, pear, and walnuts sound almost poetic, the décor exhilarates. At La Boca del Lobo the ceilings billow and sheep fly.

CLANCY'S, *Salazar 758 and Toledo. Tel. 544 252. Moderate. Credit cards accepted.*

Clancy's, in Floresta, is one of our favorite pub-style restaurants in Ecuador. With its hardwood floor, dark green walls and sofas in the bar area, it feels like a bit like England yet serves up an international menu. We end up here a lot on Sunday nights after having gone out of town for the weekend, because we like the big Greek salads and sautéed mushroom burgers. Other nice pubs include the **Reina Victoria Pub** on *Reina Victoria 530 between Roca and Carrión*, as well as the **King's Cross** behind the Swissotel in Floresta.

Italian

IL RISOTTO, *Pinto 209 y Diego de Almagro. Tel. 220 400. Expensive. Credit cards accepted.*

Il Risotto purveys what every Italian restaurant should – fresh pasta prepared with flavorful sauces, an intimate ambience, and warm hospitality without compromising professional service. Candles and roses on the table set the mood for a cozy evening of superior cuisine. If you are craving fresh salad, begin your meal with an *insalata primavera*, chock full of fresh greens, palm hearts, and olives, but split it because it is definitely big enough for two. You can match one of the pasta selections with a variety of sauces such as pesto, ragu, or four cheeses, or opt to go with one of the house specialties. The *penne alla Rusia* is prepared in a pink vodka sauce with a liberal portion of caviar. The *penne arrabiaca* might summon a few beads of perspiration to your brow, as it is truly piqued with red pepper and garlic.

IL GRILLO, *Baquerizo 535 y Diego de Almagro. Tel. 225 531. Expensive. Credit cards accepted.*

Il Grillo is an elegant option for Italian food that boasts superior service by tuxedoed waiters. A mural above a pizza oven adds playful contrast to the swank interior. We heartily recommend the spinach ravioli El Grillo upon which the chef bestows a savory abundance of perfectly browned cheese. The Cesar salads are unique and delicious especially for anchovy lovers. The one drawback to this restaurant is a wine list with the highest prices we encountered in Ecuador. Since Italian food of this caliber must be savored with a nice wine, and all are overpriced here, you may be tempted to smuggle in a bota bag filled with your favorite Chianti.

PAVAROTTI, *12 de Octubre 1955 and Cordero. Tel. 566 668. Expensive. Credit cards accepted.*

Although Pavarotti is on the expensive side, the restaurant offers some of the better Italian cuisine in Quito. The simple but elegant decor lets you focus entirely on the delicious food and professional service. Two of our favorite pasta dishes are the penne al gorgonzola and the rigatoni in vodka sauce.

LA BETTOLA, *Calama 153 and Almagro. Tel. 230 936. Moderate. Credit cards accepted.*

This is a muted, stylish *trattoria* tucked in a corner of new town. The specialties of the house are seafood and pasta.

PIZZAIOLO, *Juan Leon Mera 1012 and Foch. Tel. 543 900. Inexpensive. No credit cards accepted.*

We know very few gringo travelers who don't get the urge for a nice pizza pie every few weeks. There are hundreds of pizza joints in Quito, but Pizzaiolo is one of our favorites. The pies here are *delicioso* and feature some ingredients that you won't find in other restaurants in town. We especially like the eggplant.

If you are a brick oven fan, you'll want to keep walking a few blocks to **Le Arcate** at *Baquedano and Juan Leon Mera*. **Pizza Pizza**, uptown at *Santa María 126 and Diego de Almagro* is a total gringo hangout and good place to catch American sporting events. As strange at it sounds, our favorite pizza in the Floresta neighborhood is at the **Swissotel**, *12 de Octubre and Cordero*, where the "small" pizza can easily feed three.

Mexican

EL MERO...MERO, *Suiza N34-41 y República del Salvador. Tel. 255 152. Moderate. Credit cards accepted.*

We couldn't agree more with El Mero Mero's menu, which uses Mexican slang exclamations like *Padrísimo!* and *Barbarooo!* to describe its entrees. Housed in the Mexican cultural center, the food is so authentic and delicious that it will make you forget which side of the Panama Canal you are on. Choose from one of the *añejo* tequilas to accompany your chips and guacamole in anticipation of delectable corn tortillas that melt in your mouth. With so many enticing options, including a variety of *chiles rellenos* and tacos, you can decide not to decide by going with one of the combinations such as La Revolución Norteña. After a delicious creamy, bean soup, you will be served, not just one, but two plates loaded with enchiladas, burritos, *flautas*, and quesadillas. Even Pancho Villa would insist on a siesta after such a feast. Located on one side of Parque Carolina, this is by far the best Mexican restaurant in Quito. *Hijolee!*

LA GUARDIA DEL COYOTE, *Carrion 619 and Amazonas. Tel. 503 293. Moderate. No credit cards.*

The Guardia is not hip and doesn't have big margaritas, but the food is pretty authentic Mexican. The huge A*zteca* and *frijole* soups, when combined with chips and guacamole, are a meal in themselves. The beef can be a little chewy, so stick to chicken and veggie plates.

RED HOT CHILE PEPPERS, *Foch 713 y Juan Leon Mera. Moderate. No credit cards.*

This cantina is a decent place to get a quick Mexican flavor fix if you want something easy in New Town. The chips are good and the beers are cold. The portions are huge so consider splitting entrees such as the fajitas. The hybrid tortillas could be improved.

TEX-MEX, *Reina Victoria 847. Tel. 527 689. Inexpensive. No credit cards.*

This Mexican eatery has been around for a while, but may have difficulty facing the tough new competition in the neighborhood. Chile con carne is the locale's preferred tortilla filling. The food is just marginal.

If you just want to grab a quick, inexpensive taste of Mexico, try the **Taquería** at *Juan Leon Mera and Jorge Washington*. There's also a **Taco Bell** a few blocks north at *Juan Leon Mera and Carrión* if you're partial to chihuahuas.

Steak & Barbecue

SHORTON GRILL STEAK HOUSE, *Calama 216 and Reina Victoria. Moderate. Credit cards accepted.*

The Shorton Grill enjoys a reputation as one of the best places in New Town to satisfy that meat craving. With ten types of steaks prepared in a hundred different ways, every carnivore will be happy here.

SANTELMO, *Portugal E11-61 and 6 de Diciembre. Tel. 434 128. Moderate. Credit cards accepted.*

Santelmo, named after the funky neighborhood in Buenos Aires, offers the best Argentine beef in town. This is the place to come for a long Latin lunch. Do it the Argentine way, which means starting with a simple salad and then diving into the steak. Our favorite cut is the *bife de chorizo*, a thick filet cooked to perfection over the grill. Everything must be washed down with a good red wine so you'll be ready for that long afternoon nap.

HUNTER'S, *Av. 12 de Octubre 2517 y Muros. Tel. 504 880. Moderate. Credit cards accepted.*

Imagine a fancy pub in the Wild West and you've got Hunter's. While the main selections are wings, barbecue, beers, and ribs, the décor is like a nice suit with a bolo tie.

If you have a lower budget, you might want to try the **Texas Ranch**, *Juan Leon Mera 1140 and Calama, Tel. 557 642.* It's pretty hokey, but the steak is okay.

Asian

SAKE, *Paul Rivet N30-166 and Whymper. Tel. 524 818. Moderate. No credit cards accepted.*

Sake, in our opinion, has the freshest and most tender sushi in Quito. We simply sit down, ask the chef what fish just arrived, and eat nigiri until we're stuffed. You'll want to try some of the local seafood to give your meal a touch of Ecuador. We particularly like the *lenguado*, sole and *corvina*, seabass.

Another good option is the Japanese restaurant in the Swissotel, **Tanoshi**, *12 de Octubre and Cordero.*

HAPPY PANDA, *Cordero and Isabel La Católica. Tel. 547 322. Moderate. Credit cards accepted.*

This upscale Chinese restaurant, located behind the Swissotel in the Floresta neighborhood, is a good choice for satisfying those sweet and sour cravings. Specializing in Hunan cooking, the Happy Panda is especially popular on Sundays, when many other restaurants are closed.

SIAM, *Calama and Juan Leon Mera. Tel. 239 404. Inexpensive. No credit cards accepted.*

We call this restaurant "a hint of Thailand." The food, which is supposed to be some of the only Thai in Quito, actually tastes a bit Chinese with Thai overtones. It works for us however, when we have the urge for the flavors of old Siam. The *satay* is quite good, as are some of the soups. Stay away from the *phad thai* however, as you'll probably be disappointed.

Spanish

EL MESON ESPANOL, *Carrión 974 and Páez. Tel. 225 585. Moderate. Credit cards accepted.*

Jamón serrano, cured ham, and *pulpo a la gallega,* octopus sautéed with garlic, are just two of the many typical Spanish dishes you can find at El Mesón. Be sure to wash it down with a glass of sangria.

EL ESPANOL DELICATESSEN & SANDWICH'S, *Juan Leon Mera and Wilson. Tel. 462 946. Inexpensive. No credit cards.*

Located next door to Libri Mundi bookstore, El Español is a decent place to buy a bottle of wine, eat a sandwich or sip a coffee. With cured ham hocks hanging from the ceiling and huge jars of olives on the shelves, you certainly feel the Spanish influence. Most of the floor space is given over to high-end deli products, but there is also a small area with tables where you can enjoy your food.

Middle Eastern

ALADIN, *Diego de Almagro and Baquerizo. Inexpensive. No credit cards.*

We think that most people come here for the novelty of smoking a water pipe, but the food is not bad either if you're in need of a Middle Eastern fix. Aladin features lots of *chawarmas* as well as other sandwiches. If it's not too crowded you can sprawl on the cushioned benches while you eat your meal.

BAR CAFE SUTRA, *Calama y Juan León Mera. Inexpensive. No credit cards.*

Another in Quito's wide selection of vegetarian-oriented restaurants, the Cafe Sutra is famous for its humus. Dip into it while checking your e-mail, internet service is also offered. Look for it above the Safari Travel office.

INTERNET CAFES

Why simply surf when you can accomplish several tasks at once? The competition in the cyber cafe sector in New Town is intense, forcing rates down to about a dollar an hour and inspiring some intriguing service differentiation.

*• Rack 'em and break 'em at **Pool.net**, Calama 233.*

*• Slurp a slice or watch a movie at **Pizza.net**, Calama 354.*

*• Sip a latte, see and be seen at the hip **Papaya.net**, Calama y Juan Leon Mera.*

*• Dip into some humus at the **Sutra Bar-Cafe-Internet**, Calama 380.*

Cafes & Such

MAGIC BEAN, *Foch 681 and Juan Luis Mera. Tel. 2/566 181. Moderate. No credit cards.*

Steaming cupfuls of the freshly roasted magic bean are only one of the draws to this excellent restaurant. Owned by a couple from North Carolina, the restaurant features healthy, high quality cuisine in a laid back atmosphere. Somehow we always end up here within 48 hours of arriving to Quito after we've been on the road.

Whether you eat outside under the bamboo huts or in one of the two dining rooms inside, you're sure to walk away pleased. Staffed by hip young Ecuadorians, the restaurant has more than its share of good karma working for it. If you go to the Bean for lunch, it's hard to decide whether to try one of the tasty sandwiches or huge salads. All the fruits and vegetables are washed in purified water so you can go for it here. The thick home-style fries are an excellent addition to any entree. Save room for dessert though, because the recently baked cakes and pies are magical themselves.

If it's breakfast time, you'll have other decision-making dilemmas. The Frisbee sized pancakes are one of the Bean's specialties, but the granola with fruit is some of the best in Quito. Regardless of the time you day you'll want to start your meal with one of the tangy fresh squeezed juices or smoothies. If all you need is a cup of java to get you going, head to the Coffee To Go window outside.

CAFE CULTURA, *Robles 513 and Reina Victoria. Tel. 504 078. Inexpensive. No credit cards.*

No matter what time of day you eat at the Cafe Cultura, you'll undoubtedly be pleased. Whether it's the fresh bread or homemade muesli for breakfast, salad for lunch, or chili for dinner, this place does it right. The small cafe, set in the front room of a colonial home turned hotel, is a very pleasant place to be. With cheery sunlight streaming in the large windows in the morning and warm candlelight flickering in the evening, there's not a wrong time to visit. The food is simple but of the highest quality.

EL GRAIN CAFE, *Baquedano 332 and Reina Victoria. Tel. 565 975. Inexpensive. Master Card and Diner only.*

This restaurant, popular with both locals and travelers, is a great spot for lunch or a light dinner. Brightly painted walls, decorated with colorful masks and dried roses, add to the lively atmosphere. Once you read all the cartoons on the menu, you can get down to the food. Don't worry about ordering wrong, because it's all delicious. Quiches, safe salads, fruit drinks, pot pie, veggie dishes, sandwiches and pizza are all available, as is a daily fixed lunch special. Plan ahead though because the desserts are not to be missed.

ZOCALO, *Calama 469 y Juan León Mera. Tel. 233 929. Moderate. Credit cards accepted.*

The Zocalo offers outdoor seating in a festive atmosphere. The corner location allows for good people watching in the heart of New Town, while second floor elevation gets you out of the traffic. The menu is replete with light bar food like nachos, sandwiches, and salads, but a lot of folks come just to sip a beverage.

CREPES AND WAFFLES, *Orellana and Rábida. Moderate. No credit cards.*

As strange as it sounds, this place, featuring waffles in the name of the establishment, is not open for breakfast. They do, however, offer a delicious array of crepes, pitas, bagels, waffles and ice cream desserts starting daily at noon. With over 50 kinds of crepes and 20 kinds of waffles it's hard to choose what to enjoy.

For that bagel fix we all sometimes need you can try **American Bagel**, *Juan Leon Mera 535 and Roca, Inexpensive,* or the **Bagel Connection,** *Juan Leon Mera and Pinto.* Both serve real bagels with various types of cream cheese.

CAFE COLIBRI, *Joaquín Pinto 619. Inexpensive. No credit cards.*

You will feed like a hummingbird under a hibiscus tree in this courtyard cafe, a favorite for breakfast or just hanging out. It is one of the quieter courtyard cafe areas because of the low amount of traffic on this street. If it's cold out, the interior is a cozy, woodsy place to warm up with hot tea or coffee. The specialties of the house include decadent crepes, pastries, and German dishes.

EL MAPLE, *Calama 369, corner of Juan Leon Mera. Tel. 231 503. Inexpensive. No credit cards.*

This sleek, comfortable restaurant offers an array of dairy or soy based smoothies as well as vegetarian dishes prepared in a variety of ethnic styles, including Asian, Mexican, and Italian. El Maple also offers a good selection of sandwiches.

EL HOLANDES, *Reina Victoria and Carrión. Inexpensive. No credit cards.*

The Dutch owner of this restaurant traveled the world before he finally landed in Quito. He now offers his vegetarian favorites from around the globe at a low price. You have your choice of the Dutch, Greek, Indonesian, Hindu or Italian fixed meals. Most people choose to eat outside when the weather is nice at the umbrellaed tables.

EL CAFECITO, *Luis Cordero 1124. Inexpensive. No credit cards.*

Situated in a nicely restored, two-story house, Cafecito is a happening place to sip your favorite beverage, whether it be a hot latte or an ice-cold beer. Many homegrown twenty and thirty-somethings make this a regular hangout. Smokers freely indulge in their seductive vice here so nonsmokers should take this into consideration. Picnic benches in the front yard offer the best seating for fresh air.

SUPER PAPA, *Juan Luis Mera 741. Tel. 239 955. Inexpensive. No credit cards.*

Hungry backpackers fill themselves with stuffed baked potatoes at this easygoing locale. Take your choice of fillings, such as chicken curry, mushrooms, or broccoli in cheese, pack them into one of Ecuador's famous spuds, and you've got a meal fit to fight off hunger for the long haul. Travel tales are swapped over beers in the small, outdoor courtyard.

If you get the urge, as many do while traveling, you can find a slew of fast food joints at *Amazonas and 18 de Septiembre* as well as *Juan Leon Mera and Carrión.* There's also new **McDonalds** at *Colón and 6 de Diciembre* right in front of Parque El Ejido. **Dominoes Pizza** delivers at *Delivery Tel. 508 506.*

Quito Antigua – Old Town

LA CUEVA DEL OSO, *Calle Chile 1046. Tel. 583 826. Moderate. Credit cards accepted.*

If you are looking for a nice restaurant after a morning of getting to know Old Town, the Bear's Cave is where to head. Located just off the Plaza Independencia, Quito's business elite, often with their families, composes the cast of regulars. The design in the high ceilinged, skylit dining area is French Colonial, but the cuisine is primarily Ecuadorian, with several international dishes rounding out the menu. A tasty onion, vinegar salsa is presented with bread to take the edge off your hunger. Appetizers include *chiguiles*, corn flour tortillas stuffed with game hen, or you can choose from a variety of *empanadas*. Consider ordering either the shrimp or sea bass prepared in a delicious, rich coconut sauce. Other favorites include the onion stuffed red snapper and banana seafood chowder.

Just in front of La Cueva, in the same building, **La Zamba Teresa** is a quick, inexpensive lunch option. It looks like an ice cream parlor, but it serves much more than just desserts. The daily fixed lunch is very popular with local office workers.

CAFETERIA TIANGUEZ, *Plaza San Francisco in front of San Francisco church. Inexpensive. No credit cards.*

When the touring of Quito's colonial center becomes too much and you need a place to sit down and relax, the Tianguez is a great one for grabbing a bite and people watching. With tables both inside and out, you can enjoy the weather on a sunny day or duck out of a rainstorm on a winter afternoon. We recommend the sandwiches and big beers after one too many museums.

For your choice of fast food, try the **KFC**, **Propi Burger** or **Texas Chicken** franchises at *Guayaquil and Esmeraldas.*

SEEING THE SIGHTS

You could easily spend a week in Quito exploring the city's churches, museums and near-by attractions. If you don't have that much time, however, don't despair. You can get an excellent feel for the city in a day or two.

YOU HAVEN'T BEEN TO QUITO IF YOU HAVEN'T SEEN...

If you're extremely pressed for time and need to prioritize your visits, we recommend you try to fit these sights into your trip:

Old Town
- *Independence Plaza*
- *Government Palace*
- *Metropolitana Cathedral*
- *La Compañía de Jesus*
- *San Francisco Plaza*
- *San Francisco Church*

New Town
- *Central Bank Museum*
- *Viverium*
- *Guayasamín Museum*

Above Quito

PANECILLO VIRGIN, *Panecillo Hill. Entry $0.50 per car.*

From her privileged lookout over the city, the Virgin de Panecillo protects and blesses Quito. You too can enjoy the same hilltop views with none of her responsibilities. This is a great place to start your Quito sightseeing because it helps you get the lay of the land. Not only does all of Quito sprawl out before you, but the tops of Cayambe, Cotopaxi, and Pichincha volcanoes poke up over the surrounding hills. The red roofs of Old Town, situated just below the hill, give way to the tall buildings of New Town as you look towards the northeast. Don't miss the terraced fields on the tops of the surrounding hills that manage to cling to their ground despite urban sprawl.

The statue on the hill, erected in 1976, is a copy of **Legarda's Virgin of Quito** on the main altar in the **San Francisco Monastery**. Made from 7,000 pieces of aluminum, she shines in the morning sun. Try to visit before the clouds move in after lunch. It is not recommended to walk to the top for safety reasons, so take a cab up the curvy cobblestone streets.

LA CIMA DE LA LIBERTAD, *Los Libertadores, La Libertad neighborhood. Tuesday-Friday 8:30am-4pm, Saturday 10am-2pm. Entry $1.*

Located on the flanks of the Pichincha volcano, *La Cima de la Libertad*, or Liberty Peak, commemorates the spot where Quito's independence was won. The battle of Pichincha, fought on May 24, 1822 pitted the out-manned nationalists against the Spanish troops. The nationalist victory is outlined here in a small museum. There is also a sarcophagus with the remains of some of the battle's fallen heroes. More impressive than the museum are the large Eduardo Kingman mural and the wonderful views of the city and surrounding mountains. Save your visit here for a clear day and bring plenty of film.

Quito Antigua – Old Town

There may be a higher concentration of colonial churches and religious art in Quito's center than anywhere else in the world. That, and the fact that many of the downtown buildings have been maintained in the their colonial style, led UNESCO to name Quito a World Heritage Site in 1978.

Below you'll find an exhaustive list of all there is to do and see in the Old Town district. That doesn't mean you should try to fit it all in one day. Attempting that will make you grumpy and bleary-eyed and you won't remember anything you saw. See our sidebar, *A Nice Day in Old Town*, for a good introductory morning to Quito's colonial soul. If you've got more time, you can go back and visit the other sites that sound appealing after you knock off the biggies.

The throng of people in Old Town makes it easy for pickpockets to bump against people and grab their valuables. Be very watchful of your belongings, especially on crowded streets.

We like to start our tours of the *Quito Antigua* at **Independence Plaza**, *Venezuela and Espejo*. This is one of our favorite sites in Old Town. The tranquil plaza, with its spotless, manicured lawns, is surrounded by the classic white-washed, tile-roofed buildings that earned the area its World Heritage Site status. With two of the streets along the plaza closed to traffic, it's one of the mellower spots in downtown. People sit contentedly on the benches and we're inclined to join them every time we walk by. In the center of the plaza stands a monument to Quito's Independence. The Cathedral, on the plaza's eastern edge, and Presidential Palace, along its northern side are other spots of interest.

METROPOLITANA CATHEDRAL, *Independence Plaza. 6am-10am. No entry fee.*

Quito's Cathedral was started in 1572 and not completed until 1806. A visit is of interest more for the deaths that occurred here and bodies inside than anything else. Walk down the creaky wooden floorboards to the back of the church to get to the good stuff. Here you will find the tombs of both **Juan Jose Flores**, the first president of Ecuador, and **Gabriel García Moreno**, another president. García Moreno actually died inside here, as did one of Quito's bishops who was poisoned with strychnine-laced communion wine. On the other side of the church is the nave with the remains of **General Sucre**, the independence hero for whom Ecuador's currency is named. If you go to the very back behind the main altar, you'll come to an aquamarine altar with a plaque commemorating the actual spot where García Moreno "expired."

The Cathedral's main entrance, on the front of the plaza, is usually closed, so you need to enter around the right side on Espejo.

A CONSERVATIVE ICON

There is a plaque in the Cathedral marking the spot where **Gabriel García Moreno** *left this world. A no-nonsense dictator (Is there any other kind?) García Moreno is often credited with or accused of turning Ecuador into a theocracy during his reign. During his years in government, 1860-75, he ruled hand-in-cassock with the Catholic Church. Catholicism was a prerequisite for citizenship and the Church was given the responsibility of national education and welfare.*

Although there were many advances in the fractured country under his leadership – roads, schools, model prisons and hospitals were built and the railway was begun to link Quito and Guayaquil; his authoritarian heavy-handedness grew old in a time when liberalism was sweeping across the world.

One of his most vocal critics was Ambato's famous intellectual **Juan Montalvo**. *García Moreno's tenure was brought to a quick halt when he was hacked with a machete on the steps of the government palace. The president made his way across the plaza into the Cathedral and died inside.*

GOVERNMENT PALACE, *Plaza de Independencia.*

Although entering the palace takes some previous planning, a walk along the portico is worthwhile to continue the Gabriel García Moreno pilgrimage. A plaque marks the spot where he was attacked. A serious and decked-out color guard stands at attention outside the entrance of the palace. You can walk past them to look into the courtyard, but unless you've coordinated it before hand, that's as far as you can go. To see the murals of Francisco Orellano's trip down the Amazon, you have to drop off a written request for a tour the day before you want to visit. The request should include your full name and passport number.

QUITO OLD TOWN

1. Independence Plaza
2. Cathedral
3. Government Palace
4. El Sagario
5. Municipal Museum
6. La Merced Church
7. Museo de Arte Colonial

8. Carmen Bajo Monastery
9. Sucre National Theater
10. San Agustin Monastery and Museum
11. Casa Sucre
12. La Compania de Jesus
13. San Francisco Plaza, Monastery and Museum
14. Santo Domingo Plaza, Church and Museum

TROLE BUS LINE

To Newtown

Av. Pichincha

10 de Agusto

Venezuela

Oriente

Esmeraldas

Garcia Moreno

Manabi

Olmeda

Mejia

Chile

Espejo

Cotopaxi

Cuenco

S. de Banalcazar

Chile

A. J. de Sucre

Simon Bolivar

Garcia Moreno

S. de Banalcazar

Cuenco

Venezuela

Vicente Rocafuerte

Imbabura

Av. 24 de Mayo

El Panecillo

EL SAGRARIO CHURCH, *Espejo and García Moreno next to the Cathedral.*

The nondescript exterior doesn't even hint at the trompe l'oeil interior of this church, built at the end of the 17th century. Painted in bright colors, with interesting geometric patterns covering every inch that isn't gold leaf or faux marble, El Sagrario is worth a peek. Crane your head back to admire the colorful cupola jammed with stained glass and depictions of the saints. Lastly, on your way out be sure to notice the gallery doors, carved in 1747 by **Bernardo de Legarda**.

MUNICIPAL MUSUEM, *Espejo 1147 and Benalcázar. Tel. 283 909. Tuesday-Sunday 10am-6pm. No entry fee.*

The exterior of this large colonial edifice is in great shape after recent restoration efforts. At the time of the writing of this book, the building's interior was still under the knife. Plans for the museum's update, if the exterior work is any reflection, promise to renovate the displays of the pre-Independence religious art. We hope they don't change anything in the creepy basement display that shows wax figurines representing organizers of the first independence movement being put to death.

All the streets around Independence Plaza are filled with a crush vendors. These people are selling items for Ecuadorians, not tourists. Walk along and try to spot the *tomate de arbol*, tree tomato, or *naranjilla*, kind of a green orange.

LA MERCED CHURCH, *Cuenca and Chile. No entry fee.*

Surrounded by street markets, the walls of La Merced echo with calls of the merchants just outside its doors. Decorated in an extravagant salmon and white rococo style, the interior is reminiscent of a doll house. This church was built in the 16th century and then reconstructed in the 18th. Huge paintings by Victor Midros next to the main altar, with their funky colors, look more like something you'd find airbrushed on a T-shirt than hanging on the wall of a church. Check out the near-sighted, buck-toothed lions on the statue in front of the church.

MUSEO DE ARTE COLONIAL, *Cuenca y Mejía. Tuesday-Friday 10am-6pm; Saturday 10am-2pm. Closed Sunday and Monday. Entry $1.*

This small colonial art museum featuring religious art, can be repetitive if you have already visited the San Francisco or Central Bank Museums. There are a few worthwhile gems here if you are a fan of this type of art or want to further your understanding of the genre. Several paintings are displayed from Miguel de Santiago's dark phase, created while he resided in the San Agustín monastery. Among these are a series depicting three of the four seasons. It is so cold in the *Winter* canvas that the cherubs shiver. Also of note in this museum, are several diminutive figurines carved by one of the premiere colonial sculptors, Miguel Caspicara. Unfortunately, the dainty, recesitated Christ, *Cristo Resucitado*, that seems to frolic with joy in His rebirth, was recently stolen in broad daylight.

Walking down *Olmedo, between García Moreno and Benalcázar*, you will pass the **Casa de Benalcázar**. There is a small library inside, but really the house is only noteworthy because it has been constructed on the site where the founder of Quito lived. You might want to peer into the courtyard or just take note of it as you walk by.

EL CARMEN BAJO MONESTARY, *Venezuela and Olmedo. No entry fee.*

This convent, home to Carmelite nuns since 1745, is built on land donated by Quiteños in response to a 1698 earthquake that left the cloister with no walls to hide behind. Carmelites are an intense branch of nuns, who shave their heads and go barefoot through their secluded lives.

FUNDACION CINCO MUSEUM, *Venezuela 1302 and Esmeraldas. Tel. 514 511. Monday-Friday 9am-12pm; 3pm-5pm; Saturday 9am-1pm. Entry $0.50.*

Also called the Camilo Egas Museum, the Fundación Cinco displays some of the famous Ecuadorian artist's paintings.

SUCRE NATIONAL THEATER, *Guayaquil and Manabí. No entry fee.*

This building, reminiscent of some of the fine European theaters, has bad luck with fire. Built it 1877, it was burned by an anonymous group a few years later. Rebuilt at the end of the 19th century, it was burned again at the end of the 20th century. This time the culprit was a stray spark from the adjoining Pizza Hut restaurant. Future restoration plans are subject to the state of the economy, so you may just have to admire the building from the outside.

SAN AGUSTIN MONASTERY, *Chile and Guayaquil. Monday-Sunday, 7am-12pm and 3pm-6pm. No entry fee.*

Painted in pastels with a floral motif, the walls of this monastery look as much like a child's nursery as a monastery. This church, first constructed in 1573, was majorly damaged in a 1868 earthquake, but rebuilt at the end of the 19th century. Take a right when you enter to see the altar of San Benito Abad, the Keeper from Evil. Photos of kids, mostly drug addicts and runaways, have been plastered around the saint by their mother's in hopes of a miracle.

To your left when you walk out of the church is the **San Agustín Museum**, *Monday-Sunday, 8am-12pm and 3pm-6pm, entry fee $1.* The peaceful, large courtyard garden of the museum justifies the price of admission. After a few hours of sightseeing and walking, it's pleasant just to sit down and relax surrounded by plants and flowers.

CASA SUCRE, *Venezuela 513 and Sucre. Tel. 512 860. Tuesday-Saturday, 9am-12pm, 1pm-4pm. Entry $1.*

The Casa Sucre is a restored colonial home that the famous Independence leader **Antonio José de Sucre** owned, but never actually lived in. There's a small museum outlining the war of independence, but more interesting than that are the rooms decorated to show the good life of the aristocratic set in the 1800s.

LA COMPAÑÍA DE JESUS, *Benalcázar and Sucre. No entry fee.*

The intricate facade of La Compañía's exterior is a clue to the overstated opulence inside. Unfortunately, for the last three years, the exterior is all people have seen of the church. The drama started in 1997 when La Compañía was undergoing extensive renovation. All of the projects had been completed except for some paintings in the main cupola. While the restoration team was working on a painting of San Francisco, a faulty pump sparked, leading to a devastating fire. Both cupolas and many of the altars were ruined. They had to start over. Turning the tragedy into something positive, they have used part of the re-restoration time to reinforce the church to protect against earthquakes.

With its fusion of architectural styles, La Compañía has been called a "catholic mosque." La Compañía was founded in 1586 and moved to its present location by the Jesuit community in 1589. Its layout is very similar to that of the Gesu in Rome. The church's benefactor, Juan del Calvería, drained his entire estate in the building of the church.

If you do get to see the interior, you will be bowled over by the amount of gold leaf used in decorating the church. The seven tons that Quiteños claim is a bit dubious, but there is definitely a lot of gold. Interestingly, the original gold leaf didn't burn in the fire, but all the gold paint did, leaving no doubt for restorers as to what was original work.

QUITO'S COLONIAL TREASURES

The buildings of Quito's Old Town display some of the finest examples of Spanish colonial architecture in the world. A unique mix of European and indigenous elements marks this building style, which flourished from the 16th to early 19th centuries. The major European influences found in Quito's architecture are Flemish, Moorish, Spanish and Italian. Joined together with the indigenous, they created an art form exclusive to the continent.

The Cathedral, the San Francisco Monastery, and La Compañía de Jesus are the three most famous and magnificent architectural monuments in the city.

Walking a block up Sucre towards Cuenca, you will come to the **Plaza de San Francisco.** Quito's two main plazas have completely distinct personalities. While the Plaza de Independencia is respectful and sedate, Plaza San Francisco is the plaza of the people. Children run around and venders peddle their wares as they have done here since before the Spanish set foot on the continent. The plaza is also called the Tianguez, which means *market* in Nahuatl. You can relax here and enjoy a beer at the appropriately named Tianguez restaurant (see *Where to Eat*).

SAN FRANCISCO MONESTARY, *Plaza San Francisco.*

This gold-leafed, baroque church, founded in 1535 by Franciscan priests, is the oldest and biggest convent in Ecuador. Built on land that was originally part of an Inca ruler's estate, it covers three and a half hectares. The Italian influence is clearly seen in its architecture.

The church is a treasure trove of colonial art, with one of its most famous pieces being the original Virgin of Quito on the main altar. Sculpted by Bernardo de Legarda, her image is used throughout the country to represent Quito.

Take a look up to the choir area and notice the intricate Moorish-style ceiling and large organ. The organ, capable of playing over 5000 notes, is only played once a year because the intricate wooden ceiling over the choir, which once covered the entire church, is made without nails or glue. Should one piece of wood be vibrated loose by the sound of the organ, the whole thing will fall.

Next to the main church you can find the **Virgin de los Dolores chapter** by Francisco Cantuña. Legend has it that Cantuña, who was hired to build the temple, made a deal with the devil of his soul in exchange for meeting his construction deadline. The dark side went to work and erected the temple overnight. When the devil came calling for Cantuña's soul, Cantuña noticed that a stone was missing, allowing him to escape eternal damnation.

SAN FRANCISCO MUSEUM, *Plaza San Francisco. Tel. 581 281. 9am-6pm, Monday-Saturday; 9am-12pm Sunday. Entry $1.*

This is not a museum that you can just bop in and out of in a matter of minutes. An hour-long tour is the only way you are allowed to see this one. It is an excellent way, however, to learn about the Quito school of art and its most famous painter, **Miguel de Santiago**. Many of his works adorn the walls of the museum and you learn about them one by one by one by one.

The museum building, attached to the church, was originally used by the San Andres art school, where indigenous Ecuadorians were enrolled to learn to paint, sculpt and read. Relations between the painters and the Spanish weren't so great, as evidenced by the mural of ugly animals with European faces on the ceiling of the first salon.

In the courtyard of the museum, the main cloister, stands Quito's original fountain. The canals leading to the stone and alabaster spout were started by the Inca ruler Atahualpa and finished by the Spanish after the conquest.

The best part of tour comes at the end, when you get to enter the otherwise closed chorus area of the Iglesia San Francisco. From here you get a bird's eye view of the church and a close-up look at the Moorish ceiling.

Little is known about the life of Miguel de Santiago. He was born to mestizo parents in Quito in the 1620s, raised by a man other than his father, married, and had one surviving daughter. His daughter, Isabel, was also a professional painter and worked closely with her father.

Santiago's works stand above the rest of the Quito school due to their ambitious compositions; rich figures and landscapes; and organized, unified structures. His paintings were so outstanding for the time that in addition to being in great demand in Quito, many were sent to the Vatican in Rome.

One of Santiago's quirks was that he never sketched out his compositions first, but rather painted directly onto the blank canvas. If he didn't like the position of a limb, he would just paint over it. You see evidence of this in the San Francisco museum where over the centuries pigment has fallen off to reveal figures with two heads or three legs.

SINCHI SACHA AMAZONIAN ETHNIC ART MUSEUM AND STORE, *Plaza San Francisco. Tel. 954-326. Monday-Sunday, 9am-6pm. No entry fee.*

The Sinchi Sacha foundation was established to support the indigenous people of the Amazon and to promote and defend their rich cultures. The foundation has done that by developing a museum/store where they hope you enhance your understanding of the Amazonian culture through viewing tools and *artesanía* in the museum displays.

The museum snakes down and under San Francisco plaza in a series of exhibits highlighting the different peoples of the region. It's the perfect size to be able to take in much of the information about the various groups. The handicrafts, sold in the tradition of the San Francisco *tianguez*, or market, are bought directly from the indigenous communities, ensuring that they receive just compensation for their works. We also recommend pausing for a snack or beer in the Tianguez café after your visit. The original Sinchi Sacha museum/shop can be found at *Reina Victoria 1780 and La Niña. Tel. 230 609.*

Five blocks down Bolívar from Plaza San Francisco on the edge of Old Town you will find the **Santo Domingo Plaza**, *Bolívar and Guayaquil*. The Plaza, built in the 16th century, has seen its share of wealthy Quiteños, many of whom used to live on bordering Rocafuerte street. Famous president Gabriel García Moreno owned the house at the corner of Guayaquil and Rocafuerte.

The **church** itself, also from the 16th century, is mostly known for its huge Virgin de Rosario chapel. It is because of this chapel that the **Santo Domingo arch** was built over Rocafuerte on the side of the church. Architects devised the arch as a way to construct the chapel without blocking traffic.

The **museum**, named after the Dominican painted Pedro Bedón, is filled with Dominican works. Bedón is famous for having founded a fraternity of indigenous painters from the Quito school. It is open *Monday-Friday, 9am-4:30pm, entry $1.*

If you'd like to take a walk into the past, you can venture down to **La Ronda** or Avenida 24 de Mayo. Walking along the street lined with vintage colonial homes you can almost imagine the sound of horses' hoofs and carriage wheels on the cobblestones. Unfortunately, the threat of crime will bring you very much into the present, as the neighborhood is a bit sketchy. Don't go alone or in the evening.

A NICE DAY IN OLD TOWN

There's no reason to push yourself too hard your first day in town. The altitude will be giving you quite a work-over anyway, so you might as well take things at a manageable pace. We suggest the following itinerary to get a great feel for colonial Quito. There's lots on here, but it should leave you with enough energy to last until dinner.

You can start this tour around 10 or 10:30 am after a leisurely breakfast in your hotel or at one of the great breakfast cafes in New Town.
- *Panecillo Virgin*
- *Independence Plaza*
- *Government Palace*
- *Metropolitana Cathedral*
- *El Sagrario Church*
- *La Merced Church*
- *Lunch at La Cueva*
- *La Compañía de Jesus*
- *Plaza San Francisco*
- *San Francisco Museum*
- *San Francisco Monastery*
- *Sinchi Sacha Amazonian Ethnic Art Museum and Store*
- *Drink at Cafeteria Tianguez*

Northern Quito

As is the case with Old Town, there is too much to absorb in a single day in the New Town museums. The Banco Central museum alone is huge and, to prevent brain freeze, can really only be combined with something as small and different as the Viverium.

CENTRAL BANK MUSEUM, *Parque El Ejido. Tuesday-Friday, 9am-5pm; Saturday-Sunday, 10am-3pm. Entry $1.*

This mirrored museum looks like a giant slice of a disco ball from the outside, but houses the most extensive collection of art and archeology in the country. The expansive displays chronicle the history of the peoples of Ecuador from ancient to modern times through their art and artifacts. The Banco Central is especially user-friendly for foreign travelers because the displays are in English as well as Spanish.

The first floor of the museum contains the archeology section, with the history of pre-Hispanic America starting from the **Valdivia** culture of 3000BC and working through to the 16th century **Incas**. The displays, mostly ceramics, are too much to absorb all at once. You might want to concentrate on the groups from a certain epoch or area of the country in order to be able to appreciate what you're seeing. We especially like the copper xylophone and the **Chorrera** animal vases. The vases, called whistling bottles, reproduce the sounds of the animals they represent when water is poured into them. There are also some nice dioramas after each section representing the distinct villages of each culture.

Also downstairs is the gold exhibit, organized again by ethnic group. Be sure to read the information at the beginning about the different types of gold working in order to appreciate the difference between the filigree, relief, articulated, and lost-wax cast pieces. There are some wonderful works here, including the famous mask that is the symbol of the Banco Central museums. Our favorites are the shiny llama and caiman pendants.

The next exhibit covers colonial history and art. The Banco Central is known to have some of the best pieces from the Quito school in the country, including one of Legarda's Virgin of Quito. We prefer the racy lady in the red stockings though. Caspicara's Virgin of the Light is another of the noteworthy sculptures.

Moving upstairs, the exhibits trace the history of Ecuador through the distinct movements in painting from portraiture (yawn), to landscapes, to realism. The last part of this section, outlining the social realism movement from 1925-1945, contains striking works by Egas, Kingman and Guayasamín.

On the top floor the modern art section houses works from the 1940s through the present. If you took the train south from Riobamba you'll appreciate Muriel's *Nariz del Diablo*. We also like the Viteri pieces, which incorporate *artesanía* objects into the canvas.

This museum covers so much material that it is like more like touring an archeology, gold, colonial art and modern art museum one right after the other. There's just too much to see in one visit. We recommend the following strategy for first time visitors:

• Spend time in just a few sections of the archeology museum. Wherever you travel in the country you will find an archeology museum focusing on just that region. It's much easier to absorb the information bit by bit during your travels than to try to take it in all in a morning here. We recommend the **Valdivia** (simply because there're so old), **Chorrera** (because they are such great sculptures), **Jama-Coaque** (because they look so Asian) and **Inca** (because they are so famous) sections here. The dioramas are also nice.

• Check out the gold museum.

• Admire at the works of two of Quito's most famous sculptures in the colonial section – **Legarda** and **Caspicara**.

• Head straight to the social realism section of the modern art museum, enjoying some of the landscapes as you pass and then continue upstairs for the most recent works.

You might even want to start with the top floor and work your way down because you'll be freshest at the beginning of your visit. There are archeology museums all over the country, but few fine modern art exhibits.

MUSEUM OF THE CASA DE LA CULTURA, *Parque El Ejido. Tel. 223 392. Tuesday-Friday, 10am-6pm; Saturday, 10am-2pm. Entry $1.*

Around the left side of the building from the Banco de Central museum, the Casa de la Cultura houses art, musical instruments and indigenous clothing exhibits. While the Banco Central museum is the shining centerpiece of the El Ejido Park museum complex, the Casa de Cultural Museum merits a visit too, albeit on a different day just so you don't get museumed out.

The Casa de la Cultural is old and fraying at the edges, with big open exhibit spaces and a strange layout, but there's something comfortable and even welcoming about its old-fashioned design. The first floor houses the 19th century art exhibit, with a large collection of very nice sketches and watercolors by Joaquín Pinto at the far end of the room. Directly over this room is the modern art exhibit with some excellent pieces from the social realism or *indigenismo* school. Egas, Kingman and Guayasamín are all well represented.

From there you head down a narrow hallway that looks like one from your jr. high to the small indigenous dress exhibit with 15 display cases showing the clothing of some of Ecuador's different native groups.

Continue down the hall to reach the extensive musical instrument exhibit. This intriguing collection contains thousands of music-making treasures, including a piece from 3000BC. The display is very worthwhile, even if you're tone deaf. We like the bone flutes and the many ceramic whistles. Walk down a floor below the musical instrument section to enjoy another section of modern art and sculptures.

As you leave you'll want to check the bulletin board for upcoming events. Among other things, they usually show movies that the Ivory Merchant set appreciates.

VIVARIUM, *Reina Victoria and Santa Maria. Tuesday-Saturday, 9am-4pm. Entry $1.50.*

This museum is always a crowd-pleaser. There's just something so fascinating about Ecuador's reptiles and amphibians. Colorful poison dart frogs, stoic iguanas and the deadly fer-de-lance are just some of the highlights of this small, conveniently located museum. A visit here will arm your imagination with plenty to work with on your first dark night in the jungle.

GUAYASAMIN MUSEUM, *Bosmediano 453 and José Carbo. Tel. 446 455, 452 938. Monday-Friday 9:30am-1pm, 3pm-6:30pm. Saturday, 10am-1pm. Entry $1.*

This is one of our favorite small museums in Quito. Located in the famous painter's house in the northern suburb of Bellavista, you get a feel for the man here as well as his art. The main display features his personal art collection, which includes works from the pre-colonial era through to the present. Oswaldo Guayasamín is famous for his harsh portrayal of the realities of Ecuador's poor and marginalized indigenous peoples. You can see that in his paintings, which are also shown here. This movement, called *indigenismo*, was also shared by Camilo Egas and Eduardo Kingman, among others. Don't miss the gift shop, which has some unique items designed by Guayasamín himself.

MUSEO AMAZÓNICA, *12 de Octubre 1430 and Wilson. Tel. 506 247. Monday-Sunday 10am-4pm. Entry $1.*

This museum focuses, as you would guess, on the people of the Amazon basin. It covers their cultural ideology, including home life, hunting and myths. The museum also showcases some of the fauna of the region, with displays of stuffed animals. There's a small shop selling indigenous crafts as well as medicines made from medicinal plants.

MUSEO JIJÓN AND CAAMAÑO, *Universidad Católica de Quito, 3rd floor, Entrance near 12 de Octubre and Carrión. Tel. 529 250, extension 1317. Monday-Friday 9am-4pm. Entry $0.50.*

Ecuadorian archeologist Jacinto Jijón compiled the items in this small display during his years working and researching throughout the country. His family donated the collection of archeology pieces and colonial art to the Catholic University, which maintains the museum. Among the other notable artists displayed here are Miguel de Santiago and Joaquín Pinto.

NATURAL SCIENCES MUSEUM, *Rumipamba 341, Parque La Carolina. Tel. 449-824. Monday-Friday 8:30am-1pm; 2pm-4:30pm. Saturday-Sunday, 9am-1pm. Entry $1.*

Quite often Quito's museums, because they are located in the capital city, strive to be the biggest and the best. They have pretty much succeeded in that quest on the natural history level here. The flora and fauna of the entire country are brought together under one roof. This museum is worth a visit to see study of the things you won't get the chance to spot or will only see for a fleeting glance in the wild.

THE PLUMES OF PICHINCHA

*The **Pichincha Volcano** is one of the most striking physical landmarks in the Quito area. It's also one of the most potentially destructive. Over the years, eruptions and earthquakes have caused Quiteños to keep a watchful eye towards the snowy peak. Just recently Pichincha has stepped up its activity, with explosions spewing ash all over the city.*

If things get rough, you might want to call upon Ecuador's Saint Mariana de Paredes y Flores. In 1645 Pichincha was rumbling and scaring the city. Convinced that is was God's retribution against the evil ways of Quito's citizens, she offered herself as a sacrifice. She immediately took ill and died, which miraculously calmed the volcano.

Just Outside Quito
SANCTURIO DE GUAPULO, *Guapulo*

Just a ten minute taxi ride from New Town is the pleasant village-within-the-city of Guapulo. As you head down, down and around into the valley, you feel like you are entering another world. The main church, the **Guapulo Sanctuary**, *daily 8am-11am, 3pm-6pm*, was built in the 17th century and houses some find colonial art, especially the paintings around the altar by Miguel de Santiago. Notice the Andean landscape, which he copied with great realism. We recommend combining a visit here with a meal at the **Villa Goya Restaurant** right down the street (See *Where to Eat*).

LOS CHILLOS VALLEY, *Los Chillos.*

Twenty minutes from Quito the beautiful Los Chillos Valley is home to many of Quito's elite. With a warmer climate and fresh air, it's also favorite escape for those who aren't fortunate enough to live there. Many people choose to have a long afternoon meal or spend the night at **La Carriona**, *kilometer 2.5 on the Sangolquí-Amaguaña road, Tel. 2/331 974, Fax 2/332 005, E-mail lacarriona@accessinter.net, 28 rooms, Double $45, Restau-*

rant, Bar, tennis court, heated pool, horseback riding, credit cards accepted. This hacienda turned hotel was built 200 years ago and has now been transformed into a lovely inn. With traditional gardens, thick adobe walls and cobblestone courtyard, this is a conveniently located way to experience old Ecuador.

Tours

Some people prefer the efficiency and more in-depth information that can be provided by a private tour. Many hotels offer guide services through their own or contracted agencies. We can also recommend **Metropolitan Touring**, *Avenida República El Salvador 970, Tel. 464 780, Fax 464 702, Website: www.ecuadorable.com.* They have many different tours depending on your interests and stamina. Tour options include Old Town, the Central Bank Museum, Art Galleries, Mitad del Mundo, Scenic Quito and more.

Parks

A few of Quito's main arteries are lined with green parks. Just outside Old Town you'll find **Parque La Alameda** at the point where *10 de Agosto and Colombia* vee. Small lakes with sad looking rowboats used to be filled with aristocratic leisure seekers, but now mainly sit neglected. Unfortunately, this is not an especially safe place for gringos these days.

Continuing up 10 de Agosto, you'll come to **Parque El Ejido**, *10 de Agosto and Patria*, which features the **Casa de la Cultura and Banco Central Museums**. On weekends the park fills with picnicking families and impromptu soccer games along with an **artist market** along the sidewalk on *Patria near Amazonas*. Walking to the museums and along the sidewalk market are fine, but it is not recommended to venture into the park.

It's depressing to keep being told that it's not safe to enter a park, so luckily there's still **Parque La Carolina**, *Amazonas and Naciones Unidas*. The park, over a kilometer long, is a popular place for uptown residents to get their exercise. You'll see people jogging, playing tennis, rollerblading, skateboarding, and even horseback riding in this large park. A weekend visit is a must to get a feel for this side of Quito living.

NIGHTLIFE & ENTERTAINMENT

A *peña* is a show of live folk music. **Noches de Quito**, *Jorge Washington and Juan Leon Mera, Tel. 222 855,* is a popular one with entertainment running from 10:30pm-3am Thursday-Saturday nights. A live dance performance, the **National Ballet Folklorico** can be seen every Wednesday and Friday at 7:30pm in the *Teatro Aeropuerto*. Contact **Metropolitan**

Touring, *Avenida República El Salvador 970, Tel. 464 780, Fax 464 702, Website: www.ecuadorable.com*, for tickets.

There's a major concentration of bars and discos in the northern sector of New Town. The hopping bars always change, but you might want to try **Lennon**, *Calama and Amazonas*, **No Bar**, *Calama 380 and Juan Leon Mera*, or **Matrioshka**, *Pinto 376 and Juan Leon Mera*.

Hesitant about hitting the dance floor because you don't know the merengue from a meringue? You can drop by **Ritmo Tropical**, *10 de Agosto 1792 and San Gregoria, Tel. 227 051*, for group or private lessons in *salsa, merengue, cumbia, vallenato* and others.

If it's more of a pub atmosphere you're after, you can find real English beer and ambiance at the **Reina Victoria Pub**, *530 Reina Victoria between Roca and Carrión*, chosen by the readers of *Newsweek* as one of the World's Best Bars. Fish and chips and darts round out the experience.

The best movie theater in town is at **Mall El Jardín**, *República and Amazonas, Tel. 980 298*.

SPORTS & RECREATION
Biking
Road biking is a hazardous venture in town. We've seen some dedicated cyclers spinning along Amazonas, but that looks more like a suicide attempt than exercise.

BMX is very popular in Quito, as some young Quiteños have had success in international competitions. Many of them ride in **Parque La Carolina** on afternoons and weekends.

There are a number of adventure travel companies that offer **mountain biking** as one of their activities. Generally these trips entail taking a four-wheel drive from Quito to your destination, biking a number of kilometers (usually downhill) with the car as a support vehicle, and then returning to Quito. If this interests you, we recommend the **Biking Dutchman**, *Foch 714 and Juan Leon Mera. Tel. 543 045. E-mail: dutchman@uio.satnet.net.* The pioneer of this type of trip in Ecuador, Biking Dutchman offers one to five day trips on good bikes outfitted with RockShoks. Make sure to use the helmets, gloves and pads provided.

If you want to combine a shopping trip to Otavalo with a good day's exercise, you should look up **Ougsha Multi-Adventure**, *Atahualpa 955 and República, Tel. 462 004, E-mail: vorion@uio.satnet.net.* They have a trip that includes cycling from the Mojanda lakes, lunch at Puerto Lago and a trip to the textile market.

Golf
Golf is far more exclusive in Ecuador than in the US or Europe due to a low number of courses and high greens fees. You can try **Los Cerros**,

Juan de Salinas, Selva Alegre, Sangolquí, Tel. 331 294 for $75 per round plus $25 equipment rental charge.

Hang Gliding

Swiss transplant Christian Peclat is the hang gliding guru of Ecuador. He has founded a club in Quito called **Espacio Azul**. Members can be found taking off from Pengasí daily. Call *Tel. 09-720 258* for more information.

Hiking

Before it started sprouting new craters and erupting, the **Guagua Pichincha** was a popular day hike. Many people used it as a training climb before tackling such monsters as Cotopaxi or Chimborazo. If Pichincha has mellowed, you can make the climb. It's best to hire a guide for personal security purposes (see *Mountaineering* below).

The **Pululahua Crater**, near Mitad del Mundo, is another popular hiking spot close to town.

Horseback Riding

You can rent horses by the hour at **Parque La Carolina**. If trotting around the park is a little too tame for you, try the **Green Horse Ranch**, *Tel. 523 856*. They arrange riding trips in the Pululahua Crater near Mitad del Mundo.

Cultural Reservation Center, *Robles and Reina Victoria, Tel. 588 889, E-mail info@ecuadortravel.com,* has put together a 3-day riding school in the nearby Los Chillos Valley with overnights at the historic Hostería La Carriona.

If you're really interested in spending a lot of time in the saddle and improving your riding skills, **Hacienda Zuleta**, *Quito Tel. 569 176,* has a week-long riding program near Otavalo.

Mountaineering

Mountain climbing is a major draw to Ecuador and many people arrange their excursions out of Quito. There are a number of excellent climbing tours and guides, for people with all levels of experience, as well as outdoor equipment available for sale and rent.

Cotopaxi is probably the most popular climb. A good guide for that trip will run at least $100 per person. You can find cheaper ones, but it's really not worth the risk. Before you hire a guide, make sure he is a member of the Association of Mountain Guides of Ecuador. All ASEGUIM's guides have attended the group's basic mountaineering training course.

There are countless people and companies that offer guiding services, but the ones listed below consistently earn high ranks for their level of service, professionalism and safety record. They also provide transportation, equipment and food. Some of them even have loaner gear to help you out if you've packed more for the coast than Cotopaxi.

- **Safari**, *Calama 380 and Juan Leon Mera. Tel. 223 381.Pasaje Roca 630 and Amazonas. Tel. 220 426. US Tel. 800 434 8182. E-mail: admin@safariec.ecx.ec.* Safari is consistently given good marks for their trips. In addition to offering guiding services, they also offer instructional classes, such as their two-day glacier school.
- **Compañía de Guías**, *Jorge Washington and 6 de Diciembre. Tel/Fax 504 773. E-mail: quismontania@accessinter.net*
- **Pamir**, *Juan Leon Mera 721 and Veintimilla. Tel. 220 892, Fax 547 576*
- **Sierra Nevada**, *Joaquin Pinto 637 and Amazonas. Tel. 553 658, Fax 554 936*

If you need to buy or rent some equipment, the following stores are good bets:

- **Altamontaña**, *Jorge Washington 435 and 6 de Diciembre. Tel/Fax 558 380*
- **Camping Cotopaxi**, *Colón 942 and Reina Victoria. Tel. 521 626*
- **Kywi**, *10 de Agosto 2273 and Cordero. Tel. 221 832*

If you are looking for more information on independent climbs and hikes, Bradt's *Climbing & Hiking in Ecuador* is an excellent resource.

Multi-Sport Adventures

If you want to create your own adventure dream trip, you should check out **Adventour**, *Calama 339 and Juan Leon Mera. Tel. 223 720. E-mail: infor@adventour.com.ec.* Their grab-bag of trips includes rafting, sea kayaking, mountain biking, paragliding, horseback riding, mountaineering and motocross.

Rafting

The Blanca and Toachi rivers have some of the longest stretches of open water in Ecuador, making them perfect for rafting trips. The best company for rafting outings is **Yaca Amu Rafting**, *Amazonas N24-03 and Wilson. Tel. 236 844. E-mail: yacuma@rafting.com.ec.* They offer both single and multiple-day outings. Not only do they have an unblemished safety record, but they just do it right. Owned by an Australian, the company has excellent equipment and plans great trips, including a big lunch and beer at the end of the day. Be sure to take insect repellent.

Running

Running near most of the hotels is unpleasant due to the traffic congestion. Parque La Carolina is the favorite haunt of Quito's joggers.

The Hash House Harriers, who describe themselves as "drinkers with a running problem," alternative their weekly runs between Monday and Sunday. The group wholeheartedly welcomes visitors and new members to join in their weekly running chase of the human hare. Contact John Chick or J.M. Day at the **British Embassy**, *Tel. 560 670.*

Skating
There is an in-line and skateboard park in **Parque La Carolina** with half-pipes and other skater toys.

Tennis
The fading star of Andrés Gomez and the rising one of Nicolas Lapentti have overlapped just enough to make tennis a popular sport in Ecuador. There are public courts at **Parque La Carolina** available for a nominal fee. **Club de Tenis de Buena Vista**, *Charles Darwin and Alcabalas, Tel. 430 682* will accept reservations from non-members when their courts are not fully booked.

SHOPPING
Handicrafts
Amazonas Avenue has stores and street vendors that sell just about every Ecuadorian item available in the country. We really don't like the street, but when it's time to buy it's where we head. Leather stores, *artesanía*, T-shirts and more are all available. Juan Leon Mera is another street filled with shops for travelers that still have some space in their luggage.

For high quality *artesanía*, there are a few good choices in town. Our top choice for unique crafts is **La Bodega**, *Juan Leon Mera 614, Tel. 225 844.* **Folklore Olga Fisch**, *Colón 260, Tel. 541 315* is another store we can recommend that offers singular items from around the country. Olga died a few years ago, but not before she could expand her stores in include branches at the Swissotel and Hotel Colón.

FOLK ART'S GRANDE DAME – OLGA FISCH

"Since 1943, four years after she took refuge in Ecuador from the war in Europe, her shop, Folklore, has developed an international reputation for its wide assortment of indigenous arts and crafts. Collectors and researchers from abroad visit frequently to pay homage. The Smithsonian Institution regularly seeks her advice and exhibits her collections, including her priceless Corpus Christi dance costumes."

Tom Miller – **The Panama Hat Trail**

Galeria Latina, *Juan Leon Mera N23-69 and Veintimilla, Tel. 540 380*, has some nice things, as does **Central Artesanía** across the street. For alpaca wool clothing, try **M&V Alpaca Andina**, *12 de Octubre 1721 and Moreno, Tel. 525 830*. For high quality jewelry with an Ecuadorian flair, we can recommend **Ag**, *Juan Leon Mera 614, Tel. 550 276*, or **Artes**, *Veintimilla 560, Tel. 222 560*.

Modern Art

MarsuArte with two locations is an excellent modern art gallery carrying works from the most famous painters in the country. If you're looking for works from the giants of the social realism school, this is a good place to start. *6 de Diciembre 4475 and Portugal, Tel. 458 616*, and *Coruña 1632 and 12 de Octubre, Tel. 554 285*.

For an overview of the works of Oswaldo Viteri, as well as a chance to buy some of his pieces, check out the **Viteri Centro de Arte**, *Orellana E-11-160 and Whymper, Tel. 561 548, Monday-Friday 10am-7pm, Saturday 10am-1pm*. Viteri is best known for incorporating *artesanía* and popular culture into his canvases. If it's a Kingman in particular that you're after, try **Posada de Artes Kingman**, *Tel. 231 648*.

If you're looking for a mall, our suggestion is **Mall El Jardín**, *República and Amazonas, Tel. 980 298*; or **Multicentro**, *6 de Diciembre and La Niña, Tel. 237 949*.

EXCURSIONS & DAY TRIPS

Tour companies cover many of the excursions below. **Metropolitan Touring**, *Avenida República El Salvador 970, Tel. 464 780, Fax 464 702, Website: www.ecuadorable.com*, has many interesting options. But most of these trips you can do on your own.

North of Quito

This day trip, combining a visit to **Mitad Del Mundo, Inti Nan, Pululahua Crater** and the **Rumincucho Ruins** is probably the most popular excursion from Quito. It's fun and easily doable in a day. If you want to hike in the crater, we suggest starting your trip around 8am. You should hike the crater, visit Mitad del Mundo, return to the El Crater for lunch, run by Inti Nan and then, if you still have any stamina, see the Rumincucho Ruins. If you don't want to hike, you should leave around 11am so that you can visit Mitad del Mundo and Inti Nan, eat lunch at El Crater and again, if you have time or interest, pass by Rumincucho.

PULULAHUA CRATER, *15 minutes beyond the Mitad del Mundo. No fee.*

The Pululahua Crater is the highlight of this day trip. This extinct volcano is now a cool, lush microclimate. The crater floor is quilted with

MAY I SEE SOME I.D., SIR?

Police checkpoints are not uncommon on the roads in Ecuador. They are no big deal as long as you have your passport and tourist card with you. On buses, the officers will usually do a random identification check. For cars they will generally check everybody. If you are driving a rental car you will often be waved right through. If not, you'll have to show the car's registration papers in addition to your passport.

terraced green fields and dotted with an occasional house. The hills that were once the crater walls are now covered with shrubby green plants as the volcano had its last eruption around 400 BC. It's easy to imagine the crater as it once was while simultaneously enjoying the peaceful sight. Clouds snake stealthily over the volcano's lip, constantly changing the lighting on the crater floor.

From the edge it is about a 25-minute steep walk down to the crater floor. The obvious path is made of gravely volcanic soil that can be unstable, so make sure you're wearing proper footwear. Once at the bottom you can easily spend another hour or two hiking along the fields enjoying the scenery. The way up, a good workout at this altitude, usually takes from 45 minutes to an hour.

The crater often clouds up and even rains in the afternoon, which is why we recommend heading there early.

MITAD DEL MUNDO, *45 minutes north of Quito. 9am-6pm Monday-Friday; 9am-7pm Saturday-Sunday. Entry $1.*

The country of Ecuador derives its name from its position on the equator, so you shouldn't miss the chance to visit the hemisphere dividing line. What at first glance seems to be a kind of cheesy day trip actually turns out to be a fun and interesting outing. Not only do you get to do silly things like stand on both halves of the globe at the same time, you also learn something while you're at it.

The journey takes about 45 minutes one-way from New Town. It's not exactly the prettiest of routes, but it is interesting to notice the dramatic change in landscape as you leave Quito and enter the much drier surrounding area.

Once you arrive to the site, a wide walkway leads the way up to the Mitad del Mundo, Middle of the World, monument. The busts on each side represent the members of the French Geodesic team that mapped out the exact location of the equator from 1735-43. When you get to the end of the walkway you'll see the ticket booth on the right. Buy your ticket and head to the monument. The yellow line at your feet marks the equator. Here's your chance to take a photo kissing across hemispheres. It doesn't even take long lips.

You'll take the elevator to the top of the monument for a birds-eye view of the area. The main reason for the ride up is the trip down. A museum, **Museo Etnographico**, showcasing Ecuador's multiple ethnic groups is creatively set up on the landings of the staircase. Interesting displays highlight the clothing, tools, festival gear and even homes of the distinct peoples of the country. There's also a nice three-dimensional map of the country on the ground floor that emphasizes Ecuador's dramatic geography.

The buildings in front of the monument have been built in the same style as Old Town in Quito. There are a number of shops selling *artesanía*, multiple restaurants good for an *empanada* and cold beer, a bank, post office and even town square.

EQUATOR PARTY TRICKS

You might as well go all out and get the full equator experience:
· *Send a card postmarked "Latitude 0 0 0"*
· *Weigh yourself and see if you really are four or five pounds lighter than at home due to less gravitational pull*
· *Take a picture straddling the line*

INTI NAN SOLAR MUSEUM, *200 meters north of Mitad del Mundo Monument. Hours 9am-5pm daily. Entry $1.*

When we wandered onto this strangely sculptured plot of land visible from the Mitad del Mundo monument, we encountered such a peculiar jumble of equatorial and anthropological odds and ends, that we almost fled. Fortunately we waited to meet the perpetrator, the Mr. Science of the Equator - *Licensiado* Fabian Vera.

If you want to learn how to make poison darts, sharpening them the old fashioned way, with piranha teeth, or if you want step-by-step instructions on how to prepare a shrunken head, you'll finally learn here. After performing a few fascinating experiments to prove that we were actually smack dab at the middle of the earth, the learned one led us through a fully refurbished Indigenous hut, built up from ruins, all the while enthusiastically relating the ancient inhabitants' relationship with the equatorial sun. There's more, too much to catalogue here, but a few animal highlights include a stocked guinea pig pen, a 40-foot anaconda skin, a live centurion Galápagos turtle, and contributing the rare bit of sanity, a dachshund named Dino. This place is weird and wonderful.

RUMICUCHO RUINS, *6 km from Mitad del Mundo. Turn right at the small marker on the highway as you head towards Pululahua and follow the signs.*

Rumincucho, meaning "stone corner" is a pre-Inca site that was converted to a fort by the ruling Inca empire in the 15th century. A commanding view of the surrounding area and a steep gorge on one side made it the perfect location for a citadel. Constructed as an advance guard post, Rumincucho was a base from which the Incas could penetrate the Cayambe and Cochasquí territory to the north.

The foundation of the fort is all that remains, leaving much to the visitor's imagination. Unfortunately these ruins, so ideally situated six hundred years ago, now offer a perfect view of giant hillside scars from earth extraction for cement production. The sound of bulldozers scraping away at the hills tends to take away from the whole experience. The dusty, desolate, even desperate surroundings lead us to suggest skipping this site unless you're a real fan of ruins.

Eating at the Ruins

EL CRATER, *on the road to Pululahua Crater about 1 km before arriving to edge. Tel. 09/822 966, 09/925 867. 12pm-5pm daily. Credit cards accepted. Moderate.*

To get the most of your Mitad del Mundo experience we highly suggest lunch at El Crater. Situated on the edge of Pululahua, the restaurant enjoys a privileged view of the crater floor. The two story white building stands out dramatically against its green background of wild plants and carefully tended gardens. Inside, the hardwood floors, autumnal tones, clean lines and large picture windows work together to make this a place you'll want to sit down and stay for a while.

The walls and floors showcase the sculpture and painting of some of Ecuador's up and coming artists. If you see something you like, you should visit the small gallery on the grounds that sells more of their works. They have purposely selected pieces that are easy to take with you on the plane.

A menu featuring typical Ecuadorian food perfectly complements the setting. If you haven't had the chance to try *llapingachos* or *tortillas*, here's your opportunity. We like the *fritada* plate, which is really a kind of Ecuadorian sampler. We recommend making reservations and specifying that you want a table on the second floor overlooking the crater. This is especially necessary on weekends. If all those tables are taken there are more crater views downstairs. The view off the backside is nice, but nothing compared to the Pululahua side.

El Crater is only about 10 minutes away from Mitad del Mundo.

Other favorite excursions from Quito include the famous Otavalo markets, lovely highland lakes and interesting villages that await just two hours to the north. See the *Northern Highlands* chapter for more information.

West of Quito

As you head down the slopes of the Andes from Quito towards the west you pass through montane cloud forest before descending to the Pacific Ocean. The laid back village of **Mindo** is a perfect place from which to explore these verdant, bird-filled slopes. (See the *Northern Coast & Lowlands* chapter.)

East of Quito – On the Road to Baeza

TERMAS DE PAPALLACTA, *Quito office Foch 635 and Reina Victoria, office 4-A. Quito Tel./Fax 2/557 850. Double $40. Restaurant. Horseback riding. Credit cards accepted.*

This popular resort and thermal spa, directly east of Quito, makes for a pleasant day trip or overnight excursion. You can enjoy the swimming pools, filled with water from the nearby thermal springs, go horseback riding or hiking in the Cayambe-Coca Reserve, or just enjoy the beautiful setting and grounds of the hotel. There is a nearby lake as well. Bird watchers will want to keep an eye out for the Giant Conebill, often seen in the region.

The resort is centered around the main pool, a rock-lined lagoon filled with clear, warm spring waters. If you prefer to have a thermal bath all to yourself, you can rent one of the six cabins across the river that have their own private pools. When it's time for a meal, we recommend the fresh trout, pulled that same day from the resort's trout farm.

The resort is 65 kilometers from Quito on the "Cinnamon Route," towards Baeza. This is the same route that Francisco de Orellana took in 1542 when he crossed the Andes in search of spices and found the Amazon River instead. It takes about an hour and a half to get there.

SIERRA AZUL, *Napo Province. In Quito Paul Claudel, 41-16 y Isla Floreana. Tel. 2/264 484, Fax 2/449 464; E-mail: azul2@azul.com.ec. $55 per person full board. Cabins have electricity and hot water.*

This wonderful lodge is in a cloud forest where the jungle meets the Andes. Located at an altitude of 2,400 meters near the town of Baeza, the rustic, yet comfortable lodge offers a wide range of activities including hiking, horseback riding, and birding. You can stroll along a crystal clear stream or swim in goose-bump inspiring pools at the base of a gorgeous waterfall. There is an extraordinary variety of birds around the lodge that even non-birders enjoy.

The Sierra Azul is good for a relatively quick escape from Quito. The trip to the lodge only takes about three hours travel time from Quito.

South of Quito

Many of the points of interest along the Andes south of Quito can easily be enjoyed in a weekend or even a long day. The wonderful haciendas around **Cotopaxi** are excellent destinations for a long lunch after enjoying the park or visiting one of the picturesque market villages. See the *Central Highlands* chapter for more information.

PRACTICAL INFORMATION

Banks

You can't walk 10 meters on *Amazonas* in New Town without passing a bank. Many of them have ATM machines that accept one or more of the cards from Cirrus, Star, Plus, Diner's, Master Card, and Visa. Banks are open from 9am-1:30pm.

Books in English

• **Libri Mundi**. *Juan Leon Mera and Veintimilla. Tel. 234791*. Libri Mundi, the best bookstore chain in the country, also has branches at the hotels Oro Verde and Colón. If you can't find it here, you might not find it at all.

• **Confederate Books**, *Calama 410 and Juan Leon Mera. Tel. 527 890*. With their huge inventory of used books in English, Confederate is a required stop for travelers in need of a good read.

• **South American Explorer's Club**, *Jorge Washington 331 and Plaza. Tel. 225228*. The Club has both a lending library and book exchange. They also sell some Latin American titles.

• **Interlibro**, *Wilson and Amazonas. Tel. 567 136*. Their inventory is smaller, but their prices are better than Libri Mundi's. **Mr. Books** in the El Jardín mall is another good option.

Business Hours

Business hours generally run from 9am-5 or 6pm with an hour-long lunch at 1pm or 2pm. Retail hours are from 10am to 8:30pm. Most retailers in Quito do not close for lunch. Many Quito establishments, including banks, are open from 9am-2pm on Saturdays.

Church Services in English

With Quito's large missionary community, you can bet that there are church services in English. Try the multi-denominational one at **Advent St. Nicholas**, *Isabel La Católica 1431, near the Hotel Quito, Tel. 507 494*.

Credit Card and Traveler's Checks Offices
- **American Express**, *Ecuadorian Tours, Amazonas 339 and Jorge Washington. Tel. 560488*
- **Diners Club**, *Amazonas 4545 and Pereira. Tel. 981300*
- **MasterCard**, *Naciones Unidas 825 and Los Shyris. Tel. 262770*
- **Visa**, *Banco de Guayaquil, Colón and Reina Victoria. Tel. 566800*

Currency Exchange
It's hard to beat the exchange rates and convenience of ATM machines, but for those packing cash or traveler's checks, there are good currency exchange houses in both Old and New Town.
- **Casa Paz**, *Amazonas 370 and Robles (New Town). Tel. 563900. Sucre and Venezuela (Old Town). Tel. 511364.* They also have an office at the Hotel Colón and their airport office is open on Sundays.
- **MM Jaramillo**, *Amazonas and Colón (New Town.) Tel. 504030. Mejía 401 and Venezuela (Old Town.) Tel. 350574*
- **Multicambio**, *Amazonas and Santa Maria (New Town.), and Venezuela (Old Town)*

Embassies
- **Argentina**, *Banco Pacifico Building, Amazonas 477 and Robles, 5th floor. Tel. 562 292*
- **Brazil**, *España Building, Amazonas 1429 and Colón, 10th floor. Tel. 563 086*
- **Canada**, *Josueth Gonzáles Building, 6 de Diciembre 2816 and Orton. Tel. 543 214*
- **Chile**, *Sáenz 3617 and Amazonas, 4th floor. Tel. 249 403*
- **Colombia**, *Atahualpa 955 and República, 3rd floor. Tel. 458 012*
- **Peru**, *España Building, Amazonas 1429 and Colón. Tel. 520 134*
- **United Kingdom**, *González Suárez 111 and 12 de Octubre. Tel. 560 670*
- **United States**, *12 de Octubre and Patria. Tel. 562 890*

Emergency Phone Numbers:
- **Police** – *Tel. 101*
- **Fire Department** – *Tel. 102*
- **General Emergency** (like 911 in the US) – *Tel. 111*
- **Ambulance** – *Tel. 131*

Internet Access
There is a glut of cyber cafes in New Town, which means prices are low and computers are always available. The area around *Juan Leon Mera and Calama* probably has the highest concentration. **Equinet**, *Reina Victoria 1138 and Foch, Tel 526 957* has AOL software loaded on their computers. If you're in Floresta, **StarNet**, *12 de Octubre and Cordero at the*

bottom of the World Trade Center is a good option. Also see the *Internet Cafes* sidebar in *Where to Eat* above.

Laundry

Ask the front desk of your hotel for the nearest laundromat (*lavandería*) or dry cleaner (*lavaseco*). The full-service laundromats charge about $5 per load to wash and dry and fold your clothes for you.

Medical Service

Both the **Hospital Metropolitano**, *Mariana de Jesus and Avenida Occidental, Tel. 431520*; and the **Hospital Los Andes**, *Villalengua 267, Tel. 241540* are recommended by the American embassy. For non-emergency medical services, the embassy can provide a recommendation list for the type of specialist you need. **Farmacia Fybeca**, *6 de Diciembre 2077 and Colón, Tel. 231 263* is open 24-hours a day for pharmacy service.

National Parks

• **INEFAN**, *Ministry of Agriculture Building, Amazonas and República de Quito*

Post Office

Correos de Ecuador, *Espejo 953 and Guayaquil (Old Town by Plaza Independencia). Eloy Alfaro 354 and 9 de Octubre (New Town). Monday-Friday 7:30am-5:30pm, Saturday 8am-2pm.* Held mail can be picked up at either location. If you want to pick it up at the more convenient New Town branch, letters should be marked, *Lista de Correos, Eloy Alfaro, Quito, Ecuador.* Packages must be sent from the customs branch at *Ulloa 273 and Davalos.*

If you are going to send a package, you might want to send it through a courier. **DHL**, *República 396 and Almagro, Tel. 554177*; **Federal Express**, *Amazonas 5340 and Berlanga, Tel. 251356*; and **UPS**, *Nuñuz de Vela 470 and Ignacio San Maria, Tel. 460598* are all good choices.

Supermarkets

The best supermarket chain in the country is called **Supermaxi**. There are a number of their stores around town, one of the most convenient being in the El Jardín shopping mall at *Amazonas and Mariana de Jesus near Parque Carolina, Tel. 980 052.*

Telephone/Fax

EMETEL, *Benalcázar and Mejía (Old Town). Tel. 612112. 10 de Agosto and Colón (New Town.) Tel. 507691.* You can make international phone calls through the internet at lower prices than on a regular phone at

Equinet, *Reina Victoria 1138 and Foch, Tel 526 957.* The area code for Quito is 2.

Tourist Office/Maps
CETUR, *Eloy Alfaro 1214 and Carlos Tobar (New Town). Tel. 225101. Venezuela 976 (Old Town). Tel. 514 044. Website: www.cetur.org.* If you need topographical maps for climbing, try the **Instituto Geográfico Militar,** *Paz y Miño by Parque El Ejido, Tel. 502091.* The South American Explorer's Club has an excellent reference section of their library with maps.

13. NORTHERN HIGHLANDS

This section of the country is the most visited part of the highlands outside of Quito. Dotted with lakes and volcanoes, the landscape rolls on gentle hills to abrupt, steep fissures. **Otavalo**, the main city of the region, is home to the most famous market in the country. The textiles woven in these valleys are coveted around the world.

The indigenous society of Otavalo has managed to maintain its individuality while gaining success in the modern world. These handsome people, with their luminous black braids and distinct clothing, go about their business in a lofty almost regal manner.

The concentration of excellent hotels and haciendas in the Northern Highlands is unique in the country if not also the continent. Deciding where to stay may be one of the most difficult win-win decisions of your entire trip.

THE NORTHERN HIGHLANDS ITINERARY

Many people travel up to Otavalo on Friday night, go to the market on Saturday morning, and are back to Quito by Saturday afternoon. This strategy totally shortchanges the Highland experience. A trip here should include the following at a minimum:
- *Otavalo markets*
- *Visits to nearby artisan villages*
- *Hikes at Cuicocha or Fuya Fuya*
- *A few days unwinding at one of the incredible inns or haciendas in the area*

QUITO TO OTAVALO

The first city you hit as you head north out of town is **Calderón**. This small town on the outskirts of Quito is known principally for the marzipan figurines and Christmas ornaments you see in markets throughout

NORTHERN HIGHLANDS

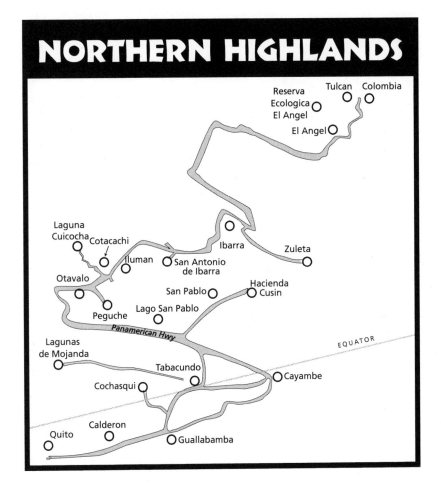

northern Ecuador. With its dusty square and tired church, Calderón isn't really worth a visit unless you are determined to get the absolute best prices on the colorful marzipan works. You can find almost as good a selection of the objects for just pennies more in both Quito and Otavalo.

If you are determined to go, the town's exit is clearly marked on the Panamericana. You'll cross back over the highway and hit the main street, Carapungo. Go left on Carapungo or else you will be fed right back out to the *Panamericana*. Just wander along the street and into the multiple stores selling their famous works.

After Calderón the highway narrows to two lanes and begins its dramatic series of climbs and descents on the way to Otavalo. The curvy road winds it way along deep valleys, demanding you pay attention to the driving rather than the terraced plots that stretch out below. If you have a driver, just sit back and enjoy the view. Dark mountains in the distance contrast with the light green shrubbery along the road. Irrigated plots stand out in the intensity of their green.

You then arrive to **Guayllabamba**, with its numerous stands plying *chirimoya* fruit and tremendous avocados. Here you'll find a weird intersection in the highway. You can either go directly to Otavalo by staying on the Panamericana, or take the worthwhile side trip to **Cochasquí** by taking the route to **Tabacundo**. This road makes a long, sinuous climb to the top of a high plain. After it crests the apex, the turn-off to Cochasquí comes up quickly on your left. Take the rough cobblestone and dirt road eight kilometers to the pyramids. It takes roughly thirty minutes from the turn-off depending on your car's suspension.

Cochasquí Ruins

It's not the 15 truncated pyramids that are the real draw to this site, but rather the gorgeous 180-degree view to the south. The pyramids, constructed by the pre-Inca Quitucara around 700 AD are quite interesting, but you have to have plenty of time and understand Spanish to appreciate the archeological aspect of the site. The hour and a half tour, with a required guide, is engaging and thorough, even though the ruins themselves are mostly just grown-over mounds.

Even if you don't understand Spanish, it's worth a visit to the site for the sweeping lookout over the valley below. It's easy to understand from this vantage point at 3,100 meters why one of the theories about the site's existence is that it was a fort to keep on eye on enemies from the south. You can see all the way to Quito and to mountains beyond. Not only are there great views of the Pichincha, Cotopaxi, Rumiñahui and Iliniza volcanoes, but you can even see the Panecillo. With binoculars you can spot both the Virgin of Quito on top of the Panecillo and the Mitad del Mundo monument. The rim of the Pululahua Crater is visible, as are most of the surrounding villages. It is really something spectacular. We recommend going as early as possible before the clouds start to move in to get the absolute best views.

Cochasquí is especially popular during the equinox and solstices. During the Fiesta de Rumiñahui shamans and healers come to absorb the special energy reputedly created by the pyramids.

There are three hypotheses for the impetus behind Cochasquí's construction. The first is that, due to it's excellent views of the valley below, the site was used as a fort to ward off attacks from enemies to the south. The second hypothesis has the Quitucara gazing the opposite direction, postulating that the site was an important astronomical observatory. The last hypothesis, and that given the most credence today, is the Cochasquí was a ceremonial site built for worshipping the sun.

The pyramids were constructed with blocks of a type of adobe made out of volcanic stone. Nine of the 15 pyramids have a unique t-shape with a ramp leading up to the platform on top of the structure. Of the buildings that have been excavated, only one has had interior passages, the rest have been solid. Skeletons with no personal objects have been found around one of the structures, leading archeologists to believe they were sacrificed to the sun god.

There are 15 funeral mounds below the pyramids.

You'll return to the highway and turn left, towards Tabacundo. Just a few kilometers down the road you pass a little blue and white church sitting on the hill. Pilgrims from all over the country make the trek here to visit its Virgin.

As you approach **Tabacundo**, you'll see signs for the **Mojanda Lakes**. This is another access point for visiting these pristine waters (see *Otavalo Day Trips & Excursions*). It takes about an hour to reach the lakes via the less-than-wonderful dirt road.

When you reach Tabacundo you'll see a road going off to the left at the gas station. You can either go left to go directly to Otavalo, or continue straight to visit Cayambe and then Otavalo. The route through Cayambe takes about ten more minutes than the other alternative.

Cayambe is a sleepy little town known for both its cheese and *bizcochos*, flaky finger-shaped biscuits. There's no real reason to go out of the way to visit here, but we really like those butter-rich *bizcochos*. The *Panamericana* runs through Cayambe, so if you didn't take the turn-off to the Cochasquí pyramids, your route from Quito will take you right through the middle of town.

If you take the direct route to Otavalo from Tabacundo, you'll drive past numerous greenhouses and flower sellers. The profusion of roses in most Northern Highland hotels is suddenly explained when you see the hectares devoted to their cultivation.

OTAVALO

Otavalo is a quaint sierra town surrounded by sumptuous lakes and volcanoes. While the countryside is gorgeous, the most inspiring aspect of Otavalo is the indigenous society that has prospered without losing a sense of cultural self. Men in long braids and fedoras nod dignified greetings. The strands of orange beads that swaddle women's necks lead to enchanting smiles that melt trepidation. Infants grasp and drool safely stowed in wraps on their mothers' backs. Flutes and drums whip up exuberant Andean melodies. All of these sights and sounds are a testament to an admirable culture, which even after a half-millennium of contact with foreigners, continues to be visible and distinct.

The markets in Otavalo are exotic, stimulating affairs. Your attention ricochets from a pig on a leash to a gunnysack of roosters, from a huge, ambulatory bunch of bananas to a rack of colorful panchos. You can explore four separate markets - big animals, small animals, food, and textiles, but we suggest loading your luggage with purchases from only one of them.

When you're not at a market, plunge into the spectacular scenery. Hike around a crater lake, ride a horse up the side of a volcano, or mountain bike to an indigenous village. One of the greatest pleasures is simply walking in the countryside from the door of your inn or hacienda. Vivid, unique images of rural life are the boon of such strolls.

For our *Best Places to Stay* chapter, we considered simply writing "See *Otavalo*". The quality and range in character of hotels here are extraordinary. You can stay in wonderful haciendas, a brilliant Relais & Chateaux resort, a mountainside inn, or a superb flower-teeming hotel in town. Everyone can find his or her image of perfect highland lodging in or around Otavalo. Many travelers hurry through here too quickly. Take some time to read over what there is to do, and where you'll be staying, then take some more time to stay a while and enjoy it.

History

Otavaleños were originally known as the Cara or Caranqui. It is thought they came from an area in present day Colombia, about a thousand years ago, because they share a similar language with an indigenous group there. Even before the Incas came on the scene, the Cara worked with textiles. They traded blankets and wraps in exchange for *achiote*, parrots, and monkeys with the jungle people to the east. They also traded their wares for cotton with the coastal people.

In 1455 the Inca Tupa Yupanqui led his armies northward along the Highlands into what is now Ecuador. The various Cara groups fiercely resisted the Incas for nearly two decades, but finally succumbed to the stronger army. The conquest was completed in 1495, three years after

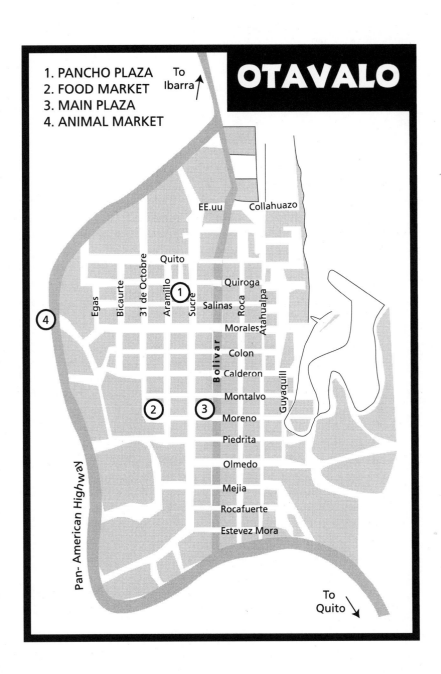

OTAVALO

1. PANCHO PLAZA
2. FOOD MARKET
3. MAIN PLAZA
4. ANIMAL MARKET

To Ibarra

EE.uu
Collahuazo
Quito
Quiroga
Egas
Bicaurte
31 de Octobre
Aramillo
Sucre
Salinas
Roca
Atahualpa
Morales
Bolivar
Colon
Calderon
Guyaquill
Montalvo
Moreno
Piedrita
Olmedo
Mejia
Rocafuerte
Estevez Mora

Pan- American Highway

To Quito

Columbus landed in the Caribbean. The Incas relocated thousands of Caras to Peru, and in their place, transferred loyal Quichua speaking subjects from other areas of the empire. To this day, the descendants of these immigrants dress differently than the Otavaleños. The Incas forced changes in language and religion, but also brought llamas to the area, the wool of which was readily adopted for textile production.

When the Spanish conquered the Incas, they were rewarded with large tracts of land and *encomiendas*, the right to collect a tribute from the local people in return for Catholocizing them. In reality the natives were indentured or enslaved. A system with the same net result, known as *huasipungo*, was later used. The landowners took advantage of the natural skills of the Otavaleños to set up mills that supplied colonial South America with textiles.

In the early twentieth century a woman from the Hacienda Cusín gave her son-in-law a poncho so finely made that he sought out the artisan. The maker, Jose Cajas of Peguche, was asked to try to replicate imported British tweeds. Cajas soon had a profitable business, the concept of which spread to other villages. Instead of following the trend of mass production, Otavalo created its niche as a cottage textile center.

OTAVALO CHIC

Otavaleño men do not cut their hair, but wear it pulled back in one long braid. A man's hair is usually braided daily by a female in the family, who sometimes weaves in colorful yarn. Men almost always wear felt fedoras, usually dark ones, but white felt hats are the style in the village of Natabuela. Shirts and pants are the modern sort manufactured in Ecuador or overseas. But these are usually covered with a pancho, also called a ruwana in Otavalo, which comes in a variety of colors and is either handmade or woven on an electric loom.

Otavalan women's dress is closer to the old Inca style than any other ethnic group in Ecuador today. Like the men, the women wear their hair long. It is worn pulled back and then wrapped in a ribbon for about a foot starting at the nape of the neck. Embroidered bloused are either purchased or made at home. Imported lace is carefully selected from the Saturday market to be added to the neck and sleeves. Shawls are usually worn over the shoulders and a rebozo, like a cotton or wool blanket, is used to carry a baby on her back. Jewelry is one of the most important accessories, particularly beaded necklaces. A woman will wear as many as fifteen strands of same-size beads so that they completely envelop her neck from chin to chest. She may wear similar beads as bracelets.

ARRIVALS & DEPARTURES

By Bus
Coorporativo Los Lagos has buses that leave from the *terminal terreste* in Quito for Otavalo every twenty minutes. The ride costs $1.50 and takes slightly over two hours. You can also take **Tran Andina** buses, which pass through Otavalo on their way to Ibarra. The bus station in Otavalo is at *Atahualpa and Jacinto Callahuazo*.

By Car
The *Panamericana* runs along the east side of Otavalo. The highway takes you south to Quito in less than two hours or north to Ibarra in a half-hour.

By Taxi
Many people prefer to be chauffeured to Otavalo from Quito rather than dealing with the hassles of a bus or a rented car. The cost is about $35 dollars one way. Most hotels in Otavalo and Quito will line this up for you. You can also consider arranging transport to or from the Quito airport because it is on the north side of the city, on the way to Otavalo.

ORIENTATION
Otavalo is nestled in the lush green hills of the Northern Highlands at 2,550 meters. Being a mere 92 kilometers north of Quito makes it a popular retreat. The most prominent physical feature nearby is the Imbabura volcano hunkering solidly above Lake San Pablo. The volcano is known at *Taita* or Father to the indigenous people. The more distance Cotacachi volcano is seen as his mate. (Whenever she has fresh snow, they say that *Taita* has visited her overnight.)

The center of Otavalo is where Parque Bolívar and Plaza Gonzalez Suarez sit cattycorner from one another. Following Sucre south four blocks takes you to Plaza de Ponchos, the artisan market.

GETTING AROUND TOWN
Otavalo is small enough to cover on foot. Part of the fun here however, is getting out and visiting the neighboring villages, lakes and mountains. Taxis are plentiful and inexpensive and are a great way to cover the area. Determine an hourly rate with the driver (around $6 an hour is standard), then sit back and enjoy the scenery. For complete freedom to explore without the clock ticking, you can also rent a car. There are no rentals available in Otavalo though, so you'll have to rent the car in Quito and drive here yourself.

WHERE TO STAY

If you can't find a hotel to make you happy in the Otavalo area, then you will never be satisfied. There are such good places to choose from here that it is difficult to decide where to lay your head.

You can either stay in Otavalo proper or slightly out of town. By staying in Otavalo, you are close to the markets and shopping and have a wide array of dining options. Our favorite places to stay in town are the **Ali Shungu** in the moderate category and the **Hostal Esther** in the inexpensive range. If you stay at out of town, you get to enjoy the solitude of the country, but will find it a little more difficult to get around. The best of the superb out-of-town options are **La Mirage**, **Hacienda Cusín**, and **Casa Mojanda**, each with a distinct perspective on how country life should be lived. All three made our *Ecuador's Best Places to Stay* chapter.

You might want to stay in town for a few nights, especially Friday night so all you have to do is roll out of bed to walk to the animal market, and then spend a few days relaxing at a hacienda or hotel in the countryside.

IN TOWN
Moderate

HOTEL ALI SHUNGU, *Calle Quito and Miguel Egas. Tel. 6/920 750; E-mail: alishungu@uio.telconet.net. 16 rooms, 2 apartments. Double $42. Restaurant. Bicycle rental. Horseback riding. Craft store. Airport transfer. Parking. No credit cards accepted.*

The Ali Shungu is our favorite place in town. Built around a lovely garden, the hotel is a wonderful oasis. You can easily spend hours lounging in a hammock with a book and their bird list, alternately napping and spying hummingbirds.

The hotel is festooned in tasteful Andean highlands decor. Local textiles adorn the comfortable rooms and thick Otavaleño blankets on the beds make for deep sleeping in the cool mountain air. Both the hot water and the water pressure in the shower deserve mention for their excellence. The real highlight of the hotel is the opportunity to interact with the self-assured Otavalan indigenous staff. These young women, all in traditional dress, confidently staff the reception desk and restaurant. The owners, Frank and Margaret, strive to work with the staff as though they were family. With 26 local godchildren, you can say they have succeeded.

The hotel is set up for whatever your activity or excursion needs. When you arrive you are given a four-page activity list and map of the area. Just three blocks from Poncho Plaza, the hotel is perfectly situated to carry home your handicraft loads. They rent mountain bikes, have access to horses, and maintain a relationship with a trusted fleet of taxi drivers that can drive you around the area for $6 an hour. They also run a Quito-Otavalo van shuttle.

The restaurant area is also a sitting room with couches around the fireplace. Plants and traditional handicrafts dot the walls, but the real draw is the gourmet vegetarian and choice meat dishes. On Friday nights the restaurant features one of the best Andean bands we've heard. (See *Where to Eat* below).

In addition to the rooms, two sunny apartment suites are also available. Accommodating up to six, each apartment has a private bedroom with a double bed, three single beds, a kitchenette with refrigerator, a dining room, a living room, stereo and a TV/VCR. With great views of both the gardens and the Imbabura Volcano beyond, they're a good option for families, a group, or couples who want more space.

Inexpensive

HOSTAL DONA ESTHER, *Juan Motalvo 444. Tel. 6/920 739. 15 rooms. Double $20. Restaurant. No credit cards.*

This beautiful colonial inn is a flower-laden niche in the heart of downtown Otavalo. Three floors of whitewashed walls and a blue railings ascend upward in the inner courtyard. The rooms are tastefully decorated with dark wood, bright bedspreads, and fresh cut flowers. Beyond the lively courtyard is the jazzy Il de Roma restaurant done up in royal blue beams and radiant yellow walls. The place settings are equally as vivacious inviting those who enter to indulge in delicious pastas and pizza. You can also relax in the cozy bar area which looks out onto the street.

EL INDIO INN, *Bolívar 904. Tel. 6/922 922, Fax 6/920 325. 40 rooms. Double $25. Restaurant. Cafe. Bar. Credit cards accepted.*

There are a couple El Indios in town, so make sure you have the right address. This hotel does not have near the personality of some other hotels in town, but it will do in a pinch. Although it falls short in the character the department, the blue and white, flower-ringed courtyards are pleasant enough, and the rooms are clean.

Budget

HOTEL OTAVALO, *Roca 504. Tel. 6/920 416, Fax 6/923 712. Website www.hotelotavalo.com.ec. 32 rooms. Double $15. Credit cards accepted.*

The Hotel Otavalo, located right in town, is the long-standing budget option. After you pass through the dark reception area, the hotel opens up to a bright covered courtyard. Tan walls with white accents offer a soothing refuge. Hardwood floors add to the ambiance. The rooms themselves are small and clean with boldly colored bedspreads. The hotel has recently changed ownership, so hopefully it will maintain its good state.

HOTEL RIVIERA SUCRE, *Garcia Moreno 380 and Roca. Tel./Fax 6/ 920 241. 27 rooms. Double with private bath $14. No credit cards.*

The Riviera Sucre is another good budget option. A sunny flower laden courtyard is surrounded by the plain, clean rooms.

OUT OF TOWN
Very Expensive
HOSTERIA LA MIRAGE, *Out 10 de Agosto just past the market. Tel. 6/ 915 237, Fax 6/915 065. US Reservations Tel. 800/327 3573. Website www.hosteria_la_mirage.com.ec; E-mail: mirage@mireage.com.ec. 23 suites. Double $220. Breakfast and dinner included. Restaurant. Bar. Tennis court. Mountain biking. Horseback riding. Heated pool. Steam bath. Jacuzzi. Massage. Conference room. Credit cards accepted.*

For absolute luxury and romance, Hosteria La Mirage, part of the esteemed Relais & Chateuax group, is one of the best spots in the country. Fragrant hummingbird-filled gardens, large exquisitely furnished rooms, impeccable service, and gourmet food comprise the package that is the La Mirage experience.

Each of the unique suites is laid out so that you gaze at the gardens instead of at the room next door. One room may be L-shaped with crimson walls, while another will be decked out with a king-sized canopy bed and gold accents. All have marble floors with throw rugs, a separate sitting area, and a fireplace. You can relax on the sofa and watch birds feed outside your window.

After enjoying your memorable dinner, your waitress will ask if you want your fire started. If you reply in the positive, it will be crackling by the time you get to your room. That toasty lump at the end of your bed is the hot water bottle placed to warm your feet. Along with the pressed flower bookmark on your pillow there is another small surprise. (We don't want to give everything away.)

The covered pool and spa area, decorated in overdone Roman style a la the Hearst Castle, should not be missed. La Mirage offers eight different types of massages including reflexology and aromatherapy. Although the spa's a must, your first activity at La Mirage should simply be a tour of the grounds. Wander through the extraordinary gardens where plants and flowers grow to prehistoric proportions. Bougainvillea, dahlias, hibiscus, roses and orchids are just a small listing of the flowers you'll find.

Our tendency at the hotel is to slow down. We like to sit in garden nooks, read and relax. If you want activity, however, there's plenty of that to be had. Horseback riding, mountain biking, hiking and shopping are all recommended.

Both dinner and breakfast are included in the price of your stay and both are memorable experiences. (For more information on dinner see *Where to Eat* below).

Selected as one of our Best Places to Stay – see chapter 11 for more details.

Expensive

HACIENDA CUSIN, *Cusín, 15 kilometers south of Otavalo. Tel. 6/ 918013, Fax 6/918003; E-mail: hacienda@Cusín.com.ec. Website haciendaCusín.com. 40 rooms. Double $98. Breakfast included. Restaurant. Bar. TV room with video library. Game room with billiards, darts, and Ping-Pong. Horseback riding. Mountain bikes. Squash court. Handicraft shop. Conference facilities. Credit cards accepted.*

To know your hacienda well, because at Cusín you really feel like you are the *patrón* of the estate, you should walk through it several times. The first time through you can get the feel for the big picture. You sense how its layout of white walls and terracotta tiles fits perfectly below the puckered green Imbabura Volcano; how the view of the local church harmonizes with the mountainside as if it were planned to be admired from the property, which it was. On the next walk-through you can study the antique tapestries, indigenous Latin American textiles, and the exquisite colonial art, which is not merely hung on the walls, but rather, ingenuously placed to create a composition.

Wander through the grounds to admire the gardens bursting with the brilliant colors found in over fifty species of flowers, which attract nearly the same number of species of birds. This may take some time, as there are about four kilometers of trails meandering through this nine hectares of Eden. These will ultimately lead you to a vegetable garden, to a llama named Pedrito, to the horse stables, and to the monastery.

The hacienda's history dates back four centuries to 1602 when land was purchased at an auction from Phillip II, King of Spain. The land was divided up among family members in the latter part of this century, and the buildings fell into disrepair until Nik Millhouse resurrected the estate, converting it into an elegant hotel. The Englishman is difficult to distinguish from the guests because he is usually having at least as much fun as they are.

The rooms retain their hacienda semblance through Andean craft furnishings, antique art, and beamed ceilings. Most of the rooms have fireplaces, as do the common areas such as the dining room, living room, and bar. Slipping into a comfortable sofa to read or chat while the fire is crackling nearby makes the grandeur almost homey. For yet more intriguing lodging, inquire about the cottage suites.

For diversion you can go horseback riding, mountain biking, or hiking in the nearby hills. Facilities on the grounds include a squash court, a well-equipped game room, and great selection movies in an extensive video library. The hacienda offers a reasonably priced Umbrella Plan, which includes a room with a fireplace, full board, and riding privileges.

Selected as one of our Best Places to Stay – see chapter 11 for more details.

HACIENDA ZULETA, *Zuleta. Tel. 2/596 176, Fax 2/596 177. E-mail: hacienda@zuleta.com. Website: www.ecuadorexplorer.com. 9 rooms. Two night/ three day package $310 per person. Includes transportation from Quito, all meals and activities. Horseback riding. Mountain biking. No credit cards.*

The Hacienda Zuleta, 110 km north of Quito, is one of the most exclusive places to stay in Ecuador. With just nine rooms and only open part of the year, the hacienda is an intimate treat. The owners of Zuleta, descendants of former president Galo Plaza Lasso, treat guests as if they were personal friends. The Plaza Pallares family still enjoys the hacienda on weekends and holiday. You feel like an invited visitor because you're sleeping in a family member's room complete with personal touches like wedding photos and the like. The rooms are very simple but comfortable and each enjoys lovely views of the garden. The linens, all hand stitched, come from the embroidery workshop on the hacienda grounds.

When mealtime comes around you won't be disappointed. Almost everything on the table comes from the hacienda. The milk, cream, cheese, butter, homemade bread, rainbow trout and organic fruits and vegetables are all produced on the 1,800-hectare working farm. You can just taste the freshness as you savor your meal. After eating you can retire to the comfortable library and living rooms.

There are plenty of activities at Zuleta. Probably the most popular is horseback riding. The Zuleteño horses are a famous mixture of Spanish-Andalusian, English and Quarter horses. In fact, many guests come specifically for the weeklong riding program. Mountain biking and hiking are also options, as are visits to Otavalo, 45 minutes away.

Because Zuleta is not a hotel, they have a minimum group size of four to six people, except for the weeklong horseback program, where the minimum is two people. The hacienda is closed to guests on most holidays.

Moderate

CASA MOJANDA MOUNTAINSIDE INN & FARM, *5 kilometers west of Otavalo. Tel./Fax 9/731 737 or via CRC in Quito 2/558 889; E-mail: mojanda@uio.telconet.net. Website casamojanda.com. 9 cabins. $45 per person including breakfast, dinner, and afternoon tea. Horseback riding. Library. Credit cards accepted.*

The extraordinary cut of the windows is the greatest homage to the mesmerizing views from the Casa Mojanda. No matter where you are, your eyes constantly drift to the vista. The hotel is surrounded on three sides by verdant folds of terrain, much of which the local farmers have tilled, against the mighty force of gravity, into a rich, undulating checkerboard of green and earthen squares.

The Casa Mojanda is an eco-tourism concern that seeks to exert minimum impact on the environment, while actively promoting local cultures and traditions. The amazing and inspiring accomplishment is that the objective is met while maintaining an extraordinary level of quality and comfort. The cabin interiors are ample and homey, finished in eucalyptus, which is grown commercially in the area. Local weavers handcraft the eye-catching wool bedspreads. Most of the furniture is either handmade or antique cedar.

While the comfort and view from your room might seem too perfect to leave, there is compelling reason to do so, both on and off the property. The cedar shelves of the library are stocked with an excellent selection of books for guests to borrow. The game room draws guests in after their active days either to relax with a movie or to challenge each other in a board games. Vegetarian meals are served in the dining room by the flickering light of the fireplace. Much of the produce comes directly from the organic garden in the back yard. Guests gather in the dining room to socialize over afternoon tea or pre-dinner drinks or simply to gaze at the landscape from the pillow-covered window niche.

You will find enough hikes and walks throughout the countryside to keep yourself busy for several days. There are crater lakes in the area, as well as Otavalo's handicraft market. A small rodeo corral was built to help beginning equestrians learn before galloping off into the hills.

Selected as one of our Best Places to Stay – see chapter 11 for more details.

HACIENDA PINSAQUI, *First left on the Panamericana north of the turn-off to Cotacachi. Tel. 6/946 116, Fax 6/946 117. Website www.ecuadortravel.com. 16 rooms. Double $76. Restaurant. Horseback riding. Bike rental. Credit cards accepted.*

The Pinsaqui is a beautiful 300-year old hacienda tucked away off the Panamericana just five kilometers north of Otavalo. The unmarked cobblestone road leads to an impressive entrance with the white hacienda anchoring the far end. The circular drive, surrounded by large blue agapantha flowers, is ringed with giant fir and palm trees. The lovely grounds, covered with more agapantha, also boast orange trees, a small pond, and hammocks to enjoy it all.

The entire hacienda, full of antiques, makes you understand why Simon Bolívar stopped to rest here for a night during his time in Ecuador.

White walls, blue highlights and dark wood are the decoration theme echoed through the house. The home has been in the family of the current owners since 1881. The stately restaurant is also excellent. (See *Where to Eat* below.)

HOSTERIA SAN LUIS, *kilometer 6 on the Tabacundo-Otavalo road. Tel. 2/360 464, Fax 2/360 103; E-mail: hosteriasanluis@accessinter.net. 32 cabanas. Double $60. Restaurant. Bar. Heated pool. Sauna. Whirlpool. Game room. Tennis courts. Volleyball court. Playground. Bicycle rental. Horseback riding. Fishing. Laundry. Excursions. Credit cards accepted.*

Hosteria San Luis is a great option if you'd like to get off the gringo track but still want high-end lodging. Located on 20 hectares in the Mt. Cayambe Valley, this family-oriented resort is a favorite getaway for city-weary Quiteños. Set up like a little whitewashed village, San Luis offers comfortable lodging in a beautiful location.

From the entrance, you pass through farmland on the eucalyptus-ringed road before arriving to the resort. Large green expanses lead your eye to Cayambe-Coca National Reserve. Family-oriented locations often suffer from overuse, but that is not the case here. The outstanding rooms, each with a small porch and fireplace, are situated so that you look out at the snowcapped-mountains rather than at your neighbor.

There are tons of activities available at San Luis. In addition to the standard biking and horseback riding, there is a fishing pond stocked with trout, a walking trail, and even a tiny bullring. Just twenty minutes from Otavalo, the *hostería* also offers excursions to all the area attractions. You can even arrange a trip to the Cayambe base lodge on the flank of the 5,790-meter mountain.

The restaurant offers both international and Ecuadorian cuisine. We recommend enjoying the smoked trout while sitting on their sunny patio.

HOSTERIA JATUNCOCHA, *Lake San Pablo south of Otavalo. Tel. 6/918 191. 25 rooms. Double $72. Restaurant. Cafe. Bar. Kayak rental. Game room. Cable TV. Credit cards accepted.*

The Jatuncocha is a place for families. It's nice enough for the parents to enjoy it and be comfortable, with cocktail hours and a fireplace in every cabin, but kids really have the run of the place. With boats, a game room, kayaks, volleyball and soccer, the Jatuncocha is set up for the large Ecuadorian families that fill it on weekends. At the foot of Imbabura on the eastern side of San Pablo Lake, it's still just 15 minutes from Otavalo.

Inexpensive

MESON DE LAS FLORES, *García Moreno near the plaza in Cotacachi. Tel. 6/915 264, Fax 915 828. 36 rooms. Double $30. Restaurant. Credit cards accepted.*

This pleasant hotel and restaurant in nearby Cotacachi is on a pedestrian walkway that leads to the town plaza. The entryway opens out to a sunny white patio highlighted with pretty blue *azulejos* tiles. Umbrellaed tables are the prime lunch time spots, but there are also more tables under the open- air covered section of the patio. Bright flowers invigorate the blue accented, whitewashed walls.

While you can order either international or Ecuadorian cuisine, we recommend sticking to the traditional fare. You can try *empanadas, llapingachos*, trout and *chicha* for the total immersion meal.

HACIENDA GAUCHALA, *near Cayambe. Tel. 2/363 042, Fax 2/362 426. E-mail: guachala@ecuadorexplorer.com. Website: www.ecuadorexplorer.com. 21 rooms. Double $35. Breakfast not included. Restaurant. Bar. Swimming pool. Horseback riding. Mountain biking. Credit cards not accepted.*

If you're dying to stay at a hacienda but don't have a very big budget, the Gauchala is for you. One of the oldest haciendas in the country (they claim it is the oldest), the Gauchala is definitely one of the most affordable.

The rooms are simple but certainly not uncomfortable. Authenticity just oozes out of the whitewash walls, hardwood floors, and deep blue window frames. There are lots of things to do for entertainment here. You can hang out by the pool, go mountain biking, or roam the range on a horse. Both horse and mountain bike riding have a reasonable $5/hour charge. In addition, Otavalo is only 30 minutes away.

You can take a bus to Cayambe from Quito and then the hacienda is just a $3 cab ride from the main plaza in Cayambe

HOSTERIA CABANAS DEL LAGO, *East side of Lago San Pablo. Quito Tel. 2/435-936. 40 cabins. Double $36. Restaurant. Credit cards accepted.*

This is a well-worn family affair complete with putt-putt golf, lots of playground equipment, and paddleboats. The cabins sleep up to seven.

WHERE TO EAT

In Town

ALI SHUNGU, *Calle Quito and Miguel Egas. Tel. 6/920 750. Moderate. No credit cards accepted.*

This is the best in town place to eat. The comfortable restaurant decorated with traditional handicrafts and plenty of plants, offers great vegetarian and meat dishes. Turquoise cloths decorate simple tables arranged around a well-tended fireplace. Otavalan women in traditional dress handle questions with aplomb, recommending a nice dry Chilean wine to accompany the smoked trout appetizer. The house salad is simply one of the best in Ecuador.

Friday nights feature a wonderful band playing traditional Andean music. Many times these type bands can be overwhelming, but this group is excellent.

The restaurant is also worth a visit for breakfast. The smoothie is a delicious way to get your fruit servings for the day and the bagel with homemade herbed cream cheese is a treat after a few weeks of traveling.

FONTANT DI TREVI, *Sucre 1205 and Morales. Moderate. No credit cards* .

If its pizza you crave, you can get it here. Located on the 3rd floor of a little shopping complex, Trevi also offers decent lasagna. (How can anything be bad with a big blob of cheese?) Friday nights they have live music.

SISA, *Calderon 409 and Sucre. Tel. 920 154. Moderate. No credit cards* .

SISA, which stands for *Sala de Imagen, Sonido y Arte*, is a little two-story complex housing a cafe, bookstore, gallery and restaurant. The blue tile floors, yellow and brick walls and blue accents make it a soothing and tranquil place to spend some time. The cafe downstairs serves some pretty wimpy sandwiches in addition to hot beverages. If you're looking for a meal, head upstairs to the restaurant where you can get chicken, beef or even some vegetarian meals.

TABASCO'S, *Pancho Plaza, Salinas 410 and Sucre. Tel. 922 475. Moderate. No credit cards* .

This was once a good Mexican food restaurant. Unfortunately, the *gringa* owner sold the place and now it specializes in both pizza and Mexican food, doing neither especially well. What it does have is an excellent location perched over Pancho Plaza. This is a great place for a beer after a day of touring. You can sit outside on the patio and watch the goings on below.

IL DE ROMA, *Juan Motalvo 444. Tel. 920 739. Inexpensive.*

You'll be enchanted by the vibrant decor in this little Italian eatery, part of the Hostal Doña Esther. Pizzas are served piping hot out of the domed shaped pizza oven. Andean musicians play here on the weekends.

PLAZA CAFE, *Jaramillo y Quiroga. Inexpensive. No credit cards.*

A mellow, earthy ambience attracts journal writers and tea sippers to this locale, as do favorite desserts like chocolate cake, brownies, and carrot cake. There is also an interesting selection of sandwiches and meals like trout with pumpkinseed sauce. Avoid the humus though, which oddly is served frozen. A similar dining option can be found at the El Otavalito next door.

ORAIBI, *Sucre 1011, corner of Color. Tel. 921 221. Inexpensive. No credit cards.*

This laid-back vegetarian restaurant features a quiet courtyard as well as inside seating. One of the rooms is outfitted with throw pillows to sit on. If you have a book you've already read, you can trade it in for a cream pie. Enjoy Andean music here on weekend nights.

QUINO RESTAURANT SABOR Y ARTE, *next to Hotel Otavalo on Roca and Moreno. Inexpensive. No credit cards.*

This small restaurant serves up a darn good piece of fish. There's nothing fancy about the décor, but they have spruced things up with the artwork.

THE PIE SHOP, *Salinas and Jaramillo on Pancho Plaza. Inexpensive. No credit cards.*

Sometimes you just need a piece of pie to make things right in the world. This is the place to go when that's the case. They also sometimes show movies at night.

Out of Town

HOSTERIA LA MIRAGE, *Out 10 de Agosto just past the market. Tel. 6/ 915 237. Very expensive.*

The *hosteria* offers an incredible dining experience about twenty minutes out of town. While it is pricey, we highly recommend this place. The restaurant, in the main building with the reception area, is decorated in French country style. The food itself is French in tone although there are many Ecuadorian highlights.

Every course at the restaurant is elegantly served to the table and beautifully presented on the plate. All plates are unveiled simultaneously by the excellent Otavaleña staff while you wait expectantly. Fresh fruit sorbet is served between courses to cleanse your palate. The fresh asparagus and shrimp appetizer is recommended, as is duck a la orange. The Tournedos La Mirage melt in your mouth. For dessert both the tangy passion fruit crepe and the apple pastry with vanilla rum sauce are well worth the calories.

HACIENDA PINSAQUI, *First left on the Panamericana north of the turn-off to Cotacachi. Tel. 6/946 116. Moderate. Credit cards accepted.*

We recommend the Pinsaqui restaurant as the best place to eat north of Cotacachi. Blue and white table clothes, dark wood floor and leather chairs, and a large picture window looking out over the lovely grounds lend the place an air of dignity. Offering both international and local cuisine, you can't go wrong with a meal here after a day on the village tour. Reservations are recommended, as the dining room is small.

PUERTOLAGO, *On the Panamericana at Lake San Pablo south of Otavalo. Tel. 920 920, Fax 920 200; E-mail: efernand@uio.satnet.net. Moderate. No credit cards.*

Puertolago is all about location. With the restaurant practically floating on the lake, it's a good spot to visit on a sunny afternoon. You're so close to the water that you can cast in a line. The food is a little bland, so go for spicier dishes, like the garlic shrimp. The *empanadas* Yamor are quite good as well. Some people opt for the evening cruises around Lake

San Pablo in a ten-meter catamaran that include music and cocktails. This restaurant is very popular with escaping Quiteños, so make reservations on the weekend.

The Puertolago is actually a *hostería* with small chalets looking out over the water. The rooms, which include a fireplace and porch, are okay, but there are many better options around.

EL LEÑADOR, *Sucre and Juan Montalvo. Tel. 915 083. Moderate. No credit cards.*

For hearty meals of grilled meats (*parrilladas*) and trout, the Leñador is the local favorite in Cotacachi.

SEEING THE SIGHTS

VASQUEZ FULLER ARCHEOLOGY EXHIBIT, *corner of Montalvo and Roca. Open daily, hours are variable. Suggested donation, $1 per person.*

When you knock on the door that says "Los Andes Residencial" or ask around thereabouts for Sr. Vasquez Fuller, be advised that you are making a commitment to spending some time with the dearest old archeologist you will ever meet. He will lead you up through the stairs of a humble residence, and then into a single room jam-packed with artifacts. He will walk you through 12,000 years of history, not moment by moment, but to some people it might seem like it. He explains a dizzying number of items in his extensive collection. Many of the pieces are quite intriguing and due to the casual nature of the place, it might be the closest you ever get to antiquities, even hands-on is permissible with some artifacts. Sr. Vasquez Fuller can wing some English, and if you can do at least the same in Spanish, you'll get comprehensive insight into the regional culture through his admirable collection.

INSTITUTO ANTROPOLOGIA, *Avenida de los Sarances. Tuesday-Friday 8am-12pm, 2pm-6pm; Saturday 8am-12pm. Entry $1.*

For detailed ethnographic information about Otavalo and the surrounding area, visit the Instituto. A bit out of the way, it is located on the western side of the highway as you head north towards Ibarra. Right before the gas station, you see a brown sign with a picture of a Greek-looking building pointing off to what appears to be a residential neighborhood. Turn left and you'll see the impressive red brick structure of the Instituto half way down the street on the left.

THE MARKETS, *various locations around town; see below.*

The most famous of the Otavalo markets is the textile market, but we actually prefer both the food and animal markets for capturing a slice of the indigenous lifestyle. If you want to shop for handicrafts however, the textile market on Poncho Plaza has enough choices to keep you busy for hours.

Both the textile and food markets are hopping daily, but the animal market only takes place on Saturday morning. The food market is also bigger on Saturday when people come from all around the surrounding area to do their weekly shopping and socializing.

If you are in Otavalo on Saturday, we recommend arriving to the **Animal Market**, *on the Panamericana by the soccer stadium*, by 6:30 am. The squeals of pigs on leashes, bleats of groomed sheep, and moos of prodded cows will lead you to the area. People stream in from all around carrying or pulling their livestock with them. Small girls will handle the piglets, while their mothers tug with all their might on sows the size of bears. Once you enter the fenced market area, it is set up according to type of animal. First come the pigs, then the sheep, then the cows and lastly, in the Cadillac showroom, the horses. Business takes place in Quichua as people bargain over the animals. Most of the Otavaleños wear typical dress. Picture taking opportunities abound, although you should ask first before taking any close-ups of people. This is one of the highlights of Otavalo and should not be missed if you can help it.

There is a **Small Animal Market**, *Quito and Jaramillo*, which is equally entertaining. All animals that fall into the wee & cute category are sold here – primarily puppies, chicks, and guinea pigs. People crowd around while a woman pulls a *cuy*, guinea pig, out of her bag and holds it up in the morning sun. Fingers inspect the flesh while bids are taken until the animal is sold and tucked into the buyer's bag for that special lunch. The kittens and puppies head for new jobs as rat catchers and animal herders. We highly recommend passing by here.

The **Food Market**, *Jaramillo between Juan Montalvo and Piedrahita*, gets going around 7am. It's perfect to walk here from the animal market on Saturday. There's as much activity happening on 31 de Octubre street leading up to the market as in the market building itself. People rush by with loads of bananas and oranges as they set up their stalls. Sugar cane, mussels, cheese, fish, and potatoes are all being hawked simultaneously. Bundles of fresh cilantro in the market's entryway imbue the area with a savory aroma. Inside the market building is more tranquil than the street. Stalls bulge with prepared foods, flowers, baskets, and beans. Old ladies waddle by doubled over by the huge loads on their backs. If you have the chance, watch a transaction take place so that you can see a woman open her blue shawl already filled with goodies, pack one more thing into it, fold it carefully and place it back on her back. You can easily spend an hour or two taking in the happenings and shooting photos. The morning light on the colorful piles of produce makes almost any picture a winner.

BAD COMPANY

Unfortunately, in addition to attracting crowds, the textile market attracts pickpockets who allegedly ride the bus up on Saturday morning with the tourists. Be careful and aware of what's happening around you at all times. It's smart to keep your bag or backpack in front of you so that you can keep on eye on it. We find it best to go out with a single objective. If our goal is picture taking, we leave most of our money in the hotel safe so that we are not distracted. If our goal is shopping, we leave the camera.

The **Textile Market**, *Plaza de Panchos on Sucre between Quiroga and Salinas*, is what attracts many visitors to the Otavalo area. All of Pancho Plaza is covered with stalls selling every type of national and even international *artesanía*. Wool sweaters, hats and gloves, cotton shirts with embroidered highlights, blankets, baskets, hammocks, dolls, and other crafts are all available. What you might want to do is scout things out the evening before and then do your shopping the next morning. You can do your best bargaining if you are the vendor's first customer of the day. You'll be able to find a gift here for everybody on your list. Our favorites are the mummy dolls and embroidered cotton shirts. There are stalls open daily on Pancho Plaza, but Saturday is the biggest day as many producers in the area close their shops and come to the market to sell their wares.

After you do your shopping you can sit and watch the locals play *pelota de mano*, handball, on the far end of the plaza.

A visit to the **Peguche Waterfall** is only worthwhile if you are just itching to see a waterfall or to get out and do something. We don't like to mix our outdoor experiences with trash viewing, and unfortunately, there is a lot of it along the trail. After the 15-minute walk along the trail from the parking lot, the 30-foot waterfall itself is pretty. You can cross over and hike up the backside for additional exercise and views. The falls are about a 45-minute walk from town. The most pleasant route is up the cobblestone road along the railroad tracks. You can find the road behind the bus station. You can also take a cab.

The **Mirador del Lechero** is a lookout spot from which you get a sweeping panoramic view of Otavalo, Lake San Pablo and the mountains beyond. Take Calle Piedrahita away from the Pan-American Highway, bearing left and heading up the hill. You can also walk to **San Pablo** this way.

NIGHTLIFE & ENTERTAINMENT

Most of the nightlife here centers around the Peñas, where you can hear live music and drink either a few coldies or some firewater. Try **Pena Amauta** on *Jaramillo* or the **Tucano Bar** on *Morales*. The music usually starts around 10pm.

The best Andean band we've heard plays at the **Ali Shungu** every Friday night starting at 8pm. Call or stop by to reserve a good table to dine and listen to the music.

SPORTS & RECREATION

Biking

A number of hotels in the area rent bikes to guests. The most popular places for bike rides are to Lake San Pablo, the weaving villages, and to the Peguche Waterfalls.

If you want to combine a shopping trip to Otavalo with a good day's exercise, you should look up **Ougsha Multi-Adventure**, *Atahualpa 955 and Republica, Tel. 462 004, E-mail: vorion@uio.satnet.net* in Quito. They have a trip that includes cycling from the Mojanda lakes, lunch at Puerto Lago, and a stroll through the textile market.

Hiking

The Otavalo area is a dreamscape for trekkers as there are many hikes in the area. You can hike around the crater at **Cuicocha** or the lakes at **Mojanda**, trek to the top of one of the area volcanoes like **Imbabura** or **Fuya Fuya**, or amble down country lanes to Indian villages. Closer to town, you can hike to the **Peguche Waterfall** or to the top of **El Lechero** for a beautiful view.

If you're up for more than just a day-trip, consider the **Golondrinas 4-Day Trek**. This walk, which starts north of Otavalo near the El Angel Reserve, passes through three distinct Ecuadorian eco-systems. It starts around 4,000 meters in the *páramo*, drops to the montane forest and then continues down to 1,500 meters and pre-montane forest. Organized by the Fundación Golondrinas, a conservation organization, the trek is a great way to enjoy the rich and varied landscape and to experience the Fundación's work first hand. Contact **Fundación Golondrinas**, *Isabel la Católica 1559, Tel. 2/226 602, Fax 2/222 390* in Quito for more information.

Horseback Riding

You can rent horses from many places in town. Riding in the nearby countryside is one of the highlight activities at the area haciendas, but tour agencies also arrange excursions to remote places like the **Mojanda Lakes**.

SHOPPING

Otavalo is best known for the shopping at Poncho Plaza, but there are many more opportunities to spend your money. Most of the weavers do not live in Otavalo, but rather in the small villages close to town. You can visit these villages, see the masters at work at looms in their homes, and buy direct.

After living and shopping here for over twenty years, Margaret Goodhart, owner of the Hotel Ali Shungu is quite an expert. She recommends the following people and places as worthwhile:

- **Jose Cotacachi** – Tapestry designer and weaver; *two galleries on the main square in Peguche.*
- **Miguel Andrango** – Famous weaver; *workshop just outside Agato.*
- **Conteron Family**– Inti Chumbi Coop weaving, handicrafts, and hats; *Iluman.*
- **San Pedro Blanket Factory** – Blankets and jackets; *just north of Otavalo*

EXCURSIONS & DAY TRIPS

You could keep yourself busy for days in the area around Otavalo. Almost all of these sights are less than an hour from town, meaning you use your time actually enjoy the places rather than in getting there an back. See the Northern Highlands map to orient yourself.

Cuicocha Lake

Emerald waters nestle in the crater of an extinct volcano at Cuicocha, which means Guinea Pig Lake in Quichua. Green hills shoot up steeply around the lake like a giant verdant bowl. Two small islands in the middle of the lake share the same flora as the surrounding hills.

There are three possible activities at Cuicocha - eating, boating or hiking. We recommend the hike. A 12-kilometer trail leads around the rim of the crater, taking about four to five hours to complete. From the top you can look off the ridge to both the lake and the valley on the other side. It's an impressive sight. If you go early, between six and seven in the morning, you'll see many birds as you hike. The walk itself is not difficult after you get up to rim level, but altitude is always a factor. The trailhead is on your right as soon as you pass through the entry gate.

If you prefer the boating option, continue down the road until it dead-ends at the El Mirador restaurant. There is a dock below the restaurant where you can buy a ticket for $1 to go on a 25-minute ride around the islands. The boat, an old outboard with wooden benches, holds about ten people. If it's not the weekend, you can negotiate your own itinerary, but you also have to negotiate a price for commandeering the entire boat.

The last option, eating, can be done at the **El Mirador Restaurant**, *Moderate, No credit cards.* Sitting right on the water, the restaurant offers great views of the lake and crater, if not the best meals. The food is not bad, it is just not noteworthy. We usually have a beer and *empanada* after the hike and then head down to eat in Cotacachi.

While there has long been a restaurant at the lake, they have just recently opened the large interpretive center. Inside you'll find information about the formation of the lake, the bio-diversity of the reserve, and the distinct indigenous groups of the area.

Lake Cuicocha is an easy 40-minute drive on paved road from Otavalo. Popular with Ecuadorian families on the weekends, it is usually very quiet during the week. You can combine a visit to the lake with an afternoon of leather shopping, as you have to pass through **Cotacachi** on your way. There is no public transport, but you can take a bus to Cotacachi and then take a cab from there if you want to cut down on your costs.

Cotacachi

Cotacachi is justifiably famous as the city of leatherworkers. Bustling leather stores line the streets of this otherwise quiet town. From the plaza, take *Bolívar to 10 de Agosto* for the highest concentration of shops. Leather jackets, suede shirts, briefcases, belts, purses, leather pants and boots are just some of the offerings. The quality varies from store to store, as does the price, so if you've come to buy it's worth shopping around. Two of the higher end stores are **Pompeii** and **Opera Design**, *both on 10 de Agosto*. Sunday is market day here and things get going a little earlier than they do any other day of the week.

Cotacachi is about twenty minutes from Otavalo. You'll go north on the Pan-American for about ten minutes before you see the turn to the left. The road, studded with welcome signs and acknowledgement of local historical figures, wanders down and over the Ambi river before climbing up to town. You can also catch the bus from Otavalo at *Calderon and 31 de Octubre*.

If you want to stay or eat here, the **Hosteria La Mirage** offers elegant lodging and cuisine, while the **Meson De Las Flores** falls into the inexpensive category. Both are excellent choices within their price ranges. See the *Where to Stay Out of Town* section above for more details.

Mojanda Lakes

These remote lakes, high in the *páramo* above the tree line, are a spectacular sight in their pristine setting. Sitting at the foot of the Fuya Fuya volcano, the three lakes, Huarmicocha, Yanacocha and Caricocha, are within a 45-minute walk of each other. If you're up for more of a workout, you can climb and descend Fuya Fuya in about two-and-a-half-hours, starting from the big lake. If you are lucky enough to have a clear day, the sweeping view from the top will be seared into your memory. Pack a lunch, bundle up against the wind, and plan on spending the afternoon in the silent stillness of the highlands.

If you enjoy hiking, we highly recommend this trip. There is no public transportation for the forty minutes ride up the bumpy cobblestone road from town. You can either hire a taxi or take the trip with a tour agency. Some companies offer horseback rides up here.

San Antonio de Ibarra

San Antonio has one of the most pleasant squares of all the villages in the Otavalo-Ibarra area. This town is known as the wood working capital of Ecuador. All of the shops on and leading to the plaza are filled with carved items. Much of the inventory is exactly the same from shop to shop, but occasionally you'll find something unique. The pieces range from the tacky copies of Michelangelo's David, to the treasured, carved chests and wooden boxes. We like the furniture stores more than those that just handle trinkets. We recommend lunch at the Hacienda Pinsaqui after your shopping excursion.

Chaltura

There's not much to see here, but popular consensus says that this is the place to go when you want to try guinea pig, *cuy*. Try to remember their ritual importance as you chew on the boney little guys.

CUY

"Cuy is guinea pig, a precious little furry animal raised on corncobs, alfalfa, grass, and lettuce, then slaughtered between six months and one year after birth. Its name comes from the squeaky noise it makes: kwee! kwee! I had to overcome severe cultural bias before finally agreeing to eat one."
– Tom Miller from his book, **The Panama Hat Trail**

Weaving Villages

Visit Peguche, Ilumán, Agato and Carabuela to see indigenous people knitting wall hangings, carpets, sweaters and other woolen items. You can buy directly from them at their workshops and get a slightly better price than you would at the market. Most people take a tour or hire a cab, but renting a bicycle is also an option.

A Drive North to La Libertad

If you are going to spend more than a few days in the area, we recommend the drive up to **La Libertad** near the **El Angel Ecological Reserve**. Although there's not much to see at the final destination, the drive is one of the more memorable in the country. Take a picnic to eat in the plaza once you get there.

After passing through Ibarra, the road climbs as it curves to the north. Slides are common, so keep alert to large rocks in the middle of the road. Dramatic, steep gorges fracture the verdant quilted landscape below. As the road drops down into the lush Chota river valley, it is like stepping through a highland looking glass directly into Cuba. Huge sugarcane plantations garnish the road and the majority of the people you see along the highway are Afro-Ecuadorian.

Right before you arrive to **Chota** take a left to **Mira**, "Balcony of the Andes", and **El Angel.** This road is in better shape but still studded with fallen rocks. After you climb out of the valley, the landscape changes to a dry, dusty gray. Suddenly, as you continue to climb, it switches again to fertile green fields. The pinched contours of the Andes in the background are dappled with clouds. Stands of eucalyptus line the road, pigs and cows are hobbled on the shoulder, and families walk along the little-used highway.

Once you reach Mira, what seems like the entire country stretches out below. There's no real reason to go into Mira, but you might want to stop and take a picture of the town statue along the highway. From Mira the road drops down to El Angel. Rammed earth walls, topped with wild grasses, line the highway. Green, yellow and black squares blanket the hills while dark mountains loom beyond.

There's not much happening in El Angel other than two sleepy squares. One fronts the church and the other has some topiary works. For a better topiary display, head on to La Libertad, where the town square has some great bush sculptures. Watch out for people and animals resting in the middle of the road. Stop the car, pull out your sack lunch, and enjoy the extremely slow pace of life.

El Angel Ecological Reserve

Only the heartiest adventurers will want to continue up the terrible, potholed, boulder-strewn dirt road to the El Angel Ecological Reserve. We suffered through the journey, and to tell you the truth, there's not much to see.

There are two access points to the park. After you leave El Angel you will see a sign pointing in two directions. One way leads to the Potrerillos and El Voladero lakes, 13 kilometers to the northeast along a bad road. The other points to Bosque El Colorado, 15 kilometers down an equally bad road on the other side of La Libertad.

The park is mainly *páramo*, highland scrub. The El Colorado section preserves thousands of Fraileon plants, which basically look like truncated palm trees. It's an interesting sight, but really not worth the beating you take to get there. There is a trail in the lagunas section that leads from El Voladero to Potrerillos lakes.

Fiesta Del Mundo (a.k.a. The Mad Hatter's)

This hotel, forever under construction, located on the *Panamericana* between the exits to Cotacachi and San Antonio de Ibarra, is, well...it is. Circular freestanding cabins are all topped with gigantic hats. There is an English bowler, a Panama hat, a fez, and an Arab headdress just to name a few. All the units have fireplaces, chairs in the shape of a human hand, and murals on the domed ceiling depicting scenes from the hat's homeland. It's just bizarre enough to make you pull over as you pass by on the highway.

PRACTICAL INFORMATION

Banks:.ATM on *Sucre and Calderon*
Business Hours:. 10am-1pm; 3pm-6pm
E-mail: Service: **Caffe.net**, *Colon and Sucre*
Laundry: **New Laundry**, *Roca 942*
Medical Service:.**San Luis de Otavalo**, *Sucre and Quito. Tel. 920 420*
Police Station: *Panamericana Norte Km 1. Tel. 920 101*
Post Office: **Pancho Plaza**, *Salinas and Sucre, 2nd Floor*
Telephone/Fax: The area code is 2. **EMETEL**, *Calderon, between Bolívar and Sucre*
Tourist Office/Maps: **CETUR**, *Calderon and Bolívar*

IBARRA

Ibarra, the government seat of Imbabura Province and a twenty minute drive from Otavalo, is a sleepy little town whose highlights you can see in about an hour. It's a pleasant enough place with whitewashed colonial buildings and two verdant plazas.

People used to overnight in Ibarra to catch the **Ibarra-San Lorenzo train**. El Niño wiped out the track, the highway opened to San Lorenzo and the train sat idle. Recently there has been talk of Hungary signing an economic cooperation agreement with Ecuador for $60 million dollars of assistance to repair the line. Who knows where Hungary is getting all that cash, but the agreement has yet to be signed.

For now, the train is only running 49 kilometers from Ibarra to Carchi. Check when you arrive to see if more of the track has been open.

WHERE TO STAY & EAT

There's really no reason to stay in Ibarra proper as the famous train to San Lorenzo no longer runs. We recommend staying in any of the fine hotels in and around Otavalo. If you're in the area and need nourishment, however, there are a few places we can recommend.

CAFE ARTE, *Salinas 543 and Flores. Tel. 950 806. Inexpensive. No credit cards.*

This coffee shop, three block east of Parque Moncayo, is a pleasant place to grab a quick nosh and rest your weary feet. You can view the paintings while you wait for your food. They also have cultural events in the evenings.

HOSTERIA CHORVALI, *Four kilometers south of Ibarra on the Panamericana. Tel. 6/932 222. Moderate. Credit cards accepted.*

Just south of Ibarra, this *hosteria* is popular with Ecuadorian families and tour groups. It's not a bad place for lunch if you're in the area. The large grounds include big plots of vegetable gardens between sections of rooms. If you're traveling with kids, they will appreciate the playground and soccer field. We recommend the Ecuadorian specialties over the international fare.

Our favorite place to eat on the highway between Ibarra and Otavalo is the **Hacienda Pinsaqui**. See *Where to Eat* in the Otavalo section.

SEEING THE SIGHTS

The city was completely destroyed in an earthquake in 1868, so most building in town date after that. The most interesting sights are downtown.

Parque Moncayo, *Flores and Bolívar*, is the prettier of the two downtown plazas. Especially clean, with flowering trees and an almost tropical feel, it is surrounded by the **Cathedral**, **El Sagraro Church** and the **Municipal Building**.

Parque La Merced, just a block west at *Flores and Olmedo*, is nice, but the buildings surrounding the plaza are not as pretty. The Virgin in the **La Merced Church** on the plaza's west side is a favorite with area pilgrims.

PRACTICAL INFORMATION

There is a shopping center on the way into town, **Supermaxi Center**, that can handle a bunch of your needs at once. There is a **bank** with a teller machine, a **KFC**, and a **Supermaxi** grocery store. You can get any picnic items you would possibly need at the Supermaxi.

If for some reason you're desperate to check your E-mail: while in town, try **Ecuahorizons**, *Bolívar 4-67 and García Moreno*. Even though it is not that helpful, there is a **CETUR** tourist office at *Olmedo 9-56*. The **post office** is on *Oviedo and Salinas*, while the phone office, **EMETEL**, is *just north of Parque Moncayo*.

TULCÁN

Tulcán, the crossing point into Colombia, is exactly what you would expect from a border town. It's a little sleazy, a little unsafe and everything you can imagine is for sale. The only curves thrown in are the altitude, 3000 meter, and the amazing topiary works in the town cemetery.

The reason travelers come here is to cross the border into Colombia. At the writing of this book the US government was advising its citizens to stay out of Colombia and even to steer clear of this Ecuadorian province. Kidnapping and extortion are not unheard of here. The Colombian guerrillas use kidnapping and the subsequent ransoms as a way to fund their organizations' fights against the government.

Many Colombians cross the border on weekends to take advance of the weak *sucre* and do some shopping.

ARRIVALS & DEPARTURES

By Air

TAME has one flight each weekday both to and from Tulcán. Their office is in the **Hotel Azteca**, *Pasaje San Francisco between Bolívar and Atahualpa, Tel. 980 675.* The airport is a couple of kilometers north of town.

By Bus

Buses all arrive to the town's bus station, *terminal terrestre*, on the south side of town. There are buses from Tulcán to Ibarra, Quito and points in between.

It's a $1 cab ride from the bus station to the center of town and a $3 ride to the border, six kilometers north of town.

By Car

The road to Tulcán from Ibarra drops into the Chota Valley before climbing again to Tulcán at 3,000 meters. The drive takes two or three hours depending on the state of the roads.

CROSSING THE BORDER

*The border, six kilometers north of Tulcán, is formed by the Rio Carchi and spanned by a bridge. Customs and immigration are open from 6am-10pm daily. Once you cross to Colombia, it's 14 kilometers to Ipiales, Colombia. The ride costs $1 in collective taxis. You should check in Quito for any visa requirements before you head north. The **Colombia consulate in Tulcán** is located at Bolívar and García Moreno just in case.*

WHERE TO STAY & EAT

There's really only one hotel in town that we can recommend. Its merit is not that it is especially good, it's just not as bad as the rest of the options.

HOTEL AZTECA, *Pasaje San Francisco between Bolívar and Atahualpa. Tel. 6/981 447, Fax 6/980 481. 50 rooms. Double $15. No breakfast included. Restaurant. Disco. No credit cards accepted.*

This is not a place you would send your mother, but it's what you've got. Try to get a room away from the disco on nights that it will be thumping until the late hours of the morning. The pizza restaurant here is pretty good for grabbing a bite to eat.

SEEING THE SIGHTS

If you only see one thing here, make it the **municipal cemetery**. It's actually the only thing to see here, but that's nitpicking isn't it? This work of art was the life project of Tulcán local Jose Franco. He's helping fertilize his works now, but he lives on through these incredible sculptures in green.

Thursday is market day in Tulcán.

EXCURSIONS & DAY TRIPS

The **Gruta de Paz**, Cave of Peace, is the biggest attraction north of Chota. Just a few kilometers up the *Panamericana* from Bolívar, the cave houses a chapel dedicated to the Virgin of Peace. There are also some thermal baths outside the cave. During religious periods like Christmas and Easter the cave is a popular destination for pilgrimages, especially with the baths waiting to soothe tired muscles.

PRACTICAL INFORMATION

Banks: Filanbanco, *10 de Agosto and Sucre on Parque Independencia*
Currency Exchange: Casa Paz, *Bolívar and Ayacucho*
Post Office: Correos, *Bolívar and Junín*
Telephone/Fax: The area code is 6. **EMETEL,** *Olmedo and Junín*
Tourist Office/Maps: CETUR, *Bolívar 5-89 and Pichincha*

14. CENTRAL HIGHLANDS

The Central Highlands, also known as the Avenue of the Volcanoes, is one of the most picturesque sections of the country. High, snow-covered volcanoes jut thousands of meters out of rolling hills tattooed with terraced fields. Colonial towns, luxurious haciendas, remote Andean villages and colorful markets offer excellent alternatives for your travel time.

As you head south out of Quito you pass through farming communities on your way to **Cotopaxi National Park**. Named after the perfectly conical Cotopaxi Volcano, the park allows you to get closer to or even summit this sacred peak. Beautifully maintained, historic haciendas make excellent bases from which to explore the area.

As you continue south through dairy farms dotted with greenhouses, you arrive to **Latacunga** where traditionally dressed women in knee socks and felt fedoras press through the active city squares. Close to here are the unforgettably authentic markets at **Saquisilí** and **Pujilí**. This is also an excellent place to head out into the lonely hills of the isolated highlands where llamas are more common than cars.

Don't forget a quick stop in **Salcedo**, where multiple ice cream stores line every street, on your way to **Ambato**. Good museums and spacious parks and gardens are highlights of the Ambato attractions.

From there you can drop down 1,000 meters through spectacular scenery to the popular city of **Baños**. This city, surrounded by green walls and waterfalls, is a wonderful base for daylong hikes and bike rides.

Returning up to the high valley between the twine spines of the Andes you reach **Riobamba**. Known as the Sultan of the Andes, this colonial city nestles in the base of **Chimborazo**, the country's highest mountain. From here you can board the roof of a train that travels along steep gorges and **The Devil's Nose** to continue on to the **Southern Highlands**.

COTOPAXI NATIONAL PARK

The perfectly conical shape of Volcán Cotopaxi is one of the most ubiquitous images of Ecuador. Standing high above the plain, its snow-

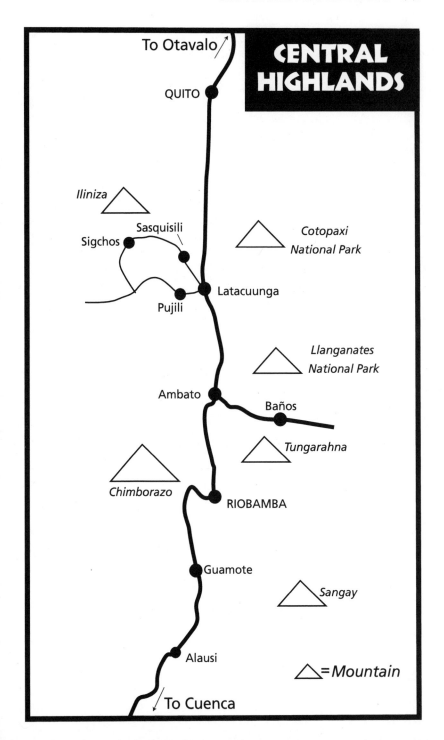

THE BEST OF THE CENTRAL HIGHLANDS

There are some experiences that are so representative of this part of the country that they need to be included on any itinerary. The freedom comes in choosing between the options for each experience.

· **Visit a very tall mountain** –*Mythical Cotopaxi and hunkering Chimborazo are symbolic of the Ecuadorian Andes.*

· **Enjoy a meal at and/or stay in a Hacienda** – *San Agustín de Callo and La Cienega are both very good options.*

· **Visit a highland village on market day** – *The markets in Saquisilí and Pujilí are justifiably famous while cities like Zumbahua and Guamote are enticingly remote.*

capped peak dominates the landscape like a preponderant inverted funnel. Once you see it, you immediately understand why the mountain is viewed as sacred to local indigenous peoples. Cotopaxi means *Cone of the Moon* in Quichua – a perfect fit given the mystic, hypnotic power of both.

The chance to get closer to and even summit this marvelous mountain is what brings many travelers to the area. Cotopaxi National Park is the most visited park on the mainland. Just hiking about the lower reaches of this large peak is a worthwhile experience, but standing over the edge of the crater as the sun rises is truly magical.

Don't worry about the volcano going off while you are in the area. Although classified as active, Cotopaxi, with just a few fumy fumaroles, has been much quieter lately than headline-grabbers like Pichincha and Tungurahua. If it does go however, it tends to wipe out entire villages. Actually, it tends to wipe out the same town, Latacunga, over and over again. Its explosion in 1877 was the 20th most deadly volcanic eruption in world history. Over 1,000 people were killed in the mudflows that followed.

Cotopaxi is a composite volcano, which are typically deep-sided, immense, symmetrical cones created from alternating layers of lava flows, volcanic ash, cinders, blocks and bombs. Many of what are considered the most beautiful mountains in the world, such as Cotopaxi, Mt. Fuji in Japan, Mt. Hood in Oregon and Mr. Rainer in Washington are composite volcanoes.

ARRIVALS & DEPARTURES

Cotopaxi is an easy trip south of Quito on the Pan-American Highway. There are two roads off the highway that lead to the entrance of the park. The first, the El Boliche entrance is 16 km south of Machachi. This rougher and longer access point passes through the picnic grounds and introduced conifers of the **El Boliche National Recreation Area** before entering the park.

The second, and main entrance, is just north of the small town of Lasso. The Lasso entrance is the most direct route into Cotopaxi National Park as well as the most trafficked. This entrance is 65 km south of Quito. It takes about an hour and a half to get to the turnoff from the *Panamericana* to the park road. From there it is another twenty minutes on dirt road to the actual park entrance.

By Bus

Any bus from Quito heading as far south as Latacunga will get you to the turnoff road that leads into the park. Just tell your bus driver ahead of time, and he will drop you off at the turn. The problem is that it's another seven kilometers to reach the entrance of the park from the highway. If you are going to try to hitch a ride to the park entrance from the highway, your best bet is to get dropped off on the busier Lasso road. Another option is to take the bus past the park to Latacunga and then cab it back north into the park from there.

Many tour companies in Quito offer day trips to Cotopaxi in small buses. If you are not going to do any extensive climbing and don't want to rent a car, this may be your best bet logistically. If you are climbing the mountain with a climbing service, transportation will be provided.

By Car

It's easy to get to the park by car. The Lasso entrance, although further south than the Boliche one, is the most direct route. The soft volcanic soil makes for a relatively smooth road, although there are some rocky and washboard spots. We recommend renting a 4WD vehicle for clearance and traction, but a normal car can probably make it. Taxis regularly make it up to the parking lot below the refuge as long is the snow line is not too low.

The best thing about having a car is that you have the freedom not only to come to and leave the park on your own schedule, but you can also explore the small market towns in the area over the course of a few days.

By Taxi

If you are staying in one of the area haciendas, they can arrange transportation to the park. You can even take a cab from Quito for about $70 round trip. From Latacunga, taxis charge $30 roundtrip to the Laguna in the park and $50 to the parking lot below the refuge. Call *Tel. 800 676.*

ORIENTATION

Located on the east side of the Panamericana, Cotopaxi National Park covers 33,400 hectares and ranges in altitude from 3400 to 5897 meters. In addition to the famed Cotopaxi volcano, the park also includes the Rumiñahui and Morurcu mountains in its boundaries.

The most visited sights in the park are the **museum**, the **lagoon** and the **climber's refuge**. The park road heads northeast, wrapping around the volcano as it leads from sight to sight. From the Lasso road off the *Panamericana*, it is seven kilometers to the actual park entrance. From there, the road leads ten kilometers further to the museum. From the museum to the lagoon is another three kilometers, and from the lagoon to the parking lot below the refuge, ten kilometers more.

GETTING AROUND THE PARK

There is no public transportation within the park. You must either have your own ride or plan to walk or hitch. Walking the park road can be a dusty prospect during the dry season when the wind blows the volcanic soil into maddening dust devils.

WHERE TO STAY & EAT

IN THE PARK

REFUGIO JOSE RIBAS, *23 kilometers into the park. 30 bunk beds. $4 per person. No credit cards.*

The most popular place to stay in the park is the José Ribas climbers' refuge. Located at 4,800 meters, it is from here that people leave shortly after midnight to make their attempts at the summit. With potable water collected from melted snow, bathrooms, and gas for cooking, it covers climbers' basic needs. You have to bring your own sleeping bag and food, which you can store in the locked secure area while you are not in the hut.

NEAR THE PARK

Expensive

HACIENDA SAN AGUSTIN DE CALLO, *Just north of Lasso on the left off the Panamericana. Tel./Fax 3/719 160. Quito Tel. 2/242 508. Quito Fax 2/269 884. 4 rooms. Double $225. Breakfast and either lunch or dinner included. Three hours horseback riding included. Restaurant. Bar. Credit cards accepted.*

The hacienda at San Agustín de Callo is one of the most memorable properties in the country with the best-preserved Inca ruins in Ecuador, gourmet food and extraordinary rooms. It's no mystery why the Inca chose this spot for building. Cotopaxi looms so big and close you feel like you can reach out and trace the contours of the mountain with your finger.

Although the hacienda merits a visit simply for the views and quality of the installations, it's the history that makes it unique. Built by the Incas in the 1400s, it was then converted by Augustan friars into a monastery. Notice as you enter the chapel, that three of the walls are the original Inca masonry. Large, perfectly chiseled stones fit together so tightly that that no mortar was necessary to keep them standing here over half a millennium. First La Condamine and then Humbolt visited to study what Humbolt called, "The House of the Inca" during their respective expeditions in Ecuador. Famous landscape painter Frederic Church captured the majesty of Cotopaxi from here in the mid-1800s. Other distinguished guests include presidents and countless well-known 20th century Ecuadorian politicians.

There's a large living area for all guests off the corner of the courtyard. With multiple fireplaces, dark wooden floors, thick exposed beams and an original Inca wall, it offers plenty of space to sit down and go over some of the books from their collection of excellent Ecuador titles. Interesting antiques and family photos make you feel as if you have been invited into the weekend home of the country's elite.

The dining room, with two original walls, is probably the most spectacular setting for a meal in the entire country. Even if you're not staying at the hacienda, a meal here is a must. (See *Where to Eat* below). Both breakfast and dinner are included in the cost of a room.

The guestrooms at the hacienda, built around the courtyard, are each unique. All however feature exposed walls with sections of painted plaster, antique country furnishings, and at least two fireplaces. A Chilean muralist has interpreted the spirit of each room with whimsical illustrations. Some of the special features in the different rooms include glass-covered excavations in the floors, sky lights over the bathtub and thick eucalyptus mantles on the fireplaces.

The Presidential Suite is just that – a place where chief executives have stayed. Ex-President Leónidas Plaza Guttierez, great-grandfather of the woman who owns the hotel, bought the hacienda in 1921. In addition, Ex-President Galo Plaza Lasso was one of her uncles. The large, comfortable suite, with two rooms and hardwood floors, has the understated luxury of a president's bedroom.

If you want more privacy or want to cook a few meals for yourself, there is also a little house on a hill above the main complex available for rent. With a comfortable kitchen and living area in addition to the master bedroom, it's the perfect country cottage. There's only one fireplace here, but it's nice and big.

There are plenty of activities to fill your days. Three hours of horseback riding are included in the cost of a room night. They can also arrange mountain bike trips, trout fishing, 4WD tours to Cotopaxi, local

Indian markets or other sights in the area, or even trekking using llamas to carry your provisions.

Selected as one of our *Best Places to Stay* – see Chapter 11 for more details.

Moderate

·**HOSTERIA LA CIENEGA,** *Just south of Lasso on the right off the Panamericana. Tel. 3/719 052. Quito Tel. 2/549 126. Quito Fax 2/549 126. 32 rooms. Double $50. Restaurant. Bar. Horseback riding. Artesanía store. Credit cards accepted.*

La Cienega is one of Ecuador's oldest haciendas and in this case, there's something to be said for age. Built in the mid-1600s, it exudes colonial stateliness while being comfortable at the same time. As if the hacienda alone weren't marvelous enough, the views from the grounds include straight shots of Cotopaxi's notched peak. Add to that the fact that it's one of the best values in the country, and you've a place tailor-made for an excellent stay in the Highlands.

There's not an entry in all of Ecuador that can compare with the grand eucalyptus-lined road leading to the big white mansion. You think it's been stolen from a Hollywood set until you realize that it's been this way for 400 years. The circular drive, set around a fountain, is framed by a colorful garden. This grandeur is only fitting for an estate that used to run all the way from Quito to Ambato.

When you enter the La Cienega your eye is immediately drawn past the reception area to the courtyard garden outside. Also set around a fountain, the featured flora includes sassy red geraniums, exploding blue agapantha and prim white daisies. Palm and pine trees offer refuge from the strong sunshine of the high plains. On the right side of the garden is the hacienda's private chapel. The white washed bell gable, sticking high above the rest of the hacienda, frames slices of blue sky and flitting clouds. The thick, intricately carved chapel doors, featuring Cienega's seal, swing open to reveal an almost monastic interior.

The original part of the house, including the main living room and guest rooms, are outfitted with furniture and decorations from previous centuries. Two-meter thick volcanic stone walls keep noise from other rooms to a minimum. Illustrious guests include La Condamine's geodesic group as well as Alexander von Humbolt and several Ecuadorian presidents.

A newer section of guestrooms and an additional garden were added when the hacienda's popularity as a weekend escape outgrew the original house. Although these rooms do not feature period pieces, they are almost like suites, with a sitting area and fireplace in addition to the bedroom. Cienega offers you the difficult choice of authenticity or a crackling hearth. (We opt for the hearth.) The very reasonably priced food at the hacienda is quite good. There's certainly no worry about being underfed here. (See *Where to Eat* below).

Inexpensive

CASA NIEVES, *42 kilometers south of Quito near Machachi. Reservations made through Cultura Reservation Center. Quito Tel. 2/558 889, Fax 2/315 092; E-mail: info@ecuadortravel.com. Website: www.ecuadortravel.com. 4 rooms. Double with bath $36. Restaurant. Horseback riding. No credit cards.*

The Casa Nieves is actually half way between Quito and Cotopaxi tucked in under Volcán Corazón. From the farm you can see Cotopaxi, Cayambe and the Illinizas. This small, intimate inn, with fireplaces and home-cooked meals, is a cozy option and a favorite for climbers working on acclimatization.

CUELLO DE LUNA, *Just north of Lasso across the Pan-American Highway from the Lasso entrance to Cotopaxi National Park. Tel. 9/700 330. Quito Tel. 2/242 744. Quito Fax 2/464 939; E-mail: cuellodeluna@exploringecuador.com. 12 rooms. Double $30. Restaurant. Bar. No credit cards.*

If you have your own transportation and want to stay in the region of a while, Cuello de Luna is an excellent value in a beautiful spot. Two kilometers down a dirt road off the *Panamericana*, the hotel looks right out at Cotopaxi.

Designed as a climber's inn, Cuello de Luna is new and comfortable. The white washed rooms, with exposed wooden beams and wooden ceilings, all include fireplaces. The spotless bathrooms are larger than ones in much more expensive hotels. The common area/restaurant in the main building has the feel of a mountain ski lodge where you can settle in for a hearty dinner around the fire.

QUINTA CUAGRA CORRAL, *turnoff to Cotopaxi Park from Panamericana. Tel. 3/485 441 or cellular Tel. 9/497 105. 1 room. $5 per person. Café. No credit cards.*

This cafeteria, located just off the highway, has four beds in a room that can come in handy if you are hiking in or out of the park. A nice Ecuadorian family runs the place. They can also provide transportation to the park entrance or points beyond.

WHERE TO EAT

In the Park

There is nowhere in the park to buy any food or drinks. You'll have to bring everything you need with you. Be sure to bring lots of water, as staying hydrated helps you acclimatize to the altitude.

Near the Park

HACIENDA SAN AGUSTIN DE CALLO, *Just north of Lasso on the left off the Panamericana. Tel./Fax 3/719 160. Quito Tel. 2/242 508. Quito Fax 2/269 884. Expensive. Credit cards accepted.*

Imagine sitting in a room with a gigantic picture window perfectly framing the snowy bulk of Cotopaxi. You look around you and notice that the walls, made of volcanic stone, are fitted together with the precise workmanship that is signature of Inca masons. Silver candelabra flicker at each end of the large antique dining table. This is not a fantasy, it is San Agustín de Callo.

We highly recommend a meal at this wonderful hacienda. In a setting like this, you would be willing to settle for much less, but it's no surprise that the staff here prepares some of the finest food in the country.

Specializing in food typical of the highlands with an international flair, San Agustín prepares Ecuadorian food the way it ought to taste. Take something as representative as the simple soup, *locro de queso*. Not content to stick to one kind of cheese, the cook here prepares the family recipe with three types of cheeses and a special cream. While everything we've ever eaten here has been delicious, you might hope for the *pay de maracuya,* passion fruit pie.

The dining room at the hacienda just has one large table, so reservations are a must. Meals cost $20 per person and are a more-than-you-can-eat fixed menu. If you can time your visit with a full moon over Cotopaxi you will remember it forever.

HOSTERIA LA CIENEGA, *Just south of Lasso on the right off the Panamericana. Tel. 3/719 052. Quito Tel. 2/549 126. Moderate. Credit cards accepted.*

Cienega's restaurant is an excellent place to enjoy a Latin-style lunch. Time your reservation so that you sit down to eat around 1:30 or 2:00 and don't get up again for hours. We recommend starting your meal in the traditional way with a round of *empanadas*. If it's a cool day you might want to include one of the delicious soups before you move on. To go all out on your main course, the *llapingachos* and *chorizo* plate is the only option. In addition to the spicy Spanish sauces and potato pancakes, it includes a fried egg and a whole avocado. Wash this down with a bottle of Chilean wine and then go fall asleep in front of the fire.

Reservations are recommended.

QUINTA CUAGRA CORRAL, *turnoff to Cotopaxi Park from Panamericana. Tel. 3/485 441 or cellular Tel. 9/497 105. Inexpensive. No credit cards.*

Located just off the Panamericana at the turn into the park, this small café offers simple food as well as a few grocery items.

SEEING THE SIGHTS

In the Park

Most people come to the park to get a closer look at Cotopaxi. That doesn't mean that's all there is to see, but it is by far the highlight. There is also a small, dark **museum**, *8am-12pm; 1pm-5pm*, with displays on the flora and fauna of the park. The stuffed museum animals are probably all you'll see of mammals in the park, but you might see birds such as the large black and white Caracara while you're out hiking.

There is also a **short trail** and **lookout point** at the museum. The self-guided trail takes about 30-45 minutes to walk and points out some of the typical vegetation of the area. The lookout point, *mirador*, offers excellent views over a deep precipice.

El Salitre is the remains of an old Inca fort. It was built to guard the mountain passes below. The walled citadel had 29 rooms for the garrison members. Excavated in 1987, it's not much more than parts of crumbling walls. The walls at San Agustín de Callo are in far better shape than the ones here, but the views are nice.

After you leave the museum you continue on the road up to an immense high plain. The lava has filled in any contours and created a tabletop. This land is flat and sparse, but loaded with pint-size life. Tiny wild flowers and plants, specially adapted to the harsh environment, cover the ground like yellow, purple, red and white confetti.

PARAMO PLANTS

*The tiny plants of the **páramo**, growing at altitudes that range from 3200-4500 meters, are perfectly adapted to their brutal surroundings. See if you can notice these characteristics:*

• They grow low to the ground in order to get heat from the soil during the day.
• They have silver leaf pigments to reflect harmful solar rays.
• Fine hairs on the leaves conserve heat and moisture.
• Their leaves are small and thick to expose less surface area to the cold.

It's on this *páramo* that you'll find **Limpiopungo Lagoon**. This small *laguna* is home to a number of water birds as well as the sparrow hawk and curunculated caracara. It's quite a surprise to see seabirds flying around at these altitudes, but many Andean gulls call the park home. You might also catch a glimpse of some hummingbirds before they zip off in search of their sugar hits.

There is a trail around the lagoon that takes about an hour to walk. Unfortunately there's some litter at the beginning of the trail, but as you hike further back it gets much cleaner. On the first part of the hike your back is to Cotopaxi as you look towards Rumiñahui. When you come around the lake, massive Cotopaxi squats like a handsome toad on the sweeping plain in front of you.

SPORTS & RECREATION
Hiking
When most people think of national parks, they think of numerous trails through the mountains. That's not the case here. The established trails are rare.

If you're not going to climb Cotopaxi you can at least start out as if you were. Many visitors like to hike the trail from the parking lot up to the climbers' refuge. If the snowline is below the parking lot, which is sometimes the case after a rain, you can hike around the **Limpiopungo Lagoon.**

If you have about a week, you can trek all the way around the base of Cotopaxi, studying the sacred mountain from every possible angle.

Mountaineering
Climbing Cotopaxi
The biggest recreational draw to the park, and one of the main reasons that many people come to Ecuador, is to climb Cotopaxi. It's a difficult but not technical climb, meaning that being in good shape and acclimating to the altitude are more important factors for success than climbing skills. Almost one in three people who attempt the climb for the first time don't make the summit because they are not adequately prepared. If you've done some lesser hikes at altitude and are in good cardiovascular condition, this can be one of the most rewarding excursions in the country.

Most people who attempt to summit Cotopaxi hire a guide through an agency in Quito. The guide service will include transportation to the park; external equipment like boots, crampons, harnesses, ice axes, headlamps and ropes; meals; and your refuge fee. You will leave Quito in the morning and drive all the way up to the parking lot below the refuge at 4,800 meters. All you have to do is walk the your stuff up from the parking lot to the cabin. Even though it looks like it's just a short hop up, it usually takes about an hour to make the trek.

Once you make it to the refuge you'll grab your bunk and get situated before heading back outside to learn how to use the ice climbing gear. For many people this is their first exposure to crampons and ice axes, so this can take a while.

When you're done, you'll have dinner and try to get to bed by dark. It will be almost impossible to sleep due to the altitude, the cold and the noise of other climbers moving around and talking. Most people are happy to get an hour's worth of good sleep before waking up at midnight to attempt the summit.

Because the snow gets unstable in the afternoon sun, you have to make sure you are up and down before it gets too warm. You'll get together with your group and head up the mountain, one by one, with your headlamp illuminating a small area in front of your feet. Take the time to look around you to watch the spooky procession of lights bobbing up the mountain.

It feels like you are going straight up. All of your concentration will be on that little patch of light in front of your feet and on trying, somehow, to get more oxygen into your lungs. You'll huff along like this in a hypnotized state until you get to the ice, where you'll put on your crampons and rope up with your group. Then you'll gasp your way, step-by-step, back into that hypnotized feeling. This will continue for anywhere from six to ten hours.

The sun will start to rise around 6am. If you have started early and made good time, you will be on or close to the summit at this point. The light dazzles as it reflects red off the ice. Watching the sun come over the white-rimmed crater after having it made it all the way to the top makes you realize that all that work was absolutely worth it.

Other Peaks in the Park

An excellent acclimatization climb in the park to 4712 meter **Rumiñahui**. You need climbing gear for some of the exposed sections, so you'll have to be content with a partial climb if you don't have your own equipment. You can reach Rumiñahui from the **Limpiopungo Lagoon**. As you walk towards the back of the lagoon you'll see the trail that head to the base of the mountain.

Another volcano, **Morurcu**, also requires climbing gear.

EXCURSIONS & DAY TRIPS

There are many excellent excursions in the area around the park. You can visit the colorful indigenous markets at **Saquisilí, Zumbahua** and **Pujilí**, enjoy a long afternoon lunch at one of the haciendas mentioned in this section, or head off into the remote, starkly beautiful highlands around **Laguna Quilotoa**. For more information on the markets and Laguna Quilotoa, see *Excursions & Day Trips* in the Latacunga section.

PRACTICAL INFORMATION

Lasso is the closest town to the park, but for a full range of services you'll have to go to Latacunga.

LATACUNGA

Latacunga, known for its dairy farms and rose greenhouses, is a town where life refreshingly does not revolve around tourists. There are services for travelers, but as the capital of Cotopaxi province, Latacunga is more about locals taking care of legal business and shopping for necessities than internet cafes and boutique hotels.

There's not much to see in terms of historical sites and buildings, as earthquakes have destroyed the city numerous times over the last couple of centuries. The worst was in 1877.

Indigenous women crowd the streets in their standard knee-socks and fedoras selling fruit, buying buckets or getting pictures taken for their national identification cards. Like walking postcards, their colorful shawls bulge with the day's shopping haul. There are plenty of things to do in the surrounding countryside, but most people choose to make these day trips while staying in one of the Cotopaxi area haciendas. If you decide instead to base out of Latacunga, you'll be sacrificing comfort to be immersed in the rhythms of this small city.

ARRIVALS & DEPARTURES

The road to Latacunga takes you through the heart of Ecuadorian flower growing country. If kilometer after kilometer of greenhouses along the Panamericana don't tip you off to the main product of the area, the billboards are a dead giveaway. "Have the most beautiful roses around" they all proclaim as they hawk their fertilizers and seeds.

If you can afford it, this is one region where having your own car really gives you freedom. You can take off on any of the excursions listed below without having the deal with bus schedules or tours. Hiring taxis for the day is another good alternative if you have the resources because then you don't have to worry about getting lost.

By Bus

Transportes Latacunga buses leave from the *terminal terreste* in Quito for Latacunga almost every ten minutes. The ride costs about $1 and takes almost two hours. You can also get on buses bound for points further south, just make sure to tell the driver you want off in Latacunga.

Local buses cover the region pretty completely, but the trick is figuring out time schedules. Most local buses depart from Calle Benavides a little north of Valencia.

By Car

Latacunga is less than 100 km south of Quito and only about 30 km from the entrance road to Cotopaxi National Park. It's an easy two-hour drive or cab ride down the *Panamericana* from Quito.

ORIENTATION

Latacunga is bisected by the Cutuchi River and the Pan-American Highway. The older and more pleasant part of town is on the east side of the highway centered around Vicente León Park.

GETTING AROUND TOWN

All of the sights in Latacunga are close enough to see on foot. If you need to grab a cab for an excursion, there are taxi stands at Vicente León Park and Plaza Chile. To phone a cab call *Tel. 800 676.*

WHERE TO STAY

Moderate

RUMIPAMBA DE LAS ROSAS, *Kilometer 100 Panamericana Sur. Tel. 3/726 128, Fax 3/727 103; E-mail: hrrosas@uio.satnet.net. 30 rooms. Double $32. Restaurant. Bar. Pool. Tennis. Volleyball. Game room. Horseback riding. Television. Credit cards accepted.*

Ten kilometers south of Latacunga at the entrance to Salcedo you'll find this ranch-style hotel, the nicest in the Latacunga area. Built on a large plot of land, the Rumipamba is designed to resemble an old hacienda. Just looking antique rather than being so means that the hotel has such modern touches as central heat and copious amounts of hot water. With rustic decorating touches like old saddles and ironworks you feel like you've stepped back into the Old West as soon as you walk into the wood-paneled lobby.

The restaurant, also in the main building, is one of the best options in the area. Locals and Quiteños pack the place on weekends, especially during the Sunday buffet.

The Rumipamba is a good choice for families due to the extensive recreational facilities. In addition to the standard swimming pool, you've got a soccer field and basketball court. The giant chess set is fun too. Each of the rooms, with fireplaces, is decorated differently, but all have the same comfortable ranch theme. Even though the hotel is on the *Panamericana*, you can find some peace and quiet if you ask for a room as far back into the gardens as possible.

HOTEL RODELU, *1631 Quito. Tel. 3/800 956, Fax 3/812 341; E-mail: rodelu@uio.telconet.net. 18 rooms. Double $22. Restaurant. Television. Credit cards accepted.*

The Rodelu is the best hotel in Latacunga proper. It is far from fancy, but is clean and offers basic services. The light wood lobby is a nice change from some of the dungeons we've walked into here. Just off Parque Vicente León, it features an eye-catching mural of Cotopaxi upstairs. We also recommend the restaurant.

HOTEL TILIPULO, *Guayaquil and Belisario. Tel. 3/810 611. 15 rooms. Double $10. Restaurant. No credit cards.*

The Tilipulo is as clean and well maintained of a budget hotel as you will find. In addition, the family that runs it offers tours of Cotopaxi, Pujilí, and Laguna Quilatoa. The only down side is that you might get some daytime traffic noise from the busy streets.

HOTEL COTOPAXI, *Salcedo and Orellana on Parque Vicente Leon. Tel. 3/801 310. 20 rooms. Double $10. Restaurant. No credit cards.*

What this place has going for it is its location overlooking the main square and the nicest desk staff you'll ever meet. It's pretty well worn around the edges though. The rooms in back are quieter than those overlooking the park.

WHERE TO EAT

RUMIPAMBA DE LAS ROSAS, *Kilometer 100 Panamericana Sur. Tel. 3/726 128. Moderate. Credit cards accepted.*

It's much more than just country cuisine at this ranch-style hotel south of town. The rustically decorated restaurant offers both typical Ecuadorian and international choices. Walk the extensive grounds and enjoy the gardens after your meal to help your digestion. They occasionally have outdoor barbecues as well.

PARRILLADA Y PIZZARIA RODELU, *1631 Quito. Tel. 3/800 956. Moderate. No credit cards.*

There's a reason this restaurant, located inside the Hotel Rodelu, is consistently full of travelers - the food is good. That seems like a simple statement, but in Latacunga it's actually an achievement. We recommend the pizza, cooked right in front of you in the wood-burning oven. The owner of the restaurant is Chilean and we tease him that we have never had pizza this good in all our travels in Chile.

PARRILLADAS LOS COPIHUES, *Down the street from the Cathedral on Quito. Moderate. No credit cards.*

What is the deal with Chileans and restaurants in this town? Founded by a Chilean, Los Copihues is named after the national flower of Chile. Scenes from that long, thin country decorate the walls and a Chilean flag hangs at the end of the restaurant. Try the grilled meats for which the restaurant is known.

RESTAURANTE LAS CANDILEJAS, *5-14 Tarqui. Moderate. No credit cards.*

This restaurant, on quiet Tarqui street behind the cathedral, draws the lunchtime office and business crowd. Go with the daily fixed meal instead of ordering off the menu.

CAFETERIA EL PASAJE, *4-50 Salcedo. Inexpensive. No credit cards.*

If you just need a quick bite, this cafe on the pleasant Salcedo pedestrian walkway is a good option. You can go for the familiar, in pizzas and sandwiches, or try the more indigenous *empanadas* and *humitas*.

ASADERO EL LENADOR, *4-31 Amazonas. Inexpensive. No credit cards.*

If *empanadas* and *humitas* are becoming old hat, you can try the true local specialties here. Pale guinea pigs roasting on the spit will catch your eye as you pass by. You can always wimp out and go for the roasted chicken.

HOTEL TILIPULO CAFETERIA, *Guayaquil and Belisario. Tel. 3/ 810 611. Inexpensive.*

This bright cafeteria is appropriate for a quick lunch or breakfast if you are staying at the hotel.

LATACUNGA POTLUCK

You may want to sample some of the typical cuisine from this part of the Highlands. You'll probably have the best luck finding these things at food stalls in the markets.

- *Chugchucaras* – *Small pieces of fried pork with miniature empanadas*
- *Plátano Frito* – *Fried bananas*
- *Cuero Reventado* – *Fried pork skin*
- *Mote* – *Cooked white hominy*
- *Chicharrón* – *Roasted pork skin*
- *Cuy* – *Guinea pig*
- *Pinol* – *Toasted barley flour, cinnamon and brown sugar*

SEEING THE SIGHTS

There's more to see in the surrounding area than in Latacunga proper, but there are enough sights to fill an afternoon if you take it slowly.

Start at the town center, **Parque Vicente León**. A green wrought iron fence surrounds the well-groomed local hangout. The shade of tall palm trees hides kissing teens while old men bask silently in the afternoon sunshine. The Moorish looking **cathedral** anchors the south side of the park while the somber **town hall** lines the park's eastern edge. Behind town hall is the smaller **Parque Bolívar** where artisans sell sweaters and other woolen items.

From Parque Vicente León you can walk along the mellow pedestrian zone on Salcedo to 2 de Mayo. Take a right on 2 de Mayo and go up two block to **Plaza Chile** where you'll find the local **market** on Tuesdays and Saturdays. Stalls selling pungent food, sensible clothing, used shoes, multi-colored livestock ropes, and bootleg CDs all battle for the consumer's attention. Don't miss the row of tailors with foot-pumped Singers fixing dresses, hemming pants and sewing up tattered bags.

MOLINAS DE MONSERRAT ETNOGRAPHICAL MUSEUM, *Vela and Salcedo. Tel. 801 221. Tuesday-Saturday 8am-12pm, 2pm-6pm. Entry $0.50.*

This museum is a nice effort on the part of Latacunga, but it doesn't quite get there. The frist trick is finding the door to the museum, down and to the right in the maze of stonework along with dirty Cutuchi River. Inside you'll see glass cases filled with dolls representing the people and customs of the area. It's a weak display, but their intentions are good. The festival costumes are the one highlight. The local library, cultural center and amphitheater are found in the same complex.

NIGHTLIFE & ENTERTAINMENT

There's not much to do here at night, as evidenced by the profusion of radical graffiti on the walls. After a pass down Salcedo you might as well call it an evening.

The only time that Latacunga really wakes up is during festivals. Their **Mama Negra Festival**, *September 22-24*, is considered one of the most vivid and interesting in Ecuador. Mama Negra, actually the Virgin de la Merced, is a small black Virgin carved in the 17th century as the guardian of Latacunga. For three days the streets are filled with costumed revelers celebrating their protectress.

MAMA NEGRA

*Very little is known about the origins of the **Mama Negra celebration**. During the annual parade, Mama Negra is represented by a costumed man with a blackened face. He rides a horse in the company of an Afro-Ecuadorian guard. Behind him, dressed to the hilt, are the highland Quichuas. There are also many other costumed people representing buffoons and sorcerers. Behind them are the formally dressed Gastadores – Big Spenders – who pay homage, and sucres, to the Virgin.*

The Carnival celebration in nearly **Pujilí** is another event not to be missed if you're in the area.

SPORTS & RECREATION

There are a number of climbs that can be done using Latacunga as a base. Cotopaxi National Park is just up the road and you can hire guides right in town. Try **Montaña Mountain Guide Service**, *Tel. 801 318.*

EXCURSIONS & DAY TRIPS

While things may be slow in Latacunga, there is enough in the surrounding area to keep you busy for three or four days.

THE LATACUNGA LOOP

There is a fantastic loop that you can do from Latacunga if you have 4WD and a couple of days. It incorporates almost all of the sites listed below. From Latacunga you go to the Hacienda Tilipulo, Pujilí, Tigua, Zumbahua, the Quilotoa Crater, the Black Sheep Inn, Sigchos, Toacazo, and Saquisilí. On this trip you jump from the modern world to another time in the remote and beautiful Andes. This is not an especially easy trip and the accommodations along the way cannot be called deluxe. We think, however, that it is one of the most interesting and rewarding things to do in all the Ecuadorian Highlands. Sturdy women in felt fedoras lead llamas across the dusty plain with tall volcanoes in the background, the wind whips the clouds across the sky and you feel as if you're on another planet.

If you don't have a car, one bus daily makes the loop, departing in the morning from Latacunga at Calle Benavides a little north of Valencia. Other buses cover portions of the loop. See the individual write-ups below for more information.

Cotopaxi National Park

Cotopaxi is easily accessible from Latacunga. For more information, see the section on Cotopaxi above.

Saquisilí Market

One of, if not the most famous indigenous markets in the country, **Saquisilí** is a must if you are in the area on Thursday. It seems like just about everything you can imagine is for sale somewhere in the town. Fried pigs heads, miracle creams, any article of clothing, kitchen wares, textiles, and every bootleg CD ever made can be found for sale if the price is right.

And then there are the animals. Don't miss the animal market, which is actually a little separated from the main activity. Just follow the moos and oinks to this wonderfully picturesque scene. Interested in a piglet? How does about twenty of them on leashes sound?

Just as interesting as all the items for sale are the people buying them. Saquisilí brings indigenous people down from high in the hills to do their weekly or even monthly shopping. Bright ponchos and felt hats dot the town everywhere you look. Just be sure to go early and beat the tourists that bus in from Quito.

The easiest way to get to Saquisilí from Latacunga is to hire a cab for a few hours. If that's not feasible, buses leave for Saquisilí from Latacunga at Calle Benevides a little north of Valencia at least twice an hour.

Pujilí

Pujilí is a pleasant little country town known for its Sunday and Wednesday markets that draw surrounding villagers by the truckload. The main avenue into town features an animated trio of statues in full festival regalia. The tiled central square, a few blocks from the market, is worth checking out as long as you're in town. A blocky neoclassical church with nicely carved doors anchors the plaza. Nearby a municipal building maintains its *Feliz Año Nuevo* greeting in Christmas lights year round.

The market is a collage of villagers in colorful panchos and felt hats. Agricultural products are the main offerings, which are displayed in stalls or spread on wool blankets. A few household odds & ends are sold here as well. An expansive metal roof has been erected to protect the market denizens from the elements. Though the Wednesday market is a smaller affair, it is still worth hitting if you are in the area.

A cab ride to Pujilí from Latacunga is about $4 each way, or $8 roundtrip including the wait. There are cabs in Pujilí if you plan on staying longer. You can also catch buses from Latacunga to Pujilí from the Texaco station on the Panamericana across the street from the train station.

Tilipulo Hacienda

A trip to check out the recently restored **Tilipulo Hacienda** is worthwhile if you are a hacienda aficionado or you would simply like a good reason to detour down pleasant country roads bordered by agave cactus fences. Elderly women herd cattle while producing yarn on hand-held spindles as they walk along. On a clear day the Iliniza Mountains shine like a frosted kiss.

Technically you are supposed to obtain a permit from the municipal authorities in Latacunga to tour the facilities. It is more practical to knock on the big blue door and ask the caretaker to make an exception and give you a tour. His effort in streamlining the bureaucracy should be rewarded with a small *propina* of course.

The estate possesses a rich history and in the near future will open as a hotel. The first structure on the grounds was built in 1720. The volcanic bricks are held in place with mortar nutritious enough to eat. It is composed of clay, blood, animal fat, molasses, and eggs. In its early days the hacienda served as a monastery and became famous for its production of cider and woven goods. The patriots of Latacunga declared independence from Spain here a century later. Most of its history as hacienda was spent in the hands of the Alvarez family, the 20th century descendents of which were known as the "Alvarez times Seven" because they had intermarried so much that the surname was Alvarez repeated seven times.

Thick whitewashed walls and pillars with intricate gray molding contain the splendor of the hacienda. A sundial in one courtyard is equipped with two needles, one for the winter solstice and the other the summer. The extensive gardens swell with blossoms and birds. There is a promenade leading from one of the gardens into the center of grassy depression that once was and will again be a pond.

The guest facilities were nearly finished at the time of our last visit. The local government will soon award the concession to a hotel operator.

There is no public transportation to the hacienda, rather you must hire a cab.

Tigua

In markets and stores all over Ecuador you've seen colorful paintings depicting scenes of rural Andean life. These small paintings, created on stretched sheepskin, are a beautiful and portable type of Ecuadorian folk art. Called **Tigua Hide Paintings**, the small town where this art form originated and still thrives is still the best place to buy them. Tigua is just 52 kilometers southwest of Latacunga on the road to Quevedo.

The best of these incredibly detailed, vibrant paintings are found in the cooperative gallery in Tigua. You'll see the sign on the right as you drive into town. The gallery is the white building up the hill. Look for works by Julio Tactaquiza, the man who invented the art form.

You can get to Tigua by bus from Latacunga. Take the Quevedo bus, *Calle Benevides a little north of Valencia,* and just ask the driver to drop you off in Tigua. Hiring a taxi from Latacunga is a good bet, as is joining up with one of the tours that visit the town. **Safari Tours**, *Quito Tel. 223 381* also has a Tigua trip out of Quito.

Zumbahua

This windy town, high up in the Andes, feels like a lonely place. Until Saturday morning that is, when it kicks into high gear with its market. Smaller than some of the more famous markets nearby, it non-the-less brings the city to life. Our favorite part of this market is the llama factor. Women in colorful shawls and knee socks use the cameloids to tote their goods into town. The llamas just look so supercilious as they stand calmly amid the blare and clatter of the commerce around them.

Zumbahua is 65 kilometers southwest of Latacunga. You can get there on bus by taking the Quevedo bus, *Calle Benevides a little north of Valencia,* and asking the driver to drop you off in Zumbahua. Hiring a taxi from Latacunga is a good bet as well. You can also join up with one of the tours that visit the town.

There are a few very modest pensions in Zumbahua around the main plaza.

Laguna Quilotoa

This trip takes the entire day, but it is worth the effort. Three hours from Latacunga, the blue-green waters of Quilotoa are as mesmerizing as the notched cone of Cotopaxi. Nestled in a slate gray crater, Laguna Quilotoa lies at 3,500 meters in the Ilinizas Reserve. There are two excellent hikes at the lake. You can either walk around the crater, a four to five hour proposal, or take an hour's walk down the scree to the water's edge. From there you can either hoof it back up yourself in about two hours or rent the service of a waiting mule. (You can only ride the mule if you weigh less than 150 pounds. If you weigh more than that, count on a long huff up.) Be sure to bring plenty of water and layered clothing for extremely variable weather.

You can get there on bus by taking the Sigchos bus, Calle Benevides a little north of Valencia, and asking the driver to drop you off at the crater (Make sure it is the Sigchos bus that passes Quilotoa as you can get to Sigchos via either Toacazo or Zumbahua). Hiring a taxi from Latacunga is a good bet as well. You can also join up with one of the tours that visit the crater along with a few of the other towns on the loop.

There are a couple of places to get something to eat, buy Tigua paintings or stay the night at the turn-off to the crater. **Cabanas Quilotoa,** *Tel. 3/812 044, Double $5,* is the best of the lot. It's extremely simple and can get very cold at night unless you ask for extra blankets.

Chugchilán

This small, isolated village is the place to go when you want to get away from it all. Luckily, there's a comfortable place to stay, which makes it a destination worthy of more than just an overnight stay.

THE BLACK SHEEP INN, *Chugchilán. Tel. 3/814 587. 8 rooms. Double $36. Dinner included. Restaurant. Horseback riding. Excursions. No credit cards.*

High in the Andes, at 3,200 meters, the inn offers spectacular scenery and plenty of activity options. It's a great place for acclimatization hikes or just meditating on the stark yet captivating landscape. You can hike to pre-Inca ruins, the Rio Toachi Canyon or even the Quilotoa Crater. The best however, is a visit to the European cheese factory, where you can sample and buy delicious cheeses. If you're not interested in doing the walking, you can make the trips on horseback or even in jeep.

Dinner, included in the price of a room, is remarkably delicious. Much of the tasty vegetarian food at the inn comes straight from their organic gardens.

The American owners of the Black Sheep Inn are very interested in experimenting with and promoting a type of agricultural method called permaculture. They are also involved in reforestation projects and community education.

The inn is about one and half hours beyond Zumbahua. You can get there on bus by taking the Sigchos bus, *Calle Benevides a little north of Valencia,* and asking the driver to drop you off at the inn. (Make sure it is the Sigchos bus that passes Chugchilán as you can get to Sigchos via either Toacazo or Zumbahua). Hiring a taxi from Latacunga is an option that will probably cost around $45 or $50.

Sigchos & Toacazo

These small towns are merely places to stop and stretch your legs as your bump your way around the loop. Sigchos has a small Sunday market.

Salcedo

South of Latacunga on the Pan-American Highway, **Salcedo** is famous for its ice cream. You have to stop here and try the frozen delight even if it's 9am. Calderón and Matta, two of the town's main streets, are jam packed with stores advertising their delicious *helados.* Frozen in cup form, they come on a stick not on a cone. You can go for a single flavor or try a multi-colored sampler. Our favorite is *mora,* blackberry.

Tuesday and Saturday are market days here if you want to stick around town and take in the local commerce.

PRACTICAL INFORMATION

Banks and **taxis** can be found on *Parque Vicente León,* although we've had a hard time getting the ATMs to accept our Cirrus card. The **EMETEL** phone office is one block behind the park on *Quevedo and Maldonado.*

AMBATO

Ambateños, known for their industriousness, leave no doubt about the purpose of their city. Poised in the center of the country, between the southern Oriente and coast, Ambato is a major commercial and transportation center. Over 300,000 call it home, in addition to the hundreds of people in town for business on any given day. The streets hum with trade, markets abound, while large homes show the results of some people's hard work (okay, and connections too).

Called the Garden of Ecuador, Ambato grows grains, sugarcane, cotton and a whole range of fruits and vegetables. It also produces footwear and textiles.

At the same time, the capital of Tungurahua province is proud of its history as an intellectual center of the country. The two most famous of these intellectuals, **Juan Montalvo** and **Juan Leon Mera**, are immortalized in statues and museums. Others, like Pedro Cevallos and Luis Martinez, have streets and parks named after them.

While the Ambato is not necessarily a destination for travelers with limited vacation time, those with a looser schedule might find it worth a short visit simply for its museums.

ARRIVALS & DEPARTURES

Ambato is only 40 km and about the same number of minutes from Latacunga. The drive snakes along the Culuchi River. There is an interesting contrast in the land as it changes from the green grass perfect for pasturing milk cows to a drier, scrubbier land as it climbs to Ambato.

You can stop at the control point between Latacunga and Ambato to peer over the edge of the canyon at **Laguna Yumbo**. It's really not all that impressive, but rather a nice place to stretch your legs.

By Bus

Buses Zaracay leave for Ambato from the main bus station in Quito every half-hour. The ride costs $2 and takes about two and a half hours. The bus station in Ambato is a few kilometers north of town.

By Car

It's an easy drive on the Pan-American Highway to Ambato from just about anywhere in the Central Highlands. Quito is two and a half to three hours north, Riobamba 45 minutes south and Baños 45 minutes southeast.

Rental Car Company
• **Localiza**, *Avenida de los Guaytambos and Montalvo, Tel. 3/849 128*

ORIENTATION

Ambato runs along the steep cliffs of the Ambato River valley. Across the river from town are the posh suburbs of Ficoa and Atocha, with their wider streets and fancy houses.

The town itself is centered around a triumvirate of parks – **Parque Montalvo**, **Parque 12 de Noviembre** and **Parque Cevallos**. On all sides of the parks you will find the town's hotels, restaurants, markets and museums.

WHERE TO STAY

Moderate

HOTEL AMBATO, *Guayaquil 0108 and Rocafuerte. Tel. 3/827 599, Fax 3/827 197. 80 rooms. Double $42. Restaurant. Bar. Cafe. Casino. Cable TV. Guarded parking. Credit cards accepted.*

The Ambato is the best hotel in town. Located on the edge of downtown, the hotel is convenient to restaurants and museums, but out of the crazy fray of the market area. The Hotel Ambato perches right over the river, so be sure to ask for a room with a view. The lights of the distant suburbs will wink you good night before you pull your blinds.

All rooms are outfitted with comfortable beds, large bathrooms and cable TV. Of course, you won't use your bed much if you find yourself with a hot hand at the casino. Slots, poker tables and blackjack tables are all waiting to take your money.

You don't have to travel far to find a good meal. The **Restaurante Ficoa**, in the hotel, is by far the number one option in town. (See *Where to Eat* below.)

HOTEL CAROLINA, *Av. Miraflores 05-175. Tel. 5/821 539. 25 rooms. Double suite $40. Breakfast included. Restaurant. Pool. Sauna. Credit cards accepted.*

The Hotel Carolina offers suites, each with a small living room outfitted with modern furnishings. It is the extra space rather than the decor that is draw. The hotel is located in the pleasant Miraflores residential area, a five minute cab ride from the city center. The small pool is indoors.

HOTEL MIRAFLORES, *Miraflores 2-27. Tel. 3/843 224, Fax 3/848 979. 35 rooms. Double $40. Breakfast included. Restaurant. Bar. Television. Credit cards accepted.*

The Miraflores used to be the best hotel of its namesake neighborhood a few kilometers from the city center. Competition from the Carolina has put the squeeze on, but it's still a fine hotel. Good-sized, comfortable rooms and garden grounds help you relax after a day of intense touring.

Inexpensive

HOTEL VILLA HILDA, *Miraflores 600. Tel. 3/845 014, Fax 3/845 571. 25 rooms. Double $24. Breakfast included. Restaurant. Bar. Pool. Credit cards accepted.*

The Villa Hilda is starting to look a little scraggly from the outside, but the large gardens are still quite pleasant. The rooms, spread throughout the complex, are definitely a bit worn, but they are a half-step above the Hotel Florida.

HOTEL FLORIDA, *Miraflores 11-31. Tel. 3/843 040, Fax 3/843 074. 50 rooms. Double $30 on weekdays, $20 on weekends. Breakfast included. Restaurant. Television. Credit cards accepted.*

If you want to stay in the nice Miraflores neighborhood but have limited funds, the Florida is a decent option on weekends when the price goes down by $10. The brown carpet and beige walls are less than inspiring, but the beds are okay and you have a phone and TV in your room.

Budget

LA CASA BLANCA, *Cordero 2-10 and Los Shyris. Tel. 3/844 448, Fax 3/844 512. 5 rooms. Double with shared bath $10. Breakfast included. Laundry. No credit cards.*

The Casa Blanca attracts budget travelers and climbers. Located in a small white house, as the name would imply, it's a good option at the lower end of the scale. Aligned with SurTrek, they also arrange climbing and trekking tours as well as multi-day expeditions.

If the Casa Blanca is full, you might want to try the **Hotel Cevallos**, *Cevallos and Montalvo, Tel. 3/847 457, Double $12,* which is popular with traveling Ecuadorians.

GRAN HOTEL, *Lalama 05-11 and Rocafuerte. 20 rooms. Double $15. Breakfast included. No credit cards.*

This blocky hotel is lacking in personality, but it is clean and centrally located. It is recommended if you are looking for an inexpensive option for a night or two.

WHERE TO EAT

RESTAURANTE FICOA, *Hotel Ambato, Guayaquil 0108 and Rocafuerte. Tel. 3/827 599. Moderate/Expensive. Credit cards accepted.*

If you're in need of flavorful, well-prepared food served in a tranquil location, head straight to the Ficoa. This restaurant far exceeded our expectations. With large windows looking out over the Ambato River, the Ficoa offers great views both night and day.

You might want to start your meal with garlic mushrooms or a bowl of their tasty French onion soup. Both are delicious. For your main course, we recommend the steak. It is cooked to perfection and accompanied with savory sauces. Chocolate lovers should save room for dessert. The Copa Tungurahua, named after the nearby snow-capped volcano, is a cascading cup of warm chocolate cake topped with ice cream and covered with chocolate sauce.

LA BUENA MESA, *Quito 924. Tel. 822 330. Moderate. Credit cards accepted.*

This French restaurant is a dinner institution with Ambato locals and the business set. Only in Ecuador can you find exquisite French cuisine so reasonably priced. Try the savory artichoke with shrimp au gratin for an appetizer. The entree selection is replete with steak and sole options, from saucy to sublime. There are several fondues to choose from as well.

PARRILLADAS EL GAUCHO, *Bolívar and Quito. Tel. 3/828 969. Moderate. No credit cards.*

El Gaucho is purely and solely for carnivores. There is nothing but beef on the menu, and there's lots of that. You can see it cooking up on the grill in the back of the restaurant from your table. All the soccer paraphernalia is explained by the fact that the owner used to play for the local professional team.

CUBA SON, *Bolívar y Guayaquil. Inexpensive. No credit cards.*

With live Cuban music every night beginning at 7 pm, this is a fun place to hit for a light meal or a slug of rum. The menu is rather limited, but does include some Cuban favorites like *ropa vieja*, black beans, yucca, and potatoes, as well as sandwiches. Che Guevera looks on approvingly from his huge portraits as patrons sip *mojitos*, a delicious concoction of crushed limes, sugar, and rum.

EL RINCON ESPANOL, *Bolívar and Quito. Tel. 824 643. Inexpensive. No credit cards.*

Office workers patronize this restaurant for its cheap fixed menu lunch, served in a flash. Try ordering something else though and you're in for a long wait.

CASA BRASILEIRA, *Rocafuerte 15-13 and Castillo. Inexpensive. No credit cards.*

This inexpensive buffet locale is popular with the town's college students. The Brazilian culinary connection is somewhat weak, but they do play taped Bossa Nova music anyway. And it's got a pool table too.

CAFE CULTURAL, *Montalvo between Rocafuerte and Bolívar. 9am-10pm. Inexpensive. No credit cards.*

This cafe, in the University Cultural Center, is a hip place to grab a sandwich before you visit the **Montalvo Museum** next door. They have live music and other events in the evenings. They also feature rotating art exhibits that although technically quite good, can push the envelope a bit when you're eating.

Quick Takes & Desserts

If you just need some fuel to continue your sightseeing, try **Choco Banana** at *Quito and Rocafuerte*. Quick sandwiches and, of course, chocolate covered bananas are the specialty here. After lunch you can stop into the **Panificadora Ambato**, *Sucre and Quito*, for an impressive and tasty display of dessert options. If it's a hot day, ice cream may be more down your alley. **Iglu** has many branches in town, but we like the one at *Sucre 5-55*.

If you've decided that today is the day for guinea pig, *cuy*, you've got plenty of options here. Head to the Ficoa neighborhood across the river where you'll find **Cuyes de Ficoa**.

SEEING THE SIGHTS

The Ambato markets, some of the largest in the country, are sometimes touted as the reason to visit here. We say skip the markets and enjoy at least two of the four museums in town. While the museums are not great on an international scale, they are interesting on the Ecuadorian level.

Start your tour of town at the **Parque Montalvo** on *Bolívar and Montalvo*. This large, fenced park is one of the fancier ones in this part of the country. A statue of Juan Montalvo stands at its center. The hideous town cathedral takes up one whole side of the park. Montalvo's home is cattycorner to the cathedral.

CASA DE MONTALVO MUSEUM AND MAUSOLEUM, *Bolívar y Montalvo. Monday-Friday 8am-12pm; 2pm-5pm. Entry $1.*

The obligatory, bilingual guided tour starts off somewhat slow due to the guide's insistence of itemizing every bust of Juan Montalvo in the world. The build is much more tolerable as you learn about the life of this intellectual who claimed he killed an Ecuadorian president with his pen. The big finale is sufficiently creepy to make the whole experience quite satisfying.

Juan Montalvo, (1832-1889) was Ecuador's foremost intellectual, most well known for his political essays, but also a playwright and poet. Exiled for most of his life, his literary attacks on the García Moreno regime were written in Colombia. When the president was assassinated outside of the presidential palace in 1875, Montalvo claimed that the murder was inspired by his prose.

After being led through several rooms of photos and personal affects, the tour winds up in the mausoleum. Juan Montalvo lays resting in a tribute that most artists will only dream of. His open, gold-plated casket is elevated on a pedestal. Meanwhile, the title of every work he penned is inscribed on the ceiling as though eternally sanctified in heaven. He could do with a manicure though. His decaying fingers poke gruesomely out of a waxy cover.

Montalvo's enraged polemical essays, directed against tyranny and dictatorship, contributed to his being banished from Ecuador. His most well-known work, *Siete tratados*, consists of seven expositions on moral and literary subjects. The most famous of these is his comparison of George Washington and Simón Bolívar. He also wrote *Capitulos que se le Olvidaron a Cervantes*, *The Chapters that Cervantes Forgot*, in the same style as the famous *Don Quijote*. Not an especially original thinker, Montalvo is recognized outside of Ecuador for his abundance of works and the vehemence of his style.

NATIONAL SCIENCE MUSEUM, *In the National College Building on Parque Cevallos. Monday-Friday 8am-12pm, 2pm-6pm. Entry $1.00.*

Okay, so maybe the subject of this isn't as high minded and noble as the works of **Juan Leon Mera** or **Juan Montalvo**, but it's pretty fun. Every kind of animal you can imagine has been stuffed and placed in here. Some taxidermist really worked overtime to bring you variety that ranges from a sagging elephant to an elongated boxer.

We especially like the extensive collection of animals from Ecuador like monkeys, jaguars and a huge vampire bat. The hundreds of stuffed birds help you identify what you saw on your walk the other morning. The last section of museum is like a freak show at the circus with two-headed sheep, goats with feet growing out of their heads and six-legged cows.

QUINTA DE JUAN LEON MERA, *Atocha neighborhood. Tuesday-Sunday 9am-4:30pm. Entry $1.*

This tribute to Ecuador's leading Renaissance man includes a small museum surrounded by an immense garden above a surprisingly pretty little piece of the Ambato River. Juan Leon Mera (1832-1894) is most well known for writing the lyrics to Ecuador's national anthem. He also wrote books of poetry and history, and was an aspiring painter. The compact museum consists of a few rooms full of the artist's personal affects, such as his writing desk, dining table, and bed. Although he is more famous for his writing than his painting, his oils on display here demonstrate his talent as an all-around artistic utility man.

Here are the first few lines of the national anthem: "Hail Oh Fatherland, one thousand times! – Oh Fatherland!, Glory to thee! Your breast swells with Joy and peace, and your radiant forehead, We behold shining brighter than the sun."

The flowerbeds burst with palm trees, blue agapantha, and red geraniums. Off to one side you can see the Ambato River churning past vegetable gardens. You can walk down a short trail through a patch of woods to reach the river. The gardens and paths are well maintained and kept almost completely litter free. The Quinta is about a ten-minute cab ride from downtown Ambato.

QUINTA MONTALVO, *Miraflores. Monday-Friday 8am-12pm, 2pm-6pm. No entry fee.*

Montalvo's country home, now smack dab in the suburb of Miraflores, is just a seven minute cab ride from downtown. While not as extensive as those of **Quinta Juan Leon Mera**, the gardens here cover at least an acre and include a small orchard. There's not much to see, but that's the beauty of the place. It's a perfect location for a market detox program among the flowers.

JUAN BENIGNO VELA PARK (PARQUE DEL AMOR), *At the edge of town on the road to Baños. No entry fee.*

This fun and whimsical park is filled with amazing topiary works. Fairy tale and Walt Disney characters appear to dance down the hillside, play guitars, and twirl in the sun. If plants can seem happy, these do. It's definitely worth a trip up here.

Markets

If you want to visit the markets here, there are plenty of them. Purely commercial, they lack much of the picturesque quality of markets in smaller cities of the Highlands. These are workaday places with a fair build-up of grime and debris. They are however, stacked with exotic fruits and vegetables, heaped with different kinds of potatoes and piled with lots of freshly butchered meat. There seems like there's one on every corner, but the main ones are the **Central Market**, *Mercado Central, on 12 de Noviembre and Lalama*; and the **Colombia Market**, *Mercado Colombia, at Cevallos and Espejo.*

Some vendors set out their small harvest of onions, leeks, and potatoes on blankets on the streets between the two markets, creating a continuous flow of wares. The flower market is a simple line of stalls to one side of the Mercado Central.

THE SALASACAS

When wandering the streets of town you might notice the distinctively dressed Salasaca Indians. The men wear white pants, white shirts and black and/or white panchos. The women wear black skirts, black blouses and brightly colored panchos fastened with a silver pin.

Both sexes wear special embroidered belts made on a backstrap loom. The patterns on the belts represent important animals and star constellations. The women often wear several belts that can measure over 20 meters long when placed end to end.

It is thought that the Incas moved the Salasacas here from Bolivia in the 15th century.

NIGHTLIFE & ENTERTAINMENT

Many people like to gamble on their luck at the **Hotel Ambato Casino**, *Guayaquil 0108 and Rocafuerte, Tel. 3/827 599*. If you're more into testing your skill on the dance floor, **El Coyote**, *Bolívar and Quito*, is a disco near Juan Montalvo Park. You can find **bars and pool halls** around *13 de Abril and Juan Leon Mera.*

Carnival in Ambato is famous for its extravagant Fruit and Flowers festival.

SPORTS & RECREATION

You can conveniently reach many of the same mountains from Ambato that you can from Baños. **SurTrek**, *Cordero 2-10 and Los Shyris. Tel. 3/844 448, Fax 3/844 512*, leads climbs to **Tungurahua**, **Chimborazo** and the **Ilinizas** among other trips. They also organize treks to Altar and the Rio Ambato. They have equipment both for rent and for sale.

SHOPPING

High quality leather clothing is a big draw to the area. You can either go to nearby **Quisapincha** on the weekends, where you shop directly from the over 100 boutiques and factories, or try a place in Ambato like **G&M Leather**, *Montalvo and Sucre*.

EXCURSIONS & DAY TRIPS

Excursions from the Ambato could be to many of the other towns in this section of the Highlands. **Latacunga**, **Baños**, **Saquisilí**, **Pujilí** and even **Cotopaxi** can all be reached comfortably in a day.

PRACTICAL INFORMATION

Rumor has it that there are 22 **banks** between the Montalvo and Cevallos Parks. We only found seven, but that's quite a few anyway. The **post office** is on *Parque Montalvo*, as is one of the many **taxi** sites in town. The **CETUR office** is in the *Hotel Ambato's parking lot*. With no maps or written material, they are limited in their helpfulness. **EMETEL** is a block off Parque Montalvo on *Castillo between Bolívar and Rocafuerte* if you need to use the phone.

BAÑOS

Baños' backdrop is absolutely stunning. Tucked into steep flanks of green, the town is shadowed by the **Tungurahua Volcano** above and the **Pastaza River** cutting a canyon below. In Baños itself, a towering waterfall shoots out of the foliage and plunges frothing into public baths. It's no mystery why both Ecuadorian and international tourists rank Baños as one of their favorite destinations. Excellent weather, beautiful scenery, plenty of activities, thermal baths and a sacred Virgin draw people from around the world.

One of the things that we like about Baños is that you are as likely to have an Ecuadorian family staying in the room next door as a German mountain climber. It's really nice to see Ecuadorians enjoying their own country.

Baños is definitely a town geared towards tourists. This can be overwhelming if you have just arrived to the country or if you just don't like the beaten path. If you've been in Ecuador a while however, it's a nice refuge from scrambled eggs and potatoes. We suggest that you travel a few other places in the country first before coming here, so that good Mexican food and brownies hold real appeal.

ARRIVALS & DEPARTURES

By Bus

The **bus station** in Baños is at *Maldonado and Espejo*. Sugar cane stands ring the streets, offering a sweet treat for your ride. **Cooperativo Baños** buses leave for Quito's *terminal terrestre* every 20 minutes. The ride costs about $2.50 and takes just over three hours. From Baños you can also catch buses for points north and south on in the Highlands as well as east to points like Puyo in the Oriente.

By Car

Baños is a relatively easy three and a half hour drive from Quito. You take the Pan-American Highway south to Ambato and then head east. From Ambato you'll drop down 1,000 meters through spectacular scenery into the greenery that cups two sides of Baños and falls off in dramatic gorges on the other two sides.

The road from the Oriente is not in as good condition as that from Ambato, but the scenery is equally if not more stunning. It takes about two hours to drive to Puyo.

If you want to rent a car in Baños to get out into the countryside, try **Cordova Tours**, *Maldonado and Espejo, Tel. 740 923.*

ORIENTATION

Baños' excellent weather is due to its location at 1850 meters. Neither highland nor jungle, it enjoys a spring-like temperature year-round (Which is kind of funny because Ecuador doesn't even have Spring.)

The terraced hillside fields around Baños seem to go straight up on two sides and straight down on the other two, making it difficult for agricultural workers to keep their footing. We once watched a man lose his balance as he was working his field. So extreme was the angle of incline that he rolled 20 meters before he could right himself. He looked up, shrugged his shoulders, and clambered back to his plot.

Baños is centered around the Cathedral and busy Ambato street. Taffy-pullers clog shop-fronts while stores sell everything from religious trinkets to goggles and bathing suits.

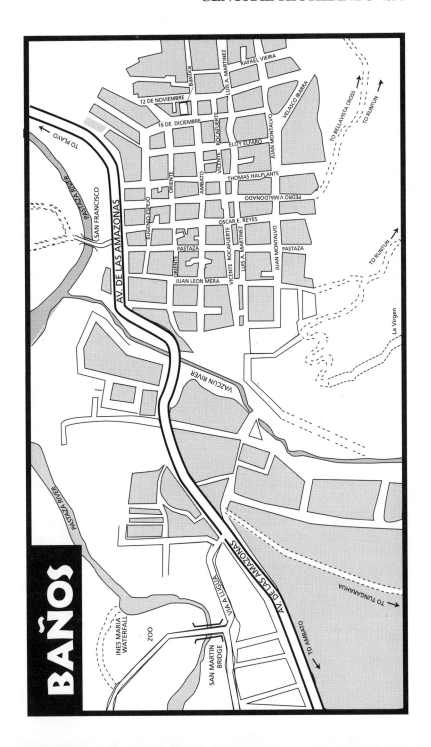

BAÑOS

INES MARIA WATERFALL

ZOO

SAN MARTIN BRIDGE

VIA A LLIGUA

AV. DE LAS AMAZONAS

PASTAZA RIVER

TO AMBATO

TO TUNGARAHUA

VAZCUN RIVER

La Virgen

TO RUNTUN

AV. DE LAS AMAZONAS

PASTAZA RIVER

TO PLAYO

SAN FRANCISCO

EUGENIO ESPEJO

ORIENTE

JUAN LEON MERA

PASTAZA

ORIENTE

VICENTE ROCAFUERTE

LUIS A. MARTINEZ

JUAN MONTALVO

PASTAZA

OSCAR E. REYES

PEDRO V. MALDONADO

THOMAS HALFLANTS

AMBATO

VICENTE

ROCAFUERTE

ELOY ELFARO

JUAN MONTALVO

VELASCO IBARRA

16 DE DICIEMBRE

12 DE NOVIEMBRE

Basilica

LUIS A. MARTINEZ

RAFAEL VIEIRA

TO BELLAVISTA CROSS

TO RUNTUN

One of the most surprising sights is the *Casacada Cabellera de la Virgin*, **Virgin's Hair Waterfall** that plunges dramatically out of the greenery and into a pool at the eastern end of town. We've never seen anything like it in a city before. You can see this sensational spectacle from just about everywhere in town.

GETTING AROUND TOWN

You can walk almost everywhere in Baños. The most distant attraction is the zoo, a couple of kilometers out of town. If you don't want to walk there, you can take a cab or go to the bus station and catch a local bus up the hill.

If you want to arrange a cab for a trip out of town, we recommend Angel at **Coopertivo El Santuario**, *Tel. 740 880*.

WHERE TO STAY

Expensive

LUNA RUNTÚN, *Caserío Runtún, Kilometer 6. Tel. 3/740 882, Fax 3/ 740 376. US Reservations, Tel. 888/217 8254; E-mail: info@lunaruntun.com Website: www.lunaruntun.com. 27 rooms. Double $135-170. Dinner and breakfast included. Restaurant. Bar. Gift shop. Horseback riding. Tours arranged. Credit cards accepted.*

The high-end hotel in Baños is not really in town, but rather appropriately perched on the edge of the steep green wall that makes the scenery from Baños so striking. The Luna Runtún, owned by a Swiss-Ecuadorian couple, offers sweeping views of town below, the Tungurahua volcano behind, and the Llanganates mountain range beyond.

The rooms of the Runtún are scattered throughout the grounds in 18 colonial houses amid abundant flower, medicinal and vegetable gardens. Tile floors, whitewash walls and thick exposed beams give the rooms a country feel. It's the details that make you feel so comfortable here – a welcome note signed by the manager, flowers on your pillow, a ceramic pitcher of water instead of a plastic bottle, and, our personal favorite, thick warm comforters for the cool mountain nights. In addition, you'll get some of the best views around from the hammock on your porch.

The Runtún takes pride in its ability to focus on ecology without sacrificing comfort. The lettuce you eat for dinner is grown organically outside your room, all trash is recycled, and you'll see very little plastic being used on the grounds.

The common areas are designed in the same colonial style as the rest of the hotel. The library, with its big fireplace and bar, is the perfect place to enjoy a cocktail before walking across to dinner.

Meals, mainly Ecuadorian fare with an international twist, are served either in the dining room or *al fresco* on the restaurant's patio. There are generally two or three entrée options for each meal.

Having your own car here is convenient, but not necessary. The steep walk down to Baños only takes about 20 minutes, while you'll need almost double that for the walk up. In a cab, the ride into town is about 15 minutes and costs $5.

Moderate

HOTEL SANGAY, *Plaza Ayora 101. Tel. 3/740917. 75 rooms. Double $35-85. Restaurant. Bar. Pool. Sauna. Game rooms. Credit cards accepted.*

With a prime position in front of the waterfall, we assumed this would be a good hotel. The most expensive rooms are nice, but exorbitantly priced considering other options in town. The cheaper rooms are shabby, so they're not worth the rate either. The facilities, such as the pool and squash court, need a fresh coat of paint.

Inexpensive

HOSTERIA MONTE SELVA, *Halflants and Montalvo. Tel./Fax 3/740 566. 12 cabins, 22 rooms. Double $30. Breakfast included. Restaurant. Bar. Pool. Sauna. Massage. Game room. No credit cards.*

The Monte Selva is our favorite in-town option. The large grounds, which head halfway up the side of the hill, are overrun with tropical plants, such as impatient ringed banana and avocado trees. There's a Polynesian feel to the buildings, which consist of guest rooms, cabanas, pool and sauna area, massage hut, restaurant and outdoor bar. Families appreciate the playground and sport court.

The cabanas are our lodging of choice. A path leads up through a profusion of flowers along a small creek that falls melodically from pool to pool in stair-step fashion. You have a bit of a climb, but when you get to your cabin it is quiet and removed, looking down at town through the large picture window. Even if you stay in one of the rooms down at the bottom, it's worth the climb through the exuberant vegetation to the lookout spot.

One of the best things about the Monte Selva is the affordable massage service available in the afternoons. It's the ultimate in relaxation after a long day in the saddle or hiking the hills.

HOTEL PALACE, *Montalvo 20-03. Tel. 3/740 470, Fax 3/740 291; E-mail: mastalir@tu.pro.ec. 32 rooms. Double $30. TV. Restaurant. Bar. Pool. Thermal baths. Game room. Credit cards accepted*

This is a great, old rambling inn with nicely decorated, refurbished rooms. The dining room serves standard Ecuadorian fare, while outside in the pool area, a grill fills the air with the mouth-watering aroma of *parrillada.* This is an excellent place for families because it has big pool with a view of the waterfall and activity-filled game rooms. There is also a garden that climbs up the hill until it merges with the jungle. There are outdoor and indoor thermal baths, much more hygienic than the public ones down the street.

CHALETS BASCUN, *El Salado Avenue. Tel 3/740 740. 15 cabins. Double $30. Breakfast not included. Restaurant. Pool. Sauna. No credit cards.*

Located on the road to the El Salado Hot Springs, these white A-frame cabins are a decent option for families, although they are a little out of the way. There's a nice pool and awesome slide for the young and young at heart.

HOSTAL ISLA DE BAÑOS, *Halflants 1-31 and Montalvo. Tel./Fax 3/ 740 609. 16 rooms. Double $18. Breakfast not included. Restaurant. Horseback riding. Tours arranged. No credit cards.*

The Isla de Baños is our recommendation as the best hotel in town for under $20. With attractive gardens, comfortable rooms (some with balconies), a staff that can arrange almost any type of excursion and hands down the tastiest breakfast in town, you can't go wrong here. The rooms have high ceilings, big windows and tons of light. The bathrooms are about what you would expect for $20, but you can get a hot shower 24 hours a day. If you just want to hang out, there are both indoor and outdoor sitting areas, as well as the gardens.

CAFÉ CULTURA, *Juan Montalvo y Pasage Velasco Ibarra. Tel. In Quito 2/564 956; E-mail: crc@ecuadorexplorer.com. 8 rooms. Double $20. Restaurant. Credit cards accepted.*

This was the original Café Cultura in Ecuador. It is under different ownership now, but has lost none of its appeal. Earthy décor and delicious fare from the café are still trademark Café Cultura qualities. Batik tapestries, dried roses, and cool murals impart a stylishly mellow ambience.

All of the rooms are unique so the prices are different for each room. It is definitely worth reserving one of the rooms that are slightly more expensive, especially those with a view of the waterfall. These rooms also have a balcony. A few of the rooms have fireplaces as well.

Be sure you indicate that it is the Café Cultura in Baños that you want when contracting the CRC for a reservation.

LE PETITE AUBERGE, *Calle 16 y Montalvo. Tel. 3/740 936. 12 rooms. Double $20. Restaurant. No credit cards.*

Le Petite Auberge is a funky, well-liked hotel with fireplaces in the rooms and a meandering courtyard garden. You can relax in a hammock next to the outdoor fireplace after a dinner at the hotel's restaurant, one of the best spots in town.

Budget

PLANTAS Y BLANCO, *Martinez and 12 de Noviembre. Tel./Fax 3/740 044. 20 rooms. Double $10. Breakfast not included. No credit cards.*

This white building surrounded by potted plants is well-known for its sunny breakfast patio. You can also get what they call a "daily morning health bath," much like a steam bath, here. This hotel has lots of nice details for a budget place. An honor bar, music, board games, movies and excellent breakfasts are all included for your Alexander Hamilton. We also like the fact that each of the simple rooms has different colored lace curtains.

EL MARQUES POSADA J, *Montalvo and Pasaje Velasco Ibarra. Tel./ Fax 3/740 616. 17 rooms. Double $10. Breakfast not included. No credit cards.*

El Marques is a pleasant budget option at the end of a quiet street. The rooms are plain, but the grounds of the hotel include nice gardens. We especially like the flagstone wall depicting the surrounding mountains.

LA FLORESTA, *Halflants y Montalvo. Tel. 3/740 457, Fax 3/740 717. 10 rooms. Double $12. Restaurant. No credit cards.*

The rooms of this tidy new hotel surround a cheerful garden embroidered with vines and orchids. The rooms are simple, but all are set up with chairs outside to contemplate the steep jungle hills.

HOSTAL EL EDEN, *12 de Noviembre and Montalvo. Tel./Fax 3/740 053. 20 rooms. Double $10. Breakfast not included. No credit cards.*

The Hostal El Eden is a red brick edifice built around a courtyard in the style of a US motel. It is completely basic, but is also clean and has hot water. You could do much worse for $10.

Outside of Baños

EL OTRO LADO, *Rio Verde, 20 km from Baños on the highway to Puyo. Tel. 09/820 367; E-mail: elotrolado@hotmail.com. Or contact the CRC, Tel. 2/ 558 889. Web site www.ecuadortravel.com. 3 cabanas. $35 per person full board. Restaurant. Spa.*

El Otro Lado might be the most unique place to sleep in Ecuador. Three beautifully designed cabins sit across a wooden suspension footbridge from a roaring waterfall, with another cascade in view in the distance. The cabanas are built of gorgeous, tawny, native wood. Each has open-air decks with hammocks, perfect for relaxing with a book or simply staring out into the dense jungle vegetation. The bathroom outside each cabin is a tall cylindrical bamboo fence wrapped around shiny ceramic fixtures. The three cabanas are situated far enough apart to provide exceptional privacy, which is what makes the accommodations distinct from even the most remote luxury jungle lodges.

The vegetarian food for the dinner table is organically grown on the premises. The owners are partial to Middle Eastern and Indian cuisine, which means healthy fare with pizzazz. The grounds of the hotel are sixty-four acres of primary and secondary forest. You can hike a two to three hour circuit where you might encounter a tropical badger or a cock of the rock.

Consider coming out to El Otro Lado with only a daypack, leaving your bags with your hotel in Baños. The fit and adventurous will ride a mountain bike out past the famous waterfalls on the highway to Puyo. You can load the bike onto a bus or prearranged taxi for the trip back uphill to Baños. Others will prefer to take a taxi both ways. In any event, you have to walk a kilometer down a trail past the waterfall to reach El Otro Lado, so minimal luggage is best. If you do want to bring you bags and stay a while, El Otro Lado will arrange for a mule to carry your load down.

WHERE TO EAT

There are some very good places to eat here. All Baños restaurants suffer from a common malady however – tardiness. Most have very small kitchens and end up making meals one by one as they are ordered. Your companion's dish may come out a full ten minutes before yours arrives to the table.

We recommend either going to dinner a little early or having a snack so you're prepared to wait up to an hour for your food to arrive. Just sit back, drink more wine and relax.

MARIANNE RESTAURANT, *Halflants y Rocafuerte. Tel. 09/837976. Moderate. No credit cards.*

Marianne conjures up some flavorful, Southern French cuisine. You can smell the moment you walk in that you are going to have a wonderful meal. There is no way the tiny kitchen can contain the mouthwatering aromas that pour out of it, or even the cooking staff. A cyclone of elbows, saucepans, and sharp knives produces delectable creations like steak *a la Mediterenee*. This savory cut is laden with onions, peppers, olives, bay leaves, thyme, and succulent grilled tomatoes. The *Poulet* in Tunis Sauce is also superb, a chicken breast in mushroom sauce with tender carrots, accompanied by tomatoes au gratin. If you've eaten your share of overcooked vegetables along the way down the *Panamericana*, you should start with the Greek salad for a fresh veggie crunch-fest.

The walls of the small locale are decorated with a hodgepodge of postcards and French memorabilia. In fact, the food is so good, and the dining area so petite that you should go early to secure a table. Service can be slow simply due to the size of the kitchen, but it is well worth the wait. Besides, it will give you more time to ponder whether to try the chocolate fondue or blackberry crepes for dessert.

LA PETITE, *16 de Diciembre and Montalvo. Tel. 740 936. Moderate. No credit cards.*

La Petite is another excellent French option in town. You enter the hotel grounds and walk down a garden pathway to the informal restaurant. They offer crepes, some vegetarian plates, and many trout preparations. Our favorite however, is the cheese fondue.

CASA MIA, *Halflants 1-31 and Montalvo. Tel. 740 609. Moderate. No credit cards.*

This is the best place in town for the full range of Ecuadorian food. With dishes such as *cocados* from the coast and *llapingachos* from the highlands, just about the entire country is represented.

This is your best chance to try *cuy*, guinea pig, prepared in a hygienic environment. You have to order ahead 24-hours, but it's worth it for a taste. Just close your eyes and think about chicken as you bite down.

Casa Mia, through the garden attached to the Hostal Isla Baños, has a daily Andean music show from 8pm-9:30pm.

INCA FLAME, *Oriente and Eloy Alfaro. Tel. 740 838. Inexpensive. No credit cards.*

One of our favorite combinations on earth is Mexican food and American desserts. We find the Inca Flame a bit of personal utopia. With excellent quesadillas, nachos, burritos and guacamole, this restaurant lives up to its Mexican side of the bargain. The flavorful shredded beef tacos are so good that we lust for them when we're traveling in other parts of the country.

When it comes time for dessert, they specialize in the two legal drugs – coffee and chocolate. The moist brownies are our favorite.

TWO HOODS IN THE HOOD

*It's impossible to come to Baños and not see flyers for, hear about, or eat at Casa Hood, Café Hood or both. Offering almost the exact menus, the restaurants are real travelers' hang-outs. They both have inexpensive vegetarian fare and comfort desserts, good tunes, book exchanges, bulletin boards, notebooks full of travel recommendations and nightly movies. So what's the deal? Apparently, Familia Hood has been divided. Ex-wife has one restaurant and ex-husband has the other. We think they're both great. Try **Casa Hood**, Martinez and Alfaro, Tel. 740 609, open through out the day but closed on Mondays; or **Casa Hood**, 16 de Diciembre and Martinez, also open all day, but closed on Tuesdays.*

EL JARDÍN, *16 de Diciembre and Rocafuerte. Inexpensive. No credit cards.*
Across the garden plaza from the Baños cathedral, El Jardín features an outdoor patio with hammocks as well as indoor seating with a bar. Open all day, they offer breakfast, salads, sandwiches and three types of lasagna.

HOSTAL ISLA DE BAÑOS, *Halflants 1-31 and Montalvo. Tel. 740 609. Inexpensive. No credit cards.*
We consider breakfast here a required Baños activity. Whether you go for the homemade yogurt, farm fresh eggs or tasty muesli, you won't be disappointed. If you're really hungry, order the fruit-filled pancake. The pancake is more like a football-sized crepe stuffed to overflowing with fresh tropical fruit.

CAFÉ CULTURA, *Juan Montalvo y Pasage Velasco Ibarra. Moderate. Credit cards accepted.*
Café Cultura is a great place to sip a coffee while nibbling on ambrosial carrot cake. The meals tend to be light, healthy, and delicious featuring an excellent selection of soups, salads, and vegetarian main courses. The place is quite laid-back and cozy, often with a fire crackling in the hearth.

RICO PAN, *Ambato across from the Plaza. Inexpensive. No credit cards.*
The dining area of this bakery mainly serves breakfast items, but they also makes great sandwiches on whole grain breads. The selection of languages on the menu board is abundant, but the items are more limited. You can ask them to make whatever you want and they might give it a try. We requested a cheese sandwich *con toda la cocina*, they ad-libbed, and it was delicious. They serve fresh pasta here too.

The **Hostal Plantas Y Blanco**, *Martinez and 12 de Noviembre, Tel. 740 044,* is another tasty breakfast option.

You can get pizza all over town, but **Sicilian**, *Alfaro between Ambato and Oriente*, is a favorite hangout for budget travelers. **Pizzeria de Paolo**, *16 de Diciembre*, is also good as is **La Campinera Pizzeria**, *Martinez y Halflants, Inexpensive, No credit cards,* made with either thin crust or deep-dish style.

If you're on crowded *Ambato street* and need a quick bite, consider **Blah Blah** or **La Abuela**. Both are small cafes with decent sandwiches.

SEEING THE SIGHTS

BAÑOS ZOO, *Off the main road into town just up from the San Martin bridge. 8am-6pm daily. Entry $2.50.*
Zoos are generally a bit depressing, especially Latin American ones, but this a good chance to see some of the many interesting animals of Ecuador. Check out the *capibara*, the largest rodent in the world, or the studious looking spectacled bear.

The best thing about the zoo is that the largest mammal in South America, the tapir, is roaming unhindered through the bird section. This awkward-looking, lumbering beast hangs-out behind cage #17. It's easy to see why they are becoming endangered as they root around blindly sniffing the air.

BASILICA, *Ambato and 16 de Diciembre.*

The Basilica in Baños is one of our favorite churches in Ecuador. The flamboyant red and gold Gothic altar is reminiscent of Las Vegas, complete with Ave Maria scrolled in glowing neon. Along the walls are giant *retablos* that recount miraculous rescues performed by the hand of the sainted Water Virgin. Whenever someone is in peril, usually swept away by the ferocious river, he calls out "Madre Mia de Agua Santa" and is mysteriously plucked from danger. The neon-wrapped Peregrina Virgin and candle-lined trough of holy water are located in a cloister through a door on the left-hand side of the church.

Upstairs is an eclectic museum, with displays ranging from the Virgin's sequined robes to reptiles preserved in brine. Check out the glass display cases that feature some wonderful tributes. These colorful buses are models of those in which pilgrims ride each year to see the Peregrina Virgin.

MUSEO HUILLACUNA, *Juan Montalvo y Pasage Velasco Ibarra. Tel. 3/740 973. 9am-12pm; 1:30pm-6:30pm.*

This small archeological museum features displays of ceramics from the coastal cultures as well as some regional antiques.

The road to the zoo passes over the **San Martin Bridge**. It's definitely worth getting out and looking over the edge of the bridge. The rushing water, forced between narrow rock walls, has dug a vertigo-inducing channel. There's also a small waterfall, **Casada Inés María** close by. Even if you're not interested in the zoo, we recommend a stroll to this bridge.

Another fun bridge to walk across is *out the end of Reyes behind the bus terminal.* The **San Francisco Bridge** is an old fashioned wooden affair suspended over the river.

A nice hike to take around 5pm is the walk up the stairs to the **Virgin Mirador**. Soft light illuminates the surrounding mountains and you get great views of the river, town and steep green hills. The path to the Virgin starts at the end of Mera. You can also walk up to the **Bellavista Cross**, high on the hill, by hiking out the end of Maldonado.

NIGHTLIFE & ENTERTAINMENT

Almost every restaurant in town offers live Andean music once a night. If that's not enough, you can hear more at the **Peña Bar Ananitay**, *16 de Diciembre and Espejo.*

One of the best bars in town is **L'ile aux Pirates**, *Eloy Alfaro and Montalvo*. Blue and orange handprints lead the way in the door where you'll find a pool table, TV, book exchange and happy hour from 10pm-11pm. There are a score of bars along *Alfaro north of Ambato*, including the trademark infringing **Hard Rock Cafe**. You can dance the night away at **La Burbuja Disco**, *Mideros and Ciudadela Rosario*.

Both Casa Hood and Café Hood offer movies nightly.

There's a local drink in Baños that for some reason has been named a "sandwich." Made with sugarcane juice and *aguardiente*, cane liquor, it is both sweet and strong. Try one on your night on the town.

SPORTS & RECREATION
Biking

The most popular bike ride is down the curving highway on the road to Puyo. Even though there is some traffic, we still consider this one of the best ways to visit the waterfalls (As long as it's not the rainy season.) Just leave early in the morning and you'll be fine. You have to change your mentality if you are expecting a workout, however, as almost the entire trip is down hill. The bike is just a way to be one step closer to the experience.

Almost all the bike shops in town offer the ride as a guided trip. Unless you are traveling alone and don't feel comfortable venturing out by yourself, there is no reason to hire a guide. Just stop by the marked sights along the way (see *Excursions & Day Trips* below) and then throw your bike in a truck or a bus at the end of the line to come back to Baños. Remember to leave early to beat most of the traffic.

There are many bike shops in town. The most important thing is that your bike is working properly. Ride it around a bit before accepting it, checking the brakes and gears. Be sure to wear your helmet also, as leaving your brains on the road can ruin your trip.

Bike Rentals
•**Hofala Rent Bikes**, *Alfaro and Oriente*
•**Taller de Bicicletas Alexander**, *Oriente and Alfaro*

Hiking

There are lots of great hikes in and around Baños. One of the most popular ones climbs up the hill behind town to the village of **Runtún**. The obvious path starts *at the south end of Maldonado*. Take a right along the ridge when the trail branches and just continue up, up, up. You'll pass the Luna Runtún Hotel and continue to climb up to the Runtún village. There is really nothing to see in the village, but the views along the way are outstanding. We suggest stopping in the Luna Runtún for a drink or a meal. To make the hike a little longer, you can go out Mera to the **Virgin Mirador** and then cut across the entire hillside behind town before climbing up to Runtún.

Another nice walk starts away from the hillside just behind the bus terminal on Reyes. A road leads down and across the swaying, wooden San Francisco Bridge to the town of **Illuchi** about two hours down the road.

There's a longer loop that you can do by going out across the San Martín Bridge and past the zoo up to the radio antenna on the **Chontilla** hill. From this vantage point at 2700 meters you have a wonderful panorama of Tungurahua, the Pastaza River and Baños. When you come down from Chontilla you hang a left and take the track to the San Francisco Bridge where you cross back into town.

You can also go through an agency in town for guided hikes to the **Sangay National Park**. (See *Mountaineering* below).

Horseback Riding

There are plenty of companies in Baños offering horseback rides. Most of them leave right from town on pathetically scrawny, abused horses. If you want to get out and ride in the surrounding countryside, we recommend **Caballos con Christian**, *Hostel Isla de Baños, Halflants and Montalvo, Tel. 740 609*. You'll leave from Baños in an old jeep and drive almost an hour up into the hills where the horses are stabled. From there, the "small" day trip goes out for about four hours, including a lunch stop, or the "full" day trip goes out for, surprise, the entire day.

The full trip climbs up to thermal springs in the cloud forest. Unless they've changed the route since we went, the small trip is out and back on a dirt road through farms. It can get a little long if you haven't spent much time in the saddle lately.

Mountaineering

The most popular peak to climb from Baños is 5023 meter **Tungurahua** (when it's not erupting). This is a long, physically exacting climb, regardless of what the tour companies might say to the contrary. True it's not too technical, but the altitude and steepness of the ascent make it a difficult slog. You'll be far better off if you've done some acclimatization climbs in the Andes before attempting this one.

This trip offers a bit of everything. You start out towards the refuge in lush, semitropical growth and end up on the rim of a snow-covered crater. The climb is usually done in two days. The first afternoon you'll hike into the **Sangay National Park** up to the Nicolás Martinez Hut at 3800 meters. The next morning you'll make your attempt at the summit.

The climb from the hut to the summit, basically straight up, takes about five hours. If you are lucky enough to have a clear day, you are rewarded for all your hard work by spectacular views that span from the Andes to the Amazon rainforest.

Only four of the many Baños travel companies are authorized to operate in the Sangay National Park. These companies have the best guides and equipment for climbing. We can recommend both Selvanieve and Julio Verne.

BETTER THAN A POWER BAR

Salasaca tradition has it that after people die they go to heaven, hauapacha, where Jesus decides if they can stay. If they have been bad, Jesus sends them to hukupacha, a hellish place full of demons and evil spirits. If they person is really bad, he or she has to stop by Tungurahua on the way to hell and eat a meal of black beetles.

Authorized Sangay Tour Companies
• **Selvanieve**, *Oriente and Maldonado. Tel. 740 335*
• **Julio Verne**, *Oriente 11-69 and Alfaro. Tel. 740 253; E-mail: julver@interactive.net.ec*
• **Rainforest Tour**, *Ambato and Maldonado. Tel. 740 743*
• **Expediciones Amazonicas**, *Oriente 11-64 and Halflants. Tel. 740 506*

There are other peaks in the Sangay National Park. **El Altar** at 5320 meters is a technically challenging climb. **Volcan Sangay**, at 5230, is extremely difficult due to continual volcanic activity and falling ash.

The dark mountains on your right as you drop down into Baños from Ambato are the Llanganates, part of mysterious **Llanganates National Park**. Popular lore has it that the remains of the vast Inca gold and silver treasures are hidden deep in this range. Although people have spent their lives looking, chances are the riches will remain lost, as access to the park is difficult and the terrain and weather even more so.

Rafting
We hate to say this, because we love rafting, but we cannot recommend hiring trips with the companies in Baños. There is no regulatory process, which means that just about anybody can buy a raft and some life jackets and call themselves a rafting company. The guides generally have very little experience and there is rarely a safety kayak along for scouting rapids or offering assistance. Just last year a boatload of tourists was killed

when their neophyte guide missed the take out spot. If that's not bad enough, many of the rivers are polluted.

Every rafting company in Baños will tell you that the rivers are safe and easy. That's just not the case. If you insist on going, **Rio Loco**, *Maldonado and Martinez, Tel. 740 929* has the best reputation in town. You should demand that a safety kayak accompany the raft.

Swimming

There is an excellent, **Olympic-size lap pool** across the street from Hotel Villa Gertrudis at *Montalvo and Alfaro.* You buy your entry ticket at the hotel and then walk across the street for your swim. Bring your own towel because they don't provide any.

Thermal Baths

Baños got its name from the thermal baths for which is it famous. When most travelers think of thermal baths they have this romantic notion of being alone in a beautiful, natural stone grotto. That doesn't happen here. The baths are like swimming pools that happen to be filled with hot bubbly water. It's just not quite the same.

If you're still into it, there are a number of options.

PISCINAS LA VIRGEN THERMAL BATHS, *below the waterfall. 4:30am-10pm. Entry $0.50.*

Even though these are the thermal baths that gave Baños its name, the hygiene here is dubious at best. Hundreds of people at a time soak in the thermal water filled swimming pools. You are much better off in the smaller, less crowded baths in the hotels.

EL SALADO HOT SPRINGS, *Via al Salado, 4:30am-5pm, Entry $0.50.*

These baths, a little more off the beaten track, aren't quite as crowded. To get to El Salado, head out the main road towards Ambato. As soon as you cross the bridge over Bascún Creek, take a left up Via al Salado. You'll pass Chalet Bascún before arriving to the baths.

SHOPPING

GALERIA CENTRO CULTURAL HUILLACUNA, *Ave. Juan Montalvo y Santa Clara, Tel. 3/740 187,* has some excellent paintings and sculptures by Ecuadorian artists.

There is an **artisan market** off *Ambato between Halflants and Alfaro.* If you're on the lookout for unique textiles, you have the chance to visit **Salasaca weavers** and buy their handiwork. Their traditional backstep loom weaving is not the same process as used for the tapestries you see in most places. Call Sr. Alanso Pilla, *Tel. 09/840 725,* to arrange the visit.

One of the most extensive offerings of **tagua nut carvings** in the country can be found at the store on *Maldonado 681 between Espejo and*

Oriente. If you are looking for a backpack or need to get yours fixed, **Mochilas Varoxi** on *Maldonado 651 and Oriente,* is an excellent store. He also can do professional tailoring jobs on your climbing clothes if you need anything repaired, which we did.

For T-shirts, sunglasses, babbles and trinkets, try the hundreds of shops along *Ambato.*

SPANISH SCHOOLS

Many people prefer Baños over Quito for studying Spanish. They like the fresh air and small town feel. There are quite a few schools for improving your language skills:

*• **Baños Spanish Center**, Oriente between Alfaro and 16 de Diciembre. Tel. 740 632*

*• **Raices**, 16 de Diciembre by the stadium. Tel. 740 090*

*• **International Spanish School**, 16 de Diciembre and Espejo. Tel. 740 612*

If you're just interested in one-on-one instruction, look for Mayra Paguay, Calle Luis Martinez and Sta. Clara, Tel. 740-470.

EXCURSIONS & DAY TRIPS
Road to Puyo Waterfalls

This trip, whether done in bike or in car, is certainly a worthwhile use of your time while in Baños. The road to Puyo runs through lush terrain striped with silky waterfalls. Water surrounds you. Falls plunge onto and sometimes over the road on your left while the Pastaza River curves along its steep banks that fall off to your right. The water is constantly eating away at the road, creating an engineering nightmare. Tunnels run blasted through dark sections of rock.

The sights along the way include the **Chamana Falls** to the right just behind the town of Ulba, the **Agoyán Dam**, and many pretty waterfalls without names. About 10 kilometers after that you reach the path to **Manta de la Novia Falls**, accessed by a suspension bridge that crosses the river. The next major waterfall is **San Jorge** on the left-hand side of the road.

A short distance further along is the *tarabita* cable car that slides across 400 meters of cable, 200 meters above the Pastaza River. The car is just a metal box covered thigh-high in wire fence. The lack of safety features definitely increases the adrenaline surge. The views and photos to be taken while dangling above the gorge are spectacular. It costs about a dollar for the ride.

The turn-around point is in the village of Rio Verde, near its magnificent, brutish waterfall **El Pailón del Diablo**, the Devil's Cauldron. You have to hike down a kilometer-long trail to reach the waterfall. The caretaker at the snack bar at the bottom asks for a donation to help cover the cost of bridge maintenance and litter removal. $1 is appropriate. You can find lodging in Rio Verde at **El Otro Lado** across the footbridge from the waterfall (see *Baños, Where to Stay*) or at the **Andillama Cabins** in Rio Verde.

Mountain bikers should start the trip as early as possible in the morning to minimize encounters with traffic. When the road narrows with a vehicle approaching from either direction, take care to pull your bike safely to the far side of the road, then resume pedaling after it passes. Most people ride their bikes in the downhill direction toward Puyo, then take a bus, prearranged taxi, or tour company vehicle from Rio Verde the 28 km back to Baños.

Almost every tour agency in town sells tickets for excursion on one of the *chivitas*, cartoon-like open-air buses that jaunt along stopping for all of the major sights. The cost is about $5 per person. You can also hire a taxi to take you for about $6 per hour.

Jungle Tours

There are several agencies in town that offer jungle trips. Avoid the tours that involve daylong bus rides to a distant destination. It is an ordeal, not an adventure, to ride for hours in a bus somewhere far, far from Baños, spend a little time in the jungle, and then ride for hours in a bus again back to Baños. If you have that much time, you are much better off picking one of the jungle destinations that we recommend in our *Oriente* chapter, and going there yourself.

If you can't get to the jungle destinations near Tena, Coca, and Lago Agrio due to time restraints, then choose a 1-2 day tour from Baños, with minimal bus time, making sure the area to be explored is no farther than Puyo. If they try to talk you into something longer, refer to the previous paragraph.

Recommended Jungle Tour Companies
• **Tsanta Tours**, *Oriente y Alfaro. Tel. 740 947*
• **Rainforestur**, *Ambato y Maldonado. Tel. 740 423*

PRACTICAL INFORMATION

Banks: Banco del Pacifico, *Montalvo and Eloy Alfaro.* This bank has an ATM.

Currency Exchange: Casa de Cambio Chimborazo, *Ambato and Halflants.*

E-Mail Service: Cafe.com, *12 de Noviembre 500*. To call this an internet café is a bit generous, as there is only one extremely slow, if functioning at all, internet line. To be fair, it's the fault of the Baños phone system, not the café. Maybe it will be upgraded soon.

Laundry: El Marques Posada J, *Montalvo and Pasaje Velasco Ibarra*; **Victor's**, *Martinez and Alfaro*.

Medical Service: Hospital, *Montalvo and Pastaza. Tel. 740 443.*

Post Office: Correos, *Halflants in front of the park*.

Supermarkets: Supermercado Carolina, *12 de Noviembre and Ambato*.

Telephone/Fax: EMETEL, *Rocafuerte and Halflants*. The area code is 3.

Tourist Office/Maps: Hola Information, *Maldonado and Espejo*.

RIOBAMBA

Riobamba is the capital of the Chimborazo province. There's not much happening here, but that's part of the appeal of this pleasant place. With pastel painted colonial-style buildings and wide cobblestone streets, it has the air of a different age. In addition, the tallest mountain in Ecuador, Chimborazo, is a big hunk of earth and ice towering over town.

Riobamba was first founded in 1530, but was completely destroyed by an earthquake in 1797. Most of the buildings in town were built after that date. Its historical claim to fame is that the convention that proclaimed Ecuador's independence from Gran Colombia met here in 1830.

ARRIVALS & DEPARTURES

By Bus

Transportes Chimborazo leave from the *terminal terreste* in Quito for Riobamba every half hour. The ride costs about $3 and takes almost four hours. You can also get on buses bound for points further south, just make sure to tell the driver you want off in Riobamba.

There are a confusing number of bus stations in Riobamba. The **main bus station** is on the northwestern edge of town near the intersection of *La Prensa and Borja*. This is the exit point for buses plying the *Panamericana* and bound for Guayaquil. A few blocks south of the main terminal you'll find the **regional terminal**, with buses bound for Guamote and Cajabamba. If you're headed for Baños or the Oriente, you'll take a bus from the **Terminal Oriental** on the east side of town at *Espejo and Córdovez*. Buses to **Guano** also leave from the east side at *Pichincha and York*.

By Car

The drive to Riobamba is a straight shot down the Pan-American Highway. If you're lucky enough to have a clear day on the four-hour drive you'll get an eyeful of Ecuadorian volcanoes.

THE DEVIL MADE ME DO IT

To take the train or not? Many people wrestle with the decision, as it's a huge time investment. The ride, barring any mechanical failures, takes six hours, and then it's at least another four-hour bus trip on to Cuenca. How do you decide?

People will rave about the views, which are nice, but the trip is not about views. It's about the excitement of riding on the roof of a train. It's exhilarating. The wind rushes by as you pass small farms watching people working their fields and travel along steep gorges with volcanoes in the background. Farmers wave and people pull over in their cars to take pictures of the spectacle of a bunch of gringos hanging off the top of a baggage car.

The roof is cold though and kind of uncomfortable. You need to think about whether or not you're prepared to take the good with the bad. If you're not going to ride on the roof, you'll probably be disappointed with the trip unless you're just a huge train fan.

By Train

The famous train used to depart from Riobamba, high in the Andes, and drop down to Durán, near Guayaquil. El Niño wiped out part of the track, so now the train only goes from Riobamba to **Alausí**. The good news is that the most famous section just past Alausí, **The Devil's Nose**, is still intact. A series of switchbacks, part of which you have to back down, The Devil's Nose isn't as scary as the name would make it out to be. The train travels 5 hours from Riobamba to Alausí, picks up passengers, goes down and up the Devil's Nose for an hour, and then heads back to Riobamba.

Most people don't take the train roundtrip, but rather ride from Riobamba down the Nose and then get off in Alausí, where there are buses waiting to go to Cuenca and back Riobamba. Other people take the bus to Alausí and just jump on for the hour-long Devil's Nose portion.

Last time we were there, the train made the trip every Wednesday, Friday and Sunday at 7am and cost $15 for foreigners. The only guarantee on departure times and days of the week is what's written on the chalkboard inside the station. We recommend checking it out personally, as even our hotel had the time wrong when we went. Tickets go on sale an hour before the train leaves, and it's a good idea to get there early.

The most famous aspect of the train is that you get to ride of the roof of the baggage car. There are perfectly comfortable passenger cars available, but most people choose the roof. It makes for a much more stimulating ride. From your high perch you'll catch picturesque and even stunning glimpses of life in the highlands.

There are a number of things you can do to make your time on the roof more comfortable:

• Sit as far back from the engine as possible to reduce noise and the smell of diesel fuel.
• Sit on the metal strip that runs along the length of the top of the baggage car for the best stability.
• Face the right side during the Devil's Nose section for the best views.
• Take food and water, but don't drink too much, as there's only one bathroom stop a couple hours into the trip.
• Rent a cushion or two because that roof is hard and cold.
• The morning cold can be brutal. Make sure you have a warm hat, gloves, and plenty of layers.
• The afternoon sun can be brutal as well. You'll want another hat to shade your eyes and plenty of sunscreen.
• It might rain as well. Take appropriate protection.
• If you don't start out on the roof, climb up at the bathroom break in Guamote. There is a mad rush in Alausí, and if you don't have your space marked out, you'll be one of the people balancing precariously on the slanted part of the roof with nothing to hang on to.

If you want to ride the train, but require a little more comfort, contact **Metropolitan Touring** in Quito, *Avenida República El Salvador 970, Tel. 464 780, Fax 464 702, Website: www.ecuadorable.com*. Their train, which is actually a first class bus on wheels, makes the trip an hour before the regular one does. They have comfortable reclining chairs in the bus as well as sturdy railing around the roof.

The train from Riobamba also goes to Quito on Saturday at 9am.

ORIENTATION

You can look down almost any street in Riobamba and see green hills at the end of the road. Downtown has a number of plazas, the most central being Parque Sucre. The main streets that run through the center of town are 10 de Agosto, Primera Constituyente and Veloz.

GETTING AROUND TOWN

You can cover almost all the sights in town by walking. You might want to take a cab to La Loma de Quito lookout point, but besides that everything else is right downtown.

WHERE TO STAY

Moderate

HOSTERIA LA ANDALUZA, *16 kilometers north of Riobamba on the Pan-American Highway. Tel. 3/904 248, Fax 3/904 223; E-mail: handaluz@ch.pro.ec. 55 rooms. Double $40. Breakfast not included. Restaurant. Bar. Business center. Auditorium. Sauna. Game room. Cable TV. Credit cards accepted.*

La Andaluza offers the nicest lodgings in the Riobamba area. Built on the site of an old hacienda, the hotel has maintained the style and feel of colonial times. Thick whitewash walls, dark wooden beams, antique decorations and many fireplaces accentuate the rustic country feel. That doesn't mean you won't be comfortable, especially if you get one of the recently remodeled rooms with central heat and king sized beds.

La Andaluza stretches across the large grounds in an intriguing maze of long hallways and staircases. Outside you'll find numerous courtyards and spectacular views of Chimborazo. The original hacienda, built in 1555, was called Chuquipoggio. Simon Bolívar slept here after his visit to Riobamba, as did all the framers of the first constitution.

Inexpensive

HOTEL MONTECARLO, *10 de Agosto between Moreno and España. Tel. 3/960 557. 17 rooms. Double $20. Restaurant. No credit cards.*

The Montecarlo, a small hotel built in an old colonial house, is our favorite option in the city center. The indoor courtyard, covered by a glass roof, is sunny and bright. An iron stairway leads to the clean rooms, all with private baths.

HOTEL CHIMBORAZO, *Argentinos and Nogales. Tel. 3/963 474, Fax 3/963 473. 36 rooms. Double $22. Restaurant. Café. Pool. Sauna. No credit cards.*

This big pink hotel looks from the outside more like something you'd find on Miami Beach than the windswept highlands of Ecuador. Its glory days are long past, but for $18 you get clean bathrooms and good views from the edge of town. It's a decent choice for the price, even if it does remind us a bit of The Shining.

Budget

HOTEL GALPON INTERNACIONAL, *Argentinos y Carlos Zambrano. Tel. 3/960 982, Fax 3/960 983. 44 rooms. Double $15. Cable TV. Restaurant. Bar. Indoor pool. Credit cards accepted.*

This hotel, located a little outside of the city center, is acceptable for a night or two. It has an odd decorating scheme including green pastel hallways and modular plastic shells as phone booths in the lobby.

HOTEL IMPERIAL, *Rocafuerte 22-15 and 10 de Agosto. Tel. 3/960 429. Double $10. Breakfast not included. No credit cards.*

This white, art deco building is in a central but loud location. The hotel offers laundry service and luggage storage, which is are unexpected services for the price level.

WHERE TO EAT

In what seems like some kind of town conspiracy, most of the restaurants are closed on Sunday night as well as all day Monday.

EL DELIRIO, *Constituyente and Rocafuerte. Tel. 967 502. Moderate/ Expensive. Credit cards accepted.*

This old home turned restaurant offers the finest fare in Riobamba. Bolívar supposedly wrote his famous poem *Mi Delirio Sobre el Chimborazo* in this house after climbing to the mountain's snowline in July 1822.

There's a nice garden and courtyard for warm, sunny days, as well as small intimate booths and a fireplace inside for when it's cooler. The Spanish bar is a great place to rehash your day's adventures over cocktails. The international menu features your standard steak and chicken plus a few Spanish dishes.

HOSTERIA LA ANDALUZA, *16 kilometers north of Riobamba on the Pan-American Highway. Tel. 3/904 248. Moderate/Expensive. Credit cards accepted.*

Another higher end option in the Riobamba area is the dining room at the **Hosteria La Andaluza**. Featuring an international menu, the restaurant serves up big plates of food in a warm country estate atmosphere.

CHARLIE'S PIZZERIA, *Garcia Moreno y 10 de Agosto. Tel. 968 231. Inexpensive.*

This is gratifying place to chew some cheese. Try the Charlie Grande with oregano, sausage, olives, mushrooms, and red bell peppers. Charlie's also serves a few good pasta dishes like lasagna and cannelloni.

CAFÉ REAL MONTECARLO, *10 de Agosto between Moreno and España. Tel. 960 557. Inexpensive. No credit cards.*

Next door to the hotel Montecarlo, this informal downtown restaurant is popular with locals. Stop in for a sandwich or the daily *menú*.

SEEING THE SIGHTS

LAS CONCEPTAS MONESTARY MUSEUM, *Argentinos and Larrea. Tel. 965 212. Tuesday-Saturday 9am-12pm, 3pm-6pm. Entry $2.*

You just don't expect to find such a well-done and pleasant museum on the windy streets of Riobamba. This is, in fact, one of the better religious museums in the country. Part of the appeal is its layout, small displays in rooms set around tranquil courtyards. The architecture can be as interesting as what is inside. Be sure to check out the massive thickness of the hand-decorated walls.

The building was founded in 1799 after the original town of Riobamba was destroyed in the 1797 earthquake. It has been a functioning monastery since then. A large part of the collection was brought as dowry by entering nuns. Other displays, such as the outstanding nativities, were created by the sisters themselves.

The objects in each room fall under common themes. Our favorite is room #3, the Nativity Room. This popular art form is absolutely intriguing. The Treasure Room, #14, is another highlight. Even if you're just passing through town, it's worth a detour to visit this fine collection.

Another small museum, the **Cordoba-Román Museum**, *Velasco 24-25 and Veloz*, houses the art collection of the Cordoba-Roman family. The colonial building is closed because it is undergoing restoration, but the work should be finished soon.

Parque Maldonado, *Veloz street between Espejo and 5 de Junio*, is full of people who aren't in a hurry. Bounded by the **cathedral** on one side and salmon-colored municipal building on another, many of the people in town seem to hang out on the benches here. The **cathedral** is surprisingly modern inside once you pass through the stone facade with relief sculptures. It is built with rich wood floors and crossbeams, and has a beautiful, muted mosaic of Jesus with the sun and moon.

Down the street from the cathedral is the **Basilica**, *Veloz and Velasco*, across the street from **Parque La Libertad**. This fabulous structure, built in 1883, features a dome painted in rust and mustard candy cane stripes. On the interior, the dome is coated in vibrant blue and green rococo style, descending to salmon colored arches and columns. The park across the street is expansive. Rest your weary soul on the benches painted with mountain scenes as you contemplate the colors of the Basilica.

Parque Sucre, *10 de Agosto and Larrea*, is edged on one side by the **Colegio Nacional Maldonado**. The park is kind of dirty, but inside the Colegio Nacional you'll find the **National Science Museum**, *Monday-Friday 8am-1pm, 3pm-6pm, Entry $0.50*. The museum houses a collection of stuffed birds and animals that is well worth the visit.

Loma de Quito is a park on the highest hill in town, which offers great views of the city and surrounding volcanoes. The best chance for a clear view is early in the morning. There is a good mural of the conquistadors as well. It's a ways from the city center, so you might consider taking a cab rather than walking here.

Ecuador hosts an array of excellent sculptures, but the striped, tiled **cow statue** at *Borga and León* outdoes most of them.

SPORTS & RECREATION
Biking
With its proximity to Chimborazo, Riobamba is really known as a climber's locale. If you're acclimatized to the altitude however, there are also some nice mountain bike rides. Talk to **Galo Bikes**, *Constituyente 23-51 and Larrea, Tel 942 468*, about renting their good bikes and hiring a guide to take you out.

Climbing
In Chimborazo's backyard, Riobamba is obviously a popular starting point for attempts on the tallest mountain in the country. While Chimborazo is only for experienced climbers, Riobamba is also in striking distance of many of the popular climbing peaks in the Southern Highlands. The best guides in town, all fully licensed, are booked through **Alta Montaña**, *Borja 35-17 and Ibarra, Tel. 963 694, Fax 942 215.*

SHOPPING
While Riobamba is not particularly known for its handicrafts, you can pick up some of the typical highland *artesanía*. We still we wish had bought the pair of wooly alpaca chaps we saw hanging in a shop between the Basilica and Cathedral last time we were there. Wool rugs from nearby Guano are another bargain here.

Thursday and Saturday are market days, with the commerce being spread all over town. It seems like almost every plaza and street has something being bought or sold. Crafts are sold at **Parque de la Concepción**, *Larrea and Orosco*; produce, pottery and baskets at **Plaza Bolívar**, *Tarqui and Argentinos*; and tagua nut products on *Primera Constituyente*.

EXCURSIONS & DAY TRIPS
Chimborazo Volcano
Chimborazo, at 6,310 meters, is the highest mountain in Ecuador. Always snow-capped, its massive summit is actually two volcanoes that have been fused together over time by snow and ice. Ecuadorians like to point out that the mountain's peak is the farthest point on earth from the center of the planet due to the equator's bulge. We have to say that's really searching for a distinction, but you'll hear that fact during your time in the country.

Chimborazo was explored by **Alexander von Humbolt** in 1802. He failed more than once to summit the mountain. **Edward Whymper** had better success, as he was the first person the reach Chimborazo's peak in 1880. Legend says that Simón Bolívar also reached the top of the mountain, after which he returned to Riobamba and wrote *Mi Delirio Sobre Chimborazo*. He really only climbed to the snowline.

Most people who stop by Chimborazo don't intend to summit, but rather just want to walk some of the lower section of the mountain. At 5,000 meters, even this is quite a workout. Many visitors attempt to hike from the lower hut at the end of the road to the Whymper Refuge and then up to the snowline.

You can stay overnight at the Whymper Refuge for $10. You must bring your own sleeping bag and all your supplies. The Refuge has kitchen facilities and a fireplace, but it can get very cold at night. Don't even think about spending the night here if you have not logged some time acclimating to the altitude.

Most of the hotels in town can arrange day trips to Chimborazo for about $35 including lunch.

Guano

Guano, a small town 15 minutes from Riobamba, is a pleasant place famous for its inexpensive wool rugs and wall hangings. Most of this *pueblo* seems to be devoted to the craft. Head to the central plaza where you can see carpet makers working in front of tall vertical looms. Tuesday and Saturday are market days for a little extra Highland color.

Cajabamba

About 20 km south of Riobamba you'll come to the small city of Cajabamba. This quiet town has a very authentic and picturesque market, with many more people speaking Quichua than Spanish. It's definitely worth a stop if you're passing through on Sunday.

Guamote

Guamote, 50 kilometers south of Riobamba on the Panamericana, is another favorite excursion. Its Thursday market is not yet on the tourist track, which means you'll see far more indigenous people going about their weekly shopping than photo-snapping gringos. The train stops through here on the way to Alausí. Guamote is actually a kilometer off the highway. If you just grab a southbound bus you will have to walk down into the valley. Buses to Guamote from the regional terminal in Riobamba go all the way into town.

Alausí

Most people end up in Alausí because they have ridden the train from Riobamba. From here they catch a bus either on to Cuenca or back to Riobamba. You can also drive or bus the 100 km to Alausí and then board the train solely for the hour-long **Devil's Nose** section. Another option is to ride the train from here back to Riobamba, but the uphill chug takes over six hours.

Alausí is also a center of weaving and ceramics.

MORE BRANDY PLEASE

"Then we went even higher, and as the train wound up the steep slopes, we sometimes saw the same landscape beneath us six or seven times from opposite windows. At one point it stopped abruptly, on the side of a precipice, and began hurtling backwards into a valley. I could already picture us being hurled into the abyss below. Then it stopped just as suddenly, and moved forward again with a jerk. This happened several times, and the train conductor, seeing me turn pale, explained that it was quite all right, we were just passing the Nariz del Diablo (The Devil's Nose). We were now some 9,000 feet above sea level, and it was bitterly cold...the hot cinnamon brandy obtainable at stations was very welcome indeed."

– Margret Wittmer in her book, **Floreana**

PRACTICAL INFORMATION

Banks: Filanbanco, *Colón and Primera Constituyente*
Currency Exchange: Casa de Cambios Chimborazo, *10 de Agosto between España and Moreno*
E-Mail Service: there's an internet café across the street from the Hotel Imperial on *Rocafuerte*
National Parks: INEFAN, *9 de Octubre at Ministry of Agriculture Building*
Post Office: Correo, *10 de Agosto and Espejo*
Telephone/Fax: The area code is 3. **EMETEL**, *Veloz and Tarquí*
Tourist Office/Maps: CETUR, *10 de Agosto 2072 and 5 de Junio*

15. SOUTHERN HIGHLANDS

It seems like life in the Southern Highlands, lower in elevation that the Central Highlands, is just a bit easier. Colonial **Cuenca**, with its wonderfully maintained buildings, marvelous art, and cobblestone streets is a perfect place to slow down and stroll for a while.

When you've gotten your fill of the city's excellent museums, head out into the surrounding valleys to experience Highland village life. Life in these small **artisan towns** doesn't appear to have changed much in the last hundred years. Traditionally dressed indigenous women weave sweaters and Panama hats just as their mothers and grandmothers did.

To travel even further back into the past, visit the country's largest Inca ruins at **Ingapirca**. The precision and fit of the stone pieces is a true marvel. You can even hike a section of the famous **Inca Trail**.

Stark buttes and hundreds of lakes await at **El Cajas National Park**. The dramatic landscape here is not to be missed, even if all you're going to do is drive through the park. Further south near **Loja**, **Podocarpus National Park** encompasses expansive high plains, lush cloud forests and over 600 species of birds.

Travelers that make it all the way down to the pleasant valley at **Vilcabamba** are rarely disappointed. This city of longevity, with its mild temperatures and moderately priced lodgings, offers endless kilometers of walks followed by inexpensive professional spa service.

CUENCA

Cuenca is our favorite metropolitan center in Ecuador. Capital of the Azuay province, it is the third largest city in the country, yet still maintains a small town feel. Its pleasantness oozes out of the beautiful colonial downtown featuring exquisite architecture, elaborate churches, excellent museums and well-preserved buildings. Some of the best restaurants in the country, along with beautifully maintained hotels, make the city especially comfortable. Charming markets overflow with flowers, hats and baskets. Add to that interesting day trips and good shopping and you've got an unbeatable combination.

Maybe it's the wrought iron balconies overlooking cobblestone streets that give the city of 330,000 its provincial atmosphere. It could also be the *chola* women with their tall Panama hats and colorful skirts walking past intricately carved heavy wooden doors. Or perhaps it's the metal boot cleaners from another era imbedded in sidewalk in front of homes. Whatever it is, you shouldn't miss it.

History

Cuenca was originally founded as an important Cañari Indian site called *Guapondélig* or Plain of Flowers. Although they defended the territory for years, the Cañari finally fell to the Inca onslaught just two generations before the Spanish arrived. The Inca changed the name of the valley to *Paucarmamba*, Plain of the Birds, and established an important city, **Pumapungo**. You can see the remains of this once grand construction behind the Central Bank Museum.

Cuenca was founded as a Spanish city by conquistador Gil Ramiro Dávalos in 1557 under the name *Santa Ana de los Cuatro Ríos de Cuenca*, or Santa Ana of the Four Rivers of Cuenca. The city, despite the density of impressive buildings downtown that might lead you to believe otherwise, grew slowly until the mid-20th century. Its distance and isolation from both Quito and Guayaquil were the key to its moderate expansion.

Since colonial times Cuenca's economy has been based on agriculture, *artesanía* and mining. Starting in the late 19th century, weaving and exporting of Panama Hats became another important Cuenca business.

SOUTHERN HIGHLAND HIGHLIGHTS

Any trip to the Southern Highlands would be incomplete if it did not include colonial **Cuenca**. *This delightful city is one of the country's true treasures. The grandeur and stark beauty of* **El Cajas National Park** *should also be covered in your itinerary as a wonderful, complementary contrast to Cuenca. If you haven't gotten a chance to visit one of the* **indigenous markets** *in another part of the country, you'll really enjoy the Sunday morning artisan towns tour. Take a shopping bag and plenty of film. For a place to unpack your bags and hang out a while,* **Vilcabamba** *is one of the most mellow and agreeable spots we've found. Long walks and spa treatments are the perfect antidote to the stresses of normal life.*

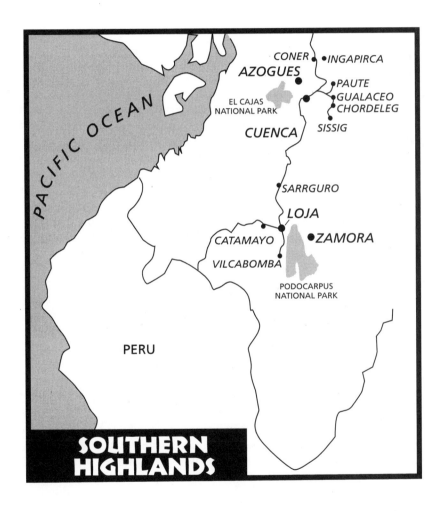

PACIFIC OCEAN

CONER • • INGAPIRCA
AZOGUES •
• PAUTE
EL CAJAS • GUALACEO
NATIONAL PARK • CHORDELEG
CUENCA SISSIG

SARRGURO

LOJA
CATAMAYO • ZAMORA
VILCABOMBA
PODOCARPUS
NATIONAL PARK

PERU

SOUTHERN
HIGHLANDS

ARRIVALS & DEPARTURES

By Air

There are daily flight to Cuenca from both Quito and Guayaquil. Austro Aero has flights from Cuenca to Macas. The airport, east of town, *Tel. 800 095*, is located at *España and Elia Liut.*

• **TAME,** *Benigno Malo 5-05 and Larga. Tel. 843 222*
• **SAN,** *Benigno Malo 7-27. Tel. 839 090*
• **Austro Aero,** *Miguel 5-42. Tel 848 659*

By Bus

If you are coming to Cuenca from the north, our suggestion is to fly if you can afford it. The Pan-American Highway from Cuenca to Riobamba is a pothole strewn, back-crunching mess. If that doesn't fit your budget or itinerary, then there are plenty of buses from all points north on the *Pana.* It takes about five hours to make the bus trip from Riobamba to Cuenca and about ten from Quito.

If you ride the train from the Riobamba to the Devil's Nose, you can catch a bus on to Cuenca when you get off the train in Alausi. The buses are waiting right outside the station. It's about a four-hour trip from Alausi to Cuenca because of all the mountains you have to climb and the condition of the highway.

The road to Cuenca from Guayaquil has its own hazards. While it's in better shape than the *Panamericana*, it winds down some very foggy mountain roads. Try to travel in the morning to avoid the fog. Depending on conditions, the trip takes about five hours. San Luis is the best bus company to take to Guayaquil. There are also regularly buses to Cuenca from Loja in the south. Again, because of the terrible state of the road, the trip takes about four or five hours.

The main bus station in Cuenca, *Tel. 823 060*, is on *Avenida España.*

By Car

There's some rough, difficult driving to get to Cuenca from all directions. The roads are in pathetic condition and there are also many foggy mountain passes. If you do drive, it's 150 kilometers from Cuenca to Riobamba, 205 km to Loja, 250 km to Guayaquil and 250 km to Macas.

It takes about five hours to get from Cuenca to Riobamba, Loja and Guayaquil depending on road conditions. The trip to Macas, via Gualaceo, takes around seven hours. It's a beautiful descent into the rainforest from the Highland *páramo.*

Car Rental Companies
•**Localiza,** *España 1485 and Granada. Tel. 863 902, Fax 860 174.*

ORIENTATION
Cuenca, located in the southern third of the Highlands, sits nestled in a fertile valley fed by four rivers, the Tomebamba, Yanuncay, Tarqui and Machángara. Lower in elevation than the Highlands to the north, the valleys around Cuenca are mild and productive. The clear Tomebamba River, draining down from **El Cajas National Park** to the west, cuts through the middle of town. On the north side of the river lies Colonial Cuenca, centered around **Calderón Park**. On the south side, Modern Cuenca sparkles with glass paneled office buildings, universities and fancy suburbs.

GETTING AROUND TOWN
You can easily walk to cover all the sights in colonial Cuenca. In fact, street reconstruction projects make it the easiest way to get around. If you prefer to ride however, taxis troll the streets and can also be found on many of the downtown plazas. After hoofing it around on cobblestone all day, we find no shame in taking a cab those six blocks to dinner.

WHERE TO STAY
Our favorite hotels in Cuenca are housed in old colonial buildings. You'll find many of them built around a roofed courtyard, a common architectural style brought over from Andalusía in Spain.

Note that it's hard to escape street noise in colonial Cuenca. Traffic sounds tend to bounce off the cobblestones and up the sides of buildings. To add to that, you've got roosters crowing in the middle of the city. When we say a hotel is quiet, that's usually a relative term, but nothing that a good pair of earplugs won't take care of.

Expensive
HOTEL ORO VERDE, *Avenida Oróñez Lazo. Tel. 7/831 200, Fax. 7/ 832 849; E-mail: ecovc@gye.satnet.net. 79 rooms. Double $160. Cable TV. Restaurant. Bar. Pool. Gym. Sauna. Conference facilities. Business Center. Credit cards accepted.*

The Oro Verde chain offers consistent excellence. The Cuenca hotel is no exception. About a five-minute cab ride from the center of town, the hotel is built over a serene lagoon. You could probably dive in from your window, but the pool might be a better choice. It shares the same view of the lagoon that the rooms do. The reception area is stylish and comfortable, featuring crosshatched exposed wooden beams and modern sculpture. The doubles are ample and finely furnished with plush reading chairs. The main restaurant here is one of the best in the city. There is also an excellent deli with whole grain breads used as a base for hearty sandwiches.

Moderate

HOTEL CRESPO, *Larga 793 and Cordero. Tel. 7/842 571, Fax 7/839 473; E-mail: hcrespo@az.pro.ec; Website: www.ecuadorexplorer.com/crespo/. 39 rooms. Double $42. Breakfast included. Restaurant. Credit cards accepted.*

The Crespo is our favorite lodging option in Cuenca. The colonial building, 130 years old, sits on the edge of the Tomebamba river in the town's historical center. The wooden highlights, high ceilings and hand painted molding in both the rooms and common areas give the Crespo a warmth and personality that other high-end hotels in Cuenca cannot match.

While the Crespo enjoys a long tradition as a first rate hotel, it hasn't rested on its laurels. Almost all of the rooms have been redecorated in the last two years, offering guests welcome comfort in a traditional setting. New carpets, sparkling bathrooms, central heat, big cable TVs and minibars make you want to settle in and stay awhile. Rooms upstairs overlooking the river enjoy some of the best views in town. You can sit on your bed and watch the light and shadows play across the green hills in the afternoon. The Crespo's restaurant shares the same good views. After dinner you might want to try some of the locally made sugarcane alcohol in the El Alambique bar.

HOTEL EL DORADO, *Gran Colombia 7-87 and Cordero. Tel. 7/831 390, Fax 7/831 663; E-mail: eldorado@cue.satnet.net. 91 rooms. Double $55. Breakfast and airport transfer included. Restaurant. Cafe. Bar. Sauna. Steam room. Massage. Credit cards accepted.*

The El Dorado, smack in the center of old Cuenca, offers all the amenities you could want in a hotel, but lacks the personality and charm of the like-priced Crespo. While the large, comfortable rooms have been updated recently, the hallways and elevator are a bit shabby. This is a nice hotel, but if you're going to stay in the historic part of town, you might as well go all the way and stay in a historic building instead of a tall box. If you do stay here, ask for a room on one of the top floors facing the cathedral for nice views.

Inexpensive

INCA REAL, *General Torres 8-40, between Sucre and Bolívar. Tel. 7/823-636 or 825 571, Fax 7/840 699; E-mail: incareal@cue.satnet.net. 25 rooms. Double $36. Restaurant. TV. Credit cards accepted.*

The Inca Real, an excellent option for your stay in Cuenca, is a beautiful converted colonial mansion dating from the 1820s. Enter the hotel through immense ornately carved wooden doors and you will tread upon equally seductive wooden stairs and floorboards. Two glass-covered inner courtyards house the comfortable rooms overlooking tidy gardens. Each of the courtyards distinguishes itself through its pastel color base of yellow or baby blue, while both share fanciful white trim. The rooms are comfortable and relatively quiet considering your location in the heart of Colonial Cuenca.

POSADA DEL SOL, *Bolívar 5-03 and Mariano Cueva. Tel. 7/838 695 or 838 995. 12 rooms. Double $30. Breakfast included. Restaurant. Credit cards accepted.*

The colors of a brilliant sunset grace the upstairs portion of the glass-covered courtyard of this colonial edifice. Indulgent yellow and red walls envelope the common area where guests lounge on the comfortable sofa in front of a crackling fire. Several of the rooms boast small wrought iron balconies overlooking Cuenca's attractive, lively streets. A delicious Hindu vegetarian restaurant, Govinda's, is on the first floor.

HOTEL CUENCA, *Borreo 10-69 and Gran Columbia. 7/833 711, Fax 7/833 819. 34 rooms. Double $22. Breakfast included. Restaurant. Cable TV. Credit cards accepted.*

The Hotel Cuenca has a promising shell in an old mansion, but the cheap, modern furnishings doom its potential. The rooms are clean and come with cable.

HOTEL EL CONQUISTADOR, *Gran Colombia 6-65 and Miguel. Tel. 7/841 703, Fax 7/831 291; E-mail: hconquis@etapa.com.ec. 43 rooms. Double $34. Restaurant. Bar. Business center. Credit cards accepted.*

The El Conquistador, in a modern building, is a popular place with mid-level Ecuadorian managers. It offers such extras as cable TV, a minibar and direct dial phones, but the rooms are quite small. They have a 24-room annex that offers the same quality lodging at *Sucre 6-78 and Borrero.*

HOTEL PRESIDENTE, *Gran Colombia 6-59 and Miguel. Tel. 7/831 066, Fax 7/842 127; E-mail: htl_pres@etapa.com.ec. 70 rooms. Double $26. Restaurant. Bar. Credit cards accepted.*

Next door to El Conquistador, El Presidente offers similar modern lodging in a similar clean but flavorless environment.

CABANAS CABOGANA, *San Miguel de Putuzhi. Tel. 7/894 044, Fax 7/894 925. Apartment with kitchen $20. Restaurant. Horseback riding. Fishing. Game room. Playground. Credit cards accepted.*

We really like the city-scene in Cuenca and can't imagine staying outside of town. If you have kids however, you might want to consider these cabins in the woods. You would need to have your own transportation, but if you stayed here you could tour town in the morning and then come back and let the kids run around here in the afternoon. You could also cook your own meals, which is sometimes nice. These apartments, in a lovely garden setting, all come with fireplaces and well-stocked kitchens. You can even catch your own trout for dinner in the stream or stocked pond. There's also horseback riding and hiking.

Budget

MACONDO, *Tarqui 11-64 and Lamar. Tel. 7/840 697, Fax 7/833 593; E-mail: macondo@cedei.org.ec. 25 rooms. Double $16 with bath, $12 shared bath. Breakfast included. No credit cards.*

This pleasant hostel is one of the best bargains in the country. The colonial style home has not only a nice covered patio, but also a large, quiet garden through the back of the house. The spacious rooms, with their traditional high ceilings, are clean and comfortable.

You get some really nice extras here that you usually don't find in budget hotels. The garden is a wonderful place to hang out and relax, the hotel can arrange tours of the surrounding area, the pancakes are delicious and kitchen is fully available to guests. Many people who can afford to spend much more money choose to stay here simply because it is so agreeable.

The rooms upstairs are a little loud, but they are large enough to stage a ballet. Any room in the main house is not a quiet as those in the back around the garden, simply because the wooden floor in the house is so well polished that it squeaks.

HOSTAL LA ORQUIDEA, *Borrero 9-31 and Bolívar. Tel. 7/824 511, Fax 7/835 844. 16 rooms. Double $13. Restaurant. TV. No credit cards.*

An exceedingly amiable place to hang your hat and a superb value, La Orquidea is set, like many Cuenca hotels, in a quaint old house. The entryway is tiled in an enchanting red, yellow, and cream colored design. The simple rooms fill up quickly so be sure to reserve in advance to assure yourself of the "aroma of comfort" as their tagline asserts.

HOSTAL CHORDALEG, *Gran Colombia 11-15 and General Torres. Tel. 7/822536 or 824611. 14 rooms. Double $15. Breakfast included. TV. Credit cards accepted.*

With gorgeous natural wood courtyard, this century old house comes in just behind the Orquidea and Macondo in terms of personality and quality for your *sucre*. It is a good choice for this price range if the other two are full.

HOTEL COLONIAL, *Gran Colombia 10-13 and Aguirre. Tel/Fax. 7/ 841 664; E-mail: hcolonial@cue.satnet.net. 12 rooms. Double $14. Breakfast included. No credit cards.*

The Colonial is another decent option in the budget category. The colonial building features a covered courtyard that has been converted into a restaurant. The rooms, although a bit dated, unexpectedly have TVs and private baths. Be warned that it can get loud when the restaurant is at full tilt.

CAFECITO, *Vásquez near Cordero. Ten rooms. Double with shared bath, $4. Restaurant. Bar. No credit cards.*

If you need to go low, low budget, this is the place for you. This popular café and bar offers a few Spartan rooms in back.

HOSTAL CARIBE INN, *Gran Colombia 10-51 and General Torres. Tel. 7/826 227. 30 rooms. Double $6. No credit cards.*

This place has some enticing neon in the entryway, but the rooms smell really bad. Go elsewhere.

WHERE TO EAT

ORO VERDE RESTAURANT, *Ave. Oróñez Lazo. Tel. 7/831 200. Expensive. Credit cards accepted.*

The Oro Verde Hotel's restaurant is a class act that serves up delicious fare. The restaurant offers Swiss specialties such as fondue; superb meat like lamb chops in mint sauce; and outstanding seafood such as shrimp in vodka sauce. If these entrees are too rich for your taste, opt for the sea bass fish sticks with tartar sauce. Vegetable lovers should try the baked ratatouille with cheese. This superb casserole is replete with vegetables, cooked without sacrificing crispness, and topped with rich, perfectly browned cheese.

VILLA ROSA, *Gran Colombia 12-22 and Montalvo. Tel. 837 944. Moderate/Expensive. Credit cards accepted.*

Villa Rosa is near the top of our "Best Restaurants in Ecuador" list. You just know when you walk into the marble-floored colonial home and sit down on the stained glass covered patio that this is going to be a meal to remember. Pewter plate chargers, freshly ironed linens and tuxedoed waiters are further signs that they do things right here.

Once you start to eat however, everything else is forgotten as the quality of the food steals the show. The international menu features enticing and unique dishes prepared to perfection. The trout, one of Villa Rosa's specials, melts in your mouth as its subtle flavors massage your palate. You just can't go wrong with anything you order.

Save room for dessert though. The mint ice cream pie with chocolate crust can only be categorized as divine. The chocolate fruit fondue is another work of art. Even the chocolates they give you with your bill at the end of the meal are worthy of savoring.

Villa Rosa is not open on weekends.

EL PEDREGAL AZTECA, *Gran Columbia 10-29 y Padre Aguirre. Tel. 7/823 652. Moderate. Credit cards accepted.*

The Mexican owner of this wonderful restaurant proudly exhibits a "No Tex-Mex" sign on the door of his truly authentic Mexican restaurant.

Photos of Golden Era Mexican film stars such as Dolores Del Rio, Cantinflas, and Pedro Infante share the walls of the main room with pop icon Luis Miguel and revolutionary Pancho Villa.

To start the dining experience as a Mexican would, dive into the salsa ranchera with homemade corn chips and sip an añejo tequila - Cuervo 1800, while washing it all back with a Corona or Tecate. We heartily endorse the *queso fundido con chorizo* as an appetizer, (a bowl of melted cheese with spicy sausage that you wrap in tortillas). After that, you might opt a for a poblano chile stuffed with your choice of chicken, beef, or cheese or the savory enchiladas verdes.

Don't miss the opportunity to sate your craving for Mexican food at El Pedregal Azteca or the owner's new restaurant **Los Chilangos,** *Crespo 3-43.*

LOS CAPULIES, *Córdova and Borrero. Tel. 832 339. Moderate. Credit cards accepted.*

Los Capulies is an excellent spot to delve into typical Ecuadorian food. A small fountain in the corner and vines growing around the upstairs balcony make it feel as if you have been invited back in time to dine on the patio of one of Cuenca's wealthier residents.

A steaming bowl of *mote*, hominy, and *ají*, chile sauce arrives to the table as soon as you sit down. Enjoy a few bites of this before looking over the menu of traditional dishes. The plates here are all quite good, but we highly recommend the *seco de chivo*, kid stew over rice, or the *ensalada mixta*, a generous portion of plump shrimp served with lettuce, avocado, tomato, bell pepper, and cheese. Attentive waiters and artful presentation enhance the experience.

Thursday, Friday and Saturday you can hear Andean music with your meal from 8:30-11:30. You might want to take a jacket if the weather is cool because the patio can be chilly at times.

CUISINE CUENQUEÑA

Try some of these traditional foods in the restaurants and markets in the province:
- **Mote** – *cooked hominy corn*
- **Mote Pillo** – *hominy with eggs and onions*
- **Mote Pata** – *thick corn soup with pork*
- **Fritada** – *fried pork*
- **Papas con Cuero** – *potatoes and roasted pork skin*
- **Ají de Cuy** – *Guinea pig with french fries and hot sauce*
- **Chicha** – *fermented corn flour drink*

EL JARDIN, *Córdova 7-23 and Borrero. Tel. 831 120. Moderate. Credit cards accepted.*

Across the street from Los Capulies, El Jardín is another decent Cuenca dining option. There are many things about the restaurant that make it top-notch. To say the service is excellent is almost an understatement. The tuxedo-clad waiters are some of the best in Ecuador. From the moment you sit down and your napkin is placed in your lap, you are well attended. We appreciate the details of El Jardín. Your water glass is full at all times, as is your wine glass if you have ordered a bottle of the Chilean nectar. Your breadbasket, brimming with tasty garlic bread, is continually refilled through out the evening. As an extra bonus, all meals come with a fresh salad that is not even mentioned on the menu.

The menu, a sheet of velum the size of bedside table top, features mainly seafood and steak options. While of high quality ingredients, the entrees lack a bit of pizzazz. We order our seafood *al ajillo*, with garlic, to give it the punch to match the outstanding service.

LA CASONA, *Larga 793 and Cordero. Tel. 842 571. Moderate. Credit cards accepted.*

The Hotel Crespo's La Casona restaurant is known in town for its tasty trout and good views over the Tomebamba River. We're just as impressed with the elaborately carved wooden doors leading into the dining area. Keep your eyes peeled for Olympic medal winner Jefferson Perez, Cuenca's most famous native son, who enjoys many meals here when he is in town.

INTI SUMAG, *Gran Colombia 7-87 and Cordero. Tel. 831 390 Moderate. Credit cards accepted.*

Located on the 6th floor of the Hotel El Dorado, the Inti Sumag offers well-prepared international food. The Sunday brunch is especially popular because you can really enjoy the nice views of Parque Maldonado and the New Cathedral. Make other plans for Saturday, however, because they are closed all day.

GOVINDAS, *Bolívar 5-03 and Mariano Cueva. Tel. 838 695. Moderate. Credit cards accepted.*

This stylish Hindu vegetarian restaurant is one of the best options in town for a lighter meal, packed with flavor. It features a long list of chutneys and curries that are a nice break from the meat and potato routine.

CASA GRANDE, *Cordero y main plaza. Inexpensive. No credit cards.*

The Casa Grande is the place to go to please a crew with diverse tastes because it has one of longest menus conceived. With everything from soups to ceviches to pastas to *humitas*, surely you can find something to suit your taste buds here. This is a student hangout with a nice interior garden to enjoy on a warm day.

PIZZARIA LA TUNA, *Gran Colombia 868 and Malo. Inexpensive. No credit cards.*

La Tuna serves good 'za with crispy crust, plenty of cheese and fresh toppings. We like to defile the vegetarian pizza by adding *salami*, pepperoni. The old west decor, with wooden benches and wagon wheels might explain why they also offer good shish kebobs, *pinchos.*

Just down the street, **Los Pibes**, *Gran Colombia 7-56*, is another pizza option, but we don't think it's as good. **Pizza Goura**, *Juan Jaramillo and Borrero,* offers palatable pizzas and vegetarian food.

CAFECITO, *Vásquez near Cordero. Inexpensive. No credit cards.*

This laid back cafe is a courtyard hangout. Mellow music, cheap beers and good sandwiches and salads make it popular with budget travelers.

DELICATESSEN EL DORADO, *Cordero y Gran Colombia. Inexpensive. No credit cards.*

This deli is a good spot to pick up sandwiches or fixin's for a picnic lunch or hike. And if you're in need of a cup of java, the **Cinema Cafe**, *inside the Teatro Casa de Cultura, Cordero and Sucre,* offers coffees, hot chocolates and appetizers to help you make it through the double features.

If it's a sweet tooth you've got, head straight to the **Heladería Holandesa**, *Malo 9-65*. The rich ice cream is the most popular item, but they also serve shakes, cookies, and cakes. For great banana splits, try **Raymipampa,** *Calderón Park*

SEEING THE SIGHTS

It's important to take note that almost everything in Cuenca closes on Saturday afternoon and stays closed on Sunday. If want to arrange any excursions for Saturday afternoon or Sunday, do it on or before Saturday morning. Many of the museums and the best restaurant are only open Monday-Friday, so you might want to plan your trip accordingly.

Colonial Walking Tour

We have outlined a half-day walking tour to introduce you to the feeling of Colonial Cuenca. Start your visit to Cuenca at **Calderón Park**, *Cordero between Sucre and Bolívar*. This park, in the center of the city, is the site of both the Old and New cathedrals as well as the town Municipal Building and elaborate Justice Building. A statue of Capitán Calderón, surrounded by tall fir trees, sits at the park's center.

Calderón, from Cuenca, was an independence fighter who distinguished himself at the important Battle of Pichincha and died of his injuries the next day. The park's red benches seem to be magnets for old men sharing stories and getting their shoes shined. Families pose for photos, kids run around playing chase, and *chola* women hurry along in their distinctive hats and skirts.

The Old Cathedral, started when the city was founded in 1557, wasn't impressive enough for Cuenca, which is the only city in Ecuador to have two cathedrals on its main plaza. The Old Cathedral, used as a measuring point for the French Geodesic Expedition, is now in the restoration process to become a religious art museum.

CHOLA FASHION

Cholas, or Cuenca mestizas, are ubiquitous sights on the streets of town. We love the way these women dress. First, perched on top of their glossy black braids, you'll see the famous Panama hats. Many of the cholas are the weavers of these celebrated chapeaus.

Next you've got their colorful skirts. They actually wear two skirts, which is what gives them that less-than-sleek profile. (That, and a few thousand potatoes in a lifetime.) The underskirt, or bolsico, is generally flannel. The falda, worn over the bolsico is the colorful skirt with embroidered trim.

NEW CATHEDRAL, *Calderón Park, Cordero and Sucre.*

Immense just doesn't seem big enough to describe the inside of this cavernous cathedral. Ten thousand people fit inside the three gigantic naves. There are quite a few things to admire here, but one of the most striking is the elaborate stained glass windows created by Basque settler Guillermo Larrazabal. Once your eyes adjust to the dim light filtering through the colored panes, you can also admire the large altar canopy covered with gold leaf. Flickering candlelight projects from the numerous side altars where people pray at all hours of the day. The faithful making their way through the building include ancient nuns, pious indigenous people and preoccupied mestizo businessmen. Echoes bounce off the marble floor traveling up and around the multiple domes. Don't miss the great central door on your way out, carved by one of Ecuador's leading sculptures.

The tawny brick building, begun in 1885, looks like a mishmash of architectural styles from the outside. A heavy, pink marble façade weights the front of the building, while incongruent but beautiful blue and white domes hover in the background above.

PLAZA DE LAS FLORES, *Sucre and Padre Aguirre.*

Just around the corner from the New Cathedral you'll see the small **Plazotela del Carmen**, overflowing with flowers. The *chola* women with their buckets of blossoms for sale are one of our favorite scenes of Cuenca. With the white backdrop of the **El Carmen de la Asunción Church** behind them, the vibrancy of the flowers and women's laughter draws us here every day we are in town. There's a small fountain in the middle of the plaza that's a favorite meeting point for the women.

The walls behind the plaza are part of the **Carmen Monastery**. The barefoot nuns in here, supposedly only six of them, live a life of constant prayer. They can't receive anybody from the outside world, not even doctors.

Plaza San Francisco lies just across the street from the flower market at *Aguirre and Sucre*. This entire plaza is a daily clothes market. Most items of interest for tourists are found along its northern edge on Sucre.

SAN FRANCISCO CHURCH, *Plaza San Francisco, Córdova and Aguirre*.

This tan and white church, with its distinctive clock tower, looks quite modern, as it has been remodeled in the 20th century. The interior is light and airy with the exception of its large baroque altarpiece. This 18th century work is the finest in Cuenca. Notice the Solomonic columns that twist elaborately up its face. In the center nook you can admire one of famous sculptor Bernardo Legarda's Immaculate Virgins.

Heading east down *Córdova to the intersection with Borrero*, you will see the unmistakable whitewashed bell gable of **La Concepción Church**. The church, built at the end of the 17th century, is the only one in Ecuador with such a front. Take a stroll down Borrero to admire the intricately carved wooden doors, a true city treasure. Across from the doors on the other side of Borrero there're some wonderfully restored colonial buildings that have been converted to shops.

Continuing down Córdova, take a right on Hermano Miguel to reach one of the finest museums of colonial religious art in the country.

MUSEO DEL MONASTERIO DE LAS CONCEPTAS, *Hermano Miguel 6-33. Monday-Friday 9am-5:30 pm; Saturday 10am-1pm. Closed Sunday. Entry $2.*

This beautiful museum in an 18th monastery may convert those lukewarm on religious art into ardent enthusiasts. The monastery, which was built with the dowries of the women who joined the convent, wraps around a quaint interior garden bedded with hydrangeas, roses, and agapantha. The rooms resonate with a solemnity of thick adobe walls and uneven brick floors. The number of pieces in each room is kept to a minimum to heighten the impact.

The **Retablo Navideño** in room eight is one of our favorite pieces of artwork in Ecuador. This energetic nativity scene is colossal, measuring one and a half meters high and three meters wide. Mary and Joseph dominate the magnificent main panel amid a flurry of gold, silver, and mirrored ornamentation. Below them is nestled a diminutive Baby Jesus. The hinged side panels represent the hills of Cuenca with several of the local churches protruding from them. In front of the panels march an eclectic procession of figurines that include cherubs, Africans in native dress, llamas, camels, and a bright green parrot.

In room nine, the **Degollación de los Inocentes** is an appropriately gruesome depiction of Herod's men following his orders to decapitate all of Egypt's infants. Other intriguing items include ancient toys that nuns donated when they joined the monastery. There is an admirable collection of carvings and paintings by leading religious artists such as Thomas del Castillo and Miguel Vásquez. Poke around downstairs or you're liable to miss a few of the areas that are open to the public.

Museums

MODERN ART MUSEUM, *Sucre and Talbot. Monday-Friday 8:30am-6:30pm. Saturday-Sunday, 9am-3pm. No entry fee.*

We quite enjoy the Cuenca MOMA. The colonial building, with impatiens and daisy-ringed courtyards, is a pleasant space to enjoy art. This building, six blocks west of Calderón Park, was once the city's House of Temperance. Citizens, most notably clergymen, came here to dry out after their binges. Interesting sculptures decorate the courtyards, making them part of the exhibition space. The paintings displayed are of varying quality, but some of the pieces are quite nice. Keep wandering back and through the building to find more and more salons.

Just a few blocks from the museum, the **Clínica Bolívar** on *Bolívar and Montalvo* is another outstanding example of the fine restoration job done on many of Cuenca's buildings.

CENTRAL BANK MUSEUM, *Calle Larga and Huyana-Capac. Tel. 831 255. Monday-Friday 9am-5pm. Saturday 9am-1pm. Entry $1.*

This is an excellent museum. While the colonial art here is superb, the landscape and *Indianismo* sections contain the most distinctive works. You can observe wonderful representations of jungle landscape, which isn't even that easy to take a picture of. Volcanoes like Tungurahua also inspired several works. The *Indianismo* movement shifted the subject matter away from religious art to a depiction of native life that was supposedly more realistic, but looks provocatively surreal in many aspects. Find where you fit in on the work entitled "La Vida del Hombre". We are between the ages of virility and discretion.

A fantastic ethnic exhibit dominates the second floor. It guides you from culture to culture by leading you through superbly replicated dwellings of each of the ethnic groups. This exhibit helps reinforce a lot of what you have learned about the Ecuadorian people and is quite entertaining.

There is also an exhibit on money in the basement. The show displays Ecuador's legal tender for the past five centuries.

In the bank's back yard are the extensive ruins of **Pumapungo**. This was one of the most important Inca sites in all South American during the half century of their active military expansion to the north. Studies of the crumbling walls show that this was a substantial religious, political and administrative center. One of the most interesting sights is a reproduction of the Convent of the Virgins of the Sun. Recent excavations have uncovered dozens of graves, including one embellished with 900 pieces of gold.

An exhibit corresponds to the ruins on the first floor, so its good to check that one out just before going outside.

TODOS LOS SANTOS PARK AND MUSEUM, *Calle Larga and Vega. Tel. 832 639. Monday-Friday 8am-12pm, 2pm-6pm. Entry $0.50.*

Todos Los Santos is really nothing more than a pleasant little garden with some very basic ruins in it, but it's the layering of these past cultures that makes it so interesting. You need all of about five minutes to walk through the place, but it's worth it. A pathway on this small site leads through vestiges of past ages. You can see fragments from 16th 17th and 20th century mills as well as Cañari and Inca walls. It's interesting to note how the Incas built over the rudimentary Cañari structures while the Spaniard then used the precisely carved Inca blocks to construct their mills. There is a small museum next door with some of the archeological pieces found on the site.

Todos Los Santos is just one long block down Calle Large from the Central Bank Museum.

REMIGIO CRESPO MUNICIPAL MUSEUM, *Larga and Borrero. Monday-Friday 9am-6pm, Saturday-Sunday 9am-2pm. Entry $0.50.*

This small museum inside the old home of one of the city's most important families offers a little bit of everything. There is a small archeology floor featuring some beautiful obsidian arrowheads, a few nice pieces of ceramics, and a floor showcasing Cuenca history. In the Cuenca section there is a display of old photos of Cuenca and some handsome old books with the town's records from 1557-1563. It's kind of quirky, but it's nice and bite-sized.

This museum is six blocks west of the Todos Los Santos Ruins on Calle Larga.

CIPAD FOLKART MUSEUM, *Miguel 3-23 and 3 de Noviembre. Monday-Friday 9:30am-1pm, 2:30pm-6pm. Saturday 9am-12pm. No entry fee.*

Right on the edge of the Tomebamba River, this museum houses a nice collection of Ecuadorian folk art as well as an excellent little crafts shop. You might have to pass by here a few times to find it open as actual working hours seem to be quite different than the times posted. They tend to open late and sometimes, especially on Saturday, not at all. This museum is right behind the Remigio Crespo Museum on the river.

From the museum you can walk *along the Tomebamba River* to enjoy what Cuenqueños call **El Vado**. This neighborhood, with its classic architecture, is the most traditional area of the city. The best time to go is in the morning when you can watch women wash their clothes along the shore and leave to dry in colorful patterns in the grass like a Cristo art work.

ABORIGINAL CULTURE MUSEUM, *10 de Agosto 4-70. Monday-Friday 9:am-12pm, 2pm-6pm. Entry $5.*

If you haven't seen enough ceramics, you can come here for a dose of 5,000 pieces of Ecuadorian archeology. The museum is actually quite well done, but it's a little overwhelming, especially if you have already been to the Central Bank Museum.

HOSPITAL MUSEUM, *12 de Abril across the river from the Hotel Crespo. Monday-Friday 8:30am-12pm, 2:30pm-5pm. Entry $0.50.*

If old instruments of torture interest you, check out this medical museum right across the river from the Hotel Crespo. Walk into the courtyard, past the rabies clinic and the entrance to the museum is next to the church.

MUSEUM OF THE ARTS OF FIRE, *Calle de la Herrerias and 10 de Agosto. Monday-Friday 8:30am-12pm, 2:30pm-5pm. Entry $1.*

This museum was still in the installation process when this book went to print, but the idea is to showcase the ceramic arts. There's a fantastic sculpture out front of a man made of steel rising out of the molten lava of a volcano. If the quality of the sculpture is any indication, this will be a great museum.

Other

TURI, *three kilometers south of colonial Cuenca up Solano.*

The small village of Turi sits high on a hill overlooking Cuenca offering spectacular views of town and the black and olive hills beyond. Only ten minutes by taxi from downtown, this is a worthwhile escape from the *centro*. There is a **lookout point** in front of the church with a neat tile map of town. If it's a nice day, we suggest taking a lunch and using the provided picnic tables.

In the **church**, on the iron grill to the left as you enter, you'll find little bags filled with hair, sand, photos and feathers. These appeals to the Virgin are an example of how indigenous religious practices have melded into their own unique version of Catholicism.

Across the street to the right, as you leave the church, you'll see some stairs that lead up to the **Grotto of the Virgin**. Hike up here for great looks down into the valleys that lead away from Cuenca.

NIGHTLIFE & ENTERTAINMENT

The Municipality of Cuenca publishes a monthly events calendar with information about art-house movies, plays and expositions. The leaflet, printed on Kraft paper, can be found in museums and hotels around town. The **Teatro Casa de la Cultura**, *Cordero between Sucre and Córdova*, specializes in double features.

The **Wunderbar**, *down the steps towards the river at Miguel and Larga*, is a popular traveler's pub. The old building has a slick brick and wood interior, with patio tables sitting over the Tomebamba River.

You might want to time your trip to be in Cuenca during **Carnival**, when the whole city turns into one big water fight interrupted only by drinking and over eating. Another excellent festival here is **Pase del Niño**, the night before Christmas. Children parade through the streets on festooned horses, donkeys, and floats.

SPORTS & RECREATION

Biking

Explorabike, *Juan Jaramillo 910 and Hermano Miguel, Tel. 883 362,* will set you up with a bike and point you in the right direction. You also have the options of hiring a guide here.

Hiking

Nearby El Cajas National Park is the most popular place for hiking. (See *Excursions & Day Trips* below).

SHOPPING

Cuenca is one of the best cities in the country to buy **religious art and antiques**. Most of the antique stores are concentrated on *Córdova between Cordero and Miguel*. If you see a piece you like, bargain hard as they will come down significantly in price if you work it.

Cuenca is also famous as the country's production center for **Panama Hats**. If you are interested in buying one, the best place in town is **Homero Ortega & Hijos**, *684 Hermano Miguel*. If they don't have the style or grade you want, try their less conveniently located main store at *Davalos 3-86, Tel. 823 429*. Remember, the closer and smaller the weave, the better the hat. You can try to buy a hat directly from the weavers at *Plaza María Auxiliadora*

If it's **jewelry** you're after, try the shops on *Gran Colombia*. Wondering why all the jewelry shops are next door to each other? Old zoning laws used to divide the city by type of commercial activity.

CUENCA & THE PANAMAS

Keep your eyes peeled as you walk through the streets of Cuenca for women carrying a few long strands of toquilla straw. If you watch their hands, many times you'll see that they are actually weaving the crown of a Panama hat. Their fingers fly without pause as they scurry around absorbed in other activities.

The best hats, known for their flexibility and extremely tight weave, can cost hundreds of dollars even in Ecuador because they take up to eight months to weave.

On the west side of Plaza San Francisco, at *Torres 7-33* is a Municipal building. Inside you'll find the *Casa de Mujer Centro Artesanal*, or **Women's Artisan Center**. The quality is hit or miss, but it's worth nosing around. Outside on the north side of the Plaza along *Sucre* you'll find sweaters and other textiles.

For **baskets and ceramics**, try the daily market at *Sangurlma and 9 de Octubre*. The baskets are not made for tourists, but rather as the means for the *chola* women to carry their purchases. That doesn't mean they are not a terrific buy. Thursday is the biggest market day in Cuenca.

EXCURSIONS & DAY TRIPS

Many tour companies in town offer trips to sights in the surrounding areas. **Expediciones Apullacta**, *Gran Colombia 11-02, second floor, Tel. 837 815, after hours cellular Tel. 9/604 870, E-mail: apu@az.pro.ec*, offers trips to El Cajas on Monday, Wednesday, and Friday and to Ingapirca on Tuesday, Thursday, and Saturday. On Sunday they make the rounds of the artisan towns (Gualaceo, Chordeleg, Sigsig, Bulcay). They provide an English-speaking guide, private transportation and a box lunch.

Ecorutas Adventure Tours, *Calle Larga y Padre Aguirre, Tel. 831 295* is for people who like to put a more active spin to their outings.

You can also try an English-speaking private guide such as **Luis Astudillo**, *Tel. 815 234*, or **Martin Aguila**, *Tel. 880 193 or cellular 09/761 356*.

Artesania Towns

This Sunday outing takes you into the valleys surrounding Cuenca to enjoy the markets and crafts of the small villages. Each village in the surrounding area is known for some type of handiwork or another – there are hat makers, weavers, guitar makers and goldsmiths. The most popular trip is the Gualaceo-Chordeleg-Sigsig route.

Gualaceo

The approximately 45-minute trip down the valley along the Gualaceo River is very scenic, with layer upon layer of hills stretching beyond the excellent paved road. Five rivers actually run through the canton, making it one of the most fertile and beautiful valleys in the Southern Highlands.

The **Gualeceo market** is just next to the Cathedral off the main square. This clean, colorful market, featuring mainly fruits and vegetables, is one of our favorites. Women wearing Panama hats and colorful embroidered shirts pile their goods into strong-handled straw baskets. Fragrant cilantro and bananas, huge sacks of grains, chunks of sugarcane and plump vegetables create a symphony of sight and smell.

Try to arrive around 10am so that you can catch the end of mass at the **Cathedral**. It's the only time you'll see the local women without their hats on. Check out the stacks of Panamas in baskets at the foot of the pews.

The small, clean **park** in front of the Cathedral has an intriguing statue of Mother Nature. If you can figure out what that thing that she's coming out of is supposed to be, please send us an e-mail.

Two blocks down Cuenca street from the fruit market you'll find the **meat market**. There are also a number of restaurants set up in here. We like to get a stack of corn *tortillas*, thick rounds that look like pancakes and taste like cornbread, to go. The roasted pigs are extremely popular with locals.

MUSEO ARTESANAL GUALACEO, *Calle Loja y Avenida del Parador. Tuesday-Saturday 8am-5pm. Sunday 8am-12pm. Closed Monday. Entry free.*

This one room museum located at the entrance of Parador Turistica Gualaceo, features intricately woven textiles from around Ecuador, with particular focus on the Cuenca region. There are few examples of pottery and other handicrafts, as well as a display on the making of Panama hats. The quality of the handicrafts in the store is excellent, but at slightly higher prices than you will find in the small towns around the area.

Chordeleg

Ten minutes up the road from Gualaceo you'll come to **Chordeleg**. The large open square features the church you can see as you come up the hill from below. *Artesanía* and jewelry stores ring this central meeting area. We're no experts, but apparently the silver filigree work done here is quite fine. There is a great *paja toquilla* store on the square underneath the *Municipalidad* where they buy and sell straw crafts and hats. There is also an excellent ceramics store at 3-19 on the main street into town as you approach the square from below. Two blocks off the main square the market, *feria*, is a smaller shabbier version of Gualaceo's.

Sigsig

Continuing on the artisan trail from Chordeleg, you'll come to **Sigsig**, with its pretty gray and white church. Another market and Panama hats are the attraction here.

LOCH NESS GODDESS

Cañari descendents were the first inhabitants of the Sigsig. Their deity was Mount Faysañán, which you can see looming overhead. They also worshipped the Ayllon Lagoon below, where tradition says a gigantic snake lived. According to the legend, this snake was the mother of all humanity.

Buses leave for Gualaceo and Chordeleg every 30 minutes from the *terminal terrestre* in Cuenca. From there you can continue by bus to Sigsig. You can also hire a taxi by the hour from Cuenca. They shouldn't charge more than $7 an hour.

Other artisan towns near Gualaceo include **Bulcay** for shawls and rugs, **Paute** for sweaters, **San Bartolomé** for guitars, and **Solano** and **Lacao** for Panama hats.

If you want to stay overnight or dine in the area, try:

HOSTERIA UZHUPUD, *Río Paute, 30 minutes from Cuenca, near Gualaceo. Tel. 7/250 339, Fax 7/250 373; E-mail: apartec@uio.satnet.net. 47 rooms. Double $28. Breakfast included. Restaurant. Bar. Pool. Poolside snack bar. Sauna. Tennis court. Billiards. Volleyball court and soccer field. Horseback riding. Convention facilities.*

The first clue that this hacienda offers endless opportunities for family fun is at the entrance. You immediately see saddled horses and a functioning oxen-driven sugar cane press. That is only the start because behind the hotel are a playground, a large swimming pool, a tennis court, volleyball court, soccer field, and a snack bar featuring *salchipapas*, ice cream, and cold beers. You can imagine that parents do not have to do much prodding with all of the activities available, but rather can spend their time relaxing by the pool.

If you don't stay here you can buy a day pass that includes use of the recreational facilities and a bottomless plate at the lengthy buffet table. You should definitely wait an hour before swimming after that meal.

HOSTERIA PARADOR TURISTICO GUALACEO, *Loja and Avenida del Parador, Gualaceo. Tel. 7/255 010, Fax 7/842 443. 22 rooms. Double $18. Restaurant. Bar. Heated pool. Volleyball and soccer. Sauna and steam bath. Credit cards accepted.*

The Parador Turistico, not as nice as the Uzhupud, is still a favorite with vacationing Ecuadorian families. The hacienda-like complex is large with colorful well-tended gardens. On warm afternoons kids tend to congregate around the pool while their parents enjoy long lunches in the adjoining restaurant. The rooms themselves are a bit worn and musty, which makes you glad the grounds are spacious.

El Cajas National Park

If you have a day to get out of the city, we highly recommend a trip to **El Cajas**. Stark buttes, dramatic landscapes, tundra-like grasses, and rivers, lakes and more lakes wait in this land of haunting beauty. A thin, ochre layer of turf covers the lumpy, rocky land where little silver discs of water appear around almost every turn. The sun breaking through the clouds is mesmerizing as it plays off the tips of black rock plateaus that shoot dramatically out of the land.

There are no established and marked trails, but rather cattle trails crisscrossing the rugged topography. You can just take off hiking from the side of the road, but you won't want to go far in case you lose your bearings. It's a good idea to explore the park with a guide to get the most out of your time there. Any of the companies listed above are fine, as is **Eduardo Astualillo**, *El Camino Explorer, Calle Sangurima 996, Tel. 826 714.* Many guides lead people to **Lake Toreadora**, one of the most beautiful in the park.

The temperature at El Cajas is always cooler than it is in Cuenca, so be sure to wear plenty of layers. If it has been raining recently you might even want to spring for a $4 pair of rubber boots. If it is raining, you can make bets on which way the droplets coming off your jacket will flow. As this range is on the continental divide, some of the drops will make an easy trip to the Pacific Ocean, while others will have to float all to way to and down the Amazon River to reach the Atlantic.

Even if you're just a casual fisher-person, you'll want to take a rod, as there are abundant trout in El Cajas lakes.

The park is about 30 minutes east of Cuenca, which is roughly a $5 taxi ride. The road actually goes right through the middle of the park and then drops down to the coast, so you'll pass this way if you travel overland to Guayaquil. If you want to take public transportation, there is one bus that leaves at 6am from the **San Sebastian Church** *on Bolívar* and comes back in the afternoon (ask the driver what time). If you want to hike away from the main road, however, a guide is your best bet. Entry $10.

Even if you have no desire to hike, a cab ride up the road through the park is more than worth the money just for the chance to admire the magnificent scenery. You could drive up, enjoy a trout lunch and then head back to Cuenca.

Most people visit the park as a guided day trip with lunch included. It is possible to stay the night, however, at the **refuge at the park**

information center. It has bunk beds and a kitchen of sorts. Just outside the park entrance, the **Hostería Dos Chorreras Fishing Lodge** is much less rustic. It's not heated, but you can pile plenty of blankets on your bed and the doubles are fine for $20. The best part of staying there or just dropping by for a meal is the excellent trout dinner. There is also a restaurant at the park office open on weekends.

It can get pretty cold and windy in the park at night, so unless you have good four-season equipment you might want to consider the lodge over camping.

Ingapirca

Ingapirca is a set of Inca ruins about two hours north of Cuenca. They're not too impressive if you've visited Peruvian masterpieces like Machu Picchu or Sacsayhuaman, but if you've never seen the exactitude of Inca stonework, it's worth the trip. The hillside setting is also quite nice.

Ingapirca served as a military and religious center for the Inca in the late 1400s, but had been a Cañari observatory before that. The ruins, mainly low stone walls, cover six hectares. The best-preserved structure is a large ellipse at highest point on the grounds that many believe served as a temple and watchtower. Note its strategic location as you check out the view and walk the three kilometers of paths.

If you take the time to get to the ruins you should be willing to spend the money to see the sight with a guide. He can help you make more sense of the walls around you. You can either contract the trip with a guide from Cuenca or drive or take the bus to the sight and hire a guide at the entrance. If you just can't deal with the constriction of a guide, there are books for sale at the entrance with information about the site. It takes about two hours to go through the ruins and small museum and spot the Inca's Face. Entry $4. Ingapirca is north of Cuenca and just east of Tambo. You take the Pan-American Highway to Tambo and then follow the marked road 10 km to the sight.

There is one bus daily that goes directly from Cuenca to Ingapirca, **Transportes Cañar**, *9am from the terminal terrestre.* Friday buses can be most crowded as it's market day in Ingapirca. You can also take a bus to **Tambo** and then hire a car or take a local bus to the ruins. Saturday is market day in Tambo.

If you want to stay overnight or dine in the area, try:

POSADA INGAPIRCA, *Half a kilometer from Ingapirca. Reservations through the Cultura Reservation Center in Quito Tel./Fax 2/588 889; E-mail: info@ecuadortravel.com; Website: www.ecuadortravel.com. 12 rooms. Double $47. Breakfast included. Restaurant. No credit cards.*

If you visit Ingapirca on your way to or from Cuenca and want to stay the night, the Posada Ingapirca is a good option. This old farmhouse just

500 meters from the ruins has been converted to a comfortable inn for guests. Heated bedrooms with rug-covered floors mean a good night's sleep is in store. You can enjoy walks along the Inca trail or just soak in the beautiful views of the valley.

Even if you're not staying here, the Posada is a good option for a meal. Specializing in traditional Ecuadorian cuisine, the restaurant serves up tasty *empanandas*, and other local treats.

HIKE THE INCA TRAIL

During their time of dominance over the western half of South America, the Inca built an impressive network of roads throughout their empire. The system was made up of two north-south roads, one running along the coast for about 3,600 kilometers, the other inland along the Andes for a comparable distance, with many interconnected links.

Use of the system was strictly limited to government and military business. Ironically, this same road system that helped them govern and control their large territory played a vital role in their conquest. The Spanish were able to quickly gain access to the entire Inca Empire along the trail.

*Although mostly trekked in Peru, there are hikeable sections of the Inca Trail all along the Andes. The best section in Ecuador starts in **Achapallas**, near **Alausi**, and ends up here in Ingapirca. The 40-45 km hike takes from 14-20 hours depending on your fitness level. Most people spread it out over three days, camping along the way. You'll ascend to 4000 meters, crossing many rivers and then head down through peaceful and quiet wide-open spaces.*

Trips can be arranged through agencies in Quito, Riobamba and Cuenca.

Azogues

Azogues, the capital of the Cañar province, is a small town about 35 km north of Cuenca on the way to Ingapirca. If you're interested in Panama Hats, this is a place where many of them are woven. You can admire them at the Saturday market. It's also worth a visit to the **San Francisco church**. The impressive cathedral watches over town from a nearby hill. The views from the church are excellent.

Cañar

Cãnar is the nearest town of any size to Ingapirca. Budget travelers will find this an easy place to stay if you want to visit the ruins and then stay the night nearby. The market on Sunday is picturesque and worthwhile if you're in the area. Descendents of the once mighty Cañari Indians come down from high in the *páramo* to do their shopping and socializing.

The Cañari Indians lived in the valleys in and around Cuenca before the expansion of the Inca Empire. They resisted the Inca advance for over fifty years. These fierce warriors, in a bit of David and Goliath story, fought off large troops and superior weapons with only slingshots and spears.

When the Cañari were finally defeated, the Inca were so impressed with Cañari combat skills that a group of them were relocated to the Inca capital in Cuzco to protect the Inca ruler.

The Cañari were never completely subdued. When the Inca nation became divided between warring brothers, the Cañari were quick to join in the attempt to overthrow their current leader, Atahualpa. They even captured him at one point. He escaped, which was bad for the Cañari, because he ordered all Cañari males killed. Atahualpa did not succeed in entirely erasing the race, but he definitely put a dent in their numbers. Spanish slavery and disease did away with many more.

Baños

Not to be confused with the major tourist city near Ambato, the **Baños** near Cuenca is much smaller and less visited. These hot springs, five kilometers southwest of Cuenca, are nice on a cold rainy day. The **Hostería Duran**, *Tel. 892 486*, is a good place to stop for a meal.

PRACTICAL INFORMATION

Banks: Banco del Pacifico, *Malo 9-75 and Gran Colombia;* **Banco Amazonas,** *Bolívar 9-74;* **Banco de Guayaquil,** *Sucre and Borrero*

Bookstores: There are a number of bookstores in the downtown area, but none of them have many, if any, books in English.

Business Hours: While Cuenca has normal business hours during the week, weekends are a different story. Many businesses, even restaurants, are not open at all on weekends. Those that are open on Saturday usually close up shop at 1:30 and don't open again until Monday morning. That includes tour agencies, so if you want to make arrangements for any outings on Sunday, do it before 1:30 on Saturday.

Currency Exchange: Cambiaria Austral, *Sucre 6-64;* **Cambidex,** *Cordero 9-73 and Gran Colombia*

E-Mail Service: Abraham Lincoln Cultural Center, *Borrero 518.* **@,** *Aguirre 1096, 2nd floor.* **Cuenc@net,** *Larga 6-02 and Miguel.* **Zon@net,** *Miguel 4-38.* **@lfnet,** *Vásquez and Borrero*

Laundry: Fastklin, *6-68 Miguel*

Medical Service: Clínica Bolívar, *Bolívar 13-14 and Montalvo, Tel. 824 126;*
  Clínica España, *Davalos 133, Tel. 809 288*
National Parks: INEFAN, *Bolívar 5-33. Tel. 827 583*
Post Office: Correos, *Borrero and Gran Colombia*
Supermarkets: Tia, *Gran Colombia and Borrero*
Telephone/Fax: The area code is 7. **EMETEL**, *Malo between Córdova and*
  Sucre
Tourist Office/Maps: Ministry of Tourism, *Córdova and Malo, 2nd floor*

LOJA

Loja, the capital of the like-named province, is a place to pass through on your way to **Vilcabamba** or **Podocarpus National Park**. There's nothing wrong per say with the town, but it's entirely mediocre. For the most part, what you have in Loja are ordinary hotels, bland restaurants and common sights.

The city is the commercial center for the agricultural products of the area. Founded in 1546, one of Loja's greatest moments came in 1820 when it was the site of the Ecuadorian declaration of Independence. Loja had another spark of world importance over 300 years ago when quinine, an alkaloid from local chichona bark, was used as anti-malarial treatment.

ARRIVALS & DEPARTURES

By Air

The **Loja** airport is forty-five minutes west of Loja in **Catamayo**. You can take a shared cab into town for $5 a person. (Shared means the tight squeeze of four people and the driver.) Another alternative is to hire the entire cab for $20.

The **TAME** office in Loja is located at *24 de Mayo and Ortega, Tel. 573 030*. When leaving Loja, it's a good idea to get to the airport an hour before your flight is scheduled to take-off. Make your taxi arrangements the night before, and be sure to specify whether you want a shared or private cab.

By Bus

The main bus station in Loja, *terminal terreste*, is located at *the intersection of Cuxibamba and the road to Catamayo* on the northern edge of town. From here you can catch buses bound for the northern locations of Cuenca, Machala, Guayaquil or Zamora. A few overnight buses make the 14-hour run all the way to Quito.

To get south to Vilcabamba, take either the **Vilcabamba Turis** minibus or the **Sur Oriente** from the main station.

Many travelers who get a far south as Loja are making their way overland to Peru. The official border crossing here is **Macará**, six hours southwest of Loja. Buses from the main station leave for Macará a few times a day.

By Car

It's only 127 kilometers to Cuenca, but the drive can take up to four hours, due to the terrible condition of the road. This is the last leg of the Pan-American Highway in Ecuador, although the word "highway" is stretching the truth a bit.

ORIENTATION

Downtown Loja is bounded by the Zamora and Malacatas Rivers and spread between the Central and Bolívar Parks. The city's main thoroughfares run along these two rivers.

GETTING AROUND TOWN

Most sights, restaurants and hotels are within walking distance of the *Parque Central*, the main plaza. If you want to go further, cabs are readily available to flag off the street or to call.

WHERE TO STAY

HOTEL LIBERTADOR, *Colón 14-30 and Bolívar. Tel. 7/560 779, Fax 7/572 119. 65 rooms. Double $35. Breakfast not included. Restaurant. Pool. Sauna. Jacuzzi. Racquetball court. Credit cards accepted.*

The Libertador is the classic downtown hotel. It's our favorite of all the Loja options. Although the hotel is older, the rooms have all been remodeled and have clean, modern bathrooms. There is also an indoor pool and game room on the top floor. Their restaurant, **La Castellana**, is one of the best in town with a *menú* that's popular with business executives. The food is good and the service is too.

GRAN HOTEL LOJA, *Aguirre and Rocafuerte. Tel. 7/575 200, Fax 7/575 202. 40 rooms. Double $30. Breakfast not included. Restaurant. Credit cards accepted.*

The Gran hotel is an impressive looking high rise hotel with comfortable rooms. Unfortunately, the hotel is right on the loud and busy Aguirre street. If you don't stay here, it's a decent choice for a meal anyway.

APART-HOTEL IBEROAMERICA, *Iberoamerica and Montero. Tel. 7/574 432, Fax 7/570 587. 16 apartments. Double $40. Breakfast not included. Restaurant. No credit cards.*

If you need a little more space or want a kitchen, these basic apartments would be your best bet. They are not at all fancy, but do deliver in the square meter department.

BOMBUSCARO HOTEL, *10 de Agosto y Avenida. Universitaria. Tel. 7/577 021; E-mail: bombus@loja.telconet.net. 35 rooms. Double $24. Cable TV. Restaurant. Credit cards accepted.*

This new hotel is a bit glitzy, but not overly so. The rooms are clean, decently furnished, and functional. The restaurant has a nice view of Loja.

RAMSES HOTEL, *Colón 14-31 and Bolívar. Tel. 7/571 402, Fax 7/581 832. 30 rooms. Double $20. Breakfast not included. Restaurant. No credit cards.*

The Ramsés is a nice, clean option for a moderately priced hotel. The rooms, arranged around an atrium restaurant, are on the small side, but they do have cable TV.

HOTEL INTERNACIONAL, *10 de Agosto 15-30 between Sucre and 18 de Noviembre. Tel. 7/578 486. 12 rooms. Double $10. Breakfast not included. No credit cards.*

The International is a notable hotel for the price. With hardwood floors and remodeled bathrooms, complete with hot water, the hotel is a great deal. Because it is located in an old colonial building, you get high ceilings and a covered atrium also.

HOTEL METROPALITANO, *18 de Noviembre y Colon. Tel. 7/570 007 or 570 244. 20 rooms. Double $10. TV. No credit cards.*

This hotel is small, clean, and centrally located. It's a decent value for the price.

WHERE TO EAT

The best places in town to eat are at the nicer hotels like the **Libertador** and **Gran Hotel**. It's not exactly exciting food, but it's solid and hygienic, the best you can expect in Loja.

JOSE ANTONIO, *Imbabura 15-30 between 18 de Noviembre and Sucre. Moderate. No credit cards.*

This is the best place in town for seafood. Located next to the Parque Bolívar, Jose Antonio serves up some of the coast's most famous dishes.

PIZZARIA ROMA, *Cuxibamba 31-91 and Gran Colombia in front of the Lea bridge. Tel. 583 520. Moderate. Credit cards accepted.*

This pizza is really not all that good, but it's the best in town. It was while dining here that we realized that "mediocre" is the best way to describe this city. If you don't feel like eating in a restaurant, this is a decent choice, as they deliver.

If you want to go healthy, try **El Jugo Natural**, with fresh fruit juices, on *Eguirren between Bolívar and Sucre.* If you want to go the other extreme, ice cream is the treat of choice at *Azuay and 18 de Noviembre.*

SEEING THE SIGHTS

There's not much to see here, but that doesn't mean it's not enjoyable taking in the limited number of attractions. The **main plaza**, *Parque*

Central, is a nicely painted hodgepodge of modern, colonial and art-deco building. The **cathedral**, with its faux marble paintings and wooden floors is a good place to sit away from the traffic noise and jumble of town.

SARAGURO STYLE

Keep your eyes out for the **Saraguro** *Indians. With a single long braid, wide-brimmed white hat, and black shorts modeled after colonial pantaloons, the men are hard to miss. They also wear a wide belt decorated with silver coins and, on formal occasions, wool chaps.*

The women wear the same white hat with a brightly colored satin blouse, black skirts and a black shawl. Notice the lovely silver tupu pins closing the shawls at their collarbones. The women also wear antique silver earrings and hand-beaded necklaces.

Interestingly, the Saraguros originally lived in southeastern Peru, but were forced by the Incas to move to this part of Ecuador. Saraguro means "Land of Corn" in Quichua, reflecting the close relationship between the land, the people and their agricultural vocation.

Cattycorner from the cathedral is the town's main museum.

BANCO CENTRAL MUSEUM, *Parque Central. Tel. 573 004. Monday-Friday 9am-1pm, 2pm-4:30pm. Entry $0.50.*

The rotating exhibits in the downstairs portion of this old colonial building are usually free. Upstairs you'll find the city's archeology exhibit, detailing the full history of Loja in Spanish. Displays include ceramics, paintings and religious art. It's worth taking a peak if you're already in town, but doesn't merit a stopover in Loja if you're just passing through.

For a good overview of the city, you can walk or cab it up to the **Virgin of Loja**. Up a hill out Rocafuerte, the Virgin watches over the entire town.

Three kilometers south from the downtown area on Aguirre you'll find the National University of Loja. Part of the university's park includes a public **botanical garden**.

The **Mercado Modelo**, public market, *18 de Noviembre and 10 de Agosto*, is unique in Ecuador in that it is almost spotless. The pleasant indoor emporium is a good place to duck out of the rain and people watch.

EXCURSIONS & DAY TRIPS

Visits to **Podocarpus National Park** are the most popular excursion from Loja; see *Vilcabamba Excursions & Day Trips*. To get to the park, take the highway south to Vilcabamba. After 15 minutes turn off to park. Seven kilometers down that road you arrive to Cajanuma where you will find the Administration Center. You can also arrange tours through the travel agency at the **Hotel Libertador**.

Another popular outing is the trip to the **Monumento Mariano de El Cisne**. This huge gothic basilica in the middle of nowhere was built in tribute to a very unique looking Virgin. We'd like to know what kind of shampoo she uses to fluff up that tremendous head of big hair. This structure, looking like a haunted house from a Scooby Doo cartoon, has been home to the Virgin de El Cisne for more than 400 years. Pilgrims come from all over the south of Ecuador to pay tribute. She has even been declared the National Patron Saint of Tourism. The most convenient time to visit El Cisne is on the way into Loja from the airport.

If you have some time, or are driving down from Cuenca, be sure to stop at **Saraguro**, the village named after the Saraguro Indians. Seventy four kilometers north of Loja, this small town has an interesting Sunday market.

PRACTICAL INFORMATION

Banks: Filanbanco, *Parque Central*
Consulates: Consulate of Peru, *Sucre 10-56 and Azuay. Tel. 571 668*
E-Mail Service: Cyber Place, *10 de Agosto between 18 de Noviembre and Sucre, Vallto Shopping Center #33*
National Parks: INEFAN, *Azuay between Olmedo and Valdivieso*
Post Office: Correos, *Colón and Sucre*
Telephone/Fax: The area code is 7. **EMETEL**, *Eguirren and Olmedo*
Tourist Office/Maps: CETUR, *Valdivieso 08-22 and 10 de Agosto*

VILCABAMBA

Vilcabamba, which means "sacred valley" in Quichua, is known for its mild climate, mellow atmosphere and lovely green hills. Hiking and relaxing are the name of the game in Vilcabamba, and luckily for travelers the combination has been raised to an art form here. The mountains surrounding town are good places to wander all day, while affordable spa services beckon around almost every corner.

Town itself is about as sleepy as it gets. Donkeys laden with sugar cane are more common in the streets than cars, and even horses roam unencumbered. Not too many people make it all the way down here, but those that do are rewarded with sweet clean air and spectacular views. You'll share the trails with cows and old women gathering medicinal herbs, but that's about it.

Vilcabamba really works its renown as an Oasis of Longevity (the name of the main road into town is translated *Eternal Youth*). Their town slogan touts this as a place where years are added to your life and life added to your years. Somewhere along the line somebody got the idea that the simple way of life here in the valley, along with the spring water, had beneficial effects on the health and life span of the people here. Studies are inconclusive, but the reputation stuck.

At 1,500 meters, the Vilcabamba has much milder weather than cities high up in the Andes. In fact, the weather here is considered by many to be the best in the country.

ARRIVALS & DEPARTURES
By Air
The closest airport to Vilcabamba is the **Loja** airport. Loja itself is only about an hour away, but the airport is another forty-five minutes from Loja, making it almost a two hour trip to Vilcabamba.

You can hire a taxi directly from the airport to Vilcabamba for $35, or you can take a shared taxi from the airport into Loja for $5 a person and then take a bus or shared taxi on to Vilcabamba.

By Bus
Buses leave for the one-hour trip to Vilcabamba from the main bus station in Loja, *terminal terreste*, every half hour. You take either the Vilcabamba Turis minibus or the Sur Oriente.

To leave Vilcabamba you can go to the plaza or just stand on the side of the highway and wait for either a bus or shared taxi for Loja to go by. You can cram into a shared taxi with four other people plus the driver, or wait for the bus.

Once you get to the *terminal terreste* in Loja, you can catch buses bound for Cuenca, Machala, Guayaquil or Zamora. A few overnight buses make the 14-hour run all the way to Quito. Many travelers who get as far south as Vilcabamba are making their way overland to Peru. See the Loja *Arrivals & Departures* section for more information on getting to the border.

By Car
The 42 kilometer road to Vilcabamba from Loja is paved and in pretty good condition relative to many in the rest of the country. The scenery is spectacular, dropping down through steep green hills. The cows that dot the hillsides appear to have been cross-bred with mountain goats as they contentedly chew their cud while standing on the steep green flanks.

ORIENTATION
The highway into Vilcabamba changes names to *Avenida Eterna Juventud*. Two of the more popular hotels, **Madre Tierra** and **Hosteria de**

Vilcabamba are situated a kilometer or two out of town on this road. The main plaza, **Parque Central**, is bounded by Fernando de la Vega, Diego Vaca de la Vega, Bolívar and Sucre streets. Diego Vaca de la Vega leads through town and then heads east to **Yamburara**, another popular hotel spot, and the zoo.

The most distinctive and highest hill around, to the west of town, is **Cerro Mandango** at just over 2,000 meters. Mandango is also known as the Sleeping God.

GETTING AROUND TOWN

You usually end up walking a lot when you're in Vilcabamba. That's just what you do here. You can hale a cab from the plaza, but people tend to do this only for long trips.

WHERE TO STAY

MADRE TIERRA RANCH & SPA, *Vilcabamba road. Tel. 7/580 269; E-mail: hmtierra@ecua.net.ec; Website: www. ecuadorexplorer.com/madretierra. 24 rooms. Double $14-$50 depending on type of lodging. Dinner and breakfast included. Restaurant. Pool. Full spa. Basketball court. No credit cards accepted.*

The Madre Tierra is a great hotel. It's the only place we've come across in all our travels that combines full spa service with inexpensive and moderately priced rooms and cabins. Who says that people with deep pockets are the only ones to enjoy facials or mud baths?

The hotel, on the edge of town and surrounded by corn fields, is set amid profuse plants and flowers. The cabins are scattered all around the thirty-two acres of grounds, with some being extremely private. All have hammocks from which you can watch the sunlight soften as the afternoon advances. Some however, are much nicer than others. The simplest ones have no windows and sketchy hot water, while the newer ones are quite agreeable with large picture windows and spacious porches.

The meals at Madre Tierra, included in the price of the room, are hearty and healthy. Homemade baked goods are standard, as is your choice of vegetarian or meat entrees. The breakfast, especially good fuel for your day's hike, includes yogurt, granola, fresh fruit, bread, eggs and potatoes.

All meals are served at long tables on the central patio. The spa is just a few steps away as are the small pool and basketball court. Fountains cascade down to the pool, creating the pleasant sound of waterfalls. The patio also serves as the central hangout spot during the day, with board games and crossword puzzles serving as good icebreakers. At night it's the spot to watch a movie on the VCR. It's hard to decide whether to spend your time exploring the surrounding hills or enjoying the spa services. It's best to come here with enough time to do both. You can enjoy a half or whole-day spa package or pick your pleasure a la carte. The spa facilities are comfortable and hygienic and the staff professional.

While the Madre Tierra is a haven for young travelers, it attracts everyone from retirees to professionals looking to get away from it all for a while. We're sure that no matter how long you have planned to stay here, you'll end up wanting to linger a few extra days.

HOSTERIA LAS RUINAS DE QUINURA, *Via a Yamburara. Tel. 7/ 580 314; E-mail: ruinasqui@hotmail.com. Web site www.lasruinasdequinara.com. 20 rooms. $10 per person full board. Cable TV. Restaurant. Bar. Pool. Sports facilities; E-mail: service. Video library and viewing room. Sauna. Massage. No credit cards.*

Considering what a bargain Las Ruinas is, you might ask yourself, "Why don't I just move in here permanently?" Not since the days of living with your parents have you gotten a deal as good as this.

For ten bucks a day, you sleep in a big double room with a hot shower and cable TV, roll into the dining room for three squares, and lounge by the pool. For fun, you can play hoops on the full court adorned with a Chicago Bulls logo, swat some Ping-Pong balls, get rich playing Monopoly, or watch one of the large selections of movies in the mini-theater video room. They also toss in 10 minutes of free e-mail service and complimentary juice and mineral water all day. The only thing they don't give you here is free laundry service, but you can use their machines to do your own at no extra charge. While Las Ruinas doesn't enjoy the tropical hillside locale and pleasant design of the Madre Tierra, it certainly evens the contest with extra services and facilities.

The *hosteria* offers a wide variety of additional services such as massages, dance classes, and Spanish classes. The staff is quite helpful in showing you the way to hiking trails or to anything else there is to do in the area. Make a reservation in advance if you can because this place frequently fills up.

CABANAS RIO YAMBALA, *Out of town past Yamburara Alto on the Yambala River. Tel. 7/580 299; E-mail: charlie@loja.telconet.net; Website: www.vilcabamba.org/charlie. 12 rooms and cabins. Double $16. Restaurant. No credit cards.*

Cabanas Rio Yambala, also known as Charlie's Cabins, are a great place to enjoy the nature that makes Vilcabamba so pleasant. The private cabins sit on the eastern edge of the Yambala River away from everything. Their restaurant serves good food, but if you want to cook your own you can also arrange kitchen access. There are both marked trails and guides, so you can go it on your own if you want or hire an escort. The guides are good to help you spot some of the more than 150 species of birds found here. They can also arrange trips to Podocarpus National Park. The cabins are an hour's walk from town.

REFUGIO SOLMACO. *Tel. 7/673 147, Fax 7/673 186. $25 per person per night, full-board. No credit cards.*

If you'd like to get into nature for a night, you can do so on horseback by riding to the Refugio Solmaco. The three-and-a-half-hour ride takes you into the sierra, past a tropical waterfall, via the Podocarpus National Park. Your home for the evening will be a rustic cabin on a lush mountainside. The sleeping quarters are dorm style rooms. Contact **Monta-Tours**, *Tel. 7/673 147*, on the plaza for more information.

HOSTERIA DE VILCABAMBA, *on the road into town. Tel. 7/580 271, Fax 7/580 273. 30 rooms. Double $15. Restaurant. Bar. Pool. Sauna. Credit cards accepted.*

The Hosteria Vilcabamba is situated amid effulgent, overflowing gardens with a stream gurgling through the middle of the property. Simple, cozy rooms reside within the attractive whitewashed bungalows. The grounds have a pool and sauna and offer massage services. While a bit more sterile than its famous neighbor Madre Tierra, some will find this aspect to be preferable.

ECO-LODGE RUMI-HUILCO or **THE POLE HOUSE**, *Out of town on Chamba river. Office on the plaza at Prima Vera Handicrafts, Diego Vaca de la Vega and Sucre. Tel. 7/673 186; E-mail: ofalcoecolodge@yahoo.com. 1 room. Double $14. No credit cards.*

If you want to feel like you're in the middle of nature, try the Pole House, an elevated cabin on the banks of the Chamba River. You have access to the fully furnished kitchen, and more importantly, the hammock on the porch. There are also good hiking trails up the adjacent hills of the Rumi Huilco Nature Reserve. The owners, Orlando and Alice Falco, have a handicraft shop on the main plaza where you can get directions for the 10 minute walk to the house. Orlando also guides trips to Podocarpus National Park.

HIDDEN GARDEN, *half a block from the square. Tel. 7/580 281; E-mail: vilca@srv8.te.conet.net. 15 rooms. Double $12 or $6 per person. Kitchen facilities. No credit cards.*

Pick herbs for your pasta or a lemon for your trout straight out of the courtyard garden. This is a laid-back place with a a small pool and tidy kitchen open for use by guests. There is definitely a mellow, communal feel here.

HOSTAL VALLE SAGRADO, *On the Parque Central. Tel. 7/580 686. 15 rooms. Double $6. Restaurant. No credit cards.*

The Valle Sagrado, right on the central plaza, is almost as cheap as they come, but surprisingly agreeable. There's hot water, a courtyard garden and a vegetarian restaurant.

HOSTAL MANDANGO, *Huilcopamba and Montalvo. 13 rooms. Double $6. Bar. No credit cards.*

The Mandango, on the western side of Eterna Juventud, is a simple hostel with small rooms and bad décor. The views from the open rooftop bar, however, are spectacular.

WHERE TO EAT

LA TERRAZA, *On Parque Central, Diego Vaca de la Vega and Bolívar. Inexpensive. No credit cards.*

La Terraza is our favorite restaurant in Vilcabamba. This bright little cantina, with gingham table clothes and cheerily painted walls, serves up almost anything a gringo could be craving. Simple Mexican, Thai and Italian dishes vie for your attention with salads and humus. Pies and brownies round out the mix. We suggest sitting at one of the outdoor tables, playing checkers or backgammon (the boards are painted right on the tables) and drinking one of La Terraza's very cold beers.

RESTAURANTE VEGETARIANO, *Diego Vaca de la Vega and Valle Sagrado. Inexpensive. No credit cards.*

The name says it all here. This vegetarian restaurant, totally plain from the outside, is set in a pleasant little courtyard garden. You can get sandwiches, salads or spaghetti, but the daily fixed price *menú* is also popular. Bring your used paperbacks, as there's a book exchange here.

Pizza & Other Fare

We call Diego Vaca de la Vega Street the Pizza Row. There are three **pizza restaurants** on the street as you head south towards Yumburara. We like the atmosphere of **Pepito's**, but **Giocconda** and the **Green Triangle** are nice too. **Craig's book exchange**, also *out Diego de la Vega on the way to Yambala*, sells tasty yogurt.

Huilcabamba offers cheap vegetarian food on the plaza. **Restaurant Katherine** also has cheap meals on the plaza.

SEEING THE SIGHTS

The town's main plaza is called the **Parque Central** or Plaza Jardín. Filled with fragrant juniper bushes, is it Vilcabamba's central meeting spot. The church, a pretty tan building with white column and blue accents, is here, as are many restaurants and tour agencies.

Vilcabamba Zoo

This small zoo houses a few of the animals typical of the region. It's a pleasant walk from town. Head east on Diego Vaca de la Vega past Yamburara Bajo. Stay on the main road as it heads right towards the river.

Just before the bridge you'll see a sign and trail to the left along the river that leads to the zoo.

Hike to the Crosses (Mandango)

As you look up over town you'll see crosses perched high on two hills to the west. The second, and higher one, sits on top of **Cerro Mandango** at 2,034 meters. The trip up takes a couple of hours, but you are rewarded with superb views of the velvety mountains in shades of green and gold. You can trace the fertile swath of the Chamba River and enjoy the contrast of Vilcabamba's red roofs against their green backdrop.

To get to the trailhead, take the highway (Avenida Eterna Juventud) south of town, past a cluster of houses on the right. After the houses you will see two cement gate posts on the right. Enter here and go up 5 meters and you'll see the trail going off to the right.

The trail at this point is just a series of cattle trails. Go right whenever you have a choice until you get to the base of the hill with the first cross and then hoof it up. Once you get to the first cross, you will see the trail continue along the ridge to Mandango. You actually go around the backside of Mandango and then up to the top.

NIGHTLIFE & ENTERTAINMENT

The **Hostal Mandango**, *Huilcopamba and Montalvo*, has an open-air rooftop bar that offers great views at sunset. It's also fun at night when they light the bonfire. There's a **disco** *on the highway below the Madre Tierra*, but it is only open on random nights.

SPORTS & RECREATION

Biking

If you want to cover more ground than you can hiking, you can rent bikes for $10 per day from the **bike shop** on *Bolivar and Agua de Hierro*. They'll give you a map of the area and send you on your way. Although the bikes are mountain bikes, the suggested routes are all on dirt roads, not single track. There's a great four-six hour loop they recommend that really gets you out into the countryside.

Hiking

Everybody you talk to at dinner will have either hiked or gone to the spa or both. The array of choices is wonderful. There are kilometers of trails that can be accessed from Vilcabamba, and then there is **Podocarpus National Park**, with its own hikes.

We suggest that you ask your hotel for directions to the nearest trail. The Madre Tierra, for example, has printed out maps for a number of nearby treks. Keep in mind that these are unsigned cattle trails, so you need to pay attention as you hike. There is a good map of Vilcabamba created by the Ministry of Tourism that shows many of the local trails. You can buy this map for $1 at most hotels.

Some of the most popular hikes are up Cerro Mandango, along the Vilcabamba River, to Las Palmas Nature Reserve and to Rumi Huilco Nature Reserve.

If you prefer guided hikes, there are plenty of people willing to show you around the area. **Monta-Tours**, *Tel. 7/673 147* is a recommended one. Ask your hotel as well, because many times you can get a discount by going through them.

See Day **Trips & Excursions** below for information on Podocarpus, where you can hike for days on end.

Horseback Riding

It seems like there is a shop on every corner advertising horse rentals, but we've found **Centro Ecuestre** in the **Avetur** office at *Diego de la Vaca between Bolivar and Valle Sagrado* to have the best horses. The price starts at $10 for four hours and goes down from there on a per hour basis. You can arrange the type of trip that suits your fancy, from one hour to three days, and then just sit back and enjoy the ride.

EXCURSIONS & DAY TRIPS

The most popular trip from Vilcabamba is to **Podocarpus National Park,** Website: *www.programapodocarpus.org.* The park, on the edge of the Andes, straddles the Nudo de Sabanilla mountain range before plunging down to the Oriente. Altitude in Podocarpus varies from 950 to 3600 meters and covers five life zones. With high *páramo,* lush cloud forests and plentiful lakes, it's a beautiful place to get out into the wilderness. The park is named after the only native species of coniferous evergreen tree in the country.

Podocarpus, covering 146,000 hectares, is the only protected area in the south of Ecuador. This amazing diverse area is home to over 600 species of birds such as the golden plumed and white breasted parakeet and the red-faced parrot. Large but difficult to find mammals in the park include such rarities as tapir, *pudu* deer and spectacled bear. Even if you don't spot all the glamour animals, you're sure to admire the huge variety of orchids.

Our favorite hike is the eight-hour (one way) trek to **Lagunas del Compadre.** You can set up camp on the banks of these lakes and enjoy the breathtaking scenery while fishing for dinner. The crystalline waters and dramatic skies make you feel as if you've plopped down in Shangri-la.

Almost every hotel or hostel in Vilcabamba can arrange guided trips to the park. Most groups access the park from the **Cajanuma Cloudforest Entrance**. Half way between Vilcabamba and Loja, the infrastructure here includes a simple refuge and administrative center. There are a few short trails here as well as the start of the 15 kilometer hike to Lagunas del Compadre. There is another administrative center in **Bombuscaro**, which you access from **Zamora**. A small orchid garden and flocks of tanagers are the highlights here.

Even if you're just taking a day trip to the park you should be prepared for sudden weather changes. The best time to visit is during the dry season from October to December. Entry $10.

PRACTICAL INFORMATION

There is an internet café, **Vilc@net**, at *Eterna Juventud and Diego Vaca de la Vega*. The **EMETEL** office is on *Eterna Juventud and Diego Vaca de la Vega*. The area code for Vilcabamba is 7. For tourist information and maps, try the tourist information office at *Bolívar and Diego Vaca de la Vega* on the main plaza. Post office is a block north of the plaza at *Agua de Hierro and Bolívar*.

MACARÁ

People heading to Peru from Loja travel south and cross at Macará. The Huaquillas crossing, on the coast, sees far more traffic than this steamy secondary border point.

ARRIVALS & DEPARTURES

A few buses a day make the six hour trip from Loja to Macará. **Transportes Loja**, *Veintimilla and Valdivieso*, returns to Loja and also makes trips to Quito and Guayaquil.

WHERE TO STAY & EAT

The only reason to stay here is if you arrive to Macará late in the day. If that happens, **Hotel Paradero Túristico**, *Panamericana and Auxiliadora, Tel. 7/694 099, Double $15,* is the best choice for room and board. At least this hotel, on the way out of town towards the border, has hot water.

PRACTICAL INFORMATION

Macará is pretty weak in the services department. You'll have to exchange money on the street if you haven't already done that before you get here. The phone office, **EMETEL** is on *10 de Agosto and Vela*.

CROSSING THE BORDER

There is no visa necessary for North Americans, but Aussie and New Zealanders need one. If you run into any problems, try the **Peruvian Consulate**, *Bolivar 127 and 10 de Agosto, Tel. 694 030. The consulate is not open afternoons or weekends. You can take either a pick-up truck or taxi to the border from the main plaza. The border is open from 8am-6pm, but closed at lunch. You'll go through official passport stamping at the border before you walk over the bridge into La Tina, Peru.*

Transportation from La Tina further into Peru is more of a sure thing in the morning, so you might want to cross earlier rather than later.

16. GUAYAQUIL & THE SOUTHERN COAST

The southern coast is home to Ecuador's largest city, **Guayaquil**, and that city's oceanside playground, the **Santa Elena Peninsula**. While Guayaquil is humid and crowded, the coastal area is arid and sparsely populated. In this chapter we cover the **coastline extending north** from the Santa Elena Peninsula as far as **Montañita** as well as the **coastline running south** from Guayaquil to the **border of Peru**.

For coastal destinations farther north than Montañita, see the *Central Coast* chapter. If you are considering travel along the coastline from Guayaquil, you should read about the destinations in both chapters because the terrain becomes much more lush and attractive along the Central Coast.

GUAYAQUIL

Guayaquil is a sweltering metropolis hugging the languid Río Guayas, a river that would have been more aptly named Río Café Con Leche, given its frothy brown flow. The vast waterway facilitated the country's largest port, spurring tremendous commercial and industrial growth. The resulting job opportunities attract hordes of migrants from the countryside. Crime, poverty, and grime are Guayaquil's most infamous characteristics. It is seedy to be sure, but also sultry at times. There is an undeniable, strangely attractive rhythm of life here that may not merit a visit in itself, but for those obliged to pass through, can provide a stimulating experience.

An intensely proud population of two million calls the capital of Guayas Province home. The conceit is historic in that, before the creation of Ecuador, Guayaquil was the first territory in South America to secure independence from Spain. When nations finally did win independence, the two revolutionary commanders, Bolívar and San Martín chose the city

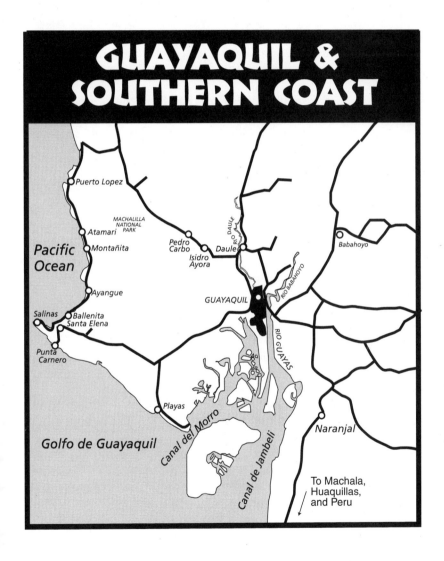

as the meeting place to decide where borders would be drawn. These days, dynamic business and political leaders constantly arise to push the city to the forefront of the nation, as Guayaquil vies with prettier Quito for distinction.

Many visitors find it makes logistical sense to spend a day or two here. The good news is that Guayaquil offers some of the finest restaurants and museums in the country. You could do worse than indulge in a day brimming with culture and a dinner plate chock-full of ceviche.

History

The Spanish conquistador **Sebastián de Benalcázar** founded Guayaquil in 1535. During the ensuing centuries it was repeatedly attacked by buccaneers and was destroyed by fires on several occasions. The liberation of the city in 1821 by patriot forces under **Antonio José de Sucre** was a major step toward South American independence.

A fateful meeting between **Simón Bolívar** and **José de San Martín** took place in Guayaquil in 1822. The two leaders, who won most of Spanish South America's independence from Spain, had never met. The results of that summit left Bolívar in control of Colombia, Venezuela, and Ecuador. San Martín, meanwhile, left empty-handed and soon ceded his presidency of Peru to Bolívar. A portion of Peru was subsequently split off and named Bolivia. San Martín headed peacefully for retirement, while Bolívar would eventually be chased from power.

Currently Guayaquil is Ecuador's largest city. Its population doubled between 1970 and 1990. Guayaquil's leading manufacturing sectors are textiles, leather goods, cement, consumer goods, and iron products. Its port is one of the most productive along Latin America's Pacific Coast. Ecuador's agricultural bounty, primarily cacao, coffee, and bananas, are loaded onto vessels here for export.

ARRIVALS & DEPARTURES

BY CAR

To enter the city from the coast, you will come in on the Via Salinas, then follow Av. Las Bomberos until it turns into Av. 9 de Octubre. This will take you into the city center. To get to the coast, follow Av. 9 de Octubre out, then follow signs indicating *Costa* or Salinas.

To enter the city from Cuenca, you will cross a bridge over the Río Babahoyo and the Río Daule. You will see airport signs until you pass the airport, then follow Avenida De Las Americas until reaching 9 de Octubre and take a left. This will take you to the city center. To leave Guayaquil for Cuenca, take 9 de Octubre to Av. Las Americas, then follow signs to the Puente De La U. Nacional or Via Duran-Tambo.

To enter the city from highway from Jipijapa or Santo Domingo, follow Francisco de Orellana until you see signs for Avenida De Las Americas, then follow that arterial. Turn left on 9 de Octubre to reach the city center. If you're heading to the Central Coast, it's very convenient to have a car. Your own wheels give you the freedom to explore different beach areas and get off the beaten path. We recommend a 4WD vehicle from a reputable rental car company, like **Budget**. We have found them to offer good cars and service.

Rental Companies
- **Budget**, *Avenida Las Americas 900 and Calle Norte. Tel. 288 510, Fax 283 656. E-mail: budgetg@gye.satnet.net. Web site: www.budgetrentacar.com.ec*
- **Avis**, *Av. De Las Americas C.C. Olimpico Tel. 285 498*
- **Colcar**, *Cordova 10-11 or airport. Tel. 288 475*
- **Hertz**, *Escobedo 1213 y Av. 9 de Octubre. Tel. 511 316*
- **Sicorent**, *Av. Arosemena Km 1.5 or airport. Tel. 206 790*

Here's an example of some car costs from **Budget** in Guayaquil. Prices will change over time, but this gives you a ballpark figure. These prices include insurance and taxes.
- **Small 2-door economy**: $27/day, 12¢/km, $220/week with unlimited mileage
- **2-door 4WD Vitara**: $43/day, 20¢/km, $615/week with unlimited mileage

BY BUS

The bus station, *terminal terrestre*, is just a bit further out than the airport, about 15 minutes by cab from the city center. It is a huge, modern facility with many shops and services. You can buy tickets in advance, which might be advisable on holidays and weekends, but usually you can just buy them at the time you want to travel. Watch your bags and be careful of pickpockets here.

Bus Companies
- **Panamericana** *Tel. 297 638*
- **Reina del Camino** *Tel. 297 040*
- **Transporte Ecuador** *Tel. 297 040*
- **Turismo Oriental** *Tel. 297 487*
- **Turismo Patria** *Tel. 297 638*

Here are some one-way fares (coach travel) to the indicated destinations:

Destination	Cost	Time
Salinas	$3	3 hours
Bahia de Caráquez	$5	6 hours
Puerto Lopez	$4	5 hours
Machala	$3	3.5 hours
Huaquillas	$4	5 hours
Cuenca	$4	6 hours
Riobamba	$4	4 hours
Quito	$8	9 hours

BY PLANE

The **Simón Bolívar Airport** is about five kilometers from the city center, which translates into a fifteen-minute cab ride to and from most hotels. The cost of the cab ride to hotels in the city is about $4. You'll find official airport taxis in front of the national and international terminals. There are currency exchange booths and ATM machines, (*cajeros automaticos*), in the airport. You can't always count on the ATM's being in service though.

National flights that you might take from Guayaquil include flights to Quito, ($40 one-way), Cuenca, ($30 one way), Ambato, ($30 one-way), and the Galápagos, ($340 round-trip). Flights to the Galápagos Islands may depart from the national or international terminal.

If you are leaving the country, there is a $25 exit fee that you pay at a window near the security entrance to the gates. If you want to pick up some last minute souvenirs, there are several shops offering their wares in the boarding area after you pass through immigration.

A separate terminal handles small commercial aircraft. This is located south of the national and international terminals.

Airlines

• **American**, *Córdova 1021 y 9 de Octubre. Tel. 564 111*
• **AeroPeru**, *Chile 329 y Aguirre. Tel. 513 691*
• **Continental**, *9 de Octubre 1911 y Esmeraldas. Tel. 453 600*
• **LanChile**, *Malecón 1401. Tel. 320 342*
• **San/Saeta**, *Vélez 226 y Chile. Tel. 329 855*
• **Tame**, *9 de Octubre 424 y Gran Pasaje. Tel. 310 305*

ORIENTATION

Greater Guayaquil stretches out on a fluvial plain. Most of its distended form is hemmed in by the **Río Guayas** on the east and the brackish fingers of the **Estero Salado** on the west. At the northern end of the city the Río Guayas is formed by the confluence of the **Río Daule** and the **Río Babahoyo**.

The fact that the city serves as Ecuador's largest port is somewhat confusing, because it nearly 100 kilometers from the coastline proper. The cargo ships traverse half the distance through the expansive Estero Salado Bay, then cover the rest by cruising 50 kilometers up the Río Guayas.

Most visitors' time is spent in the ten-block portion of the city center surrounding **Iguana Park** and buffeting the river boardwalk, **Malecón Simón Bolívar**. The airport and bus station are about five kilometers away. **Urdesa**, an exclusive residential neighborhood with attractive restaurants, is nearly the same distance.

GETTING AROUND TOWN

You can walk to all of the points of interest around Iguana Park. Your hotel is likely to be nearby, but if it isn't, this is a good drop-off point to tell your taxi driver.

Street taxis cough and sputter, but are reliable for the most part. For newer, more secure vehicles, grab a cab stationed in front of one of the nicer hotels. Of course you will pay slightly more for this comfort. Expect a 15-minute ride to the airport, bus station, or Urdesa in light traffic.

STREET SMARTS IN GUAYAQUIL

There is crime in Guayaquil, but it is not a war zone, so don't let your paranoia destroy you. As a general rule, you are safe walking in the commercial areas during the day. These include the areas around, Iguana Park, 9 de Octubre, the new portion of the Malecón, and Urdesa. You will easily sense when you stray from the areas into seedier environs. If you are going somewhere outside of these areas, ask your hotel about personal security considerations.

Leave your valuables and most of your cash in your hotel safe, taking a credit card, (easily cancelled if stolen), for bigger expenditures. Pick pocketing and bag theft are more prevalent than mugging, but if you are assaulted, politely hand the gentlemen what they want without debate.

WHERE TO STAY

Guayaquil's hotel system has been catering to the business sector for years, so it is well developed in that respect. There are some outstanding high-end hotels here, but the moderate segment is almost non-existent and the low-end suffers from personality deficiency. For budget travelers, be aware that if you try to go lower than $20 dollars or so for a double, you get pushed out into the sketchier parts of town.

From high end to low, our preferred hotels are the **Oro Verde**, **Unipark**, **Gran Hotel Guayaquil**, **Hotel Palace**, and the **Hotel Doral**.

Very Expensive

HOTEL ORO VERDE, *9 de Octubre y Garcia Moreno. Tel. 4/327 999, Fax 4/329 350. E-mail: ecovg@gye.satnet.net. Web site www.oroverde.net. 192 rooms. Double $190. Cable TV. Restaurants. Coffee shop. Deli. Bar. Pool. Gym. Shops. Business Center. Conference facilities. Casino. Travel Agency. Parking. Credit cards accepted.*

The Oro Verde is a hotel that gets it right. The hotel offers finely appointed rooms, superior service, top rate restaurants, and attractive entertainment facilities all under one roof. And yet, they continually search for new ways to satisfy their guests. Consider the thirty minutes of complimentary Internet service daily. Compare this to the policies of other five star hotels and you begin to understand the adeptness of the Oro Verde when it comes to hospitality and customer satisfaction.

Going beyond the ordinary to extraordinary means that you understand that people like options. To the Oro Verde that translates into managing one of the finest restaurants in the country, Le Gourmet, as well as one full of spunk, The Spice Grill, and another with splendid European fare, La Fondue. While the twenty-four-hour coffee shop offers an informal option, many who live in Guayaquil consider it one of the town's most solid dining spots. If you don't feel like eating in a restaurant at all, you can simply pop into the deli for excellent sandwiches and desserts.

Quality details are important in the upscale category. The Oro Verde doesn't cut corners when it comes to equipping their fitness center. Here you will find high quality machines that work - bicycles, rowing machines, and treadmills from the makers of Lifecycles. After working out, you can relax with a sauna or massage or kick back by the pool.

Executives should note that the Oro Verde has a separate tower with suites and services suited for long term stays.

HILTON COLON, *Avenida Francisco Orellana. Tel. 4/689 000, Fax 4/689 149. 290 rooms. Double $250. Restaurant. Bar. Gym; Squash Courts. Casino. Conference Rooms. Business Center. Credit cards accepted.*

The Hilton Colon Guayaquil juts from a gleaming new commercial neighborhood. The hotel offers an excellent panoramic view of the city and easy access to the airport. As the newest five star hotel, the Colon features peerless accommodations and service.

1. Oro Verde
2. Gran Hotel Guayaquil
3. Hotel Unipark
4. Hotel Continental
5. Hotel Las Americas
6. Hotel Palace
7. Hotel Ramada
8. Hotel Doral
9. Hotel Plaza
10. Sol Del Oriente

11. Rizzo Hotel
12. Hotel Alexander
13. Hotel Velez
14. Caracol Azul
15. 1822
16. Le Gourmet, Le Fondue, Spice Bar
17. Casa Basca
18. Unipark Deli
19. Iguana Park

Expensive

GRAN HOTEL GUAYAQUIL, Boyacá entre Ballén y 10 de Agosto. Tel. 4/329 690 and 4/329 918, Fax 4/327 251. E-mail: reserghg@gye.satnet.net. Web site: www.grandhotelguayaquil.com. 180 rooms. Double $100. Cable TV. Restaurants. Coffee Shop. Bar. Gym. Pool. Shops. Business Center. Conference facilities. Travel Agency. Credit cards accepted.

The Gran Hotel was built to integrate an extraordinary cathedral wall into its garden. From the interior rooms and hallways, you look across the pool area to the back façade of the historic cathedral with the stained glass windows and steeple in full view. This architectural trump endows the venerable hotel with a singular charm.

Centrally located, a block away from Iguana Park, the rooms of the Gran Hotel have been remodeled in graceful burnished wood furnishings and are on par with newer five star hotels. A noble marble stairway in the entrance maintains the historic feel.

The two restaurants in the hotel assure you of fine dining. The upscale restaurant, 1800, offers Ecuadorian cuisine with a touch of the international, while the coffee shop serves up exceptional sandwiches and breakfasts. The fitness center features a squash court and an array of functional equipment such as exercise bikes and stair climbers. Other amenities include a cozy garden-surrounded pool and an efficient business center.

HOTEL UNIPARK, Clemente Ballén 406 in front of Iguana Park. Tel. 4/327 100, Fax 4/328 352. E-mail: ecuni@satnet.net. 138 rooms. Double $145. Cable TV. Restaurant. Bar. Sauna. Business center. Credit cards accepted.

The amenities of the Unipark and its convenient location make it a favorite with both business and pleasure travelers. The recently remodeled rooms are quite spacious and comfortable and you can't beat the views of both Iguana Park and the Cathedral, especially from the 10th floor. The Unipark is located adjacent to the small mall of the same name, making grabbing a snack or replacing that lost pair of sunglasses a breeze. We like the submarine sandwiches at the **Unideli** in the mall.

From the street-level entrance you have to take the elevator up to the second level to get to the marble-floored lobby. Also on this level are the **El Parque** restaurant and **Unibar**. El Parque offers extensive breakfast and lunch buffets while the Unibar serves up fresh sushi throughout the day. Managed by Oro Verde Hotels, the Unipark displays the excellence for which the company is known.

HOTEL CONTINENTAL, Chile y 10 de Agosto. Tel. 4/329 270, Fax 4/325 454. 60 rooms. Double $140. Breakfast included. Restaurant. Bar. Cafeteria. Credit cards accepted.

Located on Iguana Park facing the Cathedral, a room in the Continental somehow has the feeling of a 1970's sitcom den. The air-conditioned rooms are comfortable and luxurious with retro-fluidity that hails from another era. It made us want to call room service for a tray of deviled eggs and a Tab. Due to the intense competition in the upscale segment, the hotel frequently offers discounts of up to 50%, throwing in breakfast and dinner buffets to boot. Be sure to ask for promotional deals, especially on weekends.

HOTEL LAS AMERICAS, *Machala 811 y 9 de Octubre. Tel. 4/291 777, Fax 4/285799. E-mail: hotameri@gye.satnet.net. 50 rooms. Double $90. Restaurant. Credit cards accepted.*

This hotel is too tacky to consider seriously for the price. You can check your part in the mirrored headboard in the Panama Suite.

Moderate

HOTEL PALACE, *Chile 214 and Luque. Tel. 4/321 080, Fax 4/322 887. 76 rooms. Double $65. Cafe. Cable TV. Minibar. Credit cards accepted.*

The Palace bills itself as the hotel with "top accommodations at affordable prices." We'd have to modify that to read, "decent accommodations at affordable prices," but it's still an okay deal. While the rooms are not exactly going to win any interior decoration awards, they are huge and have recently remodeled bathrooms. The rooms that end in x19 are extremely large with nice tall ceilings. If you're a light sleeper ask for an interior room so that you hear less street noise.

HOTEL RAMADA, *Malecon y Orellana. Tel. 4/565 555, Fax 4/563 036. 60 rooms. Double $80. Cable TV. Restaurant. Bar. Credit cards accepted.*

The Hotel Ramada shows its age, but of more dire consequence, is that its neighborhood is located far enough off the central area to be considered somewhat unsafe. This might change with the Malecón 2000 initiative meant to clean up the waterfront.

Inexpensive

HOTEL DORAL, *Chile 402 y Aguirre. Tel. 4/328490, Fax 4/327088. E-mail: hdoral@gye.satnet.net. Web site: www.hdoral.com. 60 rooms. Double $25 and $20. Breakfast included. Cable TV. Restaurant. Credit cards accepted.*

Associated with the Best Western chain, the Hotel Doral is the best option you will find near Iguana Park for under $30. Some of the doubles have been remodeled and thus are slightly more expensive. The remodeled rooms, comparable to what you would find in a US motel chain, are worth the extra money if it fits your budget. The Doral is one of the better deals in town.

HOTEL PLAZA, *Chile 414 and Ballén. Tel. 4/327 140, Fax 4/324 195. 50 rooms. Double $25. No credit cards.*

The Plaza is absolutely plain, but it's got cable, hot water, and a view of Iguana Park from the fourth floor.

SOL DEL ORIENTE, *Aguirre 603 y Esscobedo. Tel. 4/325500, Fax 4/ 329352. 45 rooms. Double $30. Restaurant. Sauna. Credit cards accepted.*

This Sol del Oriente is reasonably priced for a centrally located hotel. The rooms are big, include a mini-fridge, and some have additional furniture such as sofas and writing tables. The hotel shows its age around the edges.

RIZZO HOTEL, *Clemente Ballen 319 y Chile. Tel. 4/325 210, Fax 4/326 209. 60 rooms. Double $21. Breakfast included. Credit cards accepted.*

The Rizzo is pretty shabby, but might do in a pinch for a low-priced place near Iguana Park if the Doral and Sol de Oriente are full.

HOTEL ALEXANDER, *Luque 1107 y Pedro Moncayo. Tel. 4/532 000, Fax 4/328 474. 61 rooms. Double $25. Cable TV. Restaurant. Credit cards accepted.*

A few blocks off of Parque Centenario, the location is just getting far enough off the main drags to be a bit sketchy. The air-conditioned rooms and hotel are in pretty good shape for the price though.

Budget

HOTEL VELEZ, *Velez 1021 and Quito. Tel. 4/530 292, Fax 4/532 430. 100 rooms. Double $6. No credit cards.*

This boxy hotel, located near Centenario Park, is a great deal for budget travelers. It reminds us of a government hotel in a communist country, only it's freshly painted and the TV and phones work. There is no hot water and the neighborhood is scary at night, but it's clean and the price is right.

WHERE TO EAT

There are several extraordinary restaurants in Guayaquil. One result of the current economic situation is that a first tier restaurants in Ecuador are a bargain by international standards. This creates a great opportunity to indulge in upscale cuisine if you might not otherwise.

Ecuadorian & Seafood

CARACOL AZUL, *9 de Octubre 1918 y Los Rios. Tel. 280 361. Expensive. Credit cards accepted.*

If there is any doubt that seafood rules supreme in Guayaquil, discover the fact in its superlative form at the Caracol Azul. Like many great restaurants, the ambience of the Caracol Azul gratifies its patrons through subtleties rather than flamboyance. The restaurant is located in a classic blue house, the walls of which are decorated tastefully with modern Ecuadorian artwork.

The magnificent culinary procession begins immediately with the appetizers. Consider starting with the Macho Ceviche, a succulent trio of seabass, shrimp, and oysters. This appetizer is so bountiful it alone will satisfy many diners or you may want to split it. We highly recommend the *fondo de alcachofa gourmet*, artichoke hearts filled with shrimp simmered in white wine sauce. There is no lack of zip in the recipes here. Anything prepared *a lo macho* such as the sea bass or shrimp will please the most ardent chili lovers. Contending for our favorite entree is the *ají de cangrejo*, a spicy, delectable stone crab concoction served in a giant oyster shell. We have to agree with the *Guayaquileño* who recommended the restaurant to us. It is *fuera de serio*. Roughly translated this means "out of this world".

1822, *Gran Hotel Guayaquil, Boyaca y 10 de Agosto. Expensive. Credit cards accepted.*

The menu at the 1822 restaurant is a lesson in South American history. Outlined between the delicious main course entrees such as sliced tenderloin in English mustard sauce with mushrooms, are the exploits of the great liberators. While considering whether to order the *corvina* Boyacá, seabass in caper sauce with tiny shrimp, you will learn about the Machiavellian maneuvers that took place in 1822 when Bolívar and Martín met in Guayaquil. Don't plan on signing any treaties, however, if you order the *langostinos* Salinas. The prawns in butter brandy, with garlic, garlic, and more garlic will make face-to-face negotiations difficult, unless of course, your counterpart orders the same.

LO NUESTRO, *V. Emilio 903 y Higuera, Urdesa. Tel. 386 398. Moderate. Credit cards accepted.*

Lo Nuestro is a big restaurant with big flavor serving up favorites like *locro de queso* and *llapingachos* better than just about any other Ecuadorian establishment. The thing that Lo Nuestro does best is seafood. The *corvina al ajillo* is delicious, as is the mountainous shrimp cocktail.

A few other excellent options for Ecuadorian fare include **La Canoa**, *Mall del Sol, Tel. 692 051, moderate,* and **La Banca**, *Francisco P. Ycaza 115 y Pichincha, Tel. 565-000, moderate.*

Other tasty locales for seafood are the **Cangrejo Criollo**, *Cdla. La Garzota, Ave. Principal Villa 9, Tel. 232 018, moderate,* and **La Boulandre**, *Boliviano206 y Todos los Santos, Tel. 382 471, expensive.*

International
LE GOURMET, *Oro Verde Hotel, 9 de Octubre y Garcia Moreno. Tel. 4/ 327 999. Expensive. Credit cards accepted.*

Upon taking your table in the award-winning French restaurant, Le Gourmet, a sense of culinary anticipation builds. Something as simple as the bread and butter provides a hint of the exquisite and complex flavors to come. The bread is flavorfully enhanced with bits of olives or bacon, while the spread is subtly laced with spices like paprika. The menu is sonnet that conjures up culinary fantasies, soon to be satisfied.

Imagine a salad of baby lettuce, fresh tarragon, goat cream cheese, and spicy radish dressing. The lobster bisque, even with its rich cognac base, isn't left to fend for itself. A single duck ravioli and perfectly delicate Cornish game hen egg accent the soup.

The artistry in flavors and presentation is exquisite. With the grilled seafood, for example, the chef first prepares a grid of crunchy, tender asparagus. On top of that are layered grilled fish, lobster, and caramelized onions, all lightly bathed in vanilla sauce.

One of the things we liked best about this restaurant is that the wait staff caters expertly to novices and connoisseurs of French cuisine alike. They make wonderful, respectful recommendations to any queries that you might have. If this weren't the case, we might never have tasted the guanabana sorbet with Grand Marnier and baked oranges.

Another option in French food is the **Juan Salvador Gaviota**, *Cdla. Kennedy Norte y Orellana, Tel. 298 280.*

LA TRATTORIA DA ENRICO, *Bálsamos 507 entre Av. Las Monjas y Ebanos in Urdesa. Tel. 387 079. Expensive. Credit cards accepted.*

The Trattoria de Enrico has combined elements of whimsy and refinement to create a dining atmosphere that is too unique to pass up. You will instantly be transported from Guayaquil to Venice when you walk through the front door, as a gondolier-uniformed attendent leads you over water-filled canals to the main dining area. Here, smaller canals border the room. You can watch the golden bellies of carp as they swim above the glass ceiling of the restaurant in an overhead fish tank.

The Trattoria doesn't rely on spectacle to retain its loyal clientele, but rather, award-winning cuisine. We highly recommend the *ravioli paisana*, fresh pasta squares filled with delicately spiced meat and tender, Italian mushrooms. The menu is replete with dishes based with luscious fresh pasta as well as delicious plates of seafood and the choicest cuts of meat.

For a less formal and moderate Italian option in Urdesa, try **Casanova**, *Primera 604 y Las Manjas, Tel. 882 475.* Another excellent tratorria is **Di Carlo**, *behind the Hilton, Tel. 282 009.*

TSUJI, *Victor Emilio Estrada 813 y Guyacanes. Tel. 881 183. Expensive. Credit cards accepted.*

At Tsuji you can sample Ecuador's extraordinary fruits of the sea, sliced and prepared by a master sushi chef, in a trustworthy, hygienic environment. The *corvina* and *lenguado nigiri* melt in your mouth. The only shortcoming is that they go easy on the *wasabi* to appease local palettes, but you can remedy this by ordering extra on the side.

CIELITO LINDO, *Circonvalion and Ficus, Urdesa. Tel. 388 426. Moderate. Credit cards accepted.*

The Cielito Lindo is an odd mixture of extremely kitschy, almost cheesy décor and decent Mexican food that combine to make it one of the most popular Mexican restaurants in Guayaquil. The brightly colored eatery reminds us a bit of Cancún – not authentic Mexico, but at least in the neighborhood. The spicy salsa, for example, has excellent flavor, but you have to ignore the fact that it is served with chips in a giant sombrero. Good food bets are the fragrant chicken fajitas or one of the combo plates. This is a popular place for young *Guayaquileños* to come on dates.

CASA BASCA, *Ballén 422. Tel. 534 599. Moderate. Credit cards accepted.*

The Casa Basca, across the street from Iguana Park, is a favorite with Guayaquil businessmen. Stepping in here is like walking into one of the many basement-level *tapas* bars in Spain. The décor is simple, basically brick walls lined with bottles of wine, so the real attraction is the food.

The small restaurant is divided into two sections. The front part is a *tapas* bar, offering many Spanish appetizers like Mancheco cheese and cold shellfish. The restaurant area, with small tables, serves up fragrant and flavorful treats like garlic soup, fish prepared with peppers, and prawn sautéed in garlic. There is no menu in either section, but rather a chalkboard indicating the dishes available that day. **Tasca Vasca**, *Chile 416 and Ballén*, has the same owners and similar food.

LE FONDUE, *Oro Verde Hotel, 9 de Octubre y Garcia Moreno. Tel. 4/327 999. Moderate. Credit cards accepted.*

If the craving for cheese strikes, fondue is great way to sate it. Le Fondue also serves finely prepared steaks and other European fare. One good dip deserves another, so don't pass up the chocolate fondue for dessert.

O CASARAO, *Av. Guillermo Pareja 20. Tel. 291 213. Moderate. Credit cards accepted.*

If you have never experienced a Brazilian *churrasco*, now is your chance. Chicken, sausages, steaks, pork, and any other meat you can imagine are served crackling off the spit onto your plate in an endless, carnivorous spectacle. Vegetarians *vai embora*!

SPICE BAR, *Oro Verde Hotel, 9 de Octubre y Garcia Moreno. Moderate. Tel. 4/327 999. Credit cards accepted.*

Two things - flavor and fun - unite the menu choices at this fusion restaurant. The Spice Bar has assembled exciting recipes from around the world, usually those with a bit of piquant like Thai and Mexican favorites. If you're really hungry, join the Club 41 by eating a 41 ounce steak, and have your name engraved on a wall plaque. A lot of people like to sit on the balcony overlooking the pool for appetizers and drinks. Weekend nights are especially popular.

ORO VERDE COFFEE SHOP, *9 de Octubre y Garcia Moreno. Moderate. Tel. 4/327 999. Credit cards accepted.*

The Oro Verde's 24-hour coffee shop serves such good food that it is many Guayaquileño's preferred dining spot. The buffet spreads for breakfast and lunch are varied and enormous. The café is best place in town to get an after hours meal.

LA PEPA DE ORO, *Gran Hotel Guayaquil, Boyaca y 10 de Agosto. Moderate. Credit cards accepted.*

The Gran Hotel's 24-hour coffee shop pulls off an admirable imitation of an old American diner. The coffee counter, done up in multicolored tiles, looks out to a waterfall tumbling into the hotel pool, which has the cathedral wall and stained glass as a backdrop. You will find diner-style favorites on the menu like fried chicken, milk shakes, and grilled sandwiches oozing with cheese. The breakfast and lunch buffets are also favorites here.

ORO VERDE DELI, *9 de Octubre y Garcia Moreno. Tel. 4/327 999. Inexpensive. Credit cards accepted.*

The Oro Verde Deli offers an excellent variety of sandwiches ranging from hearty subs to healthy delights on whole grain breads. If you look, you won't be able to resist the chocolates and pastries. The Italian ices are delcious as well. At least ask for a sample of the *cerveza* flavored gelato. It really tastes like a creamy, cold brew.

UNIPARK DELI, *Clemente Ballén 406. Inexpensive. No credit cards.*

You can pick up subs at this deli across the street from the Iguana Park. It's on the ground floor of the Unipark Hotel shopping center, on the Chile street side.

For Chinese food, the best in town is **Joun Yep**, *Los Ceibos, Calle 4 102, Moderate.* Otherwise, try **Cantones**, *Guillermo Pareja y Calle 43, Tel. 236 333, Moderate.*

The fast food restaurants **Burger King**, **McDonalds**, and **KFC** clog the arterial of *9 de Octubre near the corner of Boyacá.*

SEEING THE SIGHTS

The best place to begin a walking tour is **Iguana Park**, located between *10 de Agosto and Clement Ballen*, and between *Chimborazo and Chile.* Parque de las Iguanas is also known as Parque Seminario and Parque Bolívar. We use the colloquial name because it is the most frequently heard as well as the most descriptive. This tidy little park is crawling with beefy, green iguanas. The silky, yard-long reptiles are a delight. You will find them everywhere, even in the trees. The crew of guards stationed here to protect the iguanas inadvertently makes the park one of the safer spots in the city. Many hotels, restaurants, and museums are near so we consider it to be the visitor's city center. If you want to have a lunch among the lizards, there is a deli with decent subs on the ground floor Unipark Hotel shopping center across the street.

Across from the park, on *Chimborazo Street,* is the beautiful Gothic **Cathedral**. Step inside to see the fabulous stained glass. The window high

GUAYAQUIL
SIGHTS

1. Iguana Park
2. Cathedral
3. Municipal Museum
4. Nahim Isaias Museum
5. Moorish Clock Tower
6. Municipal and Government Palaces
7. La Rotonda
8. Banco Del Pacifico Archeology Museum
9. Murals
10. Central Bank Anthropology Museum
11. Parque Centenario
12. Las Peñas
13. Crafts Market

above the altar portraying a sinuous Jesus on a crucifix against huge, single drop of blood is particularly worthy of contemplation.

MUNICIPAL MUSEUM, *corner of Chile y Sucre. Tel. 524 100. Monday-Friday 9am –5pm. Entry free.*

The Municipal Museum has archeological displays as well as paintings and contemporary sculptures. There are several good museums in town, so this might be one to skip to conserve on limited time or attention span.

From Iguana Park, walk down Clemente Ballen towards the river until you reach corner of Pedro Carbo.

MUSEO NAHIM ISAÍAS, *Clemente Ballen and Pichincha. Monday-Saturday 10am-5pm. Entry free.*

This is a superb private museum located upstairs in the Filanbanco bank. The exhibits are very well presented in air-conditioned rooms. The collection is divided into two parts. One is dedicated to archeological pieces with particular emphasis on the coastal cultures. In addition to ceramic and textiles you will find a seashells fashioned into fishhooks and jewelry. The museum also has an excellent collection of colonial art from the Quiteño school including works by such well-known artists as Luis Ribera whose works are found in Quito's most important churches. There are also several pieces by Miguel de Santiago, an artist influenced by the Flemish style, but who incorporated the local landscape into his religious paintings.

If you continue down Clemente Ballen you will reach the riverfront avenue **Simón Bolívar Malecón**. You will find parts of the Malecón to be sleekly modern, other pieces suffering dilapidation, and other sections under construction. This disparity is due to the ambitious **Malecón 2000** project in which 20 hectares of waterfront property are being completely revitalized over several years. The goal is to establish parks, museums, hotels, shops, and restaurants in a secure, arboreal environment.

The more isolated parts of the Malecón have had crime problems in recent years, but with the city renewal project, officials insist it will be made safe. We suggest you check with your hotel to see how the security situation is during your visit. The central portion, which we include on our walking tour, has always been the safest part.

Just to your right on the Malecón, you will see the **Moorish Clock Tower**. Built in 1783, it measures 23 meters tall. Turn back the other direction on the Malecón, passing the ornate **Palacio Municipal** and the simpler **Palacio del Gobierno**. Both were built in the 1920's. You will soon reach the marble **La Rotonda** monument, at the end of 9 De Octubre Street. The monument commemorates the meeting of Simón Bolívar and General José de San Martín on July 26th, 1822. The two great revolutionary leaders, who wrested much of South America from Spanish control, met in Guayaquil to discuss the fate of the new nations.

Continue down the Malecón until reaching Victor Manuel Rendon. Here you will find the Banco Pacifico Museum.

BANCO DEL PACIFICO ARCHEOLOGICAL MUSEUM, *Ycaza 113 and Pichincha. Tel. 556 010. Monday-Friday 9am-6pm. Weekends 11am-1pm. No entry fee.*

If you don't speak Spanish, this will probably be the most satisfying of the three superior archeology museums in Guayaquil. The interesting exhibits, placarded in both English and Spanish, provide an instructive background. The collection includes 650 pieces of ceramics divided into two periods - the Formative Period from 3000-300 BC and the Regional Development and Integration Period from 300 BC to 1500 AD. Each of the display cases is organized by subject matter, which we always find more interesting than purely chronological exhibitions. We especially like the exposition on the healing cults.

Head away from the river two blocks to the corner of Ycaza and Cordova to the two buildings covered with enormous **murals**. These giant replicas are a tribute to the most renowned Ecuadorian painters. Anyone who has ridden an Ecuadorian bus will appreciate *Sigan para Arriba*.

Other points of interest are farther away, so we suggest you take a taxi.

WHO THREW THE POTS?

*A trip to any museum in Ecuador, but especially those on the coast, reveals hundreds of ceramic works. Who made all these artifacts? The oldest ceramics found in the Western Hemisphere come from a fishing village on the northern Guayas coast and date back to 3200 BC. Called the **Valdivia** phase, the most prominent pieces from this period are pottery figurines with recessed flat faces, long necks, and carefully executed hair styles.*

*The **Chorrera** phase, another age of prolific pottery makers, dates back from 850 BC. Although mainly a coastal people, this is the first phase in Ecuador where the sites are not restricted to the shore. Favorite Chorrera pieces are the whistling bottles. These animal-shaped canteens were designed to make noises that sound like their representative creatures when water is poured down the spouts.*

CENTRAL BANK ANTHROPOLOGY MUSEUM, *Jose de Antepara and 9 de Octubre. Tel. 327 402. Tuesday-Friday 10am-6pm. Weekends 10am-2pm. Entry $0.50.*

There are two parts to this excellent museum. The first floor features impressive multi-media displays, in Spanish, on the peoples of the Ecuadorian coast. With some of the most interesting and intricate ceramic pieces that we have seen in Latin America, the Banco Central museum is extremely well done. In addition to the ceramic work, there are some beautiful displays of gold jewelry and a fun full-sized reproduction of a Manteño-Huancavilca sailing vessel.

The second floor features some fine 20th century contemporary art with nice background on each piece. Check the notices posted at the front door for information on art-house movies and other special events at the museum. The Central Bank Museum will be moving to the renovated Malecón at some point. Verify its present location with your hotel.

The **Parque Centenario** is on 9 De Octubre between Pedro Moncayo and Lorenzo de Garaicoa, within walking distance of the Museo del Banco Central. It is a pleasant medium-sized city park, but you will not miss much if you skip it.

Las Peñas is an artsy, colonial enclave that climbs the Cerro del Carmen hill at the far end of the Malecón. There are a few galleries in the neighborhood and plaques commemorating houses of former presidents and famous artists. **Santo Domingo**, one of the country's oldest churches, founded in 1548, is located here. Unfortunately this area is plagued by crime and we cannot recommend a visit at this point. Check with your hotel to see if the situation has improved at the time of your visit.

You should also consider a trip to the **Guayaquil Crafts Market,** *Juan Montalvo y Baquerizo Moreno, 10am-6pm.*

City & Regional Tours
• **Metropalitan Tours**, *Antepara 915 y 9 de Octubre. Tel. 4/399 931. E-mail: mgd@metropalitan.com.*
• **Oro Verde Hotel**, *9 de Octubre y Garcia Moreno. Tel. 4/327 999.*
• **RíoTours Agency**, *in the Gran Hotel Guayaquil. Web site: www.guayasnorte.com/riotours*
• **Ecuadorian Tours**, *Av. 9 de Octubre. Tel. 4/287 111, Fax 4/280 851. E-mail: ectours@gye.satnet.net.*

SHOPPING
You can find colorful panchos, tagua and balsa wood carvings, leather goods, and anything else crafted in Ecuador at the **Guayaquil Crafts Market**. There are 254 display stands on two floors. You won't go home empty-handed. The market is located at *Juan Montalvo and Baquerizo Moreno; 10am-6pm.*

The most convenient shopping centers are the **Mall del Sol** and **Policentro** in Ciudadela Kennedy.

EXCURSIONS & DAY TRIPS

BOTANICAL GARDEN, *Cerro Colorado, Las Orquideas. Tel. 417 004 or 416 975. Entry $2.*

Located on 5 hectares at the top of Colorado Hill, this botanical garden is home to over 300 species of plants, 70 species of birds, and 54 species of butterflies. Trails take you through three distinct sections of the park, one of which includes an artificial waterfall. At the top of one of the hills you can see the Daule and Babahoyo Rivers meet to form the Guayas, with the city of Guayquil spreading out in the foreground.

The trails are well marked with signs indicating the species of trees and other endemic flora of the region. One of the most vibrant attractions is a giant purple and pink orchid, the *cattleya máxima*. It will take you about 40 minutes in cab to get here. To arrange a tour in English, you should call in advance. Another good alternative is going with Metropalitan Tours, *Tel. 4/399 931, E-mail: mgd@metropalitan.com.*

Santa Elena Peninsula

About a two-hour drive from Guayaquil, the high-rise beach resort of **Salinas** punctuates the arid Santa Elena peninsula. The sparkling green ocean that laps the main beach is the primary draw here during the day, but as important to many visitors is the disco scene at night. If you prefer a more tranquil and natural beach spot, you can stay at the quirky Farallon Dillon, endowed with a gorgeous view, located near fishing village Ballenita, or opt for a hotel on a bluff above turbulent sea at Punta Carnero. The peninsula is far enough away to consider an overnight stay rather than trying to fit it in a day trip. See the *Santa Elena Peninsula* destination section below for complete information.

Playas

Other than the fact that it is an hour closer to Guayaquil than the Santa Elena Peninsula, we can't figure out why anyone would come here. This growing fishing, town located 97 kilometers southwest of Guayaquil, is not that charming from an esthetic point of view, nor is it that fun when it gets crowded on the weekends. We recommend opting for a beach spot on the peninsula or one farther up the coast.

Manglares Charute Ecological Reserve

You can take a canoe trip through a mangrove-lined fluvial lake where you will find a variety of water birds. This 87,000-hectare reserve protects one of the last remaining areas of mangroves along the southern coast. Although the reserve is only 40 kilometers away from Guayaquil, it takes well over an hour to get here in a car because it is located across the river, then south down the highway. This excursion is really only recommended to bird and flora enthusiasts.

PRACTICAL INFORMATION

Banks: There are many banks with ATM's. Near Iguana Park, there's an ATM in the Unipark Hotel mall.

Business Hours: 9am-1pm; 2pm-6pm

Currency Exchange: **Interfinsa**, *Junín 114 y Malecón*

E-mail: Service: Cafenet, *P. Icaza 113 y Malecón, Banco del Pacífico Museum, 3rd floor*

Embassies & Consulates:
• **Bolivia**, *Icaza 302 y Córdova. Tel. 564 260*
• **Canada**, *Córdova 808 y Rendón. Tel. 563 580*
• **Colombia**, *Córdova 808 y Rendón. Tel. 563 308*
• **Peru**, *9 de Octubre 411 y Chile. Tel. 322 738*
• **UK**, *Córdova 623 y Solano. Tel. 560 400*
• **USA,** *9 de Octubre y García Moreno. Tel. 323 570*
• **Venezuela**, *Chile 329 y Aguirre. Tel. 326 579*

Immigration Office: Migración del Guayas, *Av. De Las Américas, frente al terminal terrestre (bus station). 8am-11:30am; 3:00pm-5pm*

Laundry: Consult your hotel for the closest *lavanderia*

Medical Service:.Clinica Kennedy, *Ave. San Jorge y 9. Tel. 286 693*

Post Office: Correos, *Aguirre y Pedro Carbo. Tel. 514 713*

Supermarket: Economarket, *Chile y Clemente Ballen*

Telephone/Fax: The area code is 4. **Emetel** has an office on Iguana Park.

Tourist Office/Maps: Cetur, *Aguirre 104. Tel. 530 952*

SANTA ELENA PENINSULA

Two hours west of Guayaquil, the **Santa Elena Peninsula** is the favorite weekend escape for city residents. The 30 kilometer long peninsula is extensively developed into separate resort, commercial, and industrial areas.

At the tip of the peninsula, **Salinas**, the primary resort destination, is composed of a pleasant swimming beach, an emerald bay, and a beachfront row of gleaming condos. **Punta Carnero** is a quieter resort destination that sticks out like a rocky nub on the opposite side of the peninsula. We consider the most attractive option for sea and tranquility to be the odd, yet enchanting **Farallon Dillon**, near the tiny fishing village Ballenita, just at the beginning of the peninsula.

Santa Elena and **La Libertad** are the first towns on the peninsula. Both are industrial and commercial centers with La Libertad being the larger of the two.

ARRIVALS & DEPARTURES

BY BUS

You can reach Salinas by bus in three hours from the Terminal Terrestre in Guayaquil. If you are going to Punta Carnero or Ballenita, take the bus to La Libertad, then continue onward either by bus or taxi.

BY CAR

It is an easy two to three-hour drive from Guayaquil. Simply follow Av. 9 de Octubre out, then follow signs indicating *Costa* or Salinas.

You can hire a taxi to drop you off for about $35 one-way. For a day trip, to have the driver wait for you for a few hours, it would cost slightly more.

ORIENTATION

If you consider Santa Elena to be the starting point, the peninsula is only about 30 kilometers long. It has a wide base and a narrow finger that tapers quickly to only a few kilometers in width by the time it reaches Salinas. The towns are densely populated and overlap.

If you stay on the main road, which is an extension of the highway, you will first pass through Santa Elena, then along the southern edge of La Libertad, and then into Salinas.

Ballenita is northwest of Santa Elena, so you go through that town to get there. Punta Carnero is on the south side of the peninsula, so you turn left after passing La Libertad to get there.

Blessed with tame, sparkling green water and a long sandy beach, Salinas is the place where Guayaquileños seek fun and sun on the weekends. The row of shiny high-rises along the Malecón include surprisingly few hotels, but instead are primarily composed of condominiums owned by weekending families.

Baking under the sun by day and shaking to the disco beat by night is the modus operandi of this town. Sport fishing and surfing will inspire a few people to rise before noon.

WHERE TO STAY

Salinas

Salinas is the place in Ecuador where you get the least lodging value for your dollar. There is only one hotel in the high-end category, and they know it. In the moderate category, the best you can do is the **Suites Salinas** a block off the beach, or the nicer, less advantageously located **Mediterraneo**. The only recommendable inexpensive hotel is the **Yulee**.

HOTEL CALYPSO, *near the beginning of the Malecón. Tel. 4/772 425, 773 583. Tel/fax in Guayaquil 4/285 452. E-mail: calypsso@gye.satnet.net. 48* *rooms. Double $140. Cable TV. Restaurant. Bar. Disco. Pool. Parking. Credit cards accepted.*

The unsatisfactory quality for price exchange of this high-rise hotel is proof positive that Salinas is lacking competition in the upscale segment. While the location and views are superb, the so-called junior suites are about what you would expect from a nice seaside motel elsewhere. The master suites are much more comfortable and spacious, however, and would be suitable for vacationing families.

HOTEL MEDITERRANEO, *9th Avenue between 20th and 21st Streets. Tel. 4/772 313, Fax 4/772 078. 25 rooms. Double $40. Restaurant. Pool. No credit cards.*

If you don't mind walking four blocks to the beach, the Mediterraneo is a good option in Salinas. It is extremely clean and well tended, although the views are of sand flats rather than ocean. If you get a big room on the top floor in the back of the property you can get a very peaceful night's sleep. If you turn in early, stay away from the rooms around the central patio, as the restaurant, with its music, stays open until 11pm. You might want to try to *bolónes* for breakfast, big balls of cheese and plantains.

SUITES SALINAS, *Enriquez Gallo y Calle 27. Tel. 4/774 267 or 772759. Cel. 09/601 041. 50 rooms. Double $35. Cable TV. Pool. Parking. Credit cards accepted.*

The Suites Salinas is the best deal for a hotel within a block of a beach. While the rooms are not finished in sparkling tile, they are clean and big, with at least one piece of furniture to lounge on. There is a disco on the bottom floor so this will not be the quietest place you've ever stayed, but really, tranquility is not what you should come to Salinas for anyway. Do not confuse Suites Salinas with the Hotel Salinas next door.

EL CARRUAJE HOTEL, *Malecón 517. Tel. 4/774 282. 18 rooms. Double $40. Restaurant. No credit cards.*

If you just have to stay right in the center of the main boardwalk, but don't have a very big budget, El Carruaje is your only choice. A squatty hotel between towering condos, it is right across the street from the beach. Ask for a room on the top floor, but check for musty smells before you accept yours.

HOTEL YULEE, *near the Club de Yates. Tel. 4/772 028. Cel. 09/893 400. Double with private bath and A/C $30. Double with shared bath $18. Restaurant. No credit cards.*

With a good location near the far end of the beach, this is the best option for budget travelers. The rooms couldn't be more bare bones, but it can be a fun place to meet young Ecuadorian sun seekers. The exterior of the coquettish old house is painted in brilliant yellow, while the interior is done in wood weathered by the sea air.

HOTEL SALINAS, *Enriques Gallo y Calle 27. Tel. 4/ 772 179, 772 759, or 774 280, Fax 4/ 774 267. 40 rooms. Double $20. Restaurant. TV. Parking. No credit cards.*

This place is pretty run down. Go next door to Suites Salinas if you can afford it or try the Hotel Yulee if you can't.

Outside of Salinas

HOTEL DAVINCI, *On the highway from La Libertad to Salinas just past the Mall in La Libertad. Tel. 4/779 375, Fax 4/779 376. 20 rooms. Double $18. Restaurant. No credit cards.*

This avocado green hotel right on the highway has newness going for it. With cable TV, hot water and clean tile floors, everything about it is fine – except for the location. You wish it were somewhere near the beach or at least off the main road. The large restaurant serves inexpensive plates of spaghetti, rice, chicken and seafood.

Punta Carnero

The quiet side of the Santa Elena Peninsula is nearly the perfect response to brassy Salinas. You can enjoy the sights and sounds of the green sea crashing against the rocks from the swimming pool at one of the two hotels. Two flaws affect the scheme however. The first is the trash-covered road that cuts across the peninsula to the beach. The other downside, once the debris ends and the ocean beauty begins, is that the waves and undertow here are ferocious, thus the name "Mar Bravo."

HOTEL PUNTA CARNERO, *Punta Carnero, 10 km south of La Libertad. Tel. 4/775 450, 775 537, Fax 4/775 377. 35 rooms. Double $40. Restaurant. Pool. Event facilities. Credit cards accepted.*

This pretty hotel is perched on steep cliffs with long beaches pounded by turbulent waves stretching into the distance on either side. Due to the superb vista, the hotel is a favorite site for weddings. The rooms are comfortable, most of them with ocean views, and more fairly priced than the hotels in Salinas. This is also a good family place because there is a big playground for kids in addition to the ocean-view pool.

HOSTERIA DEL MAR, *Tel. 4/775370 or via Boulevard Tours Tel. 4/ 566065, Fax 4/313157. Double $35. Pool.*

On the same bluff as Hotel Punta Carnero, this is more run down than the Hotel Punta Carnero. Room G might do it for you though as it literally hangs over the edge of the ocean.

Ballencita

HOTEL FARALLON DILLON, *On the point in Ballenita. Tel. 4/785 611, Fax 4/786 643. E-mail: ddillon@gu.pro.ec. Web site: wwwpub.ecua.net.ec/ farallon. 20 rooms. Double $40. Restaurant. Museum. Credit cards accepted.*

You know this is not your standard Ecuadorian hotel as soon as you catch sight of the blue and white buildings hanging over the end of the point. The first thing you see is the on-site antique store's bell gable, a replica of Cuenca's La Concepción. Upon closer inspection of the facade you'll notice that it has been modified to include dolphins, a Star of David and the Muslim crescent.

Once you walk on-board, you have entered the fantasy land of Señor Dillon, a retired merchant marine captain who sailed the world for 33 years collecting the nautical antiques that now decorate the restaurant/ museum. Old cannons ward off pirates while sea monster lamp-fixtures keep evil spirits at bay.

A large observation deck looks out over the ocean. On clear days you can see Chimborazo in the distance, or, if the timing is right, a passing pod of humpback whales. Don't worry if you feel something strange at your feet, that's just one of the parrots playing with your shoelaces. You'll be inspired by the precision with which the Spanish-speaking parrots roll their r's...if a parrot can pronounce *corre* perfectly, you can too.

There is a $1.50 per person minimum purchase to enter the restaurant, which is also the museum. Maiden heads from around the world, ceramics and coins recovered from shipwrecks, battle axes, and a 200 year old scuba suit are just some of the treasures. We especially like the door to the men's restroom that came from a real submarine.

The crazy hotel deserves a visit if only for a quick 15-minute tour of the place on your way up the coast.

The beach below the hotel is one of the cleanest in the vicinity. During the high season there is a snack bar at the bottom of the stairs near the ocean so that you don't have to climb all the way up to quench your thirst.

WHERE TO EAT

The most highly regarded restaurant in Salinas is the boat-shaped **Mar y Tierra**, near the beginning of the Malecón. The food is not on par with the expensive pricing, but the view is nice. The restaurant in the **Carruaje Hotel** is a better value.

There are a couple of **pizzerias** about halfway down the Malecón. The weekenders from Guayaquil swear by the **cevicherias** at the market. There is a **Dunkin' Donuts** near the end of the Malecón towards the Yacht Club.

SEEING THE SIGHTS

Most people come to the peninsula to enjoy the beach. On a rainy day you can check out the archaeology museum, **Museo Amantes de Sumpa**, *Tel. 785216 or 09/866026.*

The **Farrolon Dillon**, described in the *Ballencita* section above, bills the jumble of mastheads and antique diving gear decorating its restaurant as a maritime museum. Consider planning a visit around lunch. You can check out the tide pools and swim along the stretch of beach below the hotel. There is a $1.50 minimum at the restaurant that takes the place of a museum entry fee.

SPORTS & RECREATION

Pesca Tours, *Tel. 4/772391*, offers sport fishing. The 35-foot boat can accommodate up to six passengers and costs $350 for a full day.

The **Chocolatera military base** consumes the extreme tip of the peninsula. It hosts one of the national surf competitions every year. If you want to surf or sunbathe here, you can enter the compound by registering with the guard at the gate.

PRACTICAL INFORMATION

Banks: Banks with ATM's are on the *Malecón* in Salinas and on *9 de Octubre* in La Libertad.

Post Office: Correos, *Ave. 2 and calle 17, La Libertad*

Telephone/Fax: The area code is 4. **Emetel**, *Calle 21 and Ave. 3, La Libertad*

AYANGUE

CUMBRES DE AYANGUE, *near Ayangue off the Santa Elena-Maglaralto highway. Tel. 4/916 040 or 916 042, fax 916 041. Tel. in Guayaquil 4/370115, fax 454114. 20 rooms. Double $70. Restaurant. Credit cards accepted.*

This hotel is located on an enchanting bluff where waves crash against the rocks below in a constant, soothing rhythm. The restaurant, bar, and kidney shaped pool are at the end of a point that resembles a big toe dipping into the ocean. The whitewashed railing, which borders the pool area as seen against the green ocean and rocky cliffs, makes for a view reminiscent of the Greek Isles.

The cabins are in decent shape, but are in need of some upkeep before they are worth the price. While this is definitely the nicest place to stay on the coast from Salinas to Ayangue, (about 40 km north of Santa Elena), it pales in comparison with the better-designed and maintained Hosteria Atamari, 43 kilometers farther up the coast.

MONTAÑITA

Montañita is a dusty, tired fishing village that has gained a reputation as the best surfer hangout in Ecuador. There's something about the shabbiness of the town that turns us off. Just because a place is geared towards budget travelers doesn't mean that it has to be dirty.

Just north of town, however, is the much more pleasant *La Punta de Montañita*, The Point. Montañita's best-known wave, a long right, breaks directly off the rocky point here. If you want to surf in Montañita, we highly recommend staying on The Point. You will find good lodging for each spending category, the tastiest restaurants, and the best waves.

ARRIVALS & DEPARTURES

The drive from the Santa Elena Peninsula to Montañita is not an especially pretty one. Scrubby landscapes, aqua-culture factories, litter along the highway and poor, dirty *pueblos* make you wonder whether all the hullabaloo about the coast is just empty promises from the Ecuadorian tourist board.

The road itself is not the greatest, but there are far worse ones in the country. Just don't pick up too much speed, because as soon as you do, a crater-sized pothole will threaten to suck your entire car down into the Land of the Lost.

By Bus

Buses leave regularly from Santa Elena heading up the coastal road. They stop at every village along the way though, so it ends up being almost a three hour trip. Both CITUP and Manglaralto buses travel the route.

By Car

If you travel by car, make sure it is one with good clearance. Last time we went, we rented a 4-wheel drive Vitara and were very glad we had it. The thick, sturdy tires and room under the chassis made maneuvering the potholes and unpaved sections a breeze. Until the road gets repaired, it takes just under two hours to travel the 60 kilometers from Santa Elena.

ORIENTATION

Montañita sits right on the coast, 60 kilometers north of Santa Elena. Unfortunately, it's literally about ten kilometers south of the place on the coast where things really get lush and pretty.

WHERE TO STAY & EAT

BAJA MONTAÑITA, *On the point north of Montañita. Tel. 4/901218, Fax 4/901219. 20 rooms, 15 cabins. Double $50-70. Restaurant. Bar. Pool. Jacuzzi. Credit cards accepted.*

The Baja Montañita is the nicest place to stay in Montañita. Set at the end of the beach, right in front of the break, it enjoys a privileged position over the other lodging options in town and on the point. The cabins and rooms are arranged in two story buildings around the central pool and bar. Make sure that you get an upstairs room so that you will have an ocean view from your patio.

Most guests spend their time in lounge chairs around the pool listening to the waves crash on the beach beyond. The ocean in front of the hotel is better for surfing or admiring than swimming.

There are three types of accommodations: rooms, rustic cabins, and luxury cabins. The rooms are perfect for two people. If you've got a bigger group you may want to go for a luxury cabin, which is really more like a condo. Both kinds of cabins have a bedroom with two sets of bunk beds in addition to the master bedroom and bath. The rustic cabins have no temperature control other than opening or closing the windows, while the luxury ones have both fans and semi-functioning air conditioners. Some luxury cabins have a fireplace in the master bedroom.

The restaurant here specializes in, surprise, seafood, although they have a full menu of both typical Ecuadorian and international dishes. It's a great place to watch the sunset, although you might prefer the fresh breezes around the bar on a warm night.

The busy time on the coast runs from November through March. Keep in mind that prices are generally half the rate listed above during the off-season.

CABANAS TRES PALMAS, *on the point. No telephone. 10 rooms. Double $14.*

This is a really good option for a cheap place on the point. The rooms are immaculate. Curiously, some of the rooms have a sink outside the window, which we suspect weren't in the original architectural plans. Even if you don't stay here, come by for some Mexican food and a margarita at the thatched-roof open-wall restaurant right on the beach.

EL PELICANO, *on the point. No telephone. E-mail: elpelicano27@hotmail.com. 15 rooms. Double with private bath $10. Restaurant. No credit cards.*

We love El Pelicano for the food. Great square pizzas with mushrooms plucked right from the garden lure us over here for dinner. Al fresco dining, tasty pasta and friendly proprietors don't hurt either. While the atmosphere is generally mellow, be aware that Saturday night is dance night. The rooms here are very simple, with no hot water, but you can get your own bathroom.

LA CASA DEL SOL, *on the point. Tel. 4/901 302. Cellular Tel. 9/892 896. E-mail: casasol@ecua.net.ec. 12 rooms. Double $12. Restaurant. Laundry. No credit cards.*

While not directly on the ocean, just one lot away and on the point, this is one of the cleanest and secure options you will find in the budget category.

In Town

If you really want to stay in town, there is only one hotel we can recommend.

HOTEL MONTANITA, *Malecón. Tel. 4/901296 or 284868, Fax 4/ 901299. 36 rooms. Double $12. Restaurant. Bar. No credit cards.*

This thatched-roof, waterfront fort is the dominant structure in Montañita. Three stories of rooms take up one side, while high white-washed walls complete the other facades of the expansive rectangle. A nest of hammocks upstairs gives loungers an enticing view of the sweeping surf. Most of the large interior courtyard consists of sand and a few plants. The rooms are very basic and include the electric type hot water heater.

The provisions offered in town are almost purely pizzerias and *cevecherías*, but we think El Pelicano, on the point, has the best pizza around. There is one good bakery on the street by the Hotel Montañita.

NIGHTLIFE & ENTERTAINMENT

Carnival time completely changes this place for a week. Hundreds of people, mostly young ones, flood in to party in this tiny town.

SPORTS & RECREATION

The main thing that brings people to Montañita is the waves. The best break is the right at The Point on the northern end of town. There is also a beach break directly in front of town, but the water quality is suspect.

A few places in Montañita rent surfboards. You can easily check out your options by walking the two streets of town. Most of the sticks are under 6'5", so if you're a long boarder, bring your own. There are a few balsa long boards for rent, but they are as heavy as a dining room table.

Some of the best breaks on the most beautiful beaches are another 30 kilometers up the road at places like Alandaluz and Piqueros Patas Azules. Unfortunately, they don't have any rentals available. We recommend hiring a board here for the week and then scooting up the road. You can also rent boogie boards in town.

Lots of young travelers like to just hang out on the beach. Be sure the keep on eye on your stuff both on the beach and in the cheap hotels. It's been known to walk away in somebody else's arms.

MACHALA

Most travelers who take the road south of Guayaquil are heading to the Peruvian border. Considering the other great destinations in Ecuador, there is not really much reason to come this way. **Machala**, the capital of El Oro province, is 200 kilometers south of Guayaquil. It is a pleasant enough commercial center for the banana industry, but there is not much else going on here. It is a transit point and the best place to stay near the border if you are on your way to Peru.

Each September Machala hosts the International Banana Festival. A Miss Banana competition is the spotlight event. Women from around South America are invited to participate, but smart money says place your bet on the Venezuelan entrant every year.

ARRIVALS & DEPARTURES

There are flights between Guayaquil and Machala. Tickets cost about $25 one-way. **Tame** is located at *Montalvo y Bolivar, Tel. 930 139.*

There is no central bus station. Below is a list of bus companies and destinations. If you are heading to Peru, try to change most of your money back into to dollars at a bank or currency exchange operation in Machala, otherwise you will end up dealing with the street traders in Huaquillas. North Americans and most Europeans do not need a visa for Peru, but Australians and New Zealanders have to process a visa in the Peruvian consulate in Machala, *Bolivar y Colon, Tel. 930 660,* if you haven't done so already.

Bus Companies
- **CIFA**, *Bolivar y Guayas*. To Huaquillas, Peruvian border.
- **Ecuatoriano Pullman**, *9 de Octubre y Colon*. To Guayaquil.
- **Transportes Occidentales**, *Buenavista y Olmedo*. To Guayaquil.
- **Transportes Coorpertiva Loja**, *Tarquí y Rocafuerte*. To Loja.
- **Express Sucre**, *Sucre y Colon*. To Cuenca.

WHERE TO STAY & EAT

The most luxurious place to stay and eat in Machala is **Oro Verde**, *Circunvalacion Norte y Vehicular 7. Tel. 7/933-140, Double $110*. More centrally located is the **Rizzo**, *Guayas y Bolivar, Tel. 7/921 511, Double $30*.

A moderate priced hotel with a decent restaurant is the **Hotel Oro**, *Sucres y Montalvo, Tel. 7/930 783, Double $20*. Cheaper spots include the **Hotel Inés**, *Montalvo 1509 y Boyaca, Tel. 7/932-301, Double $14*, and the **Hostal Mercy**, *Junín y Sucre, Tel. 7/920 116, Double $9*. For Chinese food try the **Chifa Central**, *Tarqui y 9 de Octubre, Tel. 7/932 761, moderate*. **Don Angelo**, *9 de Mayo y Rocafuerte, inexpensive,* has been a favorite for years.

EXCURSIONS & DAY TRIPS

The primary day trip destination from Machala is the port town of **Puerto Bolívar**, a fifteen-minute taxi ride from Machala. There are several cevicherias and seafood restaurants here. You can take a boat across the bay to the beach on **Jambelí Island** for a buck. There is sand and salt water here anyway.

Another possibility is the **Puyango Petrified Forest**. In addition to the large tree fossils, there is an abundance of bird in the scrub forest. The petrified forest is located 60 kilometers to the south via Arenillas and Palmales. You should really do this trip in a taxi or car, otherwise it will take forever to get here and back. Check with the park office in Machala, *Tel. 930 012* to check on direct transportation and tours.

PRACTICAL INFORMATION

Banks: Banco del Pichincha, *Rocafuerte y Guayas*
Consulate of Peru: *Bolivar y Colon. Tel. 930 660*
Medical Service: Clinica Metropalitana, *Buenavista y Rocafuerte. Tel. 931 517*
Post Office: Correos, *Montalvo y Bolívar*
Telephone/Fax: The area code is 7. **Emetel**, *Vela y 9 de Octubre*
Tourist Office/Maps: Cetur, *9 de Mayo y Pichincha*

HUAQUILLAS

Huaquillas is the border town about 80 kilometers south of Machala. There are a few low-end places to stay here, but you should really try to schedule not getting stuck here.

North Americans and most Europeans do not need a visa for Peru, but Australians and New Zealanders should process a visa in the Peruvian consulate in Machala or Quito.

This border crossing is about as hasslesome as they come. You should keep your passport and tourist card within reach, but in a safe spot. Immigration will stop your bus for registration even before you get to Huaquillas. You leave your tourist card and get an exit stamp with the Ecuadorian authorities at the *migración* office. You will then walk across to the Peruvian side. Ecuadorian and/or Peruvian guards may check your passport for the exit stamp as you cross.

Once on the other side of the bridge, the Peruvian *migración* office is two kilometers away. Moneychangers and porters on this side will swarm. You should be watchful of your bags and money. Knowing the exchange rate before you go will help your negotiations go smoothly. Of course you won't get the highest possible rate here so just change enough to get by.

17. CENTRAL COAST

The **Central Coast** comprises our favorite stretches of Ecuadorian beaches. Whether it's the beautiful area extending from **Atamari** to **Puerto Cayo** in the **Machalilla National Park**, or the remote section north of **Canoa**, you can find your own perfect expanse of sand.

If you need more than lounging and surfing to keep you busy, there are other very good options here. While in the area you can explore engaging animal life at the offshore island **Isla de la Plata** or delve into the fascinating archaeology at the **Chirije** dig and eco-lodge.

TOP CHOICES FOR THE CENTRAL COAST

If we only had four days to go to the beach anywhere in continental Ecuador, we would head straight for one of the resorts near Puerto Lopez, our top choices being Hostería Atamari and Hostería Alandaluz. With excellent hotels, clean beaches and beautiful blue water, we consider time spent in and around Machalilla National Park time well used.

MACHALILLA NATIONAL PARK

This section of the Ecuadorian coast, from **Atamari** to **Puerto Cayo** is worth any work it takes to get here. The vacation gods have joined forces to offer excellent hotels in all price categories, stunningly beautiful beaches, verdant hillsides and interesting animal life.

This stretch of seaside is most beautiful when the sun is shining. That happens paradoxically during the rainy season, winter, from January through May. The rains are caused by clouds that build up during the warm and sunny mornings. During the dry season, from June-December, overcast skies and cooler temperatures are the norm. That doesn't mean you won't get the occasional gloriously sunny day however.

Ecuadorian vacationers crowd to this coast from January through March, so you might want to plan accordingly.

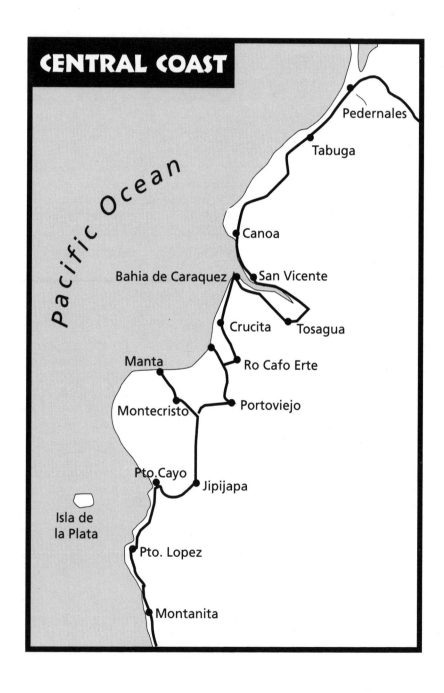

ARRIVALS & DEPARTURES

About ten kilometers north of **Montañita** the landscape abruptly changes as you head towards the Chongon-Colonche hills. Greenery blankets the rolling landscape, which serves as an excellent viewpoint to the beaches below. Along the way you catch glimpses through the fences of the Guayaquil elite's large thatched-roof mansions.

By Air

There are a couple of different airport options from which to access the area. **Manta** and **Portoviejo** are the closest and most convenient airports. TAME has daily flights to Manta from Quito and also lands in Portoviejo from Quito three days a week.

It is a two-hour car ride or three-hour bus ride from either of those towns to Puerto Lopez, the central town in the park area. A few of the hotels in the area can arrange transfers for about $30 one-way. A taxi from either of those towns should cost about the same amount.

By Bus

The Manglaralto Bus Company has buses running the length of the *Ruta del Sol* coastal highway, from **Santa Elena** in the south to **Jipijapa** in the north. There are also direct buses from Manta and Portoviejo.

By Car

This part of the coast is a great place to have a rental car. With a car you can visit different beaches and eat in a variety of restaurants; something that is difficult to do if you are dependent on the infrequent buses. We recommend a vehicle with high clearance. Four-wheel drive isn't necessary during the summer, but it can come in handy during the rainy season.

The *Ruta del Sol* highway, or Route of the Sun, starts in Santa Elena on the Santa Elena Peninsula two hours west of Guayaquil. It runs 140 kilometers up the coast before cutting inland to Jipijapa. The road is not in prime condition, but it's also not terribly poor. There are potholes and some makeshift bridges, but driving along it doesn't bump the daylights out of you. The stretch that cuts through the Machalilla Park is the best-maintained section.

ORIENTATION

This section of the country starts about 80 kilometers up the coastal highway from Santa Elena as you enter the Chongon-Colonche mountain range. Running some 50 kilometers, from **Atamari** to **Puerto Cayo**, this beautiful stretch of Ecuador also includes some islands, the most famous being **Isla de la Plata**, a bird sanctuary 34 kilometers out to sea from Puerto Lopez.

See the map of this section of coast for a layout of the land. The highway runs from Atamari north through **Ayampe**, **Puerto Rico**, **Salango**, **Puerto Lopez** and **Machalilla** before reaching Puerto Cayo.

There's really no reason to even visit any of these bedraggled towns, with the exception of Puerto Lopez. The resorts of the area are spread along the highway on the beaches. Puerto Lopez is a small tourist center with the park headquarters, a few tour agencies and cheap hotels and restaurants.

GETTING AROUND TOWN

The easiest way to get around Machalilla National Park is with a rental car. That doesn't mean, however, that it can't be done without one. If you are just coming to the area for a few days, you can easily arrange tours to **Isla de la Plata** and **Los Frailes Beach** that include pick-up and drop-off at your hotel. You can also catch one of the infrequent buses that ply the route up and down the coast.

WHERE TO STAY & EAT

One of the reasons this is our favorite stretch of coastline in Ecuador is the combination of beautiful beaches and excellent accommodations in each price category. You can't go wrong by choosing one of the following places to dine or rest your bones after a great day at the beach.

With the exception of the hotels in Puerto Lopez, these resorts are all isolated on their own sections of beach.

Expensive

HOSTERIA ATAMARI, *Kilometer 83 on the Ruta del Sol. Tel. 4/780 430. Quito tel. 2/228 470. Quito fax 2/234 075. 12 rooms. Double $60-120 depending on type of room. Restaurant. Bar. Pool. Tours arranged. Airport transfer. Credit cards accepted.*

Perched on a point high over the sea, the Atamari is one of our favorite coastal oases. Extraordinary gardens include bird of paradise plants, orange bougainvillea, plump aloe plants, and color coordinated butterflies.

From the gardens your view is automatically drawn out to sea. Waves break for kilometer after uninterrupted kilometer on the pale coast below. Turquoise waters shift to indigo as the ocean deepens. Darting frigate birds and squadrons of pelicans fly by at nose level.

One of our favorite things about the Atamari is its feeling of privacy. It's only around the pool or in the restaurant that you realize other guests are enjoying this small paradise with you. The rest of the time it's only the birds that interrupt the sound of crashing surf.

All of the buildings, with the exception of the pool and restaurant, are tucked away in the foliage. There are twelve cabins on the grounds that range from small, comfortable rooms with private but downstairs baths to large suites complete with balconies and hanging hammocks. All of the options are in excellent condition and include such luxuries as comforters and daily delivered tea.

When mealtime comes around you won't be disappointed. Specializing in seafood, the Atamari makes some of the best, albeit expensive, dishes on this section of coast. We highly recommend starting with *picaditos de cameron frito*, popcorn shrimp, outside in the bar at sunset. Because of supply issues they don't always have all the items on the menu, so ask for what's fresh and go with that as an entree.

Although the Atamari is perched above the sea, they have created beach access via a steep stepped pathway. It only takes about five minutes to get down to kilometers of flat beach, excellent for walking. Make sure you go at low tide however, because strong surf cuts the Atamari cove off from the main beach when the tide is up. You can always get back via the road, but that's about a thirty-minute walk.

Most people spend their first few days at the Atamari just unwinding, enjoying the pool and walking on the beach. When you're ready for more action however, the hotel arranges excursions to **Isla de la Plata** or **Isla de Salango**, **Los Frailes Beach**, or even mountain biking.

Selected as one of our Best Places to Stay – see chapter 11 for more details.

Moderate/Inexpensive

HOSTERIA ALANDALUZ, *Kilometer 89 on the Ruta del Sol. Tel. 5/604 103. Quito Tel. 2/505 084, Quito Fax 2/543 042; E-mail: alandalu@ecuanex.net.ec; Website: www.alandaluz.com. 40 rooms. Double $5-40 depending on type of room. Restaurant. Bar. Tours arranged. No credit cards.*

It's great to watch people walk into the main structure of the Alandaluz for the first time. Their jaws hang open as they gaze up towards the top of the huge scaffolding-like bamboo edifice and then they look at each other and say, "This place is cool."

Swiss family Robinson with an edge, the Alandaluz sets the standard for eco-tourism on the coast. Even if you're not green enough to appreciate the garbage and water recycling or compost toilets, you will applaud the long, clean beach and tasty organically grown vegetables.

The beach in front of the Alandaluz is one of the tidiest on the coast. At low tide all you want to do is lounge around on the clean white sand or enjoy the crystalline blue water. Both volleyball and soccer are available during high tide when the force of the waves on the beach is too strong for swimming.

The Alandaluz can accommodate both budget and midrange travelers with their variety of lodging options. You can set up in a simple room with bunk beds and shared bath for $5, or go for one of the private cabins for $40. The wooden cabins have hammocks, both inside and out, and come with mosquito netting. One of the most popular cabins is the Tree House, a room literally built up in the branches of a tree in front of the reception area. The bathroom is down on the ground below, so be careful about how much you drink before bed because nighttime trips to the loo are somewhat inconvenient.

The centerpiece of Alandaluz is the main building where you'll find the bar, restaurant, reception area, tour company and least expensive rooms. Hunky bamboo logs surge up three stories in a complex crisscrossed pattern like a hut on steroids. Guests tend to congregate around the bar to rehash the day's adventures or out-do each other in the "This Is How Little I Did Today" competition.

With some of the iciest, most refreshing beers in the country, the bar is a hard place to leave, but eventually the stomach over-rules and you move around the corner to the restaurant. Seafood is the mainstay of the Alandaluz menu and you really can't go wrong with anything that's fresh. Many of the vegetables are from the gardens you see all around you on the grounds and the fruits are also organically grown.

CABAÑAS DE LA TORTUGA Y IGUANA, *Ayampe. Cellular Tel.. 9/ 775 300, 9/771 306. Tel. in Guayaquil 4/203 340, Fax 4/203 340. 4 rooms. Double $10 shared bath. No credit cards.*

Located at the southern end of a long stretch of beach, this bungalow is the only place to stay in the tiny fishing community of Ayampe. A laid-back Ecuadorian couple rents four simple rooms while the kitchen and bathrooms are shared. The set-up is communal and relaxed. There is a good sandbar point-break at low tide so if you are a surfer looking for solitary waves this might be the perfect place for you. Beach walkers seeking endless sand will be equally pleased. The owners will open an 11-room hotel with ocean views for about $30 per night by the publication date of this book.

HOSTERIA PIQUEROS PATAS AZULES, *10 km south of Puerto Lopez. Tel. 5/604 135. Tel. in Guayaquil 4/383 542. 25 rooms. Double $24, ($12 per person). Restaurant. Bar. Museum. Tours to Isla de La Plata. No credit cards.*

This eco-hostel is as quirky as the blue-footed booby for which it is named. Friendly hosts with tuxedo imprinted t-shirts greet you upon arrival and attentively take care of you during your stay. To get to your room you must adventure across a swaying, slightly submerged rope and wood slat bridge traversing a stream. Don't worry, one of the workers will carry your luggage across for you. The rooms consist of four bunk beds made of concrete and shells, with a double bed in the upstairs loft. The rooms and bathrooms have a slightly institutional feel to them. They are built to last.

The real attraction of this hotel is the beach, which rivals Los Frailes as the prettiest strip of sand in mainland Ecuador. Two rocky bluffs on both points isolate the long crescent beach. The sand is kept litter-free by the hotel staff. Most of the bay is tame enough for swimming. You can retreat into the covered restaurant and bar areas for refreshments and bit of shade without giving up the view. A thick, glassy left at the south end of the bay provides a sweet ride for surfers. Boogie boards can be rented, but you must bring your own surfboard. For those who just want to use the beach, hammocks, and restaurant, the $0.50 entry fee is well worth the price. There is even a small archaeological museum to wander through.

HOSTERIA MANDALA, *northern end of the Malecón in Puerto Lopez. Tel. 5/604181. 11 cabins. Double $15. Bar. Restaurant. No credit cards.*

We had pretty much written off staying in Puerto Lopez until we ran across the Hosteria Mandala. It is run by a Swiss-Italian couple that knows how to compose a menu and make a comfortable bed. The beachfront property consists of 11 cabins, each with a hammock looking out toward the beach where three capriciously painted whale's tails jut from the sand. A deck that allows diners to enjoy the ocean breeze bands the restaurant. Sandwiches on homemade bread are ideal for a light lunch, but the seafood entrees like sole in almond sauce will at least tempt you. The hotel is located upwind from town, a few blocks from the public seafood market, at the far northern end of the beach, which makes it seem like it is not in Puerto Lopez at all.

Other options in Puerto Lopez include the **Hotel y Cabanas Pacifico**, *in hills above town, Tel. 604 147, Fax 604 133, Double $20;* and the **Hostal Villa Columbia**, *south end of the beach, Tel. 5/604105,* which charges $3 per person and has a kitchen for guest use.

For dining in Puerto Lopez we go for great Italian seafood at **Bella Italia**, run by authentic Italians. A California couple owns the coffee bar **Welcafe** that serves up extraordinary pastries and deserts.

SEEING THE SIGHTS
Visiting the Park
Much of this section of coast falls within the boundaries of the **Machalilla National Park**. This is a little confusing however, because even though the park covers 137,500 acres, there are really only three main sights for visitors to the area: **Isla de la Plata**, **Los Frailes Beach**, and the **Agua Blanca Archaeological Site and Museum**.

It costs foreigners $20 for a ticket to the park, which is good for five days. You should plan your schedule accordingly to make sure you hit all of the sights that you are interested in before your ticket expires.

Isla de la Plata

This is our favorite of the Machalilla attractions. A trip to the island is a fun day trip even if your travel plans include the Galápagos, but a must if they don't. You have the chance to see many interesting bird species as well as humpback whales, sea lions and dolphins.

The outing to the island, thirty kilometers off the coast, ends up being a full twelve-hour day. Most tour companies organize the trip for around $35 per person. That includes hotel transfers, boat transportation, food, island guides and snorkeling equipment.

WHALE'S TALES

Humpbacks, an endangered species, have been protected worldwide since the 1960s. These animals, which usually grow to lengths of 12 to 16 meters, are baleen whales, which means they strain their food out of the water by means of a filter, or baleen, in their mouths. Their diet consists of shrimp-like crustaceans, small fish, and plankton. They are known to migrate between polar oceanic waters and tropical or subtropical breeding grounds. The Central Coast area is one of their breeding grounds.

One of the most interesting things about the humpbacks is that their tails are like fingerprints – each one distinct. Many of the scientists who study the whales in the area spend much of their time sitting on top of Isla de la Plata spotting and identifying the whales by their derrieres.

The humpback is one of the most acrobatic of all whales. If you get really lucky, you might see one do a back-flip by leaping from the water belly up, arching backwards, and plunging headfirst down with a loud slapping sound. You're more likely to see a good view of one's tail before it makes a deep dive. The whale will hunch its back and roll steeply forward, bringing its tail vertically clear of the water. Have your camera ready. Their easily identifiable spouts are created by condensed air being pushed out of their lungs before they take another breath.

The tour company will pick you up at your hotel around 7:30am and take you to the Machalilla park office in Puerto Lopez to buy your park entry ticket. The ticket costs $20 over and above the cost of your tour and is good for the next five days. With it you can also enter Los Frailes Beach and Agua Blanca. The park does not accept credit cards or rumpled US currency. (Crisp US currency is happily received.)

From the park office you will go directly to Puerto Lopez's small port to board your boat. Most of the crafts are 30 footers with two outboard motors. Try to get a seat in the open air to avoid seasickness. If you visit the island from July through September you will probably see some of the 40 humpback whales that migrate to the area. There's no need to go on a separate whale watching trip as your guide and captain are in contact with other boats about sightings and are pros at spotting the animals. It takes about two hours to get to the island including stops for whale watching.

Once you get to Isla de la Plata you'll have a snack under the covered patio of the park office building before heading out on the trail. The guides stagger the groups to minimize impact so you might find yourself sitting around for a bit. That's okay though because the beach is pretty and many people feel a bit wobbly from the ride across the open ocean.

You have your choice of taking one of two hikes. Your guide will tell you what birds and animals you are most likely to see on each trail to help you make your decision. On a recent trip in early September we took the five kilometer trail and saw hundreds of frigate birds, many of the males with their flaming red pouches inflated; nesting and courting blue footed boobies; nesting masked and red footed boobies; and whales. The fearless boobies nest just a few feet off the sides of the trail (even on the trail sometimes) and are fascinating to watch.

Isla de la Plata, meaning money or silver island, was a ceremonial island for many of Ecuador's coastal populations. Archaeological excavations have uncovered signs of human presence dating back to the Valdivia period. Interestingly, groups that were antagonistic towards each other on the mainland engaged in communal rituals on the island. In the more recent past, Sir Francis Drake used the island as a safe-haven after terrorizing Spanish galleons. Some say that his treasures are buried here somewhere.

Depending on the time of year it can get extremely hot on the island in the afternoon. Although Isla de Plata is not of volcanic origin like the Galápagos, it is dry and sandy. The most important thing is to have plenty of water.

Packing up for the day trip to Isla de la Plata you'll swear you must be going out of town for a week. The weather can change drastically from morning to afternoon so it's a good idea to be prepared. It is usually warm enough that shorts and sports sandals are preferred for walking around the island. We suggest hauling all the of following (don't worry, you can leave most of it in the boat while you are on your hike):
• anti-seasickness pills
• binoculars
• camera

- water
- sunscreen
- sunglasses
- hat
- windbreaker
- fleece (if you go during the cooler dry season)
- bathing suit
- mask and snorkel (the boat provides some, but they are never as good as your own)
- towel

After the hike you'll return to the covered patio for lunch. From there you re-board your boat and travel about five minutes to the snorkeling site. Colorful parrotfish, rays, and even octopus can be seen among the coral reef. After about twenty minutes most people are pretty chilly so the boat then heads back to Puerto Lopez, which only takes a little over an hour on the return trip.

Los Frailes Beach

This beach, about ten kilometers north of Puerto Lopez, is the place we fantasize about when sitting at our computers in the dead of winter. Completely undeveloped, Los Frailes is a long crescent strand in a wide half moon bay. Palm trees sway gently in the breeze while mellow waves wash rhythmically against the shore. If you want to get away from it all for a day, this is the place to go.

From the park entrance on the highway a rough dirt road leads back 2.5 kilometers to the beach. There is absolutely no infrastructure here, so bring everything you'll need with you. Savvy Ecuadorians set up tents or umbrellas to provide a little shade - you can try to make friends with them to share a slice of *sombra*.

Because Los Frailes is part of Machalilla National Park, there is a $20 entrance fee for foreigners. Twenty dollars is a lot of money to pay to go to a beach, but if you have gone to Isla de la Plata within five days and saved your ticket you can get in for free. Many tour companies offer outings to Los Frailes combined with a visit to Agua Blanca. If you don't have a car, this is your best bet.

Agua Blanca Archaeological Site and Museum

About two kilometers south of Los Frailes, on the right hand side of the highway, you'll see the entrance to **Agua Blanca**. Here you will find the ruins of a major city from the Manteño period, thought to have sheltered over 5,000 people. All that is left today are the foundations of numerous buildings and temples that you can tell formed neighborhoods and converged in public plazas.

The recovered highlights of the Manteña culture can be found inside the on-site museum. Stone chairs, funeral urns and ritual ceramics are the major pieces of the small museum. We'll be impressed if you haul yourself off the beaches for this cultural enlightenment. Again, this site alone does not merit $20, but if you have already gone to Isla de Plata you can get in with your park ticket.

NIGHTLIFE & ENTERTAINMENT

Because of the distances between the resorts and any towns, nightlife for most people consists of whatever is happening at the bar of their hotel. There are some bars in Puerto Lopez, but they are all pretty sketchy.

SPORTS & RECREATION

Snorkeling and Scuba Diving

This section of coast has the only coral reef on the coast of Ecuador. You can arrange dive trips through your hotel or through one of the tour agencies in Puerto Lopez. Snorkeling is an activity included on your trip to Isla de la Plata.

Surfing

Other than walking or running on the beach, surfing is the main sport of the area. We consider this some of the best surf on the coast as there are some great breaks on really pretty beaches. The beach in front of Cabanas Tortuga has a nice wave at low tide that breaks both ways. There's a surfable wave in front of Alandaluz at low tide as well. Our favorite, however, is the fat left at the end of the beach at Hostería Piquero Pato Azul. There's also a beach break 15 kilometers north of Puerto Cayo that is considered one of the best in the area.

PRACTICAL INFORMATION

The only services you'll find on this stretch of coast are in Puerto Lopez. The **phone office**, **EMETEL** is *on the road through town near the bus station*. The **Machalilla National Park office** is *a block off the main road behind EMETEL*. There are no banks or exchange offices.

MANTA

Manta, the second largest port in the country behind Guayaquil, definitely has an industrial rather than vacation feel to it. Tons of Ecuadorian goods end up here before being exported around the world.

To add to the general port stench, Manta also has a thriving tuna industry. Despite this, Ecuadorians are inexplicably drawn to the beaches here during their time off. We suggest using the city solely as a transportation hub and then moving along. We can't imagine why anybody would want to stay in a dirty, crowded city that smells like rotten seafood.

ARRIVALS & DEPARTURES

The most important thing to know about Manta is how to get in and out of there quickly.

By Air

The airport is a couple of kilometers away from downtown on the east side of the Manta River. TAME has a flight to and from Quito once a day.

Airline Offices

• **TAME**, *Malecón one block north of Calle 13, Tel. 622 006*

By Bus

The main bus terminal, *terminal terrestre,* is right on front of the docks near the Manta River. There are buses to Quito, Guayaquil and all the regional cities like Bahía and Puerto Lopez. From Quito there are mainly night buses. The ride takes about eight hours and costs $7.

By Car

You can fly into Manta and rent a car to gain freedom for exploring the excellent beaches to the south. Try **Localiza**, *Malecón and Calle 16, #12, Tel. 622 026, Fax 629 375.*

It's about a two-hour drive from Manta to both Puerto Lopez and Bahía. If you are driving down the coast, the road from **Montecristi** to **Jipijapa** is quite scenic, with huge, expressive kapok trees spread along the hills. Vendors stand next to gas stoves along the highway selling delicious piping hot *tortillas de maiz,* little rounds of cornbread.

The drive from Quito is via Santo Domingo and then on through Tosagua, Rocafuerte, Portoviejo and Montecristi to Manta. There is a highway directly from Guayaquil to Manta.

WHERE TO STAY & EAT

If you get stuck staying in Manta because of airline or bus schedules, you'll be comfortable at the following hotels.

HOTEL ORO VERDE, *Malecón and Calle 23. Tel. 5/629 200, Fax 5/ 629 210. 50 rooms. Double$115 . Restaurant. Deli. Bar. Pool. Gym. Squash court. Credit cards accepted.*

The Oro Verde hotel helps make even Manta a nice place to stay.

Away from the noise and odor of downtown, this brand new hotel overlooks Murcielago Beach. You can either enjoy the beach out front or soak up the rays around the hotel's large pool. (Be careful of the undertow in the ocean.)

One of the main reasons to stay at any Oro Verde is for the excellent service. That's no exception here. Another is for the dining options. You can't go wrong with the restaurant, serving both Ecuadorian and international selections, or the deli.

HOTEL MANTA IMPERIAL, *Murcielago Beach. Tel. 5/622 016, Fax 5/623 016. 50 rooms. Double $40. Restaurant. Disco. Pool. Tennis court. Credit cards accepted..*

West of downtown and the port, the Hotel Imperial is on Murcielago Beach. The air-conditioned rooms are a little small, but comfortable, and it's nice to be away from the center of town. With a full range of facilities and an okay restaurant, this is the best mid-range choice.

HOTEL LUN FUN, *Calle 2 just off the Malecón between the bus station and the Manta River. Tel. 5/622 966, Fax 5/610 601. 20 rooms. Double $25. Restaurant. No credit cards.*

With a name like this you expect the hotel to be one big party. Unfortunately, the "fun" in Lun Fun is actually the owner's last name, but that doesn't stop it from being the best inexpensive hotel in town. It's clean and the restaurant, serving both Chinese and Ecuadorian food, is a good bet.

The restaurants at the hotels above are your good food options, but there are a few other choices if you want to get out at night. The moderately priced **Jhonny**, *Avenida 24 and Calle 17*; and **Charlat**, *Avenida 18 off the malecón,* are good alternatives for international food with a Creole touch. For pizza, we can recommend **Topi Tu**, *Malecón and Avenida 15*. There are also plenty of cheap seafood restaurants on the beaches if you just want to order something simple with a cold beer.

SEEING THE SIGHTS

There's really no reason to linger in Manta, but if you have a couple of spare hours, you might want to check out the **Banco Central Museum** *at Malecón and Calle 7, Monday-Friday 8:30am-4:30pm*, to learn more about the Manta Indian culture. They were a trading people that inhabited much of the coast when the Spanish arrived. The museum showcases some of the pottery and figurines for which they are so well known.

If you want to hit the beach, we suggest heading west along the Malecón up **to Murcielago Beach**.

PRACTICAL INFORMATION

Banks: **Banco del Pacifico**, *Avenida 2 y Calle 11*

Currency Exchange: Casa de Cambio Zanchi, *Avenida 2 y Calle 11*
Post Office: Correos, *Avenida 4 and Calle 8*
Telephone/Fax: The area code is 5. **EMETEL,** *Malecón and Calle 11*
Tourist Office/Maps: CETUR, *On the pedestrian section of Avenida 3 between Calle 10 and 11*

PORTOVIEJO

Even more so than Manta, **Portoviejo** is simply an airport as far as travelers are concerned. You fly in and then motor out. TAME, *Avenida América*, has three flights from Quito a week. The airport is a couple of kilometers west of town. From there you can either take a cab to the bus station, also on the west side of town, or to pick up your rental car at the **Hotel Ejecutivo,** *18 de Octubre and 10 de Agosto, Tel. 5/630 872, Fax 5/630 876.*

BAHÍA DE CARAQUEZ

Things have not gone well for **Bahía** over the last few years. First it was El Niño in early 1998, damaging roads, causing flooding and leaving the city without water for six months. Then in August of the same year, an earthquake measuring 7.2 on the Richter scale rocked the town again. Just as things were starting to get back on track in late 1999, a virus known as the *mancha blanca* decimated the shrimp trade, a huge source of employment for the area. The once pretty town is cracked at the seams, but through it all the enjoyable Bahians persevere.

During the late 1800s and early 1900s, Bahía was one of the most important ports on the coast. After three ships wrecked on sandbars in the bay however, Lloyds of London did some investigating and finally quit insuring boats into here in the 1950s. Manta took over as the Central Coast industrial center while Bahía became a popular beach retreat for wealthy Quiteños. In fact, most of condos in the tall buildings at the point are owned by people who live in Quito.

ARRIVALS & DEPARTURES

By Air

There's an unused airport with a long landing strip across the estuary from Bahía in **San Vicente.** Capable of handling 727s, the airport was built during native son Sixto Duran's tenure as president when there were grand plans for a resort complex there. Those plans never quite materialized, and now all flights to the region land either in **Manta,** an almost two hour drive to the south, or **Portoviejo,** about an hour away.

By Bus

The two bus companies have offices next door to each other on the *malecón* next to the municipal dock. **Coactur** and **Reina del Camino** have routes to Manta, Guayaquil, Esmeraldas, Santo Domingo and Quito.

For regional destinations, you can catch *ranchero* pick-up trucks from the plaza at *Bolívar and Aguilera one block back from the malecón*.

By Car

The drive to Bahía from Quito is via Santo Domingo and Tosagua. To get to Bahía from Guayaquil, take the highway towards Manta to Montecristi. Be sure to admire the human-looking kapok trees and sample the *tortillas de maiz* on the route between Jipijapa and Montecristi. From there go northwest through Portoviejo, Rocafuerte, and Tosagua.

You can fly into either Portoviejo or Manta and rent a car as another option.

By Ferry

The ferry from Bahía across the bay to San Vicente runs about every 15 minutes throughout the day. The dock is at *Malecón and Ante*.

ORIENTATION

This beleaguered town sits on the end of a point a little more than half way up the Ecuadorian coast. One side of the point faces the Pacific Ocean and the other the wide bay and estuary of the Chone River. San Vicente sits directly across the bay from Bahía.

The town's main street, the *malecón*, runs up and then wraps around the end of the point, where it becomes Ratti Avenue. A wide sidewalk along the street makes it a good walking route. Both the municipal and ferry docks are on the *malecón*, as are many hotels and restaurants. The wealthiest part of town, with the best hotels and big condos, is at the very end of the point.

GETTING AROUND TOWN

Most of the town's points of interest are on or near the boardwalk, *malecón*. It's a pleasant and safe walk along the ocean, but there are also lots of taxis around if you want to ride.

WHERE TO STAY

CASA GRANDE, *Viteri and Virgilio off the malecón. Reservations through Bahía Dolphin Tours. Tel. 5/692 097 Fax 5/692 088. 5 rooms. Double $55. Breakfast included. Pool. Credit cards accepted.*

This is our top recommendation for a hotel in Bahía. The Casa Grande feels about as close as you can get to staying in an upper class

364 ECUADOR & GALÁPAGOS ISLANDS GUIDE

Ecuadorian's home, because it is one. This house, tucked in between condos and hotels on the best part of the point, is an extremely comfortable place to stay. The living room, decorated with paintings by such renowned artists as Eduardo Kingman, is a great place to settle into a good book. If it's sunny outside you can enjoy the pool and patio in the backyard.

The large rooms, all with big picture windows and some with balconies, just make you feel at home. In addition, there's something so relaxing about sitting around a dining room table for your meals instead of a restaurant. Breakfast, served by a good-natured staff, features warm bread, fresh-squeezed juice, eggs and meat.

HOTEL HERRADURA, *Ratti (malecón) and Hidalgo. Tel. 5/690 446, Fax 5/690 265. 31 rooms. Double $25. Breakfast not included. No credit cards.*

The Herradura is showing some wear, but its location is great and the hotel is certainly fine for the price. White walls, wandering hallways, outdoor staircases and wagon-wheel décor give it a Spanish beach bungalow feel. We especially like room #405, with a little patio overlooking the ocean and *malecón*. If your room doesn't have its own porch, you can hang out on the wide hotel patio with its outlandish tall-backed furniture.

HOTEL LA PIEDRA, *Circunvalacion Virgilio Ratti. Tel.5/690 780 or 691 463, Fax 5/690 154; E-mail: apartec@uio.satnet.net. 25 rooms. Double $30. Cable TV. Restaurant. Pool. Credit cards accepted.*

While the La Piedra won't win any awards for interior design, the rooms are clean and newly refurbished, more comfortable than most. The pool has a view of the ocean just a few meters away.

HOSTAL SANTIGUADO, *Padre Leannen 406. Tel. 5/690 597, Fax 5/ 691 412. 8 rooms. Double $11. Breakfast not included. No credit cards.*

The Santiguado, opened in 1999, is an excellent budget option. Located in a quiet neighborhood, the hotel is clean and cheery. Run by Guacamayo Bahíatours, the Santiguado can organize many your excursions from here if you choose. There are also double rooms with shared baths available for $8.

WHERE TO EAT

MUELLE UNO, *Malecón and Ante next door to the San Vicente ferry dock. Moderate. No credit cards.*

This informal, covered pier on the waterfront is a Bahía institution. Other restaurants come and go, but *Muello Uno*, Pier One, stays in business by serving good eats at fair prices. The best dishes here are grilled over the barbecue pit at the front of the restaurant. While the steak can be hit or miss, both the chicken and sausage are excellent. All meals come with salad and a baked potato. Wash it down with a cold beer and you've got a pretty good dining experience.

HOTEL HERRADURA, *Ratti (malecón) and Hidalgo. Tel. 5/690 446. No credit cards.*

Probably the most impressive thing about this restaurant is its 17-page menu. If you're hungry ask them to bring you some of their *chiflas*, fried plantains, to tide you over while you wade through all the choices. There are two dining rooms here. We prefer the less formal garden room that looks out over the ocean to the official dining room in back. Our favorite dish is the tasty breaded and fried shrimp.

SAIANANDA, *Sixto Duran Avenue, Kilometer six on the Chone highway. Tel. 5/399 288. Moderate. No credit cards.*

Part of Saiananda Park, this vegetarian restaurant offers good food in a nice environment. At the edge of the estuary, the restaurant has a simple, natural feel. Organic foods followed by delicious desserts make it one of our recommendations.

PEPOTECA, *Malecón y Antonio Ante. Moderate. No credit cards.*

Look for the big yellow sign on the *malecón* and you will find a simple spot for good seafood. The menu features a large variety of plates including sea bass and shrimp prepared in curry or *a la Hawaina*.

SEEING THE SIGHTS

There's not that much to cover in town. The **Casa de la Cultura**, *Malecón at Peña*, has a small **museum** that's open Tuesday through Friday in the mornings. There's an archaeological collection of pre-Colombian pieces as well as a permanent exhibit of paintings and a collection of antique navigational maps.

You can look out across the bay to the Pacific Ocean from the **lookout point**, *mirador*, at the top of *Avenida Sixto Duran*. The neighborhood you pass through on your way up is a little dicey, so you might want to take a cab.

SPORTS & RECREATION

Beaches

There's a tiny strip of beach in front of the boardwalk at low tide, but it's not that pleasant. **Pellaca**, just *south of town*, is a wide, popular beach with no riptides. The best beaches around are those north of San Vicente.

Paragliding

Crucita, about an hour away near Rocafuerte, is one of the best places in the country for paragliding.

EXCURSIONS & DAY TRIPS

There are quite a few worthwhile excursions from Bahía. Both **Bahía Dolphin Tours**, *Avenida Bolívar 1004 y Riofrio, Tel. 5/692 097 Fax 5/692 088, E-mail: archtour@ecua.net.ec;* and **Guacamayo Bahíatours**, *Bolívar 906 and Arenas, Tel. 5/690 597, Fax 5/691 412, E-mail: ecopapel@ecuadorexplorer.com,* can arrange outings. Only Bahía Dolphin Tours has trips to our highly recommended Chirije.

Chirije

Chirije, one of the most important archaeological sites of coastal Ecuador, is also an eco-lodge. We think it's one of the most entertaining and educational excursions in the area. This trip is worthwhile for the archaeological aspect alone, but has even more value when you consider the clean stretch of solitary beach and kilometers of hiking trails.

Your trip starts by boarding a small open-air *chivita* bus and heading south to the site. The guide times your departure with low tide, because you're actually driving on the beach. It's a beautiful thirty minute drive along the water's edge during which you can gaze out at the ocean, watch hundreds of red crabs scurry along the beach or talk to your guide about the history of the area.

Chirije was the site of an ancient seaport from 500 BC – 500 AD. The people from here, skillful fishers and traders, have left behind a physical legacy in ceramics as well as many mysteries. The richness of the site is amazing. You can't walk around Chirije without tripping over some archaeological find.

Your day will include a tour of the current digging site and much information about Chirije's history. You will also get to visit the museum, where you'll see many of the works discovered here. The small exhibit displays wonderful treasures, including the bowl with the small bird that has become Chirije's official symbol. You can get so close to the pieces it's like having a backstage pass.

Surrounded by 250 acres of dry tropical forest and kilometers of unspoiled beaches, the site is set unobtrusively back from the beach. In fact, you're almost on top of the huts before you see them. Bougainvillea and other colorful plants and flowers cover the grounds between the thatched cabanas.

The main dining area, with its large hammock covered patio, looks out over the ocean. Meals are served outside during the day, and indoors at night when cool breezes blow off the sea. If you want to stay the night, there are five thatched A-frame cabins on the grounds. Each cabin has a master bedroom, bath, kitchen and little sitting area downstairs and up to six twin beds in the upstairs area. At the time of the writing of this book there was no generator, so there are no lights. All meals are prepared in Bahía and brought in by the staff. It's romantically rustic.

The trips to Chirije are organized by Bahía Dolphin Tours. Try to get Jacob Santos, the manager, as your guide as he is knowledgeable, funny and an all around good guy. Day trips cost $80 for four people including meal, guide and transportation. Overnight stays are $15 per person with food and transportation extra.

Frigate Islands

For an excellent chance to see the extended red pouches of the male Frigate bird up-close, you can sign on for a trip to the Bird Island Sanctuary. These small mangrove islands are home to one of the largest colonies of Frigate birds on the continent. You also have the chance to spot pelicans, herons, cormorants and other ocean birds.

Both of the tour companies listed above make the trip for $60 for four people.

Saiananda Park

Most people visit Saiananda Park, 100 hectares of dry tropical forest, to see the exotic bird collection and enjoy a nice meal. There are also trails through the forest and a Japanese garden with a "spiritual contemplation center."

Just six kilometers from Bahía, Saiananda can be reached through a boat tour that usually includes Frigate Island, or by taxi from town.

Aposentos Caves

If you're not going to make it to Isla de Plata or the Galápagos, you still have a chance to see some Blue Footed Boobies. During part of the year they migrate to these caves just a kilometer north of Canoa. They are only here from November to May.

Whale Watching

During the months of June-August, pods of humpback whales migrate to this area. You can take a tour in search of these impressive giants.

Panama Hat Tour

You know by now that the mislabeled Panama Hats originated and are still made in Ecuador. Weavers in nearby Montecristi are famous for producing the highest quality, tightest weave hats in the country. You can visit their workshops and have the opportunity to buy the hats for a fraction of what you would find them in New York or London, where many of the hats are sent.

Canoa

It would be a shame to come this far and not go to some of the beautiful beaches just a little further to the north. See the **San Vicente to Cojimíes** section below for more details.

Rio Muchacho Organic Farm

The **Rio Muchacho Organic Farm** is a working organic farm east of Canoa up the Muchacho River. If you'd like the chance to learn about and participate in the coastal *campesino* culture, this is an excellent opportunity.

The idea is for visitors to participate in the daily activities of the *montubios*, coastal farmers, in order to understand their lives. You arrive to the farm by horseback from Canoa, crossing a small mountain range to drop down into the Muchacho river valley. The picturesque scenery along the way alternates between rain forest and cropped areas.

Once at the farm you can pick out your lodgings. Your choices are a cabin along the river, or the more popular tree house, up a good 15 meters off the ground. Both are constructed of wood and thatch in the typical coastal manner with lots of open air-circulation. Hammocks are also plentiful.

It's the daily activities that are the real draw to the farm. You can plant your own tree; harvest roast and grind your own coffee; fish for river shrimp; milk the cows to make your own cheese; and make your own gourd cups and spoon. It's not all work though. You can also get a mini-spa treatment with the local clay mask and fresh aloe vera shampoo, visit the rain forest, sit around the campfire, and enjoy delicious Creole vegetarian food and homemade wine. Part of the draw the Rio Muchacho is the human interaction. Your time at the farm will be spent with a native guide and his family. You'll even have the opportunity to spend a night with them if you choose. You can also visit the elementary school and give an impromptu English lesson.

Trips to the farm are organized by **Guacamayo Bahíatours** and usually depart from Bahía. Most people visit the farm on a two-night/three day package that costs $30 per person per day for transportation, lodging, food, and activities.

PRACTICAL INFORMATION

Banks: Banco Comercial de Manabí, *Malecón and Ante.*
Post Office: Correos, *Aguilera and Bolívar.*
Telephone/Fax: The area code is 5. **EMETEL,** *Arenas and Intraigo just off the malecón.*
Tourist Office/Maps: CETUR, *Malecón and Arenas (at the edge of the playground)*

SAN VICENTE & CANOA

This section of the Ecuadorian coast is definitely off the tourist track. While that's exactly what makes it so appealing, it also means a lack of infrastructure. You can spend a lot of time hanging out here and waiting around for buses, for tides to change and for your food to come at any restaurant. On the other hand, you can be practically alone on vast stretches of white beached rimmed with stereotypical palm trees or have your own personal surf break.

Across the bay from Bahía, **San Vicente** was supposed to become the "Acapulco of South America." Somewhere along the way money and dreams ran short and now it's just a few high-rise buildings and an unused airport on the edge of a small village. We don't think that's all too tragic. Most people don't linger in San Vicente, but rather head north up the coast to some of the most isolated beaches in the country.

The sleepy fishing village of **Canoa** is a favorite for travelers who just want to hang out for a while. Clean, wide beaches, inexpensive lodging and good surf make it hard for some to break away.

ARRIVALS & DEPARTURES

By Air

The closest airports are in Manta and Portoviejo.

By Bus

If you are coming from Bahía, just take the ferry across the bay and catch a local bus to Canoa from San Vicente. Costa del Norte is the main bus company that plies this section of coast. From Manta, you can take a bus headed a bit further up the coast to Pedernales and just get off in Canoa. From Quito or Guayaquil, take the bus to San Vicente and then grab the local the 20 kilometers up the road to Canoa.

By Car

Most people visit Bahía before coming to Canoa and then drive around the estuary to San Vicente. The road from San Vicente to Canoa is a good one.

WHERE TO STAY & EAT

HOTEL BAMBU, *on the north end of the beach in Canoa. 8 rooms. Double $16. Suite $25. Restaurant. Boogie board, surfboard and bike rental. No credit cards.*

This hotel, run by Dutch guy and his Ecuadorian wife, is our favorite in Canoa. Right on the beach, the Bambu is an excellent place to chill out. It seems like there's a hammock almost everywhere you look. If you want to get more active, that's no problem either. You can play volleyball, ride bikes, or enjoy the surf.

The food here, served in their outdoor restaurant, is excellent. Try the coconut milk and fresh pineapple juice solo or mix them into a memorable piña colada. After a day on the beach, it's also nice to know you've got some of the coldest beers in the province waiting for your return. The rooms are simple but comfortable. The upstairs suite with a view of the beach is especially fine.

HOSTAL DANIEL, *Reservations through Guacamayo Bahíatours in Bahía, Bolívar 906 and Arenas, Tel. 5/690 597, Fax 5/691 412, E-mail: ecopapel@ecuadorexplorer.com. $6 per person. No credit cards.*

The Hostal Daniel features spotless cabanas with a swimming pool just 300 meters from the beach. Daniel has three surfboards for rent and will give you free surf lessons to go along with them. He can also arrange horseback riding trips.

TORBELINO, *next to the Hostal Daniel. Inexpensive. No credit cards.*

This casual restaurant, near the Hostal Daniel is a good bet for big seafood lunches. The food is fresh and well prepared and the price won't set you back a bit.

RIO MUCHACHO ORGANIC FARM, *East of Canoa. Reservations through Guacamayo Bahíatours in Bahía, Bolívar 906 and Arenas, Tel. 5/690 597, Fax 5/691 412, E-mail: ecopapel@ecuadorexplorer.com.*

The Rio Muchacho Organic Farm is a working organic farm east of Canoa up the Muchacho River. If you'd like the chance to learn about and participate in the coastal *campesino* culture, this is an excellent opportunity. (See *Bahía Excursions & Day Trips.*)

SEEING THE SIGHTS

There's not much to see in Canoa and that's the whole beauty of staying there. You've got the beach, the ocean and that's about it. At low tide you can walk up the beach half a kilometer to the **Aposentos Caves**, where you'll see nesting blue footed boobies from November to May.

SPORTS & RECREATION

Surfing is the main sport around here. There are beach and point breaks all up the coast. Many of the hostels in town rent boards. The cliffs around Canoa are also excellent for **paragliding**. There's an agency in town that will rent equipment and give lessons.

PRACTICAL INFORMATION

There are almost no services here. You'll want to have cash and take care of other business in Bahía before you leave.

NORTH OF CANOA

The seldom-visited area between Canoa and Cojimíes is where you go when you really need to get away from it all, as there's basically nothing here. An **equator monument** south of the small fishing village **Pedernales** marks the 250th anniversary of the French Geodesic Expedition. About 20 kilometers north of there is the isolated and aging **Hotel Coco Solo** with cabins and campsites right on the beach. The cabins cost $10 per person. You can make reservations through *Guacamayo Bahíatours in Bahía, Bolívar 906 and Arenas, Tel. 5/690 597, Fax 5/691 412, E-mail: ecopapel@ecuadorexplorer.com.*

Cojimíes, another fishing village further to the north, sits on the end of a sandy spit. A large bay separates it from the **Northern Coast**. From Cojimíes you can cross the bay by boat and continue on to **Muisne**.

The real thrill about this section of the country is the road itself – many times there isn't one. Traffic drives along the edge of the beach at low tide, hoping to make it all the way before the water comes up and covers the route. (This is not a good place for your car to break down.) If you've got the time, this is a wonderful adventure. If you're driving yourself, be sure to ask local drivers about the tides. You might even want to follow a bus or *ranchera*.

18. NORTHERN COAST & LOWLANDS

As you cross the Andes and head down to the coast, you pass through a number of different life zones. The subtropical cloud forests on the western flanks of the mountain range are deservedly a favorite excursion from Quito. Most commonly accessed from **Mindo**, birders especially delight in the diversity of species found in this small area.

If you take the route to the coast via **Santo Domingo de los Colorados**, you'll enter another type of environment, the tropical forest. Even though most of this land has been cleared for agriculture, a few unsullied pockets remain.

Esmeraldas, the largest town on the Northern Coast, is no more than a jumping off spot to the popular beaches just south of there. **Atacames** rocks with partying Ecuadorians almost every weekend, but especially during the summer and holidays. **Same**, cleaner and prettier, offers the best lodging on this section of coast.

If you really want to seek out the unspoiled and unique, try the **Mompiche Lodge** on the **Muisne** peninsula. Accessed only by boat, your trip to the lodge will take you through silent mangrove swamps and across open ocean before you reach the wide sandy beach and waves that surfers dream about.

LOWDOWN ON THE COAST & LOWLANDS

Mindo is a place that deserves to be on anybody's travel itinerary. There are comfortable accommodations for all budget levels and the torrents of life in the nearby cloud forests are truly impressive. Easily accessible from Quito, you can get a lot out of Mindo even if you only have 48 hours.

While the beaches of the Northern Coast are not the best in the country, they are a fun and fast getaway from Quito.

MINDO

The sub-tropical cloud forests of the Choco Bio-region, on the western slopes of the Andes, are some of the most diverse in the world. **Mindo**, only two hours northwest Quito, is one of the best places to access the area. Verdant, beautiful and dripping with moisture, the cloud forest is a bit reminiscent of the Pacific Northwest in the United States. Steep green mountains drop to gorges with pounding waterfalls and icy rivers.

The nearly constant mists at high altitude have created humid conditions within which thrive a diversity of plants that rivals that of lowland tropical forests. A thick tangle of jungle-like growth, the cloud forest has the highest bio-diversity of epiphytes in the world. Bromeliads and orchids hang in overhead gardens, attracting hundreds of species of birds.

ARRIVALS & DEPARTURES

By Bus

Buses from Quito to Mindo leave from the bus station at *Manuel Larrea and Asunción* on the west side of El Ejido Park. It used to be called Cooperativo de Cayambe, which is how the cab drivers may still know it, but now it is called Flora de Valle. Buses leave Monday-Thursday at 3:15pm and Friday-Sunday at 8am and 2pm.

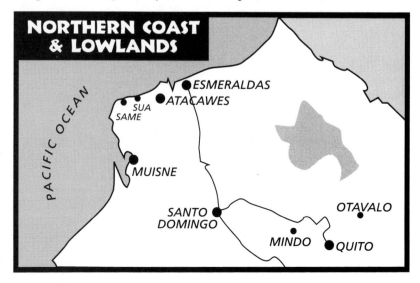

Be sure to buy your return ticket when you arrive to Mindo, as demand for seats on outgoing buses, especially on weekends, exceeds supply. The bus costs about $2 each way.

Mindo is six kilometers off the highway, down a steep road into a fertile valley along the Mindo River. Unless you take a bus directly to Mindo, you will have to be dropped off on the highway and walk the six kilometers down the hill.

Make sure you are on the bus to Quito when you leave Mindo. Other bus drivers will tell you that they can drop you on the highway and that you can hop on a bus to Quito from there. Those buses are usually full, meaning you could be waiting for hours on the side of the road.

By Car

The road from Quito to Mindo, although quite curvy, is very scenic. From Quito you head north towards Mitad del Mundo and from there, take the new highway to Esmeraldas via Calacalí. It takes about two hours from Quito. You can also hire a cab for about $30 via this route.

There is another route called the **Old Nono-Mindo Route**. It is even more scenic, but longer and not paved. The road is popular with birders who stop to spot species along the way. It takes about four hours on this route as long as there aren't any landslides or anything like that.

ORIENTATION

Mindo sits at 1300 meters on the western slopes of the Pichincha Volcano. Five rivers cut through the vicinity. Mindo itself is a very pleasant, laid-back town with about four streets and a sleepy central plaza. The Mindo River runs along its border and the cloud forests start at the edge of town. There is a road along the river that leads out of town towards the Mindo-Nambillo reserve. Along this road you will find El Monte, the Butterfly Farm and the Mindo Garden Lodge.

WHERE TO STAY

MINDO GARDEN, *On the road to the Mindo-Nambillo Reserve 4 km from town. Quito Tel. 2/ 252 488, Fax2/253 452. US Tel. 800/709 9470. Website: www.ecuadoradvent.com. 9 rooms. $55 per person. Breakfast and dinner included. Restaurant. Bar. Credit cards accepted.*

This lodge, set on 300 hectares along the edge of the Mindo River, is the nicest place to stay in Mindo. Ensconced in the cloud forest, with tall ferns and impatiens covering the grounds, it's a beautiful place to spend a few days.

The main cabin, with the dining area and game room, is a handsome wooden structure. Rustic yet attractively decorated, it is perfect for the setting. Comfortable furniture, downy sofas, and soft lighting make it especially inviting. They keep the shiny wood floors clean by asking you to remove your shoes before you enter. You might want to take a thick pair of socks for cool nights.

Each dining table is set with colorful wooden plates adorned with paintings of Ecuador's fruits and vegetables. The hearty meals, included in the price of the room, include excellent homemade bread. Service is a little slow, but the idea is to sit back and relax anyway. They are also building a pizza oven and barbecue grill to offer more food options. Many people come here from Quito simply to eat lunch and enjoy their natural surroundings.

An observation deck over the river sticks off the dining room. You can appreciate the sounds of the water crashing down the rapids while you eat. The upstairs game room includes card tables, a pool table and a TV and VCR. Guest rooms are scattered across the property in comfortable cabins. You feel fabulously isolated as you walk down the trail to your tastefully decorated room. Firm mattresses, floral bedspreads and curtains, hand-painted furniture and nice, new bathrooms make this a very comfortable place to hang out. The sounds of the river, frogs and crickets serenade you to sleep. Unfortunately, the hot water heater is the electric kind.

The lodge is next door to the Mindo-Nambillo Reserve, which means you can start hikes right from the front door. From the lodge it is 15-minute walk to the Butterfly Farm or a 45 stroll into town. If you want to spot lots of birds, something for which Mindo is famous, we recommend hiring a guide. Transportation to the lodge is an issue, as you have to cross the river to get to the lodge from town. If the river is up, taxis can't make it across. You can either try to hire a pick-up truck off the main square or walk the 45 minutes from town. On weekend afternoons you can usually hitch a ride.

EL MONTE, *On the road to the Mindo-Nambillo Reserve. Reservations through Cultura Reservation Center, Tel./Fax 2/558 889. E-mail: info@ecuadortravel.com. Website: www.ecuadortravel.com. Double $50 per person. Three meals and all activities included. No credit cards.*

Owned by an American-Ecuadorian couple, El Monte is another beautiful option in Mindo. Part of the fun of El Monte is getting to your A-frame cabana. The cabins are tucked in the forest on the far side of the river. Guests cross over on a small cable car to the comfortable cabins with hammocks and river views. Worth noting are the bathrooms, which actually include full-size bathtubs, something only found in the nicest hotels in the country.

The meals at El Monte, home cooked and delicious, never include red meat. It's really nice to know, as you enjoy your meal, that the produce and teas served at the lodge come from the lodge's own organic gardens.

This is a great place to unpack your bags and stay a while. Activities that are included with the price of the room include bird watching, white water tubing, waterfalls, swimming, horseback riding and nature walks. For an additional fee they can also organize trips to see the Cock-of-the-rock and the Butterfly Farm.

EL CARMELO DE MINDO, *1 km northwest of Mindo out the road past the town pool. Quito Tel. 2/295 831, Fax2/292 615. Email: hcarmelo@uio.satnet.net, 8 cabins. Double $40. Breakfast not included. Restaurant. Bar. Pool. Laundry. No credit cards.*

The Carmelo de Mindo, on 150 hectares of primary forest, borders the Mindo-Nambillo Reserve. It is especially known for the Cock-of-the-Rock Lek, which they guarantee can be seen here every day.

The comfortable cabins, primarily thatched A-frames, have a queen-sized bed downstairs and two twins upstairs. Two new cabins are built up like tree houses in guayabo trees, providing guests with a unique lodging experience.

The restaurant serves home-style meals, with the eggs, milk, some fruit, and vegetables all organically grown on the lodge's own plots.

There is no lack of activity options here. They have a fishing lake, soccer field, soccer court, volleyball pitch, horseback riding, inner tubing and excursions to waterfalls. Throw the pool in that mix and you've got a place that kids love.

CENTRO DE EDUCACIÓN AMBIENTAL (CEA), *in the Nambillo Reserve, at the end of the road across the river from the Mindo Gardens Hotel, Fax in Quito 2/404 037. E-mail: maldinny@yahoo.com. Double $20. Dorm $8 per person. Full board included.*

The woodsy huts on the 17-hectare nature reserve started as a biological research station that has expanded to include comfortable, rustic lodging in a pristine cloud forest. The Mindo River churns over rocks a few yards away to provide fluid percussion for the hundreds of distinct bird songs. Nearly, but not purely vegetarian meals are included in the very economically priced lodging. You'll dine family style with the young biologists stationed at the center. The cabins, while rustic, are constructed of beautiful indigenous wood, which makes them more stylish than you might expect. You can hike on several lushly vegetated trails from research station. See the *Namibillo Reserve* for more details.

Unless you have a four-wheel drive vehicle, you will probably end up walking the 45 minutes down the dirt road to the entrance of the reserve, so it is best to take only a daypack if possible. The walk is pretty and you can stop by the butterfly farm on the way.

HOSTAL ARMONIA, *Oñate and Toapanta. Tel. 2/770 114. 4 rooms without bath. Double $8. E-mail: mindo_mundo@hotmail.com. No credit cards.*

The Hostal Armonía is set in the middle of Mindo's Orchid Garden.

It's a simple place with four rooms and two shared bathrooms. The rooms are clean and the atmosphere homey. There are hammocks around the hostel for hanging out, or you can arrange tubing, horseback riding, hikes and bird watching.

GYPSY HOSTAL, *Frente al Estadio y Piscina. Tel. 2/351061 or 352805. $4 per person with shared bath.*

The Gypsy Hostal is a clean, cheap place to stay in town with a pleasant outdoor dining area.

WHERE TO EAT

MINDO GARDEN, *On the road to the Mindo-Nambillo reserve. Moderate. Credit cards accepted.*

Even if you're not staying here, you'll enjoy a appreciate in this lovely setting. The beautiful restaurant, decorated with handmade balsa figurines and tableware, sits on the edge of the river surrounded by profuse gardens. You can either enjoy the fixed meal inside, sure to satisfy, or try the outdoor pizzeria.

EL MONTE, *On the road to the Mindo-Nambillo Reserve. Moderate. No credit cards.*

El Monte is another place that's worth a visit even if you're not staying there. They offer good gringo and vegetarian food in a laid back atmosphere.

ARCO IRIS, *On the main plaza in town. Inexpensive. No credit cards.*

This simple restaurant serves up some tasty, inexpensive eats. Whether you go for the daily *menú*, which might be anything from chicken breast to pork chops, or the grilled cheese sandwich, the food is prepared fresh when you order.

SEEING THE SIGHTS

MINDO-NAMBILLO PROTECTED FOREST, *3 kilometers outside of Mindo, at the end of a road usually only for four-wheel drive vehicles.*

This is an outstanding reserve where you can experience the lush environment of a cloud forest. It helps support over 350 species of birds and 120 species of orchids found in the Mindo area. The reserve is divided up into several distinct sections; each is privately and independently managed.

The best place to begin your visit is on the trails of the Centro de Educación Ambiental (CEA) located at the end of the dirt road just beyond the Mindo Garden Lodge. The road can often only be traversed by four-wheel drive vehicle so it is probable that you will have to walk the 45 minutes to the CEA entrance. Go over the small bridge just past Mindo Garden and you will see the entrance to CEA on the right.

The CEA trails are well marked and include signs with basic commentary on the cloud forest and ecology. You will first walk along the narrow and restless Mindo River until the trail branches giving you the option of climbing the steep hill in varying degrees of difficulty, but it should be noted, that none of the hillside trails can be rated as "easy". There is one flat trail that passes along the river, through a medicinal garden, and by a marsh. This is the best option for those who prefer a less strenuous walk. Climbing one of the hillside trails to the top earns you a fantastic view of hills surrounding the fertile valley and the possibility of hiking one of two routes to the Nambillo waterfall.

If you walk left on the dirt road at the top of the CEA trail, you will soon see sign indicating *Cascada de Nambillo*. Hiking down the this route takes you across a footbridge over the Nambillo River, then to the right down another trail to the waterfall. There are some shelters set up here to camp. The caretakers will charge one to two dollars to camp or see the waterfall. The other option is to stop by the Mindo Garden Hotel before entering the CEA reserve. They charge a dollar per person to let you use the key to open the gate to their path. In this case take a right at the top of the CEA trail when it hits the dirt road. You can swim in the pool under the waterfall.

CALIGO BUTTERFLY FARM, *On the road to Mindo-Nambillo Reserve. E-mail: c_butterflies@ecuadorexplorer.com. Monday-Friday 9am-12pm, 2pm-6pm. Weekends 10am-12pm, 2pm-6pm. Entry $2.50.*

The Butterfly Farm is one of the Mindo highlights. People love to enter the greenhouses where they find hundreds of butterflies flitting about in the muted light. What's most noteable is the silence. Even the largest butterflies move softly, almost magically through the air.

Another highlight is the cocoons. The array of colors, shapes and sizes is mind boggling. It's amazing how a caterpillar turning into a butterfly can so closely resemble a green leaf, dead twig or even a piece of jewelry.

The farm is actually a commercial venture, selling live cocoons to gardens and zoos around the world. They have three huge flight areas that simulate the forest around Mindo with streams, mineral deposits, and a wide range of wild flowers in order to raise happy, healthy caterpillars.

The farm is a pleasant 30-minute walk from town.

ORCHID GARDEN, *Oñate and Toapanta. 9am-5pm daily. Entry $1.*

The Mindo area is famous for its orchids, and you can see many types of them here in the garden. Created in 1991, the idea was to protect these disappearing species. Used for research and education, it is also open to the public for pure enjoyment. It's nothing fancy, but it's a nice way to see some of the famous flowers.

RECOGNIZING ORCHIDS

The thousands of species of orchids in the world all look so different that it's hard to know when you're seeing one. The flowers vary greatly in color and shape, but they all have the same bilaterally symmetrical flower structure. These also always have three sepals, which are the modified leaves right below the petals. In many orchids one of the petals, called the lip, is distinct in both shape and color from the other petals.

The word orchid is derived from the Greek word orchis, which means testicle. This name comes from the shape of the root tubers in some species of the genus.

SPORTS & RECREATION

Birding

Mindo is famous in birding circles for its over 500 species of birds. Some of the more famous and glamorous ones include the bold red Cock-of-the-Rock, the Choco Toucan and the Golden-headed Quetzal. There are many birding guides in Mindo, but the consensus *número uno* is Vinicio Perez. He has a small hostal that offers basic lodging, but is best known for his skill at spotting and identifying birds. You can contact him once you get to town or ask your hotel to arrange his services in advance.

Hiking

There are some great, albeit steep, trails in the Mindo-Nambillo Reserve.

Horseback riding

A number of places in town offer horses for hire. Be sure to check your horse to make sure that it looks healthy before agreeing to rent. You can take a nice ride out to the butterfly farm.

Tubing

Floating in inner-tubes down the Mindo River is a favorite activity for visitors. For about $5 per person you get your tube, life jacket, helmet, a guide and transportation to and from the river. It's a fun way to see the landscape along the river, but can get cold after a while. About thirty minutes is all the time you need to spend in the water.

EXCURSIONS & DAY TRIPS

Many people, especially birders, combine a trip to Mindo with a visit to the **Bellavista Cloud Forest Reserve** 29 kilometers away. (See below).

Pahuma Reserve

Another beautiful option even closer than Bellavista is the **Pahuma Reserve**. Made up of over 1,000 hectares of cloud forest, the reserve sits on the Pacaya River. With an orchid exhibit, kilometers of trails, and beautiful pools and waterfalls, it's a great place to spend the day. There is no infrastructure for spending the night with the exception of a campers refuge located a two-hour's hike into the forest. Entrance to the reserve costs $1.

The reserve is 22 kilometers west of Calacalí on the way to Nanegalito and Mindo. There is no public transportation to the reserve, but you can get off a bus headed to Mindo from Calacalí at kilometer 22.

PRACTICAL INFORMATION

You could call the service industry in Mindo a bit underdeveloped. There are no banks, money exchangers, tourism offices or post office.

BELLAVISTA CLOUD FOREST RESERVE

The **Bellavista reserve** is also on the edge of the Choco Bio-region. Currently comprising 700 hectares, it is a magical place to discover the diversity and beauty of the cloud forest. The cloud enshrouded pre-montane forests of Bellavista range in elevation from 1600-2500 meters. You'll feel that as you hike straight up and down the mountain slopes. It is precisely this steepness that has allowed the region to escape the worst of the ravages of deforestation, as the incline is too abrupt for much farming.

People come to Bellavista to see the birds, which number 263 species. Twelve trails offer a variety of sights and terrain. Bellavista is off the beaten path, but if you take a bus to Nanegalito from the *terminal terrestre* in Quito, you can hire a truck to take you the rest of the way. Any bus for Pacto, Puerto Quito, San Miguel de los Bancos or Mindo passes through Nanegalito. You can also arrange transportation directly with the reserve.

WHERE TO STAY & EAT

BELLAVISTA DOME, *Bellavista Cloud Forest Reserve. Quito office: Jorge Washington E7-23 and Reina Victoria. Quito Tel./Fax 2/232 313. E-mail: bellavista@ecuadorexplorer.com. Website: www.ecuadorexplorer.com/bellavista/ home. 5 rooms. $55 per person. Three meals included.o Restaurant. Bar. Transportation from Quito available. No credit cards.*

There's only one place to stay at the reserve, and that's the famous British-run, four-story, geodesic dome. Located above the canopy, you can see for kilometers on a clear day. Even if it's not clear, you'll enjoy watching the wispy clouds floating silently through the valley. All of the rooms have private balconies where you can sit for hours and enjoy the sights.

The dome offers other lodging options in addition to the private rooms. There are two communal floors, with shared sleeping quarters and bathroom, for $18 per person not including meals. If you want your meals included, that will be $25 per day extra. The food offered here is vegetarian, with both Ecuadorian and international dishes.

MAQUIPUCUNA RESERVE

The **Maquipucuna Reserve**, *located next to the Choco Bio-region*, is a 4,500-hectare privately owned and managed nature reserve, surrounded by 14,000 hectares of protected forest. A large majority of the reserve's land consists of undisturbed cloud forest. Covering four different life zones, the Reserve houses a tremendous diversity of flora and fauna. Orchids, bromeliads, exotic butterflies and over 330 species of birds make the reserve a feast for the eyes as you hike its trails or swim under cascading waterfalls. Archaeological studies indicate that the area in and around Maquipucuna was home to indigenous peoples known as Yumbos. You can still find ceramics and burial sites as you explore the pathways they used to travel between the highlands and the coast.

The entrance to the Maquipucuna Reserve is a two-hour drive from Quito, accessed, like Bellavista, from Nanegalito and then an unpaved road to the north. If you take a bus to Nanegalito from the *terminal terrestre* in Quito, you can hire a truck to take you the rest of the way. Any bus for Pacto, Puerto Quito, San Miguel de los Bancos or Mindo passes through Nanegalito.

Talk to the reserve for directions if you have your own transportation. There is a rustic lodge at the reserve where you can stay if you make arrangements in advance.

THOMAS H. DAVIS ECOTOURISM CENTER, *Maquipucuna Reserve. Quito address: Baquerizo #238, E-mail: tropic@uio.satnet.net. Website: www.tropiceco.com. 5 rooms with shared bathrooms. $45 per person. Three meals included. No credit cards.*

The open-air design of the small lodge allows the breeze and sounds of the Umachaca River to pass through undisturbed. The bunk bed accommodations are Spartan, yet well designed with lots of light and even desk space. The common areas are comfortable, with plenty of hammocks for reading, resting and relaxing. The meals, served family-style, take advantage of the fresh vegetables grown in the reserve's organic garden.

There is a separate research station and laboratory for visiting scientists.

SANTO DOMINGO DE LOS COLORADOS

There are two reasons to find yourself in **Santo Domingo**. One is that you've stopped here in transit between the highlands and the coast. The other is that you are interested in seeing the birds of the lowland forests. If neither of these two reasons apply, you'll probably be disappointed that you've used your vacation time to come here.

ARRIVALS & DEPARTURES

Santo Domingo is one of Ecuador's main crossroads. Three hours from the coast, three hours from Quito, and four hours from Guayaquil, it is a town that has grown to serve the thru-traffic.

By Bus

Panamericana buses leave for Santo Domingo from the *terminal terreste* in Quito a few times a day. The ride costs $3 and takes two and a half to three hours. The main bus station in Santo Domingo is about three km north of downtown. There are buses from here to Quito, Guayaquil and Esmeraldas.

As Santo Domingo is considered a hub of the country, it makes sense that there are also buses to Bahía de Caráquez, Latacunga, Ambato, Riobamba and Cuenca.

By Car

To get to Santo Domingo from Quito, you head south on the Pan-American Highway until you arrive to Aloag. At the traffic light in Aloag you will see the westward road that takes you to Santo Domingo. (Yes, there is a traffic light in the middle of the Pan-American highway.) The road heads to the edge of the high plains and then begins a curvy, precipitous drop down through the jungle. Waterfalls crash along the side of the road, overloaded banana trucks come chugging up the other way and people pull taffy in shops along the highway.

It's a straight shot up the country through the Los Ríos and Pichincha Provinces to get to Santo Domingo from Guayaquil.

By Taxi

If you can find a taxi driver that won't take crazy chances when passing, this is a viable alternative. It costs about $40 from both Esmeraldas and Quito.

ORIENTATION

Most people never actually enter the town of Santo Domingo as they make their way across the country. Traffic circles on the highway direct people around the city, and even those spending the night usually stay at one of the hotels on the *Panamericana.*

If you do head into town, the main plaza, **Parque Zaracay**, is the center of much of the action.

GETTING AROUND TOWN

Once you get into town, you can walk just about everywhere. We're not saying it's pleasant, but its how you get around.

WHERE TO STAY & EAT

In our opinion, the best place in the northern lowlands to stay is Tinalandia. If you're just passing through however, you might want to crash in one of the hotels on the highway.

TINALANDIA, *15 km east of Santo Domingo. Tel. 2/449 028. Fax 2/442 638. 12 cabins. Double $100. Restaurant. No credit cards.*

For birders, Tinalandia is not just a place to stay, it is a titillating, ornithological paradise. Carved out of the lush, lowland jungle above the Toachi river, the retreat was built by an Ecuadorian who named it for his Russian wife, Tina. Their son Sergio currently runs the place, which includes a rarely used golf course, maintained to standards that would please officials of the British Open. The entire course is tropical rough, the sidelines of which provide the ideal location for birders to plant their tripods. Birds of all color and design, surreptitiously sing from within, then pop out from the wall of jungle growth, igniting a flurry of shutter snapping and field guide page flipping.

If you prefer to delve into the jungle, several trails have been cut into the thick of things. You might spot an emerald green toucan munching on berries, or if you look down occasionally, a snail the size of a Tonka truck. You can spend several wonderful hours admiring the gargantuan leaves and lecherous vines as you stroll under the dense green canopy.

The restaurant and service buildings are located about five hundred meters up a dirt road from the highway. The open-walled dining area looks out to the churning river through thick foliage. Hummingbird feeders are set out so the locals can dine with the guests. The fare is rib-sticking, meat and potato meals that fall into the expensive category by Ecuadorian standards.

The cabins are woodsy, comfortable, and ample, a five-minute walk up hill from the restaurant. Huge picture windows open into the jungle and occasionally a humming bird will hover there, looking in with envy at the brilliant fresh-cut tropical flowers in your room, before moving on to the ones just outside.

HOTEL ZARACAY, *Quito highway east of Santo Domingo. Tel. 2/750 316, Fax 2/754 535. 45 rooms. Double $70 suite with air conditioning and hot water, $52 room with ceiling fan. Restaurant. Bar. Pool. Credit cards accepted.*

Although located on the highway, the Zaracay is set back from the road and surrounded by trees. You enter the hotel through the reception area, which leads out to a flowered courtyard where you'll find the open-air restaurant and bar. The restaurant is also the top option in town, which is why you'll find many locals here at lunch.

The rooms come in two classes: 1) large with air conditioning, and 2) not so big with ceiling fan. The AC is not imperative here, but it helps you sleep both by cooling down the room and drowning out any noise.

HOTEL DON KLEBER, *Km 2.5 on the Quininde-Esmeraldas highway north of Santo Domingo. Tel. 2/761 956. 25 rooms. Double $18. Restaurant. Bar. Pool. No credit cards.*

If you can't afford the Zaracay, the Don Kleber is the town's next best option. It's clean and Spartan. Located up on a little hill above the highway, it gets traffic noise so you might want earplugs. Don't worry if you hear what sounds like a lady screaming bloody murder in the middle of the night, it's just one of the caged macaws by the swimming pool. The restaurant, by the pool, seems more like a patio bar, but it's what you get.

HOTEL TROPICAL INN, *Quito highway east of Santo Domingo. Tel. 2/ 761 771, Fax 2/761 775. 20 rooms. Double $20. Restaurant. Bar. Pool. No credit cards.*

The Tropical Inn, across the street from the Zaracay, will do in a pinch. It's your standard U.S. Motel Six model right on the highway. They do have some larger rooms with kitchenettes though.

CHE FARINA, *Quito highway east of Santo Domingo. Tel. 750 259. Inexpensive. No credit cards.*

This pizza restaurant, just a few doors down from the Zaracay towards town, is a decent option for a pie. It's not great, but sometimes when you're craving pizza, you'll lower your standards. Part of a national chain, it's clean and bright.

SEEING THE SIGHTS

There's really not much to see in Santo Domingo. **Parque Zaracay**, the main plaza, has just been renovated and actually looks pretty nice. The 22 benches, each representing a province in Ecuador, ring the new statue of the Colorado Indian.

Unless you count the guys on the plaza that pose for photos, the statue is about all that's left of the Colorado.

A CULTURE LOST

A common image of Ecuador is a close-up of a stoic Colorado Indian. With chili-bowl haircuts and coiffures dyed red with achiote, these men are unforgettable. The look is fast being a memory however, as Colorados become integrated into Ecuadorian society. Any of the Colorados, or Tsachilas, you see outfitted like this in Santo Domingo are doing it strictly for the chance to earn money in photos. Even nearby Chihuilpe, touted as a place to visit the Colorados in their home environment, is set up for tourists.

SPORTS & RECREATION

Birding is the name of the game. The most famous place near Santo Domingo, and one of the most renown in the country, is Tinalandia (see *Where to Stay* above). Even if you are not staying there, you can spend the day spying winged creatures for $10 per person.

EXCURSIONS & DAY TRIPS

The most gung-ho birders might want to venture further afield to some of the government and private reserves in the area. These are primarily used for research purposes, so the facilities are rustic and you must arrange your trip in advance. The remoteness of these places is what has allowed them to escape development as farmland, so access can be a problem, especially during the rainy season.

• **La Perla Forest Reserve**, *Tel. 2/725 344.* West Virginian Suzanne Sheppard came to Ecuador to farm and became a conservationist along the way. She has saved 250 hectares of wet lowland forest for the benefit of future generations. 41 km from Santo Domingo.

• **Rio Palenque Science Center**, *Quito Tel. 2/561 646.* With 100 hectares of primary lowland forest on the Palenque River, this reserve has over 360 species of birds. 50 km from Santo Domingo.

• **Bilsa Biological Reserve and Station**, *Quito Tel/Fax. 2/250 976. E-mail: jatsacha@ecuanex.net.ec. Website: www.jatunsacha.org.* Established by the Jatún Sacha Foundation, the reserve covers 770 hectares of rare tropical wet forest. 120 km from Santo Domingo.

PRACTICAL INFORMATION

Parque Zaracay is surrounded by **banks** and **taxis**. From there you walk three blocks east on Quito Avenue to the **EMETEL** phone office. The **post office** is three blocks north of the plaza on *Tsachilas and Babahoyo.*

When considering the northern coast as a destination, a clear distinction should be made between the dismal city of **Esmeraldas** and the pleasant beach area south of there.

The balmy, tropical beaches of **Atacames**, **Súa**, **Same**, and **Muisne** provide a quick, inexpensive seaside escape for Quiteños. While these beaches shouldn't be considered one of Ecuador's primary destinations, if you're in Quito yearning for some sand and sea, these will do the trick.

ESMERALDAS

In the past **Esmeraldas** was a poor but interesting city. The major business center for most of the country's Afro-Ecuadorian population, it took on tropical culture and rhythms not unlike the Caribbean. Unfortunately, the force of the El Niño storms in 1998 hit the city extremely hard.

Even more unfortunate is the fact that the money needed to make repairs to the city's infrastructure just doesn't exist. Esmeraldas today looks like a war zone. It is not the poverty per se or the misfortune wrought by El Niño that does this place in. It is, rather, a simple lack of basic sanitary services. Smoking garbage dumps ring the town and putrid debris soils the city streets. In fact, the only walls with paint are those covered with the empty promise offered by the rough cane liquor Crystal, "It makes you Happy." Only the most dedicated culture-seeking traveler can get past the fetidness to glean the vibrancy and intriguing hum of the place.

History

Esmeraldas means Emerald in Spanish. An appropriate term to describe the foliage, it is actually describing the jewel. The gems were mined here before the Spanish arrived. Try as they Spanish might, they never got the locals to divulge the mines' locations.

The province's Afro-Ecuadorian culture is documented to have begun in 1553 when a Spanish slaveship wrecked on the coast. Twenty-three Africans from the coast of Guinea attacked their captors and freed themselves. They were led by an African warrior named Antón. Other blacks began to enter the zone from neighboring areas until the group came to dominate the region.

This group was greatly admired over the years for their fighting prowess. They never submitted to the Quitus or the Incas and completely overwhelmed the local Colorado indigenous group. They then fought off many Spanish expeditions into the territory and were never conquered in over 60 years of continuous fighting with the Iberians. They were, however, finally converted to Catholicism, which led them to submit to the Spanish government as representative of the church.

AFRICAN INFLUENCE

While the hot music in Esmeraldas these days has its source in Colombia rather than Africa, there are still some strains of African culture woven into the fabric of coastal life. One of the most popular saints in the region is San Antonio, a non-white saint. He represents a transformation of the African god Legba, the trickster.

ARRIVALS & DEPARTURES

By Bus

Esmeraldas is connected by bus to other cities in all directions (except west). There are buses to Quito, Guayaquil and San Lorenzo. The best bus line is **Panamericana**, *Colon and Piedrahita*, which runs from Quito to Esmeraldas. **Transportes Esmeraldas**, *10 de Agosto between Bolívar and Sucre*, has transportation to both Quito and Guayaquil. **Occidental**, *9 de Octubre between Sucre and Olmedo*, covers local routes. **La Costeñita** bus company runs to Atacames and other points along the coast.

It takes about six hours to get to Quito through Santo Domingo. A ride to Guayaquil or Bahía de Caráquez takes about eight hours. It's four hours and 185 km to Santo Domingo.

By Car

The road most traveled is by Quiteños beating it to the coast. There are two routes from Quito. The most popular way is to access to Esmeraldas from the highlands is via Santo Domingo. There is also a new road that goes via Mindo. It's about a six-hour drive. The route to Guayaquil from Esmeraldas, eight hours, goes through Santo Domingo.

Cars can be rented in Esmeraldas at **Localiza**, *Malecón and Delgadillo, Tel. 711 761, Fax 728 666*.

By Plane

There is a TAME flight from Quito to Esmeraldas every day except Sunday. The flight, which leaves in the morning, takes thirty minutes. A one-way ticket is about $30. You can also fly to Colombia from here.

The airport is a small, one room affair. The **TAME** office in town can be found at Bolívar *and 9 de Octubre*.

There are no buses from the airport to town. A cab to Esmeraldas, 25-30 minutes on a terrible road, costs around $15. To go directly to the beaches, between 30 to 45 minutes on an equally bad road, costs $20.

ORIENTATION

Esmeraldas sits on Ecuador's northern coast at the mouth of the Esmeraldas River. South along the coast are popular weekend beach resorts. Many people fly into the Esmeraldas airport and then head directly south, skirting Esmeraldas entirely. North of the city up to the Colombian border, the coastline is primarily comprised of mangrove swamps.

The city itself is centered around the town plaza and the port. The road along the coast, the *malecón*, heads north to a section of town called **Las Palmas**. The main street in Las Palmas is Kennedy Avenue. Nicer than the downtown area, it's where we suggest staying and eating. There is also a dirty beach with lots of discos and ceviche restaurants in Las Palmas.

You should avoid walking around Esmeraldas or the beach area at night, and take care during the day.

GETTING AROUND TOWN

While walking around town is certainly feasible, many people prefer to take cabs to avoid the garbage lying in the streets. You'll also want to take cabs at night for safety reasons.

WHERE TO STAY & EAT

If you get stuck staying the night here you'll do best to head to the Costa Verde Suites, but even this place is just passable. At least it's in a quiet residential neighborhood.

COSTA VERDE SUITES, *Luis Tello 809 and Hilda Padilla. Tel 6/728 714, Fax 6/728 716. 25 rooms. Double $26. Cable TV. Restaurant. Credit cards accepted.*

This is the best of the lot in Esmeraldas, but it isn't much. The rooms are big, but the carpet is thin and the furniture is pretty worn. On the upside, they keep the place scrubbed to a shine, and the location is off the main drag in a quiet residential neighborhood. It also has a pleasant cafe style restaurant, **La Fragata**, part of which is on a terrace.

APART HOTEL ESMERALDAS, *Libertad 407. Tel. 6/728 700 or 728 701, Fax 6/728 704. 20 rooms. Double $26. Cable TV. Restaurant. Credit cards accepted.*

This is the closest acceptable hotel to the city center and it is marginal at best. You're better off heading out to Costa Verde Suites, a short distance further from town.

HOTEL CAYAPAS, *Kennedy and Valdez. Tel. 6/721 318, Fax 6/721 320. 20 rooms. Double $20. Cold water only. Restaurant. Credit cards accepted sometimes.*

You don't want to stay here unless forced to. The walls are thin, the carpets worn and the furniture old. For all of $6 more you could be at the Costa Verde. It is clean at least. The Cayapas' restaurant, **La Tolita,** is in better shape than the hotel. The menu features fish, *ceviche,* and *cocadas,* but you can also go for the chicken, steak or pasta if you have had enough seafood.

There are also a lot of small seafood joints along the short boardwalk, *malecón* in Las Palmas. Right in front of the beach, it's a decent place for a cold beer if you are in town during the day.

NIGHTLIFE & ENTERTAINMENT

Esmeraldas is sometimes referred to as Marimba Music Mecca. This xylophone-based genre of tropical music has long since been swept to the wayside in favor of hotter rhythms like *salsa* and *cumbia.* The oceanfront area near Las Palmas is host to a row of tropical music bars. Unfortunately, to sample the *sabor* you have to risk your skin. The bar area is quite sketchy at night.

EXCURSIONS & DAY TRIPS

To the North

There are a few isolated towns, many mangrove swamps and a jungle lodge between Esmeraldas and Colombia. See *North to the Border* below.

To the South

The biggest draw to this area is the beaches just south of town.

PRACTICAL INFORMATION

Banks: Pichincha, *Bolívar and 9 de Octubre.* The teller machine accepts Diners Card. **Banco Popular,** *Bolívar and Piedrahita,* has an ATM that accepts cirrus cards in theory, but we've never seen it work. It's the best bank for exchanging dollars.

Business Hours: This is the coast. 8am-11am and 2pm-4:30pm.

Medical Service: Hospital, *Libertad y Las Palmas.*

Post Office: Correos, *Montalvo y Malecón.*

Telephone/Fax: The area code is 6. **EMETEL,** above the post office at *Montalvo and Malecón.*

Tourist Office/Maps: CETUR, *Bolívar 299 between Mejia and Salinas.* It's a small office with not much information.

ATACAMES

Atacames, although described as a resort, does not exactly fit that bill. The word resort conjures up images of pristine beaches and neat waiters carrying umbrella drinks. Atacames is far more uncontrived than that. If you finally get a waiter's attention somewhere, he'll most likely have a sweaty brow and unbuttoned shirt. The beach is ringed with low-end shops and restaurants. Most of the hotels are separated from the water by a sandy thoroughfare. Loud music blares out of the seaside shacks selling cheap seafood and beer.

As the closest beach to Quito, Atacames fills up with partying *Serranos* on weekends and during holidays. Be sure to reserve in advance during the high season.

WHERE TO STAY & EAT

You shouldn't miss some of the delicious regional specialties while you're here:
• *Ceviche* – seafood with onion, lime and cilantro
• *Encocados* – seafood prepared with rich coconut sauce
• *Bolones* – big balls of plantains and cheese
• *Muchines* – yucca with sugar-cane honey
• *Cocadas* – grated coconut and brown sugar

CLUB RESORT DEL PACIFICO, *Kilometer 20 on the way to Atacames. Tel. 2/981 740. 30 apartments. Apartment $150. Breakfast included. Restaurant. Bar. Cable TV. Pool. Tennis courts. Putt-putt. Disco. Credit cards accepted.*

This resort, just north of town, is the nicest in Atacames. It is the first superior place to stay along the coast as you head south from Esmeraldas and actually one of the best on the coast. The two story apartments are arranged around the large swimming pool. Each apartment has a kitchenette, master bedroom, and bath downstairs as well as a living area, bedroom and bath upstairs. Recently renovated, the tasteful tan and blue apartments also count TV/VCRs, coffee makers, blenders and waffle irons as standard. The large grounds of the complex include two clay tennis courts, volleyball, putt-putt and a strip of beach. There is a bar and disco on the beach along with the requisite tents.

The problem is that the Resort del Pacifico is a timeshare property. They only take off-the-street clients on a space available basis. During the high season you probably won't be able to get in here even if you book in advance. What you can do is call a few days before you want to go and see if they have something available. During the low season, however, they often offer specials that include two nights for the price of one.

VILLAS ARCO IRIS, *End of Playa de Atacames, Atacames. Tel. 6/731 069, Cel. 09/787 549, Fax 06/731 437. 2-3 person cabin $35. 23 cabins. Restaurant. Pool. Credit cards accepted.*

This tropical refuge lies just beyond the hustle and bustle, crowds, and commerce of Atacama's beach strip. Twenty-three charming, thatch-roofed hut style cabins accommodate from two to six people. Each is equipped with a restful porch hammock from which you can contemplate the sway of palm leaves. You can laze away the day by the large pool surrounded by tropical flowers and greenery, or if you prefer, step outside the compound entrance onto the beach. Prices are cut nearly in half during low season.

EL MORRO, *Beach access road. Tel. 6/731 456; E-mail: elmorroatacames@yahoo.com. 25 rooms. Double $30. Restaurant. Bar. Pool. Credit cards accepted.*

This recently built hotel is unfortunately 500 meters off the beach in town. It does have nice new rooms and a decent, clean restaurant.

RESTAURANT JUAN SEBASTIAN, *on the beach, two doors south of the Arco Iris.*

Air conditioning is probably the biggest thing this place has going for it, although the food is pretty good too. Seafood is the choice of the day and week here.

PRACTICAL INFORMATION

The **bank**, **phone offices** and **buses** can all be located on the *main plaza*. At low tide you can walk all the way down to **Sua**, where you can watch fishermen bring in their haul.

SUA & SAME

Two minutes down the road from Atacames, you'll come to **Súa**, a fishing village with not much in the way of infrastructure. There are a few cheap hotels on the beach. The **Hotel Súa**, *Tel. 6/731 004, Double $8*, run by a French couple, is the best of the lot. Their restaurant is surprisingly sophisticated.

Another 15 minutes down the highway you'll reach **Same**. The beach in Same is nicer than those of Atacames and Súa and there are some good hotels here as well.

CLUB CASABLANCA, *On the road to Same. Tel. 2/252 488, Fax 2/253 452. US Reservations 800/709 9470. 43 rooms. Double $148. Breakfast, lunch and dinner included. Restaurant. Bar. Small store. Pool. Tennis. Golf. Putt-putt. Bike rental. Cable TV. Credit cards accepted.*

Casablanca, one of the nicest properties on the Northern Coast, is a place that families enjoy. There are enough activities to keep the kids busy while the parents can kick back and relax. The good thing is that nice does not mean overdone. This is not a place you will be worried about your kids putting their feet on the furniture.

We recommend setting the right tone upon arrival by trying the Piña Colada for your welcome drink - bet you'll have a few more over the course of your stay. Their secret recipe is definitely worth trying to recreate at home.

The apartments here are the way to go. With a living area, nice size kitchen, two bedrooms, two baths a porch and patio, you'll find it easy to get sucked into slowing down and relaxing. Blue and white are the theme both inside and out of these units, designed to look like the sugar cube buildings of Mikonos, Greece.

Casa Blanca is a large property with some timeshare units as well as separate sets of apartments. They have kept each set of rooms small enough that you don't feel overwhelmed, but this is definitely not a boutique hotel. Make sure you get a unit in Cabo Coral, which is closest to the surf. The rooms in Cabo Coral spread out around the pool and down to the beach. Bougainvillea covered grounds and large palm trees create a tropical atmosphere. The beach in front of the Casablanca extends down for about four kilometers. There are a few other hotels along this stretch. Crabs continuously scuttle in and out of the mellow waves. Runners and walkers ply the strip in the early morning, replaced by frolicking kids later in the day.

If it's activity you're after, there's plenty of that here as well. There are four tennis courts, two hard and two clay. We like the novelty of playing on the well-tended red clay a la Roland Garros. There is also a nine-hole golf course that is the only one is South America designed by Jack Nicolas. Unfortunately, El Niño destroyed part of it and they are still in the process of repairs. Five holes were open the last time we visited. You can also get SCUBA certified here and surf the break in front of the hotel.

The open-air restaurant is right on the beach. There is an extensive menu that includes delicious shrimp *ceviche* and whole lobster. If you get one of the rooms that is not an apartment, the price of your stay includes meals. There is a shortened menu for "everything included" guests that gets old after a while, but luckily you can always order off the regular menu. We also like the pizza.

One of the best things about Casa Blanca is their airport pick-up service. You hop off your plane into their van and are on the beach before you know it.

EL ACANTILADO, *Playas de Same-Esmeraldas. Quito Tel. 2/453 606. Cel. 09/551 459. 15 cabins. Restaurant. Pool. No credit cards.*

Several of the El Acantilado's cabins and its lookout hut literally teeter over the edge of a lushly vegetated cliff above an isolated portion of Same beach. The restaurant and small pool share the same sweeping ocean view. The rustic A-frame cabins are wrapped with ivy and bougainvillea in four spectacular colors. The entire property is a vibrant tropical garden that makes the funky, glass-walled restaurant and lounge building feel like a greenhouse turned inside out. If you can handle cold water showers for a few days, you will be more than compensated in splendor and serenity.

SEAFLOWER HOSTAL, *Same. Tel. 6/455 038, Double $25.*

This is our favorite in-town lodging. With only three rooms, you receive personal attention at this small hostel. Owned by a German/Chilean couple, the hotel is creatively decorated and serves good food as well.

MUISNE

The coastal road continues to Tonchigue and cuts inland to **Muisne**. It's about a two-hour drive from Same with the road in such a sad state. If you've got the time however, it's worth the effort.

Muisne is actually a peninsula that breaks away from the land further south. The road from Tonchigue dead-ends at a landing area from which small boats ferry people across to the town of Muisne. The town itself is unremarkable, but there is a lodge on the far side of the peninsula that is located on an absolutely gorgeous stretch of beach.

MOMPICHE LODGE, *Muisne. Quito Tel. 2/252 488, Fax 2/253 452. US Reservations 800/709 9470. 4 cabanas. Double $148. Breakfast, lunch and dinner included. No hot water. Credit cards accepted through Quito office.*

If you want to get off the beaten path on the Ecuadorian coast, this is a great place for it. After flying into Esmeraldas, you take a two-hour cab ride to Muisne. From there you get in a wooden longboat and travel for 25 minutes through mangrove forest up the estuary. Then your boat will head out to sea for 20 minutes before arriving to the 172-acre property that is Mompiche.

Here you will find four thatched cabanas built in the local *toquilla* style. Each hut has a balcony and hammocks that face out to the Pacific Ocean. There's nothing but wide, white sandy beach between the cabanas and the water.

There are a number of activities you can do while at the lodge. In addition to horseback riding, snorkeling and sailing, exploring the mangroves is a popular outing. Just a few minutes from the lodge is a fluvial lake with ducks, horned screamers, herons and woodpeckers. You can also find howler monkeys and anteaters in the area.

Many people come to Mompiche for the surf. Known as some of the best in the country, a 400-meter left breaks closed to the lodge. You can ride the two to three meter wave down the line for an entire minute before

394 ECUADOR & GALÁPAGOS ISLANDS GUIDE

dropping out on the sandy bottom. There are three surfboards available for rent.

NORTH TO THE BORDER

About 30 kilometers north of Esmeraldas the coastline is broken into a series of mangrove swamps, making transportation by road difficult. **San Lorenzo**, the country's northern-most city on the coast, is only accessible from Esmeraldas through boat/bus combinations.

A rough road from Esmeraldas forks 20 kilometers north of the city. One route stays on the coast, heading to the small fishing village of **La Tola**. The other fork heads inland to the town of **Borbón**. Borbón itself is unremarkable, but from here you can access a lodge that sit on the edge of the **Cotacachi-Cayapas Ecological Reserve**.

Steve's Lodge, 45 minutes up river from Borbón by motorized canoe, is not always open for visitors. Contact them at *e-mail: nagy@uio.satnet.net* for more information and to see if they are accepting guests.

San Lorenzo is an unattractive town very near the Colombian border. The northern-most city on Ecuador's coast, many travelers formerly reached San Lorenzo via the Highlands on the famous **Ibarra-San Lorenzo train**. The rail trip, which dropped down from the Andes to the tropical coast, is no longer functioning because of major infrastructure damage along the route caused by El Niño. There is talk of a $60 million project sponsored by the government of Hungary to get the train back on track, but that has yet to be signed.

The drop in train traffic has killed the tourism industry in San Lorenzo. It wasn't exactly booming before, but now it's dead. A highway to San Lorenzo from Ibarra has been opened, but it just does not offer the same thrill as riding the roof of a train. You can travel south from San Lorenzo to Esmeraldas via a boat/bus combination to either **La Tola** or **Borbón**.

19. ORIENTE

The **Oriente** jungle is a vast expanse of intense and tangled tropical growth reticulated by hundreds of merging rivers. Life thrives in such Neotropical rainforests like nowhere else on earth. A perpetual, silent battle for light and nutrients rages among the plants. Vines cover hectares of trees in thick green sheets. Epiphytes take root wherever they can secure a lofty nook or branch for a more advantageous lifestyle.

The flashiest and most readily encountered creatures that inhabit this exotic realm are the hundreds of species of birds. Giant colorful macaws clear their raspy throats as they cruise overhead. Toucans and parrots dress in equally ostentatious garb. Eccentric birds abound. Consider the prehistoric looking hoatzin, called stinky turkey by the locals. Sporting blue eye shadow and a spiked, orange mohawk, it tumbles through the air like a drunkard when it flies.

Mammals are more elusive, but a thrill to observe when encountered. A variety of monkeys and marmosets entertain as they cavort through the treetops, occasionally pausing to stare back at the odd voyeurs below. The dorsal fin of a freshwater dolphin rising above the flow of a river might be the most unique sight in the jungle.

When you refocus your eyes from macro to micro you begin to perceive how alive the forest is immediately around you. Leafcutter ants march by toting a bright green stream of vegetation on their backs. Walking sticks are twigs with bulging eyes and antennae. Diminutive poison dart frogs festooned in brilliant yellow, blue, and red advertise their lethality.

Melting snow and rain from the Andes create hundreds of tributaries leading into the main rivers - the Napo, Aguarico, and Pastaza - that eventually feed the great Amazon River. These primary rivers churn brown, wide, and strong. Palms and bamboo stretch out from the bank into the open air. Wherever a sandbar emerges, determined plants invade it to create a tropical isle.

The rivers are the natural highways in the Amazon Basin. Motorized canoes are used to travel long distances, picking their way along the deepest portions so their outboard propellers are not buried in the sand. Dugout canoes glide through calmer waters, often darkened with tannins from fallen leaves. Your lodge might be located one of these black-mirrored lagoons that are inhabited by caimans, piranhas, and electric eels. A stay in a jungle lodge is the best way to be completely immersed in the tropical rainforest experience. The options you have to choose from are spectacular. Often the food and service is on par with cosmopolitan hotels, even though in some cases, the employees might never have seen a car. The high-end lodges are simply extraordinary, providing comfortable beds in rustic facilities surrounded by extensive tracts of pristine, protected rainforest. There are many operations in the moderate price range as well, but the quality varies greatly. We've culled a few select lodges that do the trick of providing a complete experience in both jungle culture and nature for a reasonable price.

Currently about one half million Ecuadorians, 5% of the population, live in the huge Oriente territory that comprises over 40% of Ecuadorian land. Jungle towns are primarily utilitarian communities developed as bases for mineral and oil development. Perhaps 30,000 indigenous people still live outside of these towns, with the way of life tending to be more traditional as you move deeper into the jungle.

KNOW BEFORE YOU GO

We hope to quell your independent traveler spontaneity for a moment so that you line up your lodge or tour before you head to the jungle. As you read this chapter, try to find the option that suits you best then coordinate travel plans through the operator. We suggest the five-day/four-night packages over shorter trips.

A good jungle trip will include spectacular wildlife, knowledgeable guides, tasty vittles, and comfortable sleeping facilities. The operator normally arranges your transportation from Quito.

A bad jungle trip is usually the result of trusting a fly-by-night tour operator contacted at random in one of the jungle towns. Common complaints of dissatisfied travelers include guides getting lost, poor food, sleeping outdoors in the rain, and sexual harassment.

If you try to get it done too cheaply, you will probably shortchange yourself. Wildlife and habitat protection costs money, as does gaining professionally serviced access to those areas.

JUNGLE TRAVEL STRATEGY

The most unique thing about traveling in the jungle is that any piece of it is going to look pretty much like any other piece, even those that are

1. Flotel, Cuyabeno Lodge, Native Life
2. Sacha Lodge, La Selva Lodge, Yuturi Lodge
3. Yachana Lodge
4. Liana Lodge, Casa del Suizo, Aliñahui Butterfly Lodge
5. Kapawi Lodge

hundreds of kilometers apart. There is no benefit in trying to see as much terrain as possible. In fact, even walking the same trail twice in well-protected area will present more diversity than two distant, lesser-protected locales.

The key is heading to one pristine tract of primary rainforest where animals still roam in abundance. Macaws shout and flaunt their brilliant red feathers above towering kapok trees. Troops of monkeys leap about in the canopy. These large expanses of old growth fauna teeming with wildlife are such because the government or a private enterprise success-fully protects them.

Focus on selecting a great facility in a remote destination. Opting for one of the top jungle lodges is a superb way to experience the jungle. If you can't afford the top end, then consider one of our exceptional moderately priced recommendations. Be aware that there is a swarm of agencies out there that promise adventure and wildlife, but often deliver poor food, inept guides, and other adversity.

You should minimize time in the jungle towns. Several were built in a ramshackle manner to support the oil industry. With a few exceptions, they are just hot and dirty streets lined with cement shacks. Imagine a Mexican border town...gone downhill. You get the picture.

Tena is slowly changing out of grimy overalls into fresh khakis and a sun hat. The town now has a new zoo and biological reserve, and there are a few interesting day trips offered. This is serendipity for the most part. It still wouldn't be worth coming here instead of delving farther into the jungle. **Macas**, distant from everything, is the other more pleasant population center. Again, this is a nice aspect if you get stuck here, but not worth venturing to specifically. Towns like **Coca** and **Lago Agrio** are just plain dives. Ten minutes in either of them is enough to feel as you've spent far longer in both.

There is little satisfaction derived in bus journeys in the Oriente. Unlike the highlands where riding along the Pan-American Highway simply to gaze out at the passing countryside might be reason enough to take a bus from Quito to Riobamba, there exists no similar motivation to take a bus from Puyo to Coca. The jungle encroaches on the highway, suffocating it, and blocking any type of panoramic vista. It is bumpy and monotonous. Conversely, traveling by motorized canoe along an expansive river is a wonderful, engaging method of locomotion.

HUMAN HISTORY

The Amazon Basin is thought to have been settled by the Jíbaros around 1,000 BC. The first indigenous contact with Europeans came in the sixteenth century. Missions set up by the Salesians and other religious groups organized Amazon Basin natives into villages for the first time.

A JUNGLE OF SPECIAL INTERESTS

"There are many cannibals here (in Quito)," Moi said. *"The whole world wants to speak for the Huaorani."*

"Many of them want to help the Huaorani," I said.

"Many of them want to steal from the Huaorani."

They had prepared a speech. Moi read it to me from his notebook. *"The Huaorani are the bravest people in the world,"* he began. *"The rivers and trees are our life. We protect our life for the whole world. Now the Company is invading our land. Land where my grandfather was born and my father was born and I was born. We will fight the Company like Huaorani fight. But the Huaorani will be friends with the whole world that does not try to destroy us. We invite the whole world to come and see how the Huaorani protect the forest."*

"That is powerful," I said.

"Yes, it is," Moi said. *"But it needs more cannibal words – words they will understand. Like..."* He paused. *"Environment – that is a word that pleases them, no?"*

—Joe Kane, from his book **Savages**

While missionaries were the early reformers of indigenous communities, they were not the only group with impact. Quichua natives from the highlands fled to the Oriente to avoid European oppression. They have now been here for many generations and consider the jungle their home territory. Many Oriente natives will speak Quichua in addition to Spanish and their tribal language.

The development of oil reserves beginning in the 1950's brought the greatest change. The projects pushed natives off their land; attracted colonists from the highlands who needed additional land for homes and agriculture; created several new towns; and drew natives into the money economy.

Jungle societies have traditionally consisted of small family clans. By necessity the various regional groups have recently formed federations to negotiate with outside interests such as the Ecuadorian government, oil companies, ecological groups, and eco-tour companies. Finding a unified voice has been a challenge in a region where families had always been autonomous and individually led. Formulating a long-term strategy through tenuously supported leadership is even more difficult. For example, a company may offer money, or projects, such as medical clinic building and management, in return for the use of indigenous land. Through trial and error, it has been learned that money simply vanishes with little benefit to the people. A medical clinic has more positive impact, but resulting costs, such as environmental damage are always difficult to gage.

INDIGENOUS GROUPS OF THE ORIENTE

These days almost all of the groups have regular contact with the outside world via military outposts, religious missions, eco-tourism, and commercial ventures. Typical native dress is a T-shirt, shorts, and rubber boots. While you are not likely to see feather headdresses and tattoos, except when donned as part of a cultural presentation, several aspects of the old indigenous culture remain. These include the drinking of *chicha* (manioc beer) at social occasions, dwelling in traditional thatched-roof houses, and traveling by dugout canoe.

Rivers still play an important role in transportation. Airfields have been built in almost every part of the Oriente, but roads are nonexistent in the eastern portion. This means that in the more remote regions it is likely that the inhabitants have seen airplanes, but never a car.

If you speak Spanish and you get the opportunity to communicate with one of the indigenous people who speaks Spanish, take advantage of it. If you don't speak Spanish you can communicate through your naturalist guide. You can gain great cultural insight through such conversation. You will notice the extraordinary attention to detail. A single story can be told over several days.

NATIVE & NATURALIST GUIDES

If you stay at a jungle lodge, two guides, one native and one naturalist, will lead you on excursions. Naturalist guides are usually from the highlands and have a university degree in science or tourism. These naturalist guides speak English and other languages, organize the briefings and tours, and usually eat meals with the group.

Native guides belong to a nearby indigenous community. They are expert in negotiating rivers and streams in canoe, blazing trails, and possess extraordinary knowledge of jungle plants and animals. While they are often multi-lingual, speaking Spanish, Quichua, and their native language, rarely do they speak more than a few words of English. They certainly know bird and animal terms in English though. Their most impressive skill is the ability to detect the slightest movement in the dense jungle foliage to pick out birds and other creatures that would otherwise remain unseen.

When you are trekking through the jungle with your native guide, you will inevitably begin to see the environment through his eyes. The movements of birds that at first are undetectable become much easier to see by the end of your stay. When you look at the jungle trees, plants and animals you will begin to see them as the indigenous people do - valuable resources that serve multiple functions as food, clothing, construction material, and medicine.

The indigenous population is divided into seven principal groups, but they have many things in common. Families still live in clan groups, either independently or in missionary villages. Villages are typically composed of several huts surrounding a soccer field or an airstrip. Women usually handle agriculture while men hunt and fish, but this is not hard and fast rule. The main crops are manioc, corn, and bananas, but also include others such as *achiote*, used as a spice and temporary facial paint, chili peppers, and beans. Hunting is done with spears, poison darts and guns. Monkeys, birds, and peccaries are the principal game. The men fish with harpoons, hooks, or nets, and on the rare occasion will blast fish out of the water with dynamite, but this practice is generally frowned upon.

It is common for a local shaman to practice herbal medicine and spell casting. The shaman is usually the only one who partakes in the consumption of hallucinogens such as *ayahuasca*, which is done to have greater insight into the natural and dream world. A shaman is one of the most respected individuals in the community, but in addition to the glory the job involves a great deal of risk. When someone dies seemingly without explanation, the nearest shaman is frequently blamed for placing a curse on the deceased. The shaman might be murdered in revenge, and if he is from a different tribe, this can lead to intertribal warfare. This type of violence is quite rare though, especially when compared to what we deal with in modern cities.

Shuar

Shuar territory was originally what is now Morona-Santiago province, bordered to the west by the Andes and encasing the Upano and Santiago River systems. The Shuar fiercely resisted attempts at subjugation by the Incas. When the Spanish established colonial towns to exploit gold in the region, the Shuar overthrew them in 1599, forcing the governor to drink molten gold as a death sentence. A 1930's another gold rush brought hordes of colonizers, who established ranches once the gold fever subsided. This effectively absorbed many of the Shuar into the mestizo culture while pushing others farther into the jungle.

The Shuar believe that plants have gender. The men harvest the male plants such as corn, bananas and hallucinogens, while the women harvest the female plants such as carrots, beans, peanuts, and squash. For protein, the Shuar traditionally hunted with poison darts, but no longer depend on this type of subsistence hunting. This indigenous group, by and large, has been integrated into Ecuadorian society, particularly in Macas and surrounding towns.

Achuar

There are about 4,500 Achuars, half living in Ecuador and the other half on the Peruvian side of the border. This small population is spread out over a huge territory surrounding the Pastaza River and its tributaries. Most of the area remained unvisited by non-Achuar until the 1960's. Since then Salesian and Gospel missionaries have gained a strong foothold. The Shuar and Achuar share the *Jívara* language, so they unified into a single political federation.

Achaur are intimately familiar with the plants and animals of the region, having names for hundreds of species of plants yet to be identified scientifically. Their intricate system classifies animals according to feather or fur type, weapon used to hunt them, and potency of sting or bite. Achuar houses are elliptical in shape. The men sleep on the end pointing upstream while the women sleep on the downstream end. Even though the Achuars, like the Shuar, believe that plants have gender, the women tend to the entire harvest. Because plants possess powerful spirits the labor is dictated by a long list of rituals and taboos. The population density in Achuar territory is such that men can still productively hunt birds, wild pigs, and monkeys, as well as engage in fishing. Blow darts are still frequently used to hunt due to the advantage of silence in stalking.

Huaorani

The Huaoranis have lived most of their history with minimal contact with the outside world and their language is not related to any other in Ecuador. They inhabit a large piece of territory in the central Oriente on the southern side of the Río Napo.

The Huaorani huts are distinct in that they appear as A-frame thatched roofs that nearly reach the ground. These large communal shelters used to house up to 30 people, but now smaller versions are built in which nuclear families live. While many of the Oriente tribes wore no clothes, the Huaorani men had the unique habit of wearing a string around their waste under which they would tie the penis.

In spite of being awarded 750,000 hectares as reserve land, the oil companies presence has radically changed the lifestyle of the Huaorani over the past several decades. Most of the people now live in villages and children rarely learn to hunt. Instead, young men will seek work with "*la compañia*" the petroleum company, while wives tend to the harvest. In many cases, one of two brothers will go to work for the oil company while the other helps the wives in the fields.

Cofan

The Cofans are the group that has most been disrupted by recent oil exploitation and by colonists moving onto their territory. To distance themselves from encroaching development, they have moved from place to place. Only through determined legal battles have they recently secured five separate pieces of land around the Aguarico River.

In spite of the clash of cultures, the Cofans have held on to a few of their traditions. The shaman still plays a big role in the rituals of the community. Women spend their menstruation periods in a designated hut, then wash in a ritualistic bath before returning to the community. The hut is also used for giving birth. A long white robe made of tree bark has been replaced with regular clothing for the most part, but some of the older generation uses a long embroidered cotton robe over pants. The vibrant feather headdresses and feather placed through a pierced nose is almost no longer used. The houses are square thatched dwellings built on stilts. Game is hung over the kitchen hearth to be smoked.

Randy Borman was born to a missionary couple who lived with the Cofans for 34 years. He is recognized as a Cofan and is married to a Cofan. Through the dint of his labor and bicultural skills he organized a political group that fought for and secured 80,000 hectares of land on the Aguarico. This land is unique for the Cofans in that it can support hunting and fishing. The Cofans have also opened portions of this area to eco-tourism.

Sionas & Secoyas

Sionas and Secoyas live in a small territory in the northern part of the Oriente, primarily on the Aguarico River. Their territory has been cursed with a bounty of natural resources coveted by outsiders. First it was gold craved by the Spanish, then it was rubber sought by the Ecuadorian traders, and finally it was oil extracted by American and European developers. The indigenous labor and land was exploited ruthlessly by all outside interests. These people also have a long history of contact with missionaries and for the most part are quite integrated into the mestizo culture.

Quichua

The Quichas of the Oriente are a melting pot of indigenous people from the highlands and the Oriente. Their common bond is the Quichua language, and in fact, they are more similar to mestizo colonists than to any of the tribes in the Oriente. They mostly inhabit the area around the Napo River, but as has been their habit since pre-Inca times, they continually seek new land deeper in the jungle to settle and plant crops. With the social and economic traditions from the highlands, they are generally more aggressive in trade and commerce and tend to dominate the other indigenous groups whenever there is territorial crossover.

THE WILD JUNGLE

Tropical rainforests, such as those found in the Oriente, present the most favorable possible conditions for life on earth. Sunlight, warmth, and moisture are consistently abundant. The annual average temperature here is 77 degrees and the 140 inches of rain falls evenly throughout the year. As a result a vast number of plants and animals thrive. The numerous food webs, dispersal systems, and mutual interdependencies create a uniquely complex biological community, the single greatest source of genetic diversity on the planet.

A typical temperate forest in North America will have about 20 species of trees. You are likely to find more than 100 species in the same area in a tropical rain forest. Virtually every tree you walk by will be different. Because of fertile conditions, the struggle for survival becomes crowded and intense. Each tree finds itself in a continual battle for nutrients and sunlight.

There is little vegetation on the forest floor since the light is too dim for most plants. Other than a thin growth of tree seedlings, ferns, and dwarf palms, the forest floor presents open vistas framed by the trunks of trees that disappear into the vaulted green canopy. When one of these giant trees fall, it creates a light gap, engendering a chaotic proliferation of shrubs and vines.

The rainforest soil is actually weak and easily exhausted. Colonizers' slash and burn attempts at planting result in ever-decreasing yields. When trees are cut and the hot equatorial sun beats down on the iron-laden soil, it kills off an integrally important fungal mat. All plant life here is actually held together by this lowly fungi complex which thrives through its mutually beneficial relationships.

Despite the incredible fertility, and indeed because of it, all life must contest for survival. It is all-out warfare with many artful alliances. Every living thing must create a defense or some other hungry thing will eat it. You will find moths camouflaged as lichen, katydids that are indistinguishable from leaves right down to the vein systems, frogs that fend off predators with poison secreting glands, and some non-venomous snakes that simply mimic their poisonous cousin's bright colors. Trees grow spikes to survive by making climbing painful. Other trees accomplish the same protection by nesting vicious conga ants at their base. Other types of alliances include mutual defense packs between ants and hornets, or symbiotic relationships such as those between flowers and flying pollinators such as bats and bees.

There are five different life zones in the tropical rainforest each with a distinctive set of plant and animals that inhabit it. These are the **forest floor**, the **understory** (0-5 meters), **the middle canopy** (5-25 meters), the **canopy** formed by the treetops, and the **free air** above the forest.

Flora

Epiphytes are ferns, mosses, orchids, bromeliads, and cacti that live suspended on other plants. Living high on a tree in a tropical rainforest allows small plants to partake of strong tropical sunlight that they would be deprived of if they tried to make a go of it on the forest floor. Potential for seed dispersal by wind is another advantage. Some epiphytes, such as **tank bromeliads** act as water reservoirs. They funnel water toward a central stem and may store as much as two gallons there. The tanks also trap falling litter from which the bromeliad extracts nutrients. Other epiphytes find nutrients in the debris that surrounds them in the crotch of a tree. Most epiphytes use their host plant only as platforms and do not rob them of nutrients.

Heleconias, cousins of the ornamental bird-of-paradise plants, provide splashes of color in the rainforest foliage. These beautiful inverted flowers are named for Helicon a mountain in Greece. The vibrantly colored bract is a boat-shaped, leaf-like structure that protects a small flower deep within its recess. The bracts, which can either hang down or grow upward, use their bright red, yellow, and orange color to attract hummingbirds to the tubular flower inside. The leaves of the *heleconia* are usually like big banana leaves, and in fact, the banana plant is a type of *heleconia*.

Strangler Figs are the unhurried assassins known as *matapalos* in Spanish, which roughly translated as tree-killers. This fichus is a close relative of the ornamental house plant species, but in the tropics, is among the tallest trees in the forest. Its insidious plot begins when, as a sticky seed, it nestles into a tree crotch to nourish itself from lichens and epiphytes decaying there. Even as it grows it never taps into its host for nourishment, but rather drops vines down to the soil. In this manner, it gains access to light high in the host tree, but does not have to support a massive root structure from the outset. The strangler fig then grafts its ever-strengthening vines onto the host, covering it. This reduces the host's photosynthesizing ability and hinders the trunk's ability to carry nutrients. At maturity, the now giant fig envelops its dying host, which as it decays leaves a series of hollow nooks that geckos, bats, scorpions and other animals occupy.

Palm trees are the most useful trees to the indigenous people. The wood of various palm trees is used to build the frames for huts while the fronds are woven together to make roofs. One type of palm is the **paja**

toquilla, the leaves of which are dried and woven to make panama hats. Another palm is the **tagua** palm, which produces hard white nuts. The tagua nuts are known as vegetable ivory because they are ideal for making buttons and handicraft carvings that are found in souvenir shops all over the country. **Pambil** is a palm tree with thorny stilt-like roots. The roots of this tree are cut to make kitchen graters. This tree is also the source for hearts of palms.

The **dragon's blood** tree, (*sangre de drago*), is typical of a plant that looks nondescript to the laymen, but which the indigenous people tap for medicinal purposes. Upon puncturing the trunk of this tree, a blood-like latex sap beads out of the wound. Rubbing it on your skin creates a foamy lotion that is reputed to soothe mosquito bites when applied. It is also used as a remedy for stomach and kidney ailments when mixed with water and drunk.

Ayahuasca, which means "vine of the soul" in Quichua, is a hallucinogenic plant used in ceremonial rituals by shamans. The vine is boiled and mixed with a catalyst plant that activates its hallucinogenic properties. A shaman who drinks the mixture sees colorful visions. For example, it might open a door at the base of a giant kapok tree, shoot him up through the trunk so that he soars over the canopy and can see everything in the jungle. It is also thought to help the shaman decipher plans of the enemy and divine which sorcerer put a hex on a sick relative.

Large trees have developed two ingenuous designs that stabilize their weighty masses in wet and shallow soils – **buttresses** and **stilts**. Buttress roots are thick sheets that jut from the base of the tree in a series of right triangles to support it. Stilts shoot out from the trunks of some palms such the *pambil* like stiff, knobby dreadlocks sunk into the soil.

Birds

You will encounter a magnificent variety of bird life in the Amazon Basin. The Amazon Basin has over 1500 species, nearly twice as many as on the entire North American continent.

Toucans are among the most spectacular high canopy birds. Some toucan bills are as big as their bodies. The bill is primarily used to pry fruit from tree, but also to probe deep within even the most protective of nests to feed on eggs and nestlings. You are likely to see four or five different species of toucans including the white-throated toucan and the many-banded aracari.

Parrots spend much of their time in the upper levels of the canopy. Their approach is often indicated by noisy calls that precede their arrival. Mealy parrots are the biggest parrots you will see, while dusky-headed parrots are also quite common. You will marvel at the two types of macaws. The most common is the blue and yellow macaw. The scarlet macaw is splendid sight with its vibrant red head and brilliant wings that merge red, yellow and blue.

Hoatzins are among the strangest birds in the Amazon. These wildly coifed pheasant-sized birds are known as *pavos pestozos* in Spanish (stinky turkeys) due to their musky odor. Reminiscent of a prehistoric reptilian bird, it is born with claws on its wings, which it uses to climb when young. Even as adults the birds seem to climb better than they fly. Their awkward attempts at flight send them hurtling from one bush to crash land noisily nearby in another.

Harpy Eagles are at the top of the food chain, feeding on monkeys, sloths, agoutis, and opossums. Weighing up to 10 kilos, its short powerful wings launch it up to 40 miles an hour through the trees. You will be extremely lucky to see one of these rare, mighty predators.

Oropendulas, bright yellow and black cousins of the oriole, seem to be squawking orders with their harsh cries. The females build elaborate pouch nests that hang conspicuously like giant brown teardrops from branches.

Ant birds are dull to look at and blend in with the brown forest floor, but they have amazing feeding habits. Ant birds follow the long sinuous columns of foraging army ants. As the ants flush insects in their path, the ant birds feast. They usually stay with the same column of ants for about two weeks.

Mammals

New World monkeys look somewhat like Old World monkeys, but have evolved down a distinct path. New World monkeys have three premolar teeth, while the Old World monkeys and apes, like man, have only two. The nose construction is quite different as well, with the New World monkeys' nostrils being directed sideways rather than forward. Many Old World monkeys, baboons for example, flaunt naked, brightly colored rumps. This is never the case with American species. Several of the New World species have prehensile tails, which function as a fifth limb to grasp and propel them through the branches. Any monkey that can hang by its tail, then, is American.

You may see a half dozen species of monkeys and marmosets while in the jungle. Each species has its own delightful set of characteristics.

The **capuchin** is generally considered to be the smartest of the New World monkeys, rivaling chimps in intelligence. They are particularly good at manipulating objects into tools. Their name comes from the brown furry cap on their heads, resembling those worn by an order of Italian monks, the Capuchins.

Howlers are frequently heard and sometimes seen. The howler's roar, which are audible for over a mile, sounds like wind echoing through a large hollow tube. The sound originates in the larynx but is greatly amplified by a voice box that is 25 times as big as those of similarly sized monkeys. When two clans of howlers claim the same territory, they will have a battle of the voice boxes until one side retreats. They also use the vocalization to warn of approaching predators like big cats. You can identify the howler by its size, the second largest American species, and by its rust red coat.

Squirrel monkeys travel in large troops, sometimes consisting of more than 100 individuals. You will see these small brown monkeys following a leader through the canopy as though on a path, even when the route involves an acrobatic leap from one precarious branch to another. They usually stay close to riverbanks among creepers that are loaded with flowers and fruit. The black of their lips and their noses make the diminutive creatures look like they have just finished off a licorice ice cream cone.

Marmosets are amusing looking imps with beady eyes, prominent ears, long tails, and thick fur that gives some of them comical head tufts and enormous, droopy moustaches. Unlike other New World monkeys, marmosets have claws on their fingers and toes, rather than nails. And whereas other monkeys usually give birth to one baby at a time, marmosets habitually have two and sometimes even three babies. A further peculiarity is that the father carries the young all day except at feeding time, when he hands them to their mothers. **Tamarins** are closely related to marmosets, the main differences being larger bodies and longer limbs.

It is quite possible to see a **pygmy marmoset**, the smallest monkey in the world. This little guy has the face of a bug-eyed lion, and has a body of about 3-4 inches that weighs 100 grams. It chews woodpecker-like holes in tree trunks seeking grubs and insects for food. Its puny stature has made the pygmy marmoset less hunted than other monkeys, so they often just go about their business, hugging the side of the tree with their tiny claws as you look on.

Sloths (*perisoso*) spend most of their lives upside down hanging from tree limbs by their long, slender, hook-like claws. Renowned for their slowness, a sloth's primary defense at the paws of predators is the ability to survive a beating while throwing in a swipe or two with its sharp claws. A sloth is hard to see not only because of its slow movement, but also because in its coarse, shaggy hair lives green algae that help camouflage it. A small moth, the larva of which eats the algae, also lives there. The hair itself grows from the belly up to the back, the opposite of other animals. The sloth abandons his position in the tree every week or so to defecate in a hole at the base of the tree, which it is thought to be fertilizing.

The **tapir** (*danta*) is a herbivore like its rhinoceros and horse cousins. This rotund beast with a thick muscular neck is the largest mammal in

South America, weighing in at up to 250 kilos. In spite of its size, the tapir is an excellent swimmer and can move so furtively through the underbrush that you are more likely to see only its tracks in the wild, rather than burly, gray beast itself.

The **coati**, known as *cuchucho* in Spanish, is a member of the raccoon family, but a long rubbery snout, used for grubbing insects and other small animals, makes it infinitely cuter. It has a slimmer body and longer tail than a raccoon. If fruit is available, it will eat this almost exclusively. You are more likely to see a *cuchucho* on a leash than in a forest because the elusive creatures are frequently captured as pets.

Fresh-water dolphins are seen mainly in the more remote regions of the Cuyabeno Reserve and the Pastaza River. They swim near the surface in schools and make long, graceful leaps as high as four feet out of the water. As they age their dark gray color lightens to nearly white. They are often called pink river dolphins due to sometimes having flushed color, thought to be the result of increased blood circulation.

Other mammals you might hear or see traces of include peccaries, agoutis (bulldog-size rodents), armadillos, and kinkajous, a cat-like creature related to the raccoon. Jaguars, ocelots and jaguarundis are ferocious wild cats that are difficult to encounter, but sometime you can see their tracks. The rainforest is also home to several dozen species of bats.

Reptiles & Amphibians

The thought of encountering snakes and crocodiles send shutters down the spines of many Amazon jungle visitors. However, you will likely never see a snake. Herpetologists find an average of one or two snakes per day, and they are looking for them as a full time job. Similarly, you will find that you spend far more time looking for crocodiles than they do looking for you.

A **caiman** is a type of crocodile but one which more resembles an alligator because of its similar short, narrow snout. These reptiles simply eat everything they catch which sometimes include people and even one another. You can usually find caimans out at night by shining a strong light across a placid lagoon. The eyes of the caimans reflect the light like eerie orange light bulbs. If you are lucky enough to find one in the daylight, you might mistake its rough, motionless head for stump sticking out of the swamp.

The **anaconda** is the heaviest and longest snake in the world, as well as one of the most powerful. The longest Anaconda ever found was measured at 13 meters. They usually live close to water and coil themselves around trees from which they loop down on their prey. Being excellent swimmers, they strike from the water too. Like other boas, they kill by constriction, tightening the coils, which they throw rapidly around their victims. Their usual prey is water birds and semi-aquatic mammals like capybras, but they seldom attack people.

As many as eighty species of **frogs** may live within sight and sound of each other. The number of species found in single square mile rivals that of the entire North American continent. Most rainforest frogs are nocturnal. They emerge after dark to feed and mate and in the dark when they have little to fear from visually hunting predators. Some frogs and toads have managed to evolve effective chemical defenses. Their skin glands produce toxins instead of simple moisture. **Poison arrow frogs** flaunt their bright red, yellow, and orange patterns as they walk boldly about in daylight. One species carries enough toxins in its small skin to kill a thousand people if it were to enter the bloodstreams directly.

Fish

You will have a chance to fish for **piranhas** while in the Oriente, and even swim with them. The piranhas live in the black water lagoons and can either be herbivores or carnivores. The carnivorous species have blunt heads and powerful jaws with sharp, wedge-shaped teeth that enable them to cut the flesh from prey. They feed primarily on other fish but also on amphibians, birds, and mammals. They are sometimes known to attack cows when water levels are severely low and the fish are starved.

Giant catfish, (*bagre*) scrape algae from submerged trees or stones with their powerful sucking mouths or scratch around on the bottom for detritus. They frequently weigh in at over 50 kilos but a 30 kilo catfish would be more the norm. When our group found a worm on the forest floor about twice the size of a garden snake, our native guide put it on a huge hook and reeled in a 20 kilo catfish that we ate for days at the lodge.

THE JUNGLE GOURMET

You probably won't be offered many of the most rare jungle delicacies, but there are a few munchies commonly available. Lemon ants live in the hollow branches of the chacra del diablo tree. The branch is broken open and you consume the insects live for a tart, citrus flavor. You can sample grubs that live inside a small coconut. These fat, wriggly larva are consumed live and taste like a shot of coconut milk. Other delicacies you might indulge in include the delicious white meat of a giant catfish, piranha, and chicha, beer that is made by fermenting masticated manioc.

Insects

Butterflies are more abundant in South America than on any other continent. The most famous are the morphoes. The giant male butterflies have wingspans of up to seven inches. The iridescent blue is created by the scattering of light through thin transparent film on the butterfly's wings. You will also see *brassolidae* butterflies that are brown with striking yellow circles on their wings that look like owl eyes. While moths are usually nocturnal, there are many day flying moths in the rainforest, some of which tend to be as brightly colored as butterflies. Moths are normally distinguished from butterflies by their stout bodies, feathery antennae, and the hinge that holds the wings together.

You will find a fair number of social insects – **termites, wasps, ants**, and **bees**. Huge termite nests are found in trees packed around the limbs like big cylindrical dirt clods. You will find some of these insects, such as conga ants and paper wasps, building their nests next to each other to form a unified defense system.

Leafcutter ants carry pieces of leaves to create bright green streams that flow to their nest. The ants do not eat the leaves. They prepare a paste of chewed leaves mixed with saliva and fecal matter on which a fungus grows. They then consume this fungus which cannot grow without their existence.

Conga ants surpass snakes as the terror of the jungle in most natives' minds. These giant ants grow to the size of a little toe and have huge menacing mandibles. That is not the worrisome part though, rather it is a venomous stinger on its rump that inflicts the mother of all insect stings. The pain throbs for several days and can make lymph nodes swell. When a guide stirs up a nest of congas to demonstrate their size, he retreats to a safe distance as everyone else crowds in for a look.

Other insects of note are a variety of peculiar **walking sticks**, **centipedes**, and colorful **spiders**. You will also find a number of **katydids** and other insects mimicking leaves to an extraordinary degree of exactitude. Be sure to stop frequently and look closely at the trunks and branches around you so you won't miss the life that is right there in front of you.

JUNGLE LODGES & TOURS

Your destination in the Oriente will be the jungle lodge or tour that you select. You should pick the lodge that best fits your interests and budget before you go to the jungle, make a reservation, then follow the operator's recommendation on how to get there. As illogical as it seems, the most efficient starting point will probably be Quito because air travel is so practical to jungle destinations. In most cases, the lodge operator will handle all of your travel arrangements.

ARRIVALS & DEPARTURES

Travel to many jungle destinations starts from Quito. In most cases you fly to a regional airport, then travel onward by bus, motorized canoe, or both.

For the jungle destinations around Tena you must go overland, because there is no regular air service. You would either travel from Quito via Baeza, or from Baños if you were already in the central highlands.

By the far, the easiest way to arrange your travel into the jungle is through the tour agency that operates your lodge. They can take into account your time and location variables to recommend the most efficient way for getting to their lodge. If your trip requires air travel, the agency will purchase the tickets for you.

ACTIVITIES

All of the jungle lodges and tours offer a combination of the following activities or variations on the themes.

Motorized canoes will take you and your luggage on the journey upriver to the immediate area of the lodge. The canoes are equipped with wooden benches or seats and an awning to make the journey more comfortable. You won't see much wildlife on the wide rivers, except for the occasional kingfisher darting along the shoreline, but the is trip is wonderful for taking in the shape of the jungle at the river's edge and to see the people who live here paddle their canoes. The motorized canoes are also used when a trail or other excursions are a good distance from the base of operations.

Dugout canoes transport you through black water lakes and streams without currents. It is an awesome experience when a skilled paddler propels the canoe through glassy water barely making a sound. The dugout canoes are used for **bird watching** and **night canoe excursions** in which you search for caiman crocodiles. The caimans' eyes poised just above the water glow shiny orange when a spotlight catches them. During free time, you can paddle the dugout canoes yourself.

Jungle Walks are the most common rainforest activity. The amazing thing is that you could walk the same trail twice, and have totally different experiences according to where you look, what time of day it is, and what wildlife is present. You will don rubber boots provided by the lodge for these one to four hour treks. You will seek out wildlife with your naturalist guide, or be led on a **medicinal tour** by an indigenous guide who explains what plants the native communities use. One of the most interesting jungle walks is the **night walk**. Amazing creatures like tree frogs, walking sticks, and iridescent spiders are quite active at night and easy to spot with a good flashlight. If your naturalist guide does not have a night walk scheduled, ask for one. It's really a fantastic experience.

A **cultural visit** to an indigenous village or family home can be an intensely stimulating learning experience, a brief uncomfortable episode, or both. The most dignified exchanges are those in which the visitors are not allowed to take cameras, making it seem less of human zoo. Some communities will offer handicrafts for sale.

Local hospitality dictates that you will be served *chicha* in a wooden bowl when visiting an indigenous home. To make *chicha* the traditional way, local women chew manioc or corn then spit it into a bowl. The concoction ferments for several days to create an alcoholic beverage with the potency of light beer. In some cases the *chicha* pulp is made with a mortar and pestle rather than chewing. Your guide will let you know which you are being offered. It is courteous to act like you are sipping the *chicha* whether you want to indulge or not.

Towers are ten story high tree houses built around sturdy kapok trees allowing you to climb above the forest canopy. The normal height of 100-120 feet makes for quite a few stairs to climb on the way up. You can spend hours in this extraordinary crow's nest. On a good morning you will spot over 50 species of birds in a few hours. You may not consider yourself a birder now, but wait until you get to the Oriente. Some hit the tower on an off day when not much is happening, but persistence and keen eyes reveal remarkable sights.

Piranha fishing can be done just about any time of day from the dock of your lodge or in a dugout canoe in one of the tannin-darkened lagoons. A bamboo-fishing pole and some red meat are all you need to catch one of these razor-teethed fish. Watch how your indigenous guide reels 'em in. Slowly pulling the bait under the water to attract the fish and a quick jerk once they bite seems to be the local method.

Swimming is a great way to cool off, though you'll have to share the water with piranhas, caimans, anacondas, and electric eels. It seems absurd, but it does get awfully hot out there.

Parrot salt licks are found along the side of a few riverbanks. You will approach these natural feeding areas in a motorized canoe to see thousands of parrots from different species eating the clay to boost their salt intake. If the bright green birds are perched in the trees, you might have trouble seeing them, but their squawks and song indicate that there are thousands up there. Be sure to take a zoom lens. If the birds are feeding on the riverbank, it makes for some amazing photos.

Camping outings might be conducted from your lodge and will definitely be a part of a jungle tour. The facilities are usually open-wall, thatched-roof huts with rows of mattresses on the floor, tightly covered by a canopy of mosquito netting. It sounds rough, but it's actually quite comfortable. While camping you can really detect a noticeable difference between the wildlife sounds of day and night.

THE LODGES

We list the jungle lodges in order of price category, from most to least expensive. Within each category, we then list the lodges in order of preference.

Our favorite high-end lodges include **Sacha**, **La Selva**, and **Kapawi**. Those on a tighter budget should consider **Yachana Lodge**, **Native Life**, and **Liana Lodge**. The pricing of these operators is quite reasonable.

The top tier lodges are consistently spectacular. We try to identify differences among these so you can choose the one that best fits your personality. In particular, you should note if the lodge has hot water and electricity. Even some of the highest end lodges forgo these civilized utilities. Electricity, for example, means that a generator's motor is running. Some consider such luxuries to be necessities, while others prefer more rustic digs. Almost all lodges run a generator during the day to power the central cabin's lights and use natural gas to power the refrigerators.

The term luxury lodge should be interpreted very loosely. Luxury in no way implies five star hotel attributes, but rather superior food and service in an extraordinary natural environment. While the accommodations are quite comfortable, it would not be uncommon to find a huge bug or spider in your room. In such a circumstance, a tip would be more fitting than a complaint.

The quality of lodges and tours becomes more varied in the middle and low end segments. The jungle can be an awesome experience if you go with a good operator, but it is an ordeal if you hook up with one of the companies that doesn't quite have its act together or are just plain shysters.

We include only one tour company on our list, because many travelers who go on tours (as opposed to staying in a lodge) end up complaining about the experience. Native Life is the exception because they succeed in getting their clients into a pristine area of the jungle with respectable service for a reasonable price.

We try to standardize the pricing by listing the 4-day/3-night packages. This is for price comparison purposes only. We highly recommend the 5-day/4-night packages because you travel so far to get out to this remote, beautiful place, you might as well spend the extra day there to take advantage of the effort. We also note if the price includes transportation or not.

Most lodges provide rubber boots and rain panchos so you don't need to pack these. Moderate and low-end operators should be consulted to confirm their policy in this regard.

SACHA LODGE, *Lower Napo River, Napo Province. Quito office, Julio Zaldumbide 375 y Toledo. Tel. 2/566 090 or 509 504, Fax 2/236 521; E-mail: sachalod@pi.pro.ec; Website: www.sachalodge.com. 4 day/3 night package $577 per person including meals. Cabins have hot water and electricity. Does not include Quito/Coca roundtrip airfare of $110 per person. Credit cards accepted.*

When Tarzan dreams of his fantasy home, it must look like Sacha Lodge. Monkeys sometimes greet you upon arrival as you amble along a two-kilometer long boardwalk from the Napo River. During a short glide through a silky channel the dugout canoe rides so deep that your eyes are almost level with the water. The channel leads into a serene, ebony lagoon that spreads across four hectares. Only as you cross to the other side of this black mirror does the complex of huts slowly emerge from the lush jungle vegetation.

Sacha combines the most select ingredients of jungle adventure and native architecture then mixes in a handful of creature comforts. A day of jungle exploration - poking under leaves for frogs, trekking lush trails, swinging from vines, and paddling canoes - tends to build up a bit of dirt and sweat on your body. The natural coating feels good, but an even better sensation is scrubbing it off in a hot tiled shower. Afterwards you can relax in a bed blown cool by a ceiling fan. The rooms are big, well-lit, and just plain comfortable. Most rooms have a deck overlooking a tropically landscaped garden that hummingbirds and other bright fliers flock to. A nap in the hammock out here is divine.

A cold drink in the lofty bar overlooking the large lagoon is a nice transitional moment before dinner. Dinner itself is just right. Healthy portions of vegetables, fresh juices, and well-prepared fish and meat makes herbivores and omnivores alike content. The breakfasts are equally as good.

Sacha is an extraordinary arena for birders. It possesses the Empire State Building of tree towers, rising up 135 feet. You climb the sturdy steps thankful that you are finally going to see what the toucans and macaws see. When you reach the top gazing at the kapok trees like broccoli tops, the guide taps your shoulder indicating the telescope that he's packed with him. Through its lens you might see a pair of toucans mating, the stunning turquoise of green honey-creeper, or the silly grin of a sloth.

One of the best places to spend a few minutes after a day in the jungle is at the dock on the lagoon. You can launch yourself from the world's bounciest diving board into the refreshing water. It is an enchanting period each day as the sun sets beyond the lagoon and the surrounding vegetation turns into dark silhouettes.

The butterfly farm at Sacha is simply a wonderful place to observe these colorful creatures. While the biologist's hard work takes place in the main portion of the facility, there is well thought out area for visitors on the opposite side of the net wall. Other excursions that you have to look forward to include medicinal tours, night walks, canoe rides searching for caimans, and a trip to a parrot salt lick.

Sacha's 2,000 hectares of primary rainforest is one of the most well protected private areas on the Napo River. You have an excellent opportunity for observing a wide variety of wildlife.

Selected as one of our Best Places to Stay – see chapter 11 for more details.

LA SELVA, *Lower Río Napo, Napo Province. Quito office: 6 de Deciembre 2816. Quito Tel. 2/550 995. Quito fax 2/567 297; Website: www.laselvajunglelodge.com. 19 cabins. Four day/three night package $550 per person, all meals included. Cabins have cold water showers and gas lamps, no electricity. Does not include roundtrip airfare from Quito $110 extra per person. Credit cards accepted.*

If you want an intimate jungle experience with first class service, La Selva is one of the best. Open for 14 years now, this prototype tropical rainforest lodge gets you about as close to the jungle as you can be while still sleeping in a comfortable bed.

The layers of civilization begin to peel away as soon as you step off the dock in Coca to take a motorized canoe up the Napo River. When you arrive to La Selva, you walk on an elevated boardwalk through the rainforest to the edge of the Garzacocha Lagoon. From there you board a small dugout canoe that is paddled softly across the lake to the entrance of the lodge. An awed silence overcomes your group as you glide across the black water to the dock.

The common areas, as well as the cabins, are built in the style of the homes of the indigenous people of the region. Twin beds in the cabins are outfitted with mosquito netting and the air circulates so well through the screens that you may need to use your blanket at night. You'll have two kerosene lamps for your cabin – one to light the way outside and one to use inside. It's quite romantic to brush your teeth by the flickering light.

One of the reasons that Selva has not introduced a generator for the cabins is so guests can really immerse themselves in the natural jungle sounds. The birdcalls are especially enchanting. Their songs, which sound like stones being dropped in a bucket of water, children's slide whistles and gravely squeaks, will be your alarm clock.

The real draw to Selva is the isolation in the jungle. While there is no guarantee, you have excellent odds of spotting many exciting animals such as different types of monkeys, parrots, macaws, tanagers, and our personal favorite, pygmy marmosets. The eerie sound of howler monkeys around the lake is absolutely unforgettable, as is the sight of thousands of colorful birds flying around the parrot salt licks.

The skilled guides collaborate with you to figure out your priorities. Birders are sent out with native guides who can identify birds simply by the way the air rustles. Generalists have their choice of a wide array of activities. You should not miss the tree tower, a 45-meter wooden structure built around a beautiful kapok tree. From the excellent vantage point above the canopy you can see so many species that it will automatically make a birder out of you. Other activities include drifting slowly down black water streams wildlife, walking through the jungle to learn about medicinal plants, swimming in Garzacocha, and visits to the Butterfly Farm.

If you happen to catch a big piranha, they'll cook it up for you for dinner. If not, you're in luck anyway as the food is outstanding. When the bamboo horn signals that the meal is ready you can look forward to different fresh juices, fruit and marmalade each day at breakfast, followed by three and four course lunches and dinners. Served family-style around tables lit with kerosene lamps, the excellent flavor and variety of the food is remarkable, especially given the logistical considerations. Much of it is flown in from Quito to Coca and then brought by boat from there. Don't miss the chance to try veal Milanese a la Amazon.

Selected as one of our *Best Places to Stay* – see chapter 11 for more details.

KAPAWI, *Pastaza River, Morona Santiago Province. Guayaquil Tel. 4/ 285 711. Guayaquil fax 4/287 651; E-mail: eco-tourism@canodros.com.ec; Website: www.canodros.com. 20 cabins. Four day/three night package $750 per person including meals. Cabins have solar-heated lukewarm showers and solar electricity. Does not include roundtrip airfare from Quito, $150 round-trip per person. Credit cards accepted.*

Kapawi, the newest entry in the up-scale jungle lodge category, is a remote, marvelous place to experience the wonder and mystery of the rain forest. The facilities are spacious and comfortable, designed to fit perfectly into the jungle yet offer a haven for travelers.

The adventure begins in Quito, where you board a chartered plane to the jungle. The plane flies low along the country's spine, bringing you eye-to-crater with volcanoes. You then take a left and soar over the jungle finally to drop down onto a dusty red-dirt runway hacked out of the expanse of green. Met by your Achuar and naturalist guides, you walk 10 meters to the water's edge where you board a motorized canoe and head down the Capahuari River for one-and-a-half-hours.

Once you arrive to the lodge, an elevated walkway leads to the main buildings, which house the bar and dining areas. These buildings, as all the others on the property, are built from wood in the typical Achuar elliptical style. The bar and dining area, although built in traditional fashion, are enormous. Light and airy, with high ceilings, they are extremely comfortable and elegant in their simplicity. The bar area has plenty of low couches with comfortable pillows as well as the most extensive Amazon library we've seen in a lodge. There is a large porch out front with well-positioned hammocks.

Menus in the dining room feature homemade bread, flavorful dishes, crisp vegetables and lots of fresh fruit. Make sure that you get the chance to try their traditional Achuar meal one night, featuring fish cooked in banana leafs.

The cabins, built without nails, are rustic yet very comfortable. They are larger and lighter than the cabins at most lodges, yet very much retain a jungle feel. Mosquito netting is not necessary as large screened windows provide plenty of breeze while keeping insects at bay. A nice deck overlooking the lake has both a hammock and lounge chair. From here you can watch egrets, cardinals and hummingbirds feed among the nearby water plants. Solar power provides lighting for all the facilities.

You can plan as busy or relaxed an agenda with your guides as strikes your fancy. There are several walks, trips to lakes and other outings available. Many of Kapawi's guests look forward to the chance to be even closer to the jungle by spending one night in tents. Some activities that you can do on your own include a self-guided walk, paddling a dugout canoe around the lake, and piranha fishing. Birders will delight in the 520 species of birds found in the area. Although Kapawi has not yet built a canopy tower, one is in the works.

Another highlight is the visit to an Achuar home. Kapawi has figured out that the way to get the most out of the visit is through two-sided interaction. You really feel like an invited guest and get a chance for personal communication.

As is the case anytime except in a zoo, there is no guarantee of the animal life you'll see here. You have very good chances of finding pink river dolphins, gigantic morpho butterflies, pre-historic hoatzins and screaming macaws. You might also spot howler monkeys, squirrel monkeys, capuchin monkeys, hundreds of cobalt-winged parakeets, bats, caimans, poison dart frogs or even a kinkajou.

One of the most intriguing aspects about Kapawi is the way it has managed to produce a healthy relationship between private enterprise and the local indigenous community. In fact, the ambitious plan is to entirely hand over the lodge to the Achuar in 2012. This partnership is seen as a model for sustainable use of indigenous land throughout the country. The respect that Canodros, the owners of Kapawi, exhibits for the Achuar and their way of life is passed on to guests through every aspect of the lodge experience.

Selected as one of our *Best Places to Stay* – see chapter 11 for more details.

JUNGLE LODGE HINTS

Taking these items will make jungle life a lot easier:

• **Earplugs**. *Even though the cabins are spaced apart for privacy, if your neighbor is a raucous snorer you'll be the one with bags under your eyes.*

• **One pair of binoculars per person**. *You'll be disappointed if you miss a troop of monkeys scurrying overhead because you have to share the binoculars. Because much of the wildlife viewing is of the colorful birds, which are often small or distant, binoculars are imperative.*

• **Insect Repellent**. *This should be at least 30 DEET. The mosquitoes aren't as bad in the tropical rainforest as you'd imagine, but it's still good to have bug spray.*

• **Snacks**. *You will be fed extremely well, but your blood sugar will probably take a plunge around 5pm. Just have some portable food so you don't have to obsess on mealtime.*

• **Reading light**. *Some lodges have no electricity, some have solar power, and some have generators. The strength of your light source will vary, so take a flashlight or a headlamp so that you can finish your book (and find the bathroom in the middle of the night).*

• **Ziplock bags**. *You'll be amazed at their uses, but these primarily keep things like cameras dry as you walk in the rain. Bring a few different sizes.*

• **Silicon packets**. *Those little packets that come in boxes with most electronic gear and shoes soak up extra moisture. They are perfect to toss into your camera case.*

FLOTEL, *Cuyabeno Reserve, Aguarico River, Sucumbios Province. Metropalitan Touring, in Quito, Republica de El Salvador N36-84 y Naciones Unidas. Tel. 2/464780, Fax 2/464702; E-mail: mgd@metropolitan.com.ec; Website: www.ecuadorable.com. In the US, contact Adventure Associates, Tel. 800/527-2500 or 972/907-0414, Fax 972/783-1286; E-mail: dmm@metropolitan.com.ec. Cabins have hot water and electricity. 4 day/3 night package $490 per person including all meals. Does not include roundtrip airfare $120 Quito/Lago Agrio or $20 Cuyabeno Park Fee. Credit cards accepted.*

The Flotel is a unique concept in jungle exploration because you spend your nights in a three story high boat that resembles a vessel that you might find on the Mississippi. It actually floats on the Aguarico and Cuyabeno rivers in the heart of the extraordinary Cuyabeno Reserve.

You will be taken care of by one of the best guide teams to be found in the Oriente. They are a young enthusiastic crew that performs as superbly in dress whites as they do in jungle khakis. You will be impressed with the verve and expertise of this group. They can identify hundreds of birds by name and give in-depth background on just about any aspect of the jungle environment.

The boat anchors in advantageous positions from which its motorized and paddle canoes can explore in either direction. You have an excellent chance of seeing pink river dolphins in the Cuyabeno Reserve. Other wildlife to be observed include monkeys and scores of macaws and a variety of parrots. You will visit a Cofan reserve where the one of the indigenous leaders takes you on a medicinal tour and lectures on the intriguing aspects of their culture. There is also an excursion to a tree tower, so that you get a good look above the canopy.

You will hike into Pacuyo Camp located on a black lagoon far up the river. Drop a hook into the water hoping that a piranha bites or jump into the lagoon off a rope swing hoping one does not. Everyone who wants to camp overnight in the open-wall hut is provided with mattresses and mosquito netting. Those who want to return to the Flotel can do so as well. The barbecue dinner at the campsite is one of the gastronomic highlights of the trip.

The accommodations on board are fairly tight, but neatly designed. The beds are bunks, but there are nice details like ample reading light and lots of drawer space. It is also one of the only places in the jungle where you can get a hot shower. The upper deck is a great place for a happy hour drink. Most of the guests gather here before dinner to watch sky turn colors behind magnificent kapok trees. The open sky above the deck draws birders who scan the shoreline during the day and stargazers by night. The meals are quite varied, all include delicious soups and juices. Big breakfast eaters will be happy because they are buffet style, but you can also go light because fruit, cereal, and yogurt are in the line-up. Every night after dinner, a briefing is held to go over the next day's activities. There is a good selection of books about the jungle in the ship's library.

To get to the Flotel you fly from Quito to Lago Agrio. A bus meets you there to take you about two hours down the road to the launch point. From there, you ride in a motorized canoe down river two hours to the mother ship.

Metropalitan tours, which operates the Flotel, runs premium excursions throughout Ecuador including travel packages in the highlands and the Galápagos Islands.

Moderate

YACHANA LODGE, *Lower Napo River, Napo Province. Quito office, Francisco Andrade Marin 188 y Diego de Almagro. Tel. 2/543 851 or 541 862, Fax 2/220 362; E-mail: info@yachana.com; Website: www.yachana.com. 10 rooms and 3 cabins. 4 day/3 night package $311 per person ($245 with SAEC discount) including meals and round-trip transportation from Quito. There are*

shared showers with cold water, some cabins with private cold water showers, and
no electricity in the rooms. Credit cards accepted.

Yachana Lodge not only achieves its goal of generating benefits for the local indigenous communities, but does so while offering guests a reasonable rate for a high quality lodge. The rooms, food, and excursions are nearly on par with what you would find in lodges that cost twice as much. Meanwhile, the interaction with and support of the local indigenous communities makes the lodge about the best in the Oriente for learning about native cultures.

Your journey to the lodge will begin in Quito where you board a van that transports you on a six-hour ride to the tropical river town of Misahaullí in Napo Province. Here you board a motorized canoe, which will take you down river about halfway to Coca during a three-hour ride. The ride is the perfect opportunity to see the contours of the jungle rise up from the river. The lodge facilities are located on 400 hectares of primary and secondary rainforest near the village of Mondaña. The compound of thatched-roof huts cloaked in dense jungle foliage is a thrilling prospect to consider as your home for a few days.

Each of the rooms has two comfortable beds and a sink with fresh potable spring water. The cabins have showers while the double rooms have shared shower facilities. The water is not heated, but the outside temperature is usually warm enough that a cool shower is preferable (though not always). One of those moments that makes adventures like this seem perfect is when you sway in the hammock outside of your room, a glass of homemade lemonade in hand, ignoring your book in favor of watching the sunset paint the river sky.

Yachana will outfit you in rubber boots and a rain pancho whenever necessary to take full advantage of the 20 kilometers of rainforest trails where jungle denizens such as walking sticks, eccentric birds, and colorful frogs can be found. The one shortcoming of this area is that wild monkeys and other mammals are rarely encountered. There are an abundance of other eccentric jungle creatures to keep you occupied however. You will learn about medicinal plants that cure everything from common colds to evil spirits. Add new dimensions to your outdoor skills by paddling a dugout canoe, shooting a blowgun, and fishing for piranhas in the river.

Funedesin, a non-profit organization founded in 1991, works with local communities to create projects that balance rainforest ideals with insistent realities of regional life. The organization founded Yachana in 1992 and is involved in several other projects in the community. Your visit to the lodge will include tours of these admirable projects such as honey production and papaya farming. You can even pick your own coffee or cacao beans, roast and grind them, then sip the warm brew produced by your own hands.

Note that your South American Explorer's Club membership pays for itself with the discount received from Yachana alone.

CUYABENO LODGE, *Cuyabeno River, Sucumbios Province. Quito office, Robles 513 y Reina Victoria. Tel. 2/521 212 or 558 889, Fax 2/554 902; E-mail: neotropi@uio.satnet.net. Web site www.ecuadorexplorer.com. Four day/three night package $385. Does not include airfare of $110 roundtrip Quito/Lago Agrio or $20 Cuyabeno Reserve fee. Cabins have hot water showers and no electricity. Credit cards accepted.*

The Cuyabeno Lodge is located in the Cuyabeno Wildlife Reserve, an elaborate system of black water channels and lagoons leading to flooded forest. The lodge takes advantage of the reserve's maze of waterways by creating ample opportunities to intimately experience this lush jungle environment in dugout and motorized canoes. The native guides are from the local Siona Indigenous community. Activities include hiking, bird watching, swimming, night walks and lounging in your hammock.

The cabins are solidly constructed with thatched roofs, clean tiled bathrooms, with hot water showers. The main hut has a dining room that serves delicious Ecuadorian, Siona, and International cuisine. The lodge is located in one of the best wildlife areas in Ecuador's Amazon Basin. You have an excellent possibility of seeing several different types of monkeys and marmosets as well as pink river dolphins and caimans. More elusive animals like tapirs, ocelots, and kinkajous are occasionally spotted.

The trip begins in Quito with a jet flight to the Lago Agrio airport. From there you will drive to the river, then continue to the lodge in motorized canoe.

CASA DEL SUIZO, *Upper Napo River, Napo Province. Quito office, Julio Zaldumbide 375 y Toledo. Tel. 2/566 090 or 509 504, Fax 2/236 521; E-mail: sachalod@pi.pro.ec; Website: www.casdelsuizo.com. 40 rooms. 4 day/3 night package $298 per person including meals and transportation from Quito. Rooms have hot showers and electricity. Pool. Credit cards accepted.*

Casa del Suizo is a Swiss Family Robinson hotel in the middle of the Amazon rainforest. Nowhere else in the Oriente will you find such creature comforts as 24 hour electricity, hot showers, and overhead fans. After a day of trekking through the jungle you find the swimming pool to be a welcome and refreshing sight. Swim up to the barstools in the water, so you don't have to get out to enjoy one of the best piña coladas you've ever tasted. It feels a bit like Cancun in the jungle.

The Casa del Suizo is particularly well suited for families and groups with diverse interests. If someone in the crowd wants to trek hours into the primary rainforest while someone else wants to relax by the pool with a magazine, there is no conflict of interest.

The design of the Casa del Suizo is a creative mix of thatched roofs and jungle materials. Chandeliers are bamboo sculptures and towel holders are trapeze swings. Varnished, knotty, tree trunks support the roof of the main hut which ascends upward to a lofty lookout tower with an inspiring view. The main hut houses the reception area and dining room where meals are served buffet style. There is no doubt that the management and owners are proactive, as you will frequently see them pitching in behind the buffet line. If you have a special interest, the management will do its utmost to see that you are satisfied.

Excursions leave every morning from the hotel, and return in time for lunch. These include jungle walks and medicinal plant tours. You can build a balsa raft and float down the Napo River back to the hotel. A cultural tour and a visit to an animal rehabilitation center are other tour options. The bird life is good, but wildlife is not abundant is this area.

Many of the rooms have balconies with two hammocks from which you can gaze out at the river. All rooms have ceiling fans and about half the rooms will be equipped with air conditioning by the publication date of this book. The mini-van journey from Quito descends into the jungle and can make it to the river crossing at about five hours. Most people want to stop at the thermal springs in Papallacta at the halfway point for an invigorating dip. This adds another few hours on to the trip, but makes it go by much faster. To maintain the transportation cost in the package, a minimum of four people need to be signed up to go.

NATIVE LIFE, *Aguarico y Cuyabeno Rivers, Sucumbios Province. In Quito, Foch E4-167 y Amazonas. Tel. 2/550 836; E-mail: natlife1@natlife.com.ec. 5 day/4 night package $250 per person with SAEC discount, all meals included. Does not include park fee of $20 or transportation to Lago Agrio. Roundtrip Quito/Lago Agrio airfare is $120. Bus transport from Quito to Lago Agrio is 14 hours/$17 one-way. The cabins for two nights have shared cold water showers and no electricty. The hut for two nights camping does not have showers or electricity. Credit cards accepted.*

Native Life's tour of the Cuyabeno Reserve is the only non-lodge tour that we recommend. The company fills a niche that no one else does – getting moderate and budget travelers into the magnificent Cuyabeno Reserve for an affordable price.

From Lago Agrio you will take a bus to the Aguarico River. A motorized canoe will transport you down river to a comfortable lodge with four bunks to a room, where you spend you first and last nights of the excursion. The other nights are spent on Quichua land, deeper in the Cuyabeno Reserve. Here you sleep in a wall-less thatched-roof hut lined with rows of mattresses on the floor. Individual mosquito nets hang from the beams, covering each of the mattresses tightly. The only bathroom is a port-a-potty set-up.

The food is middlin' to delicious with emphasis on vegetarian meals. Bring snacks for the long, active hours between meals.

The thing that Native Life does most successfully is create the opportunity for budget travelers to see the incredible wildlife of the Amazon Basin. It's not that easy of a task, because wildlife preservation is a luxury good. In an ideal world it shouldn't be that way, but if you think through the hierarchy of needs, that's the reality.

You have a good chance of seeing pink river dolphins on this trip, as well as monkeys and marmosets. The company has access to a 90-foot tall tower, a giant tree house wrapped around a kapok tree, for birding. There is extraordinary bird life in the reserve and you are likely to see a hundred species or so during the time you spend here, so bring binoculars.

The number of visitors per session can be high, but they divide you up between guides for smaller excursion groups of about 10 people. Some of the Native Life guides are excellent, and others, not so good. Its pretty much luck of the draw.

Native Life isn't perfect. It receives its share of complaints from people who wish for more comfort. Because of the tight budget, sometimes things go wrong without a back-up plan, such as canoe motor breakdowns. The guides just wing it in these situations. Still, it is the most inexpensive, high probability way of seeing wildlife in a gorgeous reserve.

YUTURI LODGE, *Lower Napo River, Napo Province. In Quito, Amazonas 1324 y Colón, Tel.2/504 037 or 2/544 166, Fax 2/503 225; E-mail: yuturi1@yuturi.com.ec. Web site www.yuturilodge.com. 4 day/3 night package $288 including meals. Does not include Quito/Coca $110 roundtrip airfare. Cabins have cold water showers and no electricity. Credit cards accepted.*

Located in the Yasuni national park, 180 miles east of Coca, the Yuturi Lodge gains consistently high marks from its guests. The complex is located on the shores of a beautiful series of lakes, surrounded by magnificent rainforest. The word *yuturi* in Quichua refers to species of giant ants (*Paraponera*) commonly found in the area.

The lodge consists of 15 tropical huts built with local materials to blend into the native environment. The lodging is comfortable and the food service is excellent.

Guests partake in piranha fishing, hiking, and canoeing. One of the most popular excursion night canoe trip in search of caimans. When you go to the nearby Monkey Island you are likely to see several varieties of monkeys including capuchins and spider monkeys. Early morning bird watching is also a real treat with the chance to see dozens of species over the course of a few hours. You will see macaws, toucans, and hoatzins among other spectacular birds.

Your trip begins in Quito with a 45-minute flight to Coca. From there you will board a motorized canoe until reaching the lodge complex about 3 hours down river.

CABANAS ALIÑAHUI BUTTERFLY LODGE, *Lower Napo River, Napo Province. Quito office, Isla Fernandina N43-78. Tel. 2/ 253 267, Fax 2/ 253 266; Website: www.ecuadorexplorer.com/alinahui. Four day/three night package $250 per person including meals. Cabins have solar lights and cold water showers. Transportation to the lodge is not included.*

Cabañas Aliñahui is an eco-tourist lodge with a beautiful view (that's what Aliñahui means in Quichua) of the Napo River. Though not the most remote of lodges, it is nonetheless an engaging place to stay. The cabins are located on 270 acres of primary and secondary forest. The cabins are double, two story units, with a covered outdoor sitting area to play cards or read. You will definitely need to reserve time to lounge in one of your cabin's hammocks, and since there are two, you don't even have to fight with your mate to see who gets it. The meals here are delicious, gourmet affairs.

The Butterfly Lodge is operated by two non-profit organizations. Jatun Sacha, based out of Quito, runs a nearby biological station which studies primary forest. Guests have easy access to the trails and canopy tower at the station, (see *Tena Daytrips & Excursions*). The other organization involved is the California-based Health & Habitat. This organization's objective is to buy as much land as possible in order to protect the primary tropical rainforest. All earnings from the lodge are used to accomplish land purchase and protection. Other activities include panning for gold, a visit to the Amazoonico Animal Rehabilitation Center (see *Tena Daytrips & Excursions*) and a visit to the Jumandy Native Museum.

Inexpensive

LIANA LODGE, *Upper Napo River, Napo Province, Fax 6/887 304; E-mail: amazoon@na.pro.ec; Website: www.amazoonico.com $40 per person per night all meals included. Does not include transportation. The cabins have cold water showers and no electricity. No credit cards.*

This new lodge, set up by the Swedish-Quichua couple that runs the Amazoonica animal rehabilitation center, is an extraordinary place to stay. The cozy double occupancy huts are constructed with paja toquilla fronds and bamboo, all with views of the river. Considering the high quality of the accommodations, the reasonable pricing makes it the best deal in the jungle. In fact, it's at about the same price level as the cheap, unsatisfying jungle tours that we advise you against, so there is absolutely no reason to even consider those.

Meals are served in a beautiful, circular central hut serenaded by the trickling fountain centerpiece. The food is a delicious combination of international and native fare, which receives rave reviews from all who indulge. A premium is placed on fresh ingredients, including healthy portions of fruits and vegetables.

You will partake in activities such as cultural visits to a local Quechua home, a conversation with a shaman, a balsa raft adventure on the Napo River, as well as walks through the jungle and a petrified forest.

You can also visit the inspiring animal rehabilitation center, Amazoonica, just a short canoe ride away. Here you can see some admirable work being done to care for and return to the wild a variety of animals such as monkeys, tapirs, and snakes. See *Tena Excursions & Day Trips* for more details.

From Tena you take a public bus or taxi 9 km to Puerto Río Barantilla where you take a canoe to the lodge. Contact the lodge for more specific instructions.

CABAÑAS ANACONDA, *Lower Napo River, Napo Province*.

For the most part we avoid including purely negative reviews, but feel it necessary in this case. This lodge, located on an island in the Upper Napo River, runs a zoological slum on its grounds. The animals are in terrible shape. Don't stay here and avoid the excursion if a nearby lodge offers to take you here.

PADDLE THE JUNGLE

If the canoe rides at the jungle lodges seem to tame for you, check into a multi-day rafting or kayaking expedition.

Remote Odysseys Worldwide (ROW), *Coeur d'Alene, ID. Toll Free 800/451-6034. Tel. 208/765-0841; E-mail: rowtravel@earthlink.com; Website: www.rowinc.com. ROW offers complete tour packages that include Quito and Otavalo. The four-day rafting portion starts from Macas and covers 60-80 miles of class II-IV rapids on the Upano River. The terrain surrounding the river ranges from cultivated Shuar indigenous land to primary rainforest to tropical gorges.*

Aventour, *Calama 339 and Juan Leon Mera, Quito. Tel. 223 720; E-mail: infor@adventour.com.ec. Aventour organizes expeditions in the spectacular Cuyabeno reserve with sea kayaks. These boats are much easier to handle than white water kayaks. A support staff sets up tents along the route and prepares tasty meals. You have a good chance of seeing wildlife like fresh water dolphins, an array of parrots, and monkeys in this reserve.*

Rios Ecuador, *Hostal Camba Huasi, Via del Chofer y 15 de Noviembre, Tena. Tel. 6/887 438. In Quito 2/449 182. Rios Ecuador offers splendid one day trips from Tena.*

JUNGLE TOWNS

The most overwhelming sensation that you get while in a jungle town is simply that it doesn't belong here. Cement in the hot tropics is unpleasant terrain unless it is in the shape of a swimming pool. You may need to stay in a jungle town if you get stuck in one during transition, but you should consider a more remote area, preferably a lodge, to be your primary destination. For the most part, the lodges will advise you how to travel to their facilities or arrange the transportation for you in such a way that you will only spend the amount of time in a jungle town that is necessary to travel through it.

While some of the towns like **Coca** and **Lago Agrio** are all-around disagreeable, others like **Misahuallí** and **Macas** are obliging enough, but nowhere that you would travel to just to go there. Of all the towns, **Tena** now has enough day trips and excursions that it is almost becoming interesting as a destination in itself.

TENA

Tena is winning the battle for hub of eco-tourism in the Oriente. It is the town that jungle excursions and lodges on the Upper Río Napo use as a base. Tena is beginning to react to the needs of travelers. Services geared toward foreigners are popping up and the recently opened Amazon Park gives visitors something entertaining to do in town if they have a few spare hours. The plaza is pleasant with its bright blue and yellow cathedral adding a touch of beatitude. Just outside of town cave exploring, river rafting, and hiking are possible.

The capital of Napo Province is located where the Tena and Pano rivers merge eventually forming the Misahuallí. The Misahuallí then flows into the Napo River, one of the mightiest tributaries of the Amazon. Jungle destinations accessed from Tena are located primarily along the upper portion of the Napo River.

ARRIVALS & DEPARTURES

By Bus

The bus terminal is somewhat out of town, but in walking distance if your bag isn't too heavy. Taxi trucks only cost about a buck. The station is a kilometer south of town on the road to Puerto Napo.

Buses heading south include rides of 30 minutes to Puerto Napo (10 km), one-and-a-half hours to Misahuallí (30 km), four hours to Puyo (80 km), and eight hours to Baños (140 km). Buses north take seven hours to get to Coca (110 km) and eleven to Lago Agrio (170 km). There are two routes to Quito, 400 miles away on mostly paved road. The one northeast through Baeza is much faster, getting you there in only about six hours, while going south through Puyo takes almost twice as long. Allow yourself adequate buffer time, because the buses often take much longer than estimated due to poor road conditions and breakdowns.

By Plane
Despite its strategic location for eco-tourism, there is still no regular air service out of Tena. If you want to fly somewhere within the Oriente, you might be able to get a seat on a charter aircraft by checking at the airport.

WHERE TO STAY
HOTEL INTERNATIONAL MOI, *Sucre 432 y Suárez. Tel. 6/886 215. 20 rooms. Double $20. TV. Restaurant. Bar. Pool. Credit cards accepted.*
This is one of the better places in town. The rooms are decently furnished and comfortable. The pool makes your stay in Tena humid enough to be enjoyable.
HOSTAL LOS YUTZOS, *Agusto Rueda 190, Tena River. 8 rooms. Tel. 6/886717; E-mail: losyutzos@access.net.ec. Double $10. No credit cards.*
This pleasant little inn, overlooking the Tena River, is simply cozy and relaxing. The family that runs it is friendly and it's in a quiet neighborhood.
TRAVELER'S HOSTAL, *15 de Noviembre 438 y 9 de Octubre. Tel. 6/886 372. 20 rooms. Double $7. Restaurant. No credit cards.*
You have to like a mellow place with commodious, freshly scrubbed rooms for less than ten bucks. This is definitely the backpacker hangout, a good place for meeting people, and one of the better places to eat in town. Unfortunately it's located on the main bus route, so try to get a room in back, which is much quieter. Call for reservations in advance because the place fills up.
For cheaper digs, double $6, you can try the **Hostal Amazonas**, *Tel. 6/886 439 on the plaza*, or the **Camba Huasi**, *15 de Noviembre, Tel. 6/887 429*, but both get low marks for noise.

WHERE TO EAT
LA ESTANCIA, *15 de Noviembre y Tarquí. Tel. 886 354. Inexpensive. No credit cards.*
La Estancia is one of the better restaurants in town. Try the *tilapa rellena*, a white fish filled with cheese, hearts of palm, and rice.

TRAVELER'S HOSTAL, *15 de Noviembre 438 y 9 de Noviembre. Tel. 6/886 372. Inexpensive. No credit cards.*

This places serves everything that a gringo could yearn for in the jungle – pizzas, vegetarian dishes, good sandwiches, and back-home deserts. The also have big breakfasts and fruit plates here.

SUPER POLLO, *15 de Noviembre y Rueda. Inexpensive. No credit cards.*

This chicken joint is nothing fancy, but the food is quite good and the place is kept absolutely spotless.

CHUQUITO'S, *Plaza. Inexpensive. No credit cards.*

This is the local favorite for fish and frog legs.

A good spot for a beer is **Canu's**, a popular jungle-style bar overlooking the Tena on the plaza side, between the two bridges.

SEEING THE SIGHTS

PARQUE AMAZONICO, *Tena River. Tel. 887 597. 9am-5pm. Entry $1.*

This ecological park is located on a island in the middle of the Tena River. It features a small zoo and a short interpretive walk, as well as picnic and swimming areas. This is a good place to familiarize yourself with some mammals that are difficult to encounter in the jungle. Not all of them are caged. Spider monkeys and saddle-back tamarins roam freely in the park.

EXCURSIONS & DAY TRIPS

RIOS ECUADOR, *Hostal Camba Huasi, Via del Chofer y 15 de Noviembre. Tel. 6/887 438. In Quito 2/449 182.*

Rios Ecuador is a standout river rafting company offering class II to IV rafting and kayaking trips. The guides are first rate and riding the river amid lush jungle scenery is invigorating.

AMAZOONICO WILDLIFE REHABILITATION CENTER, *Puerto Río Barantilla canoe dock, 9 km from Tena on the road to Santa Rosa; Website: www.amazoonico.com. Entry $2.*

This is an inspiring animal rehabilitation center founded by a Swiss-Quichua couple. The tour of the center is fascinating and quite educational. Amzoonico receives a variety of animals that have been extracted from their natural environment for contraband trade or taken as domestic pets, but no longer wanted. Whenever possible the center rehabilitates the animal so it can be returned to the wild. Others are not so fortunate so they remain at the center under the care of well-trained volunteers.

The animals that are cared for here include several varieties of monkeys, snakes, coatis, and tapirs. While the primary objective of the center does not include acting as a zoo, visitors' fees help offset the costs of caring for the animals.

Amazoonico faces a myriad of challenges in addition to those of all non-profit organizations. The management never knows what type of animal will turn up next, so it is continually redesigning its spaces to lodge the animals that are brought in without warning. Funds received by the center are also used to purchase and protect the primary rainforest that surrounds it. A well-designed eco-lodge, Liana Lodge, was recently opened on the adjacent property.

FUNDACION JATUN SACHA, *Upper Napo. Quito Tel/Fax. 250 976; E-mail: jatsacha@ecuanex.net.ec; Website: www.jatunsacha.org. Monday-Sunday, 8am-5pm. Entry $6.*

Jatun Sacha, established in 1989, is a private, non-profit foundation that owns and manages three field stations and promotes biological conservation, research and education in Ecuador. The reserve covers 2,000 hectares, 80% of which are primary forest. There are trails, a tower, and even a botanical garden.

Most visitors come to walk the four kilometers of marked trails through both primary and secondary rainforest. Here among the towering trees you'll see brilliant turquoise butterflies zigzag through the still air. You can also learn a lot about the forest at your own pace on the self-guided trail. This worthwhile path, with 21 stations, offers you the chance to study the jungle without a guide. It takes about an hour to read through the booklet and hit all the stations.

While it's precisely this chance to discover the rain forest on your own that we like so much about Jatun Sacha, there are also interesting guided options. For $6, which includes lunch, you can have a park guard take you deep into the primary forest all day. Another guided option is to climb up the skinny steel observation tower to view life in the canopy from 30 meters above the ground. Both of these alternatives need to be organized before your visit.

If hooking yourself into a climbing harness and scurrying up the observation tower doesn't sound appealing, Jatun Sacha also offers a 10 meter tall bamboo tree house. While not as high as the tower, it's still a unique position from which to view the jungle.

The main facilities and hiking trails are all located at the reserve headquarters. One kilometer west of the main installations is the Amazon Plant Conservation Center. It is here that you can visit their botanical garden.

It's important to remember that Jatun Sacha's main role is a research station, not a tourist attraction. The very rudimentary cabins here are available mostly for visiting scientists and volunteers. They are open for guests however, on a space-available basis for $30 per night, which includes simple meals and your park entrance fee. They also have a volunteer program allowing interns to participate in research projects.

The internship costs $300 per month and can last from one to three months.

If you want to spend a lot of time at Jatun Sacha, our recommendation, and most people's preference, is to stay at the nearby **Aliñahui Butterfly Lodge** (see *Jungle Lodges*.) Jatun Sacha co-owns and manages the guest lodge, which is just a few kilometers down the road. Many of the other area lodges also program day-trips to Jatun Sacha.

The reserve headquarters are located on the road to Ahuano, 22 kilometers east of the Napo River Bridge. If you are coming from Tena, take a bus bound for Ahuano, not Misahuallí. Tell the driver you want to be dropped off at the Jatun Sacha station sign.

CAVE EXPLORATION. Fausto Cerda, *Tarqui 246 y 9 de Octubre. Tel. 6/886 250.*

Fausto is a competent guide who can take you to little visited caves with waterfalls and verdant grottos for a reasonable price.

CUEVAS DE JUMANDI, *10 km north of Tena, 4 km north of Archidona. 9am-5pm. Entry $2.*

Jumandi Caves is a vast cave complex with waterfalls, now turned into a tourist attraction. An area outside the caves has waterslides and a playground for kids. Big weekend crowds can flaw the experience.

PRACTICAL INFORMATION
Banks: Banco de Pinchina, *on the plaza* has an ATM
Currency Exchange: Banco de Pichincha, *on the plaza*
E-mail Service: Piraña.net, *9 de Octubre y 15 de Noviembre. Tel. 886 048*
Post Office: Correos, *Olmedo y Moreno*
Telephone/Fax: The area code is 9. **Emetel**, *Motalvo y Olmedo*
Tourist Office/Maps: Cetur, *Bolívar y Amazonas*

MISAHUALLI

Misahaullí, also known as Puerto Misahaullí due its long past importance as a river to highway transport point, is the sleepiest of jungle towns. Most of its buildings surround the only civic development – a solitary plaza with dirt streets where stray chickens make up the majority of traffic.

The town is located at the end of a rugged 20 kilometers road at the junction point of Puerto Napo, on the highway connecting Puyo to Tena. It takes almost an hour to get down this short stretch of road so you can imagine what kind of condition that it's in. If you are coming from Puyo, the turnoff is about 10 kilometers before reaching Tena, you do not need to go to Tena to get Misahuallí.

It is important to note that most jungle tours and lodge expeditions on the upper Río Napo do not leave from Misahuallí. They leave from Tena, which is over an hour away by bus. Almost all of the lodges are most easily and cheaply reached overland from Tena.

Do not expect regular or cheap motorized canoe service to get you to your lodge from here. A typical contracted canoe ride to one of the lodges down the Río Napo costs $30-50. There is no cheap "taxi canoe" as is often reported, nor is there regular river service to Coca.

There are only a few interesting things to do in the area. The trails in the primary rainforest behind the Misahualli Jungle Lodge are easy to navigate. Another outing is a walk to the waterfalls by following the Río Latas upstream from the same road that heads to Puerto Napo.

If you somehow find yourself here without heeding our advice about lining up your jungle tour or lodge before coming to the jungle, coordinate a tour or lodge stay with the folks at the Albergue Español. They are a good, reliable outfitter.

WHERE TO STAY & EAT

MISAHUALLI JUNGLE HOTEL, *Upper Napo River, Napo Province. In Quito Rmírez Dávalos 251 y Páez. Tel. 2/520 043, Fax 2/255 354; E-mail: miltour@acessinter.ent. $68 per person per night full board. 4 day/3 night package $260 meals included. Prices do not include transportation to Misahuallí..*

Located just across the river from the town of Misahuallí, the Jungle Hotel is a good place for groups and families looking for an easy, relaxing few days in the jungle. You'll enjoy meals with a lofty view of the languid Napo River. Sipping a cold beer at sunset is a refreshing end to the day.

The hotel is located on 145 hectares of mainly primary forest. A series of trails leads away from the hotel into the jungle, which you can walk by yourself or with a guide. There is also a small bird watching platform that offers active viewing during the cool morning hours. The hotel offers a variety of tours including rafting on a bamboo raft and a medicinal plant tour. A series of comfy hammocks hang beneath an open-wall hut where bon fires are lit at night. A troop of tame monkeys is usually tumbling about the grounds and cafeteria. There is no doubt that Tomasa, the biggest of them, has established her alpha role.

Guests stay in elevated wooden cabins that are protected with fine mosquito netting. All have private showers with sometimes hot water from electric showerheads.

The next best place to stay is the **Albergue Español**, *Tel. 09/558 360 or in Quito 2/221 626.* The rooms are simple but extremely well maintained and clean. A double goes for $10. **The Hotel Marena International**, *double $10,* is just a step down in quality from the Albergue, but has some rooms with views of the Napo River and a nice garden. The less fetching **Hostal Jennifer** and **La Posada** on the square charge $7 for doubles.

The best place to eat in Misahuallí is the **Le Perroquet Bleu**, which serves up some of the best pizza in the country, or maybe it just seems that way after being in the jungle for a while. The French owner must have spent some time in Italy because these pizzas are delicious. It's worth the wait it takes to get served to dig into one of these gooey pies loaded with herbs and toppings. The airy restaurant, decorated with jungle weapons and impressionist prints, also has a well-stocked bar. Other dining options include a very good restaurant at the **Albergue Español** and nice views from the one at the **Misahuallí Jungle Hotel**.

As for services in Misahuallí, there is an Anditel telephone office, a decent general store, and a few tour agencies, but no banks.

PUYO

The only reason you would stop in **Puyo**, a utilitarian jungle town of 20,000, is if you were stranded here. The town, 60 kilometers from the more intriguing civilization of Baños and 80 kilometers from the more pristine jungle near Tena, is merely a transit point between the two. You can also get to Macas from here, 130 kilometers south, on an exhausting six-hour bus ride.

For something to do here you can visit the **Los Angeles Orchid Gardens** or the **Omaerre Ethno-Botanic Park**, which has a two-hour self-guided tour. Both are a short distance from town.

About a half-hour on the road to Tena is the **Zoocriadero**, a worthwhile project to visit. The center, founded by the Chimburazo Catholic University and the Organization of Indigenous People of Pastaza, cares for wildlife that has been illegally captured as pets and abandoned. You will be able to see tapirs, crocodiles, and several varieties of monkeys here. It also develops commercial projects that can help conserve endangered species. An example is breeding giant snails so the indigenous communities won't continue to capture the threatened species in the wild for food. Even though funding is tight, the energy and commitment of the staff is inspiring.

WHERE TO STAY & EAT

HOSTERIA TUNRUNGIA, *just east of town on the road to Baños. Tel. 3/885 180 or 885 384. Restaurant. Bar. Pool.*

These prim, brown cabins with bright orange trim surround a pretty garden. There is a small pool here as well. The restaurant serves an excellent fixed menu lunch. With entrees like chicken curry, the food far surpassed our expectations. This hotel is a bright spot in Puyo, so stay here if you need a place for a night.

Other places to stay in town include the comfortable **Los Cofanes**, *27 de Febrero 629 y Ceslao Marín. Tel. 3/885 560 or 883 772. Double $10*. You can also try the **Hotel Araucano**, *27 de Febrero y Ceslao Marín. Tel. 883 834. Double $10 including breakfast.* The Auracano is an eccentric place with lots of plants and revolvers on the walls of the main dining area.

In town, there are few **banks** and a **post office** on the corner of *Atahualpa and 10 de Agosto*. The **Emetel** phone center is on *Ventimilla y Orellana*. The **bus station** is about a kilometer out of town on the *road to Baños*.

SHELL & MERA

Shell and **Mera** are two small communities a few kilometers apart usually mentioned in the same breath as though they were one. The community started as a missionary center and now has the main airstrip in Pastaza Province. You will probably not fly here, but if you do it will because you are on a chartered flight. Kapawi Lodge sometimes uses the airport to fly passengers onward to their lodge in small plane.

There is a military checkpoint here where overland passengers from Baños have to register their passport number. Puyo is about 10 kilometers down the road to the east.

MACAS

Macas, the southernmost principal town in the Oriente, is also the most agreeable. The cobblestone streets are clean, most of the businesses are set up in buildings instead of temporary shacks, and there are mountains surrounding the town so that you have something to look at. The relative prosperity when compared to other jungle towns is due to diversification of industry in lieu of complete dependence on oil. Logging, cattle ranching, farming, and mining all play important roles in supporting the 16,000 people that call the capital of Morona-Santiago province home.

Jungle excursions that depart from the town are few. The extraordinary **Kapawi Lodge** routes some of its passengers through the Macas airport then flies them onward in small plane to a remote corner of the jungle. **ROW** organizes rafting expeditions on the Upano River, but only goes about eight times per year, December through February so you should make reservations with them before coming to Ecuador (see the *Jungle Lodges and Tours* section).

You can walk to everything once you get to town, as it the commercial portion is only six by four blocks. The airport hems in the west side of town and the cathedral, four blocks away, delineates eastern limit.

ARRIVALS & DEPARTURES
By Bus

Macas is 130 kilometers south of Puyo, but it takes about five hours to get there in bus. As you can tell by the time that it takes to cover the short distance, the journey is rigorous. You have to change buses and cross a bridge over the Pastaza River on foot. Some travel 230 kilometers from Cuenca, which takes about twelve hours. Supposedly you can go overland to Loja, 430 kilometers away, but you shouldn't count on it. The dirt road is often washed out.

By Plane

The easiest way to get to Macas is by air from Quito. Tame has jet service to and from Macas Mondays, Wednesdays, and Fridays. The tickets are about $50 one-way. Tame's office in Macas is in the airport.

WHERE TO STAY & EAT

Macas hotels do not even rise to the moderate category, but the town does have a few clean, simple places to stay, adequate for a night or two. The **Peñon del Oriente**, *Domingo Comín y Amazonas, Tel. 7/700 124* is the best in town, offering doubles for $7-$10. Also good are the **Hostal Esmeralda**, *Cuenca 612 y Soasti, Tel. 7/700 130* and the **La Orquidea**, *9 de Octubre y Sucre, Tel. 7/700 970*. Both offer double rooms with private bathrooms for about $6.

For some great Chinese food, try the **Pagoda China**, *Amazonas, y Domingo Comín, Tel. 700 280, Inexpensive*. The chicken with pepper sauce is spicy and delicious. We thought the next best restaurant option was, well, the snack bar in the airport. Other than that, you might try the restaurant at the Peñon del Oriente Hotel.

You can find fresh fruit and vegetables at the market on the corner of Amazonas y Domingo Comín.

EXCURSIONS & DAY TRIPS

Sucua is frequently mentioned as a day trip because of its fame for once practicing *tsanta*, the shrinking of heads of tribal enemies. While the racial composition in this town of 6,000 is primarily indigenous, the culture is *mestizo*. There are few arts & craft shops here. You would have about the same experience if you walked to the outskirts of Macas, minus the shops. You can take a bus or taxi to Sucua, about an hour away.

The other excursion in the area is to the Oilbird Caves, **La Cueva de los Tayos**. These birds have high oil content from their diet of oil palm fruit. This attribute made them prized game for hunters who sold them to be processed into lamp fuel. The birds use ecolocation, like bats, for directional sense. The caves are over a hundred kilometers away from Macas, representing a considerable time investment.

To arrange one of these tours or check into other excursions, contact the tour agency **Tuntiac**, *Amazonas y D. Comin, Tel. 700 185*.

PRACTICAL INFORMATION

Bank: Banco del Avisoro, *24 de Mayo y 10 de Agosto*. No ATM machine
Currency Exchange: Delgado Travel, *on the plaza*
Medical Service: Hospital, *Rivdeinera*
Post Office: Correos, *9 de Octubre y D. Comín*
Telephone/Fax: The area code is 7. **Emetel**, *24 de Mayo y Sucre*

COCA

Located on the Lower Río Napo, **Coca** is the quintessential hot, muggy, oil town with streets that blind you with dust or mire you in mud depending on the weather. You are likely to find a beauty shop or a dentist office in an open wall shack. There is nothing of interest here. Even the saltines are soggy. This civilization is an unsightly mirage, a cement scar, which you can only hope that one day the jungle heals back over and mercifully puts out of its misery.

The official name of this town of 25,000 is Puerto Francisco de Orellana, but everyone calls it Coca. It's a small and everything is in walking distance. The taxis here are pick-up trucks. It's about a dollar per ride regardless of where you're going.

La Selva and Sacha Jungle Lodges route their passengers through the Coca airport. They pick you up at the airport, then board you onto a motorized canoe, barely coming into contact with town.

For budget travelers hunting for a cheap jungle tour, you are much better off trying to do this from Tena where the infrastructure is set up to handle tourists. You would spend additional time to get to Coca, a place where options are much more limited. You wouldn't necessarily get anything more remote or pristine for your effort either. You do this by selecting the right operator, regardless of which town the destination is near.

ARRIVALS & DEPARTURES

By Bus

The bus terminal is in the north end of town, about ten blocks away from the Río Napo. Some buses leave from in front of their offices in town. It's a long way to just about anywhere from here. You are looking at ten bumpy hours to Quito, seven rugged hours to Tena, or four rattling hours to Lago Agrio.

By Plane

Tame has flights to and from Quito twice a day, everyday except Wednesday and Sunday. There is only one flight on Wednesday and none on Sunday. The cost is about $50 one-way. Tame's office is on the corner of Rocafuerte and Napo. There are also flights on oil company charter planes for about the same price. Check at the airport ticket counters for schedules and availability.

ORIENTATION

Coca is located on the upper portion of the Napo River, 130 kilometers north of Tena, and 60 kilometers south of Lago Agrio.

WHERE TO STAY & EAT

LA MISION, *Malecón s/n, Tel. 6/880 544, Fax 6/ 880 547. 30 rooms. Double $15. TV. Restaurant. Pool. Credit cards accepted.*

This is the best place to stay in town and practically the only place to eat. Rooms here are very basic, but functional. Some have A/C and others just have fans. The best rooms are those with A/C that overlook the pool and the Napo River. The structure that you see across the river is not the Sydney Opera House, it's a military casino. A twisting slide corkscrews into the pool, which when launching giggling children, is the most cheery place around.

La Misión has a lock on the restaurant category in Coca as well. The food is surprisingly good, although heavy on the cream and butter. Lunch and dinner feature an international menu that includes beef, chicken and pasta. If you're looking for a lighter meal you might want to order a sandwich. Breakfast is good here as well, especially the pancakes if you've spent weeks of eating eggs every morning.

The next best place to stay and eat would be the **Hotel El Auca**, *Napo y Garcia Moreno, Tel. 6/880 127, Fax 6/880 600. 60 rooms. Double $9.* The Auca is centrally located and has a nice courtyard garden. The rooms are big, but quite worn. You can also try the **Amazonas Hosteria**, *Espejo y 12 de Febrero, Tel. 6/881 215. 10 rooms. Double $8.* It has a family style feel to it.

PRACTICAL INFORMATION

Banks: There are no banks with services for tourists, and no ATMs
Currency Exchange: **Casa de Cambio**, *Alfaro y Napo*
Post Office: **Correos**, *Alfaro y 9 de Octubre*
Telephone/Fax: The area code is 6. **Emetel**, *Alfaro y 6 de Diciembre*

LAGO AGRIO

Like Coca, **Lago Agrio** is an unattractive oil town. Fortunately, even if you use the airport to access one of the excursions into the fabulous Cuyabeno Reserve, you will probably not even see the town. Lago Agrio's official name is Nueva Loja, given to it by the early migrants who came primarily from the highland town of Loja. Texas oil workers who thought it resembled Sour Lake, Texas called it such, so Lago Agrio is the name the stuck.

Lago Agrio is the northernmost principal jungle town. It is in Sucumbios province, 60 kilometers north of Coca and just 20 kilometers from the Colombian border.

WHERE TO STAY & EAT

The best place in town to stay is the **Hotel El Cofan**, *Quito y 12 de Febrero. Tel. 830 009. Double $15*. A cheaper option is the **Hotel Lago Imperial** *Tel. 830 453. Double $8*.

The best places to eat are **D'Marios** and **Guacamayo**, both on Amazonas.

EXCURSIONS & DAY TRIPS

The **Cuyabeno Reserve** is comprised of a million hectares of mostly primary tropical rainforest. It is the most pristine publicly protected area in the Oriente that is set up for access by tourists. The reserve is renowned for its vast system of lagoons and rivers, principally the **Aguarico** and the **Cuyabeno**. The plant and animal life is abundant and varied. Its is one of the primary habitats for the pink river dolphin. Visitors often run across troops of capuchin and squirrel monkeys. It also is teeming with bird life. Cofan, Siona, and Quechua indigenous communities occupy different parts of the reserve.

You can't just wander into the park, but rather, must go with a guide-led group. Lodges and tours that visit the reserve include the **Flotel**, **Cuyabeno Lodge**, and **Native Life**. All visitors are charged a $20 fee to enter the reserve.

20. THE GALAPAGOS ISLANDS

On a **Galápagos** cruise, you will slalom through a course made up of 13 large volcanic islands, 4 smaller ones, and more than 40 islets. These islands, located nearly 1,000 kilometers from the mainland, are famous for geological and biological evolution. The slow motion exhibit is by no means over. Volcanic vents still puff sulfuric halitosis. Finch beaks wax and wane through generations. In another era a new species will flit along a branch of the family tree on an island that looks nothing like it does today.

The islands are a fire devil's tantrum, muted cinders tossed into an emerald sea. Black and red contours disintegrate into dark lava beaches, but occasionally you will sink your feet into a powdery white swath of sand. Plant life finds purchase along the salty shoreline as mangroves, climbs through desert zone as scrub and cacti, then summits the mountaintops as cloud forest kept lush by the *garua's* cool mist.

The archipelago's denizens wait on shore to bless visitors with photo opportunities of a lifetime, constantly creating one-of-a-kind poses. The marine iguanas are hideously beautiful, as still as gargoyles while they warm their blood in the sunshine. Sea lion pups clamber toward you on the beach. As soon as one gets close enough, it owns you with huge, teary, brown eyes. Sally lightfoot crabs, brilliant orange and blue hangers-on, add a dash of color.

A cruise is the only suitable manner to see the varied wildlife and beauty of the archipelago. You can choose among comfortable motorized yachts, sleek sailboats, and stable, commodious cruise ships. In addition to the cruise, if you have the time, you should consider extending your stay on Santa Cruz or one of the other islands to amble about an intriguing chunk of lava at a more leisurely (or more active) independent pace.

HUMAN HISTORY

Inca legend says that the natives sailed to the Galápagos before the Spaniards. Large balsa rafts that were in use at the time could have easily been carried to the Galápagos by the strong currents off the coast of South

THE ISLANDS AT A GLANCE

The Spanish and English adventurers called the islands by different names. We list the most common names in each language for the thirteen largest islands, ordered by size. Islands not listed measure less than two square kilometers. A review of the visitor sites and most prominent wildlife on each island can be found at the end of the chapter.

Spanish Name	English Name	Sq. Km.
Isabela	Albemarle	4588
Santa Cruz	Indefatigable	986
Fernandina	Narburough	642
Santiago	James	585
San Cristóbal	Chatham	558
Floreana	Charles	173
Marchena	Bindloe	130
Española	Hood	60
Pinta	Abingdon	60
Baltra	South Seymour	27
Santa Fe	Barrington	24
Pinzón	Duncan	18
Genovesa	Tower	14
Rábida	Jervis	5

America that sweep everything westward. It is conjectured that they could have returned to the continent by tacking the raft's sails into the wind. The legend tells of a land of volcanoes discovered by an Inca chief. The conquistadors who heard the tale organized an expedition that sailed through the islands, but did not land there, opting instead to progress to the Solomon Islands further west.

The first readily verifiable human footprints on the islands are identified in a letter to the King Charles of Spain, written in 1535. He had ordered Bishop Fray Tomás de Berlanga of Panama to travel to Peru to check on the political situation and report on the conquistadors' maltreatment of the natives. A few days into the journey, the wind ceased. With nothing to power the sails, the ship was swept off course by the strong current. The bishop tells of islands inhabited with "big tortoises, each that could carry a man". He also reported seeing iguanas, sea lions, and birds "so silly that they do not know how to flee, many of which were caught by hand". Most of the crew survived by chewing moist cactus pads, but several men and horses died from dehydration. Easter prayers were

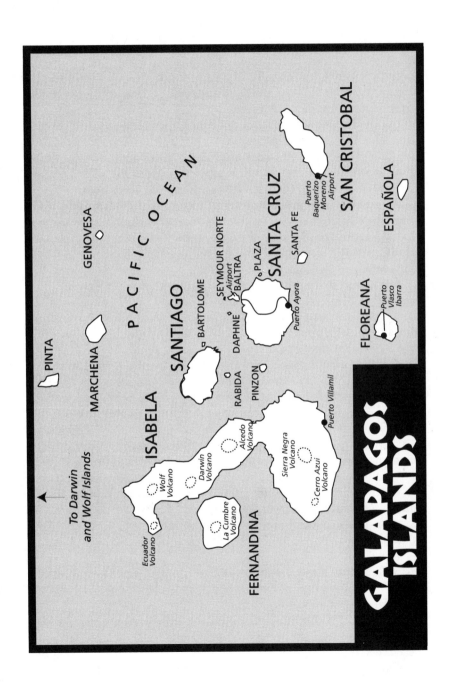

GALÁPAGOS ISLANDS

answered by the discovery of fresh water in a ravine. They could finally fill their casks and sail toward the mainland.

The islands would eventually be named for the giant tortoises that the bishop and his men found there. The Spanish word *galápago* means "saddle", referring to the shell of the huge reptile. The islands would also become known as the Enchanted Isles because of the strong and variable currents that befuddled navigators.

For the first two centuries after being mapped, the islands provided a haven for buccaneers and renegades. The pirates used the Galápagos as a refuge and base for their raids on Spanish colonial ports. They captured tortoises, which could be stacked live in the holds of the ships for up to a year, then butchered them for fresh meat as the need arose.

The abundant wildlife attracted the attention of whalers and seal fur traders who hunted among the islands. They too dined on the tortoise meat. It is estimated that in all, over 100,000 tortoises were taken from the islands, greatly diminishing several species, while eliminating others completely.

Settlement debacles ensued over the next centuries that included several disastrous attempts to found towns and penal colonies. While many industries were endeavored, including the export of moss, sulfur, lime, and tortoise oil, none were sustainable. Only fishing has survived, but this is under intense conservation pressure today.

Ecuador officially annexed the Galápagos in 1832. Both the United States and Britain attempted to purchase the islands over the next century, but to no avail. Ecuador allowed the United States to establish a military base on Baltra during World War II, which became the archipelago's main airport. The development proved to be disastrous for the native animals. The land iguana was completely extinguished from the island and now is being painstakingly reintroduced.

Ecuadorians and foreign immigrants, primarily Northern Europeans, finally established true communities on four islands in the twentieth century. The early homes were crude shelters built of volcanic rock. Life was a constant struggle for water and food, with the occasional ship from Guayaquil breaking the isolation with provisions and mail. Tourism developed into a viable enterprise with the advent of air travel, and is now the predominant employer on the island, complimented by agriculture.

The Evolution of a Theory

As a young man, **Charles Darwin** was privileged and congenial, but rather aimless. After dropping out of medical school, he opted to study the clergy. His favorite activity was bird hunting, but he so skillfully dabbled in geology and botany, which he considered to be hobbies, that he caught the attention of his professors. With encouragement from his professors, the 22-year-old Darwin accepted a position as an unpaid naturalist on a five-year scientific expedition around the world led by Captain FitzRoy. He took to the task with a diligence he had never before demonstrated.

Darwin collected thousands of animal and plant specimens and fossils in the four years before the *HMS Beagle* reached the Galápagos in 1835. He did not think the finches he saw here were very important. He did not even think they were finches. They looked like blackbirds, wrens, and warblers to him. He shot 31 finches from different islands and tossed them all in the same bag without labeling them. Only when he returned to England, working alongside other naturalists, did it come to light that the finches, as well as the tortoises and marine iguanas resembled mainland animals but were distinct from anything found there. The differences in the beaks of the thirteen finch species, now sorted by island, provided a spark to develop the theory of evolution.

After the voyage, Darwin stayed in England for good, settling into a sedate life with his cousin, Emma, whom he married. Breaking the monotony of research with long walks in his country garden and backgammon games with Emma, Darwin finished *On the Origin of the Species* twenty-three years after his return. His colleagues urged him to hasten publication just before one his peers, Alfred Wallace, was about to unveil a similar theory.

NATURAL HISTORY
Geology

The Galápagos Islands are tips of huge submarine volcanoes resting on a self-created table known as the Galápagos Platform. Darwin noticed that the major volcanoes of the archipelago were arranged in a rectilinear pattern. This alignment corresponds to fault lines, which are partly responsible for the formation of the islands.

The first islands were born a few million years ago when volcanic eruptions began to break through the ocean floor. The eruptions initiated the raising of underwater mountains. The *Hot Spot Theory* is used to explain the linear position of both the Galápagos and Hawaiian Islands. As the Pacific Plate moves eastward toward the Americas, it crosses over a point of intense heat in the earth's mantle which pressures upward through the crust to form a volcano. The plate is like fabric pushed through a sewing machine. The thrusting needle, the magma, creates a line of perforations, the volcanoes. As a result the oldest and most eroded volcanoes are to the east.

The archipelago is one of the most active volcanic regions on earth. Fifty-three eruptions from eight volcanoes have been recorded, four in the last two decades alone. Eruptions in the Galápagos are of a mild, basalt type, creating shield formations, as opposed to the more violent upheavals from conical volcanoes like Cotapaxi.

You will see two types of lava in the Galápagos:

• **Aa** lava is the rough, cindery type with sharp, loose boulders. The term *aa* comes from the Hawaiian word for "hurt".

• **Pahoehoe** lava is the rarer, smooth type that looks like a pile of rope. This term actually means "rope" in Hawaiian.

Plant Life

Because the islands lie in the Pacific Dry Belt, most of the archipelago's land is semi-desert and desert. Only the higher parts of the larger islands receive enough rain to be tropically verdant.

By virtue of their isolation for millions of years, many Galápagos plants differ from mainland relatives and even from those on neighboring islands. A relatively small number of plant species reside here, about 600 native and 200 introduced by man.

There are three major areas with distinct plant life – the coastal zone, the transitional arid zone, and in the highlands, the humid zone.

The **coastal zones** are narrow growth areas near the shore, characterized by their tolerance of salty conditions. Here you will find many plants, such as mangroves, that provide shelter for seabirds and shade for other animals like sea lions and marine iguanas.

TERMS OF ORIGIN

You will hear the terms native, endemic, and introduced to describe species in the Galápagos:

• ***Endemic*** *means that the plant species evolved in the Galápagos and grows almost exclusively here.*

• ***Native*** *means that the species arrived to the islands by natural means. Birds carrying seeds would be an example. The species is probably found in abundance elsewhere.*

• ***Introduced*** *means the species was introduced to the islands by man.*

The **arid zone** is the most extensive and widely visited zone in the Galápagos. The environment is primarily semi-desert or dry forest and the plant species are adapted to arid conditions. You will see several varieties of cacti in this zone including the lava cactus and the candelabra cactus. The giant prickly pear, (*opuntia*) is easily identified by its size and reddish, flaky bark. You can see this papery bark used to create orange-glowing lampshades in several establishments in Puerto Ayora.

In the highlands you encounter the **humid zone**, kept moist by the dense mist known as *garua*. These lush zones cover much less terrain than the desert zones. The largest trees in the islands grow here – the *scalesia,* which are actually the tallest members of the daisy and sunflower family. You can see a *scalesia* forest covering the Los Gemelos crater pits on Santa Cruz. You will also find dozens of species of ferns, moss, and lichens in this cloud forest.

Animal Life

While the islands themselves often exhibit a majestic beauty, the animals are the real stars of the show. Reptiles enjoy a particularly glamorous role. In many cases they are positioned at the top of the food chain and are the largest animals. An exotic array of seabirds resides here such as blue-footed boobies, red-chested frigatebirds, and penguins that have never seen an iceberg. Most of the mammals are ocean oriented – sea lions, dolphins, and whales, but magnificent to observe nonetheless. The spectacular marine life, renowned for color and size, will make any time spent snorkeling or diving one of the most memorable parts of your journey.

Reptiles

Reptiles are cold-blooded creatures that cannot regulate their body temperatures by sweating or panting. After a cold night they must warm themselves in the sun until they have absorbed enough heat to become active. To cool down on hot afternoons, they seek shade or remain motionless in the cool breezes. Reptiles can go long periods of time without food or water. They derive most of their water from the plants they eat. The twenty-two species of reptiles on the islands belong to five families – tortoises, marine turtles, lizards/iguanas, geckos, and snakes

Giant tortoises may weigh up to 250 kg. There might have been up to 15 species, but now there are only ten reproducing, and a last species with one remaining member alive in captivity. All of the species, usually identified by modest differences in their shell, probably evolved from a common ancestor on San Cristóbal Island. Even with protective armor, their exposed skin is vulnerable to attacks by skin-feeding parasites. They have developed mutually beneficial cleaning relationships with finches and mockingbirds. When it wants to be cleaned, a tortoise will stretch out its neck and limbs, inviting the birds to perch and dine. Though you might hear the age exaggerated to 150, the documented life span for tortoises is about 100 years. The easiest place to see giant tortoises are in the sanctuaries on Santa Cruz, but it is also possible to see them by hiking into the crater of the Alcedo Volcano on Isabela.

Marine turtles frequently pop their heads out of the open sea near your *panga*, looking much like wrinkled old men doing the breaststroke. You might see these curious creatures while snorkeling or diving, as they follow you inquisitively at a safe distance. The turtles can spend up to eight hours submerged. Some of the turtles marked in the Galápagos have been found as far away as Ecuador and Costa Rica. They feed primarily on seaweed and weigh up to 150 kilos, with the male being smaller than the female. Late in the year they mate in the quiet lagoons. The females come onto land to lay eggs once every two or three years. Up to seventy eggs may be laid by one turtle in a three-week period during several visits to the shore. The hatchlings emerge from the nests at night to avoid a horde of predators, which include ghost crabs, hawks, mockingbirds, and frigate birds. In spite of the risk many survive, returning to their native beach as adults to nest.

Lava lizards are the most frequently seen reptiles of the arid lowlands. There are seven endemic species in the archipelago, all thought to have evolved from a single ancestral species. The lizards are omnivorous predators that feed on flies, beetles, ants, spiders, and even scorpions. They depend on a keen sense of vision to capture the insects. In turn, they provide nourishment for several different types of birds.

Marine iguanas live only in the Galápagos, and you find a lot of them, up to 3,000 per kilometer. These homely creatures are famed for their swimming and diving abilities with the largest of them able to swim through breaking waves. Their dives can last up to ten minutes and can be as deep as 12 meters. To feed, marine iguanas gnaw algae from rocks with a tilt of the head, ripping off a small chunk at a time, then chew with conviction. The larger iguanas swim out and dive down for their food while the females and juveniles feed on the shoreline. To cope with the

WELCOME ASHORE

How did life get started on a scattering of volcanic rock 1,000 kilometers from the mainland?

Good swimming skills brought sea lions, sea turtles, and penguins here. Other species hitched rides on rafts made of riverbank vegetation that drifted on strong ocean currents to the islands. Reptiles and many plants can endure that two-week journey, but it's more difficult for mammals.

Air travel was the most common means of immigration. A variety of birds, some of which were simply blown off course by strong winds, found island life quite appealing and stayed. The baggage they carried with them in their feathers and guts included seeds and burrs, which found purchase in the soil and grew.

high intake of salt they must excrete most of it, which is accomplished by projecting it through the nostrils. It is quite amusing, and a bit disgusting, to watch the iguanas shoot the wads of salt, farmer-hankie style, while sunning themselves in an overlapping sprawl on the rocks.

Land iguanas grow up to a meter long and weigh up to six kilos. They are much rarer and shier than their cousins, the marine iguanas. Land iguanas have been extinguished from several islands due to hunting; competition for food with introduced animals like goats; and destruction of their eggs by rats and pigs. You may get the opportunity to see these creatures at only one visitor site on your itinerary, and you really have to search for them. The iguanas eat mainly prickly pear cactus fruits and pads, which they can swallow without removing the spines.

Their liquid needs are met by eating moist food, but after rain they drink large quantities of fresh water from puddles formed in rocks and cactus pads. Males are larger and more brightly-colored than females. They are highly aggressive and often engage in head-bashing battles. The females lay between five to fifteen eggs. While larger birds will prey upon the hatchlings, the iguanas have a mutually beneficial cleaning relationship with smaller birds.

Birds

With an abundance of coastline, lagoons, and rocky shores, the Galápagos is a perfect habitat for seabirds.

Boobies come in three varieties – blue-footed, red-footed, and masked. They are known as *piqueros* in Spanish for their lanced beaks, which lead them hurtling downward at breakneck speed to capture fish. The term "booby" is thought to have originated by sailors from *bobo*, clown in Spanish. One of the most entertaining spectacles is the courtship dance of the blue-footed booby. It is performed with the beak thrust proudly straight up, tail feathers cocked, and exaggerated high steps taken with one startlingly blue foot, then the other. The largest of the three species is the masked booby, which is white with a black mask. The red-footed booby is the smallest and the least frequently seen of three.

Flightless Cormorants seem to have traded the ability to fly for a streamlined swimming body. The bird is dark with disproportionately small wings that it stretches out to dry after swimming, creating a delightful pose. You will find the birds on low rocky spits and boulder beaches.

Frigate Birds are best known for the bright red gular sacs that the males inflate like a rubber ball. If the female is attracted by the display, the pair rocks their heads to and fro. Frigate birds are ruthless pirates that bully other birds into disgorging food in flight, then sweeping to catch it before it hits the water.

The **Galápagos penguin** is the only penguin species to live north of the equator and one of the smallest. It is estimated that about 10,000 of the birds live in the Galápagos. The Galápagos penguins choose a mate for life and take turns feeding the infants.

The **waved albatross** is a gigantic bird weighing in at up to 4 kilos, with a two meter wide wingspan. Almost the entire population nests on the island of Española.

Greater flamingoes inhabit brackish lagoons, usually just a short distance inland. The bird feeds with its head upside down, sucking in water from the front of its beak and pumping it out through the sides. The beak works like a sieve to filter out small animals that make up its diet.

Darwin finches are famous for the inspiration they have given Darwin and subsequent evolutionists. There are twelve species in the Galápagos, all thought to have evolved on the islands from a single pair blown from the mainland. The sparrow-sized birds range in color from gray to olive to pitch black.

The diversity of beak structure and feeding habits are remarkable. The size and shape of the beak determines what each species eats. Most beaks do the normal work you would expect, mainly crushing seeds for food. Then there are the oddballs. Vampire finches hop on the backs of red-footed boobies, pecking them until they can feed upon droplets of blood. This is a nuisance to the boobies, but not harmful. The mangrove and woodpecker finches eat insects from cactus. When a grub is wedged too deeply inside the cactus, the finch will search for a spine or twig, taking it in its beak to use as a tool to prod the larva out of the hole.

Mammals

Sea Lions belong to the eared seal family. The males can weigh up to 250 kg and are distinguished from the more graceful females by their size and a bump on their forehead. While the animals are often playful and curious, bulls can be aggressive and will charge if you get too close.

Fur Seals are seen less than sea lions because they prefer rockier rugged shores, with plenty of shade. The major distinguishing characteristics from the sea lion, other than habitat, are a thicker coat, bigger eyes, and a more pointed snout.

You also have a good chance of seeing a variety of **whales and dolphins** including humpback, sperm whales, orcas, pilot whales, the bottle nosed dolphin, and white-bellied dolphin.

Marine Life

The sea creatures you will see in abundance on shore are the bright orange and blue Sally lightfoot crabs. While snorkeling keep your eyes open for spotted eagle rays and mustard rays as well as white tipped sharks. There are a great number of shark species in the shallow water including reef sharks, and tiger sharks, but there has never been an attack on humans. The hammerheads are located farther out in the open seas so you have scuba dive to find them. Occasionally you will see eagle rays and manta rays from the boat measuring as much as 6 meters across. It is spectacular to watch one of these giants from your boat as it slides below the surface like a stealth bomber or rises in a sinuous vault to flash its glistening, black, quadrangular form.

CONSERVATION ON THE ISLANDS

While protective legislation had been passed a few decades earlier, the first concrete action to safeguard the Galápagos occurred in 1959. The Ecuadorian government declared all island territory, except those areas already populated, to be part of a national park. The Charles Darwin Foundation was established the same year in Brussels, shortly thereafter inaugurating a research station on Santa Cruz.

Conservation efforts put into effect by the Parks Department and supported with research by the station focus on the promotion of native and endemic species, environmental education, and the elimination of introduced species.

Protecting and repopulating native and endemic species is a commendable primary objective. In addition to sealing off certain areas from visitor contact, the government actively enforces wildlife protection. Patrolling for illegal fishing boats is one example. The foundation, meanwhile, engages in education of the local populations and visitors to lessen negative environmental impact. Scientists at the research center breed threatened and endangered species such as giant tortoises and land iguanas for reintroduction into the wild.

The most overwhelming task is a tenacious battle against introduced species, both plants and animals. Seemingly harmless plants and animals that were introduced to the islands over the past centuries have flourished. They compete for scarce food and kill the native and endemic species. The animals on the blacklist include feral cats, dogs, pigs, goats, and rats. Goats on some islands number in the tens of thousands and consume most of the vegetation sought by tortoises. Where wild pigs abound they destroy tortoise and turtle eggs, and prey upon ground-nesting birds. Plants are no less of a hazard. Blackberry vines introduced into the highlands threaten to wipe out several species of native plants.

You can appreciate the enormous amount of energy and resources necessary to protect the islands. Your national park fee helps this effort. For information on how you can offer further assistance, contact the **Charles Darwin Research Station**, *Puerto Ayora. Tel. 5/526 146, Fax 4/564 636; Website: www.polaris.net/~jpinson/welcome.html.*

THE JUDAS GOAT

Goat populations overwhelm any island on which the vigorous creatures can get a foothold. The wild beasts trod upon turtle and iguana eggs, and compete with tortoises for foliage. Isabela Island, for example, is now overrun with 100,000 goats. They have devoured much of the vegetation in the Alcedo Volcano crater where giant tortoises seek food and moisture.

To eliminate the goat populations, the parks department has put **Operation Judas Goat** *into effect on several islands. The plan consists of capturing a goat, tagging it with a radio transmitter, and painting its horns with easily identifiable, wildly colored stripes. The gregarious, unwitting traitor is reintroduced to the island and soon reveals the location of its herd. The rangers then track down the menaces for slaughter. The strategy, adopted from New Zealand, reduced the goat population on Pinta from 30,0000 to 200.*

ARRIVALS & DEPARTURES

There are two airports in the Galápagos.

The **Baltra Airport** is used for the island of **Santa Cruz**. Your tour operator may meet you at the airport to leave directly from the island. If you are going to the town of **Puerto Ayora**, you must cross a small channel by boat then traverse the island in an hour-long bus ride. **Tame** flies to the Baltra airport.

The second airport is the **Puerto Baquerizo Moreno Airport** on the island of **San Cristóbal**. The airport is just a few minutes away from the bay where the boats call. **San/Saeta** flies to the Puerto Baquerizo Moreno airport on San Cristóbal.

Be sure to clarify with your tour operator which airport you need to use if you are purchasing your airline tickets independently. Most people will purchase their air tickets through the tour operator, which eliminates any possible confusion.

There are five important variables you need to consider when selecting your Galápagos cruise:

• The **size and type of boat** will be indicative of its stability and the size of your quarters.
• The **time spent** on your cruise will generally be from three days to three weeks, with most going for seven days.
• A competent **tour operator** will be pivotal to your satisfaction.
• You may want to combine the cruise with a **special interest** such as photography instruction or diving.

• The **cost** of your cruise will be generated from the other variables, and possibly your willingness to engage in a bit of reservation roulette.

GALÁPAGOS CRUISES

The best way to see the Galápagos Islands is on a cruise on a ship, yacht, or sailboat. The ideal cruise will include comfortable cabins, delicious meals, an itinerary that guarantees a variety of wildlife and terrain, and expert, bilingual, naturalist guides. There are many vessels and tour agencies to choose from. We will help you choose the type of boat that is right for you and recommend reliable tour operators.

Most of the visitor sites are accessible only by boat so cruises are the most practical way to see the islands. While some "land-based tours" are advertised, you are really only spending your nights on land. To access the visitor sites you still have to board a boat, usually a smaller and less stable craft than one you would be on in a cruise. You do not gain much, if anything, with this strategy.

This is not to say we don't think that staying overnight on the islands is a good idea. To the contrary, we recommend that in addition to your cruise that you consider staying a few nights on Santa Cruz or one of the other islands. It is a great way to add diving, hiking, or more beach time to your visit.

Boat Size & Type

The size of your boat is perhaps the most important variable for you to consider. The size of your boat will influence its stability, speed, your level of privacy, and how many people are being shuttled to the visitor sites. Because the relative importance of each consideration will vary from person to person, it is up to you to decide what is best.

The first commandment of Galápagos boat tours is "Know Thy Belly". If you have hardy stomach and you don't easily get seasick on a rocking boat then you can choose from the full range of vessels. This includes everything from sleek 8-passenger/65-foot sailboats to the luxurious 100-passenger/300-foot Explorer II cruise ship.

If waves make you a bit queasy, however, don't kid yourself. You could spend a lot of money to be miserable for a week. Even in relatively calm conditions, the constant rolling of the boat makes some people nauseous. If you fall into the landlubber crowd, you should opt for one of the larger boats, a cruise ship of 150 feet or more that accommodates 50-100 passengers. These vessels offer greater stability and will enhance the pleasure of your trip. The largest cruise ships are steady enough that almost no one gets seasick.

If you fit in somewhere in the middle of the seasickness continuum, it's more difficult to call. Some people say that an 80-foot yacht was smoother than they imagined, while others found it dizzying. Considering the money and time to be invested in the trip, it is better to be on the conservative side. Go with a larger vessel if you are unsure.

As a general rule, with many exceptions, a bigger boat means bigger cabins. The size of your cabin will affect the amount of privacy you have because you will probably not want to spend much time in severely cramped quarters. Almost all cabins, regardless of the size of the boat, have their own bathroom and shower, but of course the size of these will vary as well. Don't take the private bathroom and shower as a given on smaller boats. Ask the tour operator to confirm this fact.

One great exception to the cabin size being consistent with boat size is when you compare yachts to sailboats. Sailboat space is much tighter due to the fact that they are narrower than yachts, and are built with fewer decks.

Vessel Terminology
For the sake of simplicity we use the following, admittedly imperfect terms to describe passenger boats in the Galápagos Islands:

Yachts are 65-125 foot vessels powered by inboard engines. They sleep 8-20 passengers. Each cabin usually has its own private bathroom with a shower. The cabins on a typical 80-foot yacht usually have enough space for a queen size bed, perhaps with a sitting nook built in. Yachts feature several comfortable common areas, often with dual functions, that include a dining room, bar, TV room with video movies, and a reference library. Meals are served family style and are casual. There is ample deck space, both covered and uncovered.

Yachts are the most commonly used tour vessels in the Galápagos and are loosely categorized from better to worse as first class, superior, tourist, and economic. There is no industry standardization so these terms can easily be misapplied.

Sailboats are 60-110 foot vessels that can be powered by wind blown sails or inboard engines. On the Galápagos cruises, sailboats almost always rely on inboard engines in order to meet schedule demands, rarely using the sails. Sailboats include catamarans. The cabins and bathrooms are much tighter than those of yachts because sailboats are narrower and have fewer decks. They feature the same common areas as yachts, but again, are less roomy. Meals are served family style and are casual. Even with the space limitations, some boat enthusiasts prefer sailboats and will not be disappointed, as there are several beauties from which to choose.

Cruise Ships are 125-300 foot vessels that accommodate 50-100 passengers. The rooms will be more like hotel rooms, some with queen size beds, sofas, writing desks, and TV's with movies on video. The cruise ships feature large common areas that include a dining room, bar, conference room, reference library, and possibly a hot tub or small pool. Meals are served either buffet style or by waiters with a fixed menu.

The larger cruise ships are faster than smaller boats, so you can reach the more distant islands on a four-day cruise rather than in seven. This is an added bonus for people who aren't thrilled by the prospect of a week at sea.

The last difference to consider among boat sizes is the corresponding size of your herd. Park regulations limit groups to 20 visitors per naturalist guide. This means that the guide per person ratio will be about the same on a yacht as on a cruise ship. However, if you go on a cruise ship, the visitor sites will necessarily have several groups roaming around at once. You will never have a visitor site to share among only a dozen people or so, which you will often be fortunate to experience with a smaller boat. Similarly, with more people to manage, cruise ship guides have to keep a tighter rein on their groups, offering less flexibility and freedom of movement than guides of smaller boats can.

Length of Cruise

The tour operator will have a standard route for its trip depending on the number of days scheduled. Occasionally visitor's sites close for maintenance or other factors force changes in itinerary. The operators are expert in their knowledge of the islands so they pick a combination of visitor sites to vary the wildlife you see. They will try to make sure your itinerary includes viewing of marine iguanas and boobies and giant tortoises and penguins and so on, within the time limits of the cruise.

The most common yacht and sailboat tours last a week composed of eight days and seven nights. Since getting to and from the islands from the mainland consumes a half-day on either side of your boat trip, the tour itself is actually seven full days and seven nights.

If you are going on a yacht or sailboat, you should consider the weeklong tour to be the minimum so you can visit the more distant sites. We do not recommend less than a week on yachts or sailboats because you just don't get very far from the port of departure. Some people might even prefer the longer cruises of 11-14 days to explore the outer islands.

On a cruise ship, the suggested minimum is the five-day/four-night package. You can cover a lot of ocean in this amount of time on a cruise ship. The weeklong trips (eight-day/seven night) on a cruise ship are also good. In this case you would add on the islands close to the port during the three-night portion. You pull into port to pick up and drop off passengers at the midweek point. We do not recommend the four-day/three-night cruise ship option alone. It's simply not enough time and you don't go very far.

Note that a half-day on either side of the cruise ship packages, like the smaller boat tours, is spent flying between the islands and the mainland.

OPERATORS, AGENCIES, & COSTS

The importance of booking your trip through a competent, experienced tour operator is critical to your satisfaction. A good tour operator will employ the most skilled naturalist guides, anticipate and resolve problems adeptly, put an excellent meal on the table three times a day, and make the entire expedition seem easy.

We provide a short list of recommended tour operators and agencies. There might be other companies that do a good job, but we have confidence in the ones we recommend.

The most frequent problems that arise when booking through an unreliable agency are poor food, unskilled naturalist guides, and broken promises. The most common deceit by the scoundrels out there is switching passengers to a smaller boat at the last minute because the original boat could not be filled. You can imagine that even with a good boat in its possession, a poor tour operator can do a lot of things wrong to blow it. For these reasons, we put more emphasis on the quality of the tour operator rather than on any specific boat.

Finally, it is important to recognize that some events, particularly poor weather and rough seas, are outside of the operator's control. Ecotourism means adventure travel in the sense that you can't always guarantee that everything will be perfect. In some rare instances, usually due to mechanical considerations, even a good operator will have to shift passengers to another boat. It should be one of equal or better quality if the operator hopes to maintain its hard-earned position above the throng of competitors.

ISLAND WEATHER

The climate of the Galápagos is unusually dry for the tropics. There are two main seasons.

•January-June is characterized by days with blues skies interrupted by brief downpours. The average temperature is 79 degrees.

•July-December, is milder. The skies are often overcast, but bright rather than dismal The season is known as garua, for the damp mist that hangs on the highest hills. The average temperature is 73 degrees.

Specialized Tours

You can combine your tour with a special interest that will slant the agenda toward one activity, such as diving, photography, or bird watching. A good attribute of these tours is that they don't exclude all other activities to engage exclusively in the special interest. For example, most dive specialized tours include hikes to volcanic lookout points and birders will get to see a marine iguana or two in addition to sharp-billed ground finches.

Specialized tours are commonly organized by an agency in the United States or Ecuador, then work through a Galápagos tour operator. A specialist guide such as a photography instructor or ornithologist, will accompany your group on the trip, in addition to the naturalist guide required by the Galápagos National Park regulation. The extra agency and additional guide mean that another cost layer is being added to your tour, so it will be more expensive. There are ways for the agency to reduce costs such as volume discounts so sometimes the specialized tours are not that much more expensive than standard tours.

We provide a list of companies offering specialized tours later in this section.

Yacht & Sailboat Tour Costs

The typical cost of a seven-day cruise, booked in advance, on a superior yacht or sailboat will be $1,200-$2,000 per person. A good rule of thumb for the boat portion, is about $200 per night, (though it goes down to almost $100/night on the cheapest boats). You must add airfare from the Ecuadorian mainland at $400 roundtrip and the Galápagos park fee of $100. That brings the total of a $1,500 cruise to about $2,000 per person including all meals while on board, excepting alcoholic drinks.

Here is the part where life seems not to be fair. Let's say you booked your trip in advance for $1,500. You are happily eating a gourmet meal on board. You almost choke on a prawn when you learn that the person sitting next to you paid only $900 for the exact same trip by waiting to book at the last minute when unreserved space was deeply discounted.

The closer you get to the date of the cruise and the closer geographically you get to the embarkation port, the cheaper you can probably acquire passage. That means if you hole up in Puerto Ayora on Santa Cruz Island waiting for the deal of the century to pop up on the day the boat sails, you just might get it. Or you might not. You might get shuffled onto a mildewy old tub reeking of diesel fumes because that's the bargain the agent found for you – or you might wait several nights at a hotel spending money to save money until the deal you've been waiting for appears. The greatest risk is that you will get stuck on a cheap, dumpy boat.

You are buying something of value with the extra money if you book in advance with a good tour operator. You purchase the security that you will be cruising on a clean, reliable craft, on the size of boat you selected, and during the timeframe you have scheduled for a vacation.

If time is not a scarce resource, but money is, we suggest you start with one of the reliable tour agencies we've listed in Quito. Tell them that you want a discounted price, that you are willing to go immediately or wait for it, but you want to go on one of their regular boats, (as opposed to shifting you to another operator's cheaper cruise). They should be able to make air arrangements to the islands from Quito on short notice if space on the boat becomes available. You give up whining rights if you don't get exactly what you want, but you might cut a pretty good deal for a high quality trip this way.

If cheap is the only thing that matters to you, we've listed a reliable deep discounter. We don't recommend you take this route, because when you consider airfare, the park fee, and the minimum cruise cost, you are going to spend a chunk of change at any rate. It would really hurt to drop $1,300 into an unsatisfactory trip because you were trying to scrimp.

A note on **tipping**: the standard for tipping in the Galápagos is $5-10 per passenger per day for the crew and $5-10 per passenger per day for your naturalist guide. Some guides split responsibilities and tips among themselves as a team.

Cruise Ship Costs

You will pay more for the space and comfort of a cruise ship. Prices on the big cruise ships at the low end can be comparable to the smaller boats. Prices range from about $250-$400 per person per night, full board, sometimes with drinks included. You must add to this your airfare from the mainland at about $400 and the Galápagos Park Fee of $100. Including airfare and park fees, an average seven night trip will cost about $3,200 per person. The four night cruise would cost on average $2,200.

Discounts for last minute bookings are not as deep on the cruise ships as they are on yachts and sailboats.

Cruise Operators & Agencies

Below is our short list of cruise operators. Among these selected operators you are sure to find a yacht, sailboat, or cruise ship to suit your needs, as well as excellent service.

Yachts & Sailboats

ANGERMEYER'S ENCHANTED EXPEDITIONS, *Foch 726 y Av. Amazonas, Quito, Ecuador. Tel. 2/569 960 Fax 2/569 956; E-mail: angermeyer@accessinter.net; Website: www.angermeyer.com.*

Angermeyer's has a rate of customer satisfaction that is simply extraordinary. The food is stellar and the boats are superb. Angermeyer operates beautiful yachts, sailboats, and offers dive-oriented trips a few times per year. They can also work as an agent to book you on other boats if theirs are full for the time frame you require and can book you on cruise ships.

ANDANDO TOURS, *Amazonas 629 y Carrion, Quito. Tel. 2/550952 or 2/548 780, Fax 2/228 519; E-mail: andando1@ecnet.ec; Website: www.andandotours.com.*

Andando operates three gorgeous sailboats. Andando passengers rave about the quality of food and service. They are simply one of the best in the business.

ECOVENTURA, *US: 7200 Corporate Center Drive, Suite 510, Miami, Fl. 33126. Tel. 800/633-7972, Fax 305/ 592-6394; E-mail: gpsnet@aol.com. In Quito: Av. Colón E9-58 y 6 de Diciembre, Quito-Ecuador, 2/ 507 408, Fax 2/ 507 409; E-mail: lmena@pi.pro.ec; Website: www.ecoventura.com.*

In addition to three superb yachts and a sailboat, Ecoventura has a 50-passenger cruise ship.

Cruise Ships

CANODROS *Guayaquil Tel. 4/285 711. Guayaquil fax 4/287 651; E-mail: eco-tourism@canodros.com.ec; Website: www.canodros.com.*

If you are leaning toward a cruise ship, check into the most luxurious first. The 300-foot *Explorer II* is a commodious, stable craft. The standard cabins are bigger than many hotel rooms, and come equipped with a queen-size bed, writing table, TV with VCR, sofa, closets, and good-sized bathroom including a full shower. Lunch and dinner is usually buffet style, with a good emphasis on fresh fruits and vegetables. Dinner is more formal, with tuxedoed waiters attending. Unlike other cruises, alcohol, except wine, is included in the price.

ECOVENTURA/GALAPAGOS NETWORK: *7200 Corporate Center Drive, Suite 510, Miami, Fl. 33126. Tel. 800/633-7972, Fax 305/ 592-6394; E-mail: gpsnet@aol.com. In Quito: Av. Colón E9-58 y 6 de Diciembre, Quito-Ecuador, 2/ 507 408, Fax 2/507 409; E-mail: lmena@pi.pro.ec; Website: www.ecoventura.com.*

Ecoventura operates the 195-foot *Corinthian*. The main advantage of the *Corinthian* is that it operates with a maximum of 48 passengers, but was built for twice that many. The dining room is spacious with a large picture window. The rates on the *Corinthian* can be as low as yachts when comparing on a per day basis.

METROPALITAN TOURING/ADVENTURE ASSOCIATES. *US: 13150 Coit Road, Suite 110, Dallas, Texas. 800/527-2500, Fax 972/783-1286; E-mail: dmm@metropolitan.com.ec. In Quito, Republica de El Salvador N36-84 y Naciones Unidas Tel 2/464 780, Fax 2/464 702; E-mail: mgd@metropolitan.com.ec; Website: www.ecuadorable.com.*

Metropaltian operates two excellent cruise ships, the 166-foot *Isabela II* and the 228-foot Santa Cruz. Metropalitan offers a wide range of superior travel services in the Galápagos and mainland Ecuador. They can put together a complete package for you that would cover your entire trip.

Diving Tours

For live aboard dive trips you can contact **Angermeyer's** or **Ecoventura** listed above or either of the following dive companies. Day dives are covered in the Santa Cruz section.

• **Scuba Iguana**, *east end of Charles Darwin, in front of the Hotel Galápagos. Tel. 5/526 296; E-mail: hotelgps@ga.pro.ec; Website: www.scuba-iguana.com.*

• **Sub-Aqua**, *Charles Darwin. Quito Tel. 2/565 294; E-mail: sub_aqua@accessinter.net*

Photography Tours

• **Galápagos Travel**, *783 Río Del Mar Blvd., Suite 47, Aptos, CA. Tel. 831/ 689-9192, Fax 831/689-9195; E-mail: galapagostravel@compuserve.com*

Birding & Other Naturalist Agencies

• **National Audubon Society Nature Odysseys**, *700 Broadway, New York, NY 10003. Tel. 212/979-3066; E-mail: travel@audubon.org; Website: www.audubon.org*

• **Cheesemans' Ecology Safaris**, *20800 Kittredge Road, Saratoga, CA 95070 Tel. 800/ 527-5330 or 408/ 867-1371; E-mail: cheesemans@aol.com; Website: www.cheesemans.com*

• **Abercrombie and Kent**, *1520 Kensington Road, Oak Brook, Illinois 60523. Tel. 800/323-7308; E-mail: info@abercrombiekent.com; Website: www.aandktours.com*

Surfing Tours

• **Galapagosurf**, *E-mail: ricardo@galapagosurf.com; Website: www.galapagosurf.com.* Ricardo Nuñez Cristiansen puts together surf expeditions that focus on outer reefs by chartering some very nice boats. As Ricardo says, "Keep it soul and rip bro."

Deep Discount Agencies

• **Moonrise Travel**, *Charles Darwin, in front of Banco del Pacifico, Puerto Ayora, Santa Cruz, Galápagos. Tel. 526 402; E-mail: sdivine@pa.ga.pro.ec.* Moonrise will find a cruise to fit your budget if that is the variable you want to focus on. They are good at what they do.

AGENDA & DAILY ACTIVITIES

The tour operator will meet you either at the airport on the mainland or on the islands. Your bags and probably you will be tagged with the company logo for easy identification. From that point on, you won't touch your bags until they are in your cabin on the ship. You should pack your sunscreen in your carry-on bag because you will probably spend some time in the sun on the way to the boat.

If you didn't meet your naturalist guide at the airport, you will meet her on the boat while sipping a welcome drink. You'll have a chance to freshen up in your cabin, then depending on the time of day, the first meal might be served. Next you will attend your first briefing, then hopefully fit in a visitor site in the afternoon.

The days begin early, normally with a wake-up call at 6:00 am for a 6:30 breakfast. The morning excursion will run from about 7:30 to noon. You will go back to the boat for lunch, with some free time for a siesta afterwards. The boat will likely cruise to the next visitor site during this mid-day period. At about 2:30 you will start the afternoon excursion, then return to the boat in the early evening. People usually gather at the bar for a beverage before dinner, then attend a briefing after the meal. After the briefing you can read something from the boat's library, watch a movie on video, socialize with the other guests, or contemplate the stars from an outside deck.

Briefings are conducted each evening to outline the next day's program. The guide will tell you which island you will visit, whether the landing will be a dry landing or a wet landing, and inform you of the specific activities possible at the visitor sites. The guides advise you at the briefing and remind you immediately before the excursion exactly what

WET & DRY LANDINGS

*Due to conservation efforts as well as difficulty navigating in shallow water, your boat cannot access the visitor sites directly. You will board a small, motorized dingy known as a panga, then head toward shore. The visitor site will be classified either as a **dry landing** or a **wet landing**. In dry landings you can wear shoes in the panga, then step onto a dock or directly onto the shoreline without getting your feet wet. In a wet landing, you ride barefoot or wear sandals, and, either shorts or pants that can be rolled up above the knee, because you will have to wade through shallow water to the beach.*

Your guide will notify you before each excursion whether the visitor site requires a wet or dry landing.

type of shoes, clothing, and additional gear, such as mask and snorkels, will be needed on the excursions.

Typical excursion activities include short hikes, swimming, snorkeling, and *panga* (motorized dinghy) rides along the shoreline. Every one of these activities will involve wildlife of one sort or another, whether it is spying on blue-footed boobies from a *panga* or staring at a sea lion mask to whiskers while snorkeling.

The hikes can involve traversing lava beds, boardwalks, sandy trails, or beaches. Since volcanic rock is quite uneven and sharp, it is a good idea to use shoes that cover your toes rather than sport sandals for walks over this type of terrain. You can use sport sandals on the sandy beach walks.

If you have physical limitations you should discuss this with your tour operator before signing onto the cruise. If the limitation isn't severe, you can review the weekly itinerary with your guide or purser at the beginning of the cruise. Pick and choose from the walks, opting to rest on board or ashore during the more rigorous ones. The most exerting walks are those that involve climbing hills of volcanic rock. Sometimes these have wooden stairs that facilitate the climb and protect the ecosystem. The larger cruise ships often have a full-time doctor on board. You should confirm this with the agency before booking your cruise if it is important to you.

Photographic opportunities are abundant on all cruises. Hikes and shoreline *panga* rides provide extraordinary photos. You will get some memorable shots without one, but a zoom lens will greatly increase your ability to take pictures of the shyer animals like penguins and boobies. Take more film than you think you will need. Ten rolls of 36 would be a reasonable amount for a week. Frequently the boats will sell film and other sundries, but you shouldn't depend on it.

All cruises offer several opportunities to snorkel and swim. Some operators include a mask and snorkel in the price of the trip while others rent the equipment. Since it is preferable to use a mask that doesn't leak and put your own snorkel in your mouth, we recommend bringing this conveniently packed equipment with you. You can snorkel pretty well without fins so packing these bulkier items is more open to debate. The water isn't frigid, but it is nippy. Packing a shorty or full wetsuit is recommended if you like to snorkel. You can't rent wetsuits on the boats. Even if you are comfortable in cold water, you can only last about ten minutes without a wetsuit. It is quite possible to see huge rays, moray eels, or penguins shooting like torpedoes through the water. The extra time in the water that a wetsuit facilitates makes bring one worthwhile.

The activity that is difficult to get enough of is cardiovascular exercise. There really isn't enough room on these boats to do anything physical except yoga. Even the exercise equipment on the nicest cruise ship leaves a lot to be desired. You can't really run at most at most of the visitor sites because of environmental impact. There would be a good chance of squashing a marine iguana with your running shoes. You might be able to get in a couple of good swims if you bring a shorty and some goggles. That's really your best bet. Another option is squeezing in a run while at one of the towns like Puerto Ayora during a shopping call.

Consider including all of the following items in your Galápagos bound luggage:

- Sunscreen, at least 30 SPF
- Sport sandals like Teva, Chaco, or other brands
- Tennis, walking, light hiking or other toe-covered activity shoes.
- A sun shading hat
- Windbreaker
- 10 rolls of 36 exposure for a week's cruise, maybe more
- An extra camera battery
- A daypack
- Snacks like gorp, granola bars, or other portable food to help between meals
- Binoculars
- A snorkel and mask
- A shorty or full wet suit for snorkeling – this is not absolutely necessary, but you'll be happy you have it

LAND DESTINATIONS

If you're not in a hurry after your cruise, why not stay a while?

The Galápagos Islands are exceptional enough to merit further exploration. The word of mouth on Galápagos cruises is so positive that people often don't consider staying for few extra days in Puerto Ayora or one of the other island towns. It's definitely worthwhile if you have the time, especially given the fact that you are already out here on these remote tropical islands with intense topography and extraordinary shorelines.

There are myriad activities in which you can partake if you stay ashore. These include hiking, biking, sea kayaking, surfing, snorkeling, diving, and cave exploring. The playground for these activities, as you would expect in the Galápagos, is uniquely beautiful. Or you can adopt the chemolian pace of the islands. Take it easy. Soak up the sun on a white sandy beach or sip a beverage while gazing at the bay.

Four islands have towns that can accommodate overnight stays. These are **Santa Cruz**, **San Cristóbal**, **Isabela**, and **Floreana**. It is Santa Cruz that offers the best choice of lodging and most diverse activities. You can reach San Cristóbal and Isabela by small plane and all islands by boat with some effort.

SANTA CRUZ/PUERTO AYORA

The island charm enraptures despite the bevy of tourists that pick through **Puerto Ayora's** boardwalk shops, which brim with colorful t-shirts and wood carved iguanas. (We opted for the wooden hammerhead shark proving that we know art when we see it). Larger tributes to the creatures that made the islands famous are resplendent statues along the main avenue. It's refreshing to see homage in the form of an enormous green iguana rather than a dandy with a sword.

You will be comfortable in one of the town's serene hotels and contentedly engaged for days. You can powder your feet on stunning white beaches, chew a weed with a giant tortoise, amble through an underground lava tube, or dive among sea turtles and rays. The main evening entertainment is volleyball on the waterfront court as the sun sets brilliant orange on the yacht-filled harbor. The pricing at hotels and restaurants, while more expensive than the mainland, is really quite reasonable considering the exotic location.

MY FATHER'S ISLAND

"I stood mesmerized as Santa Cruz appeared on the horizon, first in a low mist, then turning golden as the sun illuminated it like a painting in the Bible. Craters sat on its spine like squashed hats, tilted pots melted to one side while pouring out the earth's boiling content. I could see that the hills were just high enough to catch passing clouds giving the island a green, rain forest cap. Tied about the island's waist lay a fearful wilderness of spines, cacti and bare white trees sprouting from tangled lava churned out of the earth lifetimes ago, to hiss at the edge of the sea."
– Johanna Angermeyer from her book **My Father's Island**

ARRIVALS & DEPARTURES

By Boat

If you are on a cruise that starts and ends from Santa Cruz, it will be easy for you to tack on a few extra days. If your tour operator is arranging your air tickets, simply tell them how many extra days you want to stay on the island.

It is a bit trickier if your cruise is based out of San Cristóbal Island and you want to stay a few nights on Santa Cruz. It is possible to fly between the islands. See the inter-island air schedule. Most boats call on Puerto Ayora during the cruise, so you might be able to jump ship if it is on the last day of the cruise. There is not regular boat service between the islands at this time. You might be able get from island to island by boat. You'd have to check around the port to see if anyone is heading to Santa Cruz, then negotiate a rate.

Ingala, *Padre Julio Herrera. Tel. 526 151,* sometimes offers boat service to the other islands. You can't count on it though because they only have one boat, which tends to break down.

By Plane

The **Baltra Airport** is used for the island of **Santa Cruz**. Tame flies to the Baltra airport from Quito and Guayaquil.

To reach the town of **Puerto Ayora** from the airport requires three legs of transportation that takes just over an hour, but it's really quite easy. Just ask someone at the airport for the bus to Puerto Ayora and join the herd. The short bus ride across Baltra Island to the channel is free. They charge you about $0.25 to cross the channel on the boat, then you board a bus for an hour long ride ($2) to Puerto Ayora.

To get to the airport from Puerto Ayora, buy your ticket from the CITTEG ticket window in the patio portion of the restaurant across from the seagull statue. This is toward the west end of Charles Darwin, just up from the commercial dock. You can buy your tickets in advance, which is a good idea in the high season. You should try to get a ticket for a bus that leaves about two-and-a-half hours before your plane's departure time. You can also take a taxi across the island, but take into consideration that the boats that cross the channel are timed to meet the bus.

You can fly between the islands with Emetebe, which has service to the islands of San Cristóbal, Isabela from Santa Cruz:

• **Tame**, *Charles Darwin near the mid-point. Tel. 526 165 or 526 527*
• **Emetebe**, *Charles Darwin, office above the supermarket, near the commercial pier, Santa Cruz. Tel. Santa Cruz 5/526 177. Tel. San Cristóbal 5/ 520 036. Tel. Isabela 5/529 155. Tel. Guayaquil 5/292 492*

The plane alternates directions every other day in triangular route between three islands. The cost of the flights are $90-$100 per segment, one-way, including IVA.

Inter-Island Flight Schedule:

Monday, Wednesday, Friday: San Cristóbal to Baltra to Villamar to San Cristóbal.

Tuesday, Thursday, Saturday: San Cristóbal to Villamar to Baltra to San Cristóbal

ORIENTATION

Santa Cruz is a large centrally located island. Its main town, Puerto Ayora, the largest town in the Galápagos with a population of 8,000 is located on the south side of the island. The town fronts Academy Bay, which is the port of departure for many tour boats. The town is about an hour away from the Baltra airport, which is located on a small island, across a 200-meter channel on the north side Santa Cruz.

GETTING AROUND

Puerto Ayora is small enough that you can easily walk to all hotels, restaurants, and shops. You can also walk to several beaches.

To get to the area on the other side of the bay, known fittingly as *el otro lado*, you can hire a taxi boat for $0.25 per person.

A cab is the most convenient way to reach some points of interests, such as the tortoise reserves, lava tubes, and craters, all located in highlands. The rate is about $5 per hour if you have the cab wait.

WHERE TO STAY

Expenisve

RED MANGROVE INN, *Avenida Charles Darwin near the research station. Tel/Fax 5/526 564; E-mail: redmangrove@ecuadorexplorer.com. Website: www.ecuadorexplorer.com/redmangrove. 4 rooms. Double $88. Breakfast not included. Cafe. Bar. Hot tub. Bicycle and kayak rental. Master card only for 10% additional fee.*

The Red Mangrove is a small, extremely comfortable hotel looking out over the blue waters of Academy Bay. You can watch the waves break on the black volcanic rocks in front of the salmon-colored Mediterranean style building from almost everywhere in the hotel. The main gathering area/bar/dining room is open and airy with a touch of the Greek Islands. Lots of puffy, batik-covered throw pillows tempt you to plop down and relax right there, as do the hammocks. The welcoming fire in the evening makes it even harder to budge.

Delicious breakfast choices include fresh yogurt with granola and thick pancakes. You'll be drinking your morning brew out of beautiful ceramic mugs made by Monica, one of the owners. It's this personal touch that gives the Red Mangrove much of its charm. Both Polo and Monica are interesting, artistic people, who have decorated the hotel as an extension of their home.

The spacious rooms all have lots of windows in order to take advantage of the views and refreshing sea breezes. Even though it gets cool at night, you stay warm under the alpaca wool blankets. Rattan mats and throw pillows give the rooms an informal, mellow charm.

PUERTO AYORA

CALLE NO. 61
12 DE NOVIEMBRE
LOS PIQUEROS
LAS FRIGATAS
12 DE NOVIEMBRE
BOLIVAR NAVEDA
AV. CHARLES DARWIN
RED MANGROVE
HOTEL GALÁPAGOS
CHARLES DARWIN
RESEARCH STATION
BANCO DEL PACIFICO
Pelican
Bay
12 DE FEBRERO
TAME
AV. PADRE JULIO HERRERA
CHARLES BINFORD
DE BERLANGA
CALLE NO. 23
AV. CHARLES DARWIN
To Bahia
Tortuga
Academy
Bay
TOMAS
COMMERCIAL
PIER
To El Otro Lado

Even though the hotel is extremely relaxing, that doesn't mean there's not much to be done for the more activity-inclined. Polo is working on opening up what he calls "The Other Galápagos." By that he means the things that people on programmed boat trips don't get to see or do. He can arrange mountain biking, kayaking, scuba diving, and surfing, as well as mountain tours and trips to other islands. At the end of the day you get to come back to the hotel and sink into the hot tub while gazing at the stars.

Selected as one of our *Best Places to Stay* – see chapter 11 for more details.

HOTEL GALÁPAGOS, *Darwin Ave. near the research station. Tel. 526 330, Fax 526 296; E-mail: hotelgps@ga.pro.ec; Website: www.scuba-iguana.com. Double $100. Restaurant. Bar. Dive shop & dive tours.*

The lounge area of the Hotel Galápagos is a relaxed, funky, oceanic shrine that exhibits black lava against neon blue water through an enormous picture window. It is an airy and peaceful place to consider the intriguing, homegrown art on the walls, thumb through a Galápagos photo book, or spy a boat through the telescope. Guests congregate around the cork-covered bar for pre-dinner drinks as a prehistoric looking mobile, made from a pelican bones, drifts overhead.

The dining area, located on a split-level platform at the back of the room, shares the same intoxicating view and mellow ambience. Breakfast is particularly delightful, highlighted by warm, wholesome muffins, fresh squeezed juice, and excellent coffee.

You can relax in a hammock inside the main building or explore the grounds until you find one that suits your mood. You are likely to stumble across the oldest existing house on the island, built out of lava bricks. While the small house is uninhabited, the grounds are not. You will find a variety of finches, herons, pelicans, and other bird life.

The simple rooms feature cement floors covered with traditional woven mats and lamp shades that glow orange through the skin of the *opuntia* cactus. The ocean views and soothing sound of the breaking waves are the most attractive aspects of the rooms. In particular room number one is positioned such that at high tide diminutive waves lap against one wall. During low tide marine iguanas creep up the rocks toward the window like ghostly, salt-crusted spies.

HOTEL ANGERMEYER, *Av. Charles Darwin y Piqueros. Tel. 5/526 277. 20 rooms. Double $85. Breakfast included. Restaurant. Bar. Pool. Credit cards accepted.*

Originally owned and operated as the Residencial Angermeyer by the one of the three German brothers who were original settlers, the hotel has been remodeled and upgraded under new ownership. The centerpiece of the hotel is a tropical garden with a kidney-shaped pool. You can breakfast near the pool or in the hotel's restaurant. The air-conditioned rooms are bright, cleanly styled with attractive wooden bed frames. All of the rooms face the courtyard garden.

DELFÍN HOTEL, *Punta Estrada, el otro lado. USA 800/527-2500, Fax 972/783-1286; E-mail: dmm@metropolitan.com.ec Quito Tel. 2/464 780. Santa Cruz Tel: 5/526 297 Website: www.ecuadorable.com 25 rooms. Double $150. Breakfast included. Restaurant. Bar. Pool.*

The Delfin Hotel is run by Metropolitan Touring and is normally used as part of their Galápagos tour packages. The hotel is located on a secluded beach across the bay from Santa Cruz. The rooms are fairly simple, but the pool, views, and the beach are idyllic. You can have lunch here by calling and arranging it in advance.

Moderate

HOTEL FERNANDINA, *two blocks behind the Hotel Angermeyer. Tel 5/526 499, Fax 5/526 122. 20 rooms. Double $65. Breakfast not included. Restaurant. Bar. Pool. Hot tub. Master card only for 10% additional fee.*

If you're in search of air-conditioning and a swimming pool, the Fernandina is a good option. The quiet hotel, set a couple of blocks back from the main drag, is really the only choice in the moderate price range. The rooms, on the smallish side, are pretty blocky and generic, but the gardens and pleasant patio bar offer more than you would expect from the outside.

The main draw here, the pool, lies across the street from the guestrooms in a separate walled courtyard. Because of its size and price, the Fernandina is popular with groups.

Inexpensive

HOTEL SOLYMAR, *midway along Charles Darwin. Tel. 5/526 281. 12 rooms. Double $20-$50. Credit cards accepted.*

The Solymar is set up in two separate buildings divided by Charles Darwin Avenue. The bayside building features three distinctive rooms with ocean views, all priced differently. The most expensive room has a fantastic second floor view of the harbor, but don't expect luxury furnishings. The cheaper rooms across the street are more utilitarian. The nicest feature of the hotel is the seaside deck set up with patio furniture where you can lounge in the sunshine with marine iguanas and pelicans.

ESTRELLA DEL MAR, *12 de February y Charles Darwin. Tel. 5/526 427. 20 rooms. Double $15-$20. No credit cards.*

This cereal box hotel is worthwhile if you can get one of the rooms with a view out over the harbor, otherwise it's pretty austere.

Budget

PEREGRINA B&B, *midway along Avenida Charles Darwin. Tel 5/526 323. 4 rooms. Double $5. Breakfast not included but available for $1. No credit cards.*

This simple and clean B&B is a good budget option. The house and furnishings are small and basic, but some of the rooms have private baths. If you read Johanna Angermeyer's *My Father's Island*, you'll be interested to know that the Peregrina is owned by her stepbrother Tony.

RESIDENCIAL LOS AMIGOS, *Av. Charles Darwin, in front of Tame office. Tel. 5/526 265. $5 per person. Shared bath. No credit cards.*

Lyle Lovett would call this place plain ugly from the front. It looks like an old warehouse from an action adventure movie. Inside it is surprisingly clean and even has attractive hardwood floors.

WHERE TO EAT

Some of the food in town is quite good, especially the grilled meat and seafood. The service, however, is incredibly slow, so go to the restaurant before you are really hungry. Our theory, given the languid movement and seeming indifference of the waiters, is that they actually evolved from giant tortoises. We expect confirmation of the theory by the staff of the Darwin Research Station as soon as they get back from lunch.

ROCKY'S, *Charles Darwin, across from giant seagull. Moderate. No credit cards.*

For as simple as this open-walled restaurant looks, it sure serves up some mouthwatering grilled seafood. The entrées are accompanied by a load of veggies and a baked potato so this alone should be enough to sate most appetites. Ficus trees, whalebones, and bamboo ceilings give the place a natural feel, while cloth napkins and china add a touch of class. The restaurant is furnished with beautiful tables and chairs constructed from *cedrala*, a heavy native wood.

MEDIA LUNA, *Avenida Charles Darwin. Moderate. No credit cards.*

We don't categorize the food in very many establishments in Puerto Ayora as delicious, but it is here. The informal restaurant, set around a courtyard, offers excellent pizza. After eating ship food for a week, even if it's good, we get the craving for a cheesy pizza pie. Media Luna more than satisfies that urge. Be aware that the mediums are very big. Eating one between two people will sink you for the rest of the day.

EL PATIO, *midway along Charles Darwin. Moderate. No credit cards.*

Notice the grill as you walk into this folksy locale with fishnet ceilings. That should tip you off as to the house specialty. The "super barbecue" should sate the hardiest appetites as it includes grilled chicken, steak, pork, sausage, a salad, and potatoes. For lighter fare, try the grilled fish or ceviche.

SALVAVIDA, *west end on Charles Darwin, near commercial pier. Moderate. No credit cards.*

A popular spot for a seafood lunch or an afternoon beer. If you grab a table outside you can watch the hubbub at the small commercial pier.

CAFÉ Y LIMON, *Charles Darwin y 12 de Febrero. Moderate. No credit cards.*

This is a fun, relaxed bar that is open-walled like most establishments in Puerto Ayora. It has a pool table in the back. Most people just come here for drinks, but they serve sandwiches and grilled fish as well.

LA TRATORRIA DE PIPPO, *Avenida Charles Darwin. Moderate. No credit cards.*

This is really the only choice in town if you've got a hankering for a big plate of pasta. Unfortunately, much of the food is somewhat bland. Go for the *penne arrabiate*, with garlic and chilies, to get some flavor.

EL CHOCOLATE, *Avenida Charles Darwin. Inexpensive. No credit cards.*

Located across from the Banco del Pacifico, El Chocolate is a favorite with locals and visitors alike. The toasted sandwiches are crisp on the outside with nice gooey cheese, and the big, tangy fruit salads more than cover your vitamin C requirements for the day. If your hotel doesn't include breakfast, or even if it does, you might want to stop by here for granola with yogurt or waffles.

Capricha, *Avenida Charles Darwin*, is another restaurant serving the same type of informal, healthy food. They also have decent a bookstore and gift shop.

SEEING THE SIGHTS

The attractions in Puerto Ayora include the **Charles Darwin Research Station**, the souvenir shops along waterfront in Puerto Ayora, and a few excellent nearby beaches. You can make a day of it in the highlands by visiting the **tortoise reserves**, the **Los Gemelos pit craters**, and a **lava tube**. You should take at least a windbreaker with you to the highlands attractions, because it can be quite damp and somewhat chilly there. If you'd like to have lunch in the highlands, talk to your hotel about radioing ahead to arrange a lunch at the Furios, who own property with the lava tube or at the Narvajals. Both families provide excellent home-style meals.

Cruise itineraries frequently include a few of the visitor attractions on Santa Cruz.

Charles Darwin Research Station

Located at far east end of Charles Darwin Avenue Tel. 5/526 146, Fax 4/564 636; Website: www.polaris.net/~jpinson/welcome.html. Daily 8am-5pm. Free.

The **Charles Darwin Research Station** is a non-profit, private research facility that was founded in 1959. The main function of the station is providing information and assistance to the Galápagos National Park Service. Educational programs fortify the preservation of Galápagos' unique ecosystem. The target of these educational programs is local communities and visitors.

Your visit to the research station will begin at the exhibition center which features displays outlining the history of the Galápagos Islands and the challenging conservation goals. Particular focus is given to the impact of introduced plants and animals. The most interesting part of the public area is the **Giant Tortoise Breeding and Rearing Center**. Here you will see the tortoises in all stages of life, from youngsters about the size of a teacup, others the size of a cereal bowl, up to full grown tortoises weighing 250 kilos. You can walk into the corrals and mingle with the older tortoises.

Along the way through the breeding center, you will find the truly sad case of **Lonely George**, the last tortoise of his species. George's species inhabited only Pinta Island. Two females from another island, though not of the exact species, now share the corral with George. They have been unable to reproduce. Only time will tell if George represents the end of a branch on his evolutionary tree. An example of the extraordinary work that this research center accomplishes is the increase in the number of a giant tortoise species found on Española Island. In 1963, the biologists moved the only living tortoises of the species *elephantopus hoodensis*, which consisted of two males and twelve females, to the breeding center. To date they have repatriated more than 1,000 tortoises back to the island.

Other areas of the center's mission include marine research, quarantine consultation, and providing housing and research facilities for visiting scientists. Volunteer positions are frequently open at the center, which you can find out about through their website.

Steve Devine's Farm: Tortoise Reserve

Wandering about these clumpy hills searching for and encountering giant tortoises is a must for a Galápagos visit. It is one thing to see them in their pens at the Darwin Station, but quite another to find them roaming freely about munching on the wads of grass. Although there are fences are around the farmland, they do not hinder the tortoises, which are free to come and go as they please.

After your amble with the tortoises, enjoy a complimentary cup of hot coffee or herbal tea. The lemon grass for the tea is freshly picked from the garden. The tables on the patio make a nice place to enjoy your beverage as there is a good view of the east side of the island.

The reserve is located in the highlands, about twenty minutes in cab from Puerto Ayora. The cost to enter is $3. There is another tortoise reserve near Santa Rosa.

Los Gemelos Craters

The **Los Gemelos craters** are two 100-meter wide craters separated by the road that crosses Santa Cruz. The craters are just a stone's throw from the road. If you know you won't have time to stop, you can catch a glimpse of the one on the east side of the road as you drive to or from the airport.

These pit-craters, formed by lava subsiding into a magma fissure, are lushly vegetated by a cloud forest. The predominant species is the evergreen *scalesia* tree. The trunks and branches of the trees in this zone are covered with epiphytes, mostly mosses and liverworts, but also ferns, orchids, and some bromeliads. This type of forest occurs only in the highest points on the three largest islands. It was once extensive, but now only fragments remain. During the cool season, it is continually drenched in mist. You can hike down to the bottom of the larger, more lopsided crater on the west side by circling around to the back. If you are planning on hiking up here in the *garua* season, wear at least a windbreaker, because it is cool and very damp.

Lava Tubes

The **Furios lava tubes** are lumpy underground cylinders that run for nearly a kilometer. Floodlights positioned throughout the tunnel not only help you navigate, but also enhance the eeriness of the rough contours. The owners have built several stairways and extensive boardwalks to facilitate your subterranean stroll. Due to the dampness, some of the wood can be slick. The Furios will give you a good flashlight to use in case the power fails.

Such tubes exist because lava is a good insulator. When an outside shell hardens, it can keep the interior hot enough that its molten core continues to flow. When the lava flow from the vent tapers off, there is not enough material to fill the whole cylinder so an empty tube forms.

There is another lava tube within walking distance of the community of Bella Vista. It is open to the public, but does not have lights installed, so you should take two good flashlights, in case one goes out.

Las Grietas

Las Grietas is a deep gash in the in the rugged, orange lava above *el otro lado* point. The crevice bleeds crystal-clear, black-green water to form a perfect swimming hole. The semi-saline pool is about twenty meters long and four meters wide. It is located in the secluded desert scrub on the lava hills that rise up from the coastline. If finches are the only other creatures around, you might even venture a skinny dip.

To get Las Grietas, hire a *panga* at the pier to take you to "*el otro lado*", the other side. This two-minute ride should cost you about $0.25 or less per person. Follow the sidewalk to the Delfín Hotel, which has a nice little public beach out front. From the hotel, there are signs indicating Las Grietas. When you reach a crushed red lava path, cross it. Follow the narrow trail with the tall fence within arm's reach on your left and the salt flat on your right. You will reach a small stairway into the Grietas in less than a kilometer. The walk is interesting, you'll encounter a variety of birds along the way, but the lava is rough enough to necessitate good sport sandals or tennis shoes.

Beaches

There are some great beaches near Puerto Ayora, all within walking distance.

Turtle Bay is a dazzling, powdery, white beach. A small dune plateau, covered with red vines, buffets the backside. You shouldn't swim in the turbulent waves on the beach where the path ends. If you turn right, walk to the end of this beach, and across the spit, you will discover an equally gorgeous beach on a bay with bathtub calm water.

To get to Turtle Bay from Charles Darwin in town, head up Herrara until you reach Charles Binford, and turn left. Follow Binford as it turns from pavement into a dirt road to the entrance of the trail to Turtle Bay. You can't miss it. There is a big lookout tower at the entrance with a nice view of town and Academy Bay. It is three kilometers from town to Turtle Bay.

The **Playa del Otro Lado** in front of the Hotel Delfín has a tuft of white sand and calm water with mangroves. Surfers like the reef break a good distance from shore. To get here, hire a *panga* at the pier to take you to *el otro lado*, the other side. This two-minute ride should cost you about $0.25 or less per person. Follow the sidewalk to the Delfín Hotel. If you want to have lunch here, you have to call in advance to see if it is possible, Tel. *526 297*. The swimming hole Las Grietas is near here, so you might want to walk to that too. See the description of Las Grietas above.

The easiest beach to get to is the tiny beach on the **Charles Darwin Research Station** property. The path to the *playa* is well marked. It is located inside the entrance gate, on the opposite side of the road from the research buildings.

Media Luna & Cerro Crocker

You can hike to the crescent-shaped **Media Luna crater** from the community of Bellavista in about hour. If you want to continue the hike, head toward **Cerro Crocker**. It will take you over an hour more to reach the summit. At 864 meters, it is the highest point in the archipelago.

El Garrapatero

The road to this visitor site is scheduled to open by the publication date of this book. The beach has sea lions and excellent bird life including blue-footed boobies, flamingoes, and herons. It is a good spot for snorkeling. It will take about an hour to get here from Puerto Ayora in car. You might be able to arrange sea kayaking here with the Red Mangrove Hotel.

NIGHTLIFE & ENTERTAINMENT

The two most popular discos are **Galapsón**, just off of Charles Darwin, near the turtle statue, and **La Garrapata**, about halfway up Charles Darwin.

SHOPPING

Souvenir shops along Charles Darwin Avenue are abundant. All offer a plethora of t-shirts and woodcarvings. If you'd like to see items of higher distinction, check out the shops attached to the **Hotel Galápagos** (nice clothing) and **Red Mangrove** (beautiful ceramics) near the Charles Darwin Research Station.

SPORTS & RECREATION

Diving

Diving in the waters of the Galápagos provides big animal thrills. Enormous, shadow-like rays, eerie hammerhead sharks, and curious sea turtles can all be seen during a day dive.

There are several beginner dives offered along basaltic lava rocks that gently slope to merge with a sandy bottom. On these dives you can expect to see all of the big animals, except the hammerheads. Unfortunately, due to the presence of strong currents and surge, you need to be at least at the intermediate level to do the day-dive at Gordon Rocks, the closest site with hammerheads.

Gordon Rocks is a challenging dive. It is suggested that you have a minimum of twenty-five dives under your weight belt, are comfortable diving in currents, and have cold water diving experience. If the only one of these experiences you lack is the cold water diving, Scuba Iguana recommends that you practice in a cold lake at home with a rented 7-millimeter wetsuit. The thick skin definitely takes some getting used to. It would be okay, if that were the only adjustment. The biggest challenge, however, is the surge near the submerged tuft cone. The up and down thrust of the surge disorients your sense of buoyancy control, so it seems like you can't attain equilibrium. Consider the three factors together – a thick wetsuit with a hood, a strong current, and surge. It makes for a tough dive. If you are comfortable with the difficulty, it really is an awesome experience to see those hammerheads.

The best diving in the Galápagos is near the northern islands of Darwin and Wolf. This is where you can see multiple schools of hammerheads, as well as a multitude of other big animals. Unfortunately, the islands are too remote to access during a day dive. To dive in this area, you have to sign up for a boat tour that specializes in diving.

You can dive year round in the Galápagos and see the big fellahs. The water is colder and choppier July through October, but still has decent visibility.

A day trip with all equipment, two tanks, and lunch costs from $80-$110 per person.

We are listing only two dive shops below, which we consider to be the most reliable. These shops offer numerous day-dive options, longer trips of 5-10 days, and many other services. If you have a small group that wants to dive on your tour boat, the shop might coordinate a rendezvous, bringing with them all the necessary gear.

•**Scuba Iguana**, *east end of Charles Darwin, in front of the Hotel Galápagos. Tel. 5/526 296; E-mail: hotelgps@ga.pro.ec; Website: www.scuba-iguana.com*
•**Sub-Aqua**, *Charles Darwin. Quito Tel. 2/565 294; E-mail: sub_aqua@accessinter.net*

Horseback Riding

Juan Jose Christen and Annegret Rubsam, native islanders, offer horseback treks that begin on their farm near Bellavista. To arrange a ride, contact **Moonrise Travel**, *Charles Darwin, in front of Banco del Pacifico. Tel. 526 402; E-mail: sdivine@pa.ga.pro.ec.*

Mountain Biking

The **Red Mangrove**, *east end of Charles Darwin, Tel. 5/526 564.* rents bikes. The main place to ride is on the road up to the highlands. You can ride the bikes up to the highland attractions like the Tortoise Reserve, Lava Tube, and Los Gemelos Craters. Prepare yourself for some huffing and puffing. You can also arrange for the Red Mangrove to drop you off up there with the bikes, then cruise happily downhill.

Running & Walking

The best place for a run or a walk is on the brick path to Turtle Bay. From Charles Darwin in town, head up Herrara until you reach Charles Binford. Follow that as it turns from pavement into a dirt road to the entrance of the trail to Turtle Bay. It is three kilometers from town to this beautiful beach.

The other option is heading up Herrara and following it for as far as you want to run into the highlands. There still isn't that much traffic on the island so this is a decent route.

Sea Kayaking

The water to be paddled is mainly around Pelican Bay, and Academy Bay, to which it connects, where most of the boats are anchored. You can also paddle to a beach with mangrove trees in front of the Delfín Hotel. To rent a kayak, contact the **Red Mangrove**, *east end of Charles Darwin, Tel. 5/526 564*. They have other options in the works, so contact them to see what's new.

Surfing

There is some great surf in the Galápagos, especially if you are willing to hire a boat to take you out to the lava reef breaks. On Santa Cruz, there is a reef break that you can paddle to in front of the Hotel Delfín. Take a *panga* to *el otro lado* from the pier in Puerto Ayora for about $0.25. The hotel is just a short walk away. There are no surf shops from which to rent boards, but you will find a board of some sort to rent if you ask around.

The surf spots on San Cristóbal near Baquerizo Moreno are the best ones within walking distance of a town. Ask the local teenagers for directions. There is not much else for a kid to do here, so the sport is quite popular. Boards are tough to come by though.

If you want to arrange a surf trip on a boat, contact Ricardo Nuñez Cristiansen, *e-mail ricardo@galapagosurf.com.*

The best time of year is December-May for northwest swells. You can surf smaller southwest swells year round.

EXCURSIONS & DAY TRIPS

From Puerto Ayora, you can reach many of the visitor sites that are often included on cruises. These day excursions will appeal to those who prefer to do a land-based tour of the Galápagos, spending nights on shore, or to those who want to see additional sites after their cruise. There are well over a dozen day trips to choose from including Plazas, Santa Fe, Seymour, Isabela, and Floreana. See our *Visitor Sights* section at the end of this chapter for more information on the destinations.

A good agency to contact for day trips is Moonrise Travel. They charge about $50 per person for most of the excursions.

• **Moonrise Travel**, *Charles Darwin, in front of Banco del Pacifico. Tel. 526 402; E-mail: sdivine@pa.ga.pro.ec*

PRACTICAL INFORMATION

Banks: Banco del Pacifico, *Charles Darwin, mid-point*. The ATM is frequently out of service. You can get cash advances on Master Card inside.

Bookstores: Capricho Galeria Café, *Charles Darwin, mid-point*. Galápagos related books.

Business Hours: 9am-1pm; 2pm-6pm

Currency Exchange: Banco del Pacifico, *Charles Darwin, mid-point*

E-Mail Service: Internet service is almost non-existent due to poor phone service.

Medical Service:.Hospital, *Padre Julio Herrera. Tel. 526 129*

National Parks: Parque Nacional Galápagos, *Charles Darwin Research Station. Tel. 526 189 or 526 511*

Post Office: Correos, *Charles Binford*

Supermarket: *Near the commercial dock, west end of Charles Darwin*

Telephone/Fax: The area code is 5. **Emetel**, *Padre Julio Herrara*

Tourist Office/Maps: Ministereo de Turismo, *Charles Darwin, across from Banco del Pacifico*

SAN CRISTÓBAL

Puerto Baquerizo Moreno is the capital of the Galápagos Province and the second largest town with 6,000 inhabitants. While it is not as pleasant as Puerto Ayora, the town is sprucing up. An interpretation center was recently opened which now outclasses the one in Puerto Ayora. The cruises that leave from San Cristóbal usually begin with an orientation lecture here.

The main excursion is a half-hour drive through an agricultural zone in the highlands to the crater lake **El Junco. Frigatebird Hill**, a nesting site, is within walking distance of town. There are also several beaches in the area for soaking up the sun and the good surf. Surfers hit the point reefs on the right and left sides of the bay, as well as Canon Beach at the Navy Base.

The **Grand Hotel**, *Tel. 5/520 179* is located on a beach with great sunset views. For a place in town, try the **Hotel Orca** or the **Hostal San Cristóbal**, *Tel. 5/520 338*.

ISABELA

Isabela is the largest island in the Galápagos. Its landmass of 4,855 square kilometers is more than all other islands combined. There are two small communities on the southeastern end of Isabela where about 1,000 people live. The fishing village, **Villamil**, has a small airport. There is a road that runs 18 kilometers up the side of the **Sierra Negra Volcano** through a small agricultural community in the highlands.

The tourist infrastructure is minimal in Villamil, but that might be the very reason you want to come. If you would like to stay on the island, there is a bright, Mediterranean style bed & breakfast, **La Casa de Marita**. *Tel. 5/529 238, Fax 5/529 201; E-mail: hcmarita@pro.ec.* The rooms have kitchenettes. You also have use of the library, music room, and dining area. Ermano and Marita will assist you in lining up excursions in the area. You can also try the **Hotel Bellena Azul**, *Tel. 5/529 125.*

From Villamil you can visit long stretches of beach and lagoons with flamingoes, ride horses, or hike to the rim of the active Sierra Negra Volcano. There is an interesting tortoise breeding and rearing center that's worth a visit. You can also contract boats for excursions to other visitor sites and volcanoes.

FLOREANA

Margaret Wittmer, author of *Floreana*, runs a pension in the small community of Velasco Ibarra. The telephone number at the **Hostal Wittmer** is *5/520 150,* or you just go without a reservation. She'll almost certainly have a bed for you as well as signed copy of her book.

ISLAND BY ISLAND VISITOR SIGHTS

You will encounter marine iguanas, sea lions, lava lizards and a wide variety of seabirds on almost every island. When a particular species of seabirds is highly concentrated on one island, it is noted. The islands are listed in alphabetical order according to their most common Spanish names:
- **Baltra** island does not have any visitor sites, but it is where the airport for Santa Cruz is located.
- **Bartolomé** is a small island to the east of Santiago. There is a nice walk up to the top of a hill that offers an excellent view of the surrounding islands and of a provocative cone tuft called Pinnacle Rock. You might see white tipped sharks from the beach or while snorkeling.
- **Daphne Major and Minor** are the small islands that you can see from the Baltra airport. There are no visitor sites here, but the islands are noteworthy for the research being led by Peter and Rosemary Grant, as described in *Beak of the Finch*. The research team has studied nearly every finch born on the Daphne Major since 1971.
- **Española** is renowned for its seabirds. It is the primary habitat for the enormous waved albatross. Others found here include red-billed

tropicbirds, blue-footed boobies, and masked boobies. A walk along the bluff takes you to their nesting grounds. The visitor sites are Punta Suarez and Gardner Bay.

· **Floreana** has a nice beach and a flamingo lagoon near Punta Cormorant and a partially submerged crater, Devil's Crown, for fantastic snorkeling. You can visit Post Office Bay, where the old postal system still functions. Take a postcard from the box to deliver if it is addressed to your hometown or leave one there for someone else to do it for you. There is a lava tube cave nearby. You need a rope and a flashlight to explore it. You might also be able to visit the Wittmer residence on Black Beach, home of the author of *Floreana*.

WHERE THE COST OF POSTAGE NEVER GOES UP

Near the end of the 18th century, the first Galápagos post office was located on the island of Floreana. It was created to facilitate the delivery of mail to England and the United States. Homebound ships picked up correspondence placed in a barrel, subsequently delivering the mail to the destination. The inlet became known as **Post Office Bay**. *The original barrel has been replaced several times, but you can still drop off mail there today. Sometimes delivery is faster than through normal service. It also acts as an impromptu shrine with memorabilia from all over the world tacked onto its wooden post.*

· **Fernandina** looks like a giant barnacle protruding from the water. Penguins, flightless cormorants, and pelicans perch on black lava. It is a good place to see marine iguanas feeding on algae.

· **Genovesa** has two visitor's sites – Darwin Bay and Prince Phillip's Steps. Here you might see red-footed boobies, masked boobies, and frigate birds.

· **Isabela** is the largest island, making up over one half of the total area of the archipelago. It was formed by the united lava flow from six separate volcanoes. Its fishing village, Villamil, has a small airport. There are several visitor sites including Tagus Cove, Urbina Bay, Elizabeth Bay, and Punta Morena. Part of the shoreline consists of steep cliffs with caves that *pangas* can enter. You can find steaming fissures and giant tortoises in the bowl of the 1,100-meter Alcedo volcano. This requires a 10-kilometer trek to the rim of the volcano, and another 6 kilometers to the fissures.

· **Pinta** and **Marchena** do not have any visitor sites, but are renowned among divers for the fascinating schools of hammerheads that inhabit the surrounding waters.

- **Rábida**, a small island south of Santiago, has a brick red beach with sea lions. Flamingoes feed in a lagoon a short distance inland.
- **San Cristóbal's** town, Puerto Barquizo Moreno, is the capital of the Galápagos. It has an airport and some cruises leave from its bay. You can find souvenir shops and an interpretation center in town. You can take a road to the wet highlands and Junco Lake.
- **Santa Cruz** is the location of the port town of Puerto Ayora. Here you can visit the Charles Darwin Research Center, and shop for souvenirs along the pleasant waterfront. There are some nice beaches within walking distance of town. In the highlands you can visit giant tortoise reserves, a kilometer-long lava tube, and the Los Gemelos pit craters. Dragon Hill is accessed by boat to see land iguanas. The airport is located on Baltra Island just across a short channel. See the *Santa Cruz* destination section for more complete details.
- **Santa Fe** is about halfway between Santa Cruz and San Cristóbal. Here you might snorkel with sea lions and find land iguanas in a desert environment.
- **Santiago** is a large island with several visitor sites including Puerto Egas, Espumilla Beach, Buccaneer Cove, and Sulivan Bay. In Puerto Egas it is possible to walk to the Sugarloaf Volcano and an old saltworks operation. There is a lagoon with flamingoes near Espumilla Beach. Sulivan Bay provides good examples of pahoehoe ropey lava and horned lava formations. A popular photo subject is the volcanic islet "Chinese Hat" just off the coast.
- **Seymour**, a small island north of Baltra, has large populations of blue-footed boobies, frigate birds, sea lions, and marine iguanas.
- **South Plaza** is one of a pair of islets to the east of Santa Cruz with large sea lion colonies.

WHERE DOES YOUR $100 GALÁPAGOS PARK FEE GO?

• *Galápagos National Park Service*	$40
• *Municipalities*	$20
• *Provincial Council*	$10
• *Ingala National Institute*	$10
• *Marine Reserve*	$5
• *Wildlife & Protected Areas*	$5
• *Quarantine System*	$5
• *National Navy*	$5

INDEX

THINGS CHANGE!

Phone numbers, prices, addresses, quality of food, etc, all change. If you come across any new information, we'd appreciate hearing from you. No item is too small! Drop us an email note at: Jopenroad@aol.com, or write us at:

Ecuador & Galápagos Islands Guide
Open Road Publishing, P.O. Box 284
Cold Spring Harbor, NY 11724

TRAVEL NOTES

TRAVEL NOTES